EDWARD PREBLE

CLASSICS OF NAVAL LITERATURE
JACK SWEETMAN, SERIES EDITOR

This series makes available new editions of classic works of naval history, biography, and fiction. Each volume is complete and unabridged and includes an authoritative introduction written specifically for Classics of Naval Literature. A list of titles published or currently in preparation appears at the end of this volume.

Courtesy of U.S. Naval Academy Museum

EDWARD PREBLE, MARCH 1805, BY REMBRANDT PEALE

Preble's piercing eyes were dark blue. His coloring was that of a fair-skinned man who had spent many years at sea, and his prominent nose was characteristic of the Preble family. At the time this portrait was painted, strands of gray were beginning to appear in his light brown hair, which he combed forward in an unsuccessful attempt to conceal the baldness in front. As he posed for Peale, Preble held in his left hand a chart of his attacks on Tripoli, probably the one made by Midshipman William Lewis and reproduced elsewhere in this book.

Edward Preble

A Naval Biography
1761–1807

Christopher McKee

With a new Introduction by
the author

NAVAL INSTITUTE PRESS
Annapolis, Maryland

The latest edition of this work has been brought to publication with the generous assistance of Marguerite and Gerry Lenfest.

Naval Institute Press
291 Wood Road
Annapolis, MD 21402

© 1972, 1996 by the United States Naval Institute, Annapolis, Maryland.

All rights reserved. No part of this book may be reproduced or utilized in any form or by any means, electronic or mechanical, including photocopying and recording, or by any information storage and retrieval system, without permission in writing from the publisher.

First Naval Institute Press paperback edition published 2013

ISBN 978-1-55750-583-5 (hardcover)
ISBN 978-1-61251-497-0 (paperback)
ISBN 978-1-61251-366-9 (eBook)

A CIP record for this book is available from the Library of Congress.

♾ Print editions meet the requirements of ANSI/NISO z39.48-1992 (Permanence of Paper).
Printed in the United States of America.

9 8 7 6 5 4 3 2 1

Maps by Dorothy deFontaine

Drawings on pages 322 and 327 are reprinted from *The History of the American Sailing Navy* by Howard I. Chapelle by permission of W. W. Norton & Company, Inc.
©1948 by W. W. Norton & Company, Inc.

Our Navy at this time, when its character is to form, ought to be commanded by men who, not satisfied with escaping censure, will be unhappy if they do not receive and merit praise; by men who have talents and activity, as well as spirit, to assist a judicious arrangement for the employment of the force under their command or to cure the defects of a bad one.

> BENJAMIN STODDERT, First Secretary of the Navy, to President JOHN ADAMS
>
> 19 April 1799

Contents

List of Illustrations   xiii
Introduction   xv
Preface   xxv

Chapter 1   August 1761–April 1783   3
Will you not have more men?

2   November 1785–November 1798   30
... I sold the little wreck which had brought us miraculously over the Atlantic Ocean....

3   March 1798–September 1799   55
... I am particularly fond of naval service.

4   October 1799–January 1801   66
... I might have been left to clear the Straits of those pirates....

5   January 1801–April 1802   82
    ... *a majority of the officers of government ought to be composed of men who are firm friends to the administration.* ...

6   December 1801–September 1803   96
    ... *the Secretary of the Navy ... seems disposed to make such arrangements with respect to my future service as shall be most agreeable to me.*

7   May 1803–August 1803   123
    You have an arduous task to perform. You will have great difficulties to encounter.

8   September 1803–October 1803   139
    ... *cringing to those Barbarians will not answer.*

9   October 1803   160
    ... *it must be a pleasing reflection in the evening of his days.*

10 October 1803–February 1804   173
    But for him all places are alike. Busied with his summer's operations against Tripoli, he feels no pleasure in anything which does not forward his favorite plans.

11 February 1804–May 1804   192
    I feel extremely desirous of serving my country. Give me the means and I will do it. ...

12   August 1803–February 1805   214
You know he is not a man who commands his temper.

13   January 1804–July 1804   235
I value the national character of my country too highly to consent to a peace which the most powerful nation in Europe would blush to make.

14   July 1804–August 1804   251
... I wish to see the time when the Navy shall be supported by all ranks of our citizens. The achievement of glorious deeds will render the Navy popular. If you return to this country covered with laurels ... there will be but one pulse in America on the subject of a Navy. If, on the contrary, you should return without having seen the whites of the enemy's eye, I should not be surprised if the Navy should lose in popularity.

15   August 1804–September 1804   282
I hope to finish the war with Tripoli first, and then the sooner he [Commodore Barron] arrives the better, as I am anxious to return home.

16   October 1804–April 1807   309
The people are disposed to think that I have rendered some service to my country.

17   September 1804–June 1807   329
So powerful an opposition as appeared in Con-

gress last session may for a while check the growth of the Navy, but, unless the commercial spirit of our country dies, it must rise into consequence.

18 April 1807–August 1807   349
   That the advice of his physicians and his own hopes may not prove to be delusive must be the fervent prayer of every American. . . .

Bibliographic Notes   355
Index   377

Illustrations

Edward Preble by Rembrandt Peale	*Frontispiece*
Map of Maine	14–15
Map of Sunda Strait and Western Java	73
Mary Deering Preble	85
Eben Preble	85
Commodore Morris's Operations, May-June 1803	117
Map of Tangier	165
The *Intrepid*'s Attack on the *Philadelphia*	195
Profile of Tripoli	252–53
Movements of U.S. Squadron Between Noon and 2:45 p.m., 3 August 1804	255
Movements of U.S. Squadron Between 2:45 p.m. and 4:30 p.m., 3 August 1804	258
The Battle of Tripoli by Michel Felice Corné	264–65
Bombardment of Tripoli, 7 August 1804	273
Reconnaissance of 17 August and Bombardment of 23/24 August 1804	287

Attack on Tripoli, 28 August 1804	291
The *Intrepid*'s Attempt to Enter Tripoli Harbor, 1 September 1804	300
Attack on Tripoli, 2 September 1804	301
The *Intrepid*'s Movements, 3 September 1804	304
Preble Medal	313
Design of Gunboat No. 12	322
Design of Gunboats Nos. 29–37	327
Preble Mansion, Portland	347

Introduction

Edward Preble: A Naval Biography, 1761–1807 appeared in 1972. Republication in the Classics of Naval Literature series once again makes *Edward Preble* readily available for would-be readers. But a new edition of a book nearly twenty-five years old torments its author with temptations. If only I had known then what I know now! Rewrite here? Delete this? Add that? The danger lurking in such temptations is not unlike deciding to redecorate a single room at home. No sooner is one room done than a second, which looked just fine before, now demands redecorating too. Finish that, and a third suddenly seems shabby. And so one goes, room by room, until the whole house is redone.

Any book is shaped by the times in which it was written. It is also a child of a particular stage of the author's mental life. *Edward Preble* was written during the Vietnam War years, and I found it impossible to avoid seeing in then-contemporary events a reappearance of some old problems that the United States had met as long ago as the Tripolitan War of 1801–5: frustration of a maritime power attempting to use force against a land-based power able to tap the resources of an inaccessible interior; temptation to back a friendly pretender to power who proves, in the test, weak and lacking in essential popular support; distrust of mediators; and failure to understand, appreciate, or accept other cultures and different ways of thinking. Although far from dead, such issues—the last excepted—are less pressing in 1996 than they were twenty-five or thirty years ago. Moreover, in the years since 1972 my interest has shifted away from the stand-out-in-the-crowd leaders to the mass of men, be they officer or enlisted, who made the U.S. Navy function as an organization or who were dysfunctional within it; from the navy's quasi-mythic origins in the pre–War of 1812 years to the mature organization of the years between 1815 and the onset of the Civil War in 1861.

In 1996 it is not possible for me to return mentally to the late 1960s and be the person I then was, experiencing again the intensity of the concerns I felt and pursuing history in the particular way I did. To attempt to revise this or that paragraph or page or chapter of the *Edward Preble* of 1972 would be to compromise the book's integrity. In the end a complete rewriting in my 1996 style and with my 1996 historian's concerns, interests, and insights would be mandatory. The essential story might remain the same, but the result would be a second, and possibly quite different, biography. Consequently, a small number of now-corrected errors apart, *Edward Preble* reappears here as it was originally published. But I will take advantage of this introduction to report on Preble-related matters that I have uncovered during the past twenty-five years and to add my post-1972 thoughts on Edward Preble, the human being and the naval officer.

Preble's biographer confronts a critical problem: excellent as the documentation may be for Edward Preble the mature merchant captain and naval officer, only the skimpiest of personal records exist for the first thirty-plus years of the man's life, the time when he developed into the person known to history. One key strand in that development must have been young Edward's relationship with his powerful and remarkable if somewhat obscure father, Jedidiah Preble. A fascinating glimpse of the parent turns up in the reminiscences of a certain David Perry, who—as a young man just shy of seventeen—served in Jedidiah Preble's regiment during the abortive British attack on French-held Fort Ticonderoga in July 1758:

> It was the first engagement I had ever seen, and the whistling of balls and roar of musquetry terrified me not a little. At length our regiment formed among the trees, behind which the men kept stepping from their ranks for shelter. Col. Preble, who, I well remember, was a harsh man, swore he would knock the first man down who should step out of his ranks; which greatly surprised me, to think that I must stand still to be shot at.[1]

Like father, like son! Coming to terms with so formidable a parent as Jedidiah Preble must indeed have been a challenge. Speculation on the basis of slender evidence is often a foolhardy historical enterprise. But with Edward Preble it is hard not to interpret certain ingrained habits of the adult's behavior as the unselfconscious products of a young person's (perhaps unsuccessful) search for a difficult parent's approval. Not only does the son replicate the father's command personality, but there are also clue-bearing phrases and sentences in Edward Preble's writings; this, in a 1799 letter to his future brother-in-law, James Deering, is typical: "The *Pickering* sails as fast as anything in the West Indies, and if she was somewhat larger I should be very well satisfied with her for the present. I was much pleased with Commodore Barry, and am quite a favorite with him."[2] Here, in that last sentence, is a recurring theme in Preble's letters and diaries: the almost naive pleasure he takes in recording how well he stands in the opinions of those he perceives as superiors on the political or social ladder—whether it be President Thomas Jefferson, Secretary of the Navy Robert Smith, or Sir Alexander Ball at Malta. Old needs die hard.

Just as opaque to the historian is the private essence of Edward Preble's marriage to Mary Deering. After *Edward Preble* appeared in 1972 I serendipitously discovered the likely reason why Mary Deering was past thirty and perhaps teetering on the edge of spinsterhood when she married Edward: she had earlier been engaged to William Lithgow (1750–16 February 1796), the first United States attorney for the district of Maine, who died before they could be married.[3] But that still leaves the essential problem.

Edward's letters to Mary have survived to form one of the most important sources for this book.[4] Throughout those letters Edward writes of his love for Mary, but when he speaks of their relationship he is usually responding to something that Mary has written to him. Here is the not-to-be-overcome difficulty. Although Edward carefully saved Mary's letters, they have since vanished—almost certainly destroyed by Mary at some point during her long widowhood. To have only Edward's letters to study is akin to overhearing one-half of a telephone conversation. The eavesdropper does not know what is being said at the other end of the line and often forms an incorrect or badly distorted idea of the full two-person interaction. Another historian might have made a different decision, but I declined to speculate about the Prebles' marriage with only half of the essential evidence available. The risk of misinterpretation was too great. That is still my best judgment.

Because my research and writing since *Edward Preble* have focused on the navy's cast of supporting characters more than on the big stars, I regret that I was not better informed about some of the interesting people who have small roles in *Edward Preble,* but who deserved more lines. This regret is especially keen respecting two of Preble's key subordinates during his yearlong cruise to Java in *Essex.*

David Phipps, the frigate's second lieutenant (p. 68), had been one of the wheelhorses of the Continental Navy during the American Revolution: sailing master of *Alfred* with Commodore Esek Hopkins, and lieutenant in the sloop *Providence,* the brig *Cabot,* and the frigates *Trumbull, Warren, Raleigh, Boston,* and *Confederacy.* In the 1790s Phipps persistently sought a captain's appointment, either in a revenue cutter or a ship of the Quasi-War navy; but the evidence suggests that, in a lieutenant's berth, David Phipps had reached his level of competence. An able second- or third-in-command, he lacked the inner drive to assume successfully the lonely ultimate responsibility.

Naturally enough, Phipps preferred to attribute his exclusion from the captain's cabin to his political affiliation with the Jeffersonian Republicans rather than to any personal deficiency. He was nearly sixty years old when he served in *Essex* and possessed few, if any, financial resources apart from his naval pay. Although he was discharged as a lieutenant when the navy was downsized at the end of the Quasi-War, the incoming Jefferson administration almost immediately reappointed Phipps as a sailing master. In this capacity—more a recognition of services past than an anticipation of services future—David Phipps, his performance increasingly compromised by age and poor health, continued to serve in one low-challenge assignment or another until his death at the age of eighty-four.[5]

A sadder case was that of William Mumford, *Essex*'s purser, the money man who proved such a cross to the irritable Preble (pp. 68, 80). The reasons for Mumford's fall in the world are not entirely clear, but fall he did. A native of Newport, Rhode Island, Mumford had begun his working life before the American Revolution as deputy marshal for the vice-admiralty court in his hometown. At least by his own account, young Mumford did almost all the work the marshal was supposed to be doing because this officer actually lived in Boston. In 1772 Mumford left Newport for Providence to study law with his uncle. Once his legal training was completed, Mumford was admitted to practice in March 1775. He barely had time to bask in his new status as attorney-at-law before the incipient American rebellion went hot with the outbreak of fighting in Massachusetts. Almost immediately Mumford secured a government job as deputy to Henry Ward, secretary of state for Rhode Island. In this post, which he held from 1775 until 1783, Mumford once again claimed that he did most of the office's real work, this time because of Ward's poor health. During part of these busy and exciting years Mumford also found the time and the energy to serve as clerk to the Rhode Island Council of War and as deputy intendant of trade for the port of Providence.

At war's end a new government appointment beckoned in Philadelphia, where Mumford became principal clerk in the office of Benjamin Stelle, the commissioner for settling Pennsylvania's Revolutionary War accounts. This position kept bread on the Mumford table for about four years. Then, after what he calculated as sixteen years of government service, William Mumford found himself on the street "without any permanent employment," a situation that continued until he received his purser's warrant late in 1799. During the interval Mumford tried his hand at business and failed financially. His brother sent him money from Rhode Island until brotherly patience and pocketbook ran out. With his wife, Sarah, he eked out an existence of genteel poverty by boarding members of Congress in the Mumfords' rented Philadelphia home. All the while he was a persistent (and unsuccessful) applicant for this or that federal job until a highly placed friend suggested that he apply for a navy pursership and offered to speak to President John Adams on his behalf. Mumford drafted yet another letter of application, and his sponsor delivered it to Adams. As Mumford later told the story, "After having read it, the President observed he had heard an excellent character of Mr. Mumford but did [not] think he would have accepted of such an office or he might have had it long ago and immediately made the appointment."

At the conclusion of *Essex*'s 1800 Java cruise Mumford, whose surviving personal writings are almost invariably self-serving, unexpectedly changes character and—in a letter I wish I had found during my research for *Edward Preble*—creates a memorable record of the ship and her voyage:

> The *Essex* has been much admired at all the ports we touched at. In the Cape of Good Hope she was visited by the [British] navy officers generally, who all agreed in pronouncing her to be the most complete and beautiful frigate they ever saw, and one of the officers observed to the Captain [Preble], "If you will build such handsome frigates, you must not think hard that so many officers come on board to look at her." And, as to her sailing, she has beat every vessel she has ever had a trial with. We sailed from the Cape of Good

Hope in company with the *Rattlesnake* sloop of war, commanded by a son of Admiral Sir Roger Curtis. She got under way at the moment we did for the express purpose of beating us, but to their great mortification we ran her hull down in about four hours; and, when we arrived in the Straits of Sunda, we had a fair trial with the *Arrogant*, a 74, and the *Orpheus* frigate, two of the fastest-sailing vessels in the British navy, and we beat them above one-half. We passed the *Arrogant* so close that Captain Osborn look[ed] at us out of his quarter gallery with a degree of astonishment and observed to Captain Preble that she was the fastest-sailing vessel he ever met with.

In light of Preble's poor opinion of the man and his performance, it comes as no surprise that William Mumford was one of the pursers selected for discharge when the officer corps was cut back at the end of the Quasi-War. After Mumford's accounts were closed in the fall of 1801, the trail of historical bread crumbs becomes more difficult to follow than it is for his pre-*Essex* life. But as late as November 1820 William Mumford was still applying for—and still failing to receive—federal jobs.[6]

Since 1972 I have twice returned to Edward Preble to study aspects of his life from fresh perspectives. In "Edward Preble and the 'Boys,'" I cast a skeptical eye at Fletcher Pratt's well-known assertion that, Oliver Hazard Perry's victory on Lake Erie aside, all the American naval victories in the War of 1812 were won by Preble's former subordinates—even though Preble's junior officers from the Tripolitan War accounted for only one-third of the navy's command-rank officers in 1812. This remarkable (but misleading) statistic Pratt attributed to Preble's example. My essay questioned Pratt's numbers and his reasoning, not Preble's exemplary influence. I had explored Preble's disciplinary practices in detail in *Edward Preble* (pp. 221–24), but I came back to the subject twenty years later in *A Gentlemanly and Honorable Profession* so that I might compare Preble's discipline with that of other captains of the pre-1815 navy. The results challenged old assertions about corporal punishment—and not to Preble's discredit. Both texts are essential supplements to *Edward Preble*.[7]

How do I see Edward Preble now, after nearly twenty-five additional years of studying the nineteenth-century U.S. Navy? In the process by which the United States created (more or less out of nothing) a professional naval officer corps between 1798 and 1812, Preble was an important, an admired, and even a heroic role model for younger career officers. A harsh disciplinarian and a man of violent and poorly controlled temper—"cross, peevish and ill-tempered, surly and proud" in Sailing Master James Trant's memorable eight-word character sketch (p. 98)—Preble earned first the grudging and then the enthusiastic admiration of his subordinates by his decisiveness and vigor, by his unhesitating use of prudent discretion and initiative, by his willingness to delegate important assignments to promising younger men, by his fervent defense of what he held to be the national interests and honor of the United States, but most of all by his refusal to give up in the face of severe reverses and depressing odds.

By temperament Edward Preble was a man of action, not a military intellectual. Consumed by an intense desire to leave a famous name, he consciously sought that fame through self-sacrifice in his country's cause. I invite you to read this volume to find out how he achieved his dream.

Christopher McKee

Notes

1. David Perry, *Recollections of an Old Soldier: The Life of Captain David Perry, a Soldier of the French and Revolutionary Wars* (Windsor, Vt., 1822), 9.
2. Private collection: Preble to James Deering, 2 Apr. 1799.
3. Society of the Cincinnati, Massachusetts, *Memorials of the Massachusetts Society of the Cincinnati,* by Bradford Adams Whittemore (Boston, 1964), 372–73.
4. Rear Adm. Dundas Preble Tucker, USN (Ret.), the last direct descendant of Edward Preble, died at La Jolla, California, in October 1978. By the terms of Admiral Tucker's will, the letters from Edward to Mary—so often quoted in *Edward Preble*—together with the other Preble manuscripts in his possession were given to the Library of Congress as an addition to the Edward Preble Papers.
5. Harold C. Syrett, ed., *The Papers of Alexander Hamilton* (New York: Columbia University Press, 1961–87), 7:206; TJ Mss: R. Smith to Jefferson, received 25 Oct. 1804; NA, RG 45, Miscellaneous Letters: Jared Mansfield to James Madison, 26 Oct. 1809; NA, RG 45, Officers' Letters: O. H. Perry to Paul Hamilton, 31 May 1812.
6. LC, George Washington Manuscripts: Mumford to Washington, 9 May 1789, 1 Aug. 1789, 2 June 1790, and 7 July 1790, all partially or wholly printed in Dorothy Twohig, ed., *The Papers of George Washington: Presidential Series* (Charlottesville: University Press of Virginia, 1987–   ), 2:240–42; *Papers of Alexander Hamilton*, 12:423; NA, RG 59, Applications and Recommendations for Office, John Adams's Administration, William Mumford File: Theodore Foster to Adams, 12 Sept. 1797; Applications and Recommendations for Office, Monroe's Administration: Mumford to James Monroe, 6 Nov. 1820; Philip C. F. Smith, *The Frigate* Essex *Papers: Building the Salem Frigate, 1798–1799* (Salem, Mass.: Peabody Museum, 1974), 189.
7. "Edward Preble and the 'Boys': The Officer Corps of 1812 Revisited," in James C. Bradford, ed., *Command under Sail: Makers of the American Naval Tradition, 1775–1850* (Annapolis, Md.: Naval Institute Press, 1985), 71–96; *A Gentlemanly and Honorable Profession: The Creation of the U.S. Naval Officer Corps, 1794–1815* (Annapolis, Md.: Naval Institute Press, 1991), 237–40, 242–47, 478, 480–81, and 543. I also wrote brief sketches of Preble for two biographical reference works: Roger J. Spiller and Joseph G. Dawson, eds., *Dictionary of American Military Biography* (Westport, Conn.: Greenwood Press, 1984), and *American National Biography* (forthcoming, Oxford University Press). My retrospective assessment of Preble is taken from these two sketches.

PREFACE

During each of the distinct periods into which historians divide the development of the early U.S. Navy one officer emerged from the crowd of his fellows and became the man with whom that period will always be associated. In the Quasi-War with France, 1798-1801, Thomas Truxtun personified the professionalism and the aggressive spirit of the newly established Federal Navy. From 1807 until 1837 — years that encompassed maritime friction with Great Britain, the War of 1812, and his long service as Chairman of the Board of Navy Commissioners — John Rodgers used his influence on and control of the sources of political and administrative power at Washington to dominate the naval scene.

Between those two men, the strong figure was Edward Preble. In 1803, when President Thomas Jefferson's administration was searching for a leader who could bring the inconclusive naval war with Tripoli to an acceptable termination, Preble came from comparative obscurity to synthesize the talents of a corps of outstanding young officers and to demonstrate that, in spite of monumental handicaps, objectives could be at least partially won and honor wholly sustained. The significance of Preble's life is simple and enduring: a man's moral fibre and his actions when confronted with difficulties are more important than his failure, or his success, in overcoming those difficulties.

Edward Preble was the great naval leader of the Tripolitan War years for three reasons. First, his intellectual endowments enabled him to understand the several military, diplomatic, and commercial responsibilities of an American squadron, and to harmonize those responsibilities with the administration's policy. Second, he possessed the strength of character and force of personality to translate intellectual analysis into effective action. Third, Preble was lucky: the times in which he lived and his position in society gave him an opportunity to use his abilities in a memorable way.

But Edward Preble's biography is more than the story of an outstanding man. Early in the research for this book it became apparent that the historically important years of Preble's life, 1801-1807, could be fully understood only in conjunction with a study of the naval policy of Jefferson's presidency, and particularly the administration's objectives and strategy in the Tripolitan War. There is a well-imbedded mythology regarding President Jefferson's attitude towards the Navy. But until quite recently there has been no scholarly research into the most obvious source for learning what his naval policy really was: the correspondence between Jefferson and Secretary of the Navy Robert Smith.* Jefferson was a vigorous executive, Smith a man of strong convictions; their exchanges provide a full and fascinating record of a period in U.S. naval history that has been poorly understood.

Investigation of Jeffersonian naval policy led to extended exploration of the activities of Commodore Richard V. Morris, Edward Preble's predecessor in the Mediterranean command. Morris's failure and the administration's disgust with him prepared the way for Preble's appointment to the command of the Mediterranean squadron. Many of the tactical and diplomatic problems that Morris encountered prefigured those that Preble met — problems that suggested the limits of what American policy could expect to accomplish in the Mediterranean.

Heretofore American histories of the Tripolitan War have been one-sided. Little or nothing has been said about Tripolitan activities or attitudes. To obtain the view from the Pasha's Castle, considerable use has been made of the dispatches of Bonaventure Beaussier, the French consul at Tripoli. The attitude of cultural and moral superiority over opponents that has influenced American histories of certain U.S. wars — particularly the Indian Wars, the Mexican War, the Spanish-American War, and the Barbary Wars — is overdue for retirement. Every effort has been made to understand Yusuf Caramanli and his ministers, and to present them as subtle and skillful representatives of a different, but by no means inferior, culture.

Quoted passages in *Edward Preble* have been handled according to the rules for the "modernized method," as set down in the *Harvard Guide to*

---

* Joseph G. Henrich's Ph.D. dissertation *The Triumph of Ideology: the Jeffersonians and the Navy, 1779-1807* (Ann Arbor, Michigan: University Microfilms, 1971) became available after *Edward Preble* had been set in type.

American History (Cambridge, 1955): save for one or two cases in which it seemed desirable to follow the original, spelling, punctuation, and capitalization have been modernized; abbreviations have been spelled out; overlong sentences and paragraphs have been broken up; however, the exact words used by the person quoted have been faithfully reproduced.

Most of this book was written while I was a member of the faculty of the Edwardsville Campus of Southern Illinois University. The University provided financial support for some of the research and, more important, several periods of time, including a sabbatical leave, during which I was able to devote my full attention to the manuscript. The value of the encouragement that I received from my friend and supervisor, John C. Abbott, is greater than anyone, except perhaps the author, realizes. Rear Admiral Dundas P. Tucker, U.S. Navy (Retired), Edward Preble's great-great-grandson, has waited patiently for a long time to see this biography completed. Besides supplying me with copies of Edward Preble manuscripts in his collection, Admiral Tucker has always been enthusiastic about the project, enthusiasm that was a great stimulus to me in moments of discouragement. While I was engaged in the research for *Edward Preble* my cousin, Mrs. Margaret V. Lanahan, of Washington, D.C., had me as a houseguest for a total of several weeks. Her contribution to the completion of the book is a substantial one. Linda McKee is also a naval historian, and her help was crucial in so many ways that it is hard to enumerate them all: she aided my search for Preble manuscripts, found several elusive and important documents that would otherwise have escaped me, read the entire book many times, and offered criticisms and suggested improvements which — if not always welcome — were almost always accepted.

These persons, organizations, and institutions graciously made manuscript documents available, provided photocopies of many papers, and, when necessary, granted permission to quote: Archives Diplomatiques, Ministère des Affaires Etrangères, Paris; Boston Athenaeum; Boston Public Library; British Museum; William L. Clements Library, University of Michigan; Essex Institute; Governor Dummer Academy; Haverford College Library; Henry E. Huntington Library and Art Gallery; Library of Congress; Lilly Library, Indiana University; Longfellow House, Cambridge, Massachusetts; Maine Historical Society; Archives Division, Office of the Secretary, Commonwealth of Massachusetts; Massachusetts Historical Society; New-York Historical Society; New York Public Library; North Carolina Department of Archives and History; Nova Scotia Public Archives; Historical Society of Pennsylvania; Peabody Museum, Salem,

Massachusetts; Free Library of Philadelphia and Mrs. Marjorie Ellis; Public Record Office, London; Franklin D. Roosevelt Library; Earl Gregg Swem Library, College of William and Mary; United States National Archives; United States Naval Academy Museum; University of Virginia Library; G. W. Blunt White Library, Mystic Seaport; Collection of American Literature, Yale University, and Professor James Franklin Beard.

Quotation from the microfilm edition of the Adams Papers is by permission of the Massachusetts Historical Society; and from *The Notebooks of Samuel Taylor Coleridge,* edited by Kathleen Coburn, Volume II, copyright 1961 by the Bollingen Foundation, by permission of Princeton University Press, the Bollingen Foundation, and Routledge & Kegan Paul, Ltd.

EDWARD PREBLE

CHAPTER 1 AUGUST 1761–APRIL 1783

"Will you not have more men?"

Enoch Preble claimed that a British lieutenant named Henry Mowat and potatoes had a lot to do with it, but — really — it was inevitable that sooner or later his brother Edward would go to sea.

Those who live there probably do not notice it, but in Portland, Maine, the smells of the sea fill the air. The town itself is nearly surrounded by salt water. Portland was called Falmouth when Edward Preble was born there on 15 August 1761. The family home on Thames Street fronted on the water. Across Thames Street were the wharves. Beyond them lay Casco Bay, its islands, and the ocean.[1]

If Maine had a first citizen during the years of the American Revolution it was Edward's father, Jedidiah Preble, known to family and townsmen as "The Brigadier" from the rank he had attained in the Massachusetts provincial forces during the Seven Years' War.[2] Jedidiah was born in York, Maine, in 1707. He went to sea while still in his teens and, within a few years, had worked his way up to master and owner of coasting vessels. The elder Preble's military career began in King George's War. He participated in the capture of Louisbourg by William Pepperrell in 1745 and remained on active service until the conclusion of an uneasy peace in 1748. Some months before he was mustered out, Jedidiah Preble shifted his residence to Falmouth; earlier he had moved from York to Wells. On the approach of the Seven Years' War, he became a soldier once more, campaigning in Maine and Nova Scotia, and built a reputation as one of the ablest of the provincial officers, a distinction not lightly awarded by professional British commanders. In 1758 Colonel Preble and his regiment participated in Major General James Abercromby's disastrous campaign against Ticonderoga. The final years of the French and Indian War found him commanding Fort Pownall on the west bank of the Penobscot River, a position that involved considerable responsibility for Indian affairs. Military talent brought its rewards: by 1759 Jedidiah Preble, who had set off for war in 1745 as an ensign, was a brigadier general.

The Brigadier's military career should not conceal his economic rise. Throughout the years he steadily added to his holdings — ships, farms, backlands, houses, shops, and wharves — and by the early 1770s he was one of the wealthiest men in Falmouth. From this wealth, and the abilities which enabled him to acquire it, came social prestige and opportunities for community leadership. The most important service he rendered his town and Maine, then a district of Massachusetts, was as a member, first of the provincial legislature, and then of the Massachusetts General Court, or legislature. He started in 1753 as a representative from the town of Falmouth and, with some interruptions, ended thirty years later, as state senator from Cumberland County. The years of experience in the General Court piled up, and Jedidiah Preble became an increasingly powerful spokesman for Maine interests — an asset he did not hesitate to use to help his sons' careers.

Jedidiah's first wife, Martha Junkins of York, died in March 1753, leaving him with five children: Samuel, William, Jedidiah, Jr., John, and Lucy. About fourteen months after Martha's death, Jedidiah married, on 9 May 1754, Mehetable (Bangs) Roberts, a widow whose husband had died during the first year of their marriage. Widow Roberts was no gray-haired lady, matronly and sedate: she was only 26 years old. Jedidiah was 47, at the crest of his vigor, on his way up economically, and, clearly, looking for more than just a housekeeper and mother-substitute. Jedidiah's and Mehetable's first child, Martha, was born in November 1754. After Martha, came Ebenezer in 1757, and Joshua two years later. Edward, born in 1761, was followed by Enoch in 1763, Statira in 1767; and the baby of the family, Henry, was born in 1770. Mehetable is reported to have been an impressive woman physically. No mean businesswoman, she was fully the equal of her husband in energy. As he grew older and devoted more and more of his time to his role as a community leader, she took over the day-to-day management of his extensive properties, made capital improvements, and increased his holdings. One wonders to what extent Edward's austerity and formality, precision and efficiency, were inherited from his mother. Jedidiah's wit and joviality were traits almost wholly lacking in Edward, whose sense of humor — rarely evidenced — was sardonic. But the father's hot temper, intense determination, and talent for seamanship and military life are discernible in the son.

As a child Edward was subject to temper tantrums. One incident his brothers and sisters remembered took place when he was about ten years old. Jedidiah Preble and some of his friends were going on a hunting or fishing trip among the islands of Casco Bay. Edward kept asking to be allowed to go along. Jedidiah, anxious to cut off the nagging, told the boy that if he could get a certain chore done before the boat left, he might go. The Brigadier thought he had been clever in picking a job that Edward could not possibly do before the men got away on their junket. But Edward flew at the work, and, just as the party was shoving off from the wharf, there was Edward saying the job was done and he was ready to go. The senior Preble, still unwilling to have his outing spoiled by a boy, said there was not room in the boat. At this Edward broke into a rage. He began to pick up stones from the wharf and hurl them at father, friends, and boat until Jedidiah surrendered. Edward had shown he had the "right stuff" in him.

It was being excluded from a hunting or fishing party that put Edward in a rage. He had already developed a passion for those sports. Alone or with friends he would spend hours roaming the woods and fields near Falmouth or boating on the bay, the rivers, the ponds. By the time he was in his teens, practice had made him an expert marksman. Going out into the woods with his dogs and his guns remained a favorite form of escape all his life.

But school, not the woods, is where the Preble boys had to be most of the time. The first of Edward's teachers who can be definitely identified was his brother-in-law, Jonathan Webb, who had married Lucy Preble in 1763. Webb had graduated from Harvard in 1754 and, after failing as a businessman, had taken up schoolteaching. He lacked both ability and strength of character, and was nicknamed "Pithy" Webb by his students because, whenever he cut a quill pen, he popped the pith into his mouth and chewed on it. Edward, who cannot have been more than eight years old and was something of a troublemaker in the school, decided it would be great fun to take advantage of this disgusting habit. He removed Pithy's quills from his desk and injected something exceptionally foul-tasting — possibly excrement — into the piths. The spectacle of Webb's face and his behavior when next he put a pith into his mouth are said to have been well worth the hiding he administered to his little brother-in-law.[3]

Jedidiah Preble wanted his son to attend Harvard and prepare for one of the professions, but he knew that even if Edward did not go to college he would need a good education if he were to do well in business. There may have been some semiliterate, self-made businessmen in eighteenth century New England — but not many. Whether Harvard or countinghouse was in Edward's future, the next step was preparatory school, and Dummer

School * in Byfield, Massachusetts, was chosen. Ebenezer had already been a student there, and Enoch Preble would, in 1776, follow the tradition established by his two older brothers and enroll at Dummer.

Dummer School operated in a red, two-room schoolhouse and was run by a remarkably able and dedicated teacher, Samuel Moody. At the core of the curriculum were Master Moody's specialties, Greek and Latin, but the boys also learned French. Moody did not like mathematics, so he employed an assistant to teach that subject while he concentrated on the literary studies. Ballroom dancing was also probably part of the Dummer School program of studies while Edward was in attendance. As important as the subjects taught, were the habits of promptness, exactness, thoroughness, and intellectual independence, that Samuel Moody tried to instill in his pupils.

It is impossible to be certain of the exact dates of Edward's attendance at Dummer School. He was definitely there from 6 November 1775 through 3 April 1776, during which period he boarded with Joseph Hale, whose home served as a dormitory for students at the school. That was Edward's last year with Samuel Moody. By that time he was fourteen, the age at which most Dummer pupils completed their studies and either moved on to Harvard or went into business. The tradition that Edward did not like school and was not brilliant academically is probably exaggerated. He obviously profited from Dummer as well as from the schools he had attended earlier. It is clear that, by the time he started writing letters and keeping accounts, he had a thorough knowledge of arithmetic, spelling, grammar, and rhetoric. As an adult he certainly realized that education was the base for getting ahead socially and financially. He liked to find promising boys whose families could not afford to send them to preparatory school, informally adopt them, pay for and supervise their education. Preble helped put at least one boy through his alma mater, Dummer Academy.[4]

The Revolution began while Edward was attending Dummer School, but only one event in the early years of that war affected him personally. At the beginning of October 1775, British Vice Admiral Samuel Graves, acting on the assumption that the destruction of their homes and property would crush the spirit of insurrection in the people of New England, ordered a small squadron of warships under Lieutenant Henry Mowat to proceed north from Boston and "chastise" Marblehead, Salem, Cape Ann, Ipswich, Newburyport, Portsmouth, Saco, Falmouth, and Machias by burning the villages and seizing or destroying all the shipping in their harbors. Of this ambitious punitive program only the destruction of Falmouth was actually carried out. At 9:40 a.m., 18 October, after a warning the previous

* Now Governor Dummer Academy.

day for the inhabitants to evacuate the town, Lieutenant Mowat's squadron began firing on Falmouth. Within twenty minutes, part of the village was blazing. A landing party from the British flotilla fired other buildings. By 6:00 p.m. the job was done. More than half the houses — including the Preble home on Thames Street — were afire. Eleven merchantmen were smoking derelicts and two were prizes. Two days later the ruins of Falmouth were still burning.

Jedidiah Preble purchased a house, with adjoining shop, barn, and outbuildings, in a rural section of Falmouth called Capisic, about three miles west of the burned-out village, leased some nearby farmland, and moved his family out to the country.[5] Sixty years later Edward's brother Enoch recalled that during the summer of 1778 he and two of his brothers — Edward, 17, and Henry, 8 — were at the Capisic farm. Edward was somewhat at loose ends. He had completed the work offered by Dummer School two years before, but lacked the motivation to go on to Harvard. In wartime, subsistence farming became a necessity in Maine, and the husky Preble lads — all grew to be at least six feet tall — were expected to help out on the farm. Because Edward was the oldest boy at home, much of the management and the physical labor at Capisic fell on him.

At first farming bored Edward, and then he hated it. He was out in the hot sun all day. The woods looked cool, but he could not go there. The weeds had more vitality than the crops: it seemed as if the boys just got them out of a plot when they were shooting up again. At night, a deer or a woodchuck would slip into the garden to eat the plants so painfully tended during the daylight hours. Finally it all got to Edward. One day when the brothers were hoeing potatoes his temper exploded. He hurled down his hoe and shouted that, by God, he would do no more of this work. He started walking down the road towards Falmouth.

The next thing anyone knew Edward had signed on a ship. There was nothing new about that in the Preble family. Leaving home and going away to sea was something all the Preble boys did. By 1781, if not earlier, Ebenezer had enough experience to command his own coaster, the 30-ton schooner *Hazard*. Joshua occupied a mate's berth when he was 18 years old. Enoch made his first voyage at the age of 16, and Henry was 11 when he shipped as a boy in the Continental frigate *Deane*.

Enoch's recollection was that when Edward got to Falmouth he found a privateer brig from Newburyport, commanded by Captain Friend, looking for hands. The brig made a voyage to Europe and had an extraordinarily rough passage home when she encountered headwinds and severe cold off the New England coast. The privateer referred to by Enoch could only have been the 110-ton brigantine *Hope*, 12 guns, 40 men, commissioned 16 September 1778, and commanded by William Friend.[6]

Perhaps that was the ship in which Edward Preble first went to sea. All that can be said for certain is that he was home at Falmouth early in December 1778 when his father wrote from Boston and asked Edward to send him some papers he needed. But, beginning in 1779, there is no longer any need to depend on family memories. Edward Preble's life as a sailor became a matter of record. The articles of the sloop *Merrimack* of Falmouth, Henry Ellwell, master, show that on 22 June 1779 Edward signed on for a trading voyage to the West Indies. Then approaching 18, he was rated as a seaman in a ship's company that consisted of master, mate, and five hands.[7] It was probably in small, hometown traders, such as the *Merrimack*, that Edward Preble learned the basic seamanship that prepared him to enter the state navy of Massachusetts as an officer when opportunity came in the spring of 1780.

II

The disastrous Penobscot expedition of 1779, in which Massachusetts state forces tried to expel the British from Fort George, their newly occupied post at Bagaduce or Majabagaduce,* Maine, ended in the destruction of a number of ships, including the three oceangoing cruisers of the Massachusetts state navy. During the latter half of 1779 and early 1780 the state service was reduced to one active naval vessel, the *Lincoln Galley*, a ship used principally for inshore and errand work. But the state's high-seas navy was almost immediately reborn — and in a more glamorous form — with the launching of its largest ship and only frigate.[8] She was the *Protector*, 26 guns, 250 men, authorized by the General Court in April 1778, launched at Newburyport during the summer of 1779, and outfitted at Boston during the winter of 1779-80.[9]

John Foster Williams, who since 1776 had built a solid reputation as a wartime leader in both state ships and privateers, was chosen as her captain. At 36 years of age, he was a skilled seaman and a courageous officer. One had only to meet him or correspond with him to realize that he was no rough sea dog, but a well-educated gentleman with considerable knowledge of mathematics and nautical science. Put another way, he was a man whom gentlemen would want to train and educate their nautically-inclined sons, and there were apparently more candidates for midshipman warrants than could be satisfied. Because an important part of the midshipmen's duties would be taking command of any prizes the *Protector* might capture,

* Now Castine.

Williams decided to award warrants only to young gentlemen with considerable experience at sea. In addition to the six warranted midshipmen that the General Court had authorized for the *Protector*, Captain Williams was permitted to take along six young gentlemen who did not qualify for warrants, but who might thereby gain the experience necessary to fill any vacancies that occurred in the corps of official midshipmen. These aspirants appeared on the ship's roll as acting midshipmen.

At eighteen and with relatively little sea service behind him, Edward Preble was not considered qualified to be granted a midshipman's berth. All his father's influence could not help. The best he could get was one of the acting appointments. Even that did not come through till the last minute. Edward hurried to Nantasket Road, near Boston, where the *Protector* lay windbound, and joined his ship on 4 April 1780, only hours before she sailed. That first cruise was a short one. On 7 April the *Protector* reached Falmouth and landed Brigadier General Peleg Wadsworth, the newly appointed military commander for that section of Maine. After inspecting the defenses of the area, Wadsworth embarked in the *Lincoln Galley*, Captain Joseph Ingraham, which the *Protector* then escorted to the mouth of the St. George River. There, during the evening of 10 April, the two ships parted company, and the *Protector* sailed for the entrance to Penobscot Bay, where she was to cruise.

It looked as though the new frigate might be a lucky ship. Henry Mowat, the British officer responsible for the burning of Falmouth in 1775, was at this time the naval commander at Bagaduce, where one of two British transports that had sailed from Halifax under convoy of the sloop of war *Nautilus*, 16, anchored during the forenoon of 9 April. Mowat feared that the second transport, the *Eolus*, might be wandering among the islands at the mouth of the bay in need of a pilot, a possibility heightened by the rain, sleet, and fog that were beginning to envelop Penobscot Bay. He put the sailing master from his own sloop of war, the *Albany*, 14, and twenty-five picked men into the *Albany*'s tender, the 8-gun sloop *Bagaduce*, and sent her off to search for the *Eolus*.

The following morning the *Eolus* appeared, safe and sound, off the mouth of the Bagaduce River, but the *Bagaduce* was not with her. In the low visibility the two vessels had missed one another. Nothing was seen of the tender until nine o'clock on the morning of the 11th, when the fog lifted enough to reveal the little sloop hustling up the bay with the *Protector* hard on her heels. About an hour later there were one or two shots from the *Protector*, and Henry Mowat had the mortification of watching the *Bagaduce* strike her colors to John Foster Williams. Then frigate and prize turned and stood out to sea. Accompanied by the *Nautilus*, the *Albany* immediately came out of the Bagaduce in pursuit of the *Protector*. A light-wind chase lasted all through 12 April and into the 13th and took the pursuers past Monhegan Island before it was finally abandoned. Even though the *Protector* frequently had to heave to for her slower-moving prize, she and the *Bagaduce* easily outran the pursuing sloops of war.

Captain Williams returned to Nantasket Road on 20 April to receive orders from the Massachusetts Board of War for a longer cruise.[10] If Edward Preble had any doubts about his desire to spend his life at sea, the *Protector*'s second cruise surely erased them.

Williams was instructed to run down the Maine coast, clearing it of any armed vessels, then take station athwart the sea lanes from Europe to New York and the Carolinas. After cruising seven days in latitude 38°-39°, he was to steer for Cape Race, Newfoundland. The Board of War assumed that most ships from England bound for Canada attempted to sight Cape Race, which should make that a prime area for taking prizes. Next, after cruising to the south of the Newfoundland Banks for 20 days, Williams was to return to the Maine seaboard and patrol there before running southward as far as the route taken by vessels plying between the West Indies and England. Before returning to Boston, he was to make a third call on the Maine coast.[11]

These orders attempted to combine the protection of the state's trading vessels and coasts — particularly the vulnerable Maine seaboard — with cruises in the principal sea lanes in search of prizes. This strategy reflected a tension that runs through the history of the Massachusetts state navy. If the coasts were not protected, public unhappiness in the exposed area was quickly translated into pressure on the General Court. Yet, coastal patrol work kept the state ships away from the great sea routes where the rich prizes were to be had, and without the prospect of prize money it was difficult to recruit crews in competition with lucrative privateers.[12]

Departing Nantasket Road on 7 May 1780, the *Protector* convoyed a sloop and the schooner *Two Friends* to Machias, Maine.[13] That extreme northeast section of Maine was under Massachusetts control, but the British presence at Fort George and the privateering base at Bagaduce made the link between Boston and Machias a tenuous one. Four days after leaving Nantasket Road the *Protector* stood to the southward from the mouth of Machias Bay. Between 14 and 20 May she chased five promising-looking sail in the area of longitude 38°-39° North, latitude 61°-62° West, but three of them turned out to be friends and the other two escaped without identifying themselves. Disappointed, Captain Williams bore away for Newfoundland.

Cape St. Mary's was sighted on 26 May, and later in the day the *Protector*'s lookouts saw Cape Race, but the only ships in sight were a few small shallops close inshore. Then a period of thick, dirty weather settled in, and the *Protector* could only beat about in an apparently empty sea while boredom ate away at crew morale. After a month and two days of bootless cruising and chasing, excitement ran high on the morning of 9 June when a large ship showing British colors was sighted to windward bearing down on the *Protector*, which thereupon hoisted British colors, too. The stranger was big enough to be a seventy-four, but, as the two ships closed, her unprofessional maneuvers told Captain Williams and his first lieutenant, George Little, that she was a heavily armed merchantman. The *Protector* cleared for action.

The wind was blowing from W.S.W., and the enemy ship was running before it. Williams's *Protector* steered in a generally north or northwestward direction. The stranger approached and passed ahead of the Massachusetts frigate, then hove to under the *Protector*'s lee. Captain Williams kept under way, crossed his antagonist's stern, and came to on his lee quarter. It was about 11:00 a.m. Lieutenant Little called on the stranger to identify herself. "From Jamaica" was all the answer given — or all that could be heard. The British master demanded the *Protector*'s identity, and Little, affecting not to hear the question, put his trumpet to his ear, and signalled for a repeat. The ruse gave Williams time to determine the number of the *Protector*'s guns bearing on the enemy. Then Williams called out three orders to be executed simultaneously: Strike British colors! Raise the United States jack and ensign! Fire all guns bearing on the British ship!

The two antagonists came broadside to broadside — the *Protector* to leeward, her enemy to windward — and perhaps as close as 50 yards from one another. This short range gave the *Protector* an advantage, for her antagonist, a large and burthensome cargo ship, carried her guns so high that most of her shot went into the *Protector*'s rigging rather than her hull. The *Protector* possessed a second advantage in her marines, who displayed considerable skill in gunning down men in the enemy's tops and on her exposed deck.

Around 12:30 p.m., when the *Protector* had been slugging it out in a fairly even match with her antagonist for an hour and a half, the enemy ship was seen to be afire. The blaze spread rapidly, there was a terrific explosion, and the British ship began to sink. As fast as the carpenter's gang could patch the shot holes in them, the *Protector*'s boats were hoisted out to pick up survivors. Fifty-five men, most of them burned and wounded, were pulled from the water and from floating wreckage. Lieutenant Little recalled that many of the survivors were so excited by the bloody conflict or crazed by its macabre finale and the pain of wounds and burns that they fought the men who were trying to rescue them. Several tried to jump into the sea again from the boats that had picked them up. The only officer saved was the third mate, and from him Williams learned that his late antagonist was the letter of marque ship *Admiral Duff*, 32, bound from St. Christopher and St. Eustatius to London with a cargo of sugar and tobacco.

Damage to the *Protector* was quickly repaired, and she continued on her cruise, but Surgeon Thomas Leverett faced a major health problem. The *Admiral Duff* was infected with a West India fever and, within a month, death claimed fifteen of the fifty-five prisoners on board the *Protector*. Fever spread to the *Protector*'s crew, and the number of men on the sick list grew day by day.

At 5:00 a.m. on 1 July, the frigate's lookouts sighted two ships, one bearing S.E. and the other N.W. and both moving towards the *Protector*. Light airs were blowing from W.S.W. Williams decided to stand up towards the sail in the N.W. and have a closer look. By 10:00 a.m. the ship sighted to the S.E. had disappeared astern. An hour later the stranger in the N.W. came to life and — aided perhaps by a slightly stronger breeze than Williams enjoyed — began steering down for the *Protector*. Williams computed his noon position to be latitude 43° 34' North, with Halifax Light bearing N. by E. The stranger was figuring his noon position was latitude 43°42' North. While the two captains made their calculations, the ships held their respective courses and continued to close one another. At 2:00 p.m., Captain Williams recognized the stranger as a British frigate — one that mounted perhaps as many as 32 guns, or six more than the *Protector* carried. Furthermore, fever had cut into the number of Massachusetts men who would be able to go to quarters when the drum beat.

For these reasons, John Foster Williams decided it would be imprudent to take on the British frigate, if an engagement could be avoided. With the British ship in pursuit, the *Protector* tacked and stood away to the S.E. As she ran off she raised United States colors. About that moment she sighted two more ships, one bearing N.W. and the other W. Both were making for her. If they were consorts of the British warship, the *Protector* was in a tight spot. The wind had risen to a light westerly breeze. At 3:00 p.m. Williams altered course more to the east to run directly before this breeze and set studding sails alow and aloft. Still the British frigate came on fast. Minutes before four o'clock the enemy warship made a series of four signals. Hearts sank in the *Protector*. Those signals must be instructions to the two ships that had been sighted two hours earlier, and that still seemed to be pursuing the *Protector*. Were three British frigates closing in on the lone Massachusetts ship?

By four o'clock, the British frigate had closed the gap between herself and the *Protector* to less than 1,800 yards. She opened fire with one of her bow guns. The *Protector* had already trundled two (or perhaps four) stern chasers into position and immediately returned the British fire. During the next four hours the two ships maintained the same relative positions, the *Protector* firing to cut the enemy's masts or rigging, the British frigate replying with her bow chasers. The *Protector*'s gunnery seemed the better: several of her shot cut her antagonist's rigging, tore holes in his sails, and one broke his foreyard.

At 8:00 p.m. the British ship was working up on the *Protector*'s quarter. But the advantage was shifting to the fleeing *Protector*. It was almost dark, and night would increase her chances for escape. The enemy commander decided to take a calculated risk. He hove to and fired three broadsides at the *Protector* as she continued to run dead to leeward, answering only with stern chasers. When the British frigate was again before the wind, the *Protector* had vanished in the darkness, her only damage from the three broadsides one 12-pound shot in her mainmast. At dawn, the *Protector* sighted the two ships that had appeared to be trailing her the previous afternoon, but they did not display any interest in the Massachusetts frigate. As for the *Protector*'s old antagonist, she was nowhere to be seen. Only later did the "Protectors" learn that their enemy was His Majesty's frigate *Thames*, 32. The two mystery ships never were identified.[14]

The *Protector* spent another week or so cruising off Nova Scotia, then ran along the Maine coast and anchored in Broad Bay* on 12 July. Captain Williams wanted to refill his water casks, clean the frigate's exceptionally foul bottom, and hand over her forty remaining prisoners to the local authorities.

In later years, when Edward Preble and Midshipman Luther Little, brother of George Little, were in a reminiscent mood about their Revolutionary War adventures, they used to relate an incident which they insisted really happened while the *Protector* was anchored in Broad Bay.[15] One afternoon someone saw a great black snake emerge from the underbrush opposite the *Protector*'s anchorage, enter the water, and swim past the frigate. Perhaps 40 feet long, thick as a man's body, and able to lift his head six feet out of the water; that was how Luther Little remembered the serpent. George Little told Midshipman Preble to take the ship's barge and follow the snake — an assignment huntsman Preble found congenial, if he did not suggest it himself. The boat's crew snatched up some arms and may have put a swivel in the barge, too. Off across the bay they went, Preble driving his oarsmen on and taking occasional shots at the serpent. At the sound of each shot, the snake submerged, and the boat was not fast enough to overtake it. When the serpent had been chased for perhaps a mile and

* Now Muscongus Bay.

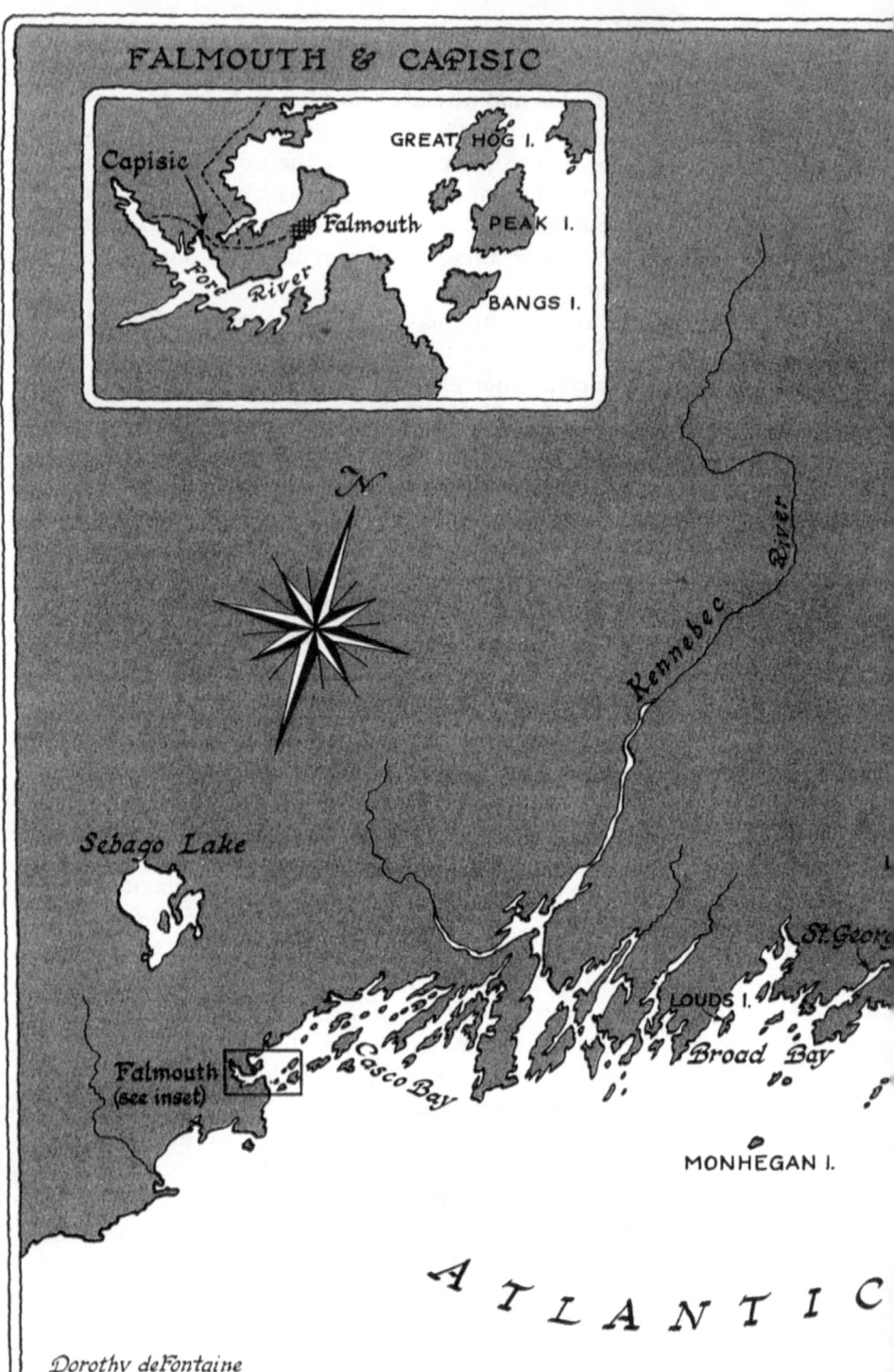

MAINE

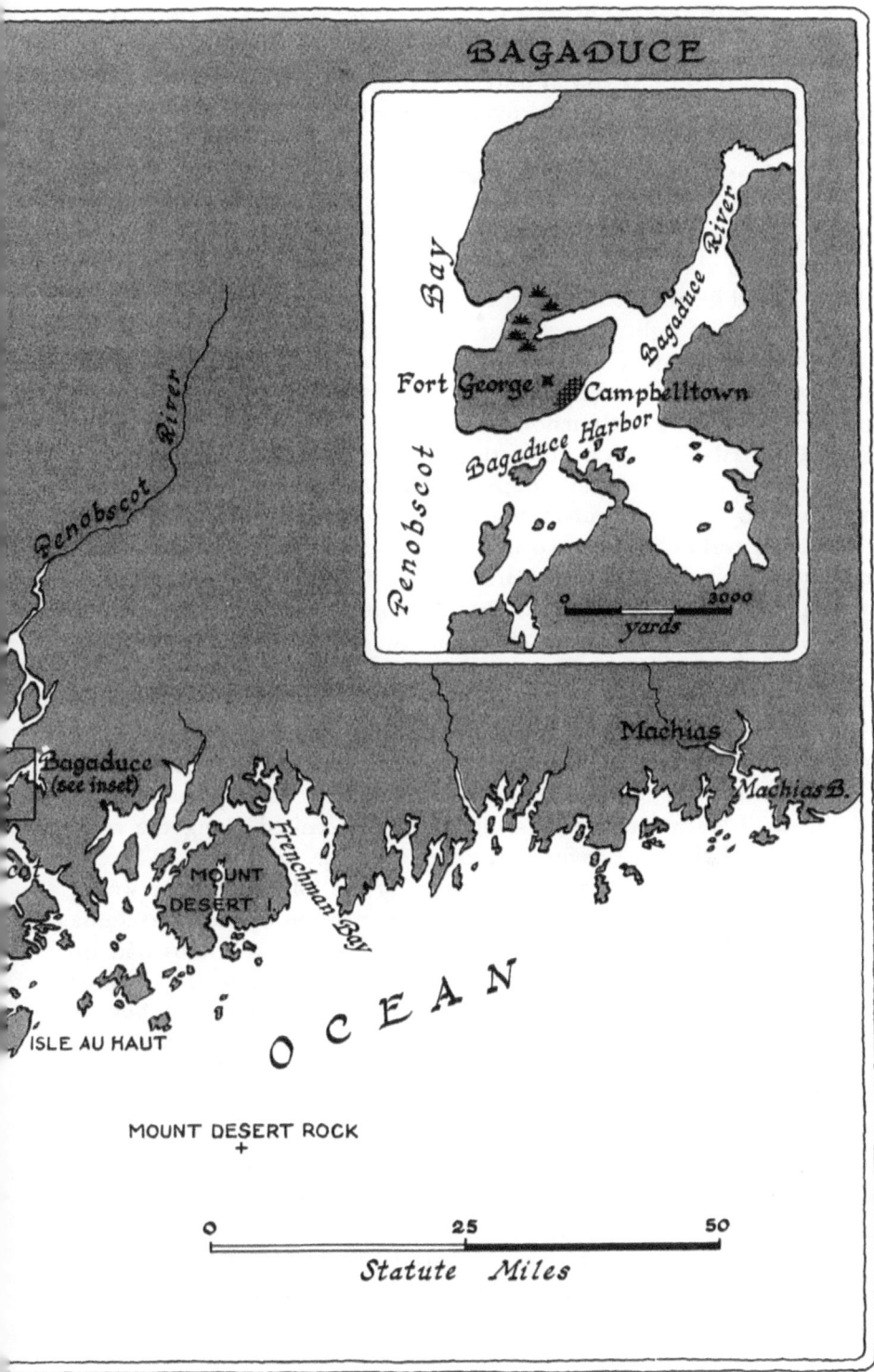

Places connected with Edward Preble's youth and the cruises of the *Protector* and the *Winthrop*

a half, it ran up on Louds Island and disappeared into the woods. Preble and his men returned disappointed to the ship with only the story to show for their efforts.

On 9 July, three days before the *Protector*'s arrival at Broad Bay, Captain Henry Mowat in the *Albany* emerged from his anchorage at Bagaduce to escort three small vessels to Lime Island in Penobscot Bay, where they were to load limestone for construction work at Fort George. While the little flotilla lay at Lime Island he armed and manned two small tenders from the *Albany* and sent them out on lightning raids against Maine's coasting trade. It was work for which small, swift vessels were much better adapted than the unhandy *Albany*: between 11 and 17 July each tender took three prizes.

Since the *Protector* lay at anchor in Broad Bay, about twenty-five miles away from Lime Island in an air line, the local magistrates pressed Williams to do something about Mowat's depredations. By 16 July Williams was making plans to sail the *Protector* and two 16-gun brigs, manned with troops from General Peleg Wadsworth's command, round to Penobscot Bay, get between Mowat's flotilla and Fort George, force an engagement, and capture or destroy the enemy craft. But for some reason, he did not act until 20 July. Too late. At ten o'clock on the morning of the 19th, the *Albany*, tenders, and prizes pulled away from Lime Island and returned to the security of Fort George. At Bagaduce Captain Mowat was not a little pleased with himself for having outfoxed John Foster Williams.

During the afternoon of 24 July the *Protector* appeared off Lunenburg, Nova Scotia, where she captured, and later released, a fishing boat. Then, causing no small alarm on shore as she went, she cruised along the coast as far as Halifax lighthouse before running off to the southward. There is little record of the *Protector*'s movements during the following three weeks, but the notable event of this period was a fresh eruption of the West India fever, picked up from the *Admiral Duff*, which Captain Williams had incorrectly assumed to be on the wane in late July. A doctor who examined the *Protector*'s crew when the frigate ended her summer patrol at Boston, 15 August 1780,[16] reported "that the ship *Protector* returned from her cruise perhaps the most sickly vessel that ever came into this port; the surgeon and his mate sick; scarce a man but what had a fever in some degree."

On the day the *Protector* entered Boston harbor Edward Preble celebrated his nineteenth birthday. Two days later, 17 August, the *Protector*'s officers and crew were formally discharged from the old roll and a new roll was begun. In spite of his youth, Preble had proved himself in John Foster Williams's eyes, and was entered in the new roll as a warranted midshipman in the navy of Massachusetts.

III

Not until mid-December did the *Protector* again sail out of Boston harbor, and when she did she had a second Preble among her young gentlemen: on 8 December 1780, Joshua Preble, already experienced as an officer in privateers, had joined the ship as an acting midshipman. The *Protector* was bound on a commerce-raiding expedition in company with the Massachusetts privateer *Deane*, Captain Elisha Hinman. The *Deane* must have been nearly equal to the *Protector* in size and armament, for she carried 30 guns and 210 men.[17] Apparently, the two ships cruised off the Newfoundland Banks for a spell, then bore away for the West Indies. On 11 February 1781 they were cruising 90 miles to windward of Antigua. Later they touched both at Martinique and at Port-au-Prince in Hispaniola. The *Deane* and the *Protector* captured no prizes near Newfoundland, but in the West Indies they took three: the sloop *Union*, a Dutch vessel in the care of an English prize crew; the brig *John*, bound from Ireland to the West Indies with a cargo of food and merchandise; and an unidentified sloop loaded with dry goods. As the *Protector* and the *Deane* ran up the American coast, homeward-bound, they bagged their biggest prize — the letter of marque ship *Polly*, twenty 9-pounders, bound from Charleston, South Carolina, to Jamaica and laden with rice, flour, and other foodstuffs.

The *Protector* and the *Deane* seem to have separated after the capture of the *Polly*. John Foster Williams entered the waters south of Long Island where, early in May, he took the 40-ton schooner *Sally*, loaded with rum. He put Joshua Preble in her as prize master and sent her off to Boston. His next prize was the 100-ton brig *Good Design*, with a cargo of Tenerife wine, which he seized during the afternoon of 4 May.[18] Midshipman Luther Little and a prize crew were sent to the *Good Design*.

Soon after daylight the following morning, when the *Good Design* was southwest of Block Island, one of Luther Little's prize crew came below to notify the master that two large ships were in sight to leeward, that is, to the northeastward. Glass in hand, Little went up into the rigging and saw that the two strangers were men-of-war. He looked to the southwest, and there was the *Protector*, unsuspectingly bearing down on the two unidentified warships. Then the *Protector* saw them. She hauled her wind to the south — but too late: the men-of-war had sighted the *Protector* and were spreading canvas in pursuit. As they passed within half a mile of the *Good Design*, Little could see that the strangers were frigates — but they ignored the brig and held their course in chase of the bigger game. Luther Little crossed the frigates' wakes and shaped a course for Boston. The last he saw of the *Protector* those two frigates were closing in on her. There was nothing he could do to help his brother and friends in the *Protector*. His duty was to make Boston and report the bad news to Governor John Hancock.

The two men-of-war that Midshipman Little had been watching were the British frigates *Roebuck*, 44, and *Medea*, 28. They had sailed from New York early on 3 May to reconnoiter the French squadron anchored off Newport, Rhode Island. At 5:00 a.m. on the 5th, they were south of Block Island when the *Medea* sighted a sail in the southwest. It was the *Good Design*. A fresh breeze was blowing from W.S.W., but the British frigates gave chase to windward. In less than two hours the *Protector* appeared over the southwestern horizon. At 1:30 p.m. the *Good Design* tacked and stood away to the eastward; the *Medea* and *Roebuck*, interested now exclusively in the *Protector*, let her sail away unchallenged. All through the day the British ships worked to the southwest, tacking against the southwesterly breeze, and steadily gaining ground on the fleeing *Protector*. By eight o'clock the *Medea* was only two miles from her, and the *Roebuck* some three miles behind the *Medea*. Night, which had befriended Williams in his escape from the *Thames*, failed him this time: he could not shake off his pursuers. Between 10:00 and 10:30 p.m., when the ships were about 60 miles southwestward from Block Island, the *Roebuck* fired a single shot. With hopeless odds against him, John Foster Williams struck his colors. Edward Preble and 179 other Massachusetts men became prisoners of war.[19]

Two days later the "Protectors," officers and men, found themselves in the notorious prison hulk *Jersey*. It looked as though Preble and his shipmates would have to adjust themselves to the prospect of months, perhaps years, of living under the most unsanitary conditions, eating inadequate, loathsome rations, being constantly threatened by disease, and with death claiming some of the *Jersey*'s prisoners each night. On 26 May Captain Williams succeeded in obtaining a ten-day permission for himself and the *Protector*'s surgeon, Thomas Leverett, to travel to Philadelphia and consult the Continental authorities about arranging an exchange for the imprisoned "Protectors." Williams found the Continental Board of Admiralty unsympathetic with the plight of men from the Massachusetts navy. From Philadelphia he wrote in dismay to the Massachusetts authorities: "I know not what we shall be exchanged for, as the Admiralty here says the State of Massachusetts has no right to give a commission, that they look on me as not a public or private officer." If the *Protector*'s company was going to be exchanged, the exchange would have to be arranged by Massachusetts. All Williams could do was go back to the *Jersey* and wait. Not surprisingly, some of the *Protector*'s sailors took the easiest route out of their hellhole by enlisting in the British Army or Navy.[20]

Edward Preble was luckier than his shipmates: he had already developed a knack for knowing the right people. William Tyng, a former sheriff of Cumberland County, Maine, was a Loyalist refugee in New York, and though he and Jedidiah Preble quarreled violently on political questions during the years immediately preceding the Revolution, the Preble and Tyng families had managed to remain on friendly terms. Tyng was an influential member of the Loyalist community at New York, and through his good offices Edward Preble was given permission to live ashore while he was waiting to be exchanged. Midshipman Preble wrote the good news to his father, who replied:

Falmouth, July 11th 1781.
Dear Child:

I recd your favour with grate Pleasure & Sattisfection to find you met with so much kindness & Frindship from Coll. Ting & Lady. Have wrot him my acknowledgments on the Subjects, & hope your futer Conduct will be Such as to render you in Sume measure worthy their further notis. As you are admited on Shore, A favour denied all the officers of the Ship, never Stain your Honr. by attempting to make your escape. I Shall do every thing, & persue every measure, that afords the least Prospect of Success to get you exchangd. in a justifyable way. Present your Mamas & my Best Compliments to Coll. Ting and Lady, & let them know Madom Ross [Mrs. Tyng's mother] was in good health yesterday. Be allways on your guard agains Temptations or giveing the least occation to any that has Shuen you favour to charge you with a breach of trust. Be kind & obligeing to all, for no man ever dose a designed injury to an other, with out doing a grater to himself. Let Reason allways govern your Thoughts & actions. Be sure write me all oppertunetys. Your mama, Brothers & Sisters joyn me in presenting their Love to you & wishing you A Speedy exchange. I am your ready Frind & affect. Father,

JEDIDIAH PREBLE[21]

Father's letter probably did not have time to reach Edward at New York. With General Preble exerting his influence at Boston and Tyng working in New York, Edward was soon on his way home. According to Massachusetts records, he was officially exchanged and discharged from the *Protector*'s roll on 24 July 1781. By the 26th, he was in Boston. Edward Preble was a privileged and fortunate young man: a year later many of his shipmates—some of them men whose years of service to Massachusetts made them worthier of prompt exchange than he was—were still in captivity.

IV

In size, in prestige, and in the excitement of the events in which she participated, the *Protector* had been the apogee of the Massachusetts state navy. However, no ship in that service was more successful in fulfilling her mission than the sloop *Winthrop*, 12, which Massachusetts fitted out during the early months of 1782.[22]

On 5 February, even before a captain had been chosen for the new sloop, Edward Preble secured the lieutenant's berth in the *Winthrop*. When a captain was appointed a month later, he turned out to be the *Protector*'s old first lieutenant, George Little. Preble and George Little made an unusually effective team. In a ship as small as the *Winthrop* they were constantly together: had they not been congenial they would soon have grown to detest one another. Though there was some difference in their ages — Little was 28 and Preble nearly 21 — they became the closest of friends.*

Governor Hancock sent the *Winthrop* out on her first cruise about 24 June 1782, in company with the Commonwealth ship *Tartar*, Captain John Cathcart. Cathcart, being the senior captain, was in command. Hancock instructed the two captains to cruise for from six to ten days in Massachusetts Bay "in quest of any vessels, not superior to you in force, that have interrupted the commerce of the merchants in Boston"; and to make a particular effort to sink or capture an annoying 16-gun vessel, apparently a privateer, known as "the Bermuda brigantine." When the *Winthrop* and *Tartar* reappeared in Boston harbor only a couple of days after they had sailed, Captain Cathcart reported that they had been forced in by the arrival in Massachusetts Bay of a 50-gun British warship. Little and, more particularly, Cathcart had to suffer the sting of derision when their "50-gun British warship" was ascertained to be an 18-gun sloop of war, probably the *Allegiance,* Commander David Phips. The laughter might just as appropriately have been aimed at John Hancock, since he had emphatically instructed Cathcart: "You are to be particularly careful not to put yourself in the way of a superior force; and should you find a force superior to you in the bay, you are immediately to return . . . into port."[23]

The *Winthrop* did not again go out with the *Tartar* but was next sent to the Maine coast. She was needed there. The big battles had ended at Yorktown the previous October, but while the negotiators slowly worked out a settlement in Paris the war went on, small and dirty, in Maine waters. The focus of the war in Maine was still Bagaduce with its garrisoned stronghold, Fort George, and the Loyalist settlement called Campbelltown. All year, except when the Penobscot and Bagaduce rivers froze over, Loyalist traders were hauling lumber to the West Indies and Bermuda. Of more immediate concern were the Loyalist privateers and whaleboats that operated out of Penobscot Bay.

Three-quarters of the Maine residents who lived to the east of Falmouth lived on the seacoast, the bays, and the navigable rivers. Before the war their support had come principally from supplying lumber and firewood

* George and Rachel Little named their son, born in 1791, Edward Preble.

to Boston and other towns to the west and south, from the sale of masts and spars abroad, and from fishing. In those prewar years there had been relatively little cultivation of the land — partly, at least, because of the infertility of the soil — and even in the best harvest years the seacoast towns had not raised more than one-half of the food they ate. The remainder was hauled in.

Their nearness to the seacoast made these people — particularly those who were loyal to the United States — vulnerable to raiders from Bagaduce. Homes were burned. Houses were robbed of arms, ammunition, provisions, clothing. Cattle and sheep were killed or carried off. Loyalist cruisers captured the lumber coasters, the fishing boats, and even the canoes of the inhabitants of the seaboard settlements. Before the Revolution, Falmouth had employed 40 vessels in West Indian and other foreign trade. By spring of 1782 her fleet had been reduced to one ship, one brig, three or four coasters, and a handful of fishing boats.

Because of the absence of naval protection for the coasters, masts, spars, lumber, and firewood lay rotting on the landings. It was imperative that protection be provided so that these cargoes might reach their markets: attempts by the people of Maine to turn more to agriculture for support had failed. A severe drought in the summer of 1781 further reduced the region's normally scanty crops. Swarms of worms attacked some of what did survive. And — that inevitable result of a dry summer — forest fires ravaged certain towns. All of this was culminating in a political crisis. Many of the region's people were not sufficiently committed to the Continental cause to be willing to suffer endlessly for it. They did the natural thing: they took the oath of allegiance to the British government and traded with Bagaduce to secure what they needed in order to live. By the summer of 1782, perhaps a majority of the inhabitants of Lincoln County favored the British government, and an index of these changed sympathies was the ability of the Loyalists to obtain decisions against Massachusetts state officials in the county courts.

Little's sailing orders, dated 8 July, instructed him first to convoy three state storeships up the coast to Maine: the sloop *Roxbury*, bound for the Kennebec, a schooner bound to Machias, and a third vessel, going to Frenchman Bay. After seeing his convoy safe to their destinations, Little was to "proceed to cruise along the eastern shore and such other parts as you shall judge most conducive to answer the principal object of your cruise: the protection of the seacoast." Whenever a number of coasting vessels were loaded and ready to make the run to Boston, he was to convoy them. "Bring your vessel to anchor in the road below," Hancock told Little, "and come up to town in your boat that I may have notice of your arrival and be made acquainted with the occurrences of your cruise." The governor's concern for the safety of the state's armed vessels was, if anything, stronger than before: "You will be particularly careful not to fall in the way of a superior force, but avoid as much as possible even the hazard of being captured." The *Winthrop* was expected to remain out four weeks at most.

Little had learned a lesson from his cruise with the *Tartar* and chose to ignore Hancock's hypercaution. When the *Winthrop* returned to Boston on 4 August her captain had made a good start on regaining any part of his reputation he might have lost in June: the *Winthrop* had three prizes with her. One was the 180-ton ship *Defiance*, commanded by James Blackie; another, the 90-ton brig *Isabella*, John Jeffry, master. No details are known about the capture of either, but the third prize was more interesting: she was the *Swallow*, Captain John Tibbets, a privateer sloop with five guns and a crew of twenty. Not long after she sailed from her home port of Portsmouth, New Hampshire, members of her crew with Loyalist sympathies mutinied, confined Captain Tibbets and the sailors who remained faithful to him, and were making for sanctuary at Bagaduce when justice, in the form of the *Winthrop*, caught up with them in an arm of the sea on the Maine coast.

There had been more to the *Winthrop*'s cruise than chases and captures. A macabre hour had been spent on 17 July when a hull was sighted floating keel-up about one mile from Mount Desert Rock. George Little, Lemuel White, the *Winthrop*'s prize master, and John Curtis, her pilot, scrambled aboard the derelict and chopped holes through her bottom with axes. There was no sign of life inside the hull. All that could be seen was lumber. By the wreck's large false keel and a distinctive patch on her bottom, Little recognized her as the schooner *Liverpool*, David Allen, master, which had sailed from Boston for Martinique on 27 February. The next day a winter storm had swept the coast; neither the *Liverpool* nor any man aboard her had been heard from since.[24]

With orders, dated 8 August, almost identical to those she had been given a month earlier, the *Winthrop* was soon on her way back to Maine. This time there were no state storeships to be shepherded up the coast, and she was to remain on station as long as her provisions held out. It was probably during this cruise that Captain Little persuaded Edward Preble's 40-year-old half-brother, John, to join the *Winthrop* in the capacity of "Eastern Pilot." John – who was an interpreter of Maine's Indian dialects as well as a coasting pilot – had spent most of the war as an officer with the state garrison around Machias. However, he had punctuated his land duty with tours as pilot in the Massachusetts state sloop *Defence* and in the Commonwealth ship *Mars*.

In the early weeks of her cruise, the *Winthrop* took a 50-ton privateer schooner, the *Hammond*, and recaptured a schooner that was prize to the *Hammond*. But on the morning of 11 September she sighted a bigger and more tempting prize: the privateer brig *Merriam*, Captain Richard Pomroy. The *Merriam*, a vessel of 120 tons with sixteen gunports, seeing herself chased, ran up Penobscot Bay towards Bagaduce with the *Winthrop* in hot pursuit. Then, to the chagrin and anger of the "Winthrops," one of those notorious Penobscot fogs came sifting in and the *Merriam* vanished in the damp, gray world in which nothing could be seen but the small circle of water immediately surrounding the *Winthrop*. Muttered oaths on board the *Winthrop* slacked off a bit when, as she came out of the bay that afternoon, she recaptured the sloop *Ceres*, a 100-ton Salem merchantman that the *Merriam* had taken a few days earlier. But Little and Edward Preble were not satisfied with the *Ceres*. They were bound they would catch the *Merriam*. During the late afternoon they worked out their plans. Forty men from the *Winthrop*'s crew were detailed as a boarding party under Preble's command. In the September twilight the *Winthrop* stood up Penobscot Bay towards Bagaduce.

Apparently the fog had lifted, and before darkness closed off visibility, the *Merriam* was spotted at anchor in the Bagaduce above Fort George, but under cover of the fort's cannon. Captain Little guided his ship towards her. It was dark when a lookout on the *Merriam* sighted the *Winthrop* close aboard and bearing down, and, perhaps mistaking her for the *Ceres* or another Bagaduce privateer, shouted out in warning:

"You will run aboard!"

"I am coming aboard," Little's strong voice boomed out in reply, and he ran the *Winthrop* alongside the *Merriam*.

"Boarders away!" ordered Preble as the bulwarks touched. His men began leaping into the *Merriam*. But the *Winthrop* had needed to make a rapid approach and still had so much way on that only Preble and fourteen of his boarding party had time to leap as she slid past the *Merriam*.

"Will you not have more men?" Little called to Preble as he maneuvered to get back alongside the *Merriam*.

The "Merriams" were confused — even panicked. Splashes on the far side of the brig announced that some of them were already abandoning ship. Preble kept cool: to reveal the weakness of his boarding party might encourage a rally.

"No," he shouted back to Little. "We have more than we want. We stand in each other's way."

Some of the *Merriam*'s crew were caught in their berths below, where Preble appeared, pistols in hand, and announced that all were prisoners.

Resistance was vain. He would kill any man who attempted it. Although it took only minutes to secure the prize, cannon and muskets opened fire from Fort George and the adjacent shore before Preble and his men could get her under way. The *Winthrop* maneuvered into position to answer the fire, then covered the *Merriam* as she stood out to sea.[25]

Captain Little brought the *Winthrop* in to Boston on 16 September and there she lay until late September or early October, when she departed on her third cruise to Maine, a cruise which lasted till near the end of November. The *Winthrop* was still a lucky ship. She recaptured the schooner *Darby*, with a lading of salt, thus netting the "Winthrops" some salvage money, and took a small privateer schooner, armed with seven 2-pounders and commanded by Loyalist Zebedee Hammond.

The latter capture shows the kind of police work in which the *Winthrop* was involved. Hammond and his men escaped from the schooner before the "Winthrops" took possession. But in the schooner Little and Preble found clothing that had been plundered from local residents who were faithful to the United States. Little then got in touch with some of the Loyalist leaders in Campbelltown — they came alongside the *Winthrop* in an open boat — showed them the stolen clothing, and said Hammond was a thief. Social pressure from these Loyalist worthies forced Hammond to investigate what his crew had been doing, while he, perhaps, had looked the other way. He then sent word to Captain Little that he could find only one plunderer among his men: a young fellow, just twenty-one, named John Daylie. Daylie had sold his share of the prize money before the schooner sailed from the Bagaduce; the only chance he stood to make anything was by covert plunder. Hammond discovered that Daylie had stolen goods from the family of one Saunders Jamisen and he tried to get the boy to make restitution. Daylie refused, whereupon Hammond sent Jamisen four guineas, and later did succeed in making Daylie return the stolen things as well.

Soon George Little learned that Richard Pomroy, captain of the *Merriam*, was already back in business and had to be silenced all over again. On 31 October the *Winthrop* sighted a former Salem privateer, the schooner *Viper*, which Pomroy had captured earlier in the month and of which he had taken command. The *Winthrop* trapped the *Viper* in shallow water, and Pomroy scuttled her. That nine-lived privateersman then escaped into the woods, eluding the landing party that Little sent to chase him. Perhaps Pomroy and his men simply concealed themselves on some nearby point of land from which they had the bittersweet satisfaction of watching the *Winthrop* men struggle in the cold October ocean to restore the *Viper*'s watertight integrity and get her afloat again.[26]

V

"First part employed getting on board stores and unmooring. Got all hands on board. At 2 a.m. got under way. At 4 a.m. got out by the lighthouse." The northwest wind was working up to a fresh gale, but the sky was clear. This was Saturday, 28 December 1782, and the *Winthrop* was setting sail from Boston on what was to be the last cruise of the Massachusetts state navy.

It is ironic that the final weeks of the Commonwealth navy are among the better-recorded periods in its short history: the *Winthrop*'s log for this cruise survives — large folios of heavy rag paper sewn into a piece of age-browned sailcloth — scarcely examined since the day George Little delivered it to Governor Hancock.[27] This log makes it possible to build a narrative of typical day-by-day operations of one of the Massachusetts navy's most active cruisers.

When the log begins, 4 December 1782, the *Winthrop* was lying in Boston harbor refitting for her cruise. A light rain was falling, and four hands were at work breaking up the hold. On succeeding days the hold was cleared out, the ballast washed, three loads of firewood were brought on board, and water casks were stowed below. At Gardner's Wharf, where the *Winthrop* was transferred on 10 December, her bottom was graved. This operation involved burning off the accretions that were fouling her hull and spreading on a fresh coating of a composition of sulphur, tallow, and resin. When her bottom had been restored, her lower sides were boot topped. Boot topping was done to the planks between the ship's light water line and her load water line: it was much the same as graving, save that the accumulated filth was scraped, rather than burned, off. Then the upper portions of the *Winthrop*'s sides were painted. While the exterior of her hull was getting all this refurbishing, thousands of pounds of bread, as well as barrels of beef, of pork, and of rum were trucked and lightered alongside for hoisting into her hold.

Edward Preble missed a lot of this preparatory ritual. He was on leave in the early part of the month, getting home to Falmouth on 1 December.[28] By the 23rd, though, he had returned to duty and the log interrupts its routine record of sails being bent and rum being received on board to note: "At 9 p.m. Mr. Preble unfortunately, as he was going to his cabin, fired off two pistols; shot one ball through his hand."

The key sentences in Governor Hancock's cruising orders for the *Winthrop*, dated 27 December, were:

> You will take under your convoy any vessels that are ready and bound to the eastward, which vessels you are hereby ordered to see safe to their several

destined ports. As soon as you have complied with your orders as to your convoy and have discharged yourself from them, you will then proceed to cruise off the island of Bermuda, and, if you shall not be so fortunate as to capture any vessels of the enemy after cruising upon that coast for three weeks, you may proceed to the West Indies and continue your cruise for two months or as long as your provisions will admit of, when you will return to the eastern shore and cruise along said shore and such other parts as you shall judge most conducive to answer the principal object of your cruise: the protection of the seacoast to Boston.

Hancock's dispatch of the *Winthrop* to Bermuda and the West Indies illustrates a divergence on maritime strategy between the governor and the House of Representatives. Of the two, the House was inclined to be more sensitive to the need for coastal patrols. On 12 November it had resolved that the governor be requested to keep the *Winthrop* cruising off the Massachusetts coast, for the protection of trade, as late in the season as weather would allow. Hancock answered that the *Winthrop* had already eliminated most of the privateers based on Penobscot Bay, and that the remaining ones could not keep the sea on the Maine coast during the winter any more than the *Winthrop* could. Moreover, Little's influential friends had been pressing the governor to let the *Winthrop* make a cruise in waters where there was an opportunity for richer prizes than could be caught off Maine. Hancock acceded to the pressure in the hope that prize money earned in the West Indies would boost the morale of officers and men in the *Winthrop* and provide income for the state treasury.[29] He may have inserted the order to provide convoy up the coast to Maine in order to placate the legislators, for the *Winthrop* did not go anywhere near Maine, but immediately ran E. by S. from Boston.

As might be expected on the ocean in winter, the *Winthrop* encountered heavy gales and heavy seas, squalls of rain and snow. She had to reduce sail; her flying jibboom pitched away; one of her anchors and some of her guns were struck below in the hold to increase seaworthiness, as waves began breaking over the sloop. "At 4 p.m. [6 January 1783] shipped a sea knocked us upon our beam-ends; split our mainsail from the balance up to the head. Righted our helm and got her before the wind." As this rugged January sea abated, the *Winthrop*'s provisions became a source of anxiety. Waves washing over the sloop and leaking scuppers had thoroughly dampened her store of bread. On two occasions, when skies cleared and the wind dropped to a moderate breeze, the *Winthrop*'s bread had to be gotten up on deck to dry. Most of it was salvaged, but 400 pounds, "entirely ruined," had to be pitched overboard.

George Little chased everything he saw. His boldness sometimes placed the *Winthrop* in what might, for a few hours, have appeared to be sticky situations. But he knew his ship's sailing qualities, and he never crossed the line that would have turned audacity into foolhardiness.

The "Winthrops" were setting up the rigging and mending the sloop's mainsail when, at 4:00 p.m., 13 January, lookouts sighted a strange sail bearing S.W. As quickly as the work could be secured Little gave chase and, shortly before 6:00 p.m., ran to within less than a mile of the stranger, then hauled his wind to stay just out of range of her guns. The stranger hoisted her colors — in the deepening darkness they could scarcely be distinguished — fired a shot at the *Winthrop*, then altered course in pursuit of her. Captain Little had no difficulty in staying beyond the enemy's shots without losing sight of her. "Dogged her all night. At daylight [14 January] run down within gunshot. Showed our colors. She gave us two guns. We returned them. Saw she was too heavy for us. She was a ship of 26 guns. Wear ship head to the southward. Left her standing N.N.E." With a top sustained speed of 11 knots and a normal cruising speed in the range of 4 to 7 knots, the *Winthrop* was so swift that few heavy ships had much enthusiasm for trying to chase her.

Little chose to ignore Hancock's order that he cruise for three weeks off Bermuda. He limited himself to passing by the island on his way to the West Indies. Antigua, the first West Indian island sighted, appeared on the southwestern horizon at 10:00 a.m. on 25 January. At eight o'clock the following morning, Antigua bearing W.N.W., a sail was sighted to the eastward of the *Winthrop*. The stranger was running before the wind on a course that would carry her across the *Winthrop*'s bow. "Down all sail and lay ahull. At 9 a.m. she hauled her wind to the southward. Made all sail and hauled up after her." During the afternoon, the *Winthrop* gradually closed on the stranger, by then identified as a brig, but at dark George Little lost her. At nine o'clock on the morning of the 27th the brig was sighted under the *Winthrop*'s lee, that is, to westward. "Set all sail" was the order in the *Winthrop*. An hour later a ship and a sloop came over the western horizon, and the brig altered course for them. Hoisting British colors, the *Winthrop* fired two shot to leeward. The brig, too, showed British colors and discharged one gun to leeward — the traditional signal that true identity had been revealed — but she refused to be taken in by the *Winthrop*'s deception: she kept running towards the ship and the sloop. When the *Winthrop* closed to within three miles of the ship and the sloop, Little could see that they were both cruising vessels. He hauled his wind to the eastward. Ship and sloop came after the *Winthrop*, but again her good sailing saved her. The pursuing sloop soon gave up the chase; at 5:00 p.m. the ship also abandoned it.

One potential prize — a merchant sloop — escaped from the *Winthrop* during the morning of 29 January by getting in under the protection of a fort on the island of Barbuda, and late that same day darkness helped another — a brig — elude the Massachusetts warship, but on 30 January at 8:00 a.m., after a three-hour chase, the *Winthrop* finally made a capture. Her prize was a schooner bound from Antigua to St. Lucia with a cargo of lumber. The schooner's crew was transferred to the *Winthrop*; Prize Master Mayhew Allen and four hands were put into the lumber ship; and Captain Little ordered Allen to get the prize in to Montserrat. The schooner secured, the *Winthrop* "made five ships ahead, standing to the northward. Hove about to the northward. Made a brig ahead. Set all sail after her. . . . [Early afternoon:] Coming up with our chase very fast. At 4 p.m. got within gunshot. Fired several shot at her. She hove to. At 5 p.m. spoke with her. She hailed from St. Augustine, bound to Antigua. Sent our boat on board. Took the prisoners out, and put Mr. Preble on board and six hands. Sent her to St. Kitts."

While Mayhew Allen and Edward Preble were taking their prizes in to the French-occupied islands of Montserrat and St. Christopher, the *Winthrop* — not yet satiated — continued her cruising, but without success. On the second day of February she joined Preble at St. Christopher. George Little sold his two prizes and supervised urgent repairs to his ship before clearing the island, 11 February 1783, for the return passage to New England. On the evening of the 26th, the *Winthrop* got soundings on Georges Bank and was immediately greeted by a heavy gale that brought snow squalls racing across the sea to sting the faces of the men standing first watch. And that was a mild prelude to what the *Winthrop* went through before she anchored at Boston. Mount Desert was sighted bearing north, 36 miles, at 7:00 a.m. on 1 March. The sky wore the look of a storm approaching from the southwest. George Little shaped a course for Isle au Haut, and Pilot John Preble guided the *Winthrop* to anchor under the shelter of the island just as the storm broke. She lay in this secure anchorage two days, dispatching parties to the shore for firewood and setting up the rigging. On 3 March the sloop went up Penobscot Bay far enough to get a look at Fort George, then dropped back down to Owls Head harbor, where she took shelter for the night. The next morning, 4 March, pushed along by "a fine breeze at north," she began a brisk day's run down to Casco Bay.

In getting from Casco Bay to Boston the *Winthrop* caught one of the worst storms of her entire winter cruise. She sailed at midmorning, 9 March, and almost instantly was struck by a fresh gale from the westward. By afternoon the storm had built up to a heavy gale. Nevertheless, 10:00 p.m. found the sloop as far down the coast as Thacher Island, off Cape Ann.

There the northwest gale was so severe that she hove to under bare poles. By 11:00 a.m. on the 10th, Cape Cod was in sight to the S.E., but not until 6:00 p.m. did the *Winthrop* succeed in reaching shelter "under the highlands of the Cape, our decks full of ice, our people jaded out, most of them frost-nipped." The storm slacked off about 6:00 a.m. on 11 March, though a fresh breeze continued to blow from W.S.W. The *Winthrop* spent the next sixteen hours working across Cape Cod Bay to an anchorage under the highlands of Marshfield. At 4:00 a.m. on 12 March she once more got under sail, but the wind, "chopping round at N.W.," shut her off from Boston, so she ran down to Plymouth harbor and dropped anchor there in a fresh N.W. gale. Finally, 13 March, the weather turned fair. A pleasant breeze was blowing from the south. With all sail spread, the *Winthrop* made the run from Plymouth to a berth off Long Wharf, Boston, in eight hours.

In the early hours of the 15th, the state government began the routine of refitting the *Winthrop* for still another cruise: overhauling rigging and sails, caulking decks, breaking up and restowing her hold, graving her bottom, paying off her crew, re-enlisting and drilling them. The government plan was to send her back to her old patrolling station on the Maine coast, where the inhabitants were once more demanding protection.[30] From 30 March till 8 April she sailed about inside Boston harbor. But the *Winthrop* would never again pass the lighthouse outward-bound as a warship. On 29 March an express from Philadelphia brought the Massachusetts government word that preliminary articles of peace had been signed at Paris. This message was followed by an order from Robert Morris, Continental Agent of Marine, recalling all vessels cruising under commissions from the United States of America.

The independence of the United States — for which George Little, Edward Preble, and their shipmates had fought right down to the last day of the war — was complete. "Friday [April] the 11. This day fine weather," says the last entry in the *Winthrop*'s log. "Hauled into the wharf. Took out our guns. Unbent our sails; sent them to the sailmaker's. Unrove our running rigging. Discharged all hands."

On 4 June 1783 the General Court voted to sell the *Winthrop* at public auction.

CHAPTER 2   NOVEMBER 1785–NOVEMBER 1798

"... I sold the little wreck which had brought us miraculously over the Atlantic Ocean...."

With the return of peace and the disbanding of the Massachusetts state navy, Edward Preble and most of his companions in the Massachusetts service joined the state's merchant marine.

There are few records on which to base the story of Preble's sixteen years in merchantmen. Only a handful of his letters and accounts for the years before 1799 remains. No diary or journal has been found that antedates 1796, the year in which he reached the age of thirty-five.[1] The earliest record of Preble's activities in the postwar years is dated November 1785, when he commanded a 60-ton, Kennebec-built schooner named *William* trading between Boston and the harbors along the Maine coast, and occasionally making runs to Halifax, Nova Scotia. The *William*'s home port seems to have been the Kennebec River.[2] Late in 1786 she made a voyage to Halifax and got back to Boston in mid-December — at the height of Shays's Rebellion in western Massachusetts. The next time the *William* cleared Boston — early February 1787, with a cargo of herring, cheese, and salt below hatches — she was bound to Edenton, headquarters of North Carolina's Port Roanoke customs district: Preble was leaving New England and moving to North Carolina. Why he went south is not known for certain. But it is probable that the intense economic depression that struck the maritime industries of Massachusetts after the Revolution, culminating with Shays's insurrection and an apparent threat of anarchy, convinced him that he would have better opportunities to make his fortune in the South, where coastal and foreign trade was booming.

At Edenton Preble went to work for Josiah Collins, Sr., a local shipowner and businessman, and he worked hard. During his first eighteen months as a Collins shipmaster he made four voyages to the West Indies.[3] On the first of these, he cleared for St. Croix, 22 March 1787, in the *William* with a cargo of lumber, hogshead staves, shingles, and barrels of fish. It may be that his ship was sold in the West Indies during this voyage, for there is no record of her return to Edenton. When Edward Preble next appears in the Port Roanoke records, it is as master of the 60-ton schooner *Elizabeth*, built in North Carolina and owned by Collins. Preble's *Elizabeth* sailed in late August 1787 with a declared destination of Tobago. But once Preble arrived in the Caribbean he may have found a better market at St. Croix, since it was from there that he brought a cargo of molasses, rum, coffee, and brown sugar in to Edenton on 29 November.

Josiah Collins's instructions to Preble for his third run to the Antilles have survived. They bear the superscription "Edenton, 9 January" and were delivered to Preble the next day at nearby Hertford, on the Perquimans River, where the *Elizabeth* was taking in her cargo of lumber and shingles for Collins's account and rice for the account of one Lawrence Baker. Collins directed his captain to sail to Martinique and, on arrival there, inquire about local markets and about those in such of the Leeward Islands as permitted U.S. ships to trade with them. "If you find that a greater price, or even as much, can be obtained for the cargo at Martinico [as] at any other of the islands mentioned, you are to dispose of it there [Martinique] to the best advantage; if not, to go where the best price can be got; provided, after estimating the expenses that will accrue in consequence of going from your destined port to another and the difference in the price of such produce as you are [to] be directed to lay in as a return cargo, you conceive it will be for the interest of the voyage." Proceeds from his sales and the specie he was carrying were to be invested in molasses and coffee. Unless Baker had given Preble different instructions, the money realized from the sale of the rice ought to be put into brown sugar.

To judge by Josiah Collins's instructions, the *Elizabeth* must have been old and decaying, for they dwelt at length on the dangers of overloading her. She should not be subjected to the strain of carrying a deck load, and if a cargo of sugar and coffee should prove to be bulkier than one made up entirely of molasses, then molasses alone must be purchased for the return cargo.

The meticulous shipowner ended with some old-fashioned advice for his young protégé: "I request you will be careful of your vessel and stores, frugal in your expenses, and to make all the dispatch in your power back to this port. Those things being attended to, you will probably make a saving voyage; but a contrary conduct will make it quite the reverse."

No sooner had the *Elizabeth* returned from Martinique on 7 April 1788 with a cargo of coffee, molasses, brown sugar, and gin, than Josiah Collins began loading her for another voyage to Martinique. She sailed down Albemarle Sound about 27 May, but before she had gone far something serious must have happened to her, because on 19 June Edward Preble was setting out from Edenton again, bound for the West Indies in Collins's 80-ton brig *Alliance*, and carrying naval stores, barrel staves, tobacco, and black walnut logs.

After this, Preble's fourth trip to the Caribbean, Josiah Collins decided to try a new market and on 1 December 1788 dispatched the *Alliance* to Lisbon, Portugal, with naval stores, pipe staves, barrel staves, corn, pork, and beeswax. When the brig returned from Lisbon in April 1789, she brought salt, white wine, madeira, hyson tea, gunpowder tea, and "sundry goods, cost £24." The records of this voyage show that the *Alliance* had been built in North Carolina, was manned by six hands in addition to Captain Preble, and carried no guns.

Collins did not attempt to repeat his European venture, but immediately put Preble back to work in the West India trade and decided to accompany him as a passenger. The *Alliance* sailed for Cap-Français, Hispaniola, on 19 May 1789, and in July returned to Edenton with a lading of molasses. Barely a month later, Preble was once again outward-bound for Hispaniola.

There is no record of Preble's return from that voyage. In fact, after the U.S. custom house was established at Edenton in 1790 — reflecting the change of control over foreign and interstate commerce from the state authorities to the new federal government — his name appears in the customs' entries only once, and that is on 3 August 1790, when he paid tonnage duties on the 31-ton coasting sloop *Hannah*. As late as April 1791 letters addressed to Edward Preble were waiting to be picked up at the Edenton post office, indicating that he was still in the area. But by then his years in North Carolina were coming to an end.

II

Newburyport was — after Portland and Boston — the Massachusetts town with which Edward Preble had the closest bonds. Dummer School was less than five miles away in South Byfield. Joshua Preble married a Newburyport girl, Hannah Cross. And it was there that Edward found his first employment after his return from Carolina.

While Preble was sailing in and out of Albemarle Sound, the state of Massachusetts was making a dramatic economic recovery, and it was probably the promise of future growth that pulled him back from the South. To no Newburyporters had returning prosperity brought more good things than to William Bartlet and Moses Brown. They had become the town's richest citizens. It was in command of Bartlet's and Brown's vessel, the *Polly*, that Preble sailed down the Merrimack and out past Plum Island about 4 October 1791. Although the *Polly* was rigged as a brigantine, her register identified her as having been built in 1785 as a schooner; it also recorded that she was 58 feet 3 inches long and 17 feet 1 inch in the beam. Her hold was 7 feet 8 inches deep, and into this small area was packed a heavy load of New England rum, chocolate, coffee, leaf tobacco, pigtail tobacco, twisted tobacco, 150 handspikes, 65 oars, two six-inch hawsers, and six anchors. Preble was bound "to the Coast of Guinea on a trading voyage" during which he was pledged to dispose of his cargo "to the best advantage and return them [his owners] the net proceed."

In his sixteen years of merchant voyaging this is the only time Preble visited a part of the world that could be called even mildly exotic or out of the ordinary. Most of his work in merchantmen took him to the ports and coasts commonly frequented by run-of-the-mill American shipmasters in the 1790s. Although some of his fellow New Englanders were making voyages up the Baltic to St. Petersburg to develop trade with Russia, or exploring the Northwest Coast, or making year-and-a-half trips to China, no desire for adventure tempted him to join these pioneers.

Perhaps his visit to Africa cooled his adventurous tendencies. Later in life, he said the venture in the *Polly* was a financial disaster because he refused, on grounds of conscience, to invest the proceeds from the sales of his outward cargo in slaves. Did he mean that Bartlet and Brown encouraged him to buy slaves and he declined? Or did he mean that he saw other New England masters insuring themselves a handsome profit by taking on slaves in the Gulf of Guinea, while he stuck to legitimate trade? It is not clear. But even if his conscience had allowed him to join the slave trade, the law of Massachusetts would not: an act passed by the General Court in 1788 made it illegal for shipowners from that state to engage in slaving. Nevertheless, some Massachusetts shipmasters and merchants openly defied the anti-slaving law; others did so covertly.

Whether because it was immoral or because it was illegal, slaving was a business in which Preble did not intend to dirty his hands. After stops at St. Croix and New York City, he was, by 31 July 1792, back at Newburyport, settling accounts with his owners. When the countinghouse clerks had added up all the credits from the sales of the *Polly*'s outward cargo and subtracted all the debits — Preble's commissions, money invested in return cargo, the *Polly*'s expenses en route — there was owing to Messrs. William Bartlet and Moses Brown the sum of £5 14s 3d.[4]

III

As 1792 came to a close, Edward Preble, who had reached the age of thirty-one in August of that year, was preparing for the first of three voyages to Spain and France for which enough records exist to give an idea of the trading and business details which engaged him during his career as a merchant captain and supercargo.

In mid-November 1792 an advertisement appeared in Boston's *Columbian Centinel:*

> FOR SALE for cash or approved credit (as she lately arrived from London) the American-built ship NEPTUNE, burthened about 240 tons, excellently calculated for freighting or the East India trade, being very burthensome, strong, well-built, and a good sailer. For inventory and conditions of sale, apply at No. 32 State Street, Boston.

For several weeks it looked as if there would be no takers, and the *Neptune*'s owner had given up hope of selling her, when, in late December, Mathew Bridge of Charlestown and Crowell Hatch of Roxbury bought the vessel and hired Edward Preble as master.[5]

Captain Preble's new command was eight years old, ship-rigged, 86 feet in length, 25 feet beam, and 12 feet 6 inches depth of hold. She was ornamented with quarter galleries but had no figurehead. Preble secured a freight of wheat and flour for Barcelona, Spain, and took on some goods Messrs. Bridge and Hatch had imported from Spain and hoped to sell in Virginia. With this cargo Preble sailed from Boston about 7 January 1793, and by the 24th was at Hampton, Virginia. There, he left his ship, crossed over to Norfolk, and went off to City Point and Richmond in search of buyers for the Spanish leather, wine, raisins, and brandy. Buyers he found, and with the proceeds of his sales he purchased pipe staves and flour to sell in Europe for the account of Bridge and Hatch.

Eight years of hard service were showing on the *Neptune* and she needed considerable overhaul — including 39 man-days of caulking — before attempting the Atlantic. While she lay in James River several of her sailors jumped ship and had to be brought back by force. By 26 March repairs had been completed, the new cargo was on board, the *Neptune* had cleared outward-bound through the custom houses at City Point and Norfolk, and Preble was making out his accounts and waiting for a fair wind to take him to sea.

May 11th found the *Neptune* anchored at Barcelona. There Preble unloaded his freight of wheat and flour and sold the 11,400 staves belonging to Hatch and Bridge. The *Neptune* sailed in ballast on 16 June and ran down the Spanish coast to Málaga. Those attempts at desertion in Virginia were symptoms of problems among the *Neptune*'s crew, and at Málaga the trouble came to a head. Michael Morphy, the U.S. Consul at Málaga, reported to Secretary of State Thomas Jefferson:

> I have also to lay before you that great abuses are committing by the American and British seamen abroad by changing their allegiance as it suits their fancy or interest when brought before the consuls of said powers or in the presence of the magistrates of the countries they are in to settle their disputes. I have a very recent proof of it of the crew of the ship *Neptune* of Boston in this port, the greatest part whereof having quarreled with the captain, Edward Preble, they called themselves British subjects (although well known to be Americans) for the sake of leaving the ship to go on board an English man-of-war that lay here. However, I found means to keep them quiet.

The difficulties were caused by a problem that produced morale crises in several of Preble's later commands: his own harsh and violent disposition. A few days after Consul Morphy had used his unspecified methods to calm the disaffected "Neptunes," Preble went ashore in Málaga and bought some canaries, a cage, and enough bird seed to see them to Boston. And that is the image of Preble as he approached the age of thirty-two: a man who could quarrel violently with his sailors, yet care lovingly for a cage of canaries in the *Neptune*'s cabin.

Before the *Neptune* left her anchorage in James River, France declared war on England and Spain. As Preble went from port to port along the Spanish coast he made his first acquaintance with the wars of the French Revolution and the Napoleonic Empire, wars that, in their impact on the United States, created the conditions under which the next fifteen years of his life were played out.

Preble loaded some wine at Málaga, then passed through the Straits of Gibraltar to Cadiz, where he picked up a load of salt for the account of Messrs. Bridge and Hatch. On 6 August 1793 Preble was finishing up his business in Cadiz; seven weeks later he sailed his ship in to her home port of Boston. He had scarcely set foot in Boston before he was telling the editor of the *Columbian Centinel* what he had seen of the war:

> Capt. PREBLE, arrived in this port from *Barcelona* via *Cadiz*, informs us that the *Spanish* fleet, consisting of 31 sail of the line and a great number of frigates and xebecks, left that port a few days before he sailed, their destination supposed to be *Toulon;* that while at *Barcelona* this fleet sailed and returned from the French island of *St. Peters,* which it captured, making the garrison, consisting of 1400 men, prisoners of war; they also took a French frigate of 36 guns and a privateer, which they brought in; that during this expedition a French fleet of merchantmen, convoyed by three frigates, left the coast of *Barbary* laden with wheat and arrived safe at *Marseilles,* although one object of the Spaniards was to intercept them; and that on the 30th June he passed,

off *Cape de Gat,* the English fleet of 26 sail of the line, 18 frigates, and a convoy of merchantmen, &c., bound to join the Spaniards; some of the boats of the fleet boarded Capt. P. but treated him with the utmost politeness.

Preble informed Mathew Bridge that during his stop at Málaga he had been impressed by a business house called Grivegnée & Co., and that Grivegnée & Co. had said that they would like to trade with Preble's Boston owners. In the late fall of 1793, Bridge, Joseph Hurd, and John M'Lean chartered the brigantine *Katy* from her owner, Samuel Barton, and placed her under Preble's command for another voyage to Spain.[6] The square-sterned *Katy* measured 70 feet 8 inches long, 20 feet 6 inches beam, and 10 feet 3 inches depth of hold. She was built in Pennsylvania in 1785 and, unlike the *Neptune,* she carried a figurehead — doubtless of a woman. For the main part of the *Katy*'s cargo Messrs. Hurd, Bridge, and M'Lean selected flour, but they also loaded into her substantial quantities of beans, beef, cheese, and pipe staves, as well as whale oil, salmon, butter, pork, tongues, and beeswax.

The owners instructed Preble to sail the *Katy* to Cadiz and sell his cargo, then take the proceeds and go overland to Málaga. From there, he was to ship to Cadiz in a Spanish coaster, for transfer to the *Katy,* 600 or 700 quarter casks of Málaga wine, 400 casks of raisins, and 200 boxes of lemons, with which Grivegnée & Co. were asked to supply him. He was reminded to "observe that the wine is of the best kind, one half three years old, the other two years, as the more ordinary kind will not stand our warm summers." On his return to Cadiz, Preble was to employ the firm of Richard Shield & Co. to secure 500 pounds of "very small and green" capers, 200 jars of olives, and, unless he found that he could make better wine purchases at Málaga, 200 quarter casks of sherry and 100 quarter casks of Rota wine. Again he was cautioned: "Be very careful that [the wines] are of the very first quality, as the ordinary kind will not by any means answer this market." To which warning Messrs. Hurd, Bridge, and M'Lean added the dig: "The wine you brought last year was very bad and of course [had a] very dull sale." As a reward for his efforts Preble was to receive a 2½ percent commission on all sales and purchases, except the Málaga wine shipped by Grivegnée & Co., and he was granted the standard privilege of carrying in the *Katy* small quantities of goods or "adventures" for his personal speculation.

After the *Katy* had cleared through customs on 13 December 1793 but before she left Nantasket Road, the Algerians abruptly entered the story. Independence from Great Britain meant that U.S. vessels lost the protection the British flag had given them against the piratical activities of the

Barbary States — Morocco, Algiers, Tunis, and Tripoli. Diplomatic relations had been established between the United States and Morocco, the least militant of the four states, in 1786. But because the United States had sold the *Alliance*, last ship of the Continental Navy, in 1785, and because a large segment of public opinion vigorously opposed the establishment of a federal navy, the only option open to the United States for coming to terms with Algiers, Tunis, and Tripoli was the payment of money. As early as 1785 two American merchantmen had been captured by cruisers from Algiers. Eight years later, as the *Katy* prepared to sail from Boston, the crews of those vessels were still in captivity, but no more Americans had been captured by the Algerians despite the fact that there were still no agreements with Algiers, Tunis, or Tripoli. War between Portugal and Algiers kept the Straits of Gibraltar closed to Algerian cruisers, and made the Atlantic coast of Spain safe enough for American merchantmen. And — as Preble did on his voyage to Barcelona in the *Neptune* — many American masters felt that, provided certain precautions were taken, the Algerian danger was not serious enough to keep them from venturing inside the Mediterranean in search of profits. Then, quite suddenly, Algiers and Portugal agreed to a one-year truce. Algerian cruisers rushed out through the Straits. In October and November 1793 they captured eleven American ships.

News that Algerians were loose in the Atlantic caused Bridge and his associates promptly to change their plans. Preble and the *Katy*'s crew indicated in unmistakable terms that they would not risk Algerian imprisonment by sailing direct to Cadiz. In orders dated 17 December 1793, Captain Preble was instructed to sail to Bilbao, inquire there how dangerous it would be for an American merchantman to approach Cadiz, and, depending on what he learned at Bilbao, adopt one of several alternatives.

"I have the pleasure to acquaint you of my safe arrival in this port on the 19th instant after a passage the most blustering I ever experienced," Preble wrote his owners from El Ferrol, 25 January 1794. "In the Bay of Biscay I met nothing but contrary gales of wind, which obliged me to bear away for this port. This is a King's port, and merchant's ships are not permitted to land and sell their cargoes here except they are loaded for account of the King of Spain. However, I have this day, after a great deal of trouble and some trifling presents to the King's officers, obtained permission to sell my cargo and deliver it here." A Portuguese ship had just arrived bearing the rumor that twenty-seven American vessels had fallen into Algerian hands, and Preble also had received a more authentic list of ten sail known to have been seized by the North African cruisers. The danger from the Algerians seemed far too great to justify taking the *Katy* to Cadiz: he had decided to dispose of his cargo at El Ferrol and nearby Corunna. The flour, whale oil, and beans sold quickly and at a good profit; the remainder of the cargo was less in demand and brought in a smaller gain for the owners. As for the butter and staves, Preble considered himself lucky to unload them at cost.

Preble loaded the *Katy* with St. Ubes salt, which he purchased out of a Portuguese ship in El Ferrol harbor, and sent her home to Boston about 20 February under command of his mate, Samuel Rider. Considering it "very necessary that two navigators should be on board," Preble had hired a Captain Bryant, of Philadelphia, to replace Rider as mate of the *Katy*. Bryant's ship had foundered at sea; he had been rescued by Captain John Wallace in the Salem brig *Francis* and taken in to El Ferrol. Preble still had to carry out the Cadiz and Málaga end of his owners' business. For this purpose he chartered the 300-ton Swedish bark *Helena* of Stockholm, Olof Lundström, master. Because the Scandinavian nations kept their relations with the Barbary States in excellent repair, the property of Hurd, Bridge, and M'Lean would be entirely safe in a Swedish bottom. The *Helena*'s charter specified that she was to carry cargo to Boston and then be freighted by Preble's owners for a return voyage to Spain.

By 17 March, the *Helena* had arrived at Cadiz where Preble, her new supercargo, purchased salt, olives, cork, and sherry. The sherry, sad to report, turned out to be "very inferior" when Messrs. M'Lean, Hurd, and Bridge examined it at Boston. Early in April the *Helena* sailed into the Mediterranean on her way to Málaga, where Grivegnée & Co. supplied more cargo in the form of mountain wine, lemons, raisins, and cork. Finding that the price of three-year-old Málaga wine had suddenly risen to the point where it would be unsalable in Boston, Preble purchased two-year-old sweet mountain wine instead, and on 22 April 1794 closed his accounts at Málaga. Six days later, with a fair wind, the *Helena* stood out for the Straits of Gibraltar and Boston.

Algerian attacks on American shipping, which had complicated Preble's business in Spain, had provoked Congress to authorize the establishment of a national navy. On 27 March 1794, while Preble was negotiating with Messrs. Richard Shield & Co. of Cadiz, President Washington was signing a bill that placed all naval affairs under the supervision of the Secretary of War, authorized the construction of six frigates, and provided for the appointment of officers for the six ships. Early in June the six men who were to superintend the building of the frigates were commissioned as captains.

Soon after the *Helena* reached Boston on 16 June, Preble decided to apply for a lieutenant's commission in the new Navy. No surviving letter explains why he was anxious to abandon his career as merchant captain and supercargo, but apparently he had found nothing in eleven years of humdrum trading voyages to match the excitement and personal satisfaction of the time he spent in the *Protector* and the *Winthrop*. Men from all sections of the union were eagerly soliciting commissions in the Navy. There were far more applicants than there were berths to be filled, and would-be appointees were seeking the support of influential friends. Preble, in determined search of a lieutenancy, managed to get an introduction to the Secretary of War, Henry Knox. Shortly thereafter, he wrote to Congressman George Thacher of Maine:

> Boston, August 16th 1794.
>
> Sir:
> Since I had the pleasure to see you here I have been introduced to General Knox by General [Henry] Jackson [Navy Agent at Boston] and have had some conversation with him respecting the appointment of officers for the ships of war of the United States, and have made application in writing for the senior first lieutenancy in the service or for the command of any ship or vessel of war that may hereafter be built for the service of this country. General Knox has made himself acquainted with my former services and reputation as an officer and is satisfied, I believe, that I ought to be appointed. He thinks it will be necessary that some of my friends should write recommendatory letters in my favor which he will lay before the President when the appointments take place. This method he thinks will insure me success although many applications have been made prior to mine. If you, Sir, will do me the honor to write a recommendatory letter to General Knox or to the President, and request the other delegates to Congress from the District of Maine to sign it with you, I think I may rest assured of an appointment that will gratify me. I will thank you to pay some attention to this business and endeavor to fix it on your next visit to the seat of government. I believe I am the only person that has made application from the District of Maine. I am bound to Europe in a few days and expect to return in about seven months, which will be before the officers will be appointed. I am, with great respect, your most obedient servant,
>
> EDWARD PREBLE[7]

A commission — should one materialize at all — would not be forthcoming for months, and Preble's immediate business was to return to Europe with Captain Lundström in the *Helena*. Once again, he was to travel as supercargo and agent for Messrs. Bridge, Hurd, and M'Lean, but this time his orders were to sell his cargo at Bilbao, Spain, where the *Helena*'s charter would expire.[8] After parting company with Captain Lundström and selling his wares, he was to take the proceeds of his sales to Cadiz or Málaga and invest them in brandy and wine.

The *Helena* cleared through Boston customs on 19 August 1794 and, almost two months later, turned up at Bordeaux, France. Undoubtedly, Preble explained the change of course to his employers, but all that remains on record is his dissatisfaction with the business methods he found in France. He had to sell his cargo to an official body, the *Comité Chargé de Traiter avec les Neutres,* and receive payment in assignats, or paper money. He also had to secure the Committee's permission to invest the assignats, one-third in brandy, one-third in wine, and one-third in "luxury articles." The rub was that he could, if permitted, have sold his cargo to merchants for the same price and received specie rather than the continually depreciating assignats — by March 1795 the paper money had dropped to a ratio of six-to-one in relation to specie and was still going down. But for the Committee, Preble told his Boston owners, "I should have made as great a voyage as I could have wished. . . . I cannot advise you to send [another] vessel here until the Committee transact business on a more liberal plan than at present."

Hurd, Bridge, and M'Lean had instructed Preble to ship one-half of the cargo he purchased in Europe to their Dutch correspondents, John Hodshon & Son. Consequently, in November 1794, he sent 233 ½ tuns of wine to Amsterdam by the Bremen brig *Mentor,* Captain Frans Tacklenborg. John Hodshon & Son shot back to Preble the complaint that "the quality of this wine is . . . exceedingly bad," and threw salt in the wound by adding, "There never came so bad a cargo to our market." This was the third cargo of poor-quality wine that Preble had purchased in less than two years. Perhaps he was not a shrewd buyer, and it may be that his desire to get back into the Navy was motivated by his own recognition of that fact. Be that as it may, in self-defense, he commented to his employers: "It is impossible for any person to be a judge of common wines unless they have been regularly bred to the business, as all wines shipped to Holland are new and shipped in the lees and in a state of fermentation." If Preble was lacking in perspicacity as a buyer, it cannot be denied that he was a persuasive negotiator. He pressured the Bordeaux firm that had secured the wine for him, Peters, Strobel & Co., into assuming the loss on the Amsterdam cargo and making other adjustments favorable to Hurd, Bridge, and M'Lean.

For the Boston market Preble made four shipments, the last of which left Bordeaux in the brig *Three Friends,* Captain Bellingham Watts, in April 1795. Hurd, Bridge, and M'Lean had to wait many months before they got their hands on *Three Friends*'s cargo. When the brig was only some 36 miles off the mouth of the Gironde River, she was captured by a two-gun privateer schooner from Bermuda, and taken to that island on the suspicion that she was carrying French property. At Bermuda, Captain Watts had to sit idle for seven weeks before his case came up for trial. When the case did get to court, he came off better than he had expected: the only thing condemned was some bottled wine in his ship's hold, which the judge ruled was French property. Watts finally reached Boston towards the end of September 1795.

Before Preble left Boston in August 1794, he and Messrs. Bridge, Hurd, and M'Lean had agreed to part company when the *Helena*'s cargo had been sold and the proceeds had been invested in return cargoes. That process was completed when the *Three Friends* sailed from Bordeaux. While he closed out his employers' accounts in France Preble talked of either going to northern Europe "in an agency of importance" or of staying on at Bordeaux for a few months, in spite of the fact that he found it "very expensive" living there. Then on the 11th of April he suddenly changed his mind and booked a passage for Philadelphia in the *Camilla*, Captain Elias Boys. With him in the *Camilla* he shipped a small cargo of capers, anchovies, olives, and claret which he hoped to sell profitably on the Philadelphia market. He got home to the United States on 19 June 1795.

IV

It is safe to assume that, when Preble disembarked from the *Camilla* at the national capital of Philadelphia, one of the first things he did was to call at the War Department offices and inquire about the status of his application for a commission in the Navy. There, he would have learned that the day when he could expect to go to sea as first lieutenant in one of the new frigates was pretty remote. Work on the six warships had barely begun and was going forward at a deliberate and craftsmanlike pace. When the lieutenants and other subordinate officers might be appointed, no one could say. And there was worse news yet to come: once a treaty with Algiers (obtained at a cost approaching one million dollars) was ratified by the United States in March 1796, Congress wanted to abandon construction of the six frigates and only with difficulty was persuaded to continue work on three of them. This compromise at least salvaged something of the Navy; the original authorization of 27 March 1794 required that the whole construction program cease on the conclusion of peace. Edward Preble would have to ply the merchant trade a while longer.

In spite of bad wine and the *Comité Chargé de Traiter avec les Neutres*, Preble made money from his voyages to Spain and France. He invested some of his newly acquired capital, and became a shipowner for the first time in his life. The vessel in question was the brig *Jason*, and Preble was one of three proprietors. The others were Eben and Gorham Parsons, Boston merchants. The three-way association was founded on the understanding that Preble was to be master as well as part owner of the brig. The square-sterned *Jason* was a new vessel, fresh from her builder's Amesbury shipyard; she was 70 feet 2 inches in length, 20 feet 3 inches on the beam, and 9 feet 7 inches deep in the hold. She had neither quarter galleries nor figurehead.

Towards the end of September 1795, Preble took command of his new ship on the Merrimack River, received a temporary register at the Newburyport custom house, and brought her around to Boston. After loading her with a heterogeneous cargo that included fish, apples, crackers, boots, nankeens, sherry, Lisbon and Málaga wine, and hogshead hoops, he cleared for Martinique on 24 October 1795. At that point the *Jason*'s trail suddenly turns cold. There is little doubt that she reached Martinique. But she never came back to Boston. Under date of 20 August 1796, her register from the Boston custom house records is cryptically endorsed: "Cancelled at Charlestown as appears by a certificate."[9] What became of her? Was she sold in some other port of the United States or abroad? Perhaps she was built as a speculation with this in mind. The fate of the *Jason* is another of the puzzles that crowd Preble's sixteen years in the merchant service.

There is not a single record to show where the master of the *Jason* was or what he did during the year following his departure from Boston.

V

If evidence were needed to prove that Yankee merchants would go anywhere to make a dollar, it could be found in the voyage on which Preble embarked on 19 October 1796.

About two months earlier, on 28 August, a French squadron of seven line-of-battle ships and three frigates, commanded by Rear Admiral Joseph de Richery, suddenly appeared on the Newfoundland Banks and bore down to attack St. John's, Newfoundland. Outnumbered at sea, the British retired behind the protecting forts and batteries of St. John's and prepared to put up stiff resistance. Richery was frightened off. Frustrated, he turned south and, a week later, destroyed the fishing settlement at Bay Bulls, twenty miles below St. John's. The next day he sent three of his ships to attack the fishing settlement at Chateau Bay, Labrador, while he led the rest of his squadron on a mission of plunder and destruction in the islands of St. Pierre and Miquelon. Not content with ravaging the shore, the French squadron destroyed upwards of eighty fishing boats and merchantmen. Then it vanished from the coast of Newfoundland.

Newspapers in Boston had few facts about this hit-and-run French raid. They had to rely on such rumors and word-of-mouth reports as came down the coast. When Gorham and Eben Parsons and Edward Preble read that St. John's and the British squadron — a 50-gun ship and two frigates — in its harbor had been captured, they put enough faith in the story[10] to risk a speculation. Into an aging schooner, the *Success,* measuring only 46 feet long, 15 feet in beam, and 5 feet 3 inches in the hold, they loaded a cargo of assorted foodstuffs, rum, and tobacco that were expected to have a brisk sale among the occupying French forces and the occupied British. The *Success* belonged to Eben Parsons; her cargo represented a three-way investment among Gorham Parsons, Eben Parsons, and Edward Preble. In titular command of the *Success* was a certain Isaac Bullock, but, in order to keep an eye on his and his associates' interests, Preble went along as supercargo. Before he left Boston Preble purchased a little memorandum book in which he kept the following diary of the voyage:

A JOURNAL OF A VOYAGE IN THE SCHOONER SUCCESS, ISAAC BULLOCK, MASTER, FROM BOSTON TO TRADE ALONG SHORE.

October 19th, 1796. At 9 o'clock in the morning we weighed anchor and sailed with the wind from the westward and the same day passed Cape Ann lighthouse.

October 20th. The wind came from the E.N.E. and blew hard with much rain. We bore away for Portsmouth and at 3 p.m. anchored in Kittery harbor, where we remained until the 23d, when, the wind changing to the N.W., we weighed anchor and sailed; and the same day we saw Portland lighthouse, when the wind again changing to the eastward with heavy rain and looking likely for a storm, we put into Portland harbor, where we remained until the 26th, with the wind from the eastward and rainy weather, when at 10 o'clock p.m. we sailed out of the harbor and stood to the eastward with the wind from the N.N.W.

October 30th. We saw the land on the coast of Nova Scotia, and at 8 o'clock the same evening we passed Halifax lighthouse about two leagues distant.

November 1st. The wind being contrary we anchored in Houlton harbor, about 25 leagues to the eastward of Halifax. This harbor is very safe with an easterly wind, and affords plenty of wood and water, and abounds with wild game. There are no inhabitants about this harbor, but I discovered many Indian wigwams in the woods which appeared to have been recently inhabited although no Indians were to be seen.

November 3d. The wind shifted to the S.W. and blew a fresh gale. We weighed anchor and steered to the E.N.E. At 2 p.m. we passed Cape Canso, the southeastward promontory of Nova Scotia, and continued to steer to the eastward [until] November 5th, when we discovered the island[s] of Miquelon and St. Peter's and at 5 o'clock p.m. anchored in St. Peter's harbor, where we experienced a heavy gale of wind from the E.S.E. I found only two families here, the town and every building on the island having been destroyed about three weeks before my arrival by a French fleet under the command of Admiral Richery and the inhabitants all sent off to Nova Scotia. This harbor is a very excellent one for small vessels and more conveniently situated for carrying on the cod fishery, either in summer [or] winter, than any of the ports in Newfoundland or the islands adjacent.

November 9th. We sailed from St. Peter's with a brisk wind from the northwestward and same day passed Cape St. Mary's, Newfoundland, abreast of which we caught a plenty of codfish.

November 10th. We passed Cape Pine and Cape Race, the southwest promontory of Newfoundland.

November 11th. Anchored in St. John's harbor. This harbor is difficult of access on account of the narrow entrance and the very high land on each side, which causes the wind to baffle in such a manner as to make it almost impossible to sail in or out without the assistance of boats; but when you are in it is perfectly safe with any wind and is perhaps as good a harbor as any in the world. The town of St. John's contains about 300 houses and about 2500 inhabitants, exclusive of soldiers. The houses in general are meanly built, and the streets very narrow and dirty beyond anything — except the houses of the lower class of people, which are more dirty than the streets. The heights above the town and at the entrance of the harbor are well fortified and capable of being defended against any force that can be brought against it. We discharged a part of our cargo here and took on board in return fish, which is the staple article of this country. During my stay in this place I was treated with great politeness and attention by Colonel Thomas Skinner (of the Royal Newfoundland Regiment which is stationed here), commandant of the island, and by the Captains [Ambrose] Crofton and [James] O'Bryen of the *Pluto* and *Shark,* men of war, and also by the officers of the Army and Navy and the inhabitants in general. We were detained here with contrary winds until the 25th.

November 25th. The wind springing up from the N.E., weighed anchor and sailed for Boston, experiencing nothing but blustering, cold, rainy weather until the 30th, when a very heavy gale of wind came on from the eastward attended by a violent storm of hail and snow. We scudded under a close-reefed foresail until 11 o'clock at night at the rate of ten miles per hour, when we lost Nicholas Bartlett of Marblehead, one of our seamen, overboard from the helm. We scudded one hour longer and then hove to, ahull, the wind blowing too violent to carry any sail.

December 1st. At 1 o'clock in the morning a heavy sea struck us on the windward quarter which threw our vessel on her beam-ends so that our mastheads were in the water. This sea carried away our main boom, gaff, and sail, our fore boom, all our quarter boards and rails, and all the quarter top-timbers level with the deck, split our pumps to pieces, and swept our decks of all our spare spars, all our oars, and some casks of water, etc., etc. And, to add to the horrors of this truly distressing night scene, we found our mainmast giving way between decks, which threatened to tear our decks up, to prevent which I cut away the mast above deck with an axe which was kept becketed by the side of the companionway, on which she righted; and very fortunately cleared the wreck by getting the vessel before the wind for some time and then bringing to on the other tack. We then with much difficulty struck a light to examine the state of our vessel below, when we found our hold about a third full of water, our [*word illegible*] shattered to pieces by the shock of the sea, and our window lockers under our cabins entirely discharged of their contents, which were thrown into the berths on the opposite side.

We were all employed until daylight in bailing water out of the hold through the cabin scuttle, and by that time had nearly freed her. In the morning the gale abated, and the light presented [us] with a prospect truly distressing, as our vessel was quite a wreck, having no spars left but our foremast and bowsprit, and our deck entirely divested of any protection to prevent a man sliding overboard. We fitted our foresail as a lugsail, and the wind being from the westward and very cold, blustering weather and the ice making fast on deck, and knowing that the N.W. winds are generally prevalent at this season of the year, we despaired of being able to gain any port on the continent, as it would be impossible for us to keep off a lee shore without a mainsail even if we could make the land. We accordingly concluded to run to the southward into milder weather and endeavor to gain some port in the West Indies, and immediately bore away from latitude 44°37' North and longitude 57°16' West, this being the angle at which our misfortune happened. The wind continued to blow violently from the N.W. quarter for several days, we steering to the southward and eastward.

December 13th. We passed the latitude of Bermuda in Longitude of 47°38' West.

December 18th. We passed the Tropic of Cancer, having sailed all this distance on one tack, with the wind from the westward, without having once shifted our foresail. We continued our course for the West India islands.

January 2d, 1797. At 4 o'clock p.m. we had the inexpressible satisfaction to see from the deck the island of Désirade and the next morning discovered the island of Guadeloupe, and at 2 p.m. came to anchor in the harbor of Pointe-à-Pitre. At this place I sold the little wreck which had brought us miraculously over the Atlantic Ocean and purchased a larger and better vessel [the brig *Fame*] in which we sailed for home.

February 17th. I left this island with pleasure, as I was daily witness of the cruel, unjust, and inhuman treatment of my fellow countrymen by that barbarous tyrant, Victor Hughes [governor of Guadeloupe], who reigns here with despotic sway. We touched at Basse-Terre the next day and proceeded from thence for America.

February 19th. We passed the islands of St. Thomas [and] Porto Rico and steered to the northward. We were frequently chased but was so fortunate as to be able to outsail all our pursuers.

March 3d. We saw Cape Ann lights about 8 o'clock in the evening and the next day anchored in Salem harbor, where we were detained with contrary winds until the 11th when, the wind being favorable, we sailed for Boston.

March 12th, 1797. We anchored in Boston harbor and moored ship.[11]

A few footnotes from other documents should be added to that account. When Preble found that the British, rather than the French, were firmly in control at St. John's, the rum in the hold of the *Success* posed a problem, since rum could not be legally imported into Newfoundland from the United States. Preble had no intention of hauling his rum back to Boston: he smuggled it ashore at St. John's and sold it.

In his diary Preble makes only passing reference to French privateers seizing American merchantmen who were trading with British ports. He was ready with more details when newspaper editors approached him for the latest news from the West Indies. "Accounts from Guadeloupe received from Capt. PREBLE, lately from thence, still wears an alarming appearance to the commerce of the *United States*," reported the *Columbian Centinel*:

> The arret of the 13th *Pluviose* (Feb. 1st) is carried into strict execution in all its points. In consequence, neutral vessels destined for either of the Islands or places of *Martinique, St. Lucia, Tobago, Demarara, Berbice, Essequibo, Port-au-Prince, St. Marks, l'Archayes,* and *Jeremie* are brought in and condemned, *vessel and cargo,* and all neutral vessels bound *to* or *from any* English port or place in the world are brought in, the cargoes *sequestered,* sold, and the money deposited in the treasury — the vessels are cleared. These spoliations extend equally to the vessels of *Sweden* and *Denmark* as to the *United States.* The greatest activity in privateering pervades all the French ports, and we are assured that the cruisers, great and small, fitted out from *Guadeloupe* alone amount to near one hundred and twenty, and that their success in the capture of English as well as neutral vessels has been equally as extensive. VICTOR HUGHES has a strong force, well armed, disciplined, paid, and fed, and exercises, with LEBAS, despotic sway. Indeed, from some accounts, he may well be styled the *"Dey of Guadeloupe,"* nominally subject to the Five *Grand Turks* of *France.*

To the *Salem Gazette* Preble gave a list of twenty-seven American vessels captured by Guadeloupe privateers:

Ship *St. Tammany,* from Liverpool for Savannah with a cargo of salt; cargo condemned, ship freed.

Snow *Two Sisters* of Portsmouth, New Hampshire; "captain brought in without his vessel and knows not where she is."

Ship *Eliza,* Captain Hambleton, from Cork for New Bedford; captain taken out and his ship lost on Marie Galante by the French prize master.

Ship *Washington,* Sigourney, from the Isle of France for Boston; blown off the coast and captured; fate not known.

One case of hardship or financial ruin after another, Preble's list marched on. He had made his first personal contact with the French attacks on American commerce that were pushing a reluctant United States towards a state of war.

VI

With advancing years, Edward Preble's childhood temper tantrums matured into fits of uncontrolled rage that were apt to erupt when he was provoked or crossed. Normally, those who encountered Preble met a man disciplined and reserved, his manners instinctively formal and courtly. But, not far below this surface personality, powerful, though obscure, emotions were working.

Of all Preble's rages, the most serious occurred on 21 March 1797, shortly after the *Fame* arrived at Boston from Guadeloupe, when he struck James Lamb, mariner, of Gorham, Maine, "a violent blow on the head" with "a musket or handgun." Although there were at least five witnesses to the attack, what led to the quarrel is not known, nor are there any other details of the fight. But Preble must have laid into Lamb viciously, because the victim was still under a doctor's care in June, and had not been able to work for most or all of the intervening weeks.

Preble was carried before Justice of the Peace John Vinall the next day and bound over for trial at the August term of the Supreme Judicial Court of Massachusetts for the County of Suffolk. Eben Parsons became Preble's surety for the $500 bail he was required to post.[12] Within twenty-four hours a deal had been arranged: Preble paid Lamb $45, and Lamb signed a document waiving any further claims. The Commonwealth of Massachusetts dropped its criminal proceedings against Preble, but as weeks went by and Lamb's recovery proved slow, Preble began to feel qualms of conscience, especially about the small amount he had paid in settlement. First, he voluntarily paid Lamb $25 more; then, he paid his medical bills; after that, he paid Lamb's room and board while the latter was out of work and convalescing; finally, he gave Lamb $200 more — not neglecting, in return for all of this, to take the precaution of securing a second full release from the injured party.

This episode seems to have served effective warning on Preble about the potential for violence within him. Not that he stopped losing his temper. There are several stories of fits of rage in later years. But after 1797 there is no evidence that, however furious he became, Preble ever again hit a man in anger.

VII

Preble's voyages in the *Jason* and the *Success* were profitable enough to leave him with new capital to invest. Part of these earnings went towards the purchase, in April 1797, of 800 acres of land on the west side of the Kennebec River, holdings to which he added another 100 acres in February 1798. This policy of investing some of his earnings in land so that some day he would be able to retire from the sea and live on the rents from his properties, was the continuation of a practice Preble had begun as early as August 1792, when he bought a lot in Portland from a Loyalist refugee, the Reverend John Wiswell.

If Preble was hedging his bets by putting some of his money into land, his primary area of investment remained ships. Shortly after his return from Guadeloupe in the *Fame* he launched out on a new venture as a shipowner.[13] With the aim of experimenting in the Boston-Havana trade, he and Stephen Codman, a Boston merchant and former Portlander, combined to purchase the schooner *Phenix*. Built in Connecticut in 1796, she measured 73 feet long, 18 feet 9 inches abeam, and 8 feet 10 inches deep. Joseph Jackson was hired as her master; Preble was to go along as supercargo. Codman and Preble laid in a stock of assorted merchandise, and Preble, having seen the activities of the Guadeloupe privateersmen on his last visit to the West Indies, took the precaution of arming the *Phenix*.

Although Secretary of the Treasury Oliver Wolcott had, only two months earlier, 8 April 1797, issued a circular instructing all collectors of customs to "restrain" any armed merchantman bound for the West Indies from sailing, the *Phenix* cleared through customs, Havana-bound, on 6 June 1797, without hindrance. Perhaps she waited until she was at sea to break out her guns; perhaps the customs officers just did not "see" them. Whatever the method, a report that Captain Preble — masters always seemed to fade out when Preble was on board as supercargo — with his guns all in place, had been spoken in longitude 67° West was considered sufficiently newsworthy to earn a mention in the *Columbian Centinel*'s nautical column.

At Havana supercargo Preble found the "markets dull." The *Phenix* was dispatched for Boston on 26 July, but he stayed in Cuba until 11 August, then returned to Boston in the ship *Mac,* Captain Parker, which he had probably freighted with Havana goods for the account of Codman and Preble. Immediately on reaching Boston, 1 September, Preble had to plunge into the task of getting the *Phenix* prepared and loaded for a second voyage to Havana. The schooner's new cargo — cables, block tin, sheet copper, bar iron, nails, white lead, Russia duck, ravensduck, sheeting, ticklenburg, osnaburg, and onions — reflected experience-bought knowledge of what would and would not sell in Cuba. The *Phenix* cleared for Havana on 19 September 1797.

Isaac Parker had replaced Joseph Jackson as master of the *Phenix,* but whether Preble was on board this time cannot be established. If he was, it is unlikely that he forgot this voyage. On her passage towards Havana, the *Phenix* fell victim to Spain's change of sides in the European war: she was captured shortly after dawn on 26 September, near 40°58′ North, 69°27′ West, by the British frigate *Ceres,* commanded by Captain Robert W. Otway, and sent in to Halifax, Nova Scotia, where her trial before the Court of Vice-Admiralty began 27 October. Part of the *Phenix*'s lading was clearly contraband, as defined by Jay's treaty of 1794, and was condemned by decree of the court, 2 November, but the *Phenix* herself was released. This unlucky schooner's troubles were not over. As she was coming into

Boston harbor from Halifax during the night of 22/23 November 1797, she struck a rock near the lighthouse. Officers, crew, and passengers were rescued by a boat that came off from Light House Island. The *Phenix* was a total loss.

The unhappy outcome of his *Phenix* venture probably strengthened Preble's desire to get out of commerce and into the Navy. That wish seemed closer to satisfaction during the fall of 1797 and the winter of 1798 than it had ever been before.

VIII

Building tensions between France and the United States were creating conditions and a national mood in America that made war between the two countries seem more and more unavoidable. The ultimate reason for the difficulty in which the United States found herself was the great war that divided Europe, a war which constantly raised the question: can any commercial nation be neutral? A more immediate cause was Jay's treaty of 1794. That had eliminated a number of issues bedeviling U.S.-British relations, but it had been negotiated at the price of U.S. abandonment of the "free ships, free goods" principle and U.S. agreement to a broad British definition of contraband. French irritation at the American-British rapprochement was exacerbated by the United States' manifest determination not to jeopardize her neutrality by fulfilling what the French considered were America's obligations under the alliance of 1778. The French method of expressing displeasure with the United States was widespread harassment of U.S. commerce by French privateers — and Preble had witnessed the results firsthand at Guadeloupe in 1797. In a final effort to head off war, in July 1797 the United States had dispatched to France two special envoys, John Marshall and Elbridge Gerry, to join C. C. Pinckney, who had been sent there the previous year as minister, but refused recognition.

Simultaneously, Congress, seeking to strengthen the United States' negotiating position, embarked on a program of modest improvements in the country's defense posture. At the end of June 1797 the national legislature passed a bill, signed into law 1 July, which gave the President discretionary power to man and employ the three frigates whose construction had continued when Congress cut the naval program from six ships to three in 1796. These frigates were in different stages of completion: the *United States* had been launched at Philadelphia on 10 May 1797; the *Constellation* went down the ways at Baltimore, 7 September; but the *Constitution*, the frigate being built at Boston, did not go afloat until 21 October.

Because the act of 1 July provided for the appointment of subordinate

officers for the three frigates, it may be assumed that Preble hastened to
bring his file up to date with additional recommendations. During the summer and early fall of 1797, John Barry, Thomas Truxtun, and Samuel
Nicholson, the men who had been appointed to command the *United States,*
the *Constellation,* and the *Constitution,* respectively, submitted to the Secretary of War their preferences for subordinate officers. Preble was aiming at
the first lieutenant's berth in the *Constitution,* since she was to be manned
and officered from the New England states. He may have known that he
was not Captain Nicholson's first choice for the appointment. Nicholson
seemed to prefer a certain Benjamin Lee of Massachusetts. Mr. Lee was a
protégé of Nicholson's, and apparently had served as a boy in the Continental frigate *Deane* when Nicholson was her captain fifteen years earlier. His
Revolutionary War record could scarcely be compared with Preble's. So
Preble waited for the War Department and President John Adams to decide
who should be the *Constitution*'s senior lieutenant. Congress adjourned 10
July 1797 without any lieutenant nominations having been sent to the
Senate for confirmation. It convened again 13 November 1797, but still no
nominations were forthcoming from the Executive.

For Preble the situation seemed about equally promising and uncertain.
The *Constitution* was still months away from being ready to go to sea.
There was no sign when the nominations would go to the Senate. Would
Preble's be among them? Or would the commission he wanted go to Benjamin Lee? Preble decided to make another merchant voyage. It would take
him out of the country for three months. By the time he got home again
the President should have made his decision.

The goal, this voyage, was the Spanish Main. The vessel was the ship
Dauphin, Edward Preble, master. The principal owners and freighters were
Edward's brother, Eben, Isaac P. Davis, and Samuel Parkman. The cargo
was the most complex Preble had ever handled: butter, beans, beef, cheese,
oil, onions, raisins, hyson and souchong tea, china (1,410 pieces in four
boxes), 10,000 board feet of lumber, bar iron, soap, brandy, gin, enough
different kinds of wine to open a small tavern, and 64 boxes, bales, trunks,
and cases enigmatically lumped together in the customs records as "merchandise," but which accounted for more than half of the cash value of the
cargo. The plan was for Preble to peddle his cargo at La Guaira and other
ports on the Spanish Main — depending on where the best markets appeared to be when he reached South America — then come home via
Havana to pick up cargo for the Boston market.[14]

On the day the *Dauphin* was ready to sail, there was one thing left for
Preble to do. He went to the office of the Boston Navy Agent, Henry Jackson, and asked for Jackson's advice: What if his commission came through

while he was gone to the Spanish Main? At Jackson's suggestion, he took a sheet of the navy agent's letter paper and one of his pens, sat down at a desk, and wrote this note to Jackson:

Boston, 12th March 1798.

Sir:
   Should I be appointed first lieutenant of the *Constitution* in my absence, I request you to do me the honor to acquaint the Secretary of War and Captain Nicholson of my acceptance. I am, with sentiments of esteem and respect, your obedient servant,
EDWARD PREBLE

Three weeks later, on 2 April, as the *Dauphin* was running down the windward side of the Lesser Antilles — Preble was giving Guadeloupe a wide berth — she was chased and captured by a Martinique-based British privateer, the *Governor Parry*, commanded by William Otty. Captain Otty put a prize crew on board the *Dauphin* and ordered her into Barbados. Immediately on his arrival at that island, on 4 April, Preble appealed to the courts and got a speedy decision: by 8 April the *Dauphin*, Preble having paid court costs and charges of $72.75, was free and on her way to La Guaira.

The La Guaira market did not promise profitable sales, but the commandant at Caracas told Preble that all South American ports were open to neutral traders. So, on 17 April, three days after arriving at La Guaira, he sailed for Cartagena. As the *Dauphin* was entering Boca Chica, one of the passages into the bay of Cartagena, 22 April, the port authorities ordered her to drop anchor and wait for further instructions. Two days later Preble was served with an order from the governor of Cartagena requiring him to depart: non-Spanish vessels could enter Cartagena only when in distress. Frustrated for a second time in his attempt to peddle his cargo, Preble weighed anchor on 27 April, bound to Portobelo, where, the Spanish assured him, he definitely would be allowed to sell whatever he wished. This information proved correct. Preble stayed at Portobelo from 29 April to 12 May, and was able to vend part of the *Dauphin*'s goods at an acceptable profit. Then he was off for Havana. There, he hoped to dispose of the remaining cargo and invest the proceeds in products that Eben Preble, Samuel Parkman, and Isaac Davis would be able either to sell in Boston or to export to other markets.

It took the *Dauphin* a month of tedious sailing to work up from Portobelo to Havana; then, on 11 June, when she was almost there — Morro Castle was less than two miles away, and Preble could see the city and the shipping in the harbor — a small schooner that had been pursuing her since earlier in the day came alongside, broke out the French tricolor, trained her swivels on the victim, and ordered Preble to surrender. The schooner was the privateer *Petite Vertu*, Captain Stephen Allies. Within two hours the *Petite Vertu*'s prize was anchored at Havana.

Once again Preble went to court. He thought he had a strong case: the capture had been made in Spanish territorial waters; Captain Allies's commission was defective; the *Petite Vertu* had been built in Havana and was manned principally with Cubans. Spanish justice was both slow and expensive. The court proceedings dragged on till 1 August and cost $2,750, but the *Dauphin* was finally freed and restored to her master.

When Preble had sold what the pilfering privateersmen had left of his cargo, his proceeds from both Portobelo and Havana totalled $39,372. This sum represented a 16 percent profit on the value of the goods at Boston. But that margin could not set him to rubbing his hands with satisfaction, for the *Dauphin*'s two seizures and her summer-long detention at Havana had turned the voyage into an expensive one.* Preble invested $14,604 of the proceeds in a Havana-Boston cargo for the *Dauphin* to carry, and freighted the schooner *Industry*, Captain Samuel S. Fisher, with $11,543 worth of goods for the account of Eben Preble and associates. What was left after his ship's expenses had been paid was to be taken back to Boston as cash and bills of exchange.

But how could Preble get out of Cuban waters without being captured again? There were said to be eight or nine French privateers operating close to Havana and using that port as a base. One solution was to arm the *Dauphin* and fight his way home. He bought six cannon and a keg of powder for $852 and was soon holding gun drills in the *Dauphin*.

He never needed to fire his guns. Much had happened in the six months since Preble left Boston. By the fall of 1798 U.S. merchant vessels were being given the protection which they had lacked only a few weeks earlier. Word of the XYZ Affair and the collapse of U.S.-French negotiations put the spur to American defense preparations. Between 27 April and 16 July Congress had, in a series of bills, authorized an increase of the Navy to thirty ships — not counting revenue cutters attached to the Navy and galleys for river and harbor defense. A separate Navy Department had been created on 30 April 1798 and, under Secretary Benjamin Stoddert, had been operating since 18 June. Congress had fought shy of a formal declaration of war against France, but had authorized the capture of French armed vessels in U.S. coastal waters and on the high seas. But to American masters at

* Because of the high danger from French privateers during a voyage to the West Indies, insurance premiums were 20 percent of the value of the policy when insurance was written on the *Dauphin* in February 1798. When the claims were settled, the insurers would pay the *Dauphin*'s freighters a loss of 8 percent to 12 percent on the amount of the policy, which meant that the investors would recover less than they had paid out in premiums.

Havana the most welcome evidence of the government's activity was the appearance on 21 September of two ships of the new Navy — the frigate *Constellation,* Thomas Truxtun, and the 20-gun ship *Baltimore,* Isaac Phillips — off the harbor entrance, and Commodore Truxtun's announcement that they were prepared to escort American traders beyond the range of the French privateers. Between 28 and 29 September, the *Dauphin,* the *Industry,* and 42 other American merchantmen came out of Havana and formed up under the *Constellation*'s and the *Baltimore*'s protection for the passage north.

Any security-induced euphoria that Preble may have experienced in the convoy was abruptly dissipated at 7:00 p.m. of 3 October in the Straits of Florida. With a shattering crash the ship *Harmony* of Charleston, South Carolina, struck the *Dauphin*. Hasty inspection showed a hole in the *Dauphin*'s hull, water rising in the pump well, rigging, spars, and sails torn loose and flapping about in the breeze. Preble hoisted a signal of distress and ran for Commodore Truxtun in the *Constellation*. When he came within speaking distance of the frigate, he called out through his trumpet that the *Dauphin* was sinking. Truxtun immediately sent two boats to her aid, though he thought Captain Preble must be overdramatizing the danger, since the only supplies he requested to initiate repairs were some pumptacks! The *Constellation* stood by the *Dauphin* all night, and in the morning sent rigging, plank, spikes, and nails to enable Preble to patch up his ship. Preble recovered his composure and at dawn, 4 October, made a cooler assessment of his damage: the *Dauphin* really was not leaking as much as he had feared the night before. Commodore Truxtun inspected the merchantman and decided she was seaworthy, though a sorry-looking mess. Judging that no French privateer would come so close to the British base at New Providence, Preble was confident that he no longer needed protection and that he could make his own repairs with the material the *Constellation* had given him. Truxtun advised him to repair his ship at Charleston or Savannah before attempting Boston, then signalled the convoy to make sail, and the *Dauphin* dropped from sight below the southern horizon.

Everyone in the convoy assumed that Preble would take Truxtun's advice and make for Charleston. But a piece of news that Preble had almost certainly received from brother Eben or from Commodore Truxtun made him anxious to get home with the least possible delay. Scorning shelter available in the southern ports, the *Dauphin* plugged along up the coast, far behind the other members of the convoy, and on 14 November anchored at Boston.

The next day Preble was handed an aging letter from the Secretary of War:

War Office, 12th April 1798.

Sir:

The President of the United States, by and with the advice and consent of the Senate, has appointed you a first lieutenant in the Navy of the United States, to serve on board the frigate *Constitution,* whereof Samuel Nicholson, Esquire, is captain and commander.

You will be pleased to signify your acceptance or non-acceptance of this appointment. In case you accept, you will immediately repair to Boston and put yourself under the orders of Captain Nicholson and conform yourself to the rules and regulations of the Marine Service and the commands of your superior officers. I am, Sir, with respect, your obedient servant,

JAMES MCHENRY

CHAPTER 3   MARCH 1798–SEPTEMBER 1799

"... I am particularly fond of naval service."

Preble nearly missed getting the duty he wanted. In the list of officers for the *Constitution* sent to the Senate for confirmation on 8 March 1798 Samuel Nicholson's protégé Benjamin Lee had, as anticipated, been nominated first lieutenant and Preble's name did not appear. But Lee declined the appointment, and on 5 April 1798 President Adams nominated Edward Preble to be first lieutenant of the *Constitution*. The Senate confirmed the appointment four days later.[1]

While Preble waited, 1,400 miles away, for the Havana courts to release the *Dauphin*, the *Constitution* went to sea on 22 July. That summer, a key Boston Federalist, Stephen Higginson, who had replaced Henry Jackson as Boston Navy Agent, wrote a series of poison-pen letters to Secretary of State Timothy Pickering about the *Constitution*'s captain and his cadre of officers. One of these letters, dated 6 June, ran:

> Captain N[icholson] is in my estimation a rough, blustering tar merely. He is a good seaman, probably, and is no doubt acquainted with many or most parts of his duty so far as relates to practical seamanship; but he wants points much more important as a commander in my view: prudence, judgment and reflection are no traits in his character, nor will he ever improve. His noise and vanity is disgusting to the sailors; but a belief that he wants courage goes much farther to render him unpopular with them, for sailors love to have brave commanders. This opinion or belief, however, may not be well founded. I suspect it is not. It may have arisen from another opinion which is, indeed, often true: that blusterers are not apt to fight. Mr. Cordis, the second lieutenant, is a young man who possesses none of the requisites. He is deficient in every point essential to a good officer. He is said to be intemperate, and he looks like it. The surgeon, Reed, is the opposite of what he ought to be in morals, in politics and in his profession. There is not a man in this town who

would trust the life of a dog in his hands. His second, Blake, is of the same cast of character as Reed, but not so highly finished. . . . Mr. Preble, the first lieutenant, is not here. He is a smart, active, popular man — judicious and qualified well for his station, or for the first command; but I do not believe he will go in the ship when he sees his associates.

Higginson's letter is more useful as a gauge of Preble's reputation in Boston countinghouses at the end of his sixteen years in the merchant trade than as an objective assessment of the *Constitution*'s officers. There is a measure of truth in Higginson's accusations, but, as the above-quoted letter implies, the real objection to Republican-oriented Nicholson was that most of the officers with whom he had staffed his ship were of a like political persuasion. During the rapid expansion of the Navy at the beginning of the Quasi-War with France, the process of officer selection was heavily influenced by the Federalists' obsessive concern with the political loyalty of the candidates. Even Preble's old Revolutionary War commander, John Foster Williams, who was a well-known partisan of the Jeffersonians, was denied a commission in the federal Navy for political reasons. He, like Nicholson, was the victim of some character assassination by Stephen Higginson:

> His feelings would dictate to him to aid the French in taking our vessels rather than restrain. He is one of the most rancorous Jacos we have. He has always been one. He cannot be altered. He thinks it quite as meritorious now to curse the British as it was in '76 and would much more cheerfully join a French privateer in capturing a British vessel than assist a British cruiser in protecting an American, more especially if she belonged to an aristocrat. He has all the feelings of '78 and cannot discern the difference between our then and present situation. The British in his view are still our enemies and the [French] our friends.[2]

When the *Dauphin* reached Boston in the middle of November, the *Constitution* was back in port. Captain Nicholson would have been glad to have Lieutenant Preble report for duty right away, but that was impossible. There were the *Dauphin*'s involved accounts to settle, insurance claims to file, and odds and ends of private business — rents, investments, and the like — needing Preble's attention. Preble wrote Secretary of the Navy Stoddert:

Boston, 15th November 1798.

Sir:

I have this day received a letter from the Secretary of War, dated the 12th April last, acquainting me that the President of the United States has appointed me a first lieutenant in the Navy, to serve on board the frigate *Constitution*. I now take the first opportunity, after an absence of more than eight months from this continent, to forward you my answer to his letter.

I feel myself highly honored by the appointment and accept it with pleasure. But at the same time I earnestly request to be allowed to be absent from the ship six weeks after the date of this letter, that time being absolutely necessary for me to arrange my private affairs in such a manner as to enable me to leave the United States for any length of time without making very important sacrifices. I am obliged in justice to myself and others with whom I have been concerned in commercial business to request this indulgence in consequence of having been captured by a French pirate on my last voyage, plundered of a considerable property, and detained abroad five months longer than I had any reason to expect when I left home. I have already put myself under the orders of Captain Nicholson and have obtained leave of absence until I can hear from the Navy Office. I hope the President of the United States will do me the honor to grant me the indulgence I ask for, as Mr. [Charles C.] Russell, who is now on board the *Constitution* acting as first lieutenant, is an able officer. I am sorry that the situation of my private concerns makes it necessary for me to require leave of absence for a moment, as I am particularly fond of naval service. I hold my existence for the service of my country and am ready at any moment to yield it in her defense. I have the honor to be with respect, Sir, your obedient servant,

E. PREBLE

Enoch Preble thought this was a gambit to avoid serving in the *Constitution*. Years later he told his son, George Henry, that Edward Preble regarded Nicholson as a coward.[3] However, it is difficult to reconcile the contention that Preble was trying to escape service as the *Constitution*'s first lieutenant with the zeal he had displayed to get the appointment — at a time when he knew perfectly well who her commander would be. More likely his attitude was that he could put up with Nicholson until he got a command of his own.

But, if it was strategy on Preble's part, it worked. Stoddert granted the requested leave on 8 December and told Preble that, when it was up, he would probably not be ordered to the *Constitution* but would be given command of either the ship *Herald* or the brig *Pickering*.

II

Stoddert's formal orders to Preble, which he received on 11 January 1799, confirmed his appointment as lieutenant commandant of the 14-gun brig *Pickering* and authorized him to recruit seventy men and boys, of whom not more than thirty-five were to be able seamen; the remainder were to be ordinary seamen, landsmen, and boys. However, the Secretary gave it as his opinion that American ships of war were overcrowded with unnecessarily large crews and suggested that Preble might wish to reduce the total number of men on board. Preble apparently had not waited for these orders to begin recruiting and fitting the *Pickering* for sea. By the 12th of January he was able to report that he had enlisted twenty men in Boston, and had sent Lieutenant Benjamin Hillar, who served in the *Pickering* under her previous commander, to the neighboring seaport towns to drum up others. He could also report that Navy Agent Higginson had agreed to supply a sergeant and thirteen Marines to make up part of his complement. Despite these efforts, however, enlistment went slowly. This Preble attributed both to the "very indifferent accommodations of the vessel" — doubtless meaning the small and crowded living space for seventy men in a brig with a fifty-eight-foot keel and a twenty-foot beam — and to the large number of armed merchantmen which were signing on crews at the same time. Even when his full complement was finally on board, Preble found that, far from being overcrowded, he was actually short-handed. "You will see by the quarter bill," he wrote the Secretary, "that seventy men will not be sufficient, as the forecastle is left with only the boatswain, one of the guns is a man short, and only the gunner and his mate to attend the magazine and pass the powder up."

In addition to recruiting a crew, Preble had to find capable persons to fill posts to which officers had not already been appointed. As sailing master, he secured Joseph Ingraham, a merchant captain of impressive reputation. During a cruise in the Pacific Ocean Ingraham had discovered some islands, now considered a part of the Marquesas group, which he named the Washington Islands. The most famous of these, Nuku Hiva, should be familiar to readers of David Porter and Herman Melville. As first mate in Robert Gray's *Columbia* and later as commander of the *Hope*, Ingraham had also been one of the pioneers in American trade with the Northwest Coast. On the last day of January 1799 Mr. Ingraham reported for duty and began to keep the *Pickering*'s journal: "Moderate breeze and cloudy, accompanied with snow at times. At 10 a.m. I joined my ship, being appointed by Captain Preble the day previous. I superseded Mr. [Isaac] Collins, late master, who was preferred to second lieutenant. Captain Preble introduced me to the officers as master of the *Pickering*."

Preble's efforts were not directed solely at enlisting a crew and appointing officers. The *Pickering* herself, although a new vessel, required some attention. When Preble took charge of her he found that she had about fifteen tons of sand ballast on board. Thinking the sand would rot the hull, he took it out and replaced it with ten tons of iron ballast. The latter lay closer to the bottom of the vessel and enabled her to carry her canvas better, without making her so deep in the water as had the sand. After a fair trial of her at sea, Preble wrote of the *Pickering*: "She will always be a very fast-sailing vessel with the quantity of ballast which she now has on board, but cannot carry more than six weeks' water and provisions without being too deep and out of trim. I am very well satisfied with all my officers, and have no doubt if I should fall in with a Frenchman of equal force I shall be able to give a good account of him."

While these routine and even tedious preparations were going forward, Preble received his sailing orders from the Secretary of the Navy. There was always a demand for protection of American commerce to Europe, where French privateers were active. However, Secretary Stoddert thought that the French would have such naval superiority over the United States in European waters that to send the little Navy to cruise there would be to risk its destruction by overwhelming force. He therefore made the protection of the American coast the first objective of his strategy. Over and above that, he saw that the European war provided an opportunity to fish in Caribbean waters, where French privateers were numerous, but the French naval force was small. By stationing most of the American Navy in that sea, he planned to make the Caribbean so secure for American shipping that a large share of the rich West Indian and Spanish American trade would be concentrated in American hands. This was the commercial objective of his strategy. Politically, Stoddert hoped that the dependence of the New World possessions on American trade would tend to make them neutral in any quarrel between the United States and the Old World nations. In the present conflict he wanted, by neutralizing her American possessions, to maneuver France into a position in which she would be forced to attack the United States from Europe rather than from the West Indies.[4]

In accord with this policy Preble's orders directed him to proceed to the island of Dominica, in the Windward Island group, to join the squadron under Commodore John Barry that was operating out of Prince Rupert Bay.

III

Stoddert's orders, which reached Lieutenant Preble in Boston on 24 January, told him to get to sea without delay. The difficulty of enlisting a crew had prolonged preparations beyond what Preble had originally expected, but the *Pickering* was able to go down to the outer harbor on the 28th and Preble planned to take her to sea on the 31st. However, he found that he would have to wait until the U.S. ship *Herald* was ready to join him in convoying the storeship *Polly*, freighted with supplies for Commodore Barry's squadron, to Prince Rupert Bay. This delay, another to receive some final communications from the Navy Department, and stormy weather kept Preble at Boston until 11:00 a.m. on 12 February 1799, when the *Pickering*, in company with the *Herald* and the *Polly*, weighed anchor for the West Indies.

The *Pickering*'s cruise was to reflect the two chief duties of the U.S. Navy during the Quasi-War with France: convoy escort and the pursuit of privateers. Even though the Navy was less than a year old and the *Pickering*'s commander had to reach back sixteen years and more to remember what he learned in the *Protector* and the *Winthrop* about the life of a ship of war, Sailing Master Ingraham's journal for the outward passage to the West Indies affords glimpses of professionalism aboard the *Pickering*: "Exercised seamen and Marines in clewing up and furling sails. Arranged a quarter bill and had affixed over each gun the names of the persons quartered at them." A later entry reads: "Drawing near the islands. Captain Preble gave orders that no top light should be shown, and that the other lights necessary in the ship should be as much concealed as possible; also that matches should be continually lighted in the night, and the gunner or his mate to be on deck to superintend them."

Navy housekeeping made its appearance: "Got up all the seamen's chests, hammocks, etc. Washed out and cleansed between decks; also sprinkled with vinegar, agreeable to the Regulations of the Navy." "Calm at 7 a.m. Careened ship to starboard. All hands employed in painting larboard side, head, headrails, blacking the bends, etc. Eleven a.m., finished painting larboard side; careened ship to port and got in readiness to paint starboard side."

And there were moments of diversion when officers and men stood back and watched Edward Preble, hunter and fisherman: "Half-past four p.m., the Captain struck with the grains [a five- or nine-pronged fish spear] and got on board two large dolphins."

Commodore Barry was not inclined to let the *Pickering* loiter in port once she reached Prince Rupert Bay, Dominica, on 14 March. By the 16th there were some thirty-six merchantmen waiting in the bay for a northward-bound convoy to see them clear of West Indian waters and the danger of privateers. Barry instructed Lieutenant Preble to act under the orders of Captain Patrick Fletcher, commanding the U.S. ship *George Washington*, and assigned the convoy duty to their two vessels. Late in the afternoon of 17 March the convoy departed Prince Rupert Bay and stood northward past Montserrat and Nevis to Basseterre, St. Christopher, where it anchored on the morning of the 19th. The next afternoon the fleet — by then increased to fifty sail, all but three of which were bound to the United States

— once more got under way and, after passing St. Eustatius, St. Martin, Dog Island, and Sombrero, laid a north-northwesterly course until 27 March when it reached the approximate latitude of present-day Palm Beach, Florida. Judging that there would be little danger from French privateers north of that latitude, Fletcher and Preble separated the *George Washington* and the *Pickering* from the merchantmen and returned to Prince Rupert Bay, the *Pickering* dropping anchor there just before midnight on 16 April 1799.

Again, little time was wasted in port. On 20 April the two ships were once more under sail, this time bound for a cruise off the French island of Guadeloupe, where they hoped to capture French privateers or to recapture French prizes being sent in to the island for condemnation. The first eight or nine days of the cruise proved unproductive. But at 5:00 a.m. on the morning of 29 April, when the ships were operating to the north of the island, the *Pickering* sighted a brig to windward; all hands were called to quarters and chase was given. Two hours later, the strange brig showed American colors, and the *Pickering* answered by hoisting hers; but when the brig did not bear away to speak the *Pickering,* Preble fired a shot at her, then a second, then a third, and at eight o'clock came up with her. She proved to be the *Fair American*, twenty-nine days out of New York. She had been bound to St. Bartholomew with a cargo of flour, rice, tobacco, soap, candles, and other goods, but at 10:00 a.m. the preceding day, when she was to the windward of Barbuda, she was captured by a French lugger. The French prize crew, which consisted of a prize master and his mate, both white men, and seven blacks, was replaced by one from the *George Washington*, and the brig was sent in to Montserrat, where the salvage on ship and cargo earned the captors $2,875.

Two days later, on 1 May, while in chase of three strange sail to the northward of Guadeloupe, the *Pickering* fell in with what appeared to be a sloop. The stranger showed American colors, but would not heave to until seven shot had been fired at her. She was in the hands of a prize crew of three whites and four blacks and all her papers had been removed, but from a passenger who had been left on board it was learned that she was the *Francis,* loaded with tobacco and flour, and had been bound to Grenada. She belonged to Messrs. Patten & Walker of Fredericksburg, and had been commanded by Edward's brother Joshua, who had by 1799 established himself in Virginia. The identification of her as a sloop was wrong; she was a schooner, but had lost her foremast and main boom in a gale when only four days out from the Capes of Virginia. In this crippled condition she made slow progress, and the day before her encounter with the *Pickering* she had been captured by two French letters of marque. Joshua Preble, his mate, and some of her crew were being carried to Guadeloupe by their captors. The *George Washington* took the disabled *Francis* in tow, and later that afternoon Preble and Fletcher left their cruising ground off Guadeloupe and began the run down to St. Pierre, Martinique, where the *Francis* and her cargo were sold, the captors again receiving a share for salvage.

The two recaptures had netted Preble and Fletcher fifteen French prisoners, whom they decided they would attempt to exchange for captive Americans on Guadeloupe. A belief that Joshua Preble was being held on the island doubtless helped make their decision. On 7 May they hired the schooner *Union* as a cartel, put her under the command of Sailing Master Ingraham, and instructed him to proceed to Guadeloupe and try to exchange the prisoners for as many Americans as General Etienne Desfourneaux, the governor of Guadeloupe, was willing to release.

The *Union* anchored at Pointe-à-Pitre, Guadeloupe, at 1:00 p.m. on the 9th, and Ingraham was promptly taken to see the governor. Desfourneaux's policy towards the United States seems to have been one of intentional ambiguity. His concern was to keep his options open. He spoke of his wish to avoid intensifying hostilities between France and the United States and of his desire to make the islands he governed neutral in the quarrel, yet he did nothing to discourage Guadeloupe-based privateers from preying on U.S. commerce.

Desfourneaux told Ingraham that he knew of no American *prisoners* on Guadeloupe. Americans, he said, were allowed to enter and leave the island unmolested. Captured American *ships* were not sold for the benefit of the captors; the proceeds from their sales were being held pending adjustment of the differences between the United States and France. Then the money would be paid to the lawful owners. The governor told Ingraham that to issue a receipt for the French prisoners repatriated in the *Union* would be tantamount to a declaration of war, and he maintained that there was no war. Later, when he spoke with William Cutter, an American merchant captain from North Yarmouth whose ship had been captured by a Guadeloupe privateer, Ingraham saw the other side of the governor's policy. Cutter told Ingraham that his captors had robbed him of his watch, quadrant, and clothing. But when Ingraham protested this to the Commissary of Prisoners, that official replied that General Desfourneaux could not be troubled with every trifling incident that took place on board the privateers.

After a friendly dinner, at which Desfourneaux forbade discussion of the political difficulties between France and the United States, the governor sent one of his officers with Ingraham to search the city of Pointe-à-Pitre for Americans and gave orders that Ingraham was to take with him any who wished to leave Guadeloupe. The sailing master could find only eleven.

Joshua Preble, he was told, had gone to St. Bartholomew under a flag of truce a few days earlier.

During Ingraham's absence, the *Pickering* made a five-day cruise to the eastward of Guadeloupe but made no captures. The next business at hand was to collect a convoy in the islands and shape a course for the United States. Thirty-four strong, the fleet sailed from Martinique on the afternoon of 16 May. The convoy put in to St. Christopher and St. Thomas for other ships to join, and the *Pickering* was detached, first to Montserrat and then to St. Bartholomew, to pick up waiting vessels and escort them to the safety of the convoy. At St. Bartholomew Preble learned that Joshua had sailed for Martinique. When it departed St. Thomas on 25 May, the assembled convoy numbered sixty-four American and nine British sail.[5]

Fletcher's and Preble's plan was that when the convoy reached latitude 34° North, approximately that of Wilmington, North Carolina, the ships bound for the Chesapeake Bay, Philadelphia, and New York would proceed under the convoy of the *Pickering*, while the vessels bound to New England ports would be escorted by the *George Washington*. But on the morning of 6 June the *Pickering* was ordered to chase a strange sail that Preble took to be a privateer — an identification that seemed confirmed when he saw that she had a tier of guns and that two sloops, which he assumed to be her prizes, were bearing down as if to her assistance. At 4:30 p.m. the supposed privateer hoisted English colors and when the *Pickering* spoke her half an hour later it was to learn, alas, that she was the British cutter *Cygnet*, 14, bound from Jamaica to Quebec. The two sloops were recognized as vessels that had parted company with the convoy three days before.

When Preble found that the chase, which had begun at 8:30 a.m. and lasted until 5:00 p.m., had carried him many miles from the convoy, he had his reasons for pursuing it so long entered in his ship's official journal: "Captain Preble judged that by capturing this vessel and her prizes he would render essential service to the fleet, as it would prevent his annoying them or making any further captures; this induced him (Captain Preble) to continue the chase." Heavy gales that struck the *Pickering* on 7 and 8 June, as she tried to rejoin the *George Washington*, scattered the convoy and Preble was left to shape his own course for Sandy Hook.

IV

"What can be the reason that the officers of the Navy from Massachusetts so soon get tired of the service?" asked Benjamin Stoddert of a Boston correspondent on 21 May 1799. "Every time a vessel arrives at Boston resignations follow. I wish the best men would enter the service and remain. Our fleet will be commanded entirely from Pennsylvania and New York if the Massachusetts officers continue their practice of resignation." One of the officers he had in mind was certainly Edward Preble. Commodore Barry, who had landed at New Castle on 10 May, had brought the Navy Department word that Preble was planning to resign when the *Pickering* came in from the West Indies. "I hope not," wrote Stoddert to Stephen Higginson. "If he does not, he will, I have no doubt, make a figure in the Navy and will soon be forward enough in rank."

The temptation that was luring Preble away from the Navy probably was an offer of the command of a large cargo carrier. She was the *Massachusetts,* a 615-ton, three-deck ship, measuring 125 feet 9 inches long, 33 feet 3 inches beam, and a 16 feet 7½ inches depth of hold, copper-bottomed and pierced for 24 guns to enable her to hold off French marauders. The *Massachusetts,* under construction at Orlando B. Merrill's shipyard in Newbury, was due to be launched in August, and to enter the Dutch East Indies trade. Her principal owners, the men to whom Preble felt so strongly obligated, were merchants with whom he had been associated in the latter days of his civilian career: James and Thomas Handasyd Perkins, Stephen Higginson, Eben Preble, Thomas C. Amory, and Ebenezer Stocker of Newburyport. Preble himself owned a one-fortieth share of the *Massachusetts* and her cargo.[6]

A far more unusual maiden voyage lay ahead of the *Massachusetts* than Edward Preble could have imagined when she was a pile of timber and copper in Merrill's shipyard. During the previous century and a half the Dutch had been the sole Western nation permitted to trade in Japan, and they were limited to the privilege of sending one or two ships annually to Nagasaki. In 1797, fear of its vessels being captured by the British led the Dutch East India Company to begin chartering neutral American bottoms to make some of the voyages to Nagasaki. When the *Massachusetts* reached Batavia she won the charter for the 1800 voyage.

Preble did not know it, but the choice he had to make was between chasing fame and honor in the Navy or setting forth on a voyage that would make him one of the minute company of Americans who, between 1797 and 1807, penetrated the closed society of Japan.

Stoddert had a high opinion of Preble and acted quickly to keep him in the Navy: he appealed to Preble's ambition. On 25 May he recommended to President Adams that Lieutenant Preble be promoted, adding that "from all the information I can receive of him [he] ought to have been a captain from the beginning." The President approved, and on 7 June Secretary Stoddert forwarded Preble his commission as a captain in the U.S. Navy, to take rank from 15 May 1799. In a covering letter he told Preble: "The President has appointed you a captain in the Navy. I hope you will accept and continue in the service; you may justly expect to rank high and soon to get a good ship."

Soon after the *Pickering* anchored inside Sandy Hook on the evening of 11 June, Preble set off for Philadelphia to report in person to the Secretary of the Navy. News of his promotion so weakened his determination to resign that he told Stoddert that he would not leave the Navy if he could possibly free himself of his business obligations. Stoddert, anxious to do anything he could to retain Preble, turned command of the *Pickering* over to Benjamin Hillar, and gave Preble permission to remain on shore, settle with his Boston friends, and wait for a larger ship.

In July Preble begged off his commitment to Messrs. Perkins & Perkins, Higginson, Preble, Amory, and Stocker. Later, he made a 25 percent profit on his original investment by selling his one-fortieth share of the *Massachusetts* to his brother Eben for $2,354.49. He had made an important decision: his future was in the Navy. In late August and early September, armed with letters of introduction and recommendation to the principal Cabinet officers from their Massachusetts allies, he traveled to Trenton, New Jersey — where the Navy Department had moved to escape an outbreak of yellow fever at Philadelphia — to press for a good command. Two months after his visit to Trenton, Captain Preble received orders which would break the pattern that had confined his voyages to the Atlantic Ocean, north of the Tropic of Capricorn.

CHAPTER 4 OCTOBER 1799–JANUARY 1801

"*...I might have been left to clear the Straits of those pirates....*"

At Salem the 32-gun frigate *Essex* had been launched on the last day of September 1799. The government intended the command for Richard Derby, one of Salem's native sons and Edward Preble's kinsman, but, unfortunately for Derby, he was out of the country when the *Essex* needed a commander. On 21 October, Secretary of the Navy Stoddert ordered Edward Preble to Salem to assume command of the *Essex* and fit her for sea.[1]

Not only was the prospective cruise going to take Preble beyond the Atlantic Ocean for the first time, it was going to carry the *Essex* farther from home than any ship of the U.S. Navy had been. Like Preble, the Navy had theretofore been a prisoner of the Atlantic. In this respect it lagged behind the American merchant marine. To the traders who sailed to China and the Northwest Coast voyages even longer than the one to be attempted by the *Essex* and Edward Preble were commonplace.

Secretary Stoddert's original plan, which accorded with his strategy of concentrating U.S. warships in West Indian waters and on the American coast, called for the *Essex* to join the frigate *Congress* at Newport, Rhode Island, from which harbor the frigates were to convoy as far as the equator a number of American merchantmen bound for the East Indies. The *Congress*'s commander, Captain James Sever, was to be senior officer of the two-frigate squadron. But on 3 December Stoddert told Preble that plans had been changed: the frigates were to go all the way to Java, so that they might convoy homeward-bound merchantmen which were expected to leave Batavia in May. Although a relatively small number of U.S. merchantmen were involved in East Indian commerce, their cargoes were extremely valuable and the trade was expanding rapidly: in 1799 American imports from the Dutch East Indies were valued at $1,446,335; by 1801 the figure had climbed to $4,432,733.[2] The merchants trading with Java feared that the principal danger to their ships would not be in the North Atlantic, but at the Sunda Strait, where French privateers from the Isle of France* would be lying in wait. These merchants were anxious that the *Congress* and the *Essex* reach the Strait before their own outward-bound vessels, and that they protect them in the Strait and at least part of the way home.

II

During November and December 1799 Captain Preble worked without letup to ready the *Essex* for her long voyage. But in thought he sometimes returned from Salem to Portland, to a long, two-story wooden house on Middle Street that was the home of Dorcas Deering, the widow of a wealthy Portland businessman. Mrs. Deering's son, James, was an old friend of Preble's, but it was her daughter, Mary, who was on the captain's mind on a snowy December day when he drafted and then carefully copied a letter to the widow:

                                          Salem, December 17th 1799.

Dear Madam:

When I last had the pleasure of seeing Mr. [James] Deering here I gave him a snuffbox for you, of which I beg your acceptance as a token of my respect. I am ordered to sail the first fair wind for Newport, and from thence for the East Indies. This order grieves me exceedingly, as it separates me for at least one year from the society of your family. You know not how very dear to my heart your amiable daughter is, but I beg leave to assure you she is infinitely more dear to me than my existence. I love her with the tenderest affection, and would sacrifice my life to promote her happiness. For heaven's sake, Madam, plead for me, and, if she should consent to be mine on my return, my whole future life shall be devoted to a tender and delicate attention to her happiness and your own. You may rely with confidence on my attention to prudence and economy, and a steady adherence to the interest of your family, for I love you all with an unfeigned affection.

You have long known of my attachment to your lovely daughter, and I feel truly sensible of the delicacy with which you have ever attended to my feelings whenever I have visited at your house. I beg you to accept my thanks for your friendship and my fervent prayers for the health, happiness and prosperity of yourself and family. Could my lovely friend know how much I suffer from the thought of so long an absence from her for whom alone I wish to live, I am sure she would pity me. Give my best love to her, and tell her the future happiness of my life rests with her; and may the God of all goodness restore me to the joys of her loved society, and bless me with her affections.

---

* Now Mauritius.

If I possessed a world, I would give it freely to pass one hour with your amiable family before I go, but that, alas, is impossible. Adieu. Yours with respect,

EDWARD PREBLE

Should Mary Deering bless another with her affections, and not me, *I am lost forever* — for heaven's sake plead for me. Adieu.

Pray pardon this hasty letter.³

III

At 8:00 a.m. on 22 December the U.S. frigate *Essex* weighed anchor, exchanged a sixteen-gun salute with Fort Pickering, and departed Salem for Newport, where she anchored on the morning of the 28th. Preble was proud of his ship's performance and wrote: "The *Essex* is a good sea boat and sails remarkable fast. She went eleven miles per hour with topgallant sails set and within six points of the wind." Even after he had been out of her for five years, Preble still remembered the *Essex* as "a prime sailer and the best model of a frigate (of her rate) in the Navy." ⁴

If the captain was happy with his ship, he was quite unhappy with some of her officers. The frigate's purser, William Mumford, he considered incompetent; having to deal with him was a continual source of irritation and annoyance. "My purser has never been of any assistance to me, nor do I expect he ever will," Preble complained. First Lieutenant Simon W. Geddes, U.S. Marine Corps, who had been ordered to join the *Essex* at Newport as senior Marine officer, came on board with a couple of sheets to the wind. Preble was greatly relieved that a scalded leg obliged the lieutenant to remain on shore when the *Essex* sailed. With the ship's second lieutenant it was a different matter. Preble had asked that an experienced and dependable officer be ordered to the *Essex*. David Phipps, who was given the berth, was certainly that: he had been a lieutenant in the Continental Navy, and had served in several ships of war during the Revolution, but, wrote Preble, "Lieutenant Phipps is very infirm and so far advanced in life, with a broken constitution, that, although he is a very worthy man, I do not expect it will be in his power to render any essential service on board, but am inclined to think, from present appearances, that he never will return." Preble proved an indifferent prophet: David Phipps lived until 1825.

IV

Final preparations kept the *Congress* and the *Essex* at Newport until the sixth day of the new year. At midmorning of that day a boat from the

Congress came alongside the *Essex;* a midshipman entered by the gangway, lifted his hat, and presented Preble a letter from his commanding officer:

                                    Frigate *Congress,* January 6th 1800.

Sir:

On the presumption that you are in readiness and unwilling to lose so favorable an opportunity of getting out of this harbor, I am to request that you will be pleased to get under way and proceed with the *Congress* to carry into effect the orders of the Secretary of the Navy. I have not completed satisfactorily the signals I wished to have arranged for our government, but those I have made out for the day I shall send you herewith. I shall endeavor, on the first favorable moment after we shall be at sea, to send on board the *Essex* the signals which shall be necessary for our government during the night. I had wished to have seen and conversed with you on this subject before I got under way, but a thousand avocations have prevented my coming on board your ship. I promise myself much satisfaction in your good company during the period of the service on which the Secretary has been pleased to employ us. Everything in my power will be attempted to render the tour a pleasant one. In case we should be unavoidably separated by stress of weather, the ships should proceed as expeditiously as possible to the Cape of Good Hope, where the ship first arriving will await the arrival of her consort to proceed together from thence. I have encouraged the merchantmen going out with us that I would remain with them a few days. This matter may be managed as circumstances may dictate. Should we wish to speak each other during the day, hoisting an American jack at the mizzen-topgallant masthead should be the signal. I have the honor to be, Sir, with great respect and esteem, your friend and humble servant,

                                      JAMES SEVER[5]

It took Preble only moments to scribble off an answer and hand it to the midshipman for delivery to Captain Sever:

                                    Frigate *Essex,* January 6th 1800.

Sir:

I have this moment been honored with your letter. Have the pleasure to inform you I shall be ready to weigh my last anchor precisely at two o'clock. My endeavors shall be reciprocal with yours in making the cruise a pleasant one. I shall, with your leave, pay you a visit the first pleasant day after we leave this, in order for adjusting any arrangements that may be thought necessary. I hope you will not carry a press of sail for this four or five days to come, as my ship is very full and not yet well secured for sea. I think the sooner we are clear of the merchant ships the better. Excuse haste. I am, with respect, friendship, and esteem, your obedient servant,

                                      EDWARD PREBLE

Pleasant weather, northerly winds, and a smooth sea: at 3:00 p.m. the two frigates began the long passage to Batavia.

The merchants' lack of interest in the outward-bound convoy was clearly demonstrated. Only two ships and a brig had come to Newport to place themselves under the protection of the frigates, and, as is unmistakable from their letters, both Sever and Preble wanted to shake them off early in the voyage. Stoddert's orders required the *Congress* and the *Essex* to reach Java as quickly as possible and by May at the latest. If they were to escort slow-moving merchantmen all the way, they would not be able to keep that schedule: the first night out, the *Essex* was obliged to run with double-reefed topsails on the caps so that the convoy could keep up. At eleven o'clock the next morning, the *Essex* came within hail of the *Congress* and the two captains decided that one night of such sailing was enough. The *Essex* spoke the nearest merchantman and told her master that he and his two companions were on their own. Godspeed and good luck!

That afternoon, 7 January, the northeasterly to northwesterly winds increased in force; there were snow, hail, and heavy seas, the *Essex* sometimes rolling and laboring and shipping a great deal of water. On the morning of the 11th the wind shifted and came out of the southwest, bringing strong gales, a lofty sea, rain — and warmer air. The *Essex*'s rigging had been fitted in colder weather, and the sudden change in temperature, together with the rough sea, slackened it so much that by mid-afternoon Preble began to fear that he might pitch out his masts. Early in the afternoon the *Essex* had been under a reefed foresail, a close-reefed main topsail, and mizzen and fore-topmast staysails. At 4:00 p.m. the captain ordered the main topsail taken in and the storm mizzen staysail set. Thirty minutes later, the wind blowing with great fury, Preble saw that the bowsprit was in real danger of snapping off and ordered the ship to bear away so that the fore-topmast staysail could be taken in, and the strain on the bowsprit eased. Simultaneously, he ordered the mizzen staysail hauled down. While sail was being shortened, the *Essex* lost sight of the *Congress*. Preble had foreseen this possibility, but, with his rigging slack, had considered it foolhardy to carry all the sail necessary to keep company with his commander. That night the *Essex* ran under reefed foresail and storm mizzen staysail, and at eleven o'clock on the morning of 12 January, in strong gales and rain, wore to the northeast and set up her starboard rigging. Thereafter, she experienced nearly a week of intermittent rough weather before fair skies gave an opportunity for doing a thorough job of setting up her rigging forward and aft, aloft and below. Nothing was seen of the *Congress* after the evening of 11 January, but Sever had provided for this contingency: the ships would proceed independently to Cape Town.

V

Sever's *Congress* was not at Table Bay, Cape Town, when the *Essex* anchored there on 11 March, but there was a squadron of British warships commanded by Vice Admiral Sir Roger Curtis, and Captain Preble enjoyed a brisk social whirl. His diaries, letters, and carefully preserved invitations all show that he took an almost naïve pride in moving in the military and political circles of which his commission made him a member. To some officers the social obligations imposed on the commander of an American frigate in a foreign port may have been a distasteful personal and financial burden. To Preble they were pure joy. Here is a résumé of the two-week round of calls and dinners at Cape Town he faithfully recorded in his diary and elsewhere:

March 12th: At 11:00 a.m. went ashore with the Captain of the Port and called on the Admiral, Sir Roger Curtis, and the Governor, Sir George Yonge. Later in the day, received congratulations on his arrival from all the British captains in port and joined the British captains at dinner with the Admiral.

March 13th: Dined with Captain S. H. Linzee of HMS *Oiseau*.

March 16th: Dined with Sir George Yonge.

March 17th: Joined the Irish officers of the garrison in celebrating St. Patrick's Day.

March 18th: Dined with Major General Francis Dundas, commander of the British troops at the Cape of Good Hope.

March 20th: Dined with the Admiral again.

March 21st: Dined with the Captain of the Port.

March 24th: Gave a dinner on board the *Essex;* guest list included John Elmslie, U.S. Consul at Cape Town, and the captains of all the British men-of-war in port. During dinner the wind increased to a heavy gale in which the frigate's launch was upset and lost, and all the guests were obliged to spend the night on board the *Essex*.

March 25th: Dined with Sir Roger for the third time.

March 26th: Dined with Captain Charles Elphinstone, Royal Navy.

March 27th: Made farewell calls on Sir Roger Curtis, Governor Yonge, General Dundas, and others.

Not that Preble was letting duty slide in a welter of parties. Contact with the British naval officers gave him an opportunity to improve himself professionally. The officers of the novice U.S. Navy admired British methods and practices, and consciously adopted and improved them. Captain Linzee of the *Oiseau* gave Preble the standing orders which Sir Roger had issued for his squadron. To judge by the way the copy has been marked up, Preble must have found this an instructive paper when he had his own squadron to command three years later. Another opportunity to study British methods was furnished by the *Instructions for Navy Surgeons* issued by the British Commissioners for Taking Care of Sick and Wounded Seamen, a copy of which Preble also picked up during his stay in Cape Town.

By the 25th of March, Preble was ready for sea again, but the *Congress* still had not appeared. Sever's orders of 6 January enjoined Preble to wait at Cape Town until the *Congress* caught up. Stoddert's orders were equally positive: "Should any unforeseen event prevent either of the frigates proceeding on this voyage, the one able to proceed must go alone." And the Secretary expected the two ships to enter the Sunda Strait by the first of May. Never one to be irresolute, Preble decided that two weeks was all the time he could afford to lose. The *Congress* must have received some serious damage to be so long delayed. Even if she reached the Cape she might be so disabled that she could go no farther. Counting on the splendid sailing of the *Essex* to make up lost time, Preble decided to push on alone to the Sunda Strait and cruise there for fifteen days. If the *Congress* did not show up in that time he would act on his own.

On the afternoon of 27 March 1800, the *Essex* sailed out of Table Bay.

VI

Java was sighted, lying north to northeast along the horizon, at 2:00 p.m. on 4 May.[6] Landfall was somewhat to the east of Trowers Island. Preble at once began to work up towards the Sunda Strait, but light breezes, sometimes falling away almost to a calm, did not allow much progress, and at one o'clock in the afternoon of the 5th, he brought the *Essex* to anchor between Kelapa Island and the Java shore. First Lieutenant Richard C. Beale and Third Lieutenant George G. Lee, acting at their captain's suggestion, took advantage of the nearby land to escape from more than five weeks of shipboard confinement and try to find some fresh fruit. They put off in the jolly boat, took soundings between the frigate and Kelapa Island, then landed to explore the island. While they were doing so, lookouts in the *Essex* sighted a ship running for Java Head and the entrance to the Strait. Two guns were fired as a signal for Beale and Lee to return to the ship. They brought back a supply of coconuts and an account of Kelapa: "This island has no inhabitants, is convenient to take wood at, and affords plenty of coconuts, but no good water."

At 5:00 p.m. Preble weighed anchor and chased the stranger. Two hours later, when he brought her to with a shot, Preble found that she was a former American merchantman, the *Friends,* out of New York, that had

SUNDA STRAIT AND WESTERN JAVA IN 1800

been captured by the French, carried in to the Isle of France, and condemned there. Flying Dutch colors, the *Friends* was being sailed by a French master, a German mate, a Portuguese boatswain, and twenty-nine lascar sailors, and she was carrying a French officer as passenger. There were two carriage guns on board, and her papers were singular: they consisted of only a copy of her condemnation and a Dutch certificate that had clearly been prepared for a vessel entirely different from the *Friends* in size, rig, and character.

Preble secured the merchantman for the night by taking the two Frenchmen on board the *Essex* and putting one of his officers and ten of his men in her. At six o'clock the following morning Lieutenants Beale and Lee were sent to examine the *Friends*. They reported that she was in ballast, had no cargo, and her hull, masts, spars, and sails were so decayed that it was not worth sending her to the United States for condemnation. The French master, Citizen Marquizeaux, assured Preble that she had been purchased in the Isle of France by a Dutchman for another Dutchman, and was bound to Batavia to be turned over to her owner. Preble suspected a ruse, but it was not worth the risk of troubling Dutch-American relations by making a prize of such a useless vessel. He took his men out of the *Friends*, released her to Captain Marquizeaux, and both ships shaped a course for the entrance to the Strait.

At noon on 6 May the *Essex* rounded Java Head and by 6:00 p.m. was abreast the northeast point of Mew Island, whence two ships of war could be seen anchored in Mew Bay. A boat from one of the ships had barely had time to come alongside and tell Preble that they were the British *Arrogant*, 74, Captain Edward Oliver Osborn, and *Orpheus*, 32, when, says Preble's journal:

> At half-past seven the ship from the Isle of France [the former *Friends*] suddenly bore down on us with studding sails out and, I supposed, for the purpose of giving himself up as a Frenchman, preferring to be captured by us, as he must unavoidably be captured by the English; in consequence of which, I fired a shot ahead of him to establish my claim, but the *Arrogant*'s boat [pushed off from alongside the *Essex* and] boarding her first took possession of her. I sent an officer on board to establish a claim, the lieutenant of the *Arrogant* took the French captain and his papers on board that ship, and the captain of the *Arrogant* demanded the prize as Dutch property.

Preble's journal ends abruptly on this strained note in Anglo-American naval cooperation during the Quasi-War, but other sources tell how the problem was resolved. By 8:30 p.m. the *Friends* was occupied by two rival prize crews: an officer and five men from the *Essex*, and four men from the *Arrogant*'s boat. The *Essex*, the prize, and the *Arrogant*'s boat then started working up to the anchorage in Mew Bay, while Preble called his officers together and told them that he had taken possession of the *Friends* on joint account with the *Arrogant*.

On the morning of 7 May, Preble had himself rowed over to the *Arrogant* in time to join Captain Osborn for breakfast. There were scarcely any French privateers in Java waters, Osborn told Preble, but the word was that a swarm of them was coming out from the Isle of France soon. When he got back to the *Essex* Preble called her officers together again and reported that he had just relinquished his claim to the *Friends* to Captain Osborn. Exactly what Osborn said to persuade Preble is not known, but the *Essex* had no authority to capture Dutch property (if such the *Friends* was) while the *Arrogant* and the *Orpheus* did. The clincher was, of course, that there was no cargo and the *Friends* herself was worthless and did not justify the expense of sending her anywhere for condemnation. And that explains her quick death: two days later, a party from the *Arrogant* ran her on shore and burnt her.[7]

Between 4:00 and 5:30 a.m., 10 May, the *Essex* hove up her anchor, sailed out of Mew Bay, and started up the Strait towards Batavia. The *Arrogant* and the *Orpheus* had gotten their anchors up and sails spread well in advance of the *Essex* and had a good lead on the U.S. frigate. "They were sure to outsail us," wrote Sailing Master Rufus Low in his journal, "as they were called the fastest-sailing ships in the English Navy." But at 9:00 a.m. the *Essex* passed close under the *Arrogant*'s lee. Captain Osborn came to his gangway, saluted Preble, and called through his trumpet that the *Essex* sailed remarkably fast: this, he said, was the first time he had been outsailed since he took command of the *Arrogant*. Late in the afternoon the *Essex* stood into Peper Bay and anchored. One or more boats were hoisted out and a party headed for land to secure some fresh provisions. As they closed the shore they found the beach lined with natives "well-armed and inclined to be hostile," reported one of the *Essex*'s diarists. "The officers did not land but returned immediately."

Batavia was reached during the afternoon of 15 May. Four days later, the fifteen days that Preble had allowed himself to wait for the *Congress* in the Sunda Strait expired, and there was no sign of Sever's frigate. Clearly on his own, Preble took command without hesitation. He notified the American merchant captains that the *Essex* would sail for the United States on 10 June, and would convoy all ships that were ready by that day.

It was 19 June before the fleet actually got under way. The convoy numbered fourteen sail: eight ships and six brigs. Of these, seven were bound to Philadelphia, two to Baltimore, two to Boston, and one each to Salem, Newport, and New York. The largest member of the convoy was the great ship *China*, commanded by James Josiah, formerly a captain in the Continental Navy. She measured 1,055 tons, carried 36 guns and a crew of 151 men, and was loaded with coffee, sugar, pepper, Japan wood, Japan ware, tea, camphor, and drugs. To judge by her armament, her owner expected the *China* to be able to fight off any privateer that might attack her, but, as will shortly be seen, she was a greater menace to herself than to anyone else. The *China* was exceptional among the merchantmen: the other thirteen ranged in size between 113 and 297 tons, their armament varied from two to ten guns — one was unarmed — and they employed crews of from eight to twenty-five men. The cargoes consisted principally of coffee, sugar, and pepper.

At 5:00 p.m. on 20 June, as the *Essex* and the merchantmen were approaching St. Nicolas Point, at the northern entrance to the Sunda Strait, a proa came alongside with word that one of the long-anticipated French privateers had struck. In the proa were the first victims — the master, the supercargo, and part of the crew of the American letter-of-marque *Alknomack*, six 4-pounders. The master, Joel Vickers, had this story to tell:

The *Alknomack* had sailed from Baltimore on 31 January and made Java Head at 7:00 a.m. on 15 June. Two hours later, as Captain Vickers came abreast of First Point, he saw a large vessel lying at anchor under the high land of Princes Island. Before long the stranger had set sail and was standing for the *Alknomack*. Vickers saw that she was armed and he ordered his crew to quarters, exhorting them to defend themselves should the strange ship prove to be an enemy. And, because the stranger appeared to be much more heavily armed than the *Alknomack*, Vickers spread all sail in an attempt to escape. For an hour and a half it looked as though he might succeed; then it fell nearly calm and his pursuer, presumably aided by her sweeps, came close up under the *Alknomack*'s lee. The stranger's men were ready to board, her tops filled with still other men armed with blunderbusses, and grapnels were ready on her yards. It was a sight calculated to terrify the merchant seamen, and the *Alknomack*'s men, including the first mate, told Vickers that since they saw no chance of making any effective resistance, they would not defend the ship. The armed stranger was already firing when Vickers sadly hauled down his colors.

His captor, it was learned, was the French privateer *Confiance*, eighteen 9-pounders and two 36-pound brass carronades, commanded by Robert Surcouf, the most famous and daring privateersman of the Indian Ocean. Surcouf dispatched the *Alknomack* to the Isle of France on 17 June and landed his prisoners on the Java shore on the 18th, but the *Confiance* lingered in the Strait looking for more fat and easy prey. Only twenty-four hours before they met the *Essex* on the 20th, the *Alknomack*'s people, who were making their way towards Batavia, had seen Surcouf's ship anchored near Anjer Point.

Here was news that quickened the pulse of the captain of the *Essex*! After a year and a half of war Preble could at last look forward to meeting his French enemy in combat. That his opponent would be the formidable Surcouf only added to Preble's eagerness to catch him. Captain Vickers, the supercargo, and the former crewmen were taken on board the ships of the convoy, and the next afternoon, 21 June, the *Essex* and her charges proceeded down the Strait — but not until Preble had made sure that everything was in readiness for Surcouf by calling all hands to quarters and exercising part of the main battery.

June the 22nd found the convoy anchored in Anjer Roads when a ship, identified as Surcouf's *Confiance*, was seen hovering around the fringes of the fleet, waiting to snatch up any vessel that drifted too far from the protection of the *Essex*. At the moment the *Confiance* was sighted, Preble sat writing a letter to a Dutch official at Batavia: "I fear this French privateer will do much mischief if I do not catch her," he wrote, "but I am determined to have her, if leaving the fleet at sea and returning to the Straits will effect it." By 1:30 p.m. the breeze had picked up enough for Preble to raise his anchor and make all sail in chase of the privateer, but he soon found that Surcouf's reputation was not lightly earned, and that his opponent was a tough seaman. During the chase the wind dropped away almost to a calm, then came ahead. This gave Surcouf an opportunity to use his sweeps to advantage. The *Confiance* showed her heels to the *Essex* and was soon nine miles to windward. At 6:30 p.m. Preble gave up, wore ship, and returned to his convoy.

Very light winds, almost a calm, prevailed on the morning of 24 June. Preble's convoy was at anchor close to the Java shore, between Anjer and Peper Bay, when at 10:00 a.m. Surcouf was again sighted coming down towards the fleet. At midday there was breeze enough for Preble to weigh and chase the *Confiance* to the northwest, towards Tamarind Island and Lampong Bay. By three o'clock Preble had so narrowed the gap between the *Essex* and the *Confiance* that he called all hands to quarters. Once again, however, the breeze was Surcouf's ally. Between 4:30 and 5:00 p.m. it fell almost calm and, for the second time, the *Confiance* got out her sweeps to make good her escape. About the same time breakers were sighted on the lee bow. Night was coming on and prudence prevailed over eagerness to make a capture. Preble abandoned the chase in keen disappointment, for at the moment the wind dropped away the *Essex* had been near enough to see the *Confiance*'s waterline: "Had there been only a moderate breeze I must have taken him."

Preble had had his fill of convoys and fruitless pursuits. To Stoddert he confessed greater ambitions: "It is singularly unfortunate for the American trade that the *Congress* did not arrive at Batavia, as in that case she could have convoyed the fleet home, and I might have been left to clear the Straits of those pirates; but now they can do as they please. They have no force to oppose them, the English squadron having left the station. I fear every merchant vessel that attempts to pass the Straits will fall a sacrifice. The necessity of a constant protection of our trade in the Straits will, I presume, be sufficiently apparent."

That was the last of the *Confiance* but, on the 25th, trouble developed with James Josiah's *China*. That morning, as the fleet was sailing down the Strait, Preble was alarmed to see her almost capsize in a breeze in which the other members of the convoy were able to carry royals. Josiah faced a dilemma. He dared not go to sea with his ship loaded as she was. Forty of his men were already sick, and, if he returned to fever-ridden Batavia to unload part of his cargo, he could expect a large number of them to die. Since the *Essex* could not leave her convoy to escort him back to Batavia, he would also have to risk meeting the *Confiance*. Josiah appealed to Preble for advice. The next day Preble, three of his lieutenants, and four masters from the convoy went on board the *China* and inspected her. The fault, said Preble speaking through the committee, was in the construction of the *China* which made it dangerous for her to stow cargo on her gundeck. It was essential that her center of gravity be lowered if she was to be reasonably seaworthy. To accomplish this, the committee recommended that Josiah abandon part of his valuable cargo at Mew Island, and transfer to the space thus vacated in the hold the ten 12-pound cannon on the upper deck and all of the water and salt provisions that he was carrying on the gundeck.

Preble's convoy lay at anchor in Mew Bay from the afternoon of 26 June until the morning of 1 July in order to fill their water casks. On the afternoon of 29 June the merchant ship *Columbia,* 109 days out from the Capes of Delaware, entered the Strait with news from the United States as recent as early March. From her Preble heard what had become of the *Congress*. The warm gale of 11/12 January that had caused him such concern had dealt heavy blows to Captain Sever. At 6:30 on the morning of the 12th Sever had found that his mainmast was sprung about eight feet above the spar deck. While a lieutenant and a handful of men were carrying out Sever's order to ease the mainmast by cutting away the main-topmast, the mainmast had given way and gone overboard, carrying with it the mizzentopmast and the head of the mizzenmast. Sever had then bent all his efforts towards saving his foremast, but, because of the loss of the other masts, the

Congress was lying in the trough of a very heavy sea and laboring hard. At 12:30 p.m. she had rolled away her fore-topmast and shortly thereafter it had been seen that the bowsprit was badly sprung. Ingenuity and muscle had been strained in an attempt to save bowsprit and foremast, but without success. At 3:30 that afternoon the bowsprit had at last given way and at the same moment the foremast had gone over the side, leaving the *Congress*, as one of her midshipmen, Henry Wadsworth, explained it to his father,

> Wrecked I suppose as completely as ever a vessel was. And after we were stript of every spar, sails, and rigging that was standing, we looked something like Noah's Ark: a large hull beating and boxing about without sail or spars. I think Noah had neither. . . . Now we are totally dismasted, rolling and straining about. Now she's down almost on her beam-ends. Now she rights again and plunges her bows into the foaming wave. . . . We broke all our household furniture. Sometimes you would see us seated at table very busy. Then would come a lee lurch and send us all to leeward, dishes, plates, table, soup, chairs, midshipmen and all. Then such scrabbling — some covered with dirt, water; some broken aback, some ahead.

Aided by calm spells Captain Sever jury-rigged his ship and eventually reached Hampton Roads at the end of February, but not before the *Congress* had experienced the humiliation of her own impotence. To quote Midshipman Wadsworth again:

> While under jury masts we were in a very mortifying condition, as we could neither run from nor to any sail that hove in sight, particularly at one time: One morning we discovered two sail ahead and standing for us, for by the lowness of our masts and not seeing our broadside they took us to be a merchantman. They came within gunshot, found what we were, and bore away. Gave chase and fired a shot. They hove to (one was a privateer, English or French, and the other her prize, American no doubt) but, finding we came up with 'em slowly, they bore away again. We fired a gun to leeward. They fired to windward in token of defiance, set their royals and away they went.[8]

Receipt of the news about the *Congress* was the last incident of Preble's cruise in the Sunda Strait. On 1 July, the *Essex* and her convoy of fourteen merchantmen passed Java Head homeward-bound.

VII

When the *Essex* entered New York harbor on 28 November 1800, Preble learned that political changes made it unlikely that his ship would be ordered to sea again in the immediate future. Secretary of the Navy Stoddert granted him an indefinite leave of absence to attend to what the Captain called "my private concerns," which were centered chiefly in

Mrs. Deering's parlor; about 16 January 1801 Preble left the frigate in the care of her four lieutenants, who were to rotate on leave, and started for Portland.

One aspect of the *Essex*'s cruise had been unpleasant. This was the display of Preble's waspish attitude towards his less able subordinates. He was dissatisfied with some of his officers even before he left Newport, and he had not hesitated to heap criticism on those who fell short of his standards. After eleven months of intimate contact at sea, he was even less prepared to tolerate mediocrity.

Purser William Mumford was the heaviest cross that Preble bore — as Preble pointed out almost every time he picked up his pen to write the Navy Department. To the Secretary of the Navy, he wrote on 25 December 1800: "I am sorry to say the officers and crew of the *Essex* are not paid off, in consequence of the confused state of the purser's accounts with them and his not being ready with his pay roll. Mr. Mumford's want of the necessary qualifications for a purser has already been attended with more expense to the government than ten times the amount of his pay and rations." Three weeks later he gave the Accountant of the Navy an instance of Mumford's want of qualifications: "I enclose you two abstracts presented me by the purser, one of undrawn rations by the crew of the *Essex*, and the other of the undrawn bread — which is a part of the very rations in the first abstract — and also his request for money to pay the amount. . . . As his account of rations due is now stated, many of the messes would receive double pay for their bread."[9] Mumford's papers show that he was much too unbusinesslike in his habits ever to have been a successful purser. He appears to have been so incompetent that a more kindly person might have felt sorry for him. But if Preble had any feeling for Mumford more charitable than contempt, he never let the unfortunate purser know it. Mr. Mumford would trouble no more captains. Not surprisingly, he was discharged from the Navy the following September.

Most interesting of the inadequate officers was Marine Second Lieutenant James Porter, because he struck back at Preble in a letter which indicates that the *Essex* was not a happy ship under her irascible captain. Porter was the sole Marine officer attached to the *Essex* after the tippling Lieutenant Geddes had been left on the beach at Newport. There is no indication that Lieutenant Porter neglected his duty during the eleven months at sea, but once the ship was moored at New York he let everything go slack. About the 15th of January, Porter — still the only Marine officer on board — fell ill, whereupon he left the ship and took up sick quarters on shore for about five days. Since the frigate had been in port the Marine detachment had, by Preble's orders, been employed in rowing the ship's boats ashore for provisions and in performing other errands. This had given the Marines opportunities to inquire about merchantmen bound to sea. Then, when their only officer absented himself from the ship for five days, the greater part of the detachment seized the opportunity to go over the hill. "The sentinels have deserted from their posts and have suffered men to go at their pleasure. Greater rascals I never heard of," reported Porter to Lieutenant Colonel Burrows, the Commandant of the Marine Corps.

Porter's letter drew a long and biting reprimand from Burrows, in the course of which the Commandant notified the unhappy lieutenant that he would soon be relieved of his command and admonished him:

> When you saw your Marines constantly doing the duty of sailors and your command taken from you, you should have remonstrated with the captain and showed him if he permitted the Marines to be rowing boats on shore and loitering about the city they naturally would desert. . . . If the captain insists on making bargemen of them, contrary to their terms of enlistment, and the men have no officer to plead their cause for them, he may give the remaining few a chance to desert, but no more Marines shall be sent till I can send an officer to protect them.

Here was an opportunity for Lieutenant Porter to divert some of the fire from himself, and he used it to present Burrows with a little sketch of Captain Preble:

> The treatment these Marines have received, [together] with the idea of having to go in the ship under Captain Preble's command, has been a sufficient inducement for them to make an elopement, and being called upon to do the duty of sailors gave them every opportunity. You have said I ought to have remonstrated with the captain of the impropriety in calling upon Marines to do sailors' duty. As a commander he ought to have known better, and my remonstrating with him would avail but little. I will venture to say there is not an officer or man of the former [ship's company] will ever go with him again.* I trust you'll be better informed of the man and his conduct from the Secretary of the Navy.[10]

But, if Preble had been a difficult commander on the long cruise to Java, there was a reason which his critics may not have known. At some point during the voyage his health had begun to fail. Now illness jeopardized his career as an officer.

---

* Floggings might have had something to do with the low morale in the *Essex*, particularly that of her Marines. The *Essex*'s journal kept by Sailing Master Rufus Low, which does not seem to include all instances of punishment in the ship, records sixteen floggings between 10 March and 7 October 1800, seven of which were awarded to members of Porter's Marine detachment, though the Marines made up less than 15 percent of the ship's company.

CHAPTER 5   JANUARY 1801–APRIL 1802

"... a majority of the officers of government ought to be composed of men who are firm friends to the administration...."

The months between December 1800 and the end of summer 1801 were a period of transition and uncertainty for the Navy. In foreign affairs the old enemy had been pacified but a new one appeared. In politics the party that had founded and supported the Navy lost power and was replaced by the party long associated with visceral opposition to a national naval force.

Preble's trip from New York to Portland was carrying him away from Washington, but he would not be cut off from news of these developments at the capital. He had struck up a warm friendship with Charles Washington Goldsborough, then a clerk to the Secretary of the Navy, but soon to be appointed Chief Clerk of the Navy Department. Goldsborough had the complete confidence of Stoddert and his successors at the Navy Department and, after his promotion to the chief clerkship, was second only to the Secretary in influence and power. The political scene, its effect on things naval, and the policies and decisions of the Navy Department — Goldsborough wrote Preble about all these in a series of long and frequent letters which ended only with the latter's death.[1]

In the winter of 1801 the naval war with France was coming to its close. A treaty ending hostilities had been signed in France on 30 September 1800 and was laid before the Senate on the 16th of December. Since the terms were not entirely satisfactory to the United States there was some doubt about what action the Senate would take. This uncertainty was reflected in a letter that Goldsborough wrote Preble on 5 January 1801:

> The Senate are still occupied with the treaty with France. The most prevalent opinion here is that their deliberations on the subject will eventuate in its

conditional ratification. Taking it for granted that this will be the case, the consequences with respect to our Navy will be the sale of the greater part of the public ships and probably the laying up of the residue, unless we should unfortunately get at loggerheads with the British. I think it is probable that the thirteen frigates, the *United States* and *Constitution, President, Philadelphia, Chesapeake, Constellation, Congress, New York, Essex, Boston, General Greene, Adams* and *John Adams,* will be retained and all the rest sold.

The recent election had resulted in a major defeat for the Federalists. Both the presidency and the control of Congress would soon pass into the hands of the Republicans, who, if the worst Federalist predictions were fulfilled, would emasculate — or possibly abolish — the Navy. But in early January it was still not known who would be President, because the two Republicans, Thomas Jefferson and Aaron Burr, had received the same number of electoral votes. The election would have to be decided by the House of Representatives — in lame-duck session and hence still Federalist-controlled. Goldsborough looked into the future and offered his prediction:

> The presidential election still occupies the solicitude of Congress and the good people of Washington. . . . My impression with regard to the future President is that Mr. Jefferson will be the man. I wish he may be. His private character certainly stands much higher than the other's, and his most violent enemies must allow him to be a true patriot. Although they may fear his head, his heart they cannot. I believe his heart is as sound as any man's.

By 20 February that prediction had been borne out and Jefferson elected; but Goldsborough, a Federalist, was still uneasy:

> Before this reaches, you will have learnt the result of the presidential election. A new order of things is now to be adopted, and those systems heretofore pursued by the administration, under which we have enjoyed protection, security, peace, and prosperity, are to be changed. Our political ship is about to be launched into the "tempestuous seas of liberty," and, as many wise and virtuous men say, with an unskillful pilot at the helm. But I forbear any reflections upon this subject, since they cannot be otherwise than painful.

Meanwhile, the Senate had approved the French treaty subject to certain modifications. As Goldsborough had forecast, Congress — though still Federalist-controlled — next moved to reduce the size and cost of the Navy. The Peace Establishment Act, approved by President Adams on 3 March 1801, "authorized" the President, "whenever the situation of public affairs shall in his opinion render it expedient," to sell all naval vessels except thirteen frigates. Of the thirteen ships retained, six were to be kept in constant service in peacetime; the other seven were to be laid up in ordinary. Frigates on active duty were allowed only two-thirds of their wartime complement of seamen and ordinary seamen. Nine captains, thirty-six lieutenants, and one hundred and fifty midshipmen were to be retained in the Navy; the President was "authorized" to discharge all other officers.

But at Portland politics were, for the moment, only a secondary interest with Captain Preble. He was pursuing Mary Deering with such vigor that he neglected his friends. "I have been waiting for the long letter you promised me from Portland," Goldsborough complained on 20 February. "From what I learn from [Captain Hugh G.] Campbell, however, you have been much better employed." No details of the courtship are known, but Mary appears to have surrendered after only token resistance, for on 17 March 1801 she became Mrs. Edward Preble.

In the Preble family, Mary Deering Preble was remembered as a strong-willed and overbearing woman, known behind her back as "The Grenadier." So formidable was she that it is reported she once subdued a burglar by pointing a hearth broom at him and convincing him it was a gun. These memories and traditions of Mary Preble date from her forty-odd years of widowhood and reflect the feelings of her dominated son and daughter-in-law.[2] About her earlier years only two things are clear: she was past thirty and on the edge of spinsterhood when she married Captain Preble; she was a retiring person who preferred books to people, except for a small circle of close friends and relatives, and had little desire to travel or to live away from Portland. "You are, I find, still pursuing the same steady, solitary course of life with your books in the snug parlor," her husband once wrote her.

Most biographers of Preble say that the Captain's marriage to Mary Deering made him a wealthy man. That is not really accurate. Not many of Edward Preble's financial records survive, but some impressions about him and money can be formed from those that do. He inherited something less than one-tenth of his father's large estate, and his voyages had always brought in enough to enable him to lead a comfortable life as a bachelor. He may not have been rich, but neither was he without money to do whatever he wanted. It is true that Mary Deering was wealthy, but such evidence as remains suggests that Edward always regarded her money and property as her money and property. He did not dip into her fortune for himself, though it may have looked to contemporaries as though he did, since he and his brother-in-law James Deering actually managed most of Mary's financial business for her.

In late March 1801 the newlyweds started on a leisurely trip towards Washington. The provisions of the Peace Establishment Act were to be carried into effect, and Preble thought that the eve of a reduction in the officer corps was the right moment for a visit to the Navy Department. A

MARY DEERING PREBLE

This miniature, attributed to Edward Greene Malbone, was probably painted at Boston in 1805. It portrays Mary with light brown, curly hair, soft blue eyes, and the pale complexion of one who rarely exposed herself to the sun's rays.

Courtesy of U.S. Naval Academy Museum

EBEN PREBLE

It is often said that the miniature to the left, by Edward Greene Malbone, is a representation of Edward Preble. However, the plump face, the heavy beard, and the powdered hair combed back — features that do not appear in Rembrandt Peale's Preble — all indicate that it is a portrait of the Commodore's brother, Eben.

Courtesy of City Art Museum of St. Louis

new Secretary of the Navy had not yet been appointed, but rumors reaching Preble indicated that the post would go to Samuel Smith, a Congressman from Maryland and a representative of the shipping and pro-naval interests in the Republican Party. As he passed through Boston on his way south, Preble prudently armed himself with a letter of introduction to Smith from James and Thomas Handasyd Perkins.

He never needed to use it. Edward and Mary arrived in New York City on 8 April, and the next day the Captain received a letter, dated 1 April, from Smith himself. Samuel Smith had declined the Cabinet post, but had agreed to perform the duties of the office on a temporary basis until a permanent Secretary could be found. Smith's letter notified Preble that the *Essex* was to be part of a squadron that the President had decided to send on a cruise under Commodore Thomas Truxtun, and directed him to ship a crew, prepare the frigate for sea, and have her at Hampton Roads by the first of May. The same letter told Preble that he had been selected as one of the nine captains to be retained under the Peace Establishment Act.

II

The *Essex* was being ordered to sea because of a new departure in American relations with the Barbary Powers — the four North African states that operated a highly successful international protection racket. Jefferson's administration was scarcely a week old when it became apparent that these predatory governments presented an immediate and pressing problem.

The chief cause for concern was Yusuf Caramanli, the Pasha of Tripoli, with whom the United States had concluded a treaty of peace and friendship in November 1796 at the initial cost of about $56,000, plus a considerable sum on the arrival in Tripoli of the American consul in 1799. However, the treaty did not require payment of an annuity or, more baldly, an annual tribute. Yusuf had grown increasingly unhappy with his bargain and had begun to mention his desire for further remuneration, say, perhaps, a brig-of-war. Finally, at an audience with the American consul, James Leander Cathcart, on 16 October 1800, he demanded that the United States pay him either an annuity or a sum in cash for keeping the peace. The Pasha said that he would wait six months for a reply — he later backed off a little from this rigid time limit — and that if he did not receive an answer to his demands in that time, or if the answer was not to his liking, he would declare war on the United States. Cathcart's dispatch to the Department of State reporting Yusuf's threats was received in Washington on 13 March 1801 and led directly to the decision that American naval forces should be sent to the Mediterranean.

The new President had long been opposed to the payment of tribute to the Barbary States. He was convinced, he said, that "it is money thrown away, and that there is no end to the demand of these powers, nor any security in their promises. The real alternative before us is whether to abandon the Mediterranean or to keep up a cruise in it, perhaps in rotation with other powers."[3] An ideal opportunity was now offered Jefferson to use the Navy to establish more stable relations with Barbary. The maritime war with France was at an end, U.S. ships could be called home from the West Indies, and a new disposition of the naval force had to be made in accord with the provision of the Peace Establishment Act which required that six frigates be kept in constant service.

On 9 March 1801 the Cabinet had tentatively decided to employ two of the frigates in the Mediterranean,[4] but it was not until about 20 March, or a week after the receipt of Cathcart's dispatch, that the President definitely determined, on the advice of both Benjamin Stoddert and Samuel Smith, to dispatch a naval force to the Barbary Coast. The six frigates were divided into two squadrons which would relieve one another annually on active cruising. Since the Peace Establishment Act authorized but did not require the President to sell all of the Navy's smaller vessels, it was decided to retain the two splendid 12-gun schooners *Enterprize* and *Experiment* and attach them to the two squadrons as tenders.[5] Between 31 March and 2 April orders were issued for the first squadron – the frigates *President*, *Philadelphia*, and *Essex*, and the schooner *Enterprize* – to assemble in Hampton Roads by 1 May.

When Thomas Truxtun begged off from the command of the squadron, Commodore Richard Dale was appointed in his place. Dale's instructions were drawn up by Samuel Smith and dated 20 May, their general terms having been determined by the Cabinet on the 15th. They made it clear that the government was sending out the squadron in the hope of preventing hostilities and promoting commerce, rather than of provoking conflict. Jefferson and his Cabinet did not intend the dispatch of Dale's squadron as the beginning of a crusade to end the traditional European policy of subsidies and presents to the Barbary States. Their aim was more limited: namely, by the presence of force in the Mediterranean, to discourage those states from periodically demanding fresh presents or more advantageous treaties, and to encourage them to honor existing agreements. For this fidelity they might be rewarded from time to time by spontaneous presents. But if any of the Barbary Powers broke the treaties and declared war they were to receive swift and memorable punishment.

On his arrival in the Mediterranean, Dale was to call at Gibraltar and there learn whether any of the Barbary States were at war with the United States. If so, he was to "chastise their insolence by sinking, burning or destroying their ships and vessels wherever you shall find them." Specific directions were given to govern Dale's disposition of his force, depending on which of the Barbary States might have declared war. If Tripoli alone was found to have initiated hostilities: "You will then proceed direct to that port, where you will lay your ships in such a position as effectually to prevent any of their vessels from going in or out." Thus the idea of a naval blockade as the effective means of bringing Tripoli to terms first appears in the government's Mediterranean strategy.

III

Preble began to ready the *Essex* for her Mediterranean cruise. But his health, which had begun to break on the long voyage to Java, was still bad. On 17 April he wrote Samuel Smith:

> I am not able to give that personal attendance I wish [to the frigate] in consequence of the present state of my health, which is very much impaired, and which a vegetable and milk diet and gentle equestrian exercise will be the most likely means of restoring. I have been advised by several eminent physicians to reside in the country for three or four months and attend particularly to my diet, and, as I really do not consider myself able at present to attend to all the necessary duties attached to my command, and which the service always requires, it would be extremely gratifying to me to obtain leave of absence until my health is restored, if it is convenient to order any other captain to command this ship for the present, without any detriment to the present arrangements of government. But sooner than the ship should be delayed one day, and by that means the service suffer, I am ready to make any sacrifice whatever and will proceed to sea.[6]

This illness, which his earliest biographer called "a debility of the digestive organs," [7] plagued Captain Preble for the remainder of his life. The vegetable-and-milk diet mentioned in his letter to Samuel Smith and his choleric disposition suggest that Preble suffered from ulcers. Smith readily granted the request for a leave of absence. All he asked of Preble was that he complete the outfitting of the *Essex*, sail her as far as Hampton Roads, and there turn over the command to Captain William Bainbridge. "I am at present quite an invalid and shall not be able to pay the necessary attention to the ship in case of stormy weather," Preble worried, but he was equal to the job, and on 29 May he gave up his ship to Bainbridge.

IV

Although Preble was a moderate Federalist, he won the confidence of the Republican administration and eventually became its most trusted naval officer. There were two principal reasons for this: the first was his ability; and the second was the fact that he was not an especially partisan person. He was intensely and emotionally patriotic, more interested in serving the country — and thereby establishing his own fame — than in forwarding the ends of his party. His ties with the administration became closer and closer.

One of the most important factors in Preble's winning of the confidence of Jefferson's Cabinet was his friendship with a fellow resident of Maine, Secretary of War Henry Dearborn. Only a few of the many letters that passed between Preble and Dearborn are now available, but there can be no question that Dearborn's confidence in Preble played a large part in the selection of the relatively junior Captain Preble as commodore of the squadron sent to the Mediterranean in the summer of 1803.

Friendship with Dearborn was also the key to Captain Preble's most questionable venture into party politics. This occurred early in 1803, but may be narrated at this point in Preble's life in connection with the change of national administrations. Nathaniel Fosdick, the Federalist Collector of Customs at Portland, was removed by the Republicans and Isaac Ilsley, a cousin of Mrs. James Deering, was appointed in his place. An error was made in the form of Ilsley's name in his nomination and commission, and the interval required to straighten out the mistake gave Fosdick an opportunity to travel to Washington and appeal his removal from office. Preble, who seems to have been the chief behind-the-scenes mover in Ilsley's nomination, saw the prize in danger and wrote to Dearborn, with whom he had been in communication before on the subject:

> I perfectly agree with you in opinion that a majority of the officers of government ought to be composed of men who are firm friends to the administration and whose political opinions correspond with the general views and measures of government, and that no man ought to hold an office under it who speaks disrespectfully of it, much less anyone who takes an active part in the opposition and makes use of his interest to its injury; for it is certainly contrary to human nature designedly to place an enemy in a situation to injure us, or to continue him in such a situation, if he should have been so placed without our consent, when it is in our power to remove him.
>
> I understand that Mr. Fosdick is at Washington to endeavor to regain his office and that he took with him a letter or remonstrance signed by a number of the inhabitants of Portland. I do not know how many signed it, but I am told most of them were his particular friends and bottle companions, and I know that many of them are in the daily habit of visiting the Insurance Office for the purpose of abusing the President of the United States and the whole administration, and I know that some of the persons who have signed the paper alluded to have said that they should prefer Mr. Ilsley for a Collector to Mr. Fosdick, but that they did not approve of the removal of Federal men

to give place to Republicans. However, Mr. F. may have recently felt it for his interest to be more modest than he has formerly been in speaking of the President, and, notwithstanding the professions he may make to regain his office, he is in my opinion what he ever has been: an enemy to the President and whole of his administration, nor do I believe that any friend to him at Portland has signed their name to any paper in recommendation of Mr. F. I know certainly that his removal has given general satisfaction to every friend of the government in the District, and that Mr. Ilsley's appointment has given very general satisfaction to all parties, and I am confident of the truth of what I observed in a former letter, that, had Mr. Fosdick been removed by death, almost every merchant in the District would have recommended Mr. Ilsley for his successor, so excellent is his character.[8]

Fosdick's friends contended that Captain Preble and Ilsley's other supporters were less concerned with getting loyal Republicans into office than they were in a Deering family vendetta against Fosdick for having apprehended one John Deering in a customs violation. Daniel Davis, the Solicitor General of Massachusetts, wrote Secretary of the Treasury Albert Gallatin a letter which, after telling the history of the quarrel, continued:

Mr. James Deering, a respectable merchant in this town and cousin to the abovementioned delinquent [John Deering], I understand has heretofore threatened the removal of Mr. Fosdick; Captain Preble of the Navy, who married Mr. James Deering's sister, is said to have embarked in the accomplishment of the same object; and Mr. William Wilson of the Army is said to have calumniated Mr. Fosdick to General [Samuel] Smith, and that General Smith has assured that gentleman that "Mr. Fosdick should be removed." . . .

It ought to be known to the President that a family connection subsists between all these gentlemen (excepting Mr. Wilson) and also between them and Mr. Ilsley, who is the person probably intended for Mr. Fosdick's successor. Mr. Ilsley and Captain Preble are the brothers-in-law of Mr. James Deering,* who is considered to be the *secret, concealed* author of Mr. Fosdick's removal. . . .

It is said that Mr. Fosdick's *political* character and conduct have been arraigned. It is impossible to defend himself against *secret accusations*. You may be assured, however, that he has it in his power, if he should be indulged with the opportunity, to give the government perfect satisfaction upon this subject. His friends and connections are among the most respectable and zealous admirers of the character of the President and of his administration. His language and deportment have been respectful and even faultless. He is well known to the Secretary of War, whose friendship he has enjoyed and which I presume still exists. The Republicans in this quarter disclaim any agency or interference in his removal, and his official industry, correctness and intelligence have heretofore deservedly acquired him the character of one of the most valuable officers in the government's service. I cannot but believe, therefore, that his removal has been brought about by the malignant agency

* Isaac Ilsley married his first cousin, Augusta Ilsley, who was the younger sister of Mrs. James Deering.

of his private enemies, to some of whom I presume the government would not readily extend their confidence.⁹

In the end Nathaniel Fosdick lost the job. Isaac Ilsley got it. And Edward Preble was the hatchet man.

V

When Commodore Richard Dale with the frigates *President, Essex,* and *Philadelphia* arrived at Gibraltar on 1 July 1801, he learned that the Pasha of Tripoli had declared war on the United States on 10 May. Also, he found in the harbor the 26-gun Tripolitan ship *Meshuda* and a 16-gun Tripolitan brig. Leaving the *Philadelphia* to watch the Tripolitans and prevent their getting out into the Atlantic, where they were believed to have been bound and where they could have done extensive damage to American trade, Dale in the *President,* accompanied by Lieutenant Andrew Sterett in the *Enterprize,* sailed on up the Mediterranean towards Tripoli. After calling at Algiers and Tunis, the *President* arrived off Tripoli on 24 July. The Pasha expressed to Dale some interest in negotiating a new treaty or at least a truce, but he would not answer Dale's pointed questions about his reasons for going to war and about the terms on which he would make a new treaty. Since Dale did not consider himself authorized to conclude either peace or a truce, the matter was dropped after a few exchanges between the two men. Except for one brief absence, the *President* continued to cruise before the port of Tripoli until 3 September, when a shortage of provisions and a sudden increase in the sick list forced Dale to raise the blockade and run down to Gibraltar.

The only important naval action of this first year of the war occurred on 1 August, when the *Enterprize,* on a passage to Malta for water, fell in with a 14-gun Tripolitan polacre and captured her after a fierce three-hour engagement. Lieutenant Sterett ordered the Tripolitan's masts cut away, her guns, anchors, and cables thrown overboard, then allowed her to proceed to Tripoli under jury rig as a cautionary example to the Pasha. President Jefferson was delighted with this successful opening to the campaign against the Tripolitans, and sent Sterett a personal letter of congratulation:

> I do myself the pleasure ... of expressing to you, on behalf of your country, the high satisfaction inspired by your conduct in the late engagement with the Tripolitan cruiser captured by you. Too long, for the honor of nations, have those barbarians been suffered to trample on the sacred faith of treaties, on the rights and laws of human nature! You have shown to your countrymen that that enemy cannot meet bravery and skill united. In proving to them that our

past condescensions were from a love of peace, not a dread of them, you have deserved well of your country, and have merited the high esteem and consideration of which I have now the pleasure of assuring you.[10]

In his Mediterranean operations Commodore Dale acted on the principle that the duties of his squadron were to observe, to convoy American merchantmen, to capture Tripolitan cruisers, and to blockade the port of Tripoli. His orders did not, Dale held, authorize him to launch an attack on the port and city of Tripoli. He did, however, develop strong views on the proper strategy to be used against Tripoli, and he made a number of recommendations to the administration for their consideration and guidance in issuing instructions to the squadron that would relieve him. In his view, two courses of action were open to the United States.

First, there was an essentially passive blockade of the port, which he described in these terms:

> Should the United States determine to carry on the war against Tripoli, it will be highly necessary to keep it closely blockaded, not to suffer any kind of vessels of any nation to go in or come out. To do this it will take two frigates and two sloops-of-war, two to be off the harbor, and two to cruise along the coast to the eastward and westward. . . . Also, I think it would be advisable to have a small vessel constructed to carry a bomb to heave a few shells in the town now and then. The more this Mr. Bey is harassed, the sooner he will be glad to make peace; and it will have a good effect on the other two powers [Algiers and Tunis]: they will then see America is not to be trifled with.

Second, the government might authorize an attack on the city and the shipping in the harbor. Such an attack would, Dale thought, require four frigates and three bomb ketches, and might be combined with a landing on the coast by light forces.[11] He personally endorsed this second course: "I would be answerable for Tripoli's being taken in two days after the force arrived off there."

This was an especially favorable time for an assault on the port because Sweden was also at war with Tripoli and had sent a force of four frigates under Rear Admiral Rudolf Cederström into the Mediterranean. Dale saw promising possibilities for joint action. In a letter to Baron Cederström, he outlined his recommendations for operations against Tripoli:

> To blockade Tripoli completely, so as to prevent all kind of communication by sea, it will be absolutely necessary to have three or four gunboats, constructed and fitted in such a manner as to carry an eighteen or twenty-four-pounder in the bow and a nine or twelve ditto in the stern, that thirty men may live on board, and to row twenty or twenty-four oars, and to sail well. Those boats would prevent all the small craft from going in and coming out; by keeping close inshore also prevent the enemy's gunboats from coming out

in a calm to annoy your ships when close inshore, which they will do if you have no boats of that kind, and may very possibly do your ships considerable damage, without having it in your power to do them any harm.

To make an attack on Tripoli, it will be necessary to have one or two bomb vessels, well fitted. With them, the gunboats, and the boats belonging to the ships, I think the place may be attacked with little doubt of success. At least, the shipping in the harbor may be burnt without much danger.

While Dale was cruising before Tripoli, the direction of American naval affairs passed into the hands of a new Secretary of the Navy — Robert Smith, Samuel Smith's brother. The squadron which would relieve Dale's ships on the Mediterranean station was the first for the success or failure of which Robert Smith would be officially responsible. It was to be made up of the frigates *Chesapeake,* flying the broad pennant of Commodore Richard V. Morris, the *Adams,* the *Constellation,* and, again, the schooner *Enterprize.*

In "An Act for the Protection of the Commerce and Seamen of the United States against the Tripolitan Cruisers," which was approved on 6 February 1802, Congress authorized the President "fully to equip, officer, man, and employ such of the armed vessels of the United States as may be judged requisite . . . for protecting effectually the commerce and seamen thereof on the Atlantic Ocean, the Mediterranean and adjoining seas." This new Act, in effect, repealed the restrictions that the Peace Establishment Act had placed on the number of officers and men in the Navy,[12] and authorized the President "to instruct the commanders of the respective public vessels aforesaid to subdue, seize and make prize of all vessels, goods and effects belonging to the Bey of Tripoli, or to his subjects . . . and also to cause to be done all such other acts of precaution or hostility as the state of war will justify and may, in his opinion, require." Finally, the term for which seamen could be enlisted was extended from one year to two, allowing the ships to operate in the Mediterranean for longer periods.

As to the squadron's operational orders, Robert Smith wrote to Commodore Morris on 20 March:

> To effectuate the great object of maintaining a squadron in the Mediterranean, which is the protection of our commerce, we must use our best exertions to keep the enemy's vessels in port, to blockade the places out of which they issue, and prevent as far as possible their coming out or going in. You will, on your arrival in the Mediterranean, make such a distribution of the force under your command as may appear, upon a full view of existing circumstances, the best adapted to the accomplishment of the views of government. Convoy must be given to our vessels as far as it can be done consistently with the plan of blockading.
>
> You will write to me by every opportunity from the Mediterranean, and give me particular information of all your movements.

In supplementary orders issued on 1 April, Smith advised the Commodore: "I shall not point out to you the ground you are to occupy in the execution of these instructions. Circumstances may arise to induce a frequent change in your position, and we have a perfect confidence that you will provide judiciously against every movement of the enemy."

Two points about these instructions deserve special notice.

First, the great degree of discretion given to Commodore Morris in the conduct of his operations. Robert Smith made it his practice to set out broad principles of policy and leave detailed strategic and tactical planning to the professional naval officers on the station. Considering the time that elapsed between an event taking place in the Mediterranean, word of it reaching Washington, and fresh instructions being received by the commodore on station, there was wisdom in the practice. It did require, though, that there be a commodore of independent and decisive temperament at the Mediterranean end.

Second, the government's choice of a blockade as the effective means of bringing Tripoli to terms. Richard Dale had offered the alternatives of a relatively passive blockade of the port, or an attack on the city and shipping, and the language of the legislation — "and also to cause to be done all such other acts of precaution or hostility as the state of war will justify and may, in his opinion, require" — authorized the latter course. The reason blockade was chosen seems to have been that an attack would require larger forces and be much more expensive than a blockade, and would thereby cripple the administration's program of fiscal retrenchment. The President summed up the government's policy succinctly when he told Congress on 15 December 1802: "To secure our commerce in that sea with the smallest force competent we have supposed it best to watch strictly the harbor of Tripoli."

The administration interpreted the overtures that Yusuf had made to Dale regarding a new treaty or a truce to mean that he was already tiring of the war and was eager for peace. Accordingly, on 18 April 1802, a month after Morris had been given his instructions, James L. Cathcart, the former U.S. Consul at Tripoli, was empowered to negotiate a new treaty with the Pasha. The terms were to be essentially *status quo ante bellum*, and Cathcart was instructed: "You are, in the most peremptory manner, to stifle every pretension or expectation that the United States will, on their side, make the smallest contribution to him as the price of peace." To support Cathcart's mission additional orders were issued to Morris on 20 April:

> It has been determined to lay all our naval force under your command before Tripoli, and Mr. Cathcart will accompany the expedition. Holding out the olive branch in one hand and displaying in the other the means of offensive operations may produce a peaceful disposition towards us in the mind of the

Bashaw, and essentially contribute to our obtaining an advantageous treaty with him. . . . You will proceed with the whole squadron under your command and lay off against Tripoli, taking every care to make the handsomest and most military display of your force, and so conducting your maneuvers as to excite an impression that, in the event of negotiations failing, you intend a close and vigorous blockade.

No new instructions were given as to the course to be followed should the negotiations fail.

CHAPTER 6   DECEMBER 1801–SEPTEMBER 1803

". . . the Secretary of the Navy . . . seems disposed to make such arrangements with respect to my future service as shall be most agreeable to me."

During the summer and autumn of 1801 Edward Preble's health began to improve. Still, he was far from complete recovery, and he faced the prospect of the long, disagreeable Maine winter. A voyage to a warmer climate sounded appealing, and he began to cast about for a way to combine his search for health with a means of making money. Brother Eben, to whom Edward wrote for advice, endorsed a tour to the south of Europe or to Madeira, but thought an attempt to make some money on the side was a bad idea:

> I should not advise you to take charge of any property where responsibility or attention is required. Public employ would not answer, and the charge of a private ship would be incompatible with the reasonableness of your request for leave of absence, as your indisposition would be considered a plea for pecuniary purposes. I advise you to take passage in some good ship to a favorable climate and leave business and care at home. Property should be a secondary consideration when in competition with health. Without the latter, the former is of little consequence.

Edward Preble did not go to Madeira, but to avoid the harm that a New England winter might do to his health, he left Portland on 22 December 1801, bound for Washington. He had gone no farther than Boston when he came down with a fever that kept him shut in his room for more than two weeks. He was getting his strength back as rapidly as his weakened health would allow when, on 27 January 1802, he received orders from Secretary of the Navy Robert Smith notifying him that he was to have a subordinate command in the new American squadron which was expected to bring the Tripolitan War to a successful conclusion. "The *Adams* requires a commander, and the President has selected you for that appointment," wrote Smith. "I have, therefore, the honor to direct that you repair immediately to New York and assume the command of that ship."

Preble thought he ought not to ask for an extension of his leave. He expected his health to improve once he got to sea — the more so since he would be on the Mediterranean station — and he supposed himself well enough to get through the irksome business of preparing the *Adams* for her cruise. The same evening that he got his orders he took passage for Portland, where he packed his baggage and arranged his financial affairs for an absence of more than a year.

Early on the morning of 31 January, he left Portland for Boston in the schooner *Greyhound,* but the wind, which had been N.N.W., soon veered to the eastward and the *Greyhound* was forced to return to port. At three o'clock the next morning another attempt was made to get to sea, but when the schooner had gone as far as the lighthouse it began to snow, and once more the *Greyhound* ran for the shelter of Portland harbor. A third attempt to sail from Portland, made on the morning of 2 February, was successful, and by sunset the *Greyhound* had run as far down the coast as Wells Bay. "Looks likely for a storm," Preble noted in his diary, and he had an experienced eye for weather: at 3:00 a.m., in a heavy snowstorm, the schooner anchored off Portsmouth lighthouse. Preble's patience was exhausted with the pace of travel in the packet, and at 10:00 a.m. he hired a small boat — so small that some of his baggage had to be left in the *Greyhound* to be brought to New York by his servant, Adam Smith — and went ashore.

From Portsmouth Preble took the stage for Boston, where he arrived on 4 February. His diary entry for the 5th reads, "Am too unwell to travel in the stage," but by the 8th he felt well enough to continue his trip and went on to Providence in the coach. On the 9th he traveled to New London, Connecticut, but that night he was so tired and sick that he could not sleep, and he lay over the whole of the 10th. Travel by packet or stage was too hard on a sick man: 11 February he hired a horse and chaise, with a boy to drive, and started for New Haven. Preble got as far as Killingworth, twenty-six miles on his way, and stopped there for the night. "Was unwell all night," he jotted in his diary. On the 12th he completed the distance to New Haven, which he reached in a heavy rain. At 7:00 a.m., 13 February, Preble boarded a New Haven-New York packet, but with rain and calms and thick weather it was not until 3:00 p.m. of the 14th that the packet got within five miles of New York City; then the tide began to run strongly against her and she made fast to a wharf. Preble disembarked and covered the last miles in a chaise. The next day he wrote Mary: "I arrived here last evening after the most painful journey I ever experienced."

The trip from Portland had shown the Captain how sick he was, and he admitted as much to Robert Smith on 20 February: "I am not able to give my personal attendance [to the *Adams*] at present, as I am confined to my room sick, but hope in a day or two to be able to go out again. My journey from Portland to this place was an undertaking greater than my state of health would justify, and I am now suffering in consequence; but have no doubt my health will be restored if I can get to sea, which I am very desirous of." Acting Lieutenant Charles Ludlow commanded on board the frigate and supervised her outfitting for sea. Preble visited the ship when his health permitted and when the weather was pleasant, or directed preparations from his room when he was too ill to leave it. Entries in his diary record the state of his health during the next two months:

> *February 16th:* Visited the ship, although quite unwell.
>
> *February 19th:* I was taken very unwell in the morning. Not able to go out.
>
> *March 1st:* Confined to my lodgings. Indisposed.
>
> *March 3d:* Confined by indisposition.
>
> *March 5th:* Very much indisposed. Took cold yesterday.
>
> *March 13th:* Unwell, but visited the ship.
>
> *March 14th:* Kept house. Very much indisposed.
>
> *March 16th:* Very unwell. Went to the ship for half an hour; returned and went to bed very sick.
>
> *March 18th:* Very unwell, but visited the ship.
>
> *April 1st:* Not well enough to attend to the ship.
>
> *April 2d:* I went on board in the morning and returned very unwell. Confined to my bed all the remainder of the day.
>
> *April 6th:* Not able to go out owing to indisposition.
>
> *April 7th:* Too unwell to go on board.

Preble's harsh disposition had created unhappiness among the officers of the *Essex*. It did the same thing in the *Adams*. Sailing Master James Trant, already dissatisfied because he had not been promoted to lieutenant, resigned his warrant, saying that he had "rather be dismissed than sail with this captain," whom he sketched in this fashion: "Captain Preble [is] seldom or ever on board, he being in a decline and cross, peevish and ill-tempered, surly and proud."[1]

This was one more indication that Preble was in no condition to assume a responsible fighting command. By mid-April he realized that he could not take the *Adams* to sea; nor, with the sharp reduction in the number of captains allowed the Navy under the Peace Establishment Act and the drive for economy in government, could he expect another extended leave of absence. The only course open was to resign from the Navy. Preble notified Secretary Smith of his decision on 13 April.

To support his resignation he enclosed statements from two physicians, which seemed to suggest that Preble's illness was closely related to, if not caused by, his emotional, choleric, driving temperament. Dr. Edward Miller, who had treated Preble a year earlier, described him as "reduced to a distressing state of debility and emaciation. . . . Repeated experience proves that he is extremely susceptible of injury from the cares and fatigue of business." Samuel R. Marshall, Surgeon of the *Adams*, made the same point in stronger language: "His health has gradually declined since his residence in this city, which circumstance I am induced to attribute to the rigid attention, zeal and anxiety which he has universally manifested in conducting the repairs of the *Adams*, and which he has pursued with unremitting industry till the last ten days, during which time he has suffered extremely from disease. The tender anxiety and care which are inseparable from his command and the activity of his mind will necessarily prove detrimental to his body."

With his resignation in the mail to the Navy Department, Edward still had to tell Mary:

> New York, April 16th 1802.
>
> My Dear Friend:
> It is now fourteen days since I have been able to go on board my ship. I have been so extremely unwell I have lately had a consultation of medical gentlemen on my case, and the result is that I have written to the Navy Office and requested permission to resign my commission in the Navy, as the cares and anxiety attending my command will counteract the good effects of change of *air* or *climate*, or any other favorable *circumstance*. I am now reduced very low, but hope, if my resignation is accepted, that I shall have strength enough to be on my way home in a fortnight from this. God only knows how much I long to see you. I shall write you again as soon as I know the result of my application to the Navy Office. In the meantime I remain your emaciated, sick, but faithful and affectionate husband,
>
> EDWD PREBLE
>
> P.S. I enclose you one of the [doctors'] certificates that you may judge of the propriety of my resignation.

Meanwhile, the letter of resignation had reached Robert Smith, who replied on the 16th with the kindness and consideration that gained him such a strong grip on the affections of the officers: "To accept your resignation under such circumstances (and under no other would you, I am persuaded, have at this season offered it) would be an act of the highest injustice to you. To insist on your continuing in the command of the *Adams* would be an act of inhumanity which no State necessity scarcely could justify. You will, therefore, hereby consider yourself released from the command of the *Adams* and on furlough until your health shall be restored." Preble received the Secretary's letter on 20 April and acknowledged it the day following.

Four days after Smith's letter had reached Preble there came a strange and private note from Goldsborough, who had been promoted to Chief Clerk of the Navy Department on the 1st of April:

> Washington, 16 April 1802.
>
> Dear Preble:
>
> Yours of the 12th instant I have received, and regret extremely the cause of your having tendered your resignation; however I cannot but think that you have acted correctly in doing so. The Secretary's answer goes by this mail, and describes to you the sensations he felt on receiving your communication. Being a man of elegant feelings, he could not permit himself to accept your resignation under the circumstances which induced you to offer it. Still, however, the service is suffering, and your continuance may produce much embarrassment and an anxiety in your mind unfavorable to your recovery.
>
> Your best plan, my dear Sir, certainly will be to divest yourself as far as possible of every care and to lead a regular and tranquil life. This, with proper medical attendance, I hope will restore you; and when perfectly recovered, if you should feel a disposition to reenter the service, from the very high opinion entertained of you by those who administer the government, there is no doubt but that they would cheerfully embrace an opportunity of benefiting their country so essentially by again accepting your services.
>
> I have not time to add anything more than my sincerest wishes that your health may be speedily restored and my hearty prayers for your prosperity and happiness. Sincerely your friend,
>
> CH: WAS: GOLDSBOROUGH

Apparently Goldsborough thought the Secretary had been carried away by his good nature and had exposed the Navy Department, of which Goldsborough had become a conspicuous official, to criticism. Certainly these were hard days for the Navy, which was under continuous fire from members of the party in power. Goldsborough, just 23 years old, greatly enjoyed manipulating the power and influence that his new office and his extensive private correspondence with the officers of the Navy gave him: there was something of the meddler and the busybody in him. Preble's reply, dated 24 April, suggested that he was politely skeptical about Goldsborough's arguments. Fortunately, he did not accept Goldsborough's advice:

> Your letter of the 16th instant, which did not pass the Post Office [at] Washington until the 21st, I have this day received, but too late to influence my answer to the letter of the Secretary of the Navy in which he has so very

handsomely desired me to consider myself on furlough until my health is restored. My answer to that letter was dictated by my feelings and I hope contained nothing improper. I presume I was actuated by the best of motives in tendering my resignation and that I have not been incorrect in accepting a furlough. However, had I supposed my continuing would have had the effect held up in your letter of the service suffering and its producing much embarrassment, I certainly should have replied differently to the Secretary's letter. It is now too late. My answer has been given, and I hope the service will not materially suffer thereby.

Five days after Preble had received Robert Smith's letter granting him a furlough, Captain Hugh G. Campbell arrived in New York to assume command of the *Adams*. Relief from the burden of outfitting the frigate was the medicine Preble needed, and almost immediately he was noting in his diary: "My health improves daily." Obviously in much brighter spirits, Captain Preble left New York on the 30th of April and, by the time he reached Portland at noon on 20 May, he was able to write, "My own health is considerably improved since I left New York."

Seven days later, he was off for Sebago Lake, perhaps intent on doing some fishing.

II

Even before Commodore Dale left the Mediterranean early in 1802 there were signs of trouble brewing with Maulay Sulaiman, Sultan of Morocco, the one Barbary ruler with whom the United States had theretofore maintained good relations. Scarcely had Commodore Richard V. Morris arrived at Gibraltar near the end of May 1802, when the Sultan indicated his intention to support the Pasha of Tripoli in his war with the United States. The Tripolitan brig that was at Gibraltar when Dale arrived in the Mediterranean the preceding July had been sold, but the *Meshuda* was still blockaded there. Now the Sultan requested U.S. permission to send a Moroccan master and crew to move the *Meshuda* from Gibraltar and navigate her under the Moroccan flag. He also asked for passports that would permit two ships loaded with wheat to enter the blockaded port of Tripoli. Both requests were denied. On 22 June James Simpson, U.S. Consul at Tangier, was notified by the Sultan that Morocco had declared war on the United States.

In early August, just as news of this declaration of war reached Washington, a merchant captain named Norman filled Congressman Samuel Smith's ear with a rumor that he had picked up in Messina, a rumor which Smith passed on to the President. According to the story, a Neapolitan frigate was being chased by a Tunisian squadron when Captain Daniel McNeill in the frigate *Boston*, a holdover from Dale's squadron, happened upon the scene. McNeill, it was said, ran between the Neapolitan and her pursuers, provoking the Tunisian commodore to fire into the *Boston*. McNeill returned the fire, and in the engagement that followed two Tunisians were sunk, two dismasted, and three chased off, leaving the victorious *Boston* badly damaged and many of her officers and men killed. On the face of it, the story was improbable, but the Navy Department had evidence indicating that McNeill was mentally deranged, and feared that he might have done so mad a thing, thereby involving the United States in war with a third Barbary state, Tunis.[2]

However, the Sultan of Morocco's declaration of war caused greater concern than the possibility of hostilities with Tunis. Morocco did not possess as many cruisers as either Algiers or Tunis, but, with ports on the Atlantic as well as within the Straits of Gibraltar, the Sultan had it within his power to threaten U.S. merchantmen in both the Mediterranean and the Atlantic trade, especially that with Madeira and the Spanish peninsula. He was known to have two galleys stationed at Tetuán. They were expected to cruise in the Mediterranean, to the east of Málaga. As American traders passed through the Gut of Gibraltar they could be attacked by these same galleys or by gunboats. Along the Atlantic coast the Sultan's oceangoing cruisers might sail from Larache, Salé, Safi, or Mogador.[3] With the prospect of the war expanding to include Morocco and Tunis, debate developed within the administration on the issue of increasing the size of the naval force on the Barbary Coast.

Secretary of the Treasury Albert Gallatin was committed to a program of rapid reduction of the debt and to the sharp restriction of naval expenditures to achieve that object. He thought U.S. resources could be better used for national development than for a wasteful and destructive war. Expansion of the war would require such an increase in the number of ships and men on active duty as to destroy his financial program. He wrote the President on 16 August:

> Our object must clearly be to put a speedy end to a contest which unavailingly wastes our resources, and which we cannot, for any considerable time, pursue with vigor without relinquishing the accomplishment of the great and beneficial objects we have in view. . . . I sincerely wish you could reconcile it to yourself to empower our negotiators to give, if necessary for peace, an annuity to Tripoli. I consider it no greater disgrace to pay them than Algiers. And indeed we share the dishonor of paying those barbarians with so many nations as powerful and interested as ourselves, that, in our present situation, I consider it a mere matter of calculation whether the purchase of peace is not cheaper than the expense of a war which shall not even give us the free use of the Mediterranean trade. . . . Eight years hence we shall, I trust, be able to

assume a different tone; but our exertions at present consume the seeds of our greatness and retard to an indefinite time the epoch of our strength.[4]

Gallatin was a man of peace. His interests were domestic. Robert Smith, anticipating America's rise to a place among the great maritime powers, used the crisis with Morocco and Tunis to advocate a vigorous policy in dealing with the Barbary States. "So far from considering that Tripoli is to be our only enemy, I am rather inclined to believe that nothing but a formidable squadron will prevent all the Barbary Powers waging war against us. A superior force in the Mediterranean will insure us an early peace and will enable us to dictate the terms that will be the most honorable and beneficial to us. A feeble force, on the contrary, will subject us to the necessity of purchasing a peace upon the same terms that have from time to time been imposed upon the small powers of Europe." The Barbary shore was extensive and the U.S. naval force there was small. The danger of American merchantmen being captured was great indeed. The taking of one merchant vessel, declared Smith, would cost the United States more than would the maintenance on the Mediterranean station of the two frigates that he thought should be added to Commodore Morris's squadron to make it strong enough to act decisively.

The United States should appear in the Mediterranean in such force that the Barbary rulers would class her with the great nations of Europe, Robert Smith contended. "A formidable force displayed at this time will make a favorable impression, will repress every disposition hostile to us, and will thus save us great trouble and much expense. It will acquire to us a character that will hereafter protect us against all such aggressions." But the chief advantage of sending out two more frigates was that the impression they would create would force Barbary to conclude peace within the year. "With a less force the war may continue for years, which would be playing a hazardous game."[5]

President Jefferson attempted to effect a compromise between these opposing programs. The basic policy toward Barbary remained unchanged: no doctrinaire break with the traditional practice of presents to the Barbary rulers. The President authorized the expenditure of as much as $20,000 at Morocco and Tunis, if it would resolve the present crises, produce a firm peace and the abandonment by those two rulers of their demands for presents at fixed periods. The United States would continue its policy of spontaneous gifts from time to time as a reward for "faithful and friendly conduct." But with Tripoli the President stood by his policy of chastisement. Not one penny was to be paid Yusuf: "It is not thought consistent with the interest or the spirit of our nation (sufficiently manifested), after a war so far successful against Tripoli, to finish by paying them a tribute. Besides the dishonor and premature abandonment of the ground our predecessors left us in possession of, it would oblige us immediately to pay a tribute to Tunis and Morocco."

War with Tunis and Morocco might make it necessary to send additional frigates to the Mediterranean, but Jefferson was unwilling to increase the size of the squadron so long as Tripoli was the only enemy. Relying on Dale's advice that two frigates could blockade Tripoli, but apparently disregarding his recommendation for small vessels to make the blockade really effective, the administration had concluded that two frigates were all it would take to bring Yusuf to terms, and Jefferson saw no reason to change that opinion. In fact, since two frigates were sufficient, the government had, before the Morocco-Tunis crisis developed, considered recalling one of the three frigates attached to the Morris squadron. To buttress the arguments against employing a larger force, Jefferson contended that he feared for the safety of frigates that remained on the Mediterranean station through the winter months; that to increase the squadron in the Mediterranean would be "an improper use of the confidence reposed in us by Congress; that, though they gave us extensive authority to arm, yet they trusted we would employ it no further than should be absolutely necessary"; and that, even if the United States were at peace with all the Barbary Powers, she would still have to keep one or two frigates cruising on that station to insure the safety of American commerce.[6]

Before it was known whether there would be war or peace with Morocco and Tunis, the President agreed to dispatch the frigates *New York* and *John Adams* to augment the Morris squadron. But in early August, before either frigate had sailed from the United States, the concentration of the *Chesapeake*, the *Adams*, and the *Enterprize* in the Straits of Gibraltar caused the Sultan of Morocco to reconsider his decision to go to war with the United States, and an uneasy peace was patched up. Word of this peace with Morocco reached Washington in the middle of October. By that time, it was known that McNeill's battle was a fiction, and there was, consequently, no new issue with Tunis. On 23 October, after the Cabinet had once again reviewed U.S. policy in the war with Tripoli,[7] Robert Smith issued orders — with which he could not have agreed — summoning home the *Chesapeake* and the *Constellation*.* This left three frigates and a

---

* An insight into the administration's strategic thought during the Moroccan crisis is provided by a personal letter from Robert Smith to an unnamed correspondent, 23 August 1802: "I have three frigates completely prepared to be put in commission, but I am inclined to believe that the *New York* only will be sent out. It is considered that the *Constellation* and the *Boston*, with the Swedish squadron, will be fully sufficient to keep the Tripolitans in check, and that the *Chesapeake*, the *Adams*, the *New York*, and the *Enterprize* will

schooner to conclude matters with the Pasha of Tripoli and watch the other Barbary rulers. In August Smith had told the President that five frigates were necessary to establish peace with Barbary. "With a less force," he had said, "the war may continue for years."

III

Edward Preble spent the summer of 1802 in travel, rest, and recuperation. So successful was this program that by mid-August he was writing to Secretary Smith about his hopes for a speedy recovery. Smith's reply was typical of that friendly and considerate man: "I derive much satisfaction [from your letter] as it relates to the favorable state of your health, which I hope may soon be perfectly restored, as well from private considerations as those of a public nature, it being not very improbable that the period is not far distant when we shall have occasion to call for your services."

The possible need for Preble's services, which Smith had only mentioned, was elaborated by Goldsborough on 22 September:

> Should the Emperor [of Morocco] fit out his whole force and employ it judiciously and actively against us, there is no doubt but that we shall be obliged to strengthen our naval armament in the Mediterranean, so as to afford protection to our commerce both there and in the Western Ocean. The Emperor will probably send several vessels to cruise in the track of our vessels to southern Europe, and that would be a quarter which would require two or three ships of considerable force to guard effectually. Should another vessel be sent out, it will most probably be the *Essex*, your old ship, and there is no doubt but that you will have the offer to command her.

The *Essex*, of course, was not sent to join the Mediterranean squadron, for only a month after the date of Goldsborough's letter the government decided to reduce the size of the force on the Barbary Coast.

Toward the last of October Preble's annual impulse to escape some of the Maine winter, the need to settle his long-outstanding accounts with the Accountant of the Navy, improving health, and a renewed interest in active

---

protect our commerce in and about the Straits [of Gilbraltar]. Our homeward-bound vessels will rendezvous at Málaga and our outward-bound vessels at Cadiz. One of our frigates stationed at the Straits will be constantly employed in convoying our merchantmen from Málaga, another in convoying them from Cadiz, and the Commodore and Sterett [in the *Enterprize*] in watching the ports of Morocco where any vessels, galleys, or boats may be. Be persuaded, Sir, that, if the whole maritime forces of the Emperor of Morocco were brought to a point, they would be unequal to the smallest frigate on the station. The principal thing to be apprehended is that some [of] our merchantmen may not rendezvous at the places appointed by the Commodore and may attempt to pass without convoy and thus may be taken by small boats. I do not believe that the Emperor will venture to send out anything excepting small galleys and boats. As to vessels of force, he has them not."[8]

service all combined to send him on a trip to Washington. It was the middle of November when Preble reached the capital, and he had been there only a few days when he received a note in the handwriting of the President:

> Thursday, November 18, 1802.
> TH:·JEFFERSON asks the favor of Captain Preble to take a family dinner with him tomorrow at half after three.

A week later he was the dinner guest of Secretary of State James Madison. Most important of all, Preble met Robert Smith for the first time. It would be hard to overemphasize the significance of these meetings with the chief members of the administration in preparing the ground for the assignment that was soon to be given Captain Preble. At the moment, Secretary Smith was beginning to plan for the squadron that would relieve the frigates under Commodore Morris when their tour of duty was up. He intended to assign the command of the relieving squadron to Richard Dale, and promised Preble one of the frigates in that squadron. Satisfaction with the result of his trip to Washington is evident in a letter that Preble sent his brother-in-law James Deering: "On my arrival here [Washington] I met with a pleasing reception from the President and Ministers of State. I am particularly pleased with the Secretary of the Navy, and he seems disposed to make such arrangements with respect to my future service as shall be most agreeable to me. I shall be here about ten days longer to assist in some business in the Navy Department, and shall then return home until the next squadron is ordered out."[9]

It may well be that the frigate promised Preble was the *Constitution,* for among his papers is the first page of a letter, dated at Boston on Christmas Eve 1802, and evidently addressed to Sailing Master Nathaniel Haraden, who had charge of the frigate in ordinary at the Boston Navy Yard: "For the preservation of the frigate *Constitution* and the health of the men employed on board her, I advise you to indent for an iron stove to be put up forward on the berth deck with a pipe to lead aft the length of the deck; also for four or five iron grates about eighteen inches square at the top to burn charcoal in for drying the magazine, storerooms, cockpit, etc. You should have a sheet iron pan of double the diameter of the grate to each to prevent the fire from injuring the deck.* Let the fire in the grates be

---

* Nathaniel Haraden's entry in the *Constitution*'s log for 2 October 1803 describes the frigate's completed system of stoves: "I have never mentioned in the logbook these stoves or grates constructed by Commodore Preble. Their effects on close, contracted air are such that I think them of a superior kind to any in the Navy, or at least to any I ever saw. The long continuation of rainy, disagreeable weather we have lately had so contracted the air between decks that it was with some difficulty that candles would burn. In consequence of which the stoves were ordered to be lighted with charcoal, and they had not been burning

well kindled on deck before it is taken below in the morning. . . ."

While Captain Preble was looking to the care of the ship chiefly associated with his fame, Commodore Morris and his squadron in the Mediterranean were engaged in operations that would cause mounting uneasiness and dissatisfaction in the administration circle at Washington.

IV

So long as there was immediate danger of the Sultan of Morocco sending his cruisers out against American trade, Commodore Morris was forced to remain near the Straits of Gibraltar. But on 16 August, when word came from James Simpson, U.S. Consul at Tangier, that the dispute with the Sultan had been resolved, he was free for operations against the principal enemy, Tripoli. Nevertheless, he had to leave the frigate *Adams* near Gibraltar to watch the Tripolitan ship *Meshuda*, still lying in that port, and to remind the Sultan that American force was close at hand.

Secretary Smith's instructions advised Morris to proceed directly to a point of rendezvous and to send the schooner *Enterprize* to Leghorn for James L. Cathcart, who was to represent the United States in negotiations with Yusuf. Morris, however, having heard that there were two or three Tripolitan cruisers near the Spanish coast, decided instead to use his frigate, the *Chesapeake*, in which his wife and young son were passengers, to convoy a number of Swedish and American merchantmen around the northern shore of the Mediterranean and call at Leghorn himself for Cathcart. Not only was Morris violating the spirit of his orders in taking this roundabout route when he sailed from Gibraltar on 18 August, but he was injecting an unfortunate domestic presence into a theater where offensive operations were supposed to be the primary concern. Whispered, but nonetheless deadly, criticism soon began to be directed at the Commodore.

Head winds and calms so delayed the *Chesapeake* and her convoy that the passage to Leghorn took nearly two months. When he arrived at his destination on 12 October, Morris found another of his squadron, the frigate *Constellation*, Captain Alexander Murray. She had left the United States ahead of the other ships in the squadron, had cleared Cape Henlopen on 14 March, passed through the Straits of Gibraltar on 29 April, and then — without waiting for the Commodore — had sailed on up the Mediterranean, arriving off Tripoli on 7 June. In company with the Swedish

---

more than one hour before the air between decks was perfectly purified and the decks perfectly dry. Their construction is this: the whole stove does not weigh more than 40 or 45 pounds, resembling in shape a common bushel basket with open latticework, supported on three legs, and standing in a receiver for the cinders and ashes."[10]

squadron under Admiral Cederström, Murray had cruised off Tripoli until early September; then he left the blockade in order to convoy some Swedish and American vessels up the Italian coast and round the northern shore of the Mediterranean to Gibraltar. He had gone as far as Leghorn when he met Morris.

During his solitary cruise off Tripoli, Murray reached some important conclusions concerning the proper way to blockade the coast of Tripoli. To Robert Smith he wrote:

> Although we keep up the blockade with all our diligence, and am myself seldom out of sight of the town, the other ships stationed in a line along the coast, yet they do contrive to get their small row galleys out in the night in defiance of us by rowing close under the land and taking shelter occasionally in the small ports with which this coast abounds. For our parts, we dare not venture too close in, on account of sudden calms and no anchorage till you are nearly on the beach. . . . If we are still to carry on this kind of warfare, be assured, Sir, that it will be necessary to increase our force with brigs or schooners, which will be fully adequate to any force they can have to encounter with belonging to Tripoli; and they can pursue their small craft in any direction where frigates cannot venture, provided they have sweeps to row after them, for few of their galleys carry more than eight guns and forty men.

At the end of the Quasi-War with France, Secretary of the Navy Benjamin Stoddert had advocated the sale of all the small vessels then on the Navy list and urged the development of a Navy consisting almost exclusively of frigates and ships of the line. In future wars, Stoddert argued, whatever need there might be for smaller vessels could be filled by privateers which a profit-hungry shipping community would be eager to fit out. Congress incorporated these recommendations in the Peace Establishment Act. Samuel Smith, while he administered the Navy Department, attempted to correct this mistaken policy to some extent by retaining the *Enterprize* and her sister ship, the *Experiment,* but the latter was sold when the influential naval architect, Josiah Fox, reported erroneously that she was not worth repairing. The *Enterprize* was then the only vessel smaller than a frigate left in the U.S. Navy.

Murray went on to present a pessimistic picture of Jefferson's Barbary policy. He disagreed with it completely. With Sweden and the United States united in war against him, Yusuf was anxious to make some kind of a settlement. So anxious, thought Murray, that he would come to very reasonable terms — if only the United States would put aside her pride and pay Yusuf a little something for making peace. Murray judged that the Pasha would not abandon his principle: no peace without a bribe.

I have turned off a number of merchant vessels since I have been on the station, but the little craft from Tunis will now and then get in, in defiance of me, by rowing close under the land, and furnishes them with many supplies. And I am not satisfied in my mind that this blockade can answer any good purpose, for it is reported here that it hath already involved us into difficulties with Morocco and will probably with all the other Barbary States. A very slight pretense for war is sufficient with them. They have nothing to lose by it; we have. . . .

I shall take the liberty of digressing further respecting our situation with all the Barbary States. America hath certainly shown a very laudable pride and dignity in her efforts to abolish the obnoxious custom of paying tribute, but unless the European nations cooperate more generally with us, and abolish that narrow-minded policy that yet prevails with some of the most potent powers much better situated than we are for keeping up perpetual warfare with them, or till they are brought to proper terms, it will be more prudent for us also to submit to the indignity at the expense of our pride. They are not a commercial people; therefore, we can make no impression upon them.

Morris ordered Murray to take the *Constellation* to Toulon to have her damaged rudder irons repaired, from there to run down to Gibraltar to pick up supplies for the squadron, and then to return to the rendezvous at Malta. At Málaga, on 10 December, Captain Murray was handed an unsealed letter from Robert Smith to Morris. This was the instruction of 23 October that required the return of the *Chesapeake* and the *Constellation* to the United States without delay. The letter had probably been left unsealed so that Murray could act on it if he should receive it before Commodore Morris did. Or so Murray argued to himself. Morris was twelve hundred miles away. It was the month of December. The enlistment of the *Constellation*'s crew would expire before she could reach the United States. Without waiting to receive orders from his immediate superior, Murray sailed for the United States.

When Murray parted from Morris at Leghorn he was under the distinct impression that Morris intended to sail for Tripoli at once and open negotiations. So convinced was Murray of the Pasha's desire for peace that he wrote the Secretary of the Navy on 30 November, "No doubt but peace is made with Tripoli ere this. There was nothing wanting but a negotiator." Whatever may have been Murray's impression, Morris did not proceed immediately to Tripoli. He remained at Leghorn from 12 October until 3 November. The Commodore claimed that southerly winds and hard weather kept him from sailing sooner, but an examination of the *Chesapeake*'s logbook at the court of inquiry that subsequently investigated his activities did not entirely substantiate his claim. The delay can hardly have seemed serious to Morris at the time, since the necessity of repairing the

Constellation and sending her down to Gibraltar for provisions, the need to leave the *Adams* in the Straits of Gibraltar to keep an eye on the Sultan of Morocco and the *Meshuda,* and the dangers to be encountered along the Tripolitan coast in November and December had all combined to convince him that he could not appear off Tripoli before January. He told Cathcart, "Nothing decisive can possibly be effected before May or June next."

It was 3 November when the *Chesapeake* cleared Leghorn and, after sheltering a few days at Palermo, she reached Malta on 20 November. There, the frigate was immobilized, first, by the urgent necessity of repairing her bowsprit, then by an outbreak of influenza which felled a large number of her company and made her captain fearful of exposing his men to the winter sea. Not until 25 December did the disease decline sufficiently for Morris to feel justified in putting to sea; that day he sailed for Syracuse to see if it was easier and cheaper to buy fresh provisions there than at Malta. He returned to Malta on 4 January 1803 to find the *New York* and *John Adams,* the two frigates added to his squadron as a result of the Moroccan crisis. He also learned of Robert Smith's order for the *Chesapeake* and the *Constellation* to be sent home and of Murray's decision to act upon it. The *John Adams* needed caulking, and the provisions she had brought up from Gibraltar had to be distributed to the other ships of the squadron. These duties were not completed until 25 January, but even then Morris could see no great urgency for him to institute a blockade of Tripoli: his intelligence indicated that all the Pasha's cruisers had returned to port, that his gunboats were about to be hauled up, and that Yusuf had no intention of sending his raiders out again before March.

At last, on 30 January, the *Chesapeake,* the *New York,* and the *John Adams* sailed from Malta for Tripoli. Cathcart, who had embarked with Morris in the *Chesapeake,* was to offer the Pasha peace terms acceptable to the United States. If, as Morris expected, these terms were rejected, the Commodore planned to send the squadron's boats into the harbor to burn all the vessels in port. At the least, such an attack would prevent the Tripolitans from molesting American commerce for some time. Morris had intended to make this attack after the vernal equinox, but because Alexander Murray had gone home instead of bringing up supplies, the squadron was so short of provisions that, although he had serious misgivings about approaching the Barbary Coast in winter, Morris could not wait for the season of better weather. His misgivings were not silly fears, for the squadron fought heavy northerly gales from the time it left Malta. After trying for about a week to get his ships in position to attack — Captain James Barron in the *New York* could not even get within sight of Tripoli — the Commodore decided that winter was not the season for an operation against Tripoli, and that his ships were far from safe on the coast. On 10 and 11 February the squadron returned to Malta.

Strong westerly winds held the squadron at Malta until the 19th of February, on which day the frigates sailed for Tunis. William Eaton, U.S. Consul at Tunis, had asked for a meeting with Morris and Cathcart. Moreover, the Bey of Tunis had lately demanded that the United States give him a 36-gun frigate, and Morris hoped to coerce him into a more reasonable attitude by appearing off Tunis with most of his squadron. Whatever might have been the effect of the visit on the Bey, its effect on Morris was to add greatly to his anxiety, since appearances indicated that Tunis was preparing for war with the United States. The Bey was having his cruisers fitted for sea, and he declared that, in spite of the American blockade of Tripoli, he would continue to trade with that port, and would resort to reprisals on American trade if any of his ships were taken or detained by the American squadron. It was equally necessary for Morris to run down the coast from Tunis and attempt to impress the Dey of Algiers, for that ruler had balked at receiving a consignment of $30,000 cash in place of the annual shipment of timber and other maritime stores specified in the U.S. treaty with Algiers. When Morris left Algiers he sailed for Gibraltar and anchored there on 23 March 1803.

Probably nothing Morris did in the Mediterranean caused more criticism than his action in taking the *Chesapeake,* the *New York,* the *John Adams,* and the *Enterprize* down to Gibraltar just when the weather made it possible to begin operations against Tripoli. At the subsequent court of inquiry Captain Rodgers was asked: "What was the earliest period of the spring 1803 when [a display of the whole squadron before Tripoli] could have been safely performed?" He answered: "At any time after the last of March 1803." James Barron also testified that "The season for bad weather had terminated some time before [6 April]. At that time and for some time preceding — how long I cannot precisely say — there was moderate and pleasant weather."

Morris argued that his orders left him no choice but to go down to Gibraltar. He had received Robert Smith's order requiring the return of the *Chesapeake* on 4 January but had not complied with it then because, in his opinion, the frigate was in no condition to cross the Atlantic in winter; it was better to keep her with the squadron until spring. When spring came he had to take the *Chesapeake* to Gibraltar and prepare her for her voyage to the United States under the command of Captain James Barron.

An even more pressing reason for going to Gibraltar, as Morris saw it, was the squadron's shortage of supplies. Provisions and stores had been sent out from the United States in ships whose charters required them to deliver their cargoes to American Consul John Gavino at Gibraltar and, through a misjudgment at the Navy Department, contained no provision for them to go beyond Gibraltar, should that be necessary. Gavino had offered the ships' masters generous additional freightage if they would take their cargoes up the Mediterranean to where the squadron was, but the masters had refused to go. The *New York* had come up the Mediterranean earlier that winter without bringing a load, and the *Constellation,* which was supposed to return to Malta with stores, had sailed for the United States instead. As a result the squadron was in real need of stores and provisions, and the sole solution Morris could see was to take the frigates down to Gibraltar, load as many supplies as they could carry, and then run back up the Mediterranean to begin his blockade of Tripoli.

On 6 April the *Chesapeake,* Captain Barron, sailed for the United States. From the information received by her, and on the events in the Mediterranean before 6 April 1803, the administration made a decision.

V

Captain Alexander Murray in the *Constellation* arrived at the Washington Navy Yard on 15 March 1803, and wasted no time in spreading his personal views on Mediterranean affairs. He chose his audience shrewdly. To Secretary of the Treasury Albert Gallatin, who was already convinced that it was better to buy peace with Tripoli than to prolong or enlarge the war, Murray said that a settlement could have been made with Tripoli during the preceding summer, when Swedish and American naval forces were informally cooperating, for $5,000 — if only Commodore Morris had not lost so much time at Gibraltar and in his passage from Gibraltar round the Mediterranean towards Tripoli. Since then, however, Murray reported, the situation had changed: Sweden had, through the mediation of France, purchased peace with Yusuf at a cost of $150,000 * and an annuity of $8,000;[11] France and Tripoli had reached a rapprochement; there was no longer any internal threat to Yusuf's rule. With all these developments so unfavorable to the American cause, Murray claimed that peace with Tripoli could be obtained only by the payment of an extravagant sum.

The internal threat to Yusuf's rule had come from his elder brother, Hamet, from whom Yusuf had stolen the pashadom some years earlier. Since the beginning of the war Consuls William Eaton and James L. Cathcart had favored a plan by which the United States would assist Hamet

* In negotiations with Barbary, the term *dollar* usually referred to the Spanish dollar, which was regarded as a standard.

in overthrowing Yusuf and establishing a government friendly to the United States. But, because Yusuf had effected a reconciliation with Hamet and had appointed him governor of Derna in Cyrenaica, hope of promoting domestic strife within Yusuf's kingdom had collapsed.

Murray's report heightened the uneasiness which the President already felt over Morris's handling of his command, and on 28 March he wrote to Gallatin: "I have for some time believed that Commodore Morris's conduct would require investigation. His progress from Gibraltar has been astonishing. I know of but one supposition which can cover him; that is, that he has so far mistaken the object of his mission as to spend his time convoying. I do not know the fact. We gave great latitude to his discretion, believing he had an ambition to distinguish himself, and [were] unwilling to check it by positive instructions." [12]

Concern over the squadron and its activities resulted in a meeting of the Cabinet on 8 April to review Mediterranean affairs. Charles W. Goldsborough's summaries of Morris's and Murray's dispatches were in the President's hands and presumably were considered by the Cabinet.[13] The President put the question: "Is there sufficient ground to recall Morris and institute inquiry into his conduct?" On the evidence before them the Cabinet concluded unanimously that there was not. Should Morris be ordered to return to the United States in the *Chesapeake* or the *Adams*, and the command of the squadron be given to Captain Rodgers? Again the decision was unanimous: No.

There the matter rested for the moment, but dissatisfaction lingered. Robert Smith's instructions had urged the Commodore to write at every opportunity and to give the Navy Department full information on all his movements. But Morris's dispatches had been disappointingly brief, uninformative, and most infrequent. At last, on 4 May, Smith took him to task for his neglect: "I have not heard from you since the 30th November 1802, but I will not permit myself to suppose that you have not written since that period. Yet it is a subject of serious concern that we have not heard from you. I presume it would be superfluous to remind you of the absolute necessity of your writing frequently and keeping us informed of all your movements."

Towards the latter part of May, the *Chesapeake* arrived home with a long dispatch from Morris, dated at Gibraltar, 30 March, in which he reported his movements since 3 November 1802 and went on to describe his plans for the future: "The *John Adams* and *Adams* shall be dispatched as soon as possible with convoy, and the *New York* will proceed direct if there should not be any American vessels wanting protection. If on the contrary, it shall be afforded. As soon as the *Enterprize* is manned she shall be employed to the best advantage in my power." The President studied the dispatch carefully, making notes as he went along.[14] His irritation with Morris's vague plans becomes apparent in the notes he made when he reached the passage quoted above: "The *John Adams* & *Adams* shall convoy. The *New York* shall proceed direct (whither?) if no Amer. vessel wants convoy. The *Enterprize* shall be employed to best advge. (how?) ."

The administration's patience had run out. As soon as the President learned that the squadron which was scheduled to relieve Morris would not sail till August, he consulted the Cabinet members at Washington and, then, on 16 June, suggested to Robert Smith, who was in Baltimore, that an order recalling Morris be sent to the Mediterranean by the newly acquired 12-gun schooner *Nautilus:* "From his inactivity hitherto I have no expectation that anything will be done against Tripoli by the frigates in the Mediterranean while under his command. If he is recalled by the *Nautilus,* and the command devolves on the others, we shall gain six weeks at least in the best season for whatever they can effect in that time against the enemy." Smith replied the next day, "I think with you that Morris ought to be recalled by the *Nautilus*";[15] and on 21 June he issued an order suspending Morris from the command of the squadron on the Mediterranean station and directing him to return to the United States without delay.

In a personal letter to Captain Rodgers, who was to succeed Morris until the relief squadron came out from the United States, Robert Smith revealed the frustration and anger he felt towards the Commodore:

> We have been for some time much displeased with the conduct of Captain Morris. He has not done anything which he ought to have done, and despairing of his doing anything, and also as a mark of our disapprobation, it has been determined to suspend him. We besides can obtain from him no information what he is proposing to do. We have generally to rely upon others with respect to his movements. Were we not informed to the contrary by others we should believe that the whole squadron was at this moment at Gibraltar. It appears that on the day of the date of his last letters he left Gibraltar with the *John Adams* and the *Enterprize* and that he had a few days before sent the *Adams* with a convoy. But none of this information did he give me. He has not informed me that he has left Gibraltar. Neither do I know where he is or what he is proposing to do.[16]

It can be seen that the reasons for the recall of Commodore Morris were his failure to communicate with the government, his apparent lack of long-range plans, and absence of energy in his operations. In brief, he was removed not for any specific deed, but rather on the administration's assessment of him as a commander, and on their judgment that he would accomplish nothing significant during his Mediterranean command.

VI

After the *Chesapeake* sailed for the United States on 6 April 1803, Commodore Morris remained at Gibraltar recruiting a crew for the *Enterprize* and loading supplies into the *New York* and the *John Adams*. Until this time Morris had been forced to leave the frigate *Adams* in the vicinity of Gibraltar to watch the Tripolitan cruiser *Meshuda* which had been lying at the Rock ever since Dale had trapped her there at the beginning of the war. The Sultan of Morocco had now formally declared that the *Meshuda* had been sold to him and he had furnished her with papers. Although he might have suspected a ruse, Morris was bound to respect the Sultan's assurances and agreed to allow the *Meshuda* to leave Gibraltar under the Moroccan flag, which she did on 8 April. Her departure freed the *Adams* for more active operations and she was sent on convoy duty around the northern shore of the Mediterranean with orders to rejoin the squadron at Malta.

James L. Cathcart, the authorized agent for negotiations with the Pasha of Tripoli, had been traveling about the Mediterranean with Commodore Morris ever since he had joined the *Chesapeake* at Leghorn the preceding fall, and during the months that they had been together the Commodore had formed a low opinion of the former consul: "Mr. Cathcart," he later wrote, "has long resided on the Barbary Coast, but has been so unfortunate as neither to command respect nor conciliate esteem. He was considered as imperious, quarrelsome and insincere. This idea of his character was, perhaps, unjust, but to treat by the agency of a person so disagreeable seemed to promise but little success." It was true that the Dey of Algiers had refused to receive Cathcart as U.S. Consul to that regency, so it would appear that Morris had reason on his side when he decided that Cathcart would add nothing to the success of negotiations with the Pasha of Tripoli. A clause in Morris's orders authorized him to negotiate with any of the Barbary Powers without Cathcart's aid — but only if circumstances made it necessary for him to act without advice and assistance. In a move that did nothing to endear him to the Secretary of the Navy, Morris took advantage of this clause and ordered Cathcart back to Leghorn in the *Adams*. He told the loudly protesting Cathcart that he could negotiate a treaty with Tripoli without his assistance, and that if he needed Cathcart he would send for him.

At last, on 11 April, the *New York*, in which Morris had been flying his pennant since Barron took the *Chesapeake* home, the *John Adams* and the *Enterprize* started up the Mediterranean with the intention of blockading the city of Tripoli. On the way, however, an explosion in the gunner's storeroom of the *New York* caused such heavy damage that Morris was compelled to stop at Malta to repair. He also found that he would have to put new copper on the *Enterprize,* take water and stores on board the schooner, and replace the supplies that had been destroyed by the explosion. The squadron was still in port attending to these details on 4 May when Captain Rodgers in the *John Adams* left Malta with orders to cruise off Tripoli.

Rodgers was more active, intense, and aggressive than his commander, and his testimony at the subsequent court of inquiry indicated that he had been fretting under Morris's relaxed approach to war:

JUDGE ADVOCATE: "Did you request of Commodore Morris to be sent on the expedition off Tripoli (on the 5th May) or was that expedition first moved by the Commodore himself?"

RODGERS: "It was spoken of at Gibraltar before we sailed for Malta. After our arrival at the latter place I expressed my opinion to the Commodore of the necessity of sending a ship off Tripoli immediately."

It took Rodgers four days to reach Tripoli, and about sunset on the 12th he captured that old nuisance of U.S. operations in the Mediterranean, the *Meshuda,* freighted with guns, cutlasses, hemp, other contraband articles, and twenty Tripolitan subjects, in the very act of trying to enter Tripoli Harbor. Rodgers left the Tripoli coast on 16 May and entered the harbor of Valletta, Malta, on the 19th. The *New York* and the *Enterprize* were still there; they were ready to sail for Tripoli, but waiting for the *Adams* to rejoin after carrying Cathcart to Leghorn. Once again, according to the transcript of the court of inquiry, it was Rodgers who nudged Morris:

JUDGE ADVOCATE: "When you returned to Malta with the prize *(Meshuda)* what communication passed between you and the Commodore relative to the necessity or propriety of blockading or cruising off Tripoli?"

RODGERS: "I recollect on rejoining the Commodore at Malta expressing my opinion that if he would display his whole force before Tripoli the Bashaw would be disposed to make peace on almost any terms. I thought he seemed to be influenced by these representations to hasten the departure of the squadron from Malta."

Morris evidently decided to wait no longer for the *Adams,* for the day after Rodgers's return, the *New York, John Adams,* and *Enterprize* sailed out of Malta. They arrived off Tripoli on 22 May, and the *Adams* joined them on the 26th. The Commodore planned a literal execution of Robert Smith's idea of simultaneous blockade and negotiation. "Holding out the olive branch in one hand and displaying in the other the means of offensive operations" was the way Smith had phrased it. Whether Morris thought his squadron was adequate in size and in type of ship to institute an effec-

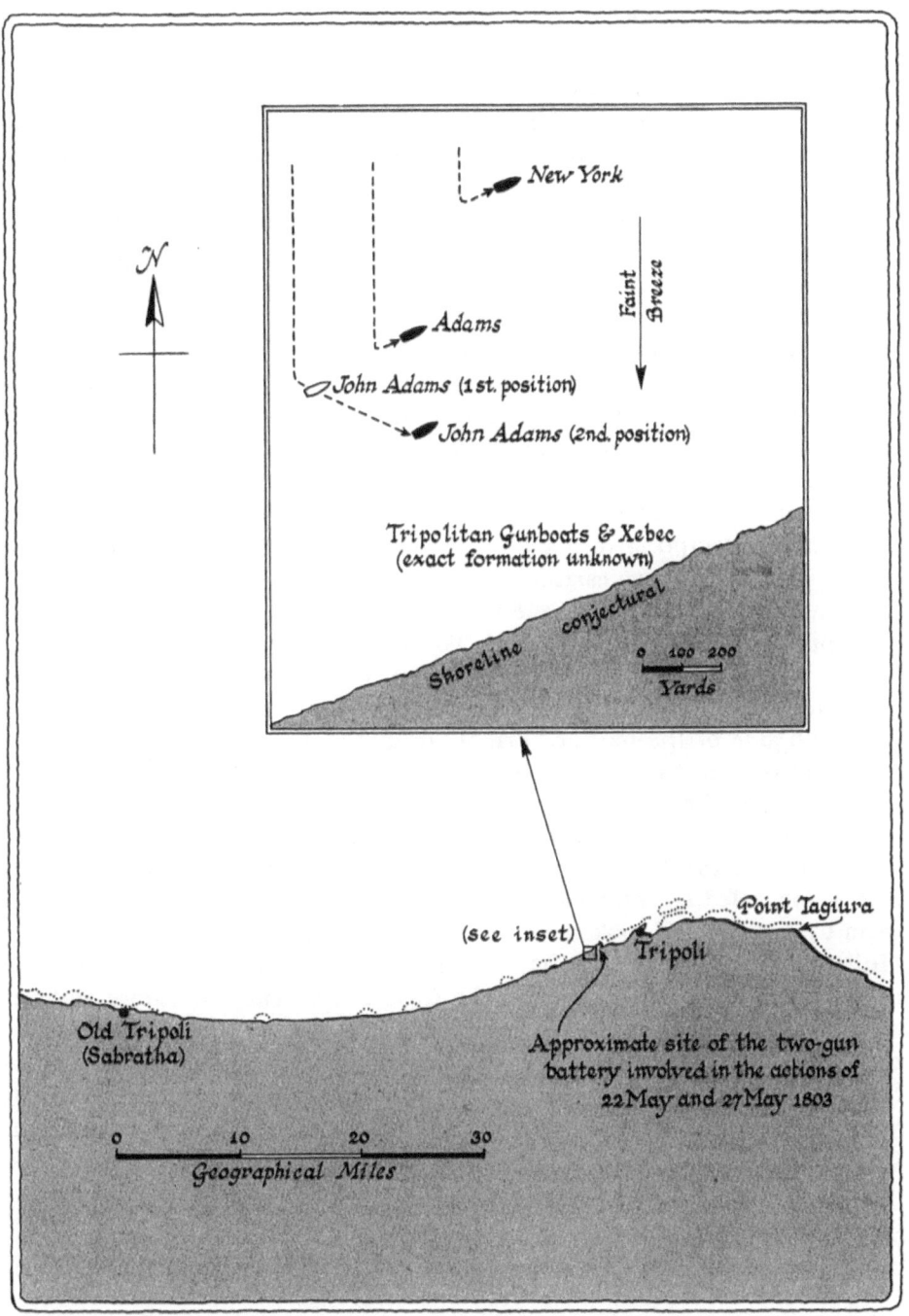

SCENE OF COMMODORE RICHARD V. MORRIS'S OPERATIONS, MAY-JUNE 1803
Inset: Battle with the Tripolitan Gunboats and Xebec, Evening, 27 May 1803

tive blockade does not appear. Certainly his second-in-command, Rodgers, did not think so. "The present force is almost too small to effect anything great," he had already written. "It is my opinion that with five frigates, two brigs or schooners, and one strong, merchant-built ship drawing twelve or thirteen feet water and constructed to carry two ten- or eleven-inch mortars, that — in two weeks after their arrival before the port of Tripoli — they would be able to force a peace on any terms our government may deem proper to dictate."

In May 1803 the Pasha's maritime force consisted of one polacre, three xebecs, two brigs, five galliots, and nine gunboats. Of these, four corsairs — including the polacre (Tripoli's largest and best cruiser), one of the galliots, and a 14-gun xebec — were somewhere at sea. The nine gunboats were used for harbor defense.

Not two hours after Morris's force appeared off Tripoli on 22 May a sail was sighted attempting to get into port from the west. It was not one of the corsairs, but a cargo carrier, a felucca of 25 or 30 tons. Morris signalled Lieutenant Isaac Hull in the *Enterprize*, which was east of the port, to attempt to cut her off from Tripoli. To intercept the felucca, the *Enterprize* had to take a course roughly parallel with the shore and was required to pass within a mile of Tripoli's fortifications and of the rocks that formed the north side of the harbor. Tripolitan gunboats rowed out through the rocks and opened fire on the *Enterprize* as she passed; the guns on the city batteries were shooting at her, too. But the schooner, aided by a fresh easterly breeze, ran through the hostile fire at seven knots without a scratch. Then, just as the "Enterprizes" were congratulating themselves on that feat, a concealed two-gun battery about four miles west of Tripoli caught them by surprise and took the schooner under fire. Return the compliment, Hull told his gunners, and he kept his vessel's head to the west. A mile or so farther along Hull came on the felucca. She had run ashore and her crew were busy carrying away everything they could. The *Enterprize* attempted to destroy the felucca by gunfire, but failed. If she was to be captured or burned, a party would have to be sent inshore in the squadron's boats. Much to the displeasure of the squadron's more ardent young officers, Commodore Morris, after a period of indecision, declined to make the attempt in the face of a body of armed men that had come riding to the rescue from Tripoli.

During the evening hours of 27 May Morris was given an opportunity that came to no other U.S. commander for the rest of the war: a chance to get between the Tripolitan gunboats and their base. At 5:00 p.m. the squadron sighted Tripoli's nine gunboats about four or five miles west of the city, escorting the 14-gun xebec into port. The enemy flotilla was directly inshore of the U.S. squadron and under the shelter of the two-gun battery. The light breeze that was blowing from the north would carry the American ships right down on the Tripolitans. As soon as the *John Adams,* which had the squadron's pilot, came up into the van from a position two or three miles astern of the *New York,* the frigates stood in to attack in a line abreast. But the wind was dying away to the faintest of breezes, and it was nearly sunset before the frigates came within gunshot of the Tripolitan gunboats. When Rodgers, in the *John Adams,* was 500 or 600 yards from the enemy (7:30 p.m.), he turned his ship's head to the east. The *Adams, New York,* and *Enterprize* executed the same maneuver — thus bringing the squadron into a line ahead, parallel with the shore — and all opened fire. Rodgers continued to work closer in towards the gunboats and xebec, while the *New York* and the *Adams* remained relatively stationary, so that ultimately the *New York* was 1,800 feet on the *John Adams*'s weather bow and the *Adams* 300 to 600 feet on her weather beam. In that position, the *John Adams* masked the fire of the other two frigates. By this time, the *New York* had gotten off two or three broadsides, but when Morris saw the *John Adams* moving into the *New York*'s line of fire he suspended shooting; somewhat later the *New York* filled away, stood off to the northwestward, and took no further part in the battle. At 7:45 p.m. the *Adams* attempted to fire over the *John Adams* at the gunboats, but her shot were cutting the *John Adams*'s rigging. In no uncertain terms John Rodgers told Hugh G. Campbell, captain of the *Adams,* to back his main topsail and drop astern of the *John Adams.* Soon afterwards the *Adams* followed the *New York*'s example and withdrew from combat. While the other frigates were hauling off, the *John Adams* kept up the fight until 8:30 p.m. — Rodgers fuming the whole time because the Commodore was going off without signalling him any instructions. By then it was so dark that the Tripolitan flotilla, under the shadow of the land, could be seen only as the flash of their guns revealed their position, and the engagement gradually fizzled out. The *John Adams* had fired 108 rounds, but there was negligible damage on either side. Before dawn the next morning, 28 May, the xebec and the gunboats slipped unseen into Tripoli harbor.

Two days later, a French cutter, the *Vaillant Bonaparte,* Captain Emmanuel Bonnevie, came out of Tripoli bound for Messina. Captain Bonnevie tipped Morris off that three Tripolitan cruisers were still out and were expected to try to run in any day. Morris deployed the *Adams* to the west of Tripoli, the *John Adams* to the east, the *New York* and the *Enterprize* directly north of the port, and waited. At ten o'clock the following morning, 31 May, the *Adams* signalled that a sail had been sighted to the west, then chased in that direction. It was once more nearly calm, but the

New York and the *Enterprize* followed as best they could, Lieutenant Hull speeding ahead with his sweeps. Between 4:00 p.m. and 6:00 p.m. the *Enterprize* caught up with the *Adams* and found that Captain Campbell had cornered, not one of the corsairs, but ten small commercial vessels at Old Tripoli.* The Americans anchored as close inshore as they dared and, to prevent the coasters being unloaded, kept them under fire all through the still, hot first day of June. Because of the lack of wind, it was five o'clock that afternoon before Morris, in the *New York*, was able to get up to Old Tripoli. There was considerable doubt regarding the national identity of the coasters. Hull was convinced that eight of them were Tripolitans and two were Tunisians. But during the day of 1 June four of the masters boarded the *Adams* and claimed they were Tunisians loaded with wheat. When Morris reached the scene, he sent the coasters a message to haul alongside the *New York* by midnight 1/2 June or he would burn them for violation of the blockade of Tripoli. But twenty-four hours had already passed since the *Adams* and the *Enterprize* had chased the vessels ashore, and this had given time for a large number of Tripolitans to gather in defense of the wheat carriers. The coasters refused to come off. Seven boats from the *New York*, the *Adams* and the *Enterprize* attempted to burn the small craft early on 2 June. The Americans succeeded in setting the vessels ablaze before they were driven off by small-arms fire from the defenders; then the Tripolitans raced down to extinguish the fires. Two of the coasters were totally destroyed; the cargoes of the other eight were saved without serious damage. No second attempt to fire the wheat was made.**

When John Rodgers was off Tripoli early in May, he had put out a peace feeler to the Pasha. Rodgers had, in the spring of 1803, little diplomatic experience and some strong, but untested, opinions on dealing with Barbary: "There is no faith to be had in the Animals we are at present contending with nor, indeed, with any of the Powers on that side of the Mediterranean." He approached Yusuf through the Danish consul, Nicholas C. Nissen, and explained that he was making inquiries about Tripolitan willingness to negotiate "in order that I may have time to prevent more decisive steps being taken." Rodgers bluffed on the size of Morris's squadron: "We have at present only two frigates on the coast, but I expect every moment to be joined by three more. We have a force arrived at Gibraltar which will certainly terminate the business this summer." And, he warned

---

* Now Sabratha.

** French consul Bonaventure Beaussier's dispatches[17] indicate that one of the three Tripolitan cruisers that Captain Bonnevie had told Morris were out slipped into port on 3 June, apparently unobserved by the U.S. squadron; that the galliot was in Tripoli harbor by 24 June; and that the polacre ran aground east of Tripoli on 22 June and was destroyed by her own crew to prevent her falling into American hands.

ominously, "Any unreasonable demands can have no effect." Up to the time Rodgers left Tripoli on 16 May to rejoin the squadron at Malta, he had received no reply.

Bluffing was a game at which Yusuf Caramanli was more skillful than John Rodgers. He did not bother to answer Rodgers until 28 May, when Nissen reported: "He [Yusuf] did not fear the forces that the United States of America might bring against Tripoli. He should know how to defend himself even if they brought all the forces of Gibraltar. And . . . by threatening, no advances to a conclusion of peace would be made."

By then Richard V. Morris had come on the coast. On 29 May he took over the diplomatic correspondence and in three days had persuaded Yusuf to agree in principle to a conference. A week later, on 7 June, Morris and a delegation of six officers landed in Tripoli and went to the French consulate. From there, Bonaventure Beaussier, the French consul and the guarantor of the delegation's safety ashore, escorted them to the residence of Sidi Mohammed Dghies, the prime minister and the negotiator for Tripoli. Morris presented his credentials, which were examined by Nicholas C. Nissen and certified to the Pasha. Then Morris handed Dghies the text of a U.S. proposal for a Tripolitan-American peace treaty.

At the second session, which took place on 8 June, each side presented its peace terms in writing. Yusuf, through Dghies, demanded from the United States $200,000 and the expenses of the war. Dghies added an unsubtle hint that this was an opening gambit, and that he expected to compromise this demand considerably in the course of negotiation. The U.S. terms constituted an ultimatum: if the treaty proposal Morris had given Dghies the day before was accepted, the United States would give the Pasha a present of $5,000 on the arrival of a new American consul; and if, at the end of five years, every article of the treaty had been strictly and faithfully observed the United States would pay the Pasha an additional $10,000. This, said Morris, was the only offer he could make other than to grant a truce of twelve months during which the Pasha could state his terms directly to the President. "I now, Sir, wait your answer to either of those proposals and will keep a boat on shore for that purpose until 12 o'clock tomorrow." The two sides were so far apart that further discussion seemed pointless. Morris prepared to return to the *New York*.

Angered by Commodore Morris's attitude, Dghies gave the American negotiator a tongue-lashing: had Morris come ashore to laugh at him? This negotiation is at an end, cried the Tripolitan. You must leave immediately. The white flag was struck.

On the afternoon of 9 June Morris sailed for Malta in the *New York*, leaving the *Adams* and the *John Adams* to keep up the blockade under

John Rodgers. No one in the squadron could have helped noticing that the Commodore's precipitate departure coincided with the time when Mrs. Morris, who was at Malta, was expected to — and did — give birth to a child. From Malta Morris sent orders to Rodgers to break up the blockade, and on 25 June all remaining American naval forces left the Tripolitan coast.

When asked his reasons for abandoning the operations against Tripoli, Morris was armed with many, almost too many, explanations:

First, there was the fear that the capture of the *Meshuda,* sailing under Moroccan colors, would lead to another declaration of war by the Sultan. Morris judged that the only way to overawe the Sultan and prevent hostilities was to move the American squadron to Gibraltar.

Second, Morris had learned that the largest warships of Tunis and Algiers were cruising in company and he feared that American shipping, or even American ships of war, might be their targets. The Dey of Algiers was displeased because he had been offered cash instead of the stores specified by the treaty, and the burning of the ten allegedly Tunisian wheat boats on 2 June had given the Bey of Tunis a pretext for war.

Third, the crew of the *Adams* had been recruited for one year only. Their term of enlistment had expired, and they were on the point of mutiny. The *Adams* had to return to the United States as soon as possible. But to send her down to Gibraltar alone might expose her to capture by the Algerian and Tunisian squadrons.

Finally, Morris thought little more could be accomplished at Tripoli as long as he had only one small vessel capable of dealing with Tripolitan gunboats in the shallow waters where they operated; and until the gunboats could be defeated, the commerce of Tripoli could not be destroyed, nor could the port be sealed off.

It was at Málaga, Spain, on 11 September 1803, while he was making his leisurely way towards Gibraltar, that Richard V. Morris received Robert Smith's letter removing him from the command of the Mediterranean squadron.

CHAPTER 7   MAY 1803–AUGUST 1803

"You have an arduous task to perform. You will have great difficulties to encounter."

Not since the end of the French war had the *Constitution* been on active service. She lay in ordinary at Boston, moored in the Charles River below the bridge that crossed to Charlestown from the foot of Prince Street and off the Charlestown Navy Yard. On 19 May 1803 Preble, who was then in Boston, received this order from Secretary of the Navy Smith: "You will assume the command of the frigate *Constitution* and have her put in a condition to sail at the shortest possible period." At ten o'clock the next morning Preble had himself rowed out to the frigate and took over command from Sailing Master Nathaniel Haraden. Then he inspected the *Constitution*'s caretaker crew — one midshipman, the boatswain, and twelve sailors — made a thorough tour of all decks and storerooms, and ordered a caulking stage brought alongside so that he would be able to examine the frigate's bottom the following day.[1] He had to decide immediately whether her hull needed recoppering and other repairs.

On Saturday, 21 May, Preble, Haraden, and Lieutenant Joshua Blake, who had been selected as the ship's first lieutenant, climbed down and began poking the frigate's bottom with boathooks and rakes. Finding that the copper was broken and full of holes from which the rakes pulled grass and sea moss, Preble decided that recoppering was necessary. There was no dry dock in the United States, and the work would have to be done by the laborious method of careening the ship. Nevertheless, Preble optimistically predicted to Robert Smith that he could complete it and be ready to sail in seven or eight weeks.

Temporary hands were hired at $1.40 or $1.32 a day, according to their experience. The hours were long. With some variations, the men were mustered at 5:15 a.m. and worked till 7:00 a.m., when they were allowed an hour off for breakfast. They worked steadily from 8:00 a.m. till 11:00 a.m., when there was a fifteen-minute break for grog, which the men provided for themselves. Dinner hour was from 1:00 p.m. to 2:00 p.m., after which work continued until 7:00 p.m., with another break for grog at 4:00 p.m. All hands went home tired when dismissal time came. After a few days on this schedule, Midshipman Ralph Izard, Jr., of South Carolina, wrote his mother:

> This day being Sunday I take the opportunity of writing to you, for on other days really we are so very busy that I have not been able to sit down for so short a time as is required to fill up a page or two. Every morning we are expected down at the wharf at four o'clock, and, excepting a few minutes that are allowed us for breakfasting and dining, we never budge from thence until about a quarter past eight in the evening. One of us sleeps on board every night, and as there are as yet but seven of us my turn comes round once a week.[2]

First, the frigate had to be moved from her mooring place in the Charles River to May's Wharf (more commonly called Union Wharf) near the foot of Whitebread Alley in northeast Boston. To reach the wharf, she would have to be kedged through a narrow channel, an operation that ought to be attempted only at flood tide and with the wind entirely still. That combination of wind and tide did not occur until Saturday, 28 May. Thomas Knox, the harbor pilot, was on board, and at 9:30 that morning the *Constitution*'s moorings were hove up and hung from one of two scows that had been brought off to her. Half an hour later, in a dead calm, the frigate began to move towards the wharf in Boston. Warping the frigate was a slow process that required great care. Most of the way it was done with small kedges and casters carried out on each bow by boats. But the second scow was at hand so that the stream anchor and 300 fathoms of hawser could be run out for the passage of especially intricate places in the channel. At seven that evening, the crew of fifty-six seamen and fourteen Marines hauled the frigate into May's Wharf and secured her.

On Monday morning the actual careening, or heaving down, began. This was no easy job with a ship as large as the *Constitution*. From the day Preble took charge of the *Constitution* Nathaniel Haraden had sensed that the forthcoming cruise was going to be worthy of a great narrative — and that narrative was going to be the *Constitution*'s log, as kept by Sailing

Master Haraden.* He was especially proud of the technical accomplishment in heaving down the frigate and recorded the whole operation with great fidelity in his log, from which much of the following account is taken.

First to be recoppered was the *Constitution*'s port, or outboard, side. Two bower anchors were carried out, one ahead and the other astern, to stabilize the ship during the careening process. Two other bowers that had been left hanging from the scow at the *Constitution*'s old mooring place were brought down by work parties and carried outboard of the frigate to serve as tripping anchors. Much of the frigate's iron ballast was removed, but the portion that was left on board, together with a number of the ship's water leaguers, was placed on the side of the ship that was to be hove under. The rudder was unhung and brought alongside the wharf; the starboard gunports, which would be under water while the port side was being recoppered, were planked in; and the frigate's upper works were overhauled and re-caulked, since every pint of water that leaked in would have to be wearily pumped out again.

A block was attached to the mainmast above the shrouds, and a similar block was secured to the foremast. These blocks, which had been specifically designed for masting and careening ships, are worth mentioning because of their unusual size. They were threefold blocks, with brass sheaves, 42 inches high — 61 inches, including the strap — 18 inches wide, and the pin alone measured 2½ inches in diameter. Two more of these gargantuan blocks were secured to May's Wharf opposite the foremast and the mainmast. The frigate's guns and the iron ballast that had been taken out of her were placed on the wharf to keep it from being torn apart and the blocks from being ripped loose by the enormous strain when the ship heeled over. Crabs or capstans were placed on the wharf inboard of the blocks. A 140-fathom purchase fall of 10-inch, white, four-strand rope was rove through the block at the head of the mainmast and the corresponding block on the wharf, then carried back to one of the crabs. Another purchase fall was rigged in similar fashion at the foremast. When the time came to careen, the men would heave on the crabs, drawing the frigate slowly over onto her starboard side.

In order to prevent the masts from being sprung or broken off, it was

---

* Haraden might never have kept his record. Some of his previous commanding officers had found Haraden, who was an old sea dog, hard to take, and Robert Smith authorized Preble to appoint another sailing master in Haraden's place, if he so wished. But Preble knew Haraden's potential value to the *Constitution* and to himself, and decided to retain him. He told Smith: "I believe he is a good sailing master, but fancy he has heretofore assumed too much, which has made him disagreeable to the officers with whom he has sailed. I am confident that he will not attempt it while under my command. I shall mark out to him a proper line of conduct which he must pursue."

essential to counterbalance the strain that would be applied to them. For this purpose, two round, rough spars, or shores, 22 inches in diameter at the butt, were inclined from shoes located close by the waterways to the mainmast, and lashed to the mast 18 inches below the trestletrees. Similar deck shores braced the foremast. On the port side of the frigate, 18-inch-square outriggers were run out of the gundeck ports until they overlapped the ship's beam by 14 feet. These outriggers were secured inboard to a long timber fixed fore and aft along the gundeck, and were lashed and braced inside the ports as well. There were five outriggers opposite the foremast and six opposite the main. From the outboard ends of these outriggers careening pendants were stretched to the mastheads. In the opposite direction martingales ran from the heads of the outriggers to gammoning bolts set near the waterline on the port side of the hull. Thus, the masts would be braced from the starboard by the deck shores, and supported from the port by the careening pendants leading from the mastheads to the outriggers, the outriggers in turn being supported by the martingales set up to the gammoning bolts in the hull.

Two other pieces of gear completed the careening apparatus: relieving tackles were hooked to the wharf, then passed under the *Constitution*'s bottom and secured to the lower tier of gunports on her outboard side. These were intended to keep her from capsizing while she was being careened, and to assist in righting her afterwards, but Haraden notes, "We found [them] to be of no use."

By 10 June preparations for careening were complete. Each day that the frigate was careened the procedure was much the same. All available hands fell to and manned the crabs, slowly turning the frigate on her side until a portion or all of the old copper was out of water. Working from stages, the carpenters began by removing the old copper. Then the seams between the planks were caulked with a thread of oakum and a thread of spun yarn. These threads were thoroughly horsed home, or hardened into the seams with a horsing iron, then payed over with a mixture of tallow, tar and turpentine; a coat of sheathing paper was laid over the planks, and the sheets of copper fastened over the whole.

Each evening the frigate was righted, then careened again the next working day. While she lay on her side, officers, seamen and carpenters worked under continual, if repressed, tension. There was always the danger that something might go awry and the ship begin to fill with water more rapidly than the pumps could free her, in which case she would settle quietly beside the wharf and would have to be laboriously raised. Everyone worked as rapidly as possible. The carpenters were not allowed to go home for dinner; they ate on the stages. Seamen took only half the usual time for dinner, and ate in two shifts.

Despite all the care that had been taken to protect them, the masts still made trouble for Preble and his officers. The mainmast was not a single stick, but a made mast, put together from twenty-eight pieces, and as the ship was careened, it began to belly downward or to starboard. Long wooden fishes had to be secured to both sides of the foremast and the mainmast. Fishing these masts caused some delay; the shrouds and careening pendants stretched under the strain and had to be set up; two days it rained, and the carpenters and caulkers could not work: it was four o'clock on Friday afternoon, 17 June, before the recoppering of the port side was completed.

There had been no major mishaps to the ship, but one serious injury had marred the careening process: while the outriggers were being secured through the gundeck ports, part of the apparatus gave way. William Hyler, a shipwright who was working on the outriggers, but inside the ship, was hurled with tremendous force up against the underside of the spar deck. His back was broken. For the remainder of his life Hyler was paralyzed from the waist down, unable to support his family, and totally dependent on charity.[3]

Sunday morning, 19 June, was spent winding the ship, or turning her end for end. The whole process of careening and recoppering was then repeated on her starboard side. At 5:00 p.m. on Saturday, the 25th of June, when the last piece of copper had been placed on the hull, the carpenters gave nine cheers and were answered with an equal number by the caulkers and the seamen. The job was done! The carpenters hauled away their stages, secured them to the head of the wharf, and went off to be paid. "The ship has considerable water in her hold, but it cannot be pumped out tonight," Haraden wrote in the day's log. "The men are receiving their weekly pay and are too much fatigued."

"They finished coppering her yesterday, which was a great relief to us all, but more particularly to Captain Preble," said one of Midshipman Izard's letters home. "It was an arduous undertaking to heave down so large a ship as the *Constitution*. A dry dock would be by far less expensive and certainly would forward the work with much greater rapidity."

II

On the 26th or 27th of May, while Preble was waiting impatiently for the *Constitution* to be moved from the Charles River to May's Wharf, he received through the mail his first official information about the composition of the new Mediterranean squadron and his position in it. He already knew, of course, that the *Constitution* would be a member of it. The other frigate would be the *Philadelphia,* commanded by Captain William Bainbridge and currently fitting for sea at the city from which she took her name. The famous schooner *Enterprize,* Lieutenant Isaac Hull, was in the Mediterranean and would remain there. That small, fast vessels were needed on the Mediterranean station had been realized by the administration, and the remaining four units of the squadron would be recent additions to the Navy, authorized under an act of 28 February 1803: the 12-gun schooner *Nautilus,* Lieutenant Richard Somers; the 16-gun brig *Syren,* Lieutenant Charles Stewart, under construction at Philadelphia; the 12-gun schooner *Vixen,* Lieutenant John Smith, on the ways at Baltimore; and the 16-gun brig *Argus,* Lieutenant Stephen Decatur, which was being built at Boston. "Reposing in your skill, judgment and bravery the highest degree of confidence," wrote Robert Smith, "the President has determined to commit the command of this squadron to your direction."

When Captain Preble was in Washington the previous November talking about his part in the new squadron, the Secretary was planning to give command of it to Richard Dale. But Dale had resigned in December because Congress had not created the rank of admiral. Smith then thought of Commodore John Barry, but that veteran was dying at his home in Philadelphia. And so the choice came down to Edward Preble.

This news made Preble a happy man. A desire to make his name famous began to be mentioned frequently in his letters. "You need not fear that I shall be too much loaded with care in commanding the squadron," he told Mary on 2 June. "I shall have enough of it, but feel that I shall acquit myself tolerable well, and I hope in a manner to acquire reputation."

In the early months of 1803 Robert Smith still held to his unpopular position: "Nothing but a formidable force will effect an honorable peace with Tripoli and repress the dispositions of the other Barbary Powers to hostility." The President could not accept this point of view. His continuing purpose was to discourage and control, rather than to eliminate, the system of payments to the Barbary States, whose ports would be even more effectively blockaded when the brigs and schooners reached the Mediterranean: "I have never believed in any effect from a show of force to those powers. They know they cannot meet us with force any more than they could France, Spain or England. Their system is a war of little expense to them, which must put the great nations to a greater expense than the presents which would buy it off. Yet nothing but the warring on them at times will keep the demand of presents within bounds. The important thing for us now is to dispatch our small vessels." [4]

In March the administration circle was deep in discouragement over the lack of activity and accomplishment by Commodore Morris. Then, Captain Alexander Murray had sailed up the Potomac with his tale of woe and criticism: Morris dawdling about the Mediterranean; Sweden paying off Tripoli; Hamet Caramanli being reconciled to his brother Yusuf; the European nations unwilling to cooperate in controlling the Barbary regencies. The Cabinet was in a mood to accept this sort of gloom at Murray's own valuation.

So far, in spite of his willingness to give occasional presents to the Barbary States, the President had always insisted that there should be no payment to Tripoli for making peace. But, when the Cabinet met on 8 April for a general review of the situation, this policy was reversed. "Shall we buy peace of Tripoli?" Jefferson asked his advisers. Their decision was, unanimously, yes. The next day, new instructions went out from Secretary of State Madison to James L. Cathcart:

> Considering that the Bashaw is no longer under the domestic distresses which at one time humbled his pretensions, that all the other nations at war with him have yielded to the customary terms of peace, and that the new terms which the concurrent policy of all civilized nations ought to force on those barbarians would now be pursued by the United States at very great expense, not only without the cooperation of a single other power, but in opposition to the example of all, and at a period in different respects critical to their affairs, it is thought best that you should not be tied down to a refusal of presents, whether to be included in the peace, or to be made from time to time during its continuance, especially as in the latter case the title to the presents will be a motive to its continuance.

Cathcart was authorized to offer the Pasha $20,000, including the consular present, for a peace settlement, and an annuity of from $8,000 to $10,000. "If these sums can be reduced, you will of course avail yourself of the opportunity. But no enlargement of them towards the example of other nations will be admissible, especially, if at the date of the negotiations, none of our citizens should be in captivity." Cathcart was also authorized to attempt to settle the slowly brewing difficulties at Tunis by offering the Bey an annual present of not more than $10,000.[5]

Commodore Morris refused to give Cathcart an adequate opportunity to carry out these instructions, but, in any event, Cathcart's day as the American negotiator with Tripoli was about up, and the execution of his orders fell to his successor. At the same time that Preble would be assuming the naval command in the Mediterranean, new hands would be taking over diplomatic affairs. Tobias Lear, who had held the difficult post of U.S. consul at Cap-Français during the attempted reconquest of Haiti by the

French, was being appointed Consul General at Algiers, with additional authority to negotiate peace with Tripoli if nothing had been concluded by the time he reached the Mediterranean. Lear and his family were to sail in the frigate *Constitution*.

Such was the background of the operational orders issued to Commodore Preble on 13 July 1803. Three paragraphs contained the essential points:

> The varying aspects of our affairs in the Mediterranean, the great distance between this country and the probable places of your operations render it improper for the government to prescribe to you any particular course of conduct. We therefore leave you unrestrained in your movements and at liberty to pursue the dictates of your own judgment, subject however to the following general regulations and instructions:
>
> It is the expectation of the President that you will without intermission maintain, during the season in which it may be safely done, an effectual blockade of Tripoli; and that you will, by all the means in your power, annoy the enemy....
>
> You will keep a vigilant eye over the movements of all the other Barbary Powers, and communicate frequently with our consuls at Algiers, Tunis and Tangier; and should any of these powers be induced to declare or wage war against the United States, it is the command of the President, and you are hereby instructed, to protect our commerce by all the means in your power against them.

News reaching Boston from Europe during the spring of 1803 indicated that the unstable Peace of Amiens, which had been concluded in March 1802, was coming to an end. Maritime war between France and Britain was about to be resumed. In this battle between giants Preble foresaw commercial gain for a neutral United States. "Rumors of an expected war in Europe are in brisk circulation here," Preble wrote to Henry Dearborn on 27 April, "and, should those expectations be verified, it will undoubtedly be for the interest of the United States to be at peace; and I am fully persuaded that the President will govern the helm of state with such wisdom and judgment as to steer the nation over which he presides clear of every difficulty and danger which the preservation of our neutrality may be attended with."[6]

By July Preble was beginning to plan his strategy along the lines of the aggressive campaign that Richard Dale had advocated. On the 16th he offered a proposition for Secretary Smith's consideration:

> I have been informed that the Tripolines have a very considerable coasting trade in which they employ a number of vessels from 30 to 150 tons, constructed and rigged in a manner peculiar to the Mediterranean. If Colonel Lear should not be successful in his mission, can I be authorized to hire or purchase three or four vessels of about 40 or 50 tons, of the above description,

either at Malta or elsewhere, for the purpose of capturing or destroying the Tripoline merchant vessels and distressing their coast? Those vessels [I] should arm as they do their coasters, say with two or four guns on deck, and should man them with an enterprising lieutenant, three or four midshipmen, a surgeon's mate, and about fifty or sixty petty officers, seamen and Marines from the squadron; only a certain number to appear on deck at a time when near the coast, or in sight of any vessel, and those to be in the Tripoline garb with the turban. This method would enable them to approach the coast without suspicion for the purpose of reconnoitering, and probably be the means of capturing some valuable prizes.

I suspect those barbarians will not be disposed to make peace with us until they feel sensible of our ability and determination to distress them by every possible means.

Robert Smith's answer must have caused Preble a twinge of disappointment, but considering the government's fiscal policy it was surely the best Smith could do. Preble's plan, the Secretary replied, was a good one, but under existing law there was no authorization for the purchase of such vessels. However, if Lear did not succeed in arranging a treaty between Tripoli and the United States, Preble would be permitted to hire one or more small vessels, provided he could man them from his squadron. Enlisting extra men for the hired vessels could not be allowed, as the expense would exceed the Congressional appropriation. Two copies of the President's formal order authorizing the capture of Tripolitan vessels were enclosed to Preble; and, since each ship that Preble hired would have to have such an authorization, this was probably a tactful hint that Robert Smith thought Preble should not hire more than two vessels.

Smith may not have been able to give Preble everything he asked, but in a personal letter which Preble probably did not receive until after his arrival in the Mediterranean, he assured the Commodore of his confidence, sympathy, and support:

Private

Baltimore, August 2, 1803.

Sir:

In an official letter I have authorized you to transfer to your squadron certain midshipmen that are in the returning ships. In this selection I have had no other object than the affording an opportunity of further improvement to young gentlemen who have been represented to me as possessing professional talents and of being ambitious of acquiring knowledge. All the officers of this cast of character are highly deserving of attention, and I shall ever interest myself in their advancement. As to those of an opposite disposition, they do not merit, and therefore will not have, the patronage of government, however respectable their friends may be....

Let not my naming to you so many midshipmen induce an opinion that all of them are to be removed to your squadron. On the contrary, I am particularly desirous that our vessels be not too much crowded with such officers, and you will, therefore, regulate this business in your discretion. If it should so happen that you should have in your ship or in any of the vessels of your squadron any midshipmen who are worthless, vicious, dishonorable in their conduct, or in any respect obviously unworthy of the rank they hold in the Navy, or who are of such a torpid, sluggish disposition as in your opinion they evidently cannot be respectable or useful officers, all such midshipmen, it is my wish, ought to be sent home in the returning vessels. You will keep it in mind that in all our Mediterranean expeditions the improvement of our officers is a favorite object. To retain in our vessels those who are not susceptible of improvement, or who are not desirous of it, would be nothing but a waste of money and time. To give to the meritorious an opportunity of acquiring knowledge is of great moment to our country as well as to themselves. It is the training and educating a highly useful class of gentlemen upon whom our country may with pride rely when she shall, as she no doubt must at some future period, be engaged in a more serious warfare than the present. Would that the gentlemen of our Navy consider what would be our situation in case we were involved in a war with the most insignificant of the European maritime powers. We could without difficulty build the requisite number of ships. We could *man* them. But could we *officer* them? Is every lieutenant qualified to command a man-of-war? How many of the midshipmen are fit for the duties of a lieutenant? And yet whence are we to select officers but from the corps of Navy officers? To take them from the merchant vessels we would subject ourselves to great vexation. These desultory remarks I make in order to evince to you my great solicitude about the improvement of all our officers.

Assured as you must be that I shall at all times be extremely happy to hear from you and greatly mortified as well as perplexed in not being kept always acquainted with your movements and objects, you will, I am persuaded, omit no opportunity of writing. And remember that the best route is through England. Write by every vessel going to England. In short, take every chance. A short letter is often of great moment in the deliberations of government.

We have received great injuries from the jarrings of Morris and Cathcart. As the head of the Navy I feel in the President's Cabinet great pain from such disasters. Your experience in affairs and your good sense and the tried merits of Mr. Lear all conspire to persuade me that you and he will move in the most perfect harmony. You have an arduous task to perform. You will have great difficulties to encounter. But if you succeed your satisfaction will be the greater and your fame will be the higher. And that you may succeed is the fervent prayer of your sincere friend,

Rt. Smith

III

Although Preble was thinking about strategy and naval policy, most of his energy was spent pressing forward on the work of getting his ship to sea.

As the frigate's officers began assembling in Boston, reactions to their new commander varied. Ralph Izard was one who liked him: "[The *Constitution*] is to be commanded by Captain Preble, to whom I made my bow this afternoon on board, and, should his future conduct towards me be as pleasing as was his first, I am sure I cannot but be very much pleased with him." Others had less happy impressions. The crew surely had little warm affection for Preble: he was remote in manner and inaccessible. Before the end of July he had a Marine sentinel posted at the door of his cabin to see that no one but the quarterdeck officers and a few others got in to see him.

When the younger officers came to know Preble better they discovered that his courtesy tended to disintegrate under stress. Wrote Midshipman Charles Morris:

> A very violent and easily excited temper was one of the prominent characteristics of Commodore Preble, from the undue expression of which, when he was greatly excited, no officer could escape. Irresolution, no less than contradiction, was an offence in his eyes, and decision of action as well as obedience of orders was necessary to preserve his favorable opinion. The ship was refitted at a wharf in Boston, while many of her former stores were in the Navy Yard at Charlestown. The Commodore one day directed me to repair to the Navy Yard daily and send to the ship such articles as should be required from time to time. As only a small part of the crew had then been collected, I inquired how many should be taken for the service; to which I received the reply, in no mild tone: "None. Get your men where you can find them." I thought best to take him at his word, and engaged ten or twelve men, and when the work was completed presented to the Commodore for approval an account for their wages. This produced another outbreak, with the inquiry as to how I had dared to incur such an expense without his orders; but on being reminded of his former conversation he gave his signature and dismissed me with courtesy.[7]

One of the irritations that kept the Commodore simmering was Captain Samuel Nicholson. In 1798 there was a rumor that Preble was looking for an excuse that would keep him from having to join the *Constitution* as Nicholson's first lieutenant. Benjamin Stoddert, who could scarcely abide Nicholson, put him on the beach in 1799, but because Nicholson was the uncle of Mrs. Albert Gallatin and of the influential congressman from Maryland, Joseph Hopper Nicholson, he survived the Peace Establishment Act of 1801 without being retired from the Navy, and was appointed superintendent of the Charlestown Navy Yard, a job which he apparently regarded as a sinecure for an old man. Preble's opinion of Samuel Nicholson had not mellowed over the years, and conditions at the Navy Yard disgusted him:

> The stores belonging to the *Constitution* when she was laid up in ordinary were landed and put into a warehouse. A kind of confused inventory was taken of them by the boatload, but the stores in the different departments were not returned separately. They were all mixed together. I cannot find

that anyone receipted for them, nor do I know of any person that considers himself responsible; and, if I may judge of the other stores by the cabin furniture, a considerable part of them will be wanting. The only furniture I can find has been delivered by Captain Nicholson. It consists of a broken set of teaspoons, a broken cruet stand, two old tablecloths, and eleven coarse homespun towels which he says have been lately made to replace those that formerly belonged to her and have been worn out in his family. There are a few chairs and a table.

This report and another one to the effect that the *Constitution*'s boats had been left lying on the ground at the yard for almost two years without any cover or protection and were consequently beyond repair, Preble gave to Robert Smith: "To communicate intelligence of this nature is as unpleasant to me as it can be to you to receive it, and I hope you will believe that no consideration but that of a sense of duty could have induced me to have touched on this unpleasant subject." Smith reassured him: "You have done what your duty as an officer required of you in making the communication to me." It is doubtful that criticism of Nicholson was as painful to Preble as he claimed. There was a harsh side to Preble, and he was inclined to show it when dealing with mediocrities. Preble had intelligence, energy, and ability, and he operated easily at an extremely high level of competence. With those who could not or did not measure up to such standards he had little sympathy or understanding. If a person lacked dedication and the ability to do a job right, Preble was willing to brush him aside roughly. However, there was no personal animosity in his criticisms. When Nicholson asked Preble to endorse his son Joseph's application for a midshipman's warrant, Preble did so cheerfully: "I do not hesitate to comply with his request, as his son appears to be a young man who promises fair to make an officer."

Serious problems developed in trying to enlist a crew for the *Constitution*. Early in June recruiting instructions had been sent to Preble, and as soon as the frigate was recoppered he began to sign on the crew. Pay for the ordinary seamen and boys was to be from $5 to $8 a month, and the wages for able seamen were to be reduced from $12 a month, which had previously been paid, to $10. As an inducement for the seamen to sign on at the lower pay, they could be given four months' advance on their wages when they signed up, instead of the two months' advance that had been allowed with the higher pay.

A good many seamen volunteered to sign up for the cruise, but most of them backed off when they heard how low the pay would be. News of the European war had set the shipping community into a flurry of activity, which caused wages in the merchant service to climb steeply, making Navy pay seem even less attractive by comparison. Also, this was the season when the fishermen were at sea, which made prospective recruits all the scarcer. In the fall, when the fishing and coasting vessels would be laid up for the winter, seamen would be plentiful and wages lower, but Preble could not wait till then to sign on a crew: he urged Robert Smith to raise the pay for able seamen to $13 and two months' advance, or $12 and three months' advance, and for ordinary seamen and boys to between $6 and $10.

Smith replied that he could not increase wages, at least until a determined effort had been made to recruit men at the lower pay and larger advance. He urged Preble to send a recruiting officer, "whose manners are well adapted to the business," to New York, where no Navy ships were fitting for sea. Smith explained that if seamen could be enlisted at the lower wages, the economy thus effected would allow him to keep one more small vessel on active service than he could if he were forced to allow the higher pay. After this letter had been copied out by Goldsborough, Smith read it over, made a correction, signed it, then, with a little pardonable hometown pride, added a postscript in his own hand: "At Baltimore the crew of the *Nautilus* have entered at ten dollars, and at the same rate will enter, without the least hesitation, the crew of the *Vixen*. I, however, have the fullest confidence that you have done, and that you will continue to do, everything practicable to effect the enlistment upon the terms proposed. The men of the same squadron [ought], you know, to be all entered [on] the same terms."

At this point, the war in Europe began to have a favorable effect on recruiting, a development welcomed by Robert Smith: "The certainty of war will invite foreign seamen, of which I expect there are a great many in New York, to enter our service, as they dare not trust themselves to the protection of the merchant service officers and they are sure of being safe from impressment in ours."[8] By the 21st of July, about 165 men had been recruited and were present for duty, and Preble wrote: "I do not believe that I have twenty native American sailors on board."

Thanks to this influx of foreign seamen, recruiting at Boston was brisk until a rise in wages in the merchant service slowed it to a trickle. Two officers went to Providence, Rhode Island, with high hopes for recruiting in that area, but their efforts were a failure. Lieutenants Joshua Blake and William Livingston, with instructions to recruit sixty able and twenty ordinary seamen, were sent to New York on 5 July. That city proved, as Robert Smith expected, to be the charm. Blake and Livingston arrived there on Saturday morning, 9 July, and found conditions very different from those in Boston. Commercial activity was slack: few merchant ships were fitting out, and those that were paid only $13 to $15 a month. Unemployed seamen were plentiful. Speculating that this was only a momentary stagnation caused by the news of war between England and France and that it would soon be followed by intense activity, Blake planned to complete his recruiting before the merchants got their new bearings, and hurried to cash in on American neutrality. The presence in the harbor of an English sloop of war was already making the sailors uneasy. "The protection of a man-of-war from impressment I shall hold up with the many other inducements," Blake assured Preble.

Early Monday morning, 11 July, Lieutenant Blake opened his rendezvous, and by eight o'clock that evening he had signed up the eighty men he was authorized to recruit. This group of recruits, less a few deserters, left New York by coaster on Friday, 15 July, in the charge of Lieutenant Livingston. Blake stayed on in New York, waiting to hear whether Preble wanted him to recruit more seamen. "At this time three hundred men could be engaged in one week," he wrote. Preble told him to recruit sixty more ordinary seamen, and sent Midshipman Ralph Izard down with additional funds. "You will please to proceed to New York in the mail stage which leaves town tomorrow morning," Preble instructed Izard. Then, probably reflecting that Izard was a young man and something of a social butterfly, he added, "I expect you to arrive in the mail you set off with." By the time Izard got to New York on Tuesday, the 19th, Blake already had a good start on his task and on 21 July, Izard sailed in the sloop *Hancock* with fifty-six recruits. After reaching Boston two days later Izard remarked dryly: "The Commodore was rather surprised at seeing me so soon, supposing it almost impossible to have returned so quickly."

IV

Preble took command of the *Constitution* on 20 May, but two months later she was still fitting for sea. In an administration already testy because of the Morris affair, criticism of Edward Preble began to be heard, criticism that probably had its roots in Robert Smith's optimistic opinion that the *Constitution* could be in the Mediterranean about ten weeks after orders were given to equip her for sea.[9] Preble was a sensitive person, and the unjustified censure cut him deeply. On 19 July he wrote to Henry Dearborn:

> I am extremely hurt that any persons should have made the observations hinted at in your letter, but it convinces me that they are not acquainted with the duty I have had to perform or the difficulties I have had to encounter. . . .
> As this is the first ship of her rate in our service that has ever been hove keel-out *in America* we had everything to create for the careening business. Ships of this size are easily handled and prepared for sea in almost any

situation when they have their proper crews on board. Four hundred men acquainted with the duty they have to perform can do much, but with the assistance I have had it is no easy task to accomplish as much as I have done in the same time. Would to God I could have done more! Zeal on my part has not been wanting. I have made use of every exertion in my power, and have devoted myself so wholly to the service as even to deny myself the pleasure of dining with a friend. Three Sundays have I hired men to work to forward the business and attended to them myself. You may rest assured I should deem myself unworthy of your friendship if I did not exert myself in the service of my country when called on. . . .

The ship had been laying by so long a time that the plank had shrunk, and it was absolutely necessary to recaulk every seam in her. The whole of the standing rigging was to strip and refit, owing to its having been fitted in cold weather. I have had much joiner's work to do. The cabin bulkheads were so placed as to prevent the guns from running out of the ports. Of course they were to be shifted. All the officers' berths and rooms in the wardroom were to remove. They were so constructed that we could not caulk under them. Midshipmen's bulkhead to build. Storerooms to finish, and magazine and filling room to copper. Bread and sail rooms to tin. Iron work to make. Cables and cordage to make. The cables are not yet finished, but will be next week. It takes a long time to spin the yarns, and it requires that they should lay in the coil, after having been tarred, two or three weeks before they are laid up. We have had the ship wholly to ballast and water with 54,000 gallons. All the yards were new and to be fitted, and the ship entirely to rig. . . .

More than has been done here cannot be done in the same time, with the same number of men, in any port of the United States. Whenever the coppering and equipping one of the 44-gun ships at Washington becomes necessary, it will be found that eight weeks is not sufficient to *build and equip a frigate for sea.*

V

"The Commodore is very anxious to get the *Constitution* to sea. He attends duty from morning until night," Nathaniel Haraden noted in the frigate's logbook early in August. By the 9th everything was ready and only an east wind kept the *Constitution* bottled up in Boston harbor.

Preble's thoughts on the eve of sailing are recorded in another letter to Henry Dearborn:

> Frigate *Constitution*, Boston Harbor,
> August 9th 1803.
>
> Dear Sir:
> I am honored with your much esteemed favor of the 30th ultimo. I am waiting for a favorable wind to proceed to sea. Everything is perfectly ready as it respects the ship and equipment. I assure you I am not in the pursuit of pleasure — excepting such as the destruction of the piratical vessels in the Mediterranean can afford me. An ardent desire to distinguish myself in the service of my country is the only inducement that could possibly take me

from the enjoyment of every domestic happiness to scenes such as I hope to be present at. If Tripoli does not make peace, I shall hazard much to destroy their vessels in port if I cannot meet them at sea. I shall endeavor to convince them that their ports are not sufficient protection for them. . . .

None but a real friend would have given me the kind advice which you have respecting the government of temper. Be assured it shall be attended to, and I most sincerely thank you for it. I am, dear Sir, with real esteem and respect, your obliged and obedient servant,

EDWARD PREBLE [10]

At daylight on Friday, 12 August, the *Constitution* weighed anchor and made sail to go to sea; but as she entered the Narrows, eight miles below Boston, the wind dropped away, and she was forced to anchor again. From there, on the 13th, Preble sent a message to Mary: "In a few hours I shall sail from this for the Mediterranean. May the Great God protect and preserve your precious life and health, and to Him do I commend both you and myself. May He in His mercy grant that we may again meet and be long happy in each other's society."

The *Constitution*'s anchors were weighed for the last time in American waters at 7:30 the next morning. Just after eight o'clock the frigate passed Boston Light, and at nine o'clock dropped the pilot. When darkness came that evening, all that could be seen of the United States was a beam from the Cape Cod Light.

CHAPTER 8   SEPTEMBER 1803–OCTOBER 1803

"... *cringing to those Barbarians will not answer.*"

Off Cape St. Vincent on 5 September 1803 the *Constitution* met the brig *Jack,* of Cape Ann, homeward bound and four days out from Cadiz. From her master Preble heard that Captain William Bainbridge, in the *Philadelphia,* had already reached the Mediterranean, and that he had sailed from Gibraltar about ten days earlier in search of two Tripolitan vessels reported to be cruising near Alicante.[1]

News of Tripolitan cruisers on the Spanish coast made Preble more anxious than ever to get to Gibraltar, but frustrating head winds and calms had set in. At noon next day, when Cape St. Vincent was still in sight and the *Constitution* was running S. by E., propelled by light, variable airs, three sail were sighted to the east. One of the strangers was a frigate under French colors; the other two could not immediately be identified, except that one of them was a ship, and she was steering down towards the *Constitution.*

This last vessel did not arouse any particular suspicion; indeed, she seemed anxious to speak the American frigate. At 1:30 p.m. the Commodore tacked to the northward and cleared for action. In reply the stranger raised a red ensign and a red flag at her main. By 2:30 the ships were close enough for the *Constitution* to shorten sail and send a boarding party to examine her.

Preble's boarding officer reported that the stranger was a Moroccan frigate, that she carried a passport from James Simpson, the American consul at Tangier, and that nothing about her appeared to be at all suspicious. Preble was less trusting, and when Tobias Lear said that he knew James Simpson's handwriting and volunteered to go on board the frigate to re-examine her papers, Preble quickly accepted.

On board the Moroccan, Lear was shown the passport, from which he found that she was the frigate *Maimona,* 30 guns and 150 men. Simpson's signature looked genuine. Speaking through an interpreter, the *Maimona's* commander told Lear that he was twenty-three days out from Salé, bound to Lisbon on the Sultan's business. Asked why it had taken him so long to come such a short distance — Lear suspected that the *Maimona* had been cruising, looking for ships to capture — the captain said that he had met head winds which had forced him to put back several times, and added that the Sultan was at peace with the whole world. Lear then asked to see the captain's commission, whereupon the latter produced an impressive-looking document, written in Arabic script and bearing a seal. Since neither Lear nor anyone in his party could read Arabic, there was nothing to do but take the captain's word that it was truly his commission, bow out graciously, and return on board the *Constitution.*

Preble and Lear were both of the opinion that, since the *Maimona's* papers appeared to be in good order, there were no legitimate grounds on which to detain her. "Indeed," Preble wrote later, "I should as soon have thought of detaining a British vessel." It was quite a wrench for Preble to let the *Maimona* go. Considering the number of guns and men she had on board and the length of time she had been out from Salé, he was worried that some deception was afoot. Lear got the impression that, had the *Maimona* still been in sight the next morning, Preble would have detained her, whatever the consequences, until he could get in touch with James Simpson at Tangier.

Four days later, on 10 September, still plagued by head winds and calms, the *Constitution* was only approaching Cadiz. During the early evening the atmosphere was hazy, but an unidentified sail could be seen to the southeast, more or less ahead of the *Constitution,* on the course the American frigate was steering. About 8:30 p.m., when darkness was complete and the breeze had dropped away, the watch suddenly discovered that the *Constitution* was close aboard the ship they had sighted at sunset. Near at hand, she looked to be a ship of war. Memory of the meeting with the *Maimona* was fresh, and the crew was called to quarters. Then Preble hailed the stranger:

"What ship is that?"

"What ship is that?" the stranger called back.

"This is the United States frigate *Constitution.* What ship is that?"

"What ship is that?" replied the uncooperative stranger.

"This is the United States frigate *Constitution.* What ship is that?"

"What ship is that?"

Preble's patience, never proverbial, was by now exhausted, and he called out, "I am now going to hail you for the last time. If a proper answer is not returned, I will fire a shot into you."

"If you fire a shot, I will return a broadside."

"What ship is that?" Preble hailed with rising exasperation.

"This is His Britannic Majesty's ship *Donegal,* 84 guns, Sir Richard Strachan, an English commodore. Send your boat on board."

That was too much for Preble who scrambled up onto the nettings and shouted, "This is the United States ship *Constitution,* 44 guns, Edward Preble, an American commodore, who will be damned before he sends his boat on board of any vessel!" And he called to the men gathered around the quarterdeck guns, "Blow your matches, boys!"

A few minutes of silence followed this last exchange. Then, a boat was heard approaching. A British lieutenant came over the side and explained that his ship was really the frigate *Maidstone,* Commander George Elliot. Captain Elliot had sighted the *Constitution* at 4:30 that afternoon, and, thinking she might be a hostile vessel, had stood towards her to investigate. The *Maidstone* had realized how close she was to the *Constitution* only moments before she was hailed by the American frigate. When Preble began hailing, Elliot had not had time to get all his crew to quarters, and, in order to gain time, he was evasive. Not until after his lieutenant had boarded her was Captain Elliot fully convinced that the *Constitution* was an American frigate.

This small incident made a strong impression on Preble's officers. The Commodore's terrible temper had made him disliked by many of them, but by standing up to the British, he made himself a hero of wardroom and steerage.[2]

II

At 10:00 a.m. on 12 September the *Constitution* hove to off Tangier, raised her colors, and fired a gun — the established signal for a consul to send a boat off to a warship. But no boat put out, and in Tangier only the Swedish consul hoisted his flag over his residence. Preble ordered another gun to be fired. Still no boat came out to the frigate. After a wait of an hour the Commodore was sure that something was wrong between the United States and the Sultan of Morocco, and he ordered the frigate to get under way for Gibraltar.

At 3:30 that same afternoon the *Constitution* anchored in Gibraltar Bay. Perhaps even before her anchor was down, Captain William Bainbridge was coming alongside in one of the *Philadelphia*'s boats. He brought the news that Morocco seemed to be at war with the United States. Bainbridge explained that his orders directed him to place himself under the command of the senior officer on the Mediterranean station, and, when he arrived at Gibraltar on 24 August, he was told that Commodore Morris could be found off Tripoli. Because of a report that there were two Tripolitan cruisers — the same ones that Preble had heard about from the master of the brig *Jack* — off Cape Gata, Bainbridge decided that, on his way up the Mediterranean, he would run close to the Spanish shore and attempt to capture them.

On the evening of 26 August, when she was nearly abreast of Cape Gata, the *Philadelphia* came upon a ship with only her foresail set, accompanied by a brig carrying the same sail. After being hailed several times, the strange ship identified herself as a cruiser from one of the Barbary States. Bainbridge ordered her to send her passports on board the *Philadelphia*. These identified her as a Moroccan cruiser, called *Mirboha*, mounting 22 guns, carrying one hundred men, and commanded by Rais Ibrahim Lubarez. Captain Bainbridge, who had concealed the *Philadelphia*'s nationality, began to quiz the Moroccan officer who brought the passports about the nearby brig. The Moroccan explained that she was an American ship, bound for some port in Spain, and had been keeping company with the *Mirboha* for three or four days. Rais Lubarez had boarded her, but had in no way detained her.

To the suspicious Bainbridge, that seemed a weird story: the brig looked more like a prize than a friendly companion. He sent his first lieutenant, John S. H. Cox, over to the *Mirboha* with orders to search the ship for American prisoners, but Lubarez would permit no search and kept Cox from going below. Now really aroused, Bainbridge dispatched a boatload of armed men to search the *Mirboha* by force, if necessary. After all this, Lieutenant Cox was probably not greatly surprised to find Richard Bowen, master of the American brig *Celia*, and most of his crew confined below the *Mirboha*'s decks. They had been prisoners since 17 August, when the *Mirboha* captured the *Celia*.

As soon as the American prisoners were discovered, Bainbridge ordered all the Moroccan officers brought on board the *Philadelphia* and sent an American prize crew to man the *Mirboha*. He abandoned his plan of going up the Mediterranean to look for Commodore Morris, and returned to Gibraltar Bay with the *Celia* and the *Mirboha*. At Gibraltar he received a report that a 30-gun Moroccan frigate — the *Maimona*, of course — was cruising near Cadiz and Cape St. Vincent. In pursuit of her, the *Philadelphia* sailed from Gibraltar on 1 September and, for ten days, cruised outside the Straits, but she took no prizes and did not even sight the *Maimona*.

After Bainbridge had captured the *Mirboha,* Rais Lubarez and his officers admitted that they had been looking for American merchantmen to seize and send to Tangier. As his authority, Lubarez offered a document written in Arabic which he said was an order from Alcayde Abd al-Rahman Hashash, the governor of Tangier. Hashash was known to be extremely hostile to the United States, and Lubarez and his officers loudly blamed him for the scrape in which they found themselves. His orders, Lubarez explained, had been delivered to him sealed and he had been instructed not to open them until the *Mirboha* was at sea. While the *Philadelphia* was cruising outside the Straits in search of the *Maimona,* John Gavino, the American consul at Gibraltar, had the orders translated and found that they did indeed authorize Lubarez to capture American ships. The orders were not signed, but the Moroccan consul at Gibraltar admitted that they were in the handwriting of either Alcayde Hashash or of his secretary.

III

Bainbridge and John Gavino soon made Preble familiar with the state of American affairs with Morocco. To recapitulate: in the spring of 1803, the Sultan of Morocco, Maulay Sulaiman, had been permitted to take possession of the old Tripolitan cruiser *Meshuda* on the strength of his declaration that she had been sold to him by the Pasha of Tripoli. But on the 12th of May Captain John Rodgers in the *John Adams* had captured this same *Meshuda* as she attempted to enter the blockaded port of Tripoli. She was carrying a contraband cargo of muskets, sabers, cannon, hemp, and other articles, was commanded by both a Tripolitan and a Moroccan captain, her complement included several Tripolitan officers and seamen, and she had nineteen more men on board than were called for in her American passport. Although it was not known at Gibraltar when Preble arrived there on 12 September, Captain Rodgers had since secured even more damning evidence of deceit and duplicity in Morocco: a declaration by part of the crew that the *Meshuda* was actually the property of the Pasha of Tripoli. This was confirmed by her Tripolitan commander, who explained that the ship had stopped at Tunis on her passage up the Mediterranean. There he had received, first, notification that the ownership of the *Meshuda* had been transferred from the Sultan back to the Pasha, and, second, orders from the Pasha which directed him to sail her to Tripoli. He had, he admitted, been sailing the *Meshuda* under the Pasha's authority when she was captured by the *John Adams.* News of this capture had reached James Simpson at Tangier on 19 June, and was immediately reported to Alcayde Hashash. The governor insisted that there had been no duplicity on Morocco's part: the *Meshuda*'s attempt to enter Tripoli was a direct violation of orders to her commander.

At the time word of the *Meshuda*'s capture reached Simpson, Morocco was making serious efforts to get some of her cruisers ready for sea. The 30-gun *Maimona*, a new ship, was completing her equipment at Salé; the *Mirboha*, 22, an ancient vessel, was outfitting at Larache. By 26 July Simpson knew that the captains of the *Maimona* and the *Mirboha* had received sealed orders which they were not to open until they were clear of the coast, and he appealed to Commodore Morris: "This measure shows a stroke against some nation is determined upon, for which reason I cannot too strongly enforce what I have before said on subject of your sending some protection to our trade in this quarter."

By the middle of August Simpson was immersed in uncertainty. Both the *Mirboha* and the *Maimona* had sailed, but nothing had been heard from them. Nor had anything been heard from the uncommunicative Commodore Morris since his letter announcing the capture of the *Meshuda*, a letter that had been sent three months earlier. On the first day of September, when Simpson received a dispatch from Captain Bainbridge describing the capture of the *Mirboha* off Cape Gata, everything became much clearer. Simpson at once carried the news of the capture to Hashash, who vehemently denied that Lubarez or any other Moroccan captain had orders from him to seize American ships. He further denied that he knew of such orders being issued by any other authority — denials that Simpson did not take seriously. Then Hashash counterattacked with repeated, badgering complaints about the American detention of the *Meshuda*.

A second meeting between Simpson and the governor was held later the same day. It was inconclusive: both sides repeated the statements made at the earlier interview. At 11:00 p.m. Hashash summoned Simpson to a third meeting. As soon as Simpson entered the governor's house the doors were shut behind him; he was told by the Alcayde's retainers that he would be held prisoner until both the *Mirboha* and the *Meshuda* were released. Simpson was kept in custody until ten o'clock the next morning, 2 September, at which time the consuls of other countries demanded his release on the grounds of diplomatic immunity. Hashash agreed to let Simpson go, but insisted that the consuls would have to be responsible for making sure that Simpson did not leave Morocco without the Sultan's permission.

On the day of his release Simpson wrote to the Sultan offering to open negotiations for an adjustment of differences between the two nations. At that moment the U.S. squadrons held both the *Mirboha* and the *Meshuda*, but, so far as was known, the Moroccans had no American ships in their power. To Simpson, this was the time to resolve the crisis and prevent it from deteriorating into a declared war. He feared that a prolonged war would result in American commerce in the Mediterranean and outside the Straits of Gibraltar being either stopped altogether or, at least, seriously curtailed: certainly insurance rates would be drastically increased. Further, Consul Simpson was convinced that, if a new treaty had to be made with Morocco, the negotiations would be tedious and expensive, and the resulting document would probably not be nearly so favorable to the United States as the current treaty, which had been made in 1786 when Sidi Muhammed ibn Abdallah was Sultan, and was rather liberal as treaties with Barbary went. The United States was not required to pay a subsidy to the Sultan, and there was provision for the exchange, instead of the enslavement, of prisoners, in the event of war. The treaty of 1786 was considered such a good one that, although the present Sultan had confirmed it in 1795, the State Department was anxious to have him ratify and confirm it again. Simpson, however, was sure that it was a fixed object of Maulay Sulaiman's policy to find an excuse to rid himself of it and to replace it with one that provided for the payment of an annuity by the United States.

It happened that the Sultan was planning to go from Mequinez to Tangier on some state business. This visit should make it possible for Simpson and Preble to deal directly with him and his minister, Mohammed Selawy, who was known to be friendly to the United States, rather than through a hostile intermediary, such as Hashash.

IV

By 13 September Preble had digested all this information on Moroccan affairs and had decided to begin by taking a tough line. He was as anxious as James Simpson was to avoid actual war, and hoped for a quick negotiated settlement with the Sultan. But he wanted the Moroccans to think he was spoiling for a fight, and late on the 13th he drafted a letter to Simpson, hoping that the consul would pass along at least its substance to the Sultan:

> The Emperor's late gross violation of our treaty . . . will justify my giving orders to the captains of the squadron under my command to capture and bring into port all vessels belonging to the Emperor of Morocco or armed vessels belonging to his subjects, as I must consider them as acting under the authority of the Emperor in capturing our vessels, knowing that they dare not act without such authority. And, if I can ascertain that the *Maimona* or any other Moorish cruiser has captured a single American vessel and should meet with her, you may acquaint the Emperor from me that it is my intention in future to sink every such vessel as a pirate, as he denies having given orders to justify their conduct. . . .
> . . . The President is extremely desirous that the United States should have peace and free commercial intercourse with all the states of Barbary, more

particularly with Morocco, but is determined neither to purchase or maintain that peace and intercourse by submitting to treatment dishonorable to our country.

Naval strength to back up Preble's hard line was rapidly concentrating in the Straits of Gibraltar. On the morning of the 13th the schooner *Vixen*, Lieutenant John Smith, had arrived after a month's passage from the Virginia Capes. That afternoon, from the opposite direction, had come the frigate *New York*. She was still commanded by Richard V. Morris, but he had already received the order suspending him from command of the squadron and had surrendered those duties to John Rodgers. As soon as the *Adams* came down the Mediterranean from Tunis, where she had gone to take James L. Cathcart to his new post as U.S. consul, Morris was to take command of her and return to the United States, leaving the *New York* in the Mediterranean as part of Commodore Rodgers's squadron. Rodgers, in the *John Adams*, rounded Europa Point early the next day. With him were his prize, the *Meshuda*, and another member of Preble's squadron, the schooner *Nautilus*, which had reached the Mediterranean at the end of July with the order recalling Commodore Morris. Moroccan plans and hopes must surely have been upset by the unexpected presence in Gibraltar Bay of six American warships: *Constitution*, 44, *Philadelphia*, 36, *New York*, 36, *John Adams*, 28, *Vixen*, 12, and *Nautilus*, 12.

At the moment, Commodore John Rodgers was the most important person with whom Preble had to deal. He outranked Preble and so was the senior officer on the station. More important, he commanded an independent squadron of two frigates, the *New York* and the *John Adams*, both of which had orders to return to the United States as soon as relieved by Preble's squadron. It was essential for Preble to gain Rodgers's cooperation in the crisis with Morocco and to keep his two frigates on station for the next few weeks, especially since the brigs *Syren* and *Argus* had not arrived from the United States.

Although John Rodgers was Edward Preble's senior in the service, he was a much younger man. Preble was 42 years old. Rodgers was only 29 or 30, and owed his seniority to having been first lieutenant of the frigate *Constellation* when she captured *L'Insurgente*. That great event had resulted in his promotion to captain, one place ahead of Preble in order of seniority. Both were ambitious, vigorous, capable, but relatively junior, officers, eager to make names for themselves in a service in which the four men above them on the list of captains — Samuel Nicholson, Richard V. Morris, Alexander Murray, and Samuel Barron — were far less qualified by either natural talents or professional training to command a squadron or direct a major operation. Given the mediocrity of the captains senior to them, both Preble and Rodgers could easily picture themselves as the most important officer in the Navy's future. There grew between them an instinctive rivalry, hostility, almost a hatred, though each was honest enough to recognize the abilities of the other.

For Rodgers, the past year had been frustrating. An activist by temperament, he had fretted at Morris's inability to act vigorously and decisively in Barbary affairs. To this had been added the cruelest blow: he had received the Mediterranean command from Morris only just in time to surrender it to Edward Preble. The orders suspending Morris and instructing Rodgers to take command of the squadron had not reached Rodgers at Málaga until 11 September, and, by the time the then-Commodore Rodgers, sailing in the teeth of head winds, reached Gibraltar, Preble was already there to relieve him. "I shall never cease to think myself unfortunate in not knowing your intentions sooner," Rodgers wrote Robert Smith, "as it has prevented me of an opportunity of erecting a lasting monument to the zeal and regard I have for my country."

Having been denied the opportunity to show how well he could succeed where Morris had failed, Rodgers was in a mood to be readily offended by the sight of a commodore's broad pennant flying on board Preble's *Constitution* in Gibraltar Bay. According to Rodgers's ideas of naval courtesy, Preble ought not to have flown his pennant in the presence of a senior officer: to keep it flying was little better than an insult. Preble contended that, since he commanded a squadron independent of the one under Rodgers, he had a perfect right to wear a pennant so that the officers of his squadron would know where to apply for orders and where to look for signals. In short, he refused to lower the offensive pennant.

Rodgers was furious. "Permit me to observe," he wrote Preble on 15 September, "[that] this is not an affair between private individuals, and that my feelings *as an officer* has been most sensibly injured. And I do (also) insist that, if the date of your commission is subsequent to mine, that it is not in the power (even) of the government to place you or any other officer in a situation which could afford an opportunity of treating me with disrespect." Here could have been the start of one of those quarrels between fellow officers that have frequently wrecked military operations more effectively than enemy action. Happily, both men were mature enough to rise above their personal dislike of one another. Preble had already told Rodgers:

> I conceive that the success of our negotiations with Morocco in a great measure depend on unanimity of sentiments and good understanding among the commanders of our ships of war. . . . I have no disposition to be on such terms with any officer of either the United States squadrons now in these seas

as to injure the interests of our country, if it possibly can be avoided. I shall with pleasure meet you to consult what measures may be best calculated to keep peace with the Barbary Powers that we are now at peace with, and what measures it will be proper to pursue to bring those powers to terms which are at war with us."

"To prevent our feelings acting in a manner that can in any [way] effect the interest of our country I drop the subject until we have more leisure to define what has passed," Rodgers replied, and he suggested an immediate meeting to form a common plan of operations. Both officers were apparently sincere and successful in their efforts to set animosity aside, though Rodgers remained piqued that Preble had taken the initiative in the Moroccan crisis without waiting for him, thus leaving Rodgers with little to do but follow along obediently behind Preble. Pointedly avoiding any reference to his rival as *Commodore* Preble, Rodgers later complained to Robert Smith: "As Captain Preble had commenced a negotiation with the Emperor through Mr. Simpson previous to my arrival, I have taken no part in them further than assent or negation and cooperative measures with the *New York* and *John Adams*." And: "I do assure you, nothing but a sincere love for my country and regard for its interests could ever have forced me to take the part I have done in this business, or voluntarily place myself in a situation which at most could afford me no more than ordinary credit."

These, however, were semiprivate thoughts in a difficult situation. In matters of action Rodgers and Preble quickly reached agreement. Rodgers would remain on the Mediterranean station with the *New York* and the *John Adams* until the *Syren* and the *Argus* arrived, or until there was some settlement with Morocco. He and Preble would cooperate as commanders of independent and equal squadrons.

V

Preble decided that, with Rodgers's help, he had more than enough force to keep Morocco under control. He instructed the *Philadelphia* and the *Vixen* to start up the Mediterranean as soon as possible, giving convoy to American merchantmen bound in that direction, and re-establish the blockade of Tripoli, which had been lifted on 25 June. Aided by the approaching winter, Bainbridge and Smith were not expected to have too much trouble keeping Yusuf's cruisers in port. For the *Nautilus*, Lieutenant Richard Somers, there was a different errand. Preble sent her off to Málaga with directions to stay no longer than twenty-four hours, and then to convoy to Gibraltar Bay eighteen American merchantmen said to be waiting at Málaga. Should Somers fall in with any Moroccan ships, he was to bring them to Preble for examination.

Drafting and delivering orders to Bainbridge and Somers kept Preble busy most of the morning of 16 September. Before noon Tobias Lear arrived on board the *Constitution* with a letter for Preble that had just come over by dispatch boat from James Simpson at Tangier. John Rodgers was in the *Constitution*'s cabin conferring with Preble, and the three men went over Simpson's communication together. Consul Simpson appeared convinced that the orders to seize American traders had originated with Alcayde Hashash, who had great discretionary authority from the Sultan, rather than with the Sultan himself. And Simpson enclosed a translation of a letter he had received from the Sultan which seemed to indicate that Maulay Sulaiman would like to negotiate his way out of the impending war.

Preble and Rodgers decided to go to Tangier right away. At the least, they would be in closer touch with Simpson; at the most, they might be able to settle the whole affair immediately by negotiation. They asked Lear to go along to advise and assist them in any negotiations that might take place. Lear was willing to go, but only in a quasi-official capacity, since his post as Consul General at Algiers gave him supervisory power over the consuls at Tunis and Tripoli, but not over James Simpson at Tangier, and he had no authority to deal with the Sultan of Morocco. Rais Lubarez and six of his officers were brought on board the *Constitution* for the trip to Tangier. Rodgers carried the Moroccan and Tripolitan captains of the *Meshuda* with him in the *John Adams*.

An east wind took the frigates along the Barbary shore at a good pace and by 7:30 the next morning, Saturday, 17 September, they were anchored in Tangier Bay. In the city, the English, French, Spanish, Danish, Swedish, and Portuguese flags could be seen flying over the official residences of the consuls, but, because of the strained relations and impending war between the United States and Morocco, the American flag had not been raised.

Both the *Constitution* and the *John Adams* had entered Tangier Bay with a white flag flying at fore-topgallant masthead. For two and a half hours nothing happened. Then, at about ten o'clock, a boat rowed by four Spaniards pulled alongside the *Constitution* and delivered a slip of paper from James Simpson. This note said only that the boat had been allowed to go off to receive any letters that the Commodore wished to send ashore. Rodgers had himself rowed over to the *Constitution*, where Preble drafted a letter to Simpson for their joint signature. The two commodores told Simpson that they had come to accommodate differences with the Sultan, if it could be done with honor and propriety on the part of the United States. They informed him that they had with them Ibrahim Lubarez, his officers, and the two captains of the *Meshuda,* and that they would permit an authorized representative of the Sultan to visit the American ships and interview the prisoners. But, Preble and Rodgers insisted, it was necessary for them to have a meeting with Simpson on board the *Constitution,* and, if there was a sincere desire for peace on Morocco's part, he would surely be allowed to come off and see them.

More waiting ensued. Most of the afternoon had slipped quietly away when, about four o'clock, another boat came out with a packet of letters from Simpson. The principal letter, addressed to Preble and Rodgers, was noncommittal: Alcayde Hashash was at Tetuán, and the functionary who commanded in his absence said he had neither authority to allow Simpson to go out to the *Constitution,* nor instructions about opening negotiations; the Sultan was due to leave Mequinez not later than Monday, 19 September, and might reach Tangier as soon as the following Friday; since nothing conclusive could be done immediately, it was suggested that Preble call in Tangier Bay again on Monday, by which time Simpson would know something more definite about the Sultan's journey and would have some word on whether the proposed negotiations were to be held with the Sultan himself or were to be conducted through Hashash: "You will believe I have but too well-founded reason to throw every objection in the way of that man [Hashash] having anything to do with our negotiations, and, if possible, it must be avoided."

Concealed in the packet was a letter addressed to "Commodore Preble, or Commanding Officer of the Ship This May Reach":

> Tangier, 17th September 1803.
>
> Sir:
>
> When the boat went this morning to you I was only allowed to send the open slip of paper you saw.
>
> In hopes of finding a conveyance for this I prepare it to acquaint you I received an express last night from Mogador with advice that in the night of the 4th instant orders were received by the governor there to seize all American vessels and property might be at that port. In consequence of which, the following morning the brig *Hannah* of Salem, Joseph W. Williams, master, arrived a few days before from thence, was taken possession of. Some part of her cargo had been landed, was carried back from the stores of the consignee to the custom house, and the master and crew put in charge of a merchant on his security for their appearance. This fresh act of hostility may be considered to throw off the mask and argue that Hashash does not alone direct this unprovoked warfare, but at same time it points out to us an additional source of danger to our commerce. I have reason to believe other American vessels may soon reach Mogador. I beg to submit, for that reason, how far it may be advisable to send one of your smaller cruisers off that port, if you have one to spare.

I have not anything else new since last wrote you. I continue in my house with two soldiers at the gate.

At return of the boat I hope to have the honor of hearing from you. I am truly, Sir, your most obedient servant,

JAMES SIMPSON

Here were further complications. If the governor of Mogador also had orders to seize American shipping, then it certainly looked as if the orders that led to the cruise of the *Mirboha* and the capture of the *Celia* had originated, not with Hashash, as Simpson had optimistically conjectured, but with the Sultan himself. The Moroccans had at least one prize in their hands to balance off against the *Mirboha*. Simpson was, to all intents and purposes, under house arrest.

Preble and Rodgers went over Simpson's letters together, then reached some new decisions. Rodgers, who had only fifteen days' water and provisions left on board his frigate, would go out into the Atlantic, cruise off Larache, Salé, and Mogador as long as supplies lasted, and warn American merchantmen against entering Moroccan ports. At the same time, he would look for Moroccan cruisers, especially the *Maimona*, which was a major cause of concern. Preble would return to Gibraltar to leave new orders for the ships of his squadron. Once those arrangements had been completed, the *Constitution* would again sail to the westward, touching at Tangier on the 19th or 20th, as James Simpson had suggested. If negotiations were still impossible, Preble would cruise in the Atlantic, in search of the *Maimona*.

As the *Constitution* ran up the Straits that night and the next morning, Preble was collecting his thoughts for a dispatch to the Secretary of the Navy: "I shall . . . endeavor by every honorable means to bring about an accommodation, but, if that cannot be done, I shall make them feel that we are sensible of the injury and injustice they have done us, but shall take no hasty steps." He referred the Secretary to the tough letter he had written Simpson on the 13th, where he would "at once discover my opinion of this business. . . . That letter was not wrote in warmth, but you may rest assured that cringing to those Barbarians will not answer. I am fully aware that it is for our interest to have peace with Morocco, but it is not necessary or proper that we should be so over-anxious as to induce them to believe we must have it on any terms they choose to dictate. I have an ardent desire to do right. I hope I shall."

VI

Preble was tired by midafternoon of 19 September. Since his arrival in Gibraltar Bay the previous morning, he had not only drafted a long dispatch to Robert Smith, but he had issued a succession of orders to the commanders of his squadron. With all those papers out of the way, he was ready to return to Tangier Bay, but the breeze had fallen off and there was a dead calm. The *Constitution* was trapped in Gibraltar Bay.

The *Mirboha*'s officers were still Preble's prisoner-guests on board the *Constitution* — rather intimate guests, since they were sharing the cabin with the Commodore and Tobias Lear. Rais Ibrahim Lubarez, Preble had learned, was a person of considerable importance, and had been at one time the Sultan's ambassador to the Spanish court. Preble was impressed by important people, whether they happened to be enemies of the moment or not, and he made all the comforts of his well-stocked cabin available to his distinguished prisoner. Besides, important or not, Lubarez was thoroughly likeable and soon became a favorite of his captors.

When dinner was over on the 19th and the Moroccan prisoners were gathered in the cabin, Preble and Lear, addressing themselves principally to Lubarez, began talking to them through a Jewish interpreter Preble had hired at Gibraltar. Lear later summarized the conversation. He did not distinguish between what he said and what the Commodore said, but it is likely that Preble did most of the talking. Certainly, the talk revolved around a number of Preble's favorite ideas.

It was most unwise, the Moroccans were told, for the Sultan to declare war on the United States, and unjust of him to do it in an underhand fashion: the passport of a consul ought to be held sacred, and never used as a cover for warlike actions. The United States wanted peace, but, if forced into war, would be formidable to the Moroccans, as the part of the American Navy which they had already seen surely demonstrated. Lubarez and his officers had been well treated, not because the United States was afraid of the Sultan and wanted to curry favor with him, but because principles of manliness and humanity led Americans always to treat their prisoners that way.

Then one of Preble's perennial themes was expounded: the Sultan would gain more from trade with the United States than he ever could from war. American shipping was numerous and powerful. American commerce extended to all nations. As a consequence, American merchantmen could bring to Morocco the products of every part of the world, and could carry away anything that Morocco had for export. Such a situation would bring prosperity to the merchants of Morocco and revenue to the Sultan.

After being assured that the United States would make every effort to keep the peace with Morocco on proper and honorable terms, the audience in the cabin was warned: "If we were obliged to go to war, we should not only destroy all their vessels, which would not require much of our force to do, but we should send ships and batter down every seaport town in the Empire."

Either the Commodore was a persuasive speaker, or the Moroccans were shrewd, for when Preble stopped talking the *Mirboha*'s officers had tears in their eyes. How just and true was everything that had been said! Lubarez replied that Maulay Sulaiman was one of the best princes Morocco had ever had: he was just and considerate, but was surrounded by bad advisers, particularly Alcayde Hashash, who had given the order to capture American shipping. If ever he returned to Morocco, Rais Lubarez went on, he personally would tell the Sultan the truth about the United States, and once the Sultan had been correctly informed about Americans, he would be disposed to keep the peace with them. He and his fellow prisoners, said Lubarez, would always remember the kind and generous treatment they had received on board the *Constitution,* and would work to encourage among their countrymen a friendly attitude towards the United States.

Shortly before or after this conversation the Moroccans learned that, although the Commodore was tough when it came to matters of national policy, he was not as hardhearted as he looked. After his first trip to Tangier Preble decided that there were too many people living in his small cabin and dining at his table. Four of the less-important Moroccan officers might just as well be sent to live on board the frigate *New York* until the *Constitution* came back from Tangier. The prisoners concerned had collected their baggage and were ready to be rowed over to the *New York* when Preble found them with tears streaming down their faces at the idea of leaving the *Constitution*. Very well, then, they could stay! But all of them except Lubarez and one other would have to move out of the cabin. Even so, their lot would not be a hard one: they could have Preble's personal servants to take care of them.

Sad to tell, these pampered guests were not familiar with what conduct was acceptable and what was unacceptable to the New England mind, and within two weeks they had scandalized the Commodore and had their liberty curtailed. According to Nathaniel Haraden's log:

> The twelve Moorish prisoners who joined the *Constitution* the 18 and 25 September last were received on board as gentlemen and for some time messed at the Commodore's table. After this they messed under the half deck and had the Commodore's servants to attend them. This method of treatment I mentioned the 27th September last. They are now under charge of the Marine officer, who is ordered to put two sentinels over them and never to suffer one of them to go in any part of the ship in the night, except under charge of a sentinel. Those last orders are actually necessary and in consequence of their attempting that unnatural crime of sodomy with the boys belonging to the *Constitution*.

During the afternoon of 20 September, while Preble was waiting for the weather to permit him to return to Tangier, the *Enterprize,* Lieutenant Isaac Hull, arrived at Gibraltar, and the Commodore had one more vessel to deploy against Morocco — a fortunate development, for there was new danger at Mogador. During the previous twenty months, a thriving trade had sprung up between the United States and Mogador, a trade conducted principally by Salem ships. In the relatively brief period from January 1802 to July 1803 American bottoms had carried $71,000 worth of merchandise to Mogador and had taken away $126,000 worth of Moroccan goods.[3] India goods were the principal import brought by the American traders, which meant that individual cargoes were valuable, and that the capture of a single American merchantman could be a heavy financial blow to her owner. The latest word from Mogador was that several American ships were expected to arrive any day. To prevent these new arrivals from sharing the fate of the *Hannah* — which they surely would if they entered the port unsuspecting — Preble ordered Hull to cruise off that port for fifteen days and warn every American vessel he met that Moroccan cruisers had orders to capture American shipping and had already seized the *Hannah.*

The calm that had prevented the *Constitution* from leaving Gibraltar on 19 September was succeeded by a westerly wind that made it impossible for a ship the size of the *Constitution* to beat through the Straits to Tangier. As frustration over his inability to reach Tangier mounted, Preble's mood deteriorated. His cautious optimism was turned into tight-lipped determination by news that the Bey of Tunis was pressing the United States to build a 36-gun frigate as a present to his government. "Should that demand be acceded to," he wrote Robert Smith,

> it will require another frigate on our own account to watch her motions. I suspect the demands of the Barbary Powers will increase, and will be of such a nature as to make it imprudent for our government to comply with. All of them, excepting Algiers, appear to have a disposition to quarrel with us unless we tamely accede to any propositions they choose to make. I believe a firm and decided conduct in the first instance towards those of them who make war against us would have a good effect. . . . The Christian Powers will have no chance with these people until they determine never to pay tribute or supply them with military or naval stores or ships, but to destroy everything they can belonging to them. They send out their cruisers, and, if they prove successful, it is war, and we must purchase peace, suffering them to keep all they have taken. But, if they are unfortunate, and we capture their cruisers before they have taken anything valuable, it is not war, although the orders for capturing our vessels are found on board and we must restore all we take from them, which enables them to commence again. I know not how long we shall be obliged to submit to this sort of treatment. The Moors are a deep, designing,

artful, treacherous set of villains, and nothing will keep them so quiet as a respectable naval force near them.

VII

Late in the evening of Saturday, 24 September, the wind came fair, and at eleven o'clock the next morning the *Constitution* entered Tangier Bay with a white flag at her fore. Two hours later, a dispatch boat rowed by Spaniards came alongside with letters from James Simpson. Preble asked the boatmen to wait, then retired to the privacy of his cabin to digest Consul Simpson's two dispatches, one of which contained numerous enclosures.

Since Preble had last heard from him, Simpson had again changed his mind on the great and puzzling question of whether it was the Sultan or Alcayde Hashash who was responsible for the war. He was inclined to exonerate Maulay Sulaiman and lay all the blame on Hashash. The most recent evidence indicated, according to Simpson, that Hashash had declared the *Meshuda* to be the Sultan's property and had obtained an American passport for her without the Sultan's knowledge. Maulay Sulaiman might not even be fully aware of the nature of the orders which Alcayde Hashash had given to Ibrahim Lubarez. Eight days previously Simpson had thought that the seizure of the *Hannah* at Mogador argued that the Sultan was directing the war. Since then, however, Hashash had hinted that he himself, in the Sultan's name, had instructed the governor of Mogador to detain American merchantmen.

There was other favorable news. Simpson had received more than one message from the Sultan and his minister, Mohammed Selawy, indicating a strong desire to terminate the affair peacefully: the seizures of the *Celia* and the *Hannah* had been intended only to force the release of the *Meshuda*, not as a declaration of war. Whatever Hashash might have done, the Sultan had not formally declared war on the United States, and without his declaration there could be no war. Maulay Sulaiman was especially anxious to recover the *Mirboha*, the loss of which had come to concern him far more than the capture of the *Meshuda*.

Although the Sultan appeared well disposed and it would probably be safe for Preble to go ashore, the Moroccans could not, at that moment, be completely trusted and it would be better to delay landing. A week earlier Simpson had written Mohammed Selawy to ask whether the Sultan wished to postpone the opening of negotiations until he himself reached Tangier, or whether Maulay Sulaiman intended to appoint someone already on the scene to represent him in dealing with Preble and Simpson. So far, no answer had come to this letter, but if Preble would return to Tangier Bay on Monday, 26 September, or Tuesday, the 27th, Simpson would probably know something definite. The Sultan ought to reach Tangier on Monday, 3 October, and Simpson surmised that he would probably send Mohammed Selawy ahead to negotiate with Simpson and Preble, and try to have the whole unpleasant business cleared up before his own arrival at Tangier.

In reply Preble summarized the terms on which he and Simpson agreed they were willing to terminate the dispute: Preble would give up the *Mirboha* and release all his Moroccan prisoners on being assured that the Sultan had not given the orders that led to the capture of the *Celia* at sea and the detention of the *Hannah* at Mogador; that the persons who did give them would be punished; and that the *Hannah* and her cargo would be released. Preble would withdraw his own orders authorizing the capture of Moroccan ships and restore any prizes he held, if Maulay Sulaiman would do the same for the United States and would agree to ratify the treaty of 1786. The *Meshuda*, however, would not be returned to the Sultan unless compensation for her were paid to the United States, as she was considered Tripolitan property and a fair prize.

At 3:00 p.m. this letter for Consul Simpson was handed to the Spanish boatmen, whereupon the *Constitution* got under way for the Atlantic. Preble had promised Simpson that he would return off Tangier in two or three days. In the meantime, the *Constitution* cruised near the entrance to the Straits in search of Moroccans. She spent most of the time between Cape Spartel and Cape Trafalgar, but did search the Moroccan coast as far south as Larache. At least ten ships were sighted and boarded or spoken. All were of Spanish, Swedish, British, or American registry. Apparently Moroccan vessels were staying in port until this trouble with the United States blew over or the Americans sailed away.

Early on the afternoon of Wednesday, 28 September, the *Constitution* escorted two Gibraltar-bound Salem merchantmen, the *Trent* and the *Rajah*, through the Straits, then hauled into Tangier Bay. Shortly after Preble had finished examining the shipping at anchor in Tangier Bay — two ships under French colors and one flying the Danish flag — through his glass, a sail was sighted to the west of Cape Spartel. The *Constitution* stood for her and soon came up with the frigate *John Adams*. Rodgers reported through his speaking trumpet that he had been cruising to the west of Cape Spartel for eleven days, looking for the *Maimona*, but had seen nothing of her.

Preble wanted to anchor in Tangier Bay that evening and get in touch with James Simpson in the morning, but, since there were signs of a bad blow from the northward, that is, directly onshore, the *Constitution* remained under sail all night. The next morning, the wind was still strong, the weather boisterous and unsettled. At 9:00 a.m. the *John Adams* parted company and steered for Gibraltar. With her water and provisions practically exhausted, it was impossible for her to remain operational much longer. Preble continued to cruise about off Cape Spartel and Tangier until early afternoon. The Commodore apparently was ill and, most of the time, was confined to his cabin. The weather showed no signs of improvement; and, as Sailing Master Haraden was at pains to explain in the log: "Between the rocks of Cape Trafalgar and Cape Spartel is a channel about fifteen miles. This is thought by all cruisers to be a very hazardous station in thick weather with a western gale. On these considerations Commodore Preble bore up in order to run through the Straits." Shortly before midnight that same day, 29 September, the *Constitution* was once more anchored in Gibraltar Bay.

VIII

It was on the 12th of September that Preble had first dropped anchor at Gibraltar and learned of the capture of the *Mirboha* and the recapture of the *Celia*. On the 29th he was at anchor there once more. The immediate future seemed reasonably clear and promising. His optimism had returned and he was pleased with what he had accomplished.

Writing to the Secretary of the Navy on 1 October, he pointed out that Morocco had the potential to be a formidable enemy: "The Emperor of Morocco has such an extensive seacoast on the Atlantic, and is so advantageously situated on the Straits for annoying our commerce, that it is very much for our interest to be on good terms with him." Despite his strong position, Preble continued, Maulay Sulaiman was eager for peace and apparently ready to settle pretty much on Americans terms; he ascribed the Sultan's interest in peace to the fact that his cruisers had been unsuccessful in the surprise war, and added, "I have no doubt but he would have discovered a different disposition if they had been otherwise."

Mainly responsible for upsetting Moroccan plans were the fortunate, simultaneous arrival of two U.S. squadrons at Gibraltar, and the fact that American warships were constantly in evidence along the Moroccan coast: Preble himself had been in Tangier Bay no less than three times in one week. Finally, Preble considered his own hard attitude to be a major cause of his success in dealing with the Sultan. "The threat I made on my arrival to sink that ship [the *Maimona*] or any other of his cruisers that I might meet with, and the active vigilance of our squadron has had a good effect on the Moors. I have no doubt but this quarrel will eventually be for our advantage, as I do not believe His Imperial Majesty will be disposed to war with us again, and we shall get clear of having anything to do with

Hashash, the former governor of Tangier, who has ever been opposed to our interest."

About the time Preble started on his last visit to Tangier, Richard V. Morris and Hugh G. Campbell exchanged commands, and the former sailed for Washington in the *Adams* on 26 September. That same day the *New York*, commanded by Campbell, passed through the Straits to take up station off Larache. The waiting, the cruising, the tedium were almost over. Soon the Sultan would be marching into Tangier. With the intention of making American naval strength as impressive to him as possible. Preble and Rodgers decided to have all available frigates concentrated in Tangier Bay during the negotiations. The *New York* would have to be recalled,* so, late in the afternoon of 2 October, Rodgers sailed from Gibraltar in the *John Adams* to find her and bring her back to rendezvous with the *Constitution* at Tangier in time for the audience with the Sultan. Rodgers, too, was optimistic: "Indeed, I am not under the smallest apprehension but that the issue will prove very favorable to the United States, as all [the Sultan's] ports at this moment are, I conceive, very effectually blockaded, and he has had reason, in this instance, to be acquainted with American capacity of active measures."

Preble's squadron was strengthened by one ship on 1 October. That afternoon the brig *Syren*, Lieutenant Charles Stewart, arrived from the United States. Work was waiting for her and her commander. American merchantmen, with cargoes of brandies, wine, and fruit, needed to be convoyed a safe distance out into the Atlantic. Stewart was ordered to sail at 6:00 p.m. on Monday, 3 October, escort the merchant vessels twenty leagues west of Cape Spartel, then rejoin Preble in Tangier Bay as quickly as possible.

Sometime during the morning of 3 October, Preble dashed off a hasty note — so hasty that he dated it 3 September — to Tobias Lear, who was still at Gibraltar: "I have received dispatches from Mr. Simpson and wish to consult you immediately. Be so good as to come in the boat which brings you this, as I cannot leave the ship at present. I shall sail this afternoon."

Simpson's new batch of letters reported that dreadful weather had delayed the Sultan's journey from Fez to Tangier. On Friday, 30 September, Alcayde Hashash was on one side of the rain-swollen river at Alcazarquivir, Maulay Sulaiman camped on the other and the only way they could communicate was by rafts supported by inflated goatskins. Now that the rains

---

* By this time Preble knew that the *Maimona*, crippled by a sprung mast, had anchored in the Tagus River on the night of 13 September, and that Alcayde Hashash had sent instructions for her to remain at Lisbon until peace was re-established between the United States and Morocco. She no longer had to be taken into consideration in Preble's disposition of his force.

had stopped, the Sultan was thought to have crossed the river on Saturday afternoon, 1 October, and was expected to reach Tangier on the 4th. Preble had no time to lose in getting to Tangier if the *Constitution* was to be at anchor in the bay when the Sultan entered the city.

Simpson had received several messages from the Sultan's minister, Mohammed Selawy, urging that Preble bring the *Mirboha* down from Gibraltar and have her at anchor in Tangier Bay before the Sultan arrived. "If His Majesty does not find there the Rais with his ship, I don't know what he may not do," Selawy had written. Why this was so important to Maulay Sulaiman, Simpson could only speculate:

> As His Majesty will not remain here more than a couple of days it may be that he is desirous of having the business settled and his people liberated under his own immediate direction, for it has been a most distressful event for him to have so many Mussulmen in the hands of Christians. Their liberty, I am fully persuaded, he has more at heart than the loss of the ship, which you will have seen is an old, good-for-nothing thing.

Preble could see no harm in gratifying the Sultan's whim: the *Mirboha* would be just as much a prize anchored among the American frigates in Tangier Bay as she was at Gibraltar. He ordered Lieutenant Joseph Tarbell to get the *Mirboha* under way the next morning and follow the *Constitution* to Tangier Bay "with all possible speed." The *Meshuda* was to remain at Gibraltar as a prison ship for the Moroccan seamen.

"We lay becalmed, drifting about Gibraltar Bay till 10 p.m.," reads the frigate's log, "at which time a breeze sprang up from the eastward. We steered over for the Barbary Shore in order to proceed to Tangier Bay."

CHAPTER 9 OCTOBER 1803

". . . it must be a pleasing reflection in the evening of his days."

National flags were flying over the consular residences in Tangier, just as on each earlier visit, when the *Constitution* and the *Nautilus* anchored in the harbor at 1:30 in the afternoon of 4 October 1803. But this time there was a difference: the American flag could be seen above the city walls.

By letter James Simpson reported that the Sultan was expected to spend the night about six hours' ride from Tangier and might reach the city by the following noon. In his reply, Preble told Simpson that he had intended to bring the *Mirboha* down to Tangier to satisfy the Sultan, but, being "an indifferent sailer," she could not make the passage from Gibraltar to Tangier, so long as the wind continued to blow out of the west. The Sultan might have to be disappointed in his desire to find the *Mirboha* at anchor in Tangier Bay when he arrived. Besides, Preble added tartly, "I cannot conceive what advantage to us or to the Emperor it can be to have her here previous to settlement of our affairs and a re-establishment of peace, as, immediately on that event taking place, I shall deliver her up in as good or better order than when detained by us, together with all the Moors in our possession. And I certainly shall not deliver up either vessel or people previous to a renewal and ratification of our treaty."

Later in the afternoon Simpson sent a second letter out to the *Constitution,* suggesting that Preble dress ship and fire a salute the next day just after the Sultan went up into the castle, or casbah, where he would have a good view of the ships in the bay. Simpson said he would signal the proper moment for the salute by hoisting a blue jack. Still in the peppery mood he had exhibited earlier in the afternoon, Preble agreed: "As you think it will gratify His Imperial Majesty, I shall salute him and dress ship; and, if he is not disposed to be pacific, *I will salute him again.*"

"In the course of the afternoon . . . Commodore Preble [received] different dispatches from the shore," Nathaniel Haraden wrote in the day's log. "How friendly they might be, I do not know. But the Commodore was very attentive to their maneuvering ashore and kept the ship all night in a perfect state of readiness for action." Throughout the night the *Constitution* was on the alert for a surprise attack from Tangier: cleared for action, guns primed, lanterns and matches lighted, hammocks left stowed in the nettings, and the crew sleeping at quarters.

At dawn on the 5th there began a spectacle on shore for Haraden to record:

> From daylight till noon we saw more than 10,000 of the Moorish inhabitants marching in from different parts of the country. They form different detachments on the sandy beach which is a little to the eastward of the town. We suppose them to be waiting for His Moorish Majesty, who is hourly expected to arrive from the country. The maneuvering [of] the different squadrons of horse was very pleasing. Commodore Preble ordered the *Constitution* to be completely dressed with colors and flags, but not to be hoisted till the arrival of the Emperor was announced, which was to be [by] a salute from the fort. . . .
>
> A little after one p.m. the different detachments formed collectively. They extended from one end of the beach to the other, which is, at the least, two miles and a half. They were all mounted on horse. At half-past one p.m. they commenced their march, with innumerable volleys of small arms, towards the town and castle. A few minutes after 2 p.m. the American colors were hoisted in the town of Tangier. They then saluted from the lower battery, eighteen guns. We immediately dressed ship and returned them an equal number.

About four o'clock, when the formalities were over and the Sultan had shut himself up in the castle, Simpson sat down to get off a note to Preble. Maulay Sulaiman probably was resting and Simpson did not plan to disturb him until the next day, which would be soon enough to open formal communications. Another good reason for not hurrying matters was that the Sultan had sent Mohammed Selawy, through whom the negotiations would probably be conducted, on a mission to Tetuán, and it was not known when he would be coming on from there to Tangier.

Before dawn of a clear, pleasant 6 October the *New York* and the *John Adams* stood in to Tangier Bay and anchored to the south of Preble's frigate. At 11:00 a.m. a highly welcome visitor reached the *Constitution:* a boat carrying Consul James Simpson came off from the city. Earlier that morning, even before he had been able to get in touch with the Sultan, Simpson had received a message from Maulay Sulaiman assuring him that he was free to go off to any of the American warships, or that the U.S.

officers could come ashore in complete safety. Preble, Lear, and Simpson had a lot to say to one another, and probably found themselves all talking at once. The most important thing Simpson reported was that Mohammed Selawy had not arrived from Tetuán, but as soon as he did — and he was expected at any moment — negotiations would begin. The Sultan wanted peace, and, with Selawy's aid, everything could be straightened out. But, warned Simpson, the Americans must not press the Sultan to open negotiations before Selawy arrived, because, if pressure were brought to bear on him, the Sultan might put the affair into the hands of some official hostile to the United States. The Consul returned to the city about noon.

Nothing much happened in the afternoon. The *Constitution* was quiet, but vigilant. Preble wrote in his diary, "The ship is constantly kept clear for battle, and all hands sleep at quarters." The idle afternoon may have put Nathaniel Haraden in a reflective mood, because in a short summary of the Moroccan affair that he entered in the log the next day, he mused: "From our first arrival at Gibraltar, September 13th, Commodore Preble has [been] very attentive in restoring peace between America and the Emperor of Morocco, and, should Commodore Preble succeed, it must be a pleasing reflection in the evening of his days."

Simpson had asked Preble to be patient in Selawy's absence, but it was wasted advice. Patience was not an easy virtue for the Commodore to practice. At 7:00 a.m. on Friday, the 7th, he fired off a letter to Simpson complaining about the delay in beginning negotiations and suggesting that the Moroccans might be up to something underhand. Consul Simpson had to repeat the advice he had given the day before: the Sultan would not transact business with Preble and Simpson personally — that was not the custom of the kingdom — and to hustle into negotiations before Selawy arrived might well result in the appointment of a Moroccan negotiator who would take a stiff line with the United States. There was no reason to worry about the Sultan's peaceful intentions: to show how much he wanted peace, he was planning to send a present of ten bullocks, twenty sheep, and four dozen fowl off to the American squadron some time that day. Such gifts normally were not sent to visiting warships until after their commanders had landed and been received in audience by the Sultan.

Shortly after noon there was another sight on shore to delight, among others, Sailing Master Haraden:

> Between one and two this afternoon the Emperor marched down on the beach, accompanied by his court, and several persons of the first distinction, and a numerous crowd of spectators. He came down to view the American squadron. Commodore Preble immediately saluted, twenty-one guns. The Emperor's band immediately played Olester, which signifies peace and friend-

ship. During this interview between Commodore Preble and the Emperor the whole shore was crowded with inhabitants [as far] as the eye could extend.

James Simpson had been watching from the city and dashed off a note to Preble: "Nothing could have been more apropos than your salute just finished. His Majesty, you no doubt saw, was on the lower battery at the end of the mole. He went there for the purpose of viewing the frigates with a stand telescope, and, I am persuaded, must have been gratified by the unexpected addition of the firing."

That afternoon two shore boats distributed the Sultan's gifts of bullocks, sheep, and fowl to the ships of the squadron. The day's events relieved some of the uneasiness that Preble had felt in the morning, and he was in a party mood: Rodgers, Campbell, and Lieutenant Isaac Chauncey of the *New York* joined him for dinner in the *Constitution*'s cabin. Another indication of relaxing tension was a visit by several Moroccans, including the captain of the port, who boarded the *Constitution* to see their friends, Ibrahim Lubarez and the other prisoners. No doubt the visitors were all the more welcome because they were, as Preble noted in his diary, "respectable Moors." That evening, for the first time since the *Constitution* had anchored in Tangier Bay, hammocks were piped down and the men did not have to sleep on the decks.

On Saturday, 8 October, Consul Simpson came off for a breakfast meeting with Preble and Lear. Mohammed Selawy had not yet arrived, Simpson reported, but the Sultan had sent for him, and he would surely be coming within a few hours. Then Preble, Lear, and Simpson settled down to a long discussion of the forthcoming negotiations with the Sultan.

When the meeting broke up, Simpson left to visit the *New York* and the *John Adams*. Before he had finished his tour, a signal, calling him back to the city, was hoisted at his residence. At home two documents from the Sultan were waiting for him. One was an order from Maulay Sulaiman instructing the governor of Mogador to release the *Hannah*, her crew, and her cargo. The second paper was a letter affirming peace and friendship between the United States and Morocco, and setting Monday, 10 October, for a meeting between Preble and Simpson and the Sultan of Morocco.

II

The party that went ashore in Tangier on the 10th was small. Besides the Commodore, there were only Tobias Lear, Noadiah Morris, and Midshipmen Ralph Izard and Henry Wadsworth. Officially Noadiah Morris was the *Constitution*'s chaplain, but he had no known connection with Holy Orders, and his real duties were those of commodore's secretary. That was the practice of the day: the nominal position of chaplain was used to provide pay and rations for someone who functioned principally as secretary to a squadron commander or as schoolmaster to a frigate's midshipmen. Midshipman Henry Wadsworth was a young man with literary ambitions who filled his off-duty hours with writing. He had already produced a lengthy manuscript diary of Commodore Morris's cruise in the Mediterranean, and was in the process of compiling a narrative of his service under Commodore Preble. His new work was in the form of a series of letters to friends in America, a literary device favored in the eighteenth century, and bore the title *Letters Written on board the United States Ship Constitution during a Cruise in the Mediterranean, Edward Preble, Esqe., Commander and Commodore of the American Squadron, to Miss Hash Tash and Others at Portland, Boston, Charlesto[w]n, Exeter and Elsewhere.*

When the five men landed at 10:30 a.m., they went directly to Consul Simpson's residence, where they were to wait until notified that the Sultan was ready to receive them. It being expected that all the consuls give gifts on the occasion of an imperial visit to Tangier, Simpson had assembled presents for Maulay Sulaiman and thirteen Moroccan officials and members of the Sultan's court, including Mohammed Selawy, the Alcayde of the Household, the Sultan's Sword-Bearer, his Umbrella-Bearer, and his Chief Groom, at a cost to the United States somewhat in excess of $1,100. About noon word came that the Sultan was ready for the American delegation, and it was time to set out through the rainy, windy afternoon for the casbah. Henry Wadsworth recorded the scene:

> We began our march from the Consul's. The company consisted of the Commodore, Consul Simpson, Consul Lear, Chaplain Morris, Midshipmen Izard and Wadsworth. Two mules and two Jews brought up the rear, carrying presents, which were several silver teapots, silks, muslins and linens; and I was much surprised when I saw among the rest a quantity of loaf sugar, tea, and coffee, for I had an idea that such articles were not such as an emperor would be in want of.
>
> We walked to the castle and entered a kind of piazza where we rested. Soon after, the Minister of State, Selawy, came in and set down on his hams against one of the pillars. He entered into conversation with the Consul, saying, "We wish for peace," etc., etc. The presents were here given to about twenty Moors, who held them uncovered and extended in their arms. A number of guards were without the castle, their guns resting against the wall.
>
> In about thirty minutes after, we made a move towards the right wing of the castle and stopped about ten yards from the door. On one side of us were drawn up in three or four crooked rows about fifty guards, dirty and lounging. Presently the Emperor came out of an alley (which led to a mosque) between us and the door. A Moor placed a morocco cushion on the step of the door, and he set down. As we expected to be ushered into the Emperor with great

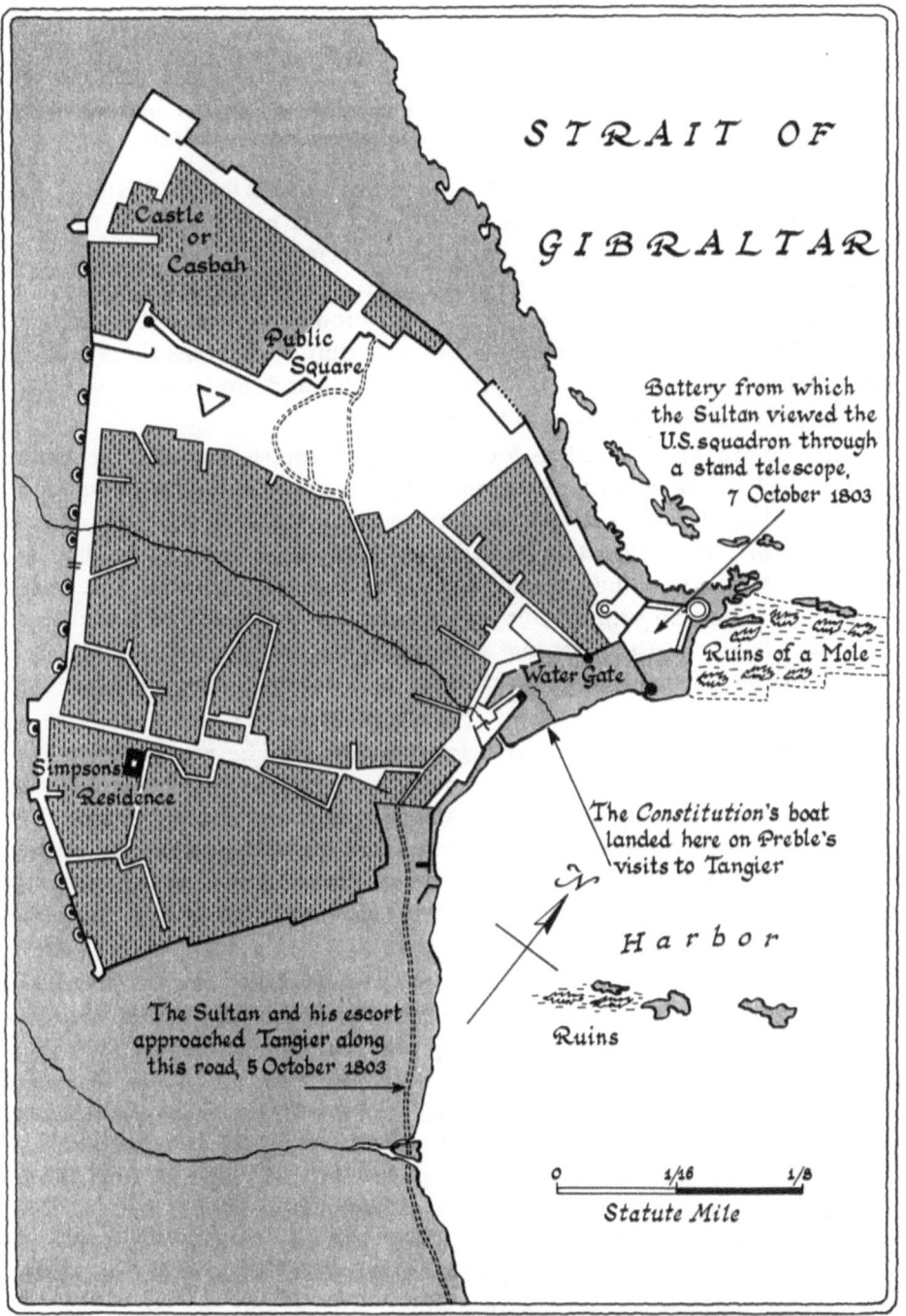

TANGIER

Adapted from a Map Drawn by Captain Burel of the Imperial Corps of Engineers, December 1809, in Archives Historiques de l'Armée, Vincennes, France

parade and state, we were much surprised when the Minister came and told us, "That is the Emperor." On this information we off hats and bowed. He made a slight inclination of his head and proceeded to business.

Ralph Izard told his mother: "We were introduced to His Majesty with very little ceremony. I had connected with the idea of Emperor of Morocco something grand, but what was my disappointment at seeing a small man, wrapped up in a woolen *haik* or cloak, sitting upon the stone steps of an old castle in the middle of the streets, surrounded by a guard of very ill-looking blacks, with their arms covered with cloth to prevent them rusting. We stood before the Emperor with our caps in hand, and the conversation was carried on by means of an interpreter."

If the Sultan had paused to look out over Tangier Bay and the Straits of Gibraltar before coming to this meeting, the scene could not have failed to impress him. Lying at anchor in front of the town were the *Constitution,* the *New York,* the *John Adams,* and the *Nautilus.* At 11:00 a.m. that day the prize *Mirboha* came in and anchored close to the American ships, giving the Sultan an opportunity to contrast her puny size with the heavy American frigates. And forming a backdrop to the picture was the brig *Syren* passing through the Straits with a convoy of six American merchantmen.

The Sultan opened the conference by saying that he was at peace with the United States and wanted the peace to continue. He regretted that differences had developed between Morocco and the United States. The orders to capture American merchantmen had not come from him, and he would surely punish those who had issued them. All American property that had been seized would be restored; all American citizens who had been captured would be released.

Having thus easily slid away from any responsibility for the hostilities, and probably caused Preble to smile inwardly, Maulay Sulaiman went on: inasmuch as he had agreed to give up the *Hannah,* he hoped that Commodore Preble would restore the *Mirboha* as well as all his Moroccan prisoners. As a particular favor, he asked that the *Meshuda* also be returned to him. If the *Meshuda*'s captain had indeed attempted to take her in to Tripoli, he had acted contrary to the orders he had received, and his disobedience would cost him his head. Since Commodore Morris had promised that the *Meshuda* would be released if she had not been acting under the Sultan's orders, Maulay Sulaiman hoped that she might be given up to him. If she were restored, promised the Sultan, she would not go out of his dominions so long as the United States was at war with Tripoli.

Simpson knew that the Sultan still hoped to avoid confirming the treaty of 1786. In their replies he and Preble bore down on the importance of ratification: the President of the United States was anxious for peace and friendship with the Sultan, provided the peace could be put on a solid and permanent foundation. What the United States wanted was a solemn and formal ratification of the treaty of 1786, coupled with assurances that it would be neither violated nor altered during Maulay Sulaiman's life. If the Sultan would ratify the treaty and give up all prizes and prisoners, Preble, on his part, promised to surrender the *Mirboha* and the Moroccan sailors, and to rescind his orders authorizing the capture of Moroccan vessels. As for the restoration of the *Meshuda*, Preble and Simpson would consider the Sultan's request and give him an answer later.

When all this had been translated, the Sultan gave his most sacred promise to ratify the treaty. His friendship for the Americans would last forever, he said, and increase in strength in consequence of their disposition to oblige him. Then the Sultan asked Simpson and Preble, who were standing about twenty paces away from him, to come closer so that they could speak more easily and informally. The rest of the American party was kept at the full respectful distance.

Simpson then spoke of his recent arrest by Hashash and his overnight imprisonment in the open courtyard of the Alcayde's residence. That incident, he submitted, was an indignity to the nation he represented as well as to himself. Preble added, doubtless with considerable force, "An insult should never be offered to a consul." Maulay Sulaiman assured Simpson that the arrest had been made without his knowledge, admitted that it was an improper and unmerited aggression, and said it would never happen again.

Preble steered the conversation to the subject of passports. The *Constitution* had the *Maimona* in her power on 6 September, but Preble had treated her as a friendly vessel because she carried Simpson's passport. In the future he would certainly put no faith in passports, unless the Sultan disavowed that deception and took steps to see that it, also, did not happen again.

Maulay Sulaiman reiterated his desire to be on the best possible terms with the United States, and said he was ready to ratify the treaty of 1786: he would write a letter to the President confirming everything he had said. He finished by telling Preble and Simpson that he had empowered Mohammed Selawy to settle all differences with the United States, and that any agreements which the minister concluded would receive his sanction. With that the audience was over.

By this time, Tobias Lear, Noadiah Morris, and the two midshipmen had left the meeting and gone back to Simpson's house. Simpson and Preble accompanied Mohammed Selawy to one of the buildings of the casbah, where the three of them went over the topics that had been covered in the meeting with the Sultan. Preble once more developed his thesis that peace was more profitable than war: "I endeavored to impress on his mind the advantages of a free commercial intercourse which they might have with all nations, and that the revenues of the Emperor arising from that source would be much greater than anything they could expect if at war with us, as I should immediately blockade all his ports and not suffer a vessel of any nation to enter or pass out." Selawy promised that documents embodying the day's agreements would be drawn up promptly. The American negotiators parted from him on the understanding that they would meet again the next day.

Preble and Simpson then joined their companions for dinner at the American consulate. While they were there, a messenger brought a document, issued in the Sultan's name, declaring that Morocco continued at peace with the United States and directing all governors, commanders of ports, and captains of Moroccan warships not to molest American vessels or merchants. This document was unacceptable because it carefully avoided any mention of the treaty of 1786, but Simpson decided that the next day would be soon enough to negotiate further on that point. After dinner the party from the *Constitution* made its way down to the landing place, where the barge had been waiting since morning. The time was nearly sundown. As they went through the streets, Ralph Izard looked around him with some distaste, and later wrote: "Tangier is a very inconsiderable place, and the natives are excessively savage. It is matter of astonishment to me that a people living so near a civilized nation as Spain should not imbibe some customs less barbarous than such as they have been accustomed to." Tobias Lear, on the other hand, noticed that the people were waving and calling out to the Americans, happy that the affair was being settled peacefully and that there would be neither war nor a bombardment of the city.

III

Early on the 11th, Simpson met with Mohammed Selawy to attempt to get a formal ratification of the old treaty. Selawy claimed that both Morocco's copy of the treaty of 1786 and the copy of the letter which Maulay Sulaiman had written President Washington in 1795 ratifying the treaty made by his father had been lost. Simpson was not so easily put off and sent to the consulate for the volume in which these documents were recorded. As quickly as the book was produced it was taken to the Sultan, and the papers in question read to him. Maulay Sulaiman then instructed

Selawy to make a brief addition to his earlier declaration: "And at last we are in peace and friendship with the said American nation as our father (to whom God be merciful) was, according to the treaty made the first day of Ramadan in the year 1200."

As they were leaving the casbah together, Simpson complained to Selawy about the way in which the ratification of the old treaty had been tacked onto the end of the declaration of peace and friendship as though it were an unimportant afterthought. Selawy assured him that the letter the Sultan was preparing to write to the President would explain the matter more fully and formally. However, added Selawy, quickly grabbing onto a good bargaining point, if the Sultan was going to tell the President that he was resolved to maintain peace with the United States, he ought to be able to give a reason for his determination. And what better reason could he give than that Preble and Simpson had agreed to hand back the *Meshuda,* as the Sultan had requested!

It had taken a contest of wills, not all the details of which are known, for Simpson to secure ratification of the old treaty. One motive that finally led the Sultan to ratify was his eagerness to get the *Mirboha* out of American hands. She was lying in Tangier Bay with no colors flying. Maulay Sulaiman knew that if he ratified the old treaty his flag would be hoisted in the *Mirboha* in full view of the large army that he had assembled, and his power and prestige would be confirmed in the army's eyes. Preble had been quite willing to return the *Mirboha* if his doing so would secure the peace. The prospect of the prize money the old ship would bring, if condemned, was certainly not enticing. She was, the Commodore had written, "such a miserable piece of naval architecture that I do not believe we have an officer in our service that would be willing to attempt to cross the Atlantic in her for ten times her value."

When Preble was notified that the ratification had been settled, he had himself rowed over to the *Mirboha* and ordered the red flag of Morocco hoisted on her. Within a few hours Rais Ibrahim Lubarez and his officers were free and back in command of their own ship. But Preble could not wait for the change of command to take place. From the *Mirboha* he had to go directly on shore because, although Simpson had already met with Mohammed Selawy that morning, the scheduled meeting between the three of them still stood. As he went, Nathaniel Haraden was writing in the log:

> The business now between the United States and Morocco is in a fair way of being settled; how honorable or dishonorable I do not know, but I am well convinced that Commodore Preble has been the chief negotiator, and there is no doubt, in my opinion, but it will be highly honorable to the American flag. The maneuvering of our squadron in this bay and its formidable appear-

ance in the night, when cleared for action, was of much service in this negotiation.

At the meeting, Mohammed Selawy again pressed for the restoration of the *Meshuda* as a favor to the Sultan. He repeated the Sultan's assurance that, if she were given up, she would not leave Moroccan waters for the duration of the war with Tripoli. Preble, convinced that exposure to American naval force had stimulated the Sultan's desire for a firm peace with the United States, decided it would be best to make him completely happy. He told Selawy that the *Meshuda* would be returned to Morocco, and the conference broke up with both sides satisfied.

It was 7:00 p.m. when the Commodore got back to the *Constitution* after a rough and dangerous trip, with thunder, lightning, rain, and waves whipped up by nearly gale-force winds. Danger and tension continued after he reached the frigate, for, in the words of the sailing master, "the night was very boisterous and perilous in an open roadstead, situated as is the Bay of Tangier." During much of the night there was rain, with flashes of lightning and the cracking and rumbling of thunder. From the look of the weather to the northward it seemed that the wind might suddenly shift to that quarter and the gale blow dead into the bay. The *Constitution*'s best bower anchor had been cut off by rocks in Tangier Bay during an earlier gale, and the recollection of this could not have added to anyone's peace of mind. Preble, his officers, and his crew spent a good part of the night on deck preparing to save the frigate should the gale swing round to the northward. Fortunately, by daylight the weather had become calmer.

If Preble got any sleep at all, it was not for more than a couple of hours. At daybreak, accompanied by Tobias Lear and Noadiah Morris, he went ashore for a final meeting with Mohammed Selawy. The Sultan, having the previous afternoon suddenly ordered his army to prepare for the march back to Mequinez, was on the point of decamping, and Mohammed Selawy would be following him shortly. There was no time to arrange for the signing by both sides of a declaration and a counter-declaration — presumably summarizing and formalizing the agreements between Morocco and the United States — that Preble and Simpson had drafted.

The omission was not serious because Mohammed Selawy handed Preble the Sultan's letter to the President, which disavowed Maulay Sulaiman's responsibility for the late hostilities and explicitly ratified and confirmed the treaty of 1786. Orally, Selawy assured Preble and Simpson that the Sultan desired peace and friendship with the United States, and was extremely pleased by the promise that the *Meshuda* would be returned to him. Selawy concluded with the announcement that the *Meshuda*'s Moroccan captain was going to lose his head for disobeying the Sultan's orders and attempting to run the blockade of Tripoli.

Simpson's account of the expenses connected with these negotiations shows that every transaction in Morocco required tips and presents. Mohammed Selawy was paid $800 for his friendly attitude towards the United States, and for services past and present. If there was a reward for Selawy, the punishment of Alcayde Hashash ultimately turned out to be much more lenient than the Sultan had promised and the Americans had expected. Neither Preble nor Simpson believed that Maulay Sulaiman's disavowals of responsibility for the war were genuine. The Commodore seems to have hinted to Nathaniel Haraden that he considered the Sultan to be the true instigator of the hostilities, for Haraden wrote: "The general report of this eventful war between America and the Emperor of Morocco is that it originated by a governor residing at Tangier, by the name of Hashash. But this report (I think) Commodore Preble suspects will leave room for question." James Simpson assumed that the idea of an attack on American commerce had come from Hashash, who had proposed his scheme to the Sultan in May and made it appear so sure of success that he had been given discretion to carry it out. Since the war had proved such a disaster, Simpson thought that Hashash would surely lose the governorship and perhaps be punished for his poor judgment. Later, however, he learned that on the evening of 9 October Hashash had saved both himself and his position by laying 50,000 Moroccan ducats — the equivalent of about $42,000 — at the Sultan's feet. So Abd al-Rahman Hashash continued as governor of Tangier. Perhaps this meant trouble for the United States in the future, but Simpson thought Hashash would thenceforth have to be more circumspect. It had cost him a large part of his personal fortune to get out of one scrape, and he could hardly afford another.

The *Constitution* lay at Tangier for two more days while Preble cleared up the tag ends of the Moroccan affair. On Thursday, 13 October, Preble, Lear, and Rodgers went ashore together to pick up the translation of Maulay Sulaiman's letter to the President as well as copies or translations of some other papers. This time Lear was no more impressed than Ralph Izard had been earlier for, when he returned to the *Constitution*, he wrote:

> The little I have seen of the place is no inducement for me to visit it often for pleasure. The very narrow and dirty streets, the wretched appearance of the inhabitants and their habitations is enough to disgust an American who has been accustomed to ample space and a tolerable degree of cleanliness. There appears to be no shops, no trade — nothing to please the eye or amuse the fancy. The departure of the Emperor has thinned the town of inhabitants,

which has made the passing in the streets (if they can so be called) more easy, but it has taken away everything worth seeing.[1]

The next morning, 14 October, Preble and Lear went ashore to say goodbye to Consul and Mrs. Simpson. The latter, especially, had to be thanked for her hospitality in providing several dinners over the preceding few days. That afternoon the *Constitution* fired a thirteen-gun salute, the garrison replied, and the frigate was on her way.

IV

Soon after he got back to Gibraltar, Edward wrote Mary:

> I have been so engaged in official duties since my arrival on this station that for many nights in succession I have slept without taking off a garment, excepting my coat, as I have often been called upon ten times in a night. I returned here from Morocco a few days since, where I have been to negotiate a peace with the Emperor, whom I found at war with the United States on my arrival here. During my stay of fourteen days at Tangier, his principal port, all the men in our ships slept at quarters, prepared for battle. It has so far been a hard service, but I have the satisfaction of having succeeded in my negotiations, and an honorable peace is established. This, I presume, will be highly gratifying to our government. A vessel will sail in a few days by which I shall write you very particularly; shall give you a description of His Imperial Majesty and of my audience. He was accompanied by an army of 10,000 men, chiefly cavalry.
>
> I have undertaken an arduous task, but hope to get honorably through and return to you, never again to separate.

CHAPTER 10   OCTOBER 1803–FEBRUARY 1804

"But for him all places are alike. Busied with his summer's operations against Tripoli, he feels no pleasure in anything which does not forward his favorite plans."

S ettlement of the Moroccan affair sent a tide of optimism through the U.S. squadron in the Mediterranean. Surely, in the spring, Tripolitan affairs could be dispatched as quickly and as decisively.[1] Preble needed all the buoyancy and satisfaction his recent success had given him, because when he returned to Gibraltar on 15 October 1803 he had to face an unpleasant situation.

In the weeks since the *Constitution* had sailed from Boston, some of her men had found that an American warship was not paradise: discipline was strict, and troublemakers were punished. In the Bay of Gibraltar the American squadron was anchored close to British warships, and some men — even some of those who had signed on in American ships to avoid impressment into the Royal Navy — thought life might be better in the British Navy after all. Tension between the Americans and the British was developing.

Six members of the prize crew aboard the *Mirboha* had managed to desert before she was brought over to Tangier on the 10th of October, and at least three of them were known to have found refuge on board the British frigate *Medusa*, Captain John Gore. Lieutenant Charles Stewart, the senior American officer present at the time, asked Gore to return the deserters to American authority. Captain Gore refused to give them up, on the grounds that, as British subjects, they claimed his protection: moreover, some of the American officers who went to the *Medusa* to claim the deserters had admitted "that they knew them [the deserters] to be His Majesty's subjects when they entered them for the service of the United States, and informed me that nearly the whole of the crews of the *Constitution* and *Philadelphia* are British seamen."[2] Gore contended that these loyal British subjects, "finding now that their Sovereign is engaged in a serious war with an inveterate foe," wanted to serve under their own flag, but were being held in the U.S. Navy by force. In conversation with American officers, Gore hinted menacingly that he might forcibly take British seamen out of the American warships.

Preble realized that he was caught in an awkward position: the British officers were correct in claiming that a large proportion of the seamen serving in the American squadron were British nationals. When he took up the controversy with Gore where Lieutenant Stewart had left it, he resorted to some verbal sleight of hand: "I know of no such person as a *British subject* on board of any [of] the ships of the squadron under my command. I know them only as *citizens* of the United States who have taken the oath of allegiance to our government and have volunteered their services."

The day Preble signed that letter to Gore two men "ran" — from the *Constitution* herself. At least one of these deserters, a man named Plover, appeared to be a bona fide American citizen, since he had allotted half his monthly pay to a sister living in Boston. Within a couple of days Preble had word that Plover and his companion could be found in the British ship *Amphion,* Captain Samuel Sutton. A lieutenant who was sent off to the *Amphion* to inquire after them was told by Sutton that the two men were indeed in his ship, that they would not be returned to the *Constitution,* and that the officers commanding the *Amphion*'s boats had been instructed to receive all American deserters who claimed their protection.

Finally, the British became insultingly bold. On 21 October the British sloop *Termagant* shifted her berth to a position about a cable's length off the *Constitution*'s port quarter; "I suppose with an intention of enticing our men to swim to them," Preble wrote in his diary. Security in the *Constitution* was tightened, and all night one of her cutters, with a detachment of armed men, was on station between the American frigate and the *Termagant*. Even so, by morning, two more men were missing and presumably safe on board the British sloop. An acting midshipman in the *Constitution,* John Bartell by name, was found to be responsible for the *Termagant*'s seductive maneuvers. For reasons that were never explained, this rascal had boarded one of the British ships and spread the word that there were Englishmen in the *Constitution*'s crew who would desert if only they had the opportunity — an opportunity the *Termagant* was supposed to provide.[3] Unfortunately, Captain Preble's words to the midshipman have not been preserved, but Mr. Bartell soon found himself discharged from the service as "unfit for duty," and homeward-bound in an American merchantman.

Harsh treatment from British naval officers with whom he wanted to be friendly hurt Preble personally, but its most important result was the Commodore's decision to change the base of his Mediterranean operations. Both Dale and Morris had used the harbor of Valletta, at Malta, as a point of rendezvous for their squadrons. Preble, too, had intended to operate out of Valletta, but if using a British port meant British naval officers enticing his men to desert, he would avoid it. He decided, instead, to base his squadron at Syracuse, in Sicily, which, though somewhat more distant from Tripoli than Malta was, did have an excellent harbor. "To be sure," wrote the Commodore in words that would have brought gloom to the hearts of his more pleasure-loving junior officers if they had read them, "[Syracuse] does not offer the public amusements and rare curiosities of many other ports, but I trust we will find amusement enough in the necessary duties of our ships."

II

Peace with Morocco meant that most of Preble's squadron could be shifted up the Mediterranean towards Tripoli. The brig *Syren,* Charles Stewart, was dispatched to Leghorn, where Stewart had to pick up some cash and jewelry belonging to the United States, then deliver them to Algiers. These valuables were to form part of the present that Tobias Lear was expected to deliver on taking up his consular duties in that regency. Stephen Decatur, who had transferred from the *Argus* to command of the *Enterprize,* was ordered to convoy a storeship to Syracuse, then repair and re-rig his schooner, by which time Preble would probably have joined him at Syracuse. Preble, in the *Constitution,* accompanied by Richard Somers in the *Nautilus,* planned to touch at Algiers long enough to land Tobias Lear, pay a few courtesy calls on Algerian officials, then show his pennant off Tripoli for a day or two, before going on to Syracuse. Isaac Hull, who had been promoted from the *Enterprize* to command of the larger *Argus,* was assigned to spend the winter in and about the Straits of Gibraltar, where Preble judged the continued presence of at least one American warship necessary to insure that Morocco remained friendly and that he would be warned if anything went amiss.

The Commodore was nevertheless aware that, when he began active operations against Tripoli, he would need the *Argus* and her commander. Already, he could see that his squadron was too small for the area of his responsibility. As he studied the strategic outlook for the year to come, Preble began a series of appeals to the Secretary of the Navy for more ships: at the least, he needed a 32-gun frigate and a brig or schooner to relieve the *Argus* at Gibraltar and allow her to come up the Mediterranean to join

Preble. He pointed out that, although the frigate and whatever small vessel was sent out would normally be stationed near the Straits of Gibraltar, if Tunis were to declare war on the United States — of which there was some fear — the frigate would be able to join the main squadron; if, on the other hand, it was Morocco that became troublesome, the frigate could stand by while the small vessel hurried off to summon aid from the main squadron. The more Preble wrote about his need for additional ships, the more convinced he became that the administration would give him what he asked.

By mid-October Preble had realized that, with the stormy season nearly on him, he could not hope to conduct any decisive operations against Tripoli before spring, and that would be soon enough for the reinforcements to arrive. All he could do in the intervening months was blockade when the weather permitted, and prepare for spring's offensive. Early in November Preble told his wife:

> I have an arduous task to perform, but hope to acquit myself honorably. I am determined to oblige the Bashaw of that regency [Tripoli] to make peace with us on terms which are admissible or to destroy his city. For the latter purpose I am in treaty with the King of Naples for a supply of gunboats to assist my squadron, which I have no doubt will be readily granted as he is the inveterate enemy of the Tripolines. I wish to close the war with the Barbarians by conduct which shall establish our naval character among them and make them have a respect for peace. . . . My duty has been hard and fatiguing since I came on this station and must expect it will be very much so at the siege of Tripoli.

A few days later he returned to the same idea: "I have a dangerous and arduous task in the siege of Tripoli, but one or the other must conquer. God grant us success."

In that frame of mind Preble got the *Constitution* under way for Algiers on the 13th of November.

III

Amid salutes from the *Constitution* and from batteries on shore, Tobias Lear, Mrs. Lear, their household, and their baggage landed at Algiers six days later. Richard O'Brien, the retiring Consul General, and his wife planned to stay on at Algiers until spring, as she was expecting an addition to their family late in December. They would be able to help the Lears adjust to life in Algiers, and O'Brien's eighteen years' experience in Barbary would be useful to Lear while he was familiarizing himself with the duties of an American consul general on the Barbary Coast. The Dey of Algiers was at his country seat and, until he returned to the city, Lear could not be received in audience, but all indications were that relations between Algiers and the United States were excellent.

The morning after the arrival of the *Constitution,* Sunday, the 20th, Preble took his favorite aides, Noadiah Morris, Henry Wadsworth, and Ralph Izard, and went ashore in the *Constitution's* barge to pay a round of ceremonial visits and to arrange for the purchase of fresh provisions. But uppermost in the minds of the Commodore and his companions was a desire to see the sights of the strange and interesting Muslim city and report them to friends and families in America. As he was at Tangier, Henry Wadsworth was equal to the occasion:

> The Commodore, Mr. Morris, Mr. Izard and myself landed at the mole at 10 o'clock; was saluted with five guns, which was returned from the ship with an equal number. We were here met by the two consuls, Mr. Lear, who came on shore yesterday, and Mr. O'Brien, and all entered the piazza where sat the Minister of the Marine, sitting cross-legged on cushions. Were here regaled with excellent coffee and sherbet, etc., severally shook hands with *his honor,* and walked up a little farther, passed the city gates, and called in to see the Port Admiral. To have passed by would have been considered an insult. We were here regaled again with coffee, etc., etc., and after a lengthy walk arrived at the consuls' house. Mrs. Lear received us with pleasure, for as she came on shore but yesterday she does not yet feel at home and a country so different from America.
>
> We walked out before dinner without the city to one of the Dey's gardens and to see his horses. The garden on the right of the city contains fruit trees of all kinds, some flowers, and culinary plants of every description; resembles a rough country garden in America — grape vines in abundance — and appears rather a garden of utility than luxury. The horses, about forty in number, were the first of the Arabian breed, the most beautiful I ever saw. The suburbs of the city to the northward, through which we passed, were entirely taken up in small burying grounds, with small stone walls about two feet high, neatly whitewashed, a great number of brick kilns, and some old ruins, such as walls, etc., etc. As we came along observed a funeral: the corpse was laying in a handbarrow, tied up in a bag, with a cover over all, and carried by four persons with a few attendants. They set down the dead and two began to dig the grave, the others ranging themselves round the brink cross-legged, in melancholy mood. We lost sight of them, and I saw no more. I suppose from appearances that they were very poor, being coarse, dirty and ragged.
>
> In another part of our walk we met eleven camels, which the drivers made to get up and down for our amusement. They are the most ugly, disgusting animal living, and, whatever their utility may be, their appearance is sufficient to banish them from every Christian country. With pleasure I observed the Commodore distribute his dollars among the slaves. There are here seven hundred slaves* lately taken under English colors. If Nelson can spare his

---

* They were Maltese mariners captured by the Algerians after the occupation of Malta by the British.

fleet from the coast of France, it is probable he will pay the city of Algiers an unwelcome visit.

Our walk afforded us much pleasure, and I set down with a voracious appetite (which my messmates say is always the case) to Consul O'Brien's dinner. And now, instead of entertaining you with table talk, I will devote this page to Mrs. Lear. An amiable, handsome woman of about twenty-three, lately married to the Colonel, his second [actually his third] wife, she is from Virginia and a distant relation to General Washington. She has that peculiar look, that cast of countenance, I may even say a likeness to my much lamented sister, Eliza. You cannot wonder, therefore, at my being attached to her, though my acquaintance is only of a few days. The Consul is a man particularly adapted to make her happy, and she to soothe his mind, troubled with the cares of government and harass[ed] with anxiety. In fact, they are each calculated to make the other amends for being deprived of the society of their friends and countrymen.

We departed at four o'clock and were saluted as before. Mr. O'Brien had supplied the barge's crew, which waited all day at the wharf, with bread, beef and wine. This I was very happy to observe, for our consular gentry in these parts generally neglect it. Mr. O'Brien, while a slave here, was very serviceable to their marine, and was made boatswain of the yard, etc., etc. He is now consulted relative to their naval affairs, and to his exertions we are indebted to their present favor and are now considered the *favorite nation* with the Dey. But damn his favor, it is too expensive!

That same evening, perhaps even at the same time that Wadsworth was working away on his narrative, the Commodore was busy drafting a letter to Mary:

I arrived here last evening and landed Colonel Lear and family at the abode of happiness as this country is called by its natives, and really from its appearance you might suppose it at least to be the abode of pleasure from the numerous pleasure-houses, gardens and country seats which surround the city of Algiers.

I went on shore this day and was received under a salute of cannon and treated in the most respectful, attentive and polite manner, introduced to all the great men of the court and each one ordered coffee and sherbet to be brought me. The custom of the country obliges one to receive more civilities than are agreeable at all times. I was only long enough on shore to visit the Dey's gardens, private walks, arbors, groves, etc., and his stables for Arabian horses and camels, and granaries and dockyards. This visit afforded me a considerable deal of pleasure, as it gratified my curiosity. The city is as large as Philadelphia, neat and handsomely built, and the houses very convenient, the streets narrow, and the houses projecting towards each other at the top so as nearly to form an arch over every street makes them very cool in summer, as passengers are continually shaded in their walks. The Dey's gardens are very extensive, cultivated with every vegetable, tree and plant that is useful and ornamental, and the whole so arranged in squares, walks, arbors, pleasure-houses, labyrinths, etc., etc., that it appeared to be the effect of enchantment.

Wealth and luxury can do much in any country, but in none more than this, as it is blessed with the finest climate and soil in the world and only wants a good government to make it an enviable situation — but the caprice of the tyrant who governs makes it a dangerous residence.

It was a pleasant, tranquil interlude; a day for sightseeing and dining with a circle of friends; a day to forget Tripoli and the concerns of command. Soon they would have to turn to harsher business: a visit to the Tripolitan coast was to be the next event of Preble's cruise up the Mediterranean. The following evening the *Constitution* made sail to the eastward.

IV

Shortly after daylight on 24 November, as the *Constitution* was passing to the south of Sardinia, her lookouts caught sight of a large sail to the northward. She changed course to speak the stranger, who identified herself as the British ship *Amazon*, 38, and gave Commodore Preble a piece of chilling intelligence: the *Philadelphia* had been captured by the Tripolitans.

All the British commander knew was that the frigate had grounded near Tripoli while chasing a hostile schooner, that the officers and crew were prisoners, and that the Tripolitans had refloated the *Philadelphia* and towed her into the harbor of Tripoli. Preble was eager to verify this dismaying report and, if possible, learn more details. With little loss of time for civilities to the British, the *Constitution* made sail for Malta. By afternoon on the 26th, the *Constitution* was off Valletta harbor. Lieutenant John H. Dent went ashore and brought back letters from Captain Bainbridge confirming the loss of the frigate and recounting the details of the disaster. From Bainbridge's letters and from accounts that he received in succeeding weeks, Preble was able to reconstruct what had happened.

Following their arrival off the coast of Tripoli on 7 October, the *Philadelphia* and the *Vixen* had spent two weeks cruising, as Bainbridge put it, "on this solitary station, without the good fortune of seeing our enemies except under the refuge of well-fortified works." It may be that the frustration of this fruitless duty had made Bainbridge less cautious than he should have been. On the 22nd he split his little squadron and sent the *Vixen* to cruise between Cape Bon and the island of Marettimo in an attempt to intercept two Tripolitan cruisers reported to be at large in the Mediterranean.[4] At last, at 9:00 a.m. on 31 October, while the *Philadelphia* was cruising alone five leagues to the east of Tripoli, a suspicious sail was sighted inshore and standing to the westward before the wind. As Bainbridge made for her, she hoisted Tripolitan colors and continued her course for Tripoli, hugging the shore as she went. The *Philadelphia* pursued her and, by half-past eleven, found herself in water only seven fathoms deep. Sensing danger, Bainbridge abandoned the pursuit, and his frigate was in the act of beating offshore when she suddenly grounded on an underwater shoal a little over three miles northeast of Tripoli.

Bainbridge's first resort was to crowd on sail in an attempt to force the frigate over the shoal, but she only became more firmly stranded. Sounding showed deeper water astern than ahead. Sails were laid aback, three anchors were cut away from the bow, drinking water was pumped out, and all the guns except those well aft were hove overboard. Finally, the foremast was cut away, and, as it fell, it carried the main-topgallant mast with it. All these attempts to back the ship off into the deep water astern proved futile. Several gunboats had already come out from Tripoli and were firing at the stranded and careening frigate from a position on which the *Philadelphia* could not bring her few remaining guns to bear. Moreover, they had made it impossible to kedge the frigate off the shoal, because they commanded the ground where the anchor would have had to be laid.

Late in the afternoon, Bainbridge concluded that the situation was hopeless. He ordered the magazine flooded, the remaining guns disabled, signal books destroyed, shot thrown into the pumps, and holes bored in the ship's bottom. When all this was done, the *Philadelphia* struck her colors. Preble never knew it, but Bainbridge did not destroy his personal papers, which thus fell into the Pasha's possession. From them Yusuf could cull intelligence on the size and composition of Preble's squadron, his problem of shorthanded crews, the extent to which the war with Morocco had tied his hands, and past as well as projected movements of the American ships.

In spite of the holes in her bottom, the ship's hull had not filled with water by the time her Tripolitan captors reached the *Philadelphia*. Some forty hours after the *Philadelphia* first grounded a westerly gale began that raised the sea enough for the Tripolitans to get the frigate off the shoal and bring her into port for repairs and refitting. The American consul at Malta passed on to Preble a report that the Pasha of Tripoli could not adequately man the 36-gun frigate and was trying to sell her to one of the other Barbary States.

There was not a single ray of good news to brighten the gloom. Preble could conjure up a large number of evils that might result from the disaster. No one knew under what flag the *Philadelphia* might soon be roaming the Mediterranean, or how much of a threat she might pose if she remained in Tripolitan hands. The prestige of the United States, only recently raised by the settlement at Tangier, would probably sink to new depths in the eyes of the Barbary regencies. Tunis, confident of being more than equal to the weakened American squadron, might declare war on the United

States. Even if Tunis remained peaceful, the U.S. squadron, with its frigate force cut by half, could not hope to compel a peace settlement with Tripoli in the spring, as Preble had so confidently expected it to do. How long the war might last he no longer could predict. With the *Philadelphia* and 307 prisoners in his hands, the Pasha was in a strong bargaining position. Preble expected him to raise his terms for a peace settlement far above anything the administration would accept. The most that Preble could expect to do was to blockade Tripoli and harass the coast, in the hope that this would encourage the Pasha to reduce his demands.

Bitter as his reflections on the loss of the *Philadelphia* might be, Preble tried to avoid saying or writing anything critical of Captain Bainbridge. But sometimes his emotions got the better of his self-control: "Would to God that the officers and crew of the *Philadelphia* had, one and all, determined to prefer death to slavery!" he burst out on one occasion. "It is possible such a determination might save them from either." As he brooded over Bainbridge's accounts of the disaster, the Commodore could not help wondering why the frigate had not been completely disabled before she was surrendered to the Tripolitans. The speed and ease with which the enemy had refloated her did not seem to speak well for the attempt to scuttle her.

In January 1804 Henry Preble wrote from Paris that he had just heard of the loss of the *Philadelphia,* "a most unfortunate event as it will render your projects in the Mediterranean fruitless. I find some slight censure falls on you for having sent this frigate to blockade Tripoli without a consort." His brother's letter drew from Edward a criticism of Bainbridge that he had hitherto kept to himself. "If I am censured for sending the *Philadelphia* to blockade Tripoli *alone* it is unjust and proceeds from want of correct information," he replied. "I sent the *Vixen* of sixteen 18-pounders, carronades, in company with her and wholly under the control of Captain Bainbridge, but he thought proper to send her to look out off the island of Lampedusa. If he had kept her with him, it is probable he would have saved his ship."[5]

The tone of all Preble's official letters about the *Philadelphia,* whether addressed to Washington or to his correspondents in the Mediterranean, was cautiously optimistic, and exemplified magnificently his self-control. His personal appraisal was filled with foreboding, but it came out only in a letter he wrote to his wife from Syracuse on 12 December:

> I have now to inform you of a most distressing event: the loss of the frigate *Philadelphia,* Captain Bainbridge. She ran on the rocks near Tripoli while in chase of one of the Barbary corsairs and was obliged to surrender to a host of

savages who attacked her. Captain Bainbridge, together with all his officers and crew, amounting to 307 men, are slaves and are treated in the most cruel manner, without a prospect of ever again beholding their friends. I hope to God such will never be my fate! The thought of never again seeing you would drive me to distraction. I will not indulge it. May Heaven preserve us both, and may its choicest blessings be yours. The loss of the *Philadelphia* deranges the plans I had formed for the reduction of Tripoli at present, but I expect government will send me an additional force in the spring. I most sincerely pity the cruel fate of poor Bainbridge. I know not what will become of them. I suspect very few will ever see home again.

If Edward Preble ever came close to despair it probably was in this crisis. His dream of being famous had gone. No massed force would repeat the triumph of Tangier. There was no hope for a brilliant solution of the Tripolitan War. The United States would, in the end, ransom the captives. What could Preble, with one 44-gun frigate and a handful of small vessels, do?

V

One immediate change in Preble's plans resulted from the altered situation. Instead of sailing for Tripoli at once, he made for Sicily to establish his base at Syracuse and refit the *Constitution* for winter cruising.

When the Americans arrived on 28 November, the governor of Syracuse, Marcello de Gregorio, welcomed them to his city hospitably and even eagerly. Preble accepted his offer of the free use of the arsenal, where he could store his extra boats and spars, as well as magazines that would hold 5,000 barrels of provisions. Gregorio candidly explained that he was anxious to have the American squadron based at Syracuse, since its presence would probably discourage Tripolitan cruisers from raiding the nearby coast, which the lackluster Neapolitan navy was incapable of protecting effectively. Naturally, the governor's friendly and cooperative attitude could not be allowed to go unrewarded, and Preble presented him with twelve bottles of attar of roses, two English cheeses, two dozen bottles of port, two dozen bottles of madeira, a barrel of mess beef, a keg of butter, and a round of beef.[6] And the Syracusans engaged in a little bribery of their own: Preble was obviously flattered when, as he reported in his diary, the "nobility and gentlemen of the place" called on board the *Constitution* "with offers of their friendship and services." In his letter of 12 December to Mary, he wrote:

> I arrived in this place about a fortnight since, and, although surrounded by the ruins of ancient magnificence and splendor, I have been so constantly occupied in my attention to the squadron and in forming an establishment

here for a general rendezvous that I have not had time to visit them. I am now writing in full view of Mount Etna, covered with snow from its summit to its base, and the cold breeze which blows from it chilling my fingers so as to make it difficult to write. You are well acquainted with the history of this part of the world, and I will attempt to give you a general account of its present situation when I return from a cruise off the coast of Tripoli which I shall sail on this evening. I expect to be out about three weeks and shall return and spend the winter here. The celebrated temple of Minerva is yet standing and is converted into a cathedral. Some remains of Diana's temple is yet to be seen. I fill all my water at the fountain of Arethusa, and purchase my fresh butter from the farm which was given to Timoleon by the Syracusans for driving out Dionysius the Tyrant. When I return here and have time to visit the antiquities I shall have quite a history to give. . . .

The climate here is delightful in summer, but the weather I have experienced since the 1st of October has been much worse than any we have on the coast of America in the midst of winter. I have to expect much worse on my present cruise than any that I have yet experienced.

While the *Constitution* was undergoing her refitting, Preble drafted a dispatch notifying Washington of the capture of the *Philadelphia*. Several copies of the letter were made, to be sent by various routes. If possible, word of the setback must reach Washington while Congress was still in session, since an increased appropriation would be needed if the *Philadelphia* was to be replaced and the squadron strengthened. Preble repeated his earlier request for a frigate to cruise near the Straits of Gibraltar, thus releasing the *Argus* for service nearer Tripoli, and asked that one or two frigates replace the *Philadelphia*. He estimated that, with a force of such size, he would be able to blockade Tripoli completely and harass the Tripolitan coast so severely that the Pasha, who seemed to have had the upper hand since the capture of the *Philadelphia,* would drastically reduce his price for ransom and a peace treaty. If all went well, it might be possible to force Yusuf to ask for peace without requiring the United States to ransom the *Philadelphia*'s crew.

On 15 December the *Nautilus* sailed from Syracuse with instructions to waste no time in getting down to Gibraltar. She carried two sets of the dispatches reporting the capture of the *Philadelphia*; one was to be forwarded to the United States from Gibraltar, the other from Cadiz. Midshipman Christopher Gadsden, Jr., bound home on sick leave, was a passenger in the *Nautilus* and he carried additional copies of the dispatches that he was to mail or deliver personally to Robert Smith when he landed in the United States.

Two days after the departure of the *Nautilus*, the *Constitution* and the *Enterprize* sailed for the coast of Tripoli, where Preble expected to remain so long as the weather was mild enough for the Tripolitan cruisers to be at sea. He did not intend, however, to risk the *Constitution* in a continuous, and probably unnecessary, blockade during the stormy winter months. "Should any accident happen to this ship and any of the other Barbary Powers should break out upon us, the consequences may be dreadful to our commerce in these seas," he explained. There was special work for the *Enterprize* to do at Tripoli. Lieutenant Stephen Decatur was instructed to run close in with the coast, reconnoiter the port, and determine the position of the *Philadelphia*. Preble had already written Robert Smith: "I do not believe the *Philadelphia* will ever be of service to Tripoli. I shall hazard much to destroy her. It will undoubtedly cost us many lives, but it must be done."

VI

At 8:30 a.m., 23 December, the *Enterprize* signalled that to the southwest she could see the Tripolitan coast. Almost at the same moment, on the southwestern horizon, the *Constitution* sighted a strange sail standing away from the land with an offshore breeze. She immediately made sail for the stranger and signalled the *Enterprize,* which was closer to her than was the *Constitution,* to chase to the southwest also. Preble had scarcely begun his pursuit when the wind veered to the southwest, bringing the stranger dead to windward. The *Constitution* was flying English colors, and the stranger, apparently suspecting nothing, continued to steer towards the American frigate until she fell in with the *Enterprize,* which escorted her down to the Commodore.

Close at hand, the frigate's officers could see that the stranger was a ketch-rigged vessel of some 60 or 70 tons and perhaps 60 feet in length. Preble immediately sent a boat to bring her master and his papers to the *Constitution* for examination. Almost all the papers were in Arabic and Turkish and there was no translator on board. The Commodore glanced through them, then questioned the master. When he had finished his questioning, he ordered his English colors struck and the American run up. Panic broke out in the ketch. Men who earlier had been huddled together in conversation could be seen running about the deck in confusion. But they had no chance to get away: the ketch was directly under the *Constitution*'s guns. Preble gave the order to seize her, and within a few minutes his large cutter had been hoisted out and was on its way to the ketch with a prize crew.

Preble was not being high-handed. He had grounds for detaining the ketch as a suspicious vessel. Apparently she was an Ottoman ship; at least she was navigating under the Ottoman flag and her master was a Turk.

Greeks and Cretans made up her crew, and she was carrying an Ottoman official from Tripoli to Constantinople. All that was unexceptionable, but she also had on board as passengers two Tripolitan officers, ten Tripolitan soldiers, and forty-two negro slaves, some of whom belonged to the Pasha and some to Tripolitan merchants. She had sailed from Tripoli the night before, was bound to another Tripolitan port, Benghazi, and thence to Constantinople.

If that had been all there was to it, Preble would have netted a nice haul of Tripolitan prisoners; the ship, her master and crew, and their distinguished Turkish passenger would have been released to continue their voyage. But Preble had further suspicions, and he had recently acquired a new source of intelligence about Tripoli. When, on his passage from Syracuse to Tripoli, he had called off Malta, the American consul there had brought out to the frigate an Italian physician, Dr. Pietro Francisco Crocillo. Until a few weeks before, Crocillo had been Yusuf Caramanli's personal physician, but the two of them had come to a falling out. Anxious to retain a man who had a fund of useful information from inside the Pasha's court, Preble offered Crocillo an appointment as surgeon's mate in the *Constitution,* and the offer had been accepted.

A search of the ketch turned up some side arms and other property which could be identified as having belonged to officers of the *Philadelphia.* More important, Crocillo knew both the Tripolitan officers in the ketch and explained their rank and importance to the Commodore. He also told Preble that the ten Tripolitan soldiers had been attached to the gunboats that attacked the *Philadelphia* when she grounded. Most interesting of all, the doctor reported that the ketch's Turkish master had been in one of the gunboats that captured the *Philadelphia* and had acted a prominent role in the boarding of the frigate, seizing prisoners, and stealing their clothing. It was all highly questionable. Very well, let the prize crew take the ketch to Syracuse. There Preble could examine her at leisure, have all her papers translated, and determine whether she was a lawful prize.

VII

Stormy weather off Tripoli drove the *Constitution* back to Syracuse on 29 December. Preble was greatly interested in getting the papers he had taken from the Ottoman ketch translated, but there was no one in Syracuse who could do the job and he could not get a translator from Malta to make the journey to Syracuse. He was beginning to think the Sicilian port was something of a backwater. Since the *Constitution* was in need of some repairs and alterations, Preble and a small staff — Ralph Izard, Henry

Wadsworth, and Noadiah Morris, the last recently promoted to purser — embarked in the *Vixen,* 13 January 1804, and set sail for Valletta.

No sooner had the 12-gun *Vixen,* boldly flying a commodore's broad pennant, arrived at Malta the next day, than the Commodore's party was swept into the busy social whirl of government and garrison. "I now for the first time in two years enjoyed a few days of uncontrolled liberty, for the Commodore did not trouble us excepting to inform us where we were to dine," wrote Midshipman Wadsworth. "We therefore gave ourselves up to all the pleasures of the Carnival season; but I will not break my narrative here. . . . At some future period you shall have the *Memoirs of a Masquerade* or the *Intrigues of Carnival Times.*" In a letter to his friend David Porter, Wadsworth told a little of those intrigues: "Met a bouncing English girl at the masquerade last night. She said she was married, but I might cuckold her husband. Nice bit!"[7]

Preble's pleasures were more sedate. He immediately called on Sir Alexander John Ball, the governor; on Rear Admiral Sir Richard Bickerton, second in command in the Mediterranean under Lord Nelson; on Major General William A. Villettes, commander in chief of the troops on Malta; and on Brigadier General Hildebrand Oakes. The following morning all these officers returned Preble's courtesy by calling on him on board the *Vixen.* In contrast to the somewhat hostile atmosphere at Gibraltar, at Malta cordial relations with the British officials were quickly and easily established. That same day Preble, Ball, and Bickerton rode out together to see something of the island, and upon their return Preble was Ball's guest at dinner. There was a Garrison Ball, a formal dinner with General Villettes on the Queen's birthday, the Governor's Ball in honor of the same occasion, dinner with General Oakes and many of the field and staff officers of the army, and formal calls by generals of the army and captains of the navy.

Preble loved it all. And the friendly atmosphere soon showed up in more practical matters: Admiral Bickerton told Preble that he disapproved of the business of enticing Preble's seamen to desert at Gibraltar; Preble could bring the *Constitution* into Valletta harbor with Bickerton's personal assurance that his men would not be lured into desertion. Equally important, Sir Alexander Ball gave Preble oral permission to enlist Maltese pilots, sailors, and boys to fill up gaps in the American crews.

Day after day Preble waited impatiently while a Turk he had hired took his own time about producing a translation of the ketch's papers. Impatient or not, he kept himself busy at Malta. Part of his time was occupied by conferences with two agents of Hamet Caramanli, the former Pasha of Tripoli, who had been deposed by his younger brother Yusuf. After seven years of exile at Tunis Hamet had, in the fall of 1802, accepted Yusuf's offer of the governorship of Derna and had taken up his duties in Cyrenaica. However, the reconciliation between the brothers was barely surface deep: neither trusted the other. Yusuf apparently made his conciliatory move only because he feared Hamet would ally himself with the United States and Sweden in an attempt to recover the pashadom. Indicative of Yusuf's attitude towards Hamet was his refusal to release Hamet's wife and five children whom he had been holding hostage ever since he had driven Hamet out of Tripoli. On his part, Hamet Caramanli, although governor of Derna, had been intriguing with Commodore R. V. Morris for aid in overthrowing Yusuf. By the summer of 1803, Hamet had moved into open revolt against his brother. Early in the fall of that year Yusuf made a supreme effort to rid himself of Hamet once and for all by sending loyal troops to Derna by sea. This small army, aided by those of the inhabitants who opposed Hamet Caramanli's rule, was to defeat and capture Hamet after Yusuf's cruisers had seized control of Derna harbor and the adjacent coast, cutting Hamet off from his friends and supporters at Malta. But Hamet had seen the shape of the future. He declined to wait, fight it out with Yusuf's army, and risk capture and the loss of his head. Instead, he had decamped to Alexandria in Egypt.

Almost immediately on Preble's arrival at Syracuse in November he received letters from Hamet's agents in Malta. The first to approach him was Richard Farquhar, a merchant who traded with Tripoli and Derna, and seems to have served as Hamet's English-language secretary during the latter's intrigues with Commodore Morris. Farquhar put Preble in touch with one Salvatore Busuttil, Hamet's immediate representative at Malta. After some preliminary exchanges of correspondence Preble took advantage of his trip to Malta for long meetings with both Busuttil and Farquhar to hear their proposals for cooperation between Preble and Hamet Caramanli.

Busuttil explained that Hamet was at Alexandria, where he might easily assemble a large army of Arabs and Mamelukes; but before he could organize his army he would need eighty or ninety thousand dollars, some fifty barrels of powder, and six fieldpieces. If Preble could supply these necessities, Hamet would march overland and capture Derna and Benghazi, then go on to Tripoli, which he would assault by land while Preble's squadron bombarded it from the sea. Alternatively, Preble might send a ship to Alexandria, pick up Hamet and a group of his followers, and transport them to Derna or Benghazi, where Hamet was supposed to have support among the population and where he would be joined by the rest of his troops from Egypt. In return for American aid in regaining the pashadom Hamet was prepared to offer the United States perpetual peace, to allow her to hold

Tripolitan hostages and garrison the principal fort in the harbor of Tripoli to insure this peace, or to permit the United States to set its own terms for a new treaty. He further pledged to release all American and all other Christian slaves in Tripoli.

Hamet's desire to overthrow his usurping brother seemed to open up real chances for a strong campaign against Yusuf, especially in combination with Preble's plan to employ light vessels in attacking Tripoli. The Commodore encouraged Farquhar and Busuttil. He told them that he expected his squadron to be reinforced and, when it was, he would be strong enough to attack Tripoli. Preble also agreed, or Richard Farquhar understood him to agree, to make arrangements for sending Busuttil and some of Hamet's followers from Malta to Alexandria. There they would unite with the deposed Pasha and his other supporters for a move against Derna and Benghazi. Those towns seized, Hamet would be in position to march against Tripoli during the summer months. Moreover, in Hamet's control, Cyrenaica would be a source of fresh provisions for the American squadron. Preble promised to ask Washington for instructions on how far he could go in supporting Hamet's revolution with money and supplies. He sought this guidance from Robert Smith at once:

> I wish earlier notice had been taken of this man and his views. In fact, I am astonished that the first or second squadron did not oblige the Bashaw of Tripoli to sign any treaty they pleased. I have less force than either, with ten times the force to contend with. The Tripolines by May will have nineteen gunboats, and unless we have boats to fight them in their own way we shall not be likely to succeed. If you will allow me to expend one hundred thousand dollars in such additional naval force as I think proper, I will take Tripoli or perish in the attempt. I am confident that it may easily be destroyed or taken in the summer with gun and mortar boats protected by our cruisers.

Hamet's agents were not the only ones who sought out Preble at Malta. After the capture of the *Philadelphia,* there was a report abroad that the Pasha of Tripoli intended to demand $3,000,000 from the United States for ransom and a peace settlement. Preble had not been at Valletta long before he was contacted indirectly by Gaetano Andrea Schembri, Yusuf Caramanli's consul at Malta, who said he was authorized by the Pasha to open preliminary negotiations looking towards a peace treaty. Schembri first proposed a ten years' truce between Tripoli and the United States. The Commodore rejected this flatly. Next, Schembri suggested that Yusuf would be willing to trade the *Philadelphia,* which Tripoli could not use, for a schooner, and would surrender his American prisoners for $500 apiece. However, this proposal was linked with the payment of an annuity to Tripoli by the United States, and Preble was adamant in turning it down:

the United States, he told Schembri, would never agree to pay one cent for peace or tribute. After further negotiation Preble and Schembri agreed on what, considering the reverse the United States had suffered in the loss of the *Philadelphia*, seemed to be attractive terms: the United States would accept the Pasha's offer to exchange the *Philadelphia* for a schooner, and Yusuf would accept $100,000 ransom for all his American prisoners.

Apparently the Pasha was worried and even frightened by the vigorous preparations Preble was making for his summer campaign. But tempting as the proposals by Schembri might appear, Preble did not attempt to close the deal. The Turk had finally finished translating the ketch's papers, and, at the moment, getting back to Syracuse was uppermost in Preble's mind. If the Pasha was willing to talk peace now, the Commodore thought that he would be anxious to do so after Preble had executed a plan that he had been forming for the past several weeks.

When the *Vixen* sailed for Sicily on January 23rd, Henry Wadsworth was sad to leave the gay life of Valletta in her wake: "In ten days, the Commodore having finished his business, we reluctantly departed for Syracuse. But for him all places are alike. Busied with his summer's operations against Tripoli, he feels no pleasure in anything which does not forward his favorite plans."

VIII

Edward Preble returned to Syracuse on 25 January determined to consummate without delay the seizure of the Turkish ketch he had detained on 23 December, and to send her immediately thereafter on an expedition, whose purpose must be kept a closely held secret. For nine days these objectives had first call on his attention and energy. Even a sad letter from Eben Preble, with word of the sudden death of their brother Joshua at Savannah, Georgia, neither slowed nor diverted him.

Fortunately for Preble, at this juncture there appeared a mariner who had the precise information needed to secure the ketch's condemnation, and Preble hired him as a pilot for the *Constitution*. He was a thirty-two-year-old native of Palermo, named Salvador Catalano, who had formerly commanded one of Richard Farquhar's small ships trading between Malta and Tripoli. Catalano was in Tripoli the day the *Philadelphia* was lost. He had seen the ketch haul down her Ottoman colors, raise Tripolitan colors, take on board Tripolitans armed with muskets and sabers, then slip her cables and sail out towards the stranded *Philadelphia*. She did not actually go alongside the frigate, but her launch carried her master and the Tripolitans to where the *Philadelphia* lay, and the former participated eagerly in removing the American prisoners to Tripoli and in robbing them.

That was all the evidence Preble needed. The ketch's character as an Ottoman vessel was forfeit. She was either a Tripolitan or a pirate. Preble retained her for legal condemnation and held prisoner all but eight of the people on board: the Ottoman official was permitted to continue his trip to Constantinople, and seven Greek crewmen were allowed to enlist in the U.S. Navy as ordinary seamen. Although orders from the Navy Department plainly required Preble to send all prizes to a port in the United States for condemnation, he merely promised Robert Smith that he would forward all the papers necessary to insure the ketch's condemnation and explained that he was not sending her because "she is not a proper vessel to cross the Atlantic at this season of the year." He was aware that, should the Department take exception to what he had done, it would be months before a rebuke could reach the Mediterranean. By then he might have ended the war. But it was probably transparent to Robert Smith that Preble needed his prize.

As soon as her month's quarantine was over, and her prisoners had been removed, the ketch was alive with bustle and activity. Officers from the *Enterprize* could be seen getting her under way and towing her to the mole for repairs; Lieutenant Stephen Decatur was in charge and was directing all the work; the *Constitution*'s large cutter was busy carrying muskets and side arms to the ketch; the Commodore was referring to her as the *Intrepid*.

The expedition that Preble was planning was one that would suggest itself to a man who had first attracted public attention by boarding and capturing the *Merriam* under the British guns at Bagaduce: he was going to send a party to board and destroy the *Philadelphia* at her moorings in Tripoli harbor. Intelligence indicated that all the frigate's guns were mounted but there was no ammunition on board, and she was normally guarded by about thirty men.

Lieutenants Charles Stewart, in the *Syren,* and Stephen Decatur, in the *Intrepid*, were to command the expedition. Except for Catalano, one other pilot, and some midshipmen from the *Constitution*, the *Intrepid* was manned by volunteers from the *Enterprize*. The *Intrepid* was the key to success: her Mediterranean appearance would allow her to enter the harbor without creating suspicion. Since the *Syren* had never been off Tripoli, she was not likely to be recognized as an American vessel: on the way to Tripoli Stewart was to disguise her as a merchantman by repainting her, sending down the topgallant masts, rigging in the flying jibboom, shutting in her ports, and raising quarter-cloths. The two ships were to approach their goal after dark, the *Intrepid* running well ahead of the *Syren* to avoid any possibility of arousing Tripolitan suspicions. Boarding was to be done from the *Intrepid;* the role of the *Syren* was to be principally one of support. Preble assigned only one mission to Decatur: destroy the *Philadelphia*.

At 5:00 p.m. on 2 February 1804 the *Syren* and the *Intrepid* sailed out of Syracuse harbor. If Sailing Master Haraden guessed where they were going, he was discreet: "They stood out to the southward and are bound on some secret expedition."

CHAPTER 11 FEBRUARY 1804–MAY 1804

*"I feel extremely desirous of serving my country.
Give me the means and I will do it...."*

Once the *Syren* and the *Intrepid* were under way, Preble could only wait and keep busy with the routine of the squadron and with working out the details of his strategy for the summer. He was sure that the strategy he planned — blockade of the Pasha's harbors, destruction of Tripolitan cruisers and commerce, and attacks on the city of Tripoli — was one by which "Tripoli would soon be brought to any terms we might please to dictate," but it was one for whose execution he would have to have more ships.

If he could buy, hire, or borrow three or four gunboats and two or three bomb ketches, they, in company with two frigates and a schooner, would be able to seal off Tripoli from the sea and bombard the town and harbor. A brig or a schooner would have to be stationed off Cape Misurata to intercept Tripolitan cruisers and traders attempting to avoid the blockade by slipping along the African shore on their way to or from the eastern Mediterranean. Another brig or schooner would be needed to cruise between Derna and Benghazi and disrupt the commerce of those two Tripolitan ports. Between Cape Bon and the western end of Sicily, a brig and a schooner should be on patrol in order to deny Tripolitan cruisers access to the western half of the Mediterranean; or, at least, to insure that, should any Tripolitans get into that part of the sea, they and their prizes would be captured on their return. Finally, he wanted to have a brig cruising off the Calabrian coast, presumably in case any Tripolitans raided Sicily or southern Italy or headed up the Adriatic.

Consequently, besides gunboats, bomb ketches, and any vessels that might have to be kept near Gibraltar, one more frigate and one more small vessel had to be added to Preble's present squadron of one frigate, two brigs, and three schooners. Preble's strategy depended on the arrival of the additional ships he had requested from the United States.

Prospects were favorable. Midshipman Christopher Gadsden, carrying dispatches reporting the capture of the *Philadelphia*, might have reached the United States already. At Gibraltar, on 3 January 1804, he had taken passage in the schooner *Mary*, Captain Sinclair, bound to Georgetown, South Carolina, and in a last-minute note to Preble had assured the Commodore, "You may depend upon my not losing a moment in going to Washington." Consul John Gavino had written Preble, "The wind is now coming round to the east, and Captain Sinclair with Mr. Gadsden are gone off in order to proceed for America." Equally encouraging was a widely circulated, but unofficial, report that early in the fall Lieutenant Andrew Sterett had been recruiting men in Baltimore for Preble's old frigate, the *Essex*, and it was generally assumed that she was being readied to join the Mediterranean squadron. Preble gathered that the administration was going to strengthen his squadron promptly, and he expected he would soon have word that not only the *Essex*, but two other small frigates, the *Congress* and the *Boston*, were on their way to the Mediterranean.

It was a question of waiting: waiting for reinforcement; waiting for the *Syren* and the *Intrepid*.

II

By Sunday, 19 February, the *Syren* and the *Intrepid* had been absent for two and a half weeks — much longer than it should have taken them to execute a quick attack and get back to Syracuse. Each passing day increased Preble's anxiety, and, after a four-day hard gale that lasted from the 6th through the 9th of February, the Commodore was unable to conceal his fear that the *Intrepid* and the *Syren* had been driven on the Tripolitan shore and lost. Beginning about 12 February, Preble had ordered a lookout for Stewart's and Decatur's vessels to be maintained at the *Constitution*'s masthead.

At ten o'clock on the morning of the 19th the two ships came into sight off the entrance to Syracuse harbor. Immediately the *Constitution* made signal number 227 to the *Syren:* "Business or enterprize, have you completed, that you was sent on?" There followed a minute or two of tense expectation on the *Constitution*'s quarterdeck, while the answering flags were hoisted — two . . . three . . . two. Surely Preble did not have to look in his signal book to know the meaning of number 232. This was the message he had been hoping for: "Business, I have completed, that I was sent on."

It was 7 February when the *Syren* and the *Intrepid* approached Tripoli, the *Intrepid* anchoring off the harbor entrance before 9:00 p.m.[1] Foul odors rising from the old ketch's hold, rats and vermin that swarmed through the vessel, salt provisions so decayed and smelly that no one could bear to walk to leeward of the cook's pots while the rotten mess was boiling — none of these had dampened morale among the *Philadelphia*'s would-be destroyers on the passage from Syracuse. Then came a keen disappointment. A heavy swell that had been setting from the northeast all afternoon was breaking all the way across the harbor entrance, and the breeze, which had been blowing fresh from the westward, showed signs of soon increasing to gale force. The attempt must not be made that night. Even if the *Intrepid*'s and the *Syren*'s boats got in with impunity, they would never be able to get out through those breakers. Decatur, anxious to be out of sight of Tripoli by daylight, made sail.

By the time this gale — the same storm that had caused Preble to worry about the fate of the *Syren* and the *Intrepid* — had blown itself out late on the 10th, the two ships had been carried so far to the east that it took them five days to get back to the vicinity of Tripoli. Point Tagiura, to the east of Tripoli, was sighted at 5:30 p.m. on 15 February. After this sighting the two ships stood somewhat off the land — presumably to avoid detection — then at 9:30 p.m. tacked in the general direction of Tripoli. However, since they had neither sighted Tripoli nor managed to get a bearing on the town during daylight, they could not locate the harbor in the dark.

Prospects for success seemed none too promising. The element of surprise might have been lost. Twice, they had spent several hours hovering off the Tripolitan coast. There was a good possibility that the ships had been observed from shore, and it was not improbable that the Tripolitans had seen through their disguises and recognized them as hostile ships of war. Morale — high a few days earlier — sagged. The men were grousing: old *Philadelphia* might be so well defended by now that only fools would attempt to capture her. This sudden collapse of self-confidence tested Decatur's leadership severely, but he was able to project a mood of resolution and assurance that soon had the situation under control.

How sanguine Stewart and Decatur really were about a third try after the first two had failed is unknown, but they went ahead with their plan for the *Intrepid* to stand in towards Tripoli about five miles ahead of the *Syren* and anchor after dark near the eastern end of the chain of rocks that formed the harbor of Tripoli. There the *Intrepid* was to wait until the *Syren* came up or boats from the *Syren* joined her. After midnight the

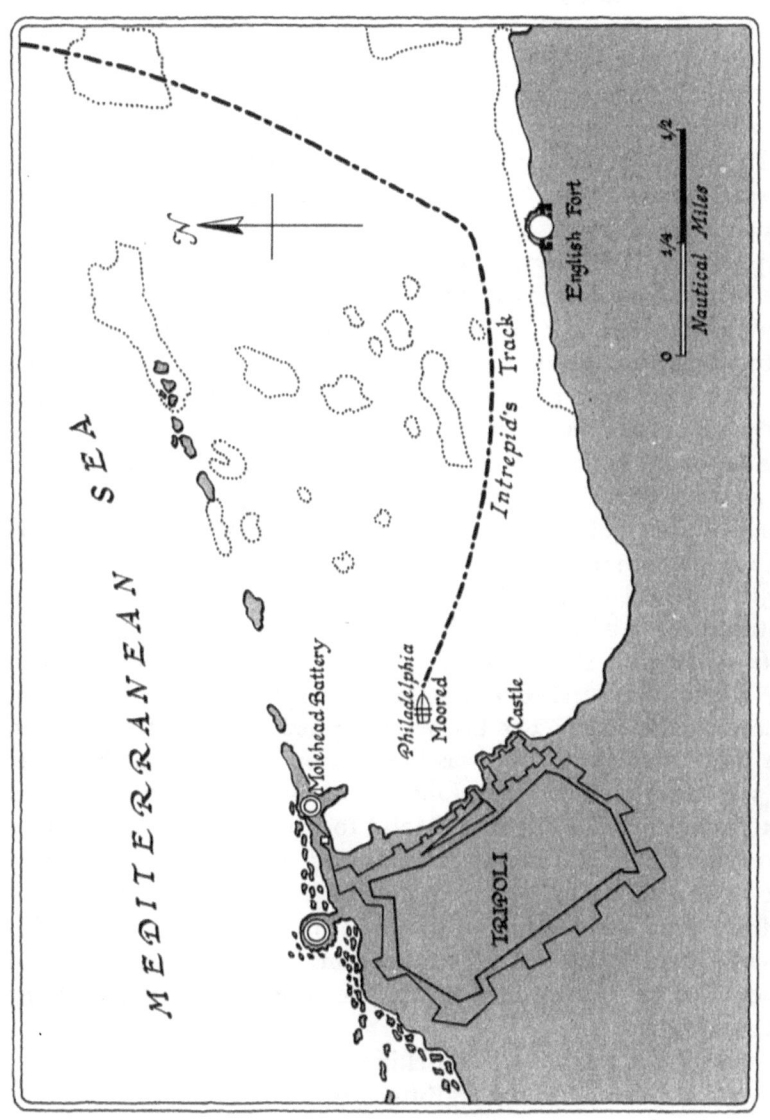

THE *INTREPID*'S ATTACK ON THE *PHILADELPHIA*, 16 FEBRUARY 1804
Redrawn from a Chart made by Midshipman William Lewis
Depth of water along the *Intrepid*'s route over the submerged shoal at the
N.E. corner of the chart varies between eleven and fifteen feet.

Intrepid and the *Syren*'s boats would head for the place where the *Philadelphia* lay anchored within 400 yards of the Pasha's castle and about 700 yards from the Molehead Battery.

February 16th was a pleasant, clear day with a fine breeze. At 11:00 a.m. the *Intrepid* stood in towards Tripoli for the third time. A drag made of ladders, lumber, and extra spars was out astern to hold the ketch back, while a lubberly-looking spread of canvas created the illusion that the *Intrepid* was straining to reach the harbor before dark. Her appearance was that of a small trader from Malta. She was flying English colors. Only six or eight men were allowed on deck at a time, and they were dressed as Maltese. Apparently the disguise was working: answering colors were raised over the British consulate in the town.

It was already dark when the *Intrepid* approached the harbor entrance. Perhaps two and a half or three hours would still be required to reach the *Philadelphia*. The wind had grown fainter, and Decatur, fearing that, if he waited several hours for the *Syren*'s boats to join him, it might die away entirely before he could reach his target, decided to abandon the original plan and go ahead alone. If a calm forced the *Intrepid* to get out her sweeps, the large number of men concealed on board — seventy-odd officers and men plus a midshipman and nine men from the *Syren* who had joined her on the 15th — would be revealed. He would risk trying to carry out the mission without the rest of the men from the *Syren*.

The *Intrepid* sailed into the harbor at 7:00 p.m. Except for the men in Maltese dress, all hands stretched out on the deck to conceal themselves. Absolute silence was the order. The breeze continued light. As the *Intrepid* bore down on the *Philadelphia*, she was hailed from the frigate: the Tripolitan guard was on the alert. Speaking in Arabic, Salvador Catalano explained that the ketch had come from Malta to load cattle for the island's British garrison[2] and had lost her anchors during the recent gale. Might she make fast to the *Philadelphia* until morning? Permission granted. A boat put out from the *Philadelphia* with a line; the *Intrepid*'s boat carried a line out towards the *Philadelphia*. The two lines were tied together, and the *Intrepid* began to haul in towards the frigate. Slowly the distance closed between ketch and frigate.

One of the Tripolitan guards was watching the approaching ketch over the *Philadelphia*'s bulwarks. A light glinted off some cutlasses concealed under the *Intrepid*'s thwarts. *"They are Americans! They are Americans!"* shouted the guard. The captain of the Tripolitan guard called out to ask if there were any Americans in the ketch. No, answered Catalano coolly, this is a Maltese vessel and has only Italians and Englishmen on board.

The line was hauled in farther. Once more the suspicious guard shouted:

"They are Americans! They are enemies!" At last the guard's fears convinced his captain, and the latter shrieked for the tow line to be cast loose. This crisis was too much for Catalano, and his self-possession snapped for a moment. "Board, Captain! Board!" he yelled at Decatur. If the men had acted on Catalano's impulse, most of them would have fallen into the water between ketch and frigate. Decatur refused to panic. His voice boomed out: *"No order to be obeyed but that of the commanding officer."* Discipline was restored for the few critical seconds till the ketch was almost touching the *Philadelphia*.

"Board ! ! !" shouted Decatur as he jumped for the frigate.

"The effect was truly electric," recalled Surgeon's Mate Lewis Heermann years later. "Not a man had been seen or heard to breathe a moment before; at the next, the boarders hung on the ship's side like cluster bees; and, in another instant, every man was on board the frigate." No shots were fired. Everything was handled with edged weapons. Resistance was feeble: there were only seven or eight guards on board the frigate.[3] Two Tripolitans escaped over the side, four or five were killed, and one guard was taken prisoner at the end of the action.

Each boarder carried a three-inch piece of sperm candle, the wick of which had been charred and soaked in spirits of turpentine. Four of the men had been equipped with two lanterns apiece. These lanterns were lighted before the boarding began and were carried aboard the *Philadelphia* in double bags, joined by a strap which passed over one shoulder and connected under the other arm, thus leaving the sailor with both hands free for combat. All the boarders had, during the planning for the attack, been assigned to squads. Each squad, operating under its officer-leader, was to ignite its candles from one of the lanterns and set fire to a designated section of the frigate — but not until Decatur gave the order.

As soon as the Americans were in complete possession of the *Philadelphia*, prepared combustibles were passed on board from the *Intrepid*.

> The gun deck was all of a sudden beautifully illuminated by the numerous candles of the crew [wrote Surgeon's Mate Heermann]. The squads, supplied with combustibles, repaired to their stations. After the lapse of a few minutes Captain D[ecatur] demanded at every hatchway, from forward to aft, whether they were ready, and — on being answered in the affirmative from below — returned to the hatchways as before, giving the word succinctly at each, "Fire!" — in order of insuring the simultaneousness of setting fire to every part of the ship alike.
>
> Enveloped in a dense cloud of suffocating smoke, the officers and men jumped on board the ketch, and Captain D., bringing up the rear, was literally followed by the flames, which issued out of the hatchways in volumes as large as their diameters would allow, and, seizing soon after on the rigging, ran up

to the mastheads and presented a column of fire truly magnificent. Every haste was now made to get from alongside. The bow was shoved off with long sweeps, and the jib hoisted. But the jib took the wrong way, and the ketch fell to again. The flames now rushed with great violence from every gunport and scupper hole alongside to within a few feet of the sails of the ketch, which were of cotton. The same efforts were at several times repeated — and with the same result each time. The main boom likewise had got entangled in the quarter gallery. But, notwithstanding the most imminent danger of being consumed by the devouring element they had kindled, the crew were so delighted with the "bonfire" that, perfectly careless of danger, they indulged in looking and laughing and casting their jokes. But Captain D., seeing the utmost peril of his situation, leapt upon the companion and, flourishing his sword, threatened to cut down the first man that was noisy after that. This uncommon effort restored order. Boats were got ahead to tow the ketch round, and, the main boom being cleared, she escaped after a considerable detention — with the loss, however, which was sustained in the bustle, of the Tripoline flag taken by Captain D. on board the frigate and one of the frigate's boats, which had been secured and got adrift afterwards.

In laying the ketch on the lee side of the ship every precaution had been taken that, nautically considered, was calculated to pay off her head with ease. But the phenomenon of combustion had been entirely lost sight of until practically demonstrated that the consumption of air to support combustion must be drawn alike from every part of the periphery of a circle toward the column of fire in the center.

The escape was complicated, too, by the gunners in Tripoli and on the nearby cruisers. During the critical part of the attack — when the frigate was boarded and captured — they had remained quiet. But about the time the firing of the *Philadelphia* was consummated and the raiders were beginning their retreat, the Tripolitans began a harassing fire with cannon and muskets on the Americans, who could be heard giving three hearty cheers over their own success. American luck held: only one of Decatur's men had been wounded in boarding and capturing the frigate; now the only harm done the escapees was a shot that passed through the topgallant sail of the *Intrepid*.

As the *Intrepid* pulled out of the harbor, Decatur, the young officers, and the crew could look back on the spectacular sight of the *Philadelphia* afire from one end to the other and up to her tops. About midnight her cables burned through, and the hulk drifted into shallow water where it continued to blaze furiously. During the retreat from the harbor, the *Intrepid* met the *Syren*'s launch and barge with the reinforcements that were supposed to have taken part in the action, but had never caught up with the *Intrepid* because of Decatur's decision to begin the attack well ahead of schedule. Between 12:30 and 1:00 a.m. the *Intrepid* and the boats rejoined the *Syren*, which welcomed them with repeated cheers, and both ships made sail for Syracuse. At 6:00 a.m. the two were forty miles away from Tripoli and the light of the burning *Philadelphia* could still be seen from the *Syren*'s deck.

III

The destruction of the *Philadelphia* made Preble more optimistic about future operations. "My heart is fixed on obliging him [the Pasha of Tripoli] to sue for peace, and I hope yet to make him consent to sign a treaty as favorable as ours with Morocco without a cent for peace or tribute," he wrote the Secretary of the Navy, as soon as he learned of Decatur's success. "I hope before the end of next summer to make him give me the officers and crew of the late frigate *Philadelphia* without a ransom."

Almost immediately a fresh crisis blew up to mock his optimism. Three days after he arrived at Malta in the *Constitution,* on 3 March, to transact some squadron business before going off Tripoli, three Tunisian warships came in to repair and equip for a cruise against an unidentified enemy. Within hours of their arrival, Preble heard a rumor that the Bey of Tunis was about to declare war on the United States.

Circumstances gave credibility to the rumor. On the evening of 5 March, Charles Stewart in the *Syren* had hailed a stranger flying the flag of one of the Barbary States. She replied, truthfully enough, that she was from Tunis and bound to Malta. However, when Stewart asked permission to board her to verify her identity — as the treaty of 1797 between Tunis and the United States authorized him to do — she refused to cooperate. Stewart's suspicions were aroused. But, since the stranger and the *Syren* were of nearly equal strength, he decided not to attempt to enforce his rights. Instead, he dogged her to Malta, and reported her hostile attitude to the Commodore. Preble wrote Robert Smith:

> Had I met with her, I certainly should not have suffered her to pass without asserting the right our treaty gives us of examining passports, as Tripoline vessels often visit Tunis, and wear similar colors to the Tunisian vessels. You may rely with confidence that I shall do all in my power to protect our commerce and punish those who infringe on our rights. I hope I shall not be accused of a want of prudence in the measures I adopt.

About a week later, a boat from the principal Tunisian cruiser brought some officers alongside the *Constitution*. One of the officers asked for Preble, and, as the Commodore later told it,

> in a haughty, imperious tone demanded that I should turn all our prisoners up for his inspection to enable him to judge if there were any Tunisians

among them. I replied to him that I had released the only one of his nation that had fallen into my hands. . . . This was not satisfactory, and, as I did not think the request or the manner in which it was made very decent or proper on their part, I refused to gratify them or degrade ourselves by a compliance. They then moved off, but observed that it would not be long before they should have plenty of us.

A traveler returning from Tunis repeated the rumor that the Bey was planning to declare war on the United States early in the spring. Ships were said to be hurriedly fitting for sea in Tunisian ports. Difficulties with Tunis were not unexpected. As early as September Preble had known that the Bey was in a mood to make trouble. When James L. Cathcart had arrived in Tunis to take up his duties as U.S. consul, the Bey had declared he was unacceptable in that capacity and had refused to receive him. More important, the Bey had boldly asked the President to make him a present of a 36-gun frigate. It had been rumored that Tunis would declare war if the President did not comply. Apart from the request for a frigate, the most serious irritant in Tunisian-American relations was Tunis's claim that the U.S. squadron under Commodore Morris had captured about four thousand Spanish dollars' worth of Tunisian property and sold it at Malta. The goods in question had been taken, together with some Tripolitan property, from the Austrian polacre *Paulina* near Malta in January 1803. Every aspect of the seizure was irregular and questionable, and it had soured understanding between Tunis and the United States all out of proportion to the amount involved.

Under the threat of war by Tunis, Preble saw the strategic situation thus: from the best intelligence that he could collect, it appeared that Tunis, a far more dangerous maritime power than Tripoli, had one 36-gun frigate ready for sea, one frigate pierced for either 36 or 42 guns under construction, thirty-two xebecs mounting between 6 and 36 guns each, thirty galleys armed with 1 or 2 guns, and ten gunboats. Preble had two brigs, three schooners, and a frigate with which he had to attack Tripoli, watch Tunis as a potential enemy, and keep an eye on Morocco. If Tunis were to declare war, her cruisers could be expected to capture many American merchantmen, not only because Preble had so few ships with which to protect them, but also because, since individually or in small detachments his brigs and schooners could be overwhelmed by the large Tunisian cruisers, he would have to keep his squadron united.

If Preble was to deal with Tripoli and the Tunisian threat, he would have to have more ships. Writing privately to his friend Secretary of War Dearborn, he said he ought to have two more frigates and two more brigs if he was to beat the Tripolitans so that "we never shall have occasion in future to pay them a cent for peace or tribute. This I pledge myself to do, or perish in the attempt." [4]

Officially, Preble asked the Secretary of the Navy for a minimum of two frigates and a vessel to relieve the *Argus* at Gibraltar, and assured him that, with this small addition to its Mediterranean squadron, the United States would be able to dictate peace terms to Tripoli before July, and to deter Tunis from going to war. He pointed out that all the Barbary Powers were strengthening their naval forces, and unless something was done to check their ambitions, they would soon become an even more serious problem in the Mediterranean. For this reason, it would be better if the administration were to add three frigates to his squadron: "If you send three, be assured we shall eventually be gainers by it, as it will give us a consequence with the Barbary States which we want."

After surveying American interests in and around the Mediterranean, Preble told Robert Smith: "Our commerce in the Mediterranean is immensely valuable and daily increasing; and, should the war continue between the European Powers, we may engross nearly the whole business by keeping up a respectable force to protect our vessels. I hope we never shall consent to pay Tripoli for peace or tribute; and, should Tunis make war, that we never shall have peace with them but on the same terms. If we are now too economical with our naval force, it will only lead to greater expenses in future."

"I feel extremely desirous of serving my country," he concluded one of his appeals for reinforcement. "Give me the means and I will do it, by rendering the purchase of peace or payment of tribute totally unnecessary in this Eastern World. In the meantime, everything shall be done that our little squadron is competent to, and, I hope, more than can be reasonably expected from it."

Late in March Preble sailed for Tripoli. From there, he intended to go to Tunis: he must try to deal with the Tunisian problem before it deteriorated into war.

IV

About this time, a new element was injected in the diplomatic situation vis-à-vis Tripoli. When Robert R. Livingston, the American minister at Paris, learned of the grounding and capture of the *Philadelphia,* he solicited — without instructions or authorization from Washington, and, indeed, contrary to the President's wishes[5] — French assistance in freeing the American prisoners and in negotiating a new treaty between the United States and Tripoli. In response to Livingston's request, Talleyrand, the Minister of Foreign Relations, instructed Bonaventure Beaussier, French consul at

Tripoli, to act as mediator between the two warring countries. Preble had been officially notified on 18 March of French willingness to intervene, and the most important purpose of his call off Tripoli was to establish contact with Beaussier and investigate the possibilities of a negotiated settlement with Yusuf Caramanli.

But was Preble in a mood to make the most of French mediation? The destruction of the *Philadelphia* had reinforced his uncompromising attitude towards the Barbary States. French goodwill might be helpful in negotiations with the Pasha, Preble thought, but he intended to rely chiefly on American strength. He was not yet ready to open his campaign. When reinforcements, which he expected from the United States within the next few weeks, arrived, and he had borrowed or hired some gunboats and bomb ketches, then, beginning with Derna, he would capture and destroy the towns and settlements along the coast. The refugees would be driven into the city of Tripoli, which Preble would blockade and bombard, while his smaller vessels were destroying the gunboats and cruisers in the harbor. He was sure that by the end of July these harsh measures would have forced Yusuf to accept the only principles on which Preble was willing to negotiate a new treaty: peace without the payment of money or the promise of regular stipends, and release of the American prisoners without ransom.

Nor was the Tripolitan government ready for realistic negotiations at that moment. In January Gaetano Andrea Schembri, the Tripolitan consul at Malta, had approached Preble — not in person, but using Patrick Wilkie, Agent Victualler for the British fleet at Malta, as a go-between — and represented himself as authorized by Yusuf Caramanli to open exploratory talks with the United States. After Wilkie had carried several messages back and forth between commodore and consul, Schembri indicated that peace could be secured if the United States gave Tripoli a schooner in exchange for the *Philadelphia* and paid $100,000 for the release of all the prisoners. Preble considered these terms close to acceptable, and gave Schembri tacit, indirect encouragement to continue the negotiation. But by late March Preble was convinced that Schembri had been spinning a complicated web of intrigue of which he, Schembri, was to be the principal beneficiary. As with all Preble's quasi-secret dealings during his Mediterranean command, records are fragmentary, vague, and contradictory, but it is certain that Schembri was playing his position two or three ways, any one of which could have resulted in personal profit for him.

Before Decatur destroyed the *Philadelphia*, negotiations between Tripoli and Tunis over her future had reached an advanced stage. Since Yusuf could not use her effectively, he was to trade her to the Bey of Tunis for two 24-gun xebecs. The Bey was to send a crew to Tripoli and bring the

Philadelphia out under Tunisian colors. Even if Preble had been alerted, he could not have touched her. Meanwhile, the two xebecs, manned by Tripolitans, were to sail from Tunis and go after American shipping in the western Mediterranean before Preble was aware of what had taken place. If the Pasha did, indeed, ask Schembri to approach Preble in January with the peace feelers, including the proposal to exchange the *Philadelphia* for a schooner, he may have done so in order to lull Preble's activity and frustrate any plans he might be making to destroy the frigate. Schembri seems to have had a different idea. He had hoped to buy the *Philadelphia*, using a large sum of money owed to him by Yusuf as part or all of the purchase price, and sell her to Preble. In one transaction, he would have collected the debt the Pasha owed him and, no doubt, made a profit on the sale of the frigate.

Whether or not Schembri had really been asked by Yusuf to approach Preble in January, on 20 February, four days after the destruction of the *Philadelphia*, he arrived at Tripoli and announced that he was authorized by Commodore Preble to negotiate for peace and for the ransom of the American prisoners. Preble was aware of Schembri's mission and had persuaded Sir Alexander Ball, the governor of Malta, to ask Brian McDonogh, British consul at Tripoli, to cooperate with Schembri in bringing the Pasha to propose an amicable settlement or to accept reasonable conditions for peace.[6]

Schembri explained to Yusuf that he had come because of the vital interest he took in the Pasha's glory and to counsel him to make peace with the United States. He described Preble's squadron (perhaps even exaggerated its strength), the additional vessels he was assembling for his summer campaign, his substantial cash resources, and his continuing contacts with the exiled ex-pasha, Hamet Caramanli. The United States cared little whether it went on fighting or made peace, Schembri maintained. He even claimed that Preble was not too interested in redeeming the captive officers and sailors, especially since he planned to punish them for surrendering the frigate by executing them as soon as they were freed!

It was in Tripoli's interest to negotiate a peace settlement without delay, argued Schembri. Peace would thwart Preble's plan of assisting Hamet to overthrow Yusuf. When Preble had disbanded the force he was collecting for the summer campaign, and the American squadron had left the Mediterranean, Tripoli could start the war all over again with a greater chance of success and, thus, exact a fitting revenge for the burning of the *Philadelphia*. Despite his contention that Preble had small interest in ransoming the *Philadelphia*'s crew, Schembri sought to persuade the Pasha that the best plan would be to conclude a treaty that did not call for the payment of a lump sum of money for the peace settlement or for an American annuity, but did include a heavy ransom for the prisoners. In Preble's name, Schembri offered first a ransom of $150,000, then $200,000, and gave the impression that he was prepared to go up to $300,000 — even though he had led Preble to think $100,000 or $120,000 would be acceptable.

Schembri, the negotiator, made a bad impression on the Tripolitans. They judged him inept; they thought his arguments shot through with absurdities, contradictions, and falsities: at one moment he contended that Preble planned to shoot the crew of the *Philadelphia,* and at another that he would pay up to $300,000 to redeem them. Nevertheless, Yusuf called his council into session. After some discussion, the council decided to decline Schembri's mediation and ransom offers on the grounds that, since he was in the Pasha's service, it would look as though Tripoli had made the overtures, and that would compromise the dignity of the regency. But, as if to show that he was not dissatisfied with Schembri's services, Yusuf presented him with a valuable breast pin.

While these discussions with Yusuf were going forward, Schembri had been lining his own pockets and serving his employer, the Pasha, in a far more practical manner. Preble had issued passes to the British authorities at Malta permitting them to send merchantmen to Tripoli in ballast to purchase and take away a thousand bullocks to feed the garrison and inhabitants of Malta. In his character as a Maltese merchant, Schembri contracted to carry some of the cattle in his ships. Having thus secured some of Preble's passes, he attempted to use them as a cover for carrying cargoes, including military stores, into Tripoli and bringing merchandise out through the American blockade. Thanks, in part at least, to a tip from Richard Farquhar, Preble's small vessels intercepted and captured three of Schembri's ships engaged in this illicit operation, and Preble had the satisfaction of having deprived Schembri of the personal profits from some of his underhand dealings.

When all of Schembri's intrigues had been unraveled, the only serious damage was found to be that while Yusuf Caramanli was thinking of the generous sum of $300,000 he believed Preble was prepared to pay to ransom the *Philadelphia*'s crew, Preble was nearing the Tripolitan coast convinced that, in a few months, he would be able to dictate a peace treaty that involved no payment whatsoever, either for peace or for ransom.

V

A five-gun salute, full shipboard ceremonies, and a dinner concocted from Preble's choicest private stores — the Commodore liked to have such delicacies as partridge in his larder — greeted Bonaventure Beaussier when he boarded the *Constitution* at 2:00 p.m. on 27 March. But in spite of the cordial atmosphere, Preble and Beaussier soon knew that they were far apart on what constituted an equitable settlement of the war between Tripoli and the United States.

Yusuf Caramanli welcomed French mediation, Beaussier began, and had said that because of his regard for First Consul Bonaparte, he would not press for all the advantages which the course of his war with the United States had given him. Preble, on his part, indicated that he was willing to pay a reasonable ransom for the immediate release of the *Philadelphia*'s crew. When that had been done, he said, and he had released the Tripolitan prisoners he held, the war would continue until Tripoli was willing to agree to a new treaty acceptable to the United States. What price would the Pasha expect for ransom alone?

No, replied Beaussier, it could not be done that way. The United States would have to negotiate for peace and ransom at the same time; the Pasha would never give up his American prisoners until he had received money for peace as well as for ransom. Nor would Yusuf be at all interested in exchanging some of his American prisoners for Tripolitans captured by Preble. As for the cost of a settlement: some of the small European powers had recently paid large sums for peace with various of the Barbary States; Portugal had paid the Dey of Algiers one million dollars for the ransom of 374 captives. Gaetano Andrea Schembri had told Yusuf that Preble was prepared to pay, perhaps, $300,000 to ransom the American prisoners. The Pasha had been at great expense preparing his defenses against American attacks. For all these reasons, Beaussier supposed he might demand between $250,000 and $500,000 to negotiate a new treaty and release the prisoners.

Beaussier probed: "What is the maximum sum that you can offer to conclude a treaty of peace and to obtain a deliverance of the prisoners?" Preble declined to answer. He informed Beaussier that he was assembling a formidable squadron and, in six weeks, would return to Tripoli, reinforced with gunboats and bomb ketches. Then he showed Beaussier models of the gunboats and bomb ketches he planned to employ.[7] If there was no hope for a reasonable negotiated settlement, this squadron would attack the city of Tripoli. More than that, he was going to send one of his ships up to Alexandria and bring Hamet Caramanli back to Benghazi, where he would be established and supported by American power. The terms of a new treaty? The United States did not intend to pay anything for a peace settlement, and would not agree to pay an annuity of any kind. He wanted, Preble said, to free the American prisoners in Tripoli, but would rather sacrifice them all than agree to peace terms "incompatible with the honor and dignity of the nation."

Beaussier took the position that, however successful Preble's naval campaign might be, however much shipping he sank and destroyed, the war would be expensive for the United States to support and would only add to the cost of the ultimate settlement. The American prisoners would remain securely locked up in the Castle, from which Preble could not release them by naval means. The more damage Preble did to Tripoli, the higher the price Yusuf would demand for making peace. Besides, could Preble be sure his attacks would be successful? Rumors had already reached Tripoli that the American squadron was preparing to bombard the city. Yusuf had been energetically and effectively strengthening his defenses. Since the French consul was fond of reusing his more effective prose passages, he probably touched on these defensive preparations in words not too different from those he had written his own government earlier in the month: "The Pasha is ready to receive the enemy, whatever type of hostilities the enemy wishes to attempt. His port bristles with cannon, quite independent of the twelve gunboats that defend the approaches. Now [since the burning of the *Philadelphia*] this prince does not rely on the vigilance of anyone: he shows himself day and night and inspects everything." [8] At the end of three hours of discussion, Preble and Beaussier parted without having reduced the differences that separated them.

Preble was discouraged. As he judged the French consul, the mediator, far from being impartial, was entirely on Yusuf's side. It seemed to Preble that all the consuls in Tripoli were intriguing against the United States: they were aware that if Yusuf made peace with the United States, he would immediately select one of their nations as his next victim. Preble was sure that France wanted the United States to be at war with both Tripoli and Tunis, since an American blockade of those ports would seal off the source of provisions for the British on Malta. Summing up his talk with Beaussier, Preble wrote in his diary: "We must, therefore, depend wholly on our own exertions for effecting a peace, which can only be done by an increase of our force and a number of gun and mortar boats to batter down his [the Pasha's] castle and town."

Preble's assessment of the French government's attitude was wide of the mark. France seems to have been sincerely willing to use its influence to bring about a peace treaty between the United States and Tripoli. Apart from the spirit of détente in French-American relations arising from the American purchase of Louisiana, French self-interest lay in the maintenance of American trade with Italy and the south of France, and that trade was being hampered by fear of Tripolitan cruisers and the uneasy state of

American relations with Tunis. The United States was a major neutral carrier whose services were necessary to France during the current European war. The French Foreign Ministry believed the chief difficulty in mediating the Tripolitan war would be the American negotiating position: the United States wanted to make peace with Tripoli through French influence, but appeared unwilling to pay anything for a settlement. On the whole, the war had gone badly for the United States, which fact, according to the established customs of the Barbary States, would cause Yusuf to think that the United States should pay him well for peace and would make him strongly resist a gratuitous settlement. French influence could probably procure a gratuitous settlement, but the resulting peace would be insecure and short-lived. Talleyrand had authorized Beaussier to use Bonaparte's name, wishes, and influence to bring pressure to bear on Yusuf to make peace, but to do it adroitly enough to avoid placing France in the position of having to take action or suffer loss of prestige if Yusuf refused to fall in line with Bonaparte's desires.[9]

While Preble waited for some indication from shore of a desire for further discussions, he cruised off Tripoli for two more days, amusing himself by racing the *Constitution* against the *Syren*. However, on the evening of 29 March a northwest gale suddenly sprang up and forced the *Constitution* out to sea for maneuvering room. Instead of returning to Tripoli, Preble, taking the *Syren* with him, steered for Tunis and his problems there.

VI

Full precautions against a surprise attack went into effect when the *Constitution* and the *Syren* anchored in Tunis Bay on the evening of 3 April. The *Syren*'s Marines were armed, boarding pikes and battle axes were close at hand. In the *Constitution* all hands slept at battle stations. Springs were ready on the anchor cables. Tompions were removed, and the guns cast loose and primed. In this state of readiness Preble's squadron spent a quiet and uneventful night.

When Chargé d' Affaires George Davis boarded the *Constitution* the next day he told Preble that Tunis was still preparing her cruisers for war, but that the situation looked slightly less gloomy than it had a few weeks earlier. For one thing, the destruction of the *Philadelphia* had made the Tunisian government more cautious in dealing with the United States. But the possibility of trouble had not vanished: the Bey was still demanding settlement of the claim for the Tunisian merchandise captured in the *Paulina* by Morris's squadron.

Preble had to grasp another nettle. According to Davis, the Bey would be insulted if Preble did not pay him a formal call, yet if he or any of his officers went ashore, the Bey would almost certainly arrest them to force a settlement of the *Paulina* claim. This was no idle fear: about a year earlier Commodore Morris had gone ashore in Tunis and found himself forcibly detained to insure the payment of a debt owed by the former U.S. consul, William Eaton.[10] Davis offered no advice; he handed the dilemma to Preble to solve.[11]

Preble's conciliatory mood was ascendant. He wrote the Bey and explained that he was not feeling at all well and was anxious to sail from Tunis Bay as quickly as might be, since he had urgent business to transact elsewhere. For these reasons he hoped the Bey would excuse him from landing for an audience. Since the *Paulina* affair had occurred under Commodore Morris, he knew little about it and had absolutely no authority to settle the claim: Consul General Tobias Lear, who did have power to deal with it, was expected from Algiers shortly and, Preble told the Bey, he hoped Lear would be able to negotiate a settlement that would be satisfactory to Tunis.

Davis spent the night in the *Constitution,* returned to Tunis on 5 April, and delivered Preble's letter to the Bey on the 6th. When the Bey said he would not even read Preble's communication until the *Paulina* claim had been settled, Davis told him what it contained. But the Bey was unyielding. "Speak with more reason," he told Davis:

> One commodore takes my property and sells it, makes me promises of restitution which he never performs. A new one arrives who knows nothing of the affair, and the one who will succeed him must certainly know less. I know nothing of your old or new commodore. It is not these I am to seek: it is the flag that plunders me. You say he has not the power to make me restitution. Then I must assume the authority of capturing your vessels and paying myself. But let us not discuss this subject any farther: it will only lead to warm remarks which may have consequences I wish to avoid. Apprize the admiral that the affair must be closed before he leaves the harbor. His answer will guide my conduct.

Preble's attitude, when, late that afternoon, he learned of the Bey's threats, was that he had done all he had the power to do by way of conciliation. "If he should declare war, as he threatens," Preble wrote Davis, "I am confident he must have already resolved on it without this frivolous pretext." While Preble was writing, a storm that made it dangerous for the *Constitution* to remain at anchor in Tunis Bay was gathering to the northward. Preble finished his letter quickly, and ordered the *Syren* to await any developments that might take place on shore. The *Constitution* secured her guns, weighed anchor and, with the wind blowing heavily from the northwest, headed for open water.

When the *Syren* rejoined the *Constitution* three miles north of the island of Zembra on 10 April she brought news of a relaxation of tensions at the Tunisian court. The morning after Preble had sailed, 7 April, George Davis had again called on the Bey and on the Sapitapa, the Bey's prime minister and seal-bearer, to encourage them to be patient until Lear could come to Tunis and resolve the *Paulina* crisis. Although the Bey and the Sapitapa grumbled ominously about the United States forcing Tunis into war, and about how hostile and suspicious appeared Preble's refusal to come on shore, they were in a much less belligerent mood. The Bey had read Preble's letter, and the Sapitapa announced that Tunis was willing to grant the United States six weeks' grace before it must pay the *Paulina* claim.

That reprieve at least gave time for Lear to arrive from Algiers or send instructions on how the *Paulina* affair should be handled. It came at a time when Preble probably needed good news, for he was suffering his first serious illness since he took command of the *Constitution* at Boston. A fever kept him in his cabin, and presumably in bed, from the 6th of April through the 11th. On the morning of the 12th he was strong enough to go on deck as the *Constitution* sailed into Valletta harbor, and by the 14th he had resumed his regular place on the quarterdeck. If Eben Preble had known about this illness he would have been worried, for in earlier years he had seen Edward take unnecessary chances with his health, and had recently written him: "I hope you enjoy your health. You must be attentive to it, as of the first consequence to yourself and important to your country."

VII

A storeship from the United States, the *Woodrop Sims,* was anchored in Syracuse harbor when Preble arrived there from Malta on 14 April. She brought a letter dated 24 January in which Robert Smith notified the Commodore that the Navy Department was sending the frigate *John Adams* to the Mediterranean as a transport with stores and some additional men for the squadron, and that she could be expected to reach Syracuse about the end of April. Unfortunately, the *John Adams*'s usefulness to Preble in his operations would be minimal, since she was coming out armed *en flûte*, that is to say, without her full complement of guns.*

The *Argus,* Isaac Hull, having escorted the *Woodrop Sims* up the Medi-

---

* The term *en flûte* was used because empty gunports made the side of a vessel look like a flute.

terranean, was also at Syracuse, and Preble decided not to let her go back to Gibraltar. He needed a vessel in the Straits to remind Morocco that he was watching, but the touch-and-go situation with Tunis made it even more important to have the *Argus* in the central Mediterranean. Preble intended to send all his small vessels to establish a strict blockade of Tripoli and to keep them cruising off the port until summer, when the *Constitution*, with the gunboats and bomb ketches, would launch an attack on the city. And because he needed more ships for his blockade, Preble reinforced his own squadron by commissioning one of Gaetano Andrea Schembri's ships, the brig *Transfer*, which the U.S. squadron had captured for violating the conditions under which she had been given a pass to enter the blockaded port of Tripoli. The *Transfer* came equipped with sixteen 6-pounders, muskets, blunderbusses, cutlasses, pistols, and everything else required for a man-of-war brig. Preble renamed her *Scourge* and gave the command to Lieutenant John H. Dent.

Ever since his visit to Malta in January, Preble had been edging into negotiations with Tripoli, but Consul General Lear was the person authorized by the administration to negotiate a new treaty with Tripoli. Consequently, in late February Preble had sent the *Vixen* off to Algiers with dispatches asking Lear to return to Syracuse in the *Vixen* to be on hand for any negotiations that might develop, and suggesting that, if he could not come, he send instructions by the schooner.

As Preble had half expected, Lear was unable to leave his post in Algiers but the former Consul General in that city, Richard O'Brien, went back in the *Vixen* to assist Preble as a negotiator. Owing to his long residence on the Barbary Coast, O'Brien could be expected to be thoroughly at home in dealing with the Tripolitans. Moreover, because O'Brien was fluent in the languages of Barbary, his presence eliminated the necessity for interpreters. On 22 April Preble sent O'Brien to Tunis in the *Enterprize* to advise George Davis on negotiations there and on the settlement of the *Paulina* claim, which Lear had authorized to be paid. Preble intended to follow in the *Constitution* in a few days, pick up O'Brien, check into the state of Tunisian-American relations, then sail for Naples where he hoped to secure gunboats and bomb ketches for his summer campaign against Tripoli.

Three days later, the *Constitution* sailed from Syracuse. On the way to Tunis, she called at Malta. The most significant thing Preble did there was to let Hamet Caramanli's agents know that he had abandoned his plan to cooperate with them in helping the deposed pasha overthrow Yusuf. From the time of their meetings in January until his recent decision to drop the scheme, Preble had continued to encourage Richard Farquhar and Salvatore

Busuttil and had led them to think he would support and cooperate with Hamet. Since January a third man, Clemente Fama, or as he was usually called, Mr. Clemente, had entered the conspiracy. Like Hamet's other agents, he was an obscure figure, a young man who apparently had commanded small merchantmen in the Mediterranean trade. He spoke French, but little, if any, English. His uncle, who lived in Tripoli, probably was a supporter of Hamet's; certainly he was busy supplying intelligence to the conspirators.

The plans for joint operations that Preble formed with these three agents of Hamet's varied in their details from time to time during the winter and spring of 1804, but they involved these principal elements: if Preble could spare one of his small cruisers he was to send it to Alexandria, take Hamet on board, and bring him to Derna or Benghazi where the deposed pasha was supposed to have enough of a following to establish himself with the support of one or more of Preble's ships; simultaneously, the army which Hamet was alleged to be able to raise in Egypt would march overland to Benghazi. In an alternate version of this plan Hamet was to march with his army to Derna, where one of Preble's brigs would assist him in securing control of Cyrenaica. From Benghazi Hamet's army was to march against Tripoli while Preble attacked the city from the sea. All of these land movements would have to be completed before the summer heat dried up the springs along the route. In March Preble had considered a plan to attack Derna and Benghazi with his squadron about the middle of May and capture the two towns. If Hamet and his followers had succeeded in marching from Egypt to Cyrenaica by that date, Preble would turn Derna and Benghazi over to them; if they had not, he would destroy the towns and proceed with the attack on Tripoli.

To prepare for Hamet's coming or to lay the groundwork for Preble's occupation of Benghazi and Derna, Busuttil, Farquhar, and Clemente Fama had planned to go to Benghazi under the cover of a trading voyage. A merchantman had been chartered, a cargo for the Benghazi market had been purchased, and thirty or forty men had signed up to go to Cyrenaica in the merchantman to further the conspirators' plans. Preble had been deeply involved in the formation of this plan: he was to send one of his brigs to convoy the merchantman to Benghazi, and he had instructed Hamet's three agents to have everything ready to go on short notice. This small group of revolutionaries presumably intended to capitalize on existing political unrest in Cyrenaica. They and Preble probably knew that when Hamet's successor in the governorship of Derna tried to enter the town, he had been attacked and wounded, and three members of his suite had been killed. It was said that most of the people of Derna were opposed to the new Bey's appointment and wanted to name their own governor.[12] That must have seemed a promising hour for an armed band to land and announce that it had come to restore Hamet Caramanli as pasha of Tripoli.

Shortly before his visit to Malta Preble decided to drop all these plans for joint operations with Hamet. Why, he never explained in writing. He had always told Farquhar and Busuttil that his cooperation depended on the reinforcement of his squadron: there was no word of any from the United States, except the partially armed *John Adams*, and he had not succeeded in finding any gunboats and bomb ketches locally. These facts and his preoccupation with the Tunisian crisis were probably the main reasons why he abandoned the plans he had been making to work with Hamet Caramanli. In addition, there was no evidence that the deposed pasha was actually raising any troops or was in any way preparing to march into Cyrenaica. If Preble decided not to follow through with the schemes of Farquhar, Busuttil, and Clemente Fama, he did not forget the tempting opportunity Hamet Caramanli offered for overthrowing Yusuf and setting up a Tripolitan government dependent on and favorable to the United States.

Late in the afternoon of 1 May the *Constitution* anchored in Tunis Bay, and the next morning Davis and O'Brien came out to her to report the progress of their negotiations with the Tunisian government. The *Paulina* claim had been settled amicably, as Preble had hoped it would be, but the Bey had proved more unreasonable than George Davis had anticipated, and no other progress had been made: the Bey was just as testy as he had been during Preble's last visit to Tunis Bay. Davis had delivered to the Bey a letter from the President. Its tone was friendly and conciliatory, but it politely rejected the Bey's request for a 36-gun frigate. Davis considered himself authorized by Lear to offer Tunis an annual stipend of from $8,000 to $10,000 if Tunis would abandon all other claims on the United States — such as the gift of a frigate — and would guarantee to remain at peace. Although the Sapitapa had given Davis to understand in no uncertain terms that he considered the proffered annuity a paltry one, and had hinted that the Bey intended to refuse it, the Tunisian government had so far neither accepted nor formally rejected the proposition.

In spite of this report, Preble was certain there was no immediate danger of war. The Tunisian ports were so exposed to attack from the sea that the Bey would not dare to begin hostilities as long as the United States had a squadron cruising the Mediterranean. To remind the Bey of the U.S. presence it would be necessary to divert the *Constitution* every so often from the operations against Tripoli. If only he had more frigates! No word from Washington of the substantial reinforcement he had been expecting so confidently. In Barbary affairs everything now depended on the outcome of Preble's campaign against Tripoli. "It has become absolutely necessary to our national and naval character in the Eastern World that we humble that regency and bring the Bashaw to our own terms." To do this, Preble must have gunboats and bomb ketches; to get them, he sailed on 3 May for the Bay of Naples.

CHAPTER 12 AUGUST 1803–FEBRUARY 1805

"You know he is not a man who commands his temper."

As the *Constitution* stood towards Naples, the life of the ship followed its daily routine — a routine established by the customs of the service and Edward Preble's orders.[1]

At dawn sailors tumble out of their hammocks on the berth deck. During the winter months they dress in blue jackets and trousers. For hot summer weather their uniform is white duck trousers and frocks, to which, in the cooler weeks of spring and fall, they add white duck jackets. As daylight increases, sails are trimmed, ropes hauled taut, lines that have been trailing in the water unseen during the night are taken up, and the ship's livestock and poultry are fed. Sailors pull off their shoes and stockings, turn up their trousers, and begin washing down the spar and gun decks, the gun carriages, portsills, quickwork, ladders, chains, and the outside of the ship. "The operation of washing decks generally employs all the watch," writes Nathaniel Haraden in the *Constitution*'s log, "and no other duty can be carried on while the decks are washing." Forward in the head, men are carefully scrubbing down the whole area, particularly the seats, and a half-hearted attempt is under way to clean the cables below the head. Soon after 7:00 a.m., if the day is fair, sailors are spreading the awnings over the spar deck. Half an hour later Boatswain John N. Cannon and his mates pipe hammocks up, and the men swarm down the ladders to the berth deck. They move quickly, for they have only twelve minutes to take down their hammocks, fold them portmanteau-fashion as prescribed by regulations, bring them topside, and stow them in the nettings.

Precisely at eight o'clock, the end of the morning watch, boatswains' pipes summon the men to breakfast, and seamen, ordinary seamen, and Marines break up into their messes of six for an hour of food and rest.* At 9:00 a.m. the duty officer sends a midshipman to notify Boatswain Cannon that the breakfast hour is over and to ask him to call the crew immediately and start them on the day's work. From that time until four o'clock in the afternoon the men, working under the supervision of Cannon and his mates (who are armed with rattan canes to bestir the sluggard), are busy at dozens of jobs. The most important duties are taking in or making sail and otherwise working ship. A large part of the forenoon is devoted to more cleaning, this time the berth deck and lower regions of the frigate. During the winter months these spaces are scraped rather than washed, because the *Constitution*'s surgeon, Dr. James Wells, considers the combination of damp decks, enclosed hard-to-dry areas, and cold weather dangerous to health. Nathaniel Haraden meditates in the log: "It is very evident that the necessary duty of cleaning between decks can never be dispensed with over two or three days, but so frequent a repetition of scraping is very injurious to the decks. Yet it is my opinion that frequent washing between decks is worse than scraping. The innumerable inlets between decks, which lead the water to every part of the ship's frame, may be considered (in my opinion) as a reason why all the ships of our Navy have become rotten."

Other tasks are waiting to be done, some one day, some another: mending or altering sails; setting up rigging; cleaning and airing sails to control mildew; restowing booms;** unbending torn sails and bending new ones; scraping down topmasts; making wads; reeving halyards and tackles; painting ship; rousing up, splicing, and rounding a cable; whitewashing between decks; tarring down rigging; blacking yards and bends. And, when all other sources of employment fail, the crew can always be set to the unending task, recorded day after day in the frigate's log, "working up junk"; that is, making gaskets, mats, sennit, points, and other sorts of ropework from pieces of condemned cable.

Entries in the ship's log testify that accidental death is never far away: "Departed this life by falling from the booms into the hold, David Darling, boy. In the first watch committed his body to the deep." And: "At 2 p.m. Charles Berryman, seaman, fell overboard. Brought the ship to, lowered down a boat, and used every means to save him, but in vain, as he sunk

---

* Individual sea chests are not used in the *Constitution* according to Sailing Master Haraden: "Served out canvas bags to the ship's company. These bags were made out of the old foresail which was split on our passage from America to Gibraltar. There are six men to each mess. Each mess is allowed one chest which is considered as belonging to the mess. The other chests, belonging to individuals, are stove up and hove overboard. This arrangement with the chests is actually necessary for the health of the ship's company."

** Nathaniel Haraden comments: "The *Constitution*'s upper deck is very badly constructed for stowing the booms, so that if the boats are stowed low the spars extend so far out in the gangway as to prevent working the gangway guns."

before the boat could reach him." Ironically, many sailors do not know how to swim.

As day officer of the *Constitution,* First Lieutenant Charles Gordon supervises her daily business. He directs the work of the warrant officers — boatswain, carpenter, sailmaker, master-at-arms, gunner; assigns recruits to their watches, stations, guns, and berths; sees that the sailors are properly clothed and equipped; and commands the quarterdeck and forecastle guns when the *Constitution* goes to quarters. During the morning Lieutenant Gordon scrutinizes every part of the ship, penetrating deep into the hold in search of things out of order. When he is finally satisfied that all is clean and nothing amiss to catch Preble's cold eye, he goes aft to the cabin and reports the *Constitution* ready for her captain's inspection.

Surgeon Wells submits to Preble his daily report on the health of the crew. He identifies the men on sick report, their complaints — fevers, diarrhea, rheumatism, hemoptysis, fractures, contusions, abscesses and ulcers, an occasional case of ophthalmia — and gives the names of the convalescents and men discharged from the sick list. About the same time, Captain John Hall fills out a printed form, "Morning REPORT of a Detachment of MARINES, commanded by Captain JOHN HALL, on board the United States Frigate CONSTITUTION, Commodore EDWARD PREBLE, Commander." This document gives the Commodore a summary of the condition of his Marines: it shows how many men are fit for duty, on leave, absent without leave, sick, and confined in irons.

As the morning wears on, women are to be seen about the deck.* Henry Wadsworth wrote his friend David Porter, a prisoner in Tripoli, that he was sending him a bundle of books collected from the gentlemen of the steerage, Wadsworth's old flute and paint box, and Midshipman William Lewis's violin, then added: "I believe you are neither *piper* or *fiddler,* but there must be some among you who can pipe and others who can 'dance at the sound of a lute.' But what are you to do for partners? We could send Mrs. Cannon for one. By the bye, she would cut a figure presiding at your tea board. Can't you laugh at the idea?"[2] Mrs. Cannon must have been the wife of Boatswain John N. Cannon, and it is highly unlikely that he was the only man who had brought his wife along.

At least one lieutenant (or the sailing master), two midshipmen, and a quartermaster are on the quarterdeck, day and night. The weather side

* In Preble's time women, most of them the wives of warrant and petty officers, were present in U.S. warships more frequently than is generally realized. Whether or not to allow wives on a cruise was a matter that the Navy Department left to the discretion of individual squadron commanders. Official and semiofficial records simply did not "see" these women; hence, although their presence was probably the rule rather than the exception, there are precious few mentions of them.

of the quarterdeck is reserved for the officer of the watch, so long as Preble is not on deck. But, when the Commodore appears, it is quickly vacated and becomes his exclusive domain, wherein he may pace forward to the mainmast and back to the taffrail in isolated grandeur. No officer or seaman will enter that side of the quarterdeck unless he needs to speak to Preble. Then, if an officer, he will be careful to lift his hat before speaking; if a petty officer or seaman, he will remove his hat altogether and remain uncovered during the conversation. When the Commodore goes below, he is secure in the knowledge that a midshipman will be sent to notify him and request his orders if strange sails are sighted or the weather changes.

When Preble chooses to visit a passing British frigate or has other occasion to leave the ship, ceremony attends both his departure and his return on board: at least two lieutenants and the frigate's midshipmen are on the quarterdeck; six sidesmen attend the gangway; Boatswain Cannon pipes the side; the Marine detachment is drawn up on the quarterdeck under the command of Captain John Hall or Second Lieutenant Robert Greenleaf, and its drummer marks the Commodore's departure or return with three rolls on the drum.

Each half hour, as the last grains of sand run into the bottom of the watch glass, the quartermaster calls the time, the watch glass is turned, and the ship's bell is struck. Every hour, on the hour, the officer of the watch notes in chalk on the log board the speed and course of the ship, the wind direction, and the events since the previous entry. At noon Preble, Sailing Master Haraden, the lieutenants, and the midshipmen appear on deck, instruments in hand, to calculate the frigate's position. When this piece of information has been recorded, Haraden takes the log board and retires to a quiet corner to write up the log for the preceding twenty-four hours. This is Haraden's hour of glory. At one o'clock, his burst of creativity over, he goes to the cabin and presents the logbook for Preble's inspection.

Warrant officers, petty officers, seamen, ordinary seamen, boys, and Marines break off work at noon and take an hour for their ration of pork or beef, bread, rice or peas or cheese. At noon, too, they get the first half of their daily grog ration. The *Constitution*'s regulations require them to drink this standing at the grog tub. This rule aims to prevent the men from trading grog rations among themselves, a practice that contributes to the Navy's greatest discipline problem — drunkenness.* Commissioned officers

---

* Water is issued to the crew on a different basis than is grog. Nathaniel Haraden reports in the log: "Put the ship's company on allowance of water of two quarts per man and served them out kegs, one man in each mess receipting for them. . . . The water is served out to the ship's company under the immediate inspection of one of the master's mates. They are allowed water for boiling their peas and rice and third water to grog, exclusive of the two quarts per day. This allowance is fully sufficient for any man and prevents noise and confusion round the scuttlebutts."

will not sit down to dinner in the wardroom until 2:00 p.m. and, when they do, the senior officer at the table will, as prescribed by Navy regulations, "see that politeness and decency be preserved. He will also pay particular attention to prevent any sort of gaming."

The day's work ends at four o'clock, the sailors gather for their second serving of grog, and then the time is usually their own. Those who want to smoke go under the forecastle, the only place in the ship where burning tobacco is permitted. One or two fiddles and perhaps a fife appear; some of the sailors begin dancing on the spar deck; others start up games of one kind or another; still others assemble around one of the berth deck's better raconteurs.[3]

Somewhat before sunset the crew is mustered at quarters, chiefly for the purpose of discovering if anyone is intoxicated. But the officers are also looking for dirty or slovenly men, men with long, untied hair, and men in ragged clothing. Offenders are admonished to mend their ways, or reported for punishment. Muster over, the livestock is fed, decks are swept, and the *Constitution*'s sides are wetted. Hammocks are piped down. Each man moves to the nettings to reclaim his — they are numbered for identification — and goes below to sling it.

First watch is called at 8:00 p.m. The duty lieutenant checks the roll to make sure all his men are present, and the watch disperse to their posts. Although it is a violation of law for seamen to sleep during their watch, most captains of the Navy permit them to doze off when they are not needed to alter sail or perform other duty. But Preble, having discovered during the spring of 1804 that men who sleep in the heavy dew that wets the deck at night soon turn up on the surgeon's report, orders his watch officers to keep the seamen constantly in motion during their watch.

Promptly at eight o'clock the *Constitution*'s glasses are reset by Preble's watch. The officer of the watch requests Preble's orders for the course to be steered and sail to be carried during the night. Lights are put out at eight o'clock in fall and winter, at nine o'clock during the spring and summer months. The fire in the galley is extinguished except for enough flame to light the matches and lanterns, should it be necessary to go to quarters during the night. Silence is the rule of the ship: the watch goes about its work as quietly as possible to avoid disturbing sleepers. On the quarterdeck alertness and vigilance hold sway. The old *Marine Rules and Regulations* warn: "An essential part of [the officer of the watch's] duty is to keep the sailors always ready, and never to believe himself so secure as to have no accident to fear. . . . The captain shall not suffer the officers of the watch to occupy themselves in any situation in reading or in any other amusement which might interrupt in any manner the continual attention which they owe to the ship and their duty."

II

Aided by only a tiny staff — Purser Noadiah Morris, Chaplain Peter Leonard, and Ship's Clerk John Thompson — Preble carried a great burden of military and diplomatic responsibility. This burden was compounded by his preference for drafting all his own letters, and by his day-to-day involvement in the administration of the *Constitution*. Still, whether his ship was at sea or waiting in port, Preble might find a certain amount of leisure in his day. He could retire to his cabin, select a title from his well-stocked private library of more than one hundred and ten volumes,[4] and read for an hour or two.

Preble's shipboard library, like his mind, was primarily practical and related to his immediate concerns. Seamanship and naval affairs formed the largest category among his books. Carington Bowles's *Universal Display of the Naval Flags of All Nations in the World,* David Steel's *The Elements and Practice of Rigging and Seamanship,* two volumes of *The Naval Chronicle,* the unofficial journal of the Royal Navy, *The Art of Defence on Foot with the Broad Sword and Sabre,* by C. Howorth, as well as the English translation of Jacques Bourdé de Villehuet's *The Manoeuverer or Skilful Seaman, Being an Essay on the Theory and Practice of the Various Movements of a Ship at Sea as well as of Naval Evolutions in General* — all British publications, it should be noted — indicated that he had a respectable professional library. The worn condition of his first American edition of John Hamilton Moore's *New Practical Navigator* showed that it had been heavily used.[5] Robert Liddel, *The Seaman's New Vade Mecum, Containing a Practical Essay on Naval Book-keeping, with the Method of Keeping the Captain's Books and Complete Instructions in the Duty of a Captain's Clerk,* apparently was never far from Preble's desk; that is, when it was not being used by Noadiah Morris, Peter Leonard, or John Thompson. As the title indicates, the *Vade Mecum,* another British publication, was a complete and thorough handbook to navy paper work — a tome of more than 400 pages that included instructions and sample forms for preparing sick books, lists of convoys, lists of killed and wounded, instructions on the preparation of a purser's accounts, examples of a letter to the captain requesting a survey on spoiled provisions and of an affidavit to be made in the event of shipwreck, as well as the method for making a signal book. John Malham's two-volume *The Naval Gazetteer* provided geographical information needed by a navigator: descriptions of ports, straits, and islands of the world; sailing directions; and instructions for anchoring in different roadsteads. *A Treatise on Practical Navigation and Seamanship*, by William Nichelson, was the work of a British sailing master who, like Haraden, had a good opinion of his own skills; naming names, he explained how ignorance, carelessness, and poor seamanship had led to disasters at sea, and contrasted them with his own experiences in saving ships from perilous situations.

Emmerich de Vattel's *The Law of Nations* stood on Preble's shelf, though the Commodore's five-volume set of the *Laws of the United States* was probably consulted more frequently, since it included the treaties between the United States and foreign powers.

History was represented by David Hume's *History of England*, by Vincent Mignot's *The History of the Turkish or Ottoman Empire from Its Foundation in 1300 to the Peace of Belgrade in 1740*, and by Jean Jacques Barthélemy's *Travels of Anacharsis the Younger in Greece during the Middle of the Fourth Century before the Christian Era*, the last a description of ancient Greece written as if it were a travel narrative by a fictitious Scythian named Anacharsis. *The Naval, Commercial, and General History of Great Britain*, by John Payne, with its emphasis on British naval history and the rise of British sea power, whose five volumes were on loan to Lieutenant John Smith of the *Vixen*, also belonged to Preble.

As in most eighteenth-century libraries, travel was well represented. John Barrow's *An Account of Travels into the Interior of Southern Africa in the Years 1797 and 1798* was there, as were the two best-known English accounts of Sicily, Henry Swinburne's *Travels in the Two Sicilies* and Patrick Brydone's *A Tour through Sicily and Malta*. These works served as guidebooks to the American officers when they explored Sicilian cities and the surrounding countryside. Two accounts of Egypt — Thomas Walsh's *Journal of the Late Campaign in Egypt* and Dominique Vivant Denon's *Travels in Upper and Lower Egypt . . . during the Campaigns of General Bonaparte* — were products of the recent French and British campaigns in that region, but Preble may have acquired them because they contained descriptions of Malta.

Belles lettres interested Preble much less than did history or travel, and he had but slight acquaintance with the current English literary scene. Samuel Taylor Coleridge arrived at Malta in May 1804 and shortly thereafter became private secretary to Sir Alexander Ball, the governor. Coleridge and Preble met many times, but if Preble was aware that Coleridge was a rising young figure in English letters, he seems to have been unimpressed. Literature was represented in the Commodore's collection only by Alexander Pope's translations of Homer, by some Bernardin de Saint-Pierre, and by the works of Laurence Sterne.

One book was saved for the moment when Preble and his dinner guests pushed back from the oval table in the cabin and were ready to entertain themselves for an hour by singing. While the waiter filled the glasses once more, Preble would go to his bookshelf and take down *A Collection of Songs, Selected from the Works of Mr.* [Charles] *Dibdin, to Which are Added the Newest and Most Favourite American Patriotic Songs*. Preble's voice was strong and he sang well. He loved naval and patriotic songs.

III

"On his first entrance in a ship of war every midshipman has several disadvantageous circumstances to encounter," wrote Thomas Truxtun in one of his essays on the training of naval officers:

> These are partly occasioned by the nature of the sea service and partly by the mistaken prejudices of people in general respecting naval discipline and the genius of sailors and their officers. No character, in their opinion, is more excellent than that of the common sailor, whom they generally suppose to be treated with great severity by his officers, drawing a comparison between them not very advantageous to the latter. The midshipman usually comes aboard tinctured with these prejudices, especially if his education has been amongst the higher rank of people. . . . Blinded by these prepossessions, he is thrown off his guard and very soon surprised to find, amongst these honest sailors, a crew of abandoned miscreants, ripe for any mischief or villainy. Perhaps, after a little observation, many of them will appear to him equally destitute of gratitude, shame or justice, and only deterred from the commission of any crimes by the terror of severe punishment. He will discover that the pernicious example of a few of the vilest in a ship of war is too often apt to poison the principles of the greatest number, especially if the reins of discipline are too much relaxed, so as to foster that idleness and dissipation which engender sloth, diseases, and an utter profligacy of manners.[6]

Truxtun's convictions about the foundations of discipline in a ship of war were shared by almost all naval officers of Preble's day: most members of a ship's crew were inclined to good behavior, but there was always a hard core of dedicated troublemakers, if not criminals. A somewhat larger group of men was just as ready for mischief as was the hard core, but was deterred from breaking the rules by fear of severe punishment. The criminal element could corrupt the behavior of the entire crew. Strict discipline was the only way to hold these unruly forces under control. Although Preble never had much of a theoretical nature to say about discipline, his practice shows that he, too, shared these convictions: to maintain discipline he relied about equally on two punishments — confinement in irons and flogging.

On an average day in the *Constitution*, Master-at-Arms John Burchard would have under his charge two or three men in irons. Sometimes the number would be as low as one or as high as eight.[7] More men were confined for drunkenness than for any other single violation. One particular morning found seven members of the *Constitution*'s Marine detachment in irons, sobering up after a spree. The next most common offenses were probably desertion and whatever might be covered by the phrase *neglect of duty*. One crew member was locked up for accidentally dropping a marlinspike from the rigging, another for slashing a man with a knife. Usually, prisoners were confined in irons for periods ranging from a few days up to two or three weeks. One of the longest sentences on record was that of Hugh McCormick, seaman, who spent fifty days in irons after attempting to desert. In some cases confinement in irons was a man's whole punishment; for others a flogging climaxed a week or two in confinement. The sternest punishments were those of repeaters, men who appeared to be confirmed troublemakers. On 16 December 1803 a Marine, George Crutch, was flogged twenty-four lashes for embezzling a pair of shoes and selling them. Seven weeks later Crutch was in trouble again. This time he had stolen a watch while on his post, thrown it overboard to escape detection, and then lied about the theft. His punishment was one of the severest Preble ever ordered — forty-eight lashes followed by four months in irons.

The basic legislation under which the U.S. Navy operated, "An Act for the Better Government of the Navy," passed in 1800, forbade any commanding officer on his own authority to flog a sailor more than twelve lashes; whippings in excess of that were supposed to be awarded by courts-martial. Despite the intent of the law, Preble, and most other captains, had a device for getting around the twelve-lash limit: since crime usually involved violation of several regulations, Preble would award twelve lashes for each offense. For instance, a sailor found guilty of drunkenness was also guilty of stealing his beverage from the ship's stores or of smuggling it into the *Constitution*; because of his inebriation, he would be unable to do his job and could be charged with neglect of duty, too. By assigning twelve lashes for each offense — drunkenness, theft or smuggling, neglect of duty — Preble could raise the punishment to thirty-six lashes.

Floggings were held at irregular intervals in the *Constitution*. Sometimes a month or more would go by between punishments. But in one eight-day period, all hands were summoned to witness punishment on three occasions. Unless there was urgent need to inflict exemplary punishment on a flagrant violator, as in the case of Marine George Crutch, Preble usually waited until there were from two to five offenders awaiting punishment before ordering the floggings to take place. Just as drunkenness was the most frequent cause for men being confined in irons, so it was the most frequent offense for which men were flogged; neglect of duty was the second most common, then theft, followed by desertion. Preble normally ordered floggings of twelve, twenty-four, and thirty-six lashes, twenty-four lashes being the most common punishment; twelve lashes were given somewhat less frequently, while thirty-six were awarded regularly but sparingly. Rarely would Preble order as few as six lashes, and the forty-eight-lash punishment was an extreme reserved for the most intractable offenders.

The harshest flogging Preble ordered or approved was that of Thomas Ayscough, seaman, who was punished for drunkenness, embezzlement, disobedience, and neglect of duty, with forty-eight lashes administered on 23 November 1804. A week later, 29 November, the ship's sheep were found to have been fed poison. Four of them died at once. The "smooth-faced villain" (Nathaniel Haraden's phrase) who had committed the crime was not immediately identified, but Ayscough gave himself away by attempting to desert a few days later. Caught and accused, he admitted his guilt. On 4 December Ayscough was given sixty-four lashes for the poisoning of four sheep, attempted desertion, and drunkenness; 15 December he received forty-eight additional lashes for the sheep-poisoning incident; and a final twenty-four on 28 December rounded out a total of one hundred and thirty-six lashes.

Preble's temper was as notorious as ever. One evening Stephen Decatur received this note from the Commodore: "Your men on shore for the purpose of fitting your rigging were this afternoon most of them drunk. This must undoubtedly have happened in consequence of the negligence of the officers in charge of them. I request you to make the necessary enquiry respecting this neglect on their part, as I shall most certainly take notice of it. One of your men is in irons on board this ship for impertinence to me." But Preble seems rarely to have ordered a flogging while he was angry. He usually gave himself a couple of days to cool down before deciding the punishment. An exception occurred about ten o'clock one morning when that most dreaded of all cries in a wooden ship, "Fire!" swept through the *Constitution*. But when the investigating officers reached the source of the smoke — one of the officers' cabins adjoining the gunroom — they found the cause of the alarm to be the ship's corporal, James Wallace, who was fumigating the cabin without the permission of the first lieutenant. This incident must have made Preble truly furious, for he ordered Wallace to be punished with an immediate thirty-six lashes "for attempting to fumigate any part of the ship without regular orders, for neglect of duty, and for suffering the rope yarns to blaze."

It is a risky business to compare Preble's discipline with that of his contemporaries. Some officers, Isaac Hull for one, made much less use of the lash than did Preble. By contrast, Preble was more lenient than John Rodgers, who, when he presided at courts-martial, sometimes awarded floggings through the fleet (in hundreds of lashes) and brandings. Preble might be rated as an extremely strict disciplinarian, but not a vindictive or brutal one.*

IV

Three principles governed Preble's handling of disciplinary problems with officers. First, he had a low threshold of tolerance for courts-martial and courts of inquiry. He thought it a waste of time for valuable officers to sit listening to the sordid details of petty quarrels and uninteresting crimes when they should have been busy with more important duties. Invariably Preble sought to resolve disputes or handle disciplinary matters without convening courts. There were no courts-martial in the Mediterranean squadron during his command; only one matter had to be examined before a court of inquiry. Second, if Preble considered the offender a promising officer who had simply made a bad mistake, then counsel, a reprimand, or a minor administrative punishment — say, a couple of weeks under arrest with nothing for the offender to do but think about his misdeed — were the Commodore's preferred courses of action. Third, should the offender appear to be incurable and undesirable as a naval officer, then Preble would try to maneuver him into resigning, using as a club the threat of a court-martial.

* In connection with the comparative strictness of the different captains and their use of flogging, there is, among Preble's papers, an interesting letter from Lieutenant Charles Gordon to Preble, 15 August 1805. Gordon had been ordered to the *Adams* as first lieutenant under Alexander Murray. En route from his home on the Eastern Shore of Maryland to Washington, Gordon stopped at Baltimore to call on Secretary of the Navy Robert Smith. Reported Gordon:

> We had a very lengthy conversation. He gave me every assurance that this should be the last cruise I should be in a subordinate station and appeared, from his conversation, to be disposed to promote me [to master commandant] this cruise in consequence of Commodore Murray's deafness and inactivity, supposing it would require an officer invested with power equal to a captain to discipline his crew and maneuver the ship. The Secretary observed that Murray's ship had always appeared to his discredit in point of discipline and cleanliness, the cause of which had always been attributed to his first lieutenants. "Now," said he, "that cannot be an excuse, as *you* have already established your character." I thanked him for the compliment and felt myself particularly obliged to you. As your ship was the only one I had ever any command over the men, I concluded he had formed his opinion from your report of me. A first lieutenant is generally disagreeably situated with Murray in consequence of his easy disposition; he will not allow his officers to chastise the men. Notwithstanding, I have a very high opinion of him as a brave and experienced officer. He is a cousin of mine, I believe.

One day in May 1804, when the *Constitution* was at Naples, the pinnace was sent in to the mole to wait for Lieutenant Charles Gordon and certain other officers who had Preble's permission to go ashore on liberty on the condition that they be back on board by sundown. Octavius A. Page, the midshipman in charge of the pinnace, wandered off into the city and permitted the pinnace's crew to do likewise. After sundown, when the Commodore happened along, he found the pinnace still waiting at the mole for Gordon and his friends and two of her crew missing. Taking advantage of Page's permissiveness, Gordon's tardiness, and the approach of night, the two sailors had deserted. Preble, highly irritated, arrested Page for neglect of duty, and threatened in no uncertain terms that he would answer for his conduct before a court-martial. Ten days after the incident Page wrote Preble, asking him to overlook his imprudence and release him. Midshipman Page was either shrewd or well-advised in choosing grounds for his appeal that Preble would find difficult to reject: "When you deliberate coolly on my conduct and hear my defense you will, I am confident, acknowledge it not so culpable as you at first thought it, but release me from a confinement which is particularly distressing at this time, on the eve of our expedition to Tripoli, the only opportunity for a long time an officer in our service will probably have of distinguishing himself." Preble's solution was to keep Mr. Page under arrest for five weeks, then transfer him to the smaller *Vixen*.

A disciplinary problem that was handled by the giving of counsel and the administration of a mild private reprimand involved Lieutenant Samuel Elbert of the *Constitution*. Mr. Elbert and another lieutenant had agreed to trade watches for the night of 4/5 July. But the lieutenants and their messmates and friends had arranged a party in honor of the Glorious Fourth, and wine flowed freely. By 8:00 p.m., when Lieutenant Elbert was supposed to appear on deck to take charge of the first watch, he was in such a happy frame of mind that he forgot he had the duty. He apologized to the Commodore, reminded him that it was the first time Preble had ever had to discipline him, and promised it would be the last. Because the 4th of July was the biggest holiday in Edward Preble's year, he was probably willing to forgive a lot committed in the name of celebrating what he called "that great event . . . the anniversary of American Independence." Elbert's apology was accepted and he was restored to duty with the admonition: "The charge of the ship and responsibility for whatever may take place resting with you when in command of a watch, and the general printed instructions absolutely forbidding the deck ever to be left without a lieutenant, etc., should impress your mind strongly with the impropriety of being absent when it is your tour of duty."

Midshipman Thomas Baldwin was a source of distress to Preble from the day he joined the *Constitution* at Boston on 16 June 1803. His conduct was "in the highest degree ungentlemanly, being frequently intoxicated and *always* vulgar in his conversation and deportment." The *Constitution* had scarcely reached Gibraltar in September 1803 before Baldwin committed an act serious enough for Preble to get rid of him.

Baldwin went ashore at Gibraltar on liberty. After visiting one or more dram shops he ran into his shipmate, Midshipman Joseph Nicholson, and Midshipman John B. Nicholson, of the *John Adams*. Together they entered a store, and while John Nicholson was selecting a dirk, Thomas Baldwin shoplifted a sword knot. The trio had left the store and were walking down the street when the shopkeeper came running after them and accused John Nicholson of stealing the sword knot. Indignant, Nicholson denied the charge. A search was made. The stolen knot was found on Baldwin. Nicholson called Baldwin a "damned rascal," or, as Preble put it, "reproach[ed] him with the stigma his conduct had cast on the American officers," whereupon Baldwin drew his sword to attack Nicholson right there on the public street.

At last, Preble had Baldwin where he wanted him. As an alternative to court-martial, he drafted a letter of resignation from the Navy, had it neatly copied by one of his secretaries, and presented it to Baldwin. All Baldwin had to do was sign and hand over his warrant. In reporting the incident to Robert Smith, Preble said he hoped a court-martial could be dispensed with and Baldwin's resignation accepted, because, "I studied the feelings of his family and friends, who are of the first respectability and I think entitled to consideration, especially when the service does not suffer too much by the indulgence." He did not add that, by forcing Baldwin to resign, he was choosing an infallible method of getting him out of the Navy. Convening a court-martial carried the risk of Baldwin being awarded a much milder punishment than dismissal from the Navy.

Sometimes a few cutting words from the Commodore were all that was needed to restore discipline and order. In April 1804 Preble and Charles Stewart became involved in a hot-tempered dispute revolving around whether the *Syren*'s regular sailing master, Alexander C. Harrison, was incompetent, whether the fact that he was in sick quarters on shore had been officially reported to the Commodore, and whether the *Syren*'s acting sailing master, Samuel B. Brooke, should be transferred to the *Argus*, as Preble intended. The disagreement culminated when Stewart, who had something of a reputation for quarreling with his commanding officers, angrily wrote Preble: "It has much surprized me that you are determined to deprive me of Sailing Master Brooke, notwithstanding all I have said to you respecting Mr. Harrison, and I now inform you that if you take him from me you will leave the *Syren* without one." Dipping his pen in ice, Preble replied: "Two masters cannot be allowed to one vessel, nor did I know that two orders for the removal of one was necessary until I received your note of this moment. Mr. Brooke must comply with the order I gave him this morning immediately." And he did.

V

"It is truly melancholy to think of the dismal contrast that [Syracuse's] former magnificence makes with its present meanness," recorded Purser John Darby, who was writing a book on his travels in the Mediterranean:

> The mighty Syracuse, the most opulent and powerful of all the Grecian cities, which by its own proper strength alone was able at different times to contend against all the power of Carthage and Rome, which is recorded (what the force of united nations is now incapable of) to have repulsed fleets of two thousand sail and armies of two hundred thousand men and contained within its own walls what no city ever did before or since, fleets and armies that were the terror of the world — this haughty and magnificent city, reduced even below the consequence of the most insignificant burgh! . . . All their warlike spirit is lost at this day. The present inhabitants are the most lazy, idle, indolent people on the face of the earth and don't deserve the name of a nation.

The officers of Preble's squadron saw in their base ancient grandeur and modern degeneracy.[8] On liberty, they wandered over the sites of the old quarters of Tyche, Neapolis, and Achradina: "Almost the whole space which we passed over are now converted into rich vineyards, cornfields, and orchards, the walls of which are indeed everywhere built with broken marble full of engravings and inscriptions, but most of them defaced and spoiled." A beautiful Roman statue of Venus had been recently discovered by the Sicilian archaeologist, Saverio Landolina, and had to be seen by anyone with the smallest interest in the classical world. The Roman amphitheatre and the Greek theatre might be visited. Or, armed with torches and led by an antique Capuchin with a long white beard, the Americans would explore the catacombs and hear with skepticism their guide assert that one passage ran all the way to Catania, forty miles away! Everyone had seen the Arethusa Fountain, for the ships filled their water casks at this great fresh-water spring by the harborside. More likely to attract the officers' derisive attention, according to Washington Irving who visited the U.S. squadron at its base during the winter of 1804-05, was the stream below the Fountain that was "generally crowded by a great number of half-naked nymphs busily employed in washing, and all the stones in the brook are nearly worn through by the custom of beating their clothes on them. These females are seldom remarkable for beauty nor do I think the chaste Diana would deem any of them worthy of being enrolled in her immaculate train."

In the Latomia dei Cappuccini, an ancient quarry whose floor was covered by a luxuriant garden and orchard, they saw the grave of their fellow officer, eighteen-year-old William R. Nicholson. Above the marker proclaiming that Nicholson was "cut off from society in the bloom of his youth and health," some monks had erected a cross. Midshipman Nicholson was killed in a duel with Midshipman F. Cornelius de Krafft during the afternoon of 18 September 1804. Legend was to grow up that they had fought over a Syracusan beauty, but the real cause of the duel was an insignificant quarrel: an alleged insult by de Krafft to Nicholson.[9] From the Latomia the touring officers might climb to the Capuchin monastery on the rock above, where the monks — again according to Washington Irving — would offer them "a small pitcher of wine, making at the same time very strong exhortations to sobriety and temperance, observing that a little wine was good but to drink much was both injurious and sinful. I do not know how far their advice would have been followed had not the execrable taste of the wine forced us to comply with it. It surely carried its persuasions to sobriety along with it."

And there was urban Syracuse: "But heavens! What a change!" cried Irving. "Streets gloomy and ill-built, and poverty, filth, and misery on every side. No appearance of trade or industry. No countenance displaying the honest traits of ease and independence. All is servility, indigence, and discontent."

The nobility were ostentatious and indigent. Over and over again the Americans told the story of the grand party given by Stephen Decatur at which one of the guests, a certain Baron Cannarella, attempted to steal two silver spoons, a glass, and some sugar. He was thwarted by the alertness of one of Decatur's servants who, as the Baron was about to secrete the articles on his person, stepped up to him, held out his tray, and said: "When you have done looking at them, Sir?" Priests were everywhere; it seemed as though churches must occupy one-third of the city. "In one," wrote Purser Darby, "we were shown some ancient relics which they told us were of Our Savior and several of the saints, and they pretended to show us a piece of dried flesh set in rich diamonds, which they said was a part of Our Savior's hand. And many such stories they tell you and pretend to be facts, and they no doubt believe them. But we are not quite so superstitious." From the terraces of convents and the galleries of convent churches beautiful young nuns peeped, giggled, waved their handkerchiefs, called, and blew kisses to Preble's officers as they walked through the streets and visited the churches. And the Americans railed at mores that sent these lovely, eager young girls unwillingly off to convents because their fathers could not afford to allow them to marry.

Among the lower classes poverty took a harsher form. One observer said that five-sixths of the population would be better off out of existence. Another described them as poor, servile, dishonest, and abominably filthy. Ralph Izard said that he knew of more than twenty men, women, and children who had starved to death in the streets. A noisy crowd of beggars followed the Americans as they walked the city. With darkness came the danger of crime. During the first weeks after Preble established the base at Syracuse, his officers were frequently attacked in the streets at night. But the would-be attackers soon learned that the Americans were armed and fully capable of defending themselves. It came to be said that anyone could walk the streets any time of night in safety — provided he spoke English. That was an exaggeration: in October 1804 the naval shore hospital was attacked by thugs. Windows were smashed; Dr. John W. Dorsey, the surgeon, was assaulted; two patients were robbed; and a third, who attempted to defend himself, was stabbed seven times. Only one of the attackers was captured; the others sought and obtained sanctuary in a church.

Life at Syracuse did have its pleasant side. Sicilian women made the American officers feel welcome. "Gallantry here is pretty much upon the same footing as in every other part of Sicily," Purser Darby reported from Palermo. "If anything, it is carried to greater lengths. However, a breach of the marriage vow is no longer looked upon as one of the deadly sins, and the confessor falls upon easy and pleasant enough methods of making them atone for it. . . . The ladies of Palermo are certainly not excelled by any in the world for their fondness for gallantry, and it is a fact that they not only at Palermo, but in every part of Sicily and Malta, give the preference to the American officers to any other nation in the world, their own not excepted." And "one of the most beautiful women in Naples and a princess . . . said that she had rather be the friend and companion of a brave American officer than the wife of the first prince of the blood."

Preble's establishment of his base at Syracuse rejuvenated the city economically. Merchantmen called at the port in growing numbers. More money was in circulation. Two new hotels in the English style of innkeeping had opened to take advantage of the American trade. The Syracuse opera boasted the best company of singers in all Sicily, for the word had gone out to opera houses throughout the island that the U.S. officers were in the habit of throwing money on the stage for their favorite performers.

The prima donna, Cecilia Fontana Bertozzi, was supported "in a very handsome manner" by the *Scourge*'s commander, Lieutenant John H. Dent.

For all of that, the officers in the squadron would rather have taken their liberty at Malta. Everything was better there. The opera company, for example, was superior to the one at Syracuse. The music was finer and the performance better. As Darby saw it:

> Their dancers are capital performers. . . . [The] dress of the female dancers are white silk drawers [that con]fine and fit them as tight as their skin, over which is thrown a loose thin muslin dress, which reaches only as low as their knees, their whole form and shape exposed to view as much so as if they were in nature's dress, and their actions and gestures are very wanton indeed. I think they would by no means (at first view) be pleasing to the delicacy of the American ladies. I must confess I was very much struck with their appearance at first and looked with astonishment at some of the ladies who sat [nearby], but they appeared not to be affected.

The U.S. squadron's all-important role in the reviving economic life of Syracuse armed Preble with enormous power and influence over the government of the city. It would be too harsh to say that he used his power in a callous and brutal manner, but it is true that he was utterly without subtlety in forcing the local authorities to conform to his will.

Preble's irritation with, and contempt for, governor Marcello de Gregorio grew hand-in-hand. He claimed that Gregorio begged him for some beef as a present, then turned around and sold it to a Danish sea captain for half its value. Excitable, impatient, vacillating, voluble, aggravating to deal with, Gregorio was the sort of weak person calculated to bring out the worst kind of aggressiveness in Preble. Poor Gregorio! In his behalf it should be said that even before Preble first anchored at Syracuse, Gregorio was cast in the role of a little guy caught in the middle of a fight between two big brawlers, France and England, and trying to placate first one and then the other. After Preble's appearance he had also to deal with the smaller, but equally cocky, United States, whose agents were armed with those seductive and corrupting dollars.

The culminating incident between Preble and Gregorio occurred in April 1804. Some weeks earlier a seaman had deserted from the *Enterprize* and enlisted in a French privateer anchored in Syracuse harbor. Because the officers of the French vessel had promised to protect the deserter, he made no secret of his whereabouts — in effect thumbing his nose at the U.S. officers and telling them, "You can't get me now." Preble was away at sea at the time, and Lieutenant John Smith of the *Vixen*, the senior officer present, could not persuade the governor to force the deserter's restoration. In due time the privateer sailed, and later sent a prize in to

Syracuse. In that prize was the American deserter. Stephen Decatur sent an armed boat to search the captured vessel, and seize his runaway seaman. The last thing Gregorio wanted to do was to give the French any pretext for taking offense, for the air was full of rumors that they were about to occupy Syracuse. So, when the French prize master protested Decatur's action, Gregorio declared that the latter had violated Sicilian neutrality. He ordered the city gates shut and detained Richard Somers and eight other American officers who were on shore. Gregorio's aide-de-camp and another officer, a member of the governor's council, came off to the *Constitution* to announce the governor's action to Preble and explain that the American officers would be permitted to return to their ships when the deserter was put back on the French prize.

"This was ten o'clock at night, and the Commodore in bed," wrote Henry Wadsworth. "You know he is not a man who commands his temper. So in the rage the tables and chairs and Neapolitan officers' hats flew about the cabin, and when the light was again brought in it was some time before these unfortunate messengers could be found. They were detained on board all night frightened out of their senses." Preble made the night signal to clear for action, and the *Constitution, Nautilus, Syren, Enterprize* and *Scourge* remained at quarters throughout the night.

As soon as it was light Preble sent off a letter to Gregorio. He was still so agitated that he neglected to keep a copy of his note, but he is reported to have demanded the immediate and unconditional release of his officers, threatened to appear before the King at Naples to complain about Gregorio's conduct, and promised to blow the town about Gregorio's ears if the shore batteries fired on any of his ships. Gregorio was forced into an undignified retreat: the gates were opened to the nine American officers; the matter of the deserter was dropped; a delegation came off to try to calm the storm, and the governor wrote Preble at least two letters of apology that could be described only as obsequious. Not content to leave it at that, he enlisted the aid of Mrs. Gould Francis Leckie, wife of the most prominent British resident of Syracuse, and she wrote Preble:

> The situation of his [the Neapolitan] court with the French government is such that, without disobeying the orders received, he [Gregorio] could not act otherwise than he has done, though on all occasions it is his wish to convince you of the very high esteem and regard which he entertains for your person and the American nation, the interest of which it will ever be his desire to promote. Let me, therefore, beg of you that if you go to Naples you will not represent his conduct in such a manner as to injure or perhaps entirely ruin a man whose weakness is ever the cause of those disputes which arise more from the bad advice of those about him than from any evil intention of his own. You will have the goodness to answer the present as soon as possible

that I may calm the fears of the governor who, though he affects indifference, is terribly frightened.

At this point Preble judged that what he termed his "humiliation" of the governor had gone far enough, but he rumbled to Mrs. Leckie: "I am confident the governor could not have received any orders from his court to protect deserters from the United States squadron to oblige the French government or to insult our flag by forcibly detaining our officers on shore. . . . He certainly has a very singular way of discovering that attachment to the American nation which he professes to have for it." Having achieved his purpose, he no longer had any intention of mentioning the matter at Naples. He was prepared to dismiss the affair forever with one grand gesture to Mrs. Leckie: "The governor, in having prevailed on you to become his advocate, has acted wisely for once in his life; for be assured, Madam, it will ever afford me the highest satisfaction to have it in my power to oblige you." *

But it did not end there. The sour fruit of this incident was an increas-

* Did Preble's difficulties with the governor of Syracuse bring him to advocate the acquisition of permanent overseas naval bases by the United States? In a letter to his old friend Stephen Decatur, 12 October 1819, Gould Francis Leckie wrote:

> You may remember how intimate a footing I was on with Commodore Preble. . . . I believe he used often to communicate to you the conversations we had together on various political subjects. Shortly after your successful return from Tripoli, where you burnt the frigate which had had the misfortune to run ashore on that coast, the Commodore obtained the loan of a flotilla of gunboats from the Neapolitan government. The following year, on a request being made to have the use of them as last year, he met with a refusal. C[ommodore] Preble was very much disappointed at this business, and it was the cause of the United States sending a flotilla to Syracuse, but you lost nearly the whole summer.
> On this subject I often had many conversations with Preble, and it was on this occasion that I endeavored to gather from him the motives which had induced your government to send an armament into the Mediterranean. It was then he began to see the causes which had prompted the British to possess islands and posts in various quarters of the world. It was then he felt that the United States must either abandon foreign commerce to more enterprising nations and become simply an agricultural state like the Chinese or tread in the steps of the British and Dutch. The subsequent misunderstandings which took place at Syracuse showed him that to depend on a friendly port on every occasion was not quite eligible. The want of a place for stores obliged him often to purchase them with great trouble, expense, and delay, besides having to contest with all the caprices and bad faith of the agents of the arsenals as well as the bad choice of articles.
> On this subject Commodore Preble was, I remember, fully impressed; and I am not sure if he ever showed you a memoir which I wrote him on the necessity of the United States having a port or island of their own in the Mediterranean if they chose to be feared or respected. He thanked me very much for the trouble I had taken and was shortly after succeeded by Commodore Barron.10

This letter was written fifteen years after the Preble-Leckie conversations, and whether it truly presents Preble's thoughts or whether Leckie was projecting his own opinions is impossible to tell. None of Preble's surviving correspondence mentions the idea, and the memoir that Leckie prepared for Preble is not now among the Edward Preble Papers.

ingly blatant disregard for any of the laws and regulations of Syracuse that did not please Preble's subordinates. And subversion of law and order was carried out in Preble's name. "Although we had great power at Syracuse before, yet now we are uncontrolled," said Henry Wadsworth. "We never perform quarantines, and, if any of the squadron in the Commodore's absence are refused pratique [clearance by the health authorities], they have only to observe, 'I shall inform the Commodore,' which has the desired effect. We disarm their guards, and open their gates, and break their laws with impunity." American evasion of the quarantine regulations is more fully explained by Samuel Taylor Coleridge, who reported to Sir Alexander Ball that he was surprised to see how quickly a certain English gentleman had reached Syracuse from Malta in spite of the eight-day quarantine on ships from Valletta. That is, he was surprised until he learned that the Englishman had come over as a passenger in one of the U.S. warships, which performed no quarantine, but "have all pratique instantly. . . . It is said that the Americans give false accounts of themselves, but this is not true. No questions are asked that can draw out a true account, and even when, by some accident, the truth is said, the Pratique Master is deaf to all but the answers to the previously concerted questions."

Overburdened with responsibility and work, Preble was unaware of many of the excesses that his subordinates were practicing in his name. The scales were at last struck from his eyes when, after a two-month absence from Syracuse, he received an appeal from Gregorio: "Your presence is very necessary here. It is with the utmost regret I am constrained to acquaint you that the discipline which you enforced is no longer maintained, for which reason continual applications of the inhabitants here are made to *me* for redress. I have waited for your arrival with the utmost anxiety, fully persuaded that the event would restore things to their former good order." By the time Preble became aware of the situation his term of command in the Mediterranean was ending. He could only report to his successor that "great irregularities have been committed [at Syracuse] by some of our officers, for which I hope they may suffer severely. I suspect you will find it necessary to make an example, and the sooner the better."

But if Preble was honest with himself he must have known that ultimate responsibility for the contempt in which his officers held Syracuse's law and order was the example that he, Edward Preble, had set as early as the end of December 1803, when the *Constitution* returned to Syracuse with the captured ketch that subsequently became the *Intrepid*.[11] Because of her contacts with a vessel from Barbary, the *Constitution* was placed in quarantine by the port's health officers. With so much to be done, quarantine was the last place Preble wanted to be. Luckily, an English gentleman named George Dyson, who had lived for some time in another part of Sicily, was making a short stop in Syracuse en route home to Great Britain. When he realized Preble's plight Dyson came alongside the *Constitution* in a boat and told him that, as an old Sicily hand, he knew how to get around irksome quarantine regulations. Preble climbed down into Dyson's boat, and the two of them went on shore where they arranged for the Baron San Marco, head of the local health office, to receive a gift: a carriage and harness costing $250. The U.S. squadron had no more problems with quarantine. Obviously, Mr. Dyson was a good man to have around. Preble appointed him acting U.S. navy agent for Syracuse; his trip to England was forgotten.

CHAPTER **13** JANUARY 1804–JULY 1804

"I value the national character of my country too highly to consent to a peace which the most powerful nation in Europe would blush to make."

Preble had been thinking about gunboats and bomb ketches for his attack on Tripoli almost constantly since the settlement of the Moroccan crisis. "I am in treaty with the King of Naples for a supply of gunboats to assist my squadron," he wrote Mary in November 1803. That was not exactly true: he did not approach the Neapolitan government until several months after the date of that letter. But he seems to have felt a need to build himself up in Mary's eyes and to have filled it by supplying her with analyses of how well he was doing, by descriptions of praise he was receiving from the administration, and by exaggerations like this one. Undoubtedly, the reality on which his statement was based was a meeting between Richard V. Morris and Sir John Acton, prime minister of the Kingdom of the Two Sicilies, which occurred around the end of July or the first of August 1803. Morris had inquired whether Naples would be willing to loan or charter gunboats and bomb ketches to the American squadron if such were needed to terminate the war with Tripoli. Acton had indicated that the Neapolitan government would be willing, but no agreement had been concluded.[1]

Preble's efforts to acquire some small vessels did not begin until January 1804, when he asked American agents at Leghorn to investigate the possibilities for purchasing or chartering two or three bomb ketches and three or four gunboats. These initial soundings in northern Italy and in the south of France proved unpromising. Nothing could be done at Toulon or Marseilles without permission from Paris, and to forward his request there would be time-consuming. Furthermore, it was doubtful that France would jeopardize her relations with Tripoli by allowing the United States to fit out vessels of war in French ports. Suitable boats could be built at Leghorn, but, from the signing of the contract, it would require four and a half months to complete four boats — and that was probably nothing more than a contractor's optimistic estimate. The foundry at Florence would need a year to make four mortars of the kind Preble wanted to arm the ketches he hoped to purchase or hire. And when one of Preble's agents contacted a Jew at Leghorn who owned four second-hand mortars, that gentleman promptly broke them up and sold them for old brass. It was said he feared Yusuf would retaliate against the Tripolitan Jews if he learned that a Jew had sold arms to the United States.

Even before these discouraging reports were all in, Preble had decided that the Neapolitan government was still the most likely source of gunboats and bomb ketches. Since the Kingdom of the Two Sicilies existed in a state of chronic, if neither active nor spectacular, warfare with Barbary, Naples should have no qualms about supplying the United States with arms. Early in February Preble asked his agents in Palermo and Messina, where flotillas of gun and bomb vessels were stationed, to find out if any of the boats could be hired or purchased. Simultaneously, he sent Lieutenant John H. Dent, who was commanding the *Enterprize* while Decatur was absent on the expedition to destroy the *Philadelphia*, up the coast to Messina with orders to "examine the gun and mortar boats there, and endeavor to know if any of the largest size are for sale. Inquire what guns or mortars can be procured, what vessels suitable for gunboats or light cruisers are for sale or charter and at what rate." Hopeful of securing gunboats somewhere, Preble was already enlisting Maltese sailors and pilots. He was looking for men who were familiar with the lateen rig and would be able to train the American sailors in handling it.

Back from Palermo and Messina came word that the sort of boats Preble wanted were indeed stationed in those ports, but that the local authorities had no power to sell or lend them to the Commodore: Preble would have to apply to the central government at Naples. Every person Preble consulted seemed certain the Neapolitan government would let him have the vessels he needed, but by the middle of March he realized that he would have to go to Naples if he wanted to get them.

Preble had no instructions authorizing him to embark on his policy of buying, hiring, or borrowing gunboats and bomb ketches; he did not even have authority to incur the expense of manning and outfitting vessels gratuitously loaned to the United States. In fact, before he sailed for the Mediterranean, he had been warned by Robert Smith against making unauthorized purchases of vessels and taking on enlistments that would exceed the Congressional appropriation. But he would not permit such warnings to paralyze him. He judged that the administration was so anxious for decisive action in the Mediterranean that it would condone what he had done. At Sir Alexander Ball's dinner table in early June Preble claimed that he was having the gunboats and bomb ketches prepared at his own expense, and that he would seek reimbursement only if his attack on Tripoli succeeded — but success was certain.[2] In a sense, the boast was justified, for, whether he was successful or not, the Accountant of the Navy might refuse to accept his account for gunboat expenses on the grounds that Preble had no authority to incur the bills. The event proved Preble a shrewd judge of the administration's mood and of the proper moment to use his own discretion: he did not know it, but Congress had already authorized the chartering or borrowing of gunboats in the Mediterranean for the war against Tripoli.

At 10:00 a.m. on 9 May Preble landed in Naples and immediately called on Sir John Acton.* Prime Minister Acton was sympathetic to Preble's request but explained that, since he could not act on an oral application, Preble would have to prepare a memorial for Acton to lay before the King: if Preble would come to dinner the next day, he could present his formal application then.

As suggested, Preble returned armed with an application for eight gunboats, two mortar boats, supplies of powder, shot, shells, muskets, and sabers, plus eight long brass cannon, 24- or 32-pounders, mounted on ship carriages. In the application, he outlined his campaign. He proposed to mount the brass cannon on two chartered merchantmen and use them as floating batteries. His gunboats and small cruisers would capture or destroy the dozen or more Tripolitan gunboats. That accomplished, the gunboats and floating batteries would enter Tripoli harbor and, from positions so near the shore that the guns in the Tripolitan forts could not be brought

---

* In Naples Preble found, as he had in some other Mediterranean ports, that U.S. diplomatic representation on the consular level was weak and ineffective. The American consul there, John S. M. Mathieu, "a man without energy and without influence," was the bane of American merchant captains and supercargoes trading at Naples. Mathieu was not a citizen of the United States and did not bother to conceal his lack of attachment to the country that employed him: he treated American citizens with hauteur and rudeness. Since his primary job was that of clerk to a merchant of Naples, he devoted only a small part of his time to his consular duties. This resulted in inordinate delays in the transaction of official business — delays compounded by his extreme punctiliousness. He was incapable of making up his mind, and whenever, in his consular capacity, he had to make an important decision, he appealed to this or that Neapolitan or to one of the other consuls to tell him what to do. Rather than approach the Neapolitan government through such an incompetent, Preble depended heavily on Frederic Degen, a Prussian merchant who for many years had handled the business of most of the American firms and ships trading with Naples. Degen was well-informed on the affairs of the United States, and — most important of all — had easy access to Sir John Acton.[3]

to bear on them, open fire on the Castle and the city. The *Constitution* and the bomb ketches, out at sea, would join in the bombardment. The assault on Tripoli was to be preceded by a series of quick strikes on the lesser Tripolitan ports. He would attack Benghazi first, since he understood that Yusuf planned to build and equip light cruisers in that port while Tripoli was blockaded. The tactics would be the same as for Tripoli — gunboats and floating batteries would enter the harbor and bombard the town — and once Benghazi had been destroyed, they would be repeated against Derna and other seacoast towns.

Preble submitted his request; then he waited. "I was so much engaged while at Naples that I did not see Pompeii, Herculaneum, or any of the curiosities for which that country is so much celebrated and so much visited," he wrote Mary later. For the next couple of days perhaps it was not so much a press of duties as the suspense of waiting for Acton's reply that put Preble out of the mood for sightseeing. "The city of Naples is perhaps the most populous in the world for the ground it covers. The houses are five and six story high, and each floor generally inhabited by families that have no acquaintance with each other. The population is estimated at a million of inhabitants for the city and suburbs. It is probable I may visit it again when we have peace with the Barbarians, and I shall be more at leisure to gratify my curiosity by seeing, and yours by describing, whatever may be interesting."

The 11th went by without any word. On the 12th Preble sent General Forteguerri, the Neapolitan minister of marine, a gift of twenty-four small and four large bottles of attar of roses. In his pocket notebook, the expenditure of $56.00 was explained as: "Secret service. Presents to the M^{tr} M^{e} at Naples." [4] Perhaps not coincidentally, on 13 May he was informed by Acton that the King had decided to lend the United States six long 24-pounders,* six gunboats, and two bomb ketches, as well as shot, shells, match, powder, and other supplies and equipment.

For Preble, the next few days were filled with activity as the *Constitution* took on guns, powder, cartridges, round shot, grapeshot, ladles, worms, sponges, and rammers from the arsenal at Naples. Shortly after 1:00 a.m. on 19 May, the loading completed, the *Constitution* got under way for Messina, where she was to pick up the gunboats and bomb ketches. The passage from Naples to Messina was tediously slow and frustrating, but Preble was fascinated by Stromboli, which was sighted as they neared their destination: "This island has a volcano which is continually burning. In

---

* Hardly had Preble received these cannon when, for reasons which he did not explain, he abandoned his plan of mounting them on chartered merchantmen and decided to place them on the upper deck of the *Constitution*.

the day a vast column of smoke is seen continually rising, and in the night the blaze and cinders which it vomits forth are seen at a great distance."

It was 6:00 p.m. on 24 May when the *Constitution* anchored at Messina, and at daylight the next morning Preble was out inspecting the boats that were to be loaned to him. As he had expected, he found the gunboats ready for sea. They were lateen-rigged, roughly 60 feet long, and mounted one long 24-pounder at the bow. This gun pivoted slightly, but essentially it could fire only in the direction in which the bow was pointing. Each bomb ketch mounted a 26-pound cannon forward, and carried a 14-inch brass mortar which, when charged with American powder, could throw a shell, perhaps, two miles, but with the much weaker Neapolitan powder, its range was only a mile and a half. The ketches were in disarray and, although Sicilian carpenters and workmen were displaying encouraging signs of energy in making them seaworthy, they would not be available for active service for three weeks. Preble would have to come back later to get them.

Manned by ninety-six Neapolitan sailors — loaned to and paid by the United States — and by officers and men from the *Nautilus*, whose overhaul at Messina had not been completed, the borrowed gunboats hoisted U.S. colors and weighed for Syracuse on 30 May. Preble followed them down the Strait of Messina in the *Constitution*. Two days before sailing he had written: "If I can reach Tripoli with this force, added to our own vessels, I think it probable the Bashaw's gunboats and cruisers may meet the fate they long since ought to have met with, and his old walls rattle about his ears."

II

Preble's optimism soon wilted. By the time he wrote Mary from Syracuse on the 1st of June he had lapsed into a gloomy mood:

> I arrived here yesterday from Naples and Messina with six gunboats which I borrowed of the King of Naples for an attack on Tripoli. I have also procured from him two bomb vessels which will be ready in about three weeks. I shall then attack the Bashaw's city and castles and hope with this additional force to our little squadron to be able to effect an honorable peace, although I by no means place too much dependence on success. The city of Tripoli is strongly fortified and defended by a large force of gunboats. I am astonished that our government have not sent out a reinforcement of ships. It is now nearly eight months since the loss of the *Philadelphia* and nothing has arrived to replace her. The season for action has already arrived, and, as the fine weather continues but about three months so that gunboats can navigate these seas with safety, I shall be obliged to attack Tripoli under many disadvantages for want of more ships or I shall lose the season by letting it pass off without attempting anything. This I am determined not to do.

To sit idle in that frame of mind while he waited for the bomb ketches would be intolerable for Preble. On 4 June the *Constitution* sailed from Syracuse on one more round of calls at Malta, Tripoli, and Tunis. Preble intended to make a last attempt to negotiate with the Pasha before bringing up his gunboats and bomb ketches for the attack. The imminence of his assault might make Yusuf interested in a peace treaty. If Preble could release the *Philadelphia*'s crew by paying a moderate ransom, he would do so. He was afraid that, otherwise, if he destroyed the ships in the harbor of Tripoli and his attacks were gradually reducing the city to ruins, the Pasha might retaliate by massacring the prisoners. Better a moderate ransom than that.

Preble approached negotiation with a divided mind, an ambivalence distilled in a sentence of his letter to Mary: "I wish to be able to establish peace without the shedding of blood, but, if an honorable one cannot be settled without, some sacrifices must be made." He was anxious to free the American prisoners, but he did not really expect that the terms he was willing to offer would be accepted by the Pasha until Preble's squadron had carried out a destructive attack on Tripoli. The Commodore had set a high standard for the settlement: "I value the national character of my country too highly to consent to a peace which the most powerful nation in Europe would blush to make."

Consul General Lear's formal commission to negotiate peace with Tripoli had been issued before the administration knew about the loss of the *Philadelphia* and the three hundred Americans in Tripolitan prisons. Consequently, he was determined not to come up from Algiers to conduct any negotiations until he received instructions based on the changed situation. But he did authorize Preble to offer terms which he, Lear, thought would be acceptable to the government: ransom of $600 for each prisoner Yusuf held and a small present on the arrival of a new American consul at Tripoli, but no money for the peace treaty itself, and no annual tribute. Assuming that Preble would exchange the Tripolitans he held for an equal number of Americans, settlement on those terms would cost about $140,000, or something more when gifts to cooperative Tripolitan ministers had been figured in.

Lear knew that Preble was independent and relied on his own judgment. He also knew that Preble desired a crushing military defeat of Yusuf Caramanli that would display the United States as a naval power to be reckoned with; that he preferred this solution to a compromise negotiated settlement; and that he was willing to set a higher standard for Barbary relations than was the administration. He tried to caution Preble: "To tell you, my dear Sir, what I think of your conduct since you have been in this sea would appear too much like flattery. I hope and trust you will find our country ready to pay the tribute due to your talents, your patriotism, and your activity. Ardent as I know you would be to gather laurels in your profession, yet I am equally certain that the love of your country would never permit you to sacrifice her peace and interest when they can be preserved with honor and propriety."

But Preble was already committed to the course dictated by his own judgment. For the first time since his arrival in the Mediterranean he put aside the guidance of the diplomatic agents and set out to achieve what he thought should be the policy objectives. Convinced that if he offered the $140,000 authorized by Lear, not only would the Pasha quickly accept it, but the other Barbary Powers would be stimulated to make trouble in the hope of a similar pay-off, Preble refused to offer anything like that amount.

Tripoli looked even stronger on 12 June than it had on 26 March, when the *Constitution* last called there. An armed brig and schooner rode at anchor inside the harbor entrance, and seventeen gunboats were visible. The diplomatic situation seemed no more promising than it had when Beaussier and Preble conferred on 27 March. After that meeting, the French consul had told Yusuf Caramanli that Preble was determined neither to buy peace nor pay tribute, would pay only a moderate ransom for the American prisoners, and was willing to sacrifice all the prisoners rather than negotiate a peace incompatible with national dignity and honor. Beaussier passed on to the Pasha what Preble had said about the forces he was gathering and about his plan to form a united front with Hamet Caramanli.

Yusuf was not impressed. Beaussier hinted that if Yusuf refused to consider terms that would be acceptable to the United States, he might displease Bonaparte. Yusuf dismissed that idea: he respected the First Consul, but he refused to believe that Bonaparte wanted him to throw away all the advantages he had gained in three years of war. Preble's threatened attack? He was ready to defend himself. Hamet Caramanli was no danger: he had no money, could collect no large band of followers, and was well down the road towards alcoholism. Beaussier knew that was an accurate sketch of Hamet. Yusuf began showing signs of ennui, so the audience ended.

Beaussier saw these first conferences as attempts by the two sides to put their maximum demands on record. Only with the next round of meetings would serious negotiation begin, and it promised to be difficult: Yusuf expected so much; Preble was willing to offer so little. But Beaussier was convinced that Preble was temporizing until he received instructions from Washington based on a knowledge of the loss of the *Philadelphia*. He hoped that when those were received Preble would modify his stand and offer a larger settlement.⁵

At 9:00 a.m. on 13 June a white flag was hoisted on board the *Constitution* and when it was answered from the Castle, Preble sent Richard O'Brien ashore in the barge. As the barge approached the landing, its occupants could see some of the *Philadelphia*'s officers walking on the terrace of the Castle. The prisoners waved their hats to O'Brien and his companions, whereupon their guards hustled them out of sight.

A new round of negotiation was about to begin, and Preble's principal interest was in ransoming the *Philadelphia*'s crew. He had instructed O'Brien to offer $40,000 for that purpose and to promise $10,000 in cash presents to the ministers who cooperated in effecting it. In the unlikely event that the Pasha was interested in ending the war, Preble advised O'Brien, he would sign a treaty, "but I cannot pay one cent for peace." The only reward Preble was willing to promise Yusuf for signing a new treaty was a present of $10,000 when a new American consul was appointed.

There is ample reason to think that Preble regarded O'Brien's mission as nothing more than a pro forma attempt to deal peacefully with Yusuf Caramanli, and did not expect any agreement to be reached before he began his attacks. However, if that is not the case, then a series of unfortunate errors was made.

First, the white flag that was hoisted at the Castle only gave Preble permission to send a boat on shore; it did not authorize him to land an emissary. He should have sent an officer ashore to request permission for O'Brien to land and parley. As it was, O'Brien had the humiliation of arriving unannounced and being kept waiting beside the barge for more than an hour while Yusuf and his ministers adjusted to his unexpected apparition and hurried around preparing to receive him.

Second, O'Brien went the wrong way about entering into negotiation. A serious negotiator was expected to come on shore prepared to stay for several days, and to spend the first two or three of them in private discussions with Sidi Mohammed Dghies, the Pasha's powerful and influential prime minister. Dghies would be likely to oppose any negotiator who attempted to bypass him: for one thing, he would expect to be informed, in a discreet manner, that he would be monetarily rewarded for receiving the negotiator's overtures favorably. There was a jarring air of haste about O'Brien's visit. Consul O'Brien made no attempt to see Dghies privately.

Third, Preble had given O'Brien a letter to Beaussier asking him, as official mediator, to support O'Brien in his negotiation, but O'Brien made no effort to contact Beaussier. He contented himself with handing Preble's letter for Beaussier to Mohammed Dghies, and proceeded to conduct the parley with the Pasha on his own.

O'Brien made his offer of $40,000 to ransom the prisoners. The Pasha was insulted: his circle had been telling the Jewish bankers of Tripoli that they expected to squeeze from $600,000 to $800,000 out of the United States in the peace settlement.[6] Those figures were undoubtedly inflated above what Yusuf really expected to receive. On the other hand, when Citizen Beaussier heard about O'Brien's offer, he described it as a niggardly, insulting, and indecent proposal, one that might have been made after a prolonged bombardment had inflicted considerable damage on the city and its inhabitants, but was clearly inappropriate under the circumstances. Yusuf was convinced that Preble's real purpose in landing an envoy to make patently unacceptable propositions was espionage; an offer of $40,000 could only be a ruse to cover a more sinister purpose. Angry though he might be, the Pasha was relatively self-controlled when he told O'Brien that he rejected the $40,000 because he had every right to expect more, and that O'Brien would not be allowed to go into the city, or to see any of the American prisoners or any of the foreign consuls. If that was the only offer O'Brien was prepared to make, Yusuf concluded, there need be no further communication between them. The audience was over in an hour and a half,[7] and by 2:30 p.m. O'Brien was back on board the *Constitution*. Preble summed up the day in his diary: "Thus ended this attempt to release our countrymen and restore peace. We have now nothing to expect from the justice or humanity of the tyrant of Tripoli but must endeavor to beat and distress his savage highness into a disposition more favorable to our views than what he at present possesses."

About the time that Yusuf was terminating the audience, Beaussier broke the seal on his letter from Preble and read:

> I am honored with your letters of the 28th March and 24th of May, which were received but a few days since. Otherwise, I should have replied to them sooner. I shall immediately send copies of them to my government and to our minister at Paris in order that they may be acquainted that the intervention of the First Consul, through the Chargé d'Affaires of the French Republic at Tripoli, is not likely to have the effect which (I believe) they might have expected. I cannot but suppose the First Consul will feel somewhat mortified that through his influence you have not been able even to obtain permission to land the necessary clothing and stores which the American prisoners are suffering for want of. It is probable the First Consul expected his mediation would have had more weight with the Bashaw of Tripoli than it appears to have had.

Beaussier, still viewing the meetings of 27 March as mere preliminaries to serious negotiation, was not a little surprised by what he read. Why should

Preble have turned so violently against him? Preble, on the other hand, had decided by 13 June that French mediation was going to accomplish nothing, at least as long as Beaussier was the mediator. He considered the Frenchman so prejudiced in favor of Yusuf as to be useless in that role.

For his part, Beaussier regarded Preble's approach to the difficult negotiation as abrupt, and his offers to the Pasha as paltry and insulting. It seemed to him that Preble wanted French mediation to result in the delivery of the American sailors on the payment of a token ransom and the conclusion of peace without a cash settlement, and that was expecting too much. Yusuf would not accept such terms, because token ransoms and gratuitous peace settlements would strike at the very foundation of his power: his ability to blackmail the smaller and weaker maritime powers, which found it cheaper to pay him off from time to time than to bear the cost of mounting a war that would eliminate the Barbary States as a threat to their shipping. Furthermore, Beaussier was convinced that Preble had been prejudiced against him by Brian McDonogh, the former British consul at Tripoli, whom Beaussier described as "an evil man, vindictive, an enemy of peace, who — suspecting above all the intervention of France — will seek to take revenge on the regency, on the Americans, and on us by perfidious counsel and insinuations." Preble had met McDonogh after the British consul left Tripoli in March, but whether McDonogh contributed to Preble's disillusionment with Beaussier is not known.

How to unravel this tangle of mistrust? Beaussier did have high regard for Yusuf Caramanli; the Pasha was a strong and efficient ruler, a man of ability. But there is no evidence that Beaussier failed to do all he could to mediate the war. It is to Beaussier's credit that, while Preble lost his temper and wrote more than one scourging letter to the French consul, Beaussier remained in control of his emotions, and, after receiving these missives, immediately sought to reestablish good relations with Preble and to get negotiations, which he considered Preble had broken off unilaterally, started again. Probably, as things stood in June 1804, the situation was beyond the help of mediation. The Pasha would never accept what Preble was willing to offer, unless it were forced on him by a military defeat; and Preble considered mediation pointless unless it could bring about release of the prisoners for a token ransom and a gratuitous peace treaty, "for if we should incline to accede to the Bashaw's demands, we may have peace whenever we choose without the assistance of any other agent than our dollars."

Both Preble and Yusuf Caramanli were ready to let battle settle the issue between them. Three days after O'Brien's abortive meeting with the Pasha, the *Constitution* steered northwestward from Tripoli towards the passage between Kerkenna and Lampedusa. Before he sailed away Preble told Henry Wadsworth, who was acting lieutenant in the *Scourge*, that he would return with his gunboats and bomb ketches in time to begin the bombardment of Tripoli on the Fourth of July.

III

On 19 June the *Constitution* entered Tunis Bay for the third time since April. The Commodore's policy of watching the Tunisians closely had been a success so far: Tunis had not attacked the United States. But his visits there contributed little to his peace of mind, since the omens were as difficult to decipher as ever. The Bey appeared dissatisfied, threatening, and hostile. But what were his intentions?

For two weeks after Preble had sailed from Tunis on 3 May affairs moved along fairly calmly. The Bey continued to insist that he be paid an annuity equal to that given to Algiers, but he did not irrevocably reject Chargé d'Affaires George Davis's offer of from $8,000 to $10,000. Then on the 17th of May he sent for Davis, and, when the American chargé appeared before him, he cried: "Go. Leave instantly my regency. You wish war with all the world, and, since you have resolved to force me into [war], I am contented." This new crisis revolved around the alleged capture of two sandals from Djerba by cruisers of the U.S. squadron, and the failure of the blockaders off Tripoli to honor a passport issued by George Davis. After discussion of the matter, Davis was of the opinion that the Bey did not actually want to go so far as to expel him and commence hostilities with the United States — at least not at that moment: he would be content if Davis would write Preble, insisting that his passports be respected, and relaying the Bey's demand for restoration of the captured craft and compensation of the owners for all damages sustained. Should Preble not comply immediately, the Bey warned Davis, he, the Bey, would pay himself. He would accept no excuses for delays in settling the claim, and if Tunisian subjects were ever again molested by the U.S. squadron he would expel Davis from the regency without a hearing.

Davis faithfully repeated the Bey's complaints to Preble. The matter of the passport proved to have been nothing more than a mistake which Preble had already rectified. But the question of the captured craft puzzled Preble. He could not learn that his squadron had made any prizes similar to the vessels the Bey claimed had been seized. At last, he decided that the Bey must be talking about a small open boat that the *Argus* had captured on 29 April near Old Tripoli and which Lieutenant Isaac Hull, finding her cargo to be only cheap earthenware, had later cut adrift. Preble declined to take the Bey's demand for restoration and damages seriously: when captured, the boat was on her way to Tripoli in violation of the blockade, and she had been defended by Tripolitan troops. Clearly, she was legitimate prey for the U.S. squadron.

During the afternoon of 21 June Preble sailed out of Tunis Bay, bound for Malta and Syracuse, and with his departure the Bey lapsed into silence about the captured vessel — a silence that George Davis considered more ominous than his threats. But Preble was not as fearful of imminent war with Tunis as Davis, in his more pessimistic moods, tended to be. The Commodore continued to think that Tunis would not declare war if his attacks on Tripoli were successful or if the United States reinforced its Mediterranean squadron. Although he maintained that his frequent appearances in Tunis Bay had made the Tunisian government more cautious than it might otherwise have been, Preble could not take all the credit for forcing Tunis to walk modestly. A Neapolitan squadron was already at sea, and there were reports that the Russian and Ottoman fleets were about to appear in the Mediterranean. Tunisian officials feared that any one of those three fleets might be planning an unfriendly visit to their port. At the same time, an internal crisis made it desirable for Tunis to avoid international entanglements. Much of the previous year's grain crop had been lost because of drought. Such grain as was available had tripled in price. Famine threatened. Discontent was rising: assassinations and robberies were occurring in the countryside around Tunis. All of this suggested that Preble would be left undisturbed for the summer to concentrate on Tripoli.

IV

By mid-June Preble had heard that the frigates *Congress, Essex,* and *John Adams* were on their way to join his squadron. News that the *President,* Captain Samuel Barron, and two brigs were also said to be coming out was not entirely welcome, because Barron was senior to Preble in rank and would automatically take command of the Mediterranean squadron if he joined it. However, Preble's qualms on this point were eased by his understanding that the *President* and the brigs were to form an independent squadron under Barron, based at Gibraltar and cruising in the Atlantic, while he continued to command in the Mediterranean.

On 16 July Preble received a copy of the April 19th issue of the *Boston Gazette* and, under the heading IMPORTANT NEWS, he read:

> Commodore Preble's squadron will consist, when the intended reinforcement arrives, of the *Constitution, President* and the *United States* of 44 guns; *Congress* and *Constellation* of 36; *John Adams,* 32; *Syren,* Capt. Stuart of 16;

Argus, Hull of 16; *Nautilus,* Summers of 16; *Enterprize,* Decatur of 14; and *Vixen,* Smith of 14 guns. — In all eleven vessels.

There was nothing about a separate squadron at Gibraltar; it looked as though all the additional frigates were to be under Preble's command.

But Preble had no word, official or unofficial, on when he could expect these ships. With one or two more frigates, success in his attacks on Tripoli would be certain. Of his present squadron only the *Constitution* had guns large enough to batter down the walls and silence the forts of Tripoli. Yet, to wait for reinforcements was unthinkable. Writing from Messina on 5 July, he told Mary:

> I came here a few days since for some bomb vessels and sail tomorrow morning for Tripoli to make a general attack on the town. No addition has arrived to our squadron from the United States since the loss of the *Philadelphia,* although anxiously expected for a long time past. A frigate or two at the present moment would be of great service and insure us success, but as the season will soon be over in which our gun and mortar boats can keep the sea with safety, I have determined to wait no longer. If we succeed with our small squadron, the more honor for those concerned; and I hope we shall, for on that depends the liberation of our unfortunate countrymen and the restoration of peace, which will afford us some leisure moments. Be assured I have experienced none yet.

V

While Preble had spent the spring and early summer taking care of his responsibilities elsewhere and gathering forces to attack Tripoli, his small cruisers *Syren, Argus, Enterprize, Vixen,* and *Scourge* had been maintaining a day-to-day presence of American warships off Tripoli and preventing traffic from entering or leaving the harbor.

Only occasionally would a blockade-runner, usually a small boat, be seen slipping along close under the land. But at daybreak on 7 July the one serious battle of the spring and summer blockade began when the *Scourge* sighted a large galliot close inshore and standing for Tripoli. Hoisting the signal "Discovering strange ships S.S.W.," the *Scourge* gave chase and was joined by the *Argus,* the *Vixen,* and the *Syren.* When the galliot saw that she was being pursued, she put before the wind and ran herself on shore about nine miles to the west of Tripoli. The American ships fired several shots at her, but the Tripolitans and the crew, who had already begun unloading, continued calmly salvaging her cargo of wheat. By this time the wind had died away, leaving the pursuers about 800 yards from the galliot and unable to close the shore. Lieutenant Charles Stewart instructed the American ships to arm and man their boats; from the *Syren* he sent the launch, armed with a 12-pound carronade, and the barge, armed with a heavy swivel, to capture the galliot and bring her off. But the Tripolitans had hauled the galliot up on a reef that prevented the armed boats from getting close to her and made it impossible to bring her off. A large number of defenders, hidden among the rocks and sand hills along the shore, were firing at the boats. While the *Syren*'s launch and barge were replying with carronade and swivel, other boats were towing the *Vixen* within gunshot of the stranded galliot. The *Vixen* opened fire on the coaster but was unable to destroy her. As the morning wore on the number of defenders on shore increased. The battle became a stalemate. Finally, at 11:00 a.m., Stewart signalled the boats to return and tow off their respective ships.

Optimistically, Stewart reported that the galliot had been "cut to pieces," and Henry Wadsworth said she had been "made a riddling sieve" by the *Vixen*'s fire. But the next day she was afloat; the *Syren* and *Vixen* stood in again and opened a brisk fire on her and on the great crowd that had collected on shore. More damage was done the galliot and a number of her defenders were wounded, but the Americans were not able to prevent the Tripolitans from saving the entire cargo.

Most of the time the blockade was dull duty. If it was working properly, ships stayed away and nothing happened. But incidents occurred, or were provoked, that helped keep morale high. Sometimes a blockader would stand in towards one of the forts near Tripoli, or perhaps the battery at Old Tripoli; a brisk exchange of cannon fire would follow — usually doing little damage on either side. Tiring of this, the blockader might run past Tripoli itself, firing a couple of desultory shots as she went. Once in a while, the Tripolitan gunboats would be provoked into getting under way: they would come out to the rocks that formed the northern side of the harbor and trade a few shots with the blockaders, but if the action showed any signs of getting serious, they would prudently retire.

More thrilling for the youthful blockaders was to take a boat and crew on shore at a distance from Tripoli to get a supply of sand for scouring decks before the inhabitants and Tripolitan troops drove them off. A larger invasion occurred on 13 May when Lieutenants Stewart of the *Syren* and John Smith of the *Vixen* set out on a plundering expedition with two or three boatloads of men and landed about twenty miles east of Tripoli. A few coastal guards tried to oppose the landing but were quickly driven off. For a couple of hours Stewart and Smith prowled about on shore without doing any recorded damage, then retreated when armed inhabitants began gathering in force.

On the occasion of his visit off Tripoli in mid-June — the visit during which Richard O'Brien had gone ashore for his audience with the Pasha —

Preble became aware of some of the more irresponsible adventures. As befitted his superior age and wisdom, he was not happy about them, and skirmishes between the blockaders and the Tripolitan batteries and gunboats drew his particular disapproval. They were accomplishing no important purpose, and were using up ammunition, accustoming the Tripolitans to American attack, and giving them an opportunity to practice gunboat maneuvers under fire. Preble forbade the blockaders to become involved in any more pointless shooting matches.

While Richard O'Brien was ashore an old friend hinted that the Tripolitans kept a small schooner and a four-gun galliot constantly manned and ready to sweep out in company with the gunboats to attack any blockader that might get becalmed alone near the coast. Desire to be revenged for the burning of the *Philadelphia* would spur the Tripolitans to act boldly. The *Scourge* was thought to be the most probable target: she had proved to be a dull sailer and had only a few sweeps. Preble warned that none of the blockaders should ever approach Tripoli alone, and that the *Scourge* must be kept at a safe distance from the city. No risks, he said, were to be run "for the sake merely of destroying or cutting off a market or fish boat." This cautious policy was prompted by Preble's faith in his coming attack on Tripoli as the principal measure for ending the war. He would need his small cruisers to participate in that attack. And the last thing he wanted was more American prisoners in the Pasha's hands.

But the important question is: How effective was the blockade? This is difficult to answer. Consul Beaussier said that a blockade of Tripoli could be effective only during the spring and summer months when the blockaders could keep the coast under close surveillance, and even then a vessel could slip through from time to time. Then, too, there was no blockade of the eastern ports of the regency, and some gunpowder and other war supplies from the Levant were being unloaded at Misurata and carried to Tripoli by land. Still another weakness of the blockade was that most of Tripoli's normal trade was concentrated in the hands of a few Jewish merchants, and the Pasha was not averse to seeing the Jews suffer a little by the blockade.

On the other hand, the American officers on blockade duty — who were certainly too sanguine — told themselves that seaborne commerce to Tripoli had been completely interrupted, that such goods as were coming part of the way by sea were being landed at Djerba and carried overland to Tripoli along a route where there was great danger of robbery by Arabs from the interior.

Preble did not regard the blockade as a panacea for the war with Tripoli, but it was an important element in his strategy. To get ahead of the story, the blockade was, by the late summer and fall of 1804, having an effect —

and this in spite of all its defects. The same grain shortage that was producing internal disturbances in Tunis was distressing Tripoli. The city was tottering on the edge of famine, and the blockade made it impossible for Tripoli to import wheat in sufficient quantities to meet its needs. Moreover, as the summer wore on, the Tripolitans made heavy inroads on their stock of powder, and the blockade kept them from fully replenishing the supply and from securing enough military stores from their usual sources in the Levant, even though the route through Misurata provided partial relief.

And so the blockade went on into July — just as essential as ever, but more monotonous since Preble had taken away the occasional excitements. At 1:00 a.m. on 25 July the *Syren* sighted a sail to leeward, and bore away to speak her. She was the *Constitution,* coming down for the attack on Tripoli, and with her were the *Vixen,* the *Nautilus,* six gunboats, two bomb ketches, and a storeship.

CHAPTER 14 JULY 1804–AUGUST 1804

"... I wish to see the time when the Navy shall be supported by all ranks of our citizens. The achievement of glorious deeds will render the Navy popular. If you return to this country covered with laurels ... there will be but one pulse in America on the subject of a Navy. If, on the contrary, you should return without having seen the whites of the enemy's eye, I should not be surprised if the Navy should lose in popularity."

Some five hours after the *Constitution* was spoken by the *Syren* on 25 July, Tripoli came into sight from her masthead, bearing S.W. some 15 or 18 miles, but a northeast wind and a heavy sea setting on shore made it imprudent for Preble's squadron to approach the city immediately. The next day the unfavorable weather moderated, and by noon of 27 July the entire squadron — the *Constitution,* three brigs, three schooners, six gunboats, and two bomb ketches — was twelve miles N.E. ½ E. of Tripoli and standing down towards the city. The moderate breeze from the southeast was right for approaching the port, and the sea was smooth, save for a heavy swell running towards the shore. At 1:00 p.m. Preble counted nineteen Tripolitan gunboats pulling out of the harbor towards his advancing squadron. Apparently they were willing to stand and fight. Preble's ships prepared to cast loose the gunboats and ketches they were towing as soon as the Commodore judged they were close enough to the enemy. But the word did not come. Suddenly the wind shifted from S.E. to N.N.W. Preble held his course to the southwestward until 3:00 p.m. when the squadron, then two and one-half miles north of Tripoli, dropped anchor, and began its final preparations for battle.[1]

From the *Constitution*'s deck Preble could see a troop encampment that had sprung up along the south side of the harbor since his last visit to the town. The defending batteries and forts showed 115 pieces of ordnance covering the seaward approaches to the harbor and city. Unlike the guns in Preble's ships, they had the advantage of being mounted on stable platforms and being protected by masonry fortifications. Several of the Pasha's small cruisers were in the harbor, but the nineteen gunboats that had come

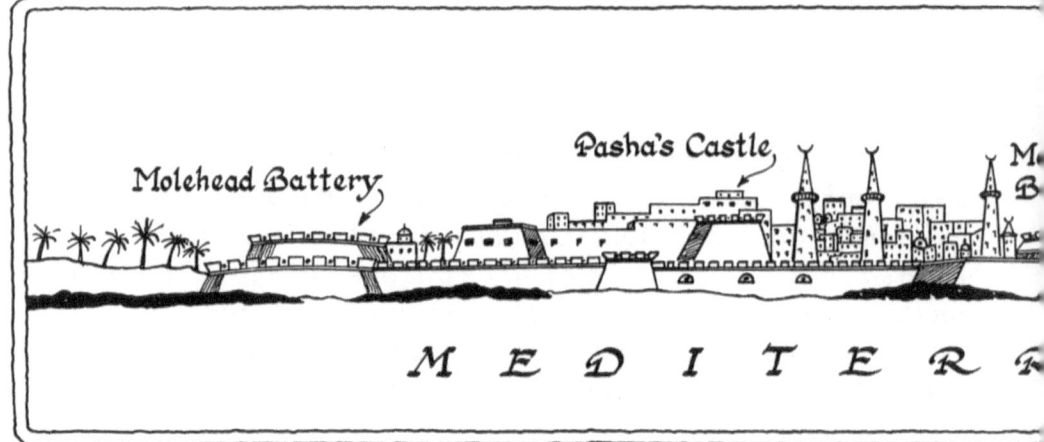

A VIEW OF TRIPOLI IN BARBARY

out as Preble's squadron bore down for the city were to provide Tripoli's chief defense afloat. If these gunboats chose to shelter behind Kaliuscia and Ra's al Zur reefs, the long line of partly submerged rocks that formed the north side of the harbor, it might be difficult for Preble to get at them. And, should gunfire drive them from that refuge, they might still withdraw near the shore and under the guns of Tripoli's fortifications.

Preble was not contemptuous of the city's defenses. His force might not be a match for them. The Neapolitan gunboats had been constructed for harbor defense. They were flat-bottomed and heavy. On the passage across from Sicily, Preble had found them unwieldy and unsafe, unless tethered to larger vessels. His brigs and schooners might be useful for covering the gunboats and extricating them from critical situations, but they would not be much use for the serious work of attacking Tripoli, since they were, to quote Nathaniel Haraden, "considered as vessels rather of show than force." The explosive shells of the bomb ketches were expected to inflict great damage on the city, and the *Constitution*'s guns might prove a match for an equal number of cannon on shore, but the frigate could not attack simultaneously all parts of the city's extended defenses. Preble's difficulties are plain, but his tactical plan of attack is not; although it must have been discussed at length in his almost daily conferences with his senior officers, Preble left no detailed record of it. Clearly, he proposed to have the ketches

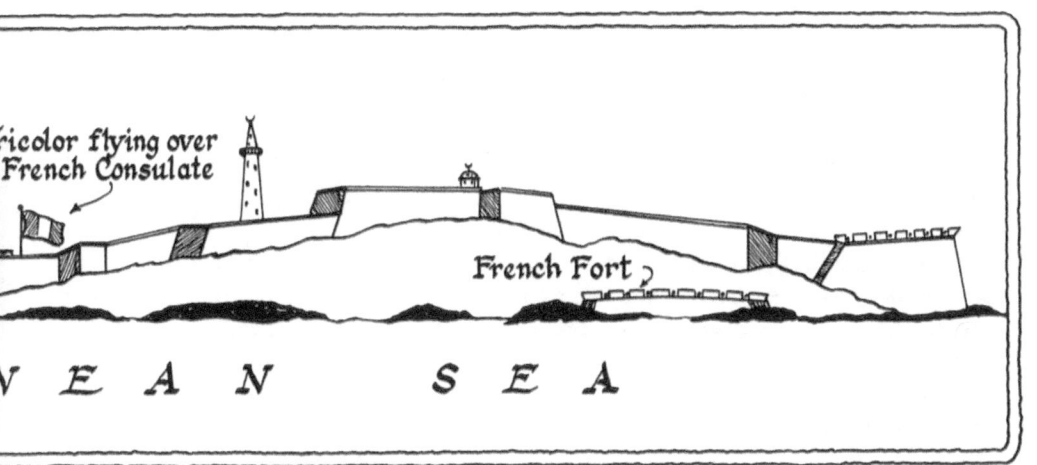

Adapted from Profiles Drawn by Midshipmen F. Cornelius de Krafft and William Lewis

bombard the city while the *Constitution* attacked the batteries. Preble evidently intended, if the enemy gunboats could be destroyed, to send his shallow-draft vessels into the harbor to bombard the city from close range. That might be all the planning he did: he might have intended to see how the Tripolitans responded to his display of force, and develop his tactics as events dictated.

While Preble's vessels were proceeding to their assigned positions and anchoring, the wind, which was still blowing directly on shore, was increasing in velocity. The Tripolitan gunboats had retired to the calmer waters of the inner harbor. By 5:00 p.m. the wind, N. by E., was kicking up such a rough sea that both the *Syren* and *Vixen* had been compelled to let go a second anchor to keep from drifting. Riding at anchor under such conditions was growing increasingly dangerous, and by eight o'clock all the ships of the squadron had raised anchor and were standing to the N.N.W.

For a week the weather prevented the squadron from again approaching Tripoli.

II

Running before fresh breezes from E. by N., Preble's squadron spent the morning of 3 August 1804 approaching Tripoli on a S.S.W. course. At noon the *Constitution* was almost two miles N. by E. from the Molehead Battery. The air was clear, and with his glass Preble could see that the flotilla of Tripolitan gunboats had taken up stations outside the harbor rocks. Flags were flying on the Castle, the batteries, the cruisers anchored in the harbor, and the gunboats outside the rocks. The fortifications were filled with men; roofs and terraces in the city were crowded with spectators, eager to see the anticipated chastisement of the tiny American force.

Preble signalled the squadron to come within hail, wore the *Constitution*, and stood offshore on the starboard tack. While executing this maneuver the *Constitution* cleared for action, distributed water to every part of the ship as a precaution against fires that might be started by hot shot from the enemy batteries, and hoisted the signal: Prepare for battle. As the brigs and schooners, with their gunboats in tow, came within speaking distance, Preble told them of his intention to attack the Tripolitan batteries and gunboats. His plan was simple and flexible: the U.S. gunboats were to stand in and commence firing at the Tripolitan flotilla, and thereafter the action would develop as circumstances and opportunity dictated. Immediately, the gunboats, which had been organized in two divisions, and bomb ketches were manned and made ready to cast loose from their mother ships.

	Gunboats and Bomb Ketches	Commanding Officers	Mother Ships
First Division	Gunboat No. 1	Richard Somers	*Nautilus*
	Gunboat No. 2	James Decatur	*Argus*
	Gunboat No. 3	Joshua Blake	*Argus*
Second Division	Gunboat No. 4	Stephen Decatur	*Enterprize*
	Gunboat No. 5	Joseph Bainbridge	*Syren*
	Gunboat No. 6	John Trippe	*Vixen*
	Bomb Ketch No. 1	Thomas Robinson	*Constitution*
	Bomb Ketch No. 2	John H. Dent	*Constitution*

At about 12:30 p.m. the *Constitution* tacked inshore and stood for the batteries. Within a few minutes Preble saw that the preceding maneuvers had thrown the squadron into confusion and the ships were widely separated. The *Constitution* backed her main topsail to allow the squadron to re-form, but the *Nautilus*, with Gunboat No. 1 in tow, had fallen far to leeward and astern and was having so much difficulty in getting to windward to join the other brigs and schooners, that at 1:15 p.m. Preble impatiently signalled her to make more sail. The afternoon was creeping away; the fickle weather might change for the worse, as it had on the 27th of July. Preble decided that he could lose no more time waiting for the *Nautilus*

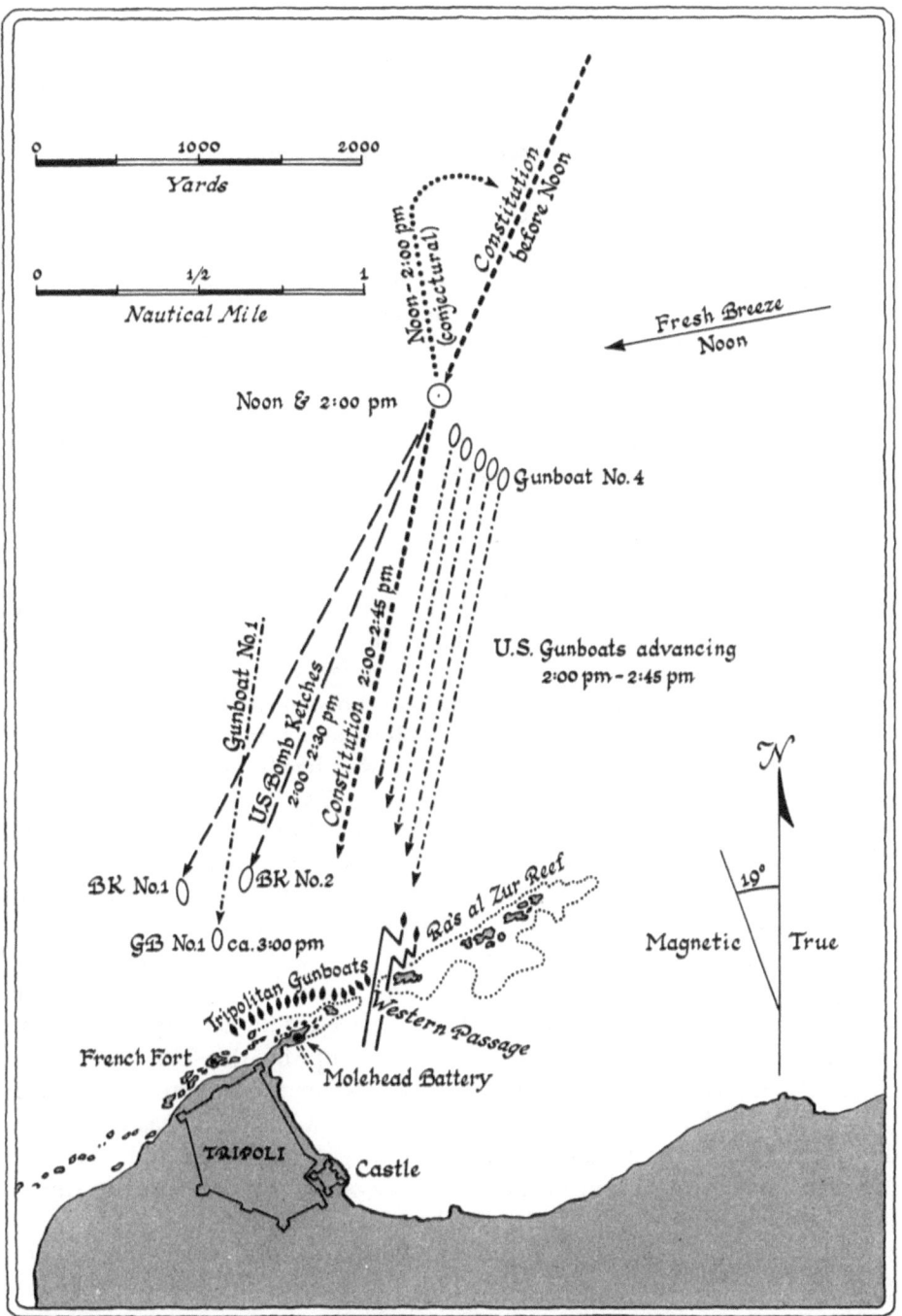

3 August 1804: Movements of the U.S. squadron and the Tripolitan gunboats between noon and about 2:45 p.m.

to close. He signalled the squadron to follow his motions, filled the main topsail, and stood in towards Tripoli once more.

By two o'clock the *Constitution* was perhaps two miles N. by E. from the Molehead Battery. The *Nautilus* was astern of her, and the *Syren, Vixen, Enterprize,* and *Argus* were spread out to the eastward of the *Constitution.* Preble hoisted the signal to cast off the gunboats and bomb ketches. After allowing fifteen minutes for the gunboats to get clear of their mother ships, he signalled them to advance and attack the enemy's ships and batteries. Few, if any, of the gunboats saw the signal. They had taken the signal to cast off as the signal to attack and were already advancing towards the Tripolitan flotilla. The gunboat commanders seem to have neglected to station any specific subordinates to look out for signals from the Commodore, and they themselves were too absorbed in other duties to watch for signals. For the ensuing two and a half hours, the gunboats were out of touch with the *Constitution.* Their commanders were either acting at their own discretion or following the lead of one of their fellows. The outcome of the battle rested on the individual commanders' initiative and discretion.

While the gunboats were advancing on the enemy the ketches were also steering down towards Tripoli on a course roughly parallel to, but west of, the gunboats. At 2:30 p.m. the Commodore hoisted at the mizzenmasthead signal number 179, a blue flag, above a yellow and blue flag, over a red and blue flag, the general signal for battle. Followed by the brigs and schooners, the *Constitution* stood in towards the batteries. The ketches were in position to heave shells into the city; Bomb Ketch No. 1 fired first (2:45 p.m.) and No. 2 followed suit a few moments later. One of these shells exploded close to the Molehead Battery. The other fell in the town. Up to this moment the Tripolitan cannon had remained silent; but as the first shell burst, the batteries and gunboats opened a rapid fire on the U.S. squadron, concentrating most of it on the ketches and the *Constitution,* which had run within less than a mile of the Molehead Battery. The ketches were almost hidden behind the curtain of spray thrown up by the Tripolitan shot. Under the *Constitution*'s starboard bow, the water was agitated to foam by falling balls; although one shot cut the line that a leadsman was using from the port chains, the Tripolitans had yet to get the range and the three American vessels remained unscathed. It was three o'clock and the *Constitution* was maneuvering to bring her batteries into play.

The numerically superior Tripolitan flotilla against which the six U.S. gunboats were advancing was formed up just outside the harbor rocks in a line running roughly northeast-southwest. At the eastern end of the formation, two enemy gunboats under sail were standing off and on the land. In the western passage, or entrance to the harbor, five gunboats were at anchor.

Still farther west and somewhat offshore of them, eleven gunboats were anchored in a crescent formation under the Molehead Battery. Inside the harbor three or four small cruisers were positioned so that their guns covered the principal passages through the chain of rocks.

When the signal was made for the brigs and schooners to cast off their tows, four of them were to the east of the *Constitution* and their gunboats were cast off within a quarter mile of one another. But the *Nautilus* was so far to leeward that Richard Somers in Gunboat No. 1 could exercise no control over the other two boats of his division. In the absence of their assigned commander, No. 2 and No. 3 turned to Stephen Decatur for leadership. As Decatur stood in towards the enemy, four boats, No. 2, No. 3, No. 5, and No. 6, fell in behind him and formed a line extending from southeast to northwest. This little flotilla bore down on the two gunboats under sail outside the rocks, and when Decatur had closed to within point-blank range, opened with round shot. After they had fired eight or nine balls, one of the shot appeared to find its target, for the Tripolitans retreated behind the rocks, where they were inaccessible to Decatur's gunboats.

Stephen Decatur, followed by his brother James in Gunboat No. 2, William Bainbridge's brother Joseph in Gunboat No. 5, and John Trippe in Gunboat No. 6, then bore up and ran to leeward, towards the moored Tripolitan gunboats. Instead of following Stephen Decatur's lead, Joshua Blake in Gunboat No. 3 remained to windward, and so began a series of strange activities that later made him a subject of controversy. A few minutes before three o'clock, Decatur's gunboats closed to within about twenty yards of the five Tripolitan boats anchored in the western passage. Each of the U.S. boats fired a round of canister shot and a volley of musketry. The blast caused the Tripolitans to cut their moorings and pull back into the harbor. The Americans, unable to do anything more with those boats, kept on towards the eastern wing of the eleven Tripolitan gunboats under the Molehead Battery. These Tripolitans did not cut and run. The four American boats closed, firing round shot until they were close enough to deliver a "boarding *dose*"—a canister of 432 musket balls; musket and pistol fire were reserved until the opponents were almost touching gunwales. In a rash move, the Tripolitans fruitlessly discharged their handguns before the U.S. boats were in range, and had not finished reloading by the time the battle broke up into a series of boarding actions.

Stephen Decatur and nineteen men armed with boarding pikes, pistols, cutlasses, and tomahawks, boarded the windward Tripolitan boat, where thirty-six defenders awaited them. The battle was bloody. Decatur was not disposed to give quarter. By the time the Tripolitan flag was hauled down sixteen Tripolitans had been killed, fifteen wounded, and only five cap-

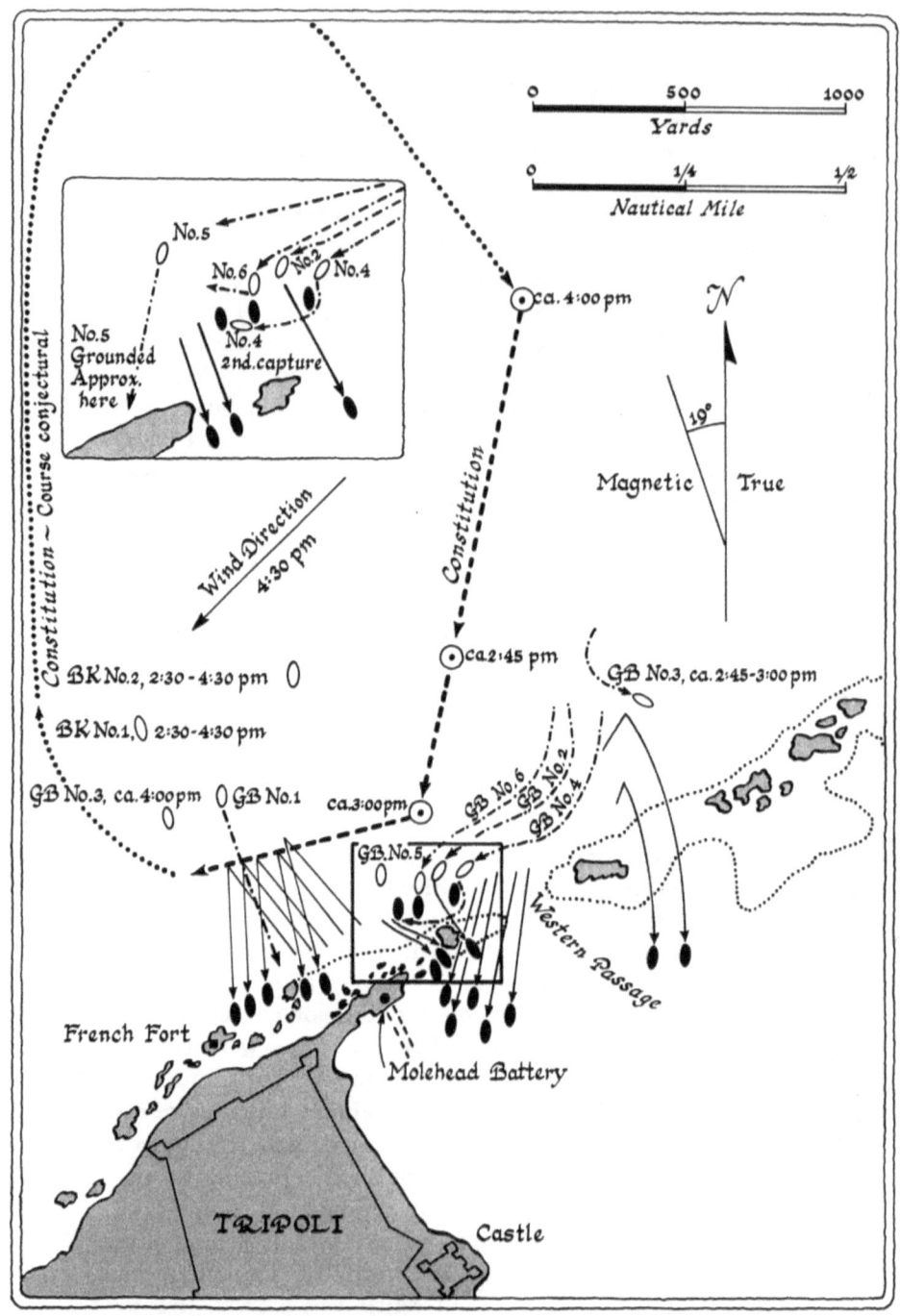

3 August 1804: Movements of the U.S. squadron and the Tripolitan gunboats between about 2:45 p.m. and 4:30 p.m. *Inset:* Detail of the boarding actions.

tured unwounded. "I find hand-to-hand is not child's play. 'Tis kill or be killed," boasted Decatur. "Some of the Turks died like men, but much the greater number like women."

At one point in the battle, Stephen Decatur found himself fighting alone against five Tripolitans, including the gunboat's commander, armed with scimitars. He managed to hold his own until the Tripolitan commander broke Decatur's cutlass with a blow from his better-tempered weapon. Decatur grappled with the Tripolitan, but his opponent, being bigger and stronger, forced Decatur across the gunwale of the boat, fell on top of him, drew a yataghan, and prepared to dispatch him. Decatur, having somehow managed to draw his pistol, discharged it through the Tripolitan's kidneys. Fortunately for Decatur, his servant with fixed bayonet and a Marine private armed with cutlass and tomahawk advanced upon his other four assailants and dispatched them.

James Decatur in Gunboat No. 2 ran down towards the second boat in the line, discharging a few 24-pound round shot, but relying principally on close-range musket and blunderbuss fire to subdue the enemy. The Tripolitan hauled down her colors: it looked as though all but three of her crew had been killed. No. 2 came alongside, and as James Decatur leaped on board to take possession of his prize, Tripolitan muskets were raised and fired. A ball struck Decatur in the head, and he fell into the sea between the boats. His second in command, Midshipman Thomas Brown, confused by the enemy's ruse, allowed his men to turn their attention to pulling their dying commander from the water. The diversion was just long enough to permit the Tripolitan boat to sheer off and pull towards the harbor. Brown did not pursue her. After beating off another gunboat that came up to menace him, he tacked to the northward and away from the battle. When, later in the day, Preble learned of the Tripolitan ruse, he ordered that in future hand-to-hand combats no quarter was to be granted.

Sailing Master John Trippe in Gunboat No. 6 attacked a third Tripolitan gunboat, and there followed a combat in which Preble took special interest — perhaps because it reminded him of the *Winthrop*'s capture of the *Merriam* during the Revolution. As the stern of No. 6 touched the Tripolitan, Trippe, Midshipman John D. Henley, and nine men leapt on board. Before any more men had time to follow, the American gunboat fell off, and Midshipman David Deacon, left in command on board No. 6, could not maneuver his unwieldy craft back alongside the enemy. Trippe and his party were stranded — eleven Americans against thirty-six Tripolitans. Shouting words of encouragement to his men, he and Henley led them in a rush against the enemy.

The Tripolitan captain was considerably more than six feet tall, while

Trippe was a little man. Nothing daunted, Trippe lunged for his opponent and, as he did so, his cutlass shattered against the Tripolitan's scimitar. He grabbed the Tripolitan, who easily threw him to the deck. In the scuffle Trippe managed to wrestle away his enemy's scimitar, cutting his own hand in the process. Other Tripolitans cut at Trippe with their swords, and he was bleeding from eleven wounds. But, with the scimitar in his hand, he had the advantage over his assailant. Twice, three times, he wounded the Tripolitan. Admiring his antagonist's bravery so much that he wanted to save his life, Trippe repeatedly signalled him to surrender — but the Tripolitan fought on until Trippe fell or fainted from loss of blood, whereupon an American sailor ran the Tripolitan through with a boarding pike. Even as the Tripolitan collapsed to the deck, he shouted to his men to revenge the death of their leader.

In spite of fierce resistance, the outnumbered attackers soon had the upper hand. Trippe was more generous than Decatur when it came to giving quarter and, once he was on his feet again, prevented his men from slaughtering the routed Tripolitans. He even rescued two who had fallen overboard and were begging to be saved. When the prize was finally secured, fourteen Tripolitans were dead, and seven of the twenty-two prisoners were wounded.

While Gunboat No. 5, Midshipman Joseph Bainbridge, was running to leeward with the other gunboats for the attack, a Tripolitan shot cut off the upper third of her lateen yard. Handicapped by this blow, she became even more ungainly than usual. She attempted to close with the enemy, but they were able easily to elude her. Moreover, with her yard broken off and sail and lines sagging in disarray, No. 5 tended to drift to leeward, regardless of her oarsmen's efforts. The best Bainbridge could do was to keep within 300 or 400 yards of the area where No. 4, No. 2, and No. 6 were engaged with the six Tripolitan gunboats that formed the east wing of the eleven-boat line, and harass the Tripolitans with round shot and grape from his bow gun. There were a few anxious moments when No. 5 stranded under the Molehead Battery, but Bainbridge managed to extricate her and escape capture.

Richard Somers in Gunboat No. 1 fought an isolated action with the west wing of the Tripolitan crescent of gunboats. Spurred by Preble's 2:00 p.m. signal to the brigs and schooners to cast off their tows, the *Nautilus* made more sail and attempted to overtake the other gunboats as they advanced towards the Tripolitans under Stephen Decatur's leadership. When the Commodore hoisted his general signal for battle, Somers cast off from the *Nautilus* and, with his sweeps out, struggled for at least half an hour to catch up with his division. By that time the gunboats had opened fire on the five Tripolitans moored in the entrance to the western passage, and it was apparent that he would not be able to fetch to windward to join them. At about 3:00 p.m. he passed between the bomb ketches and was standing in the general direction of the French Fort. The five gunboats forming the west wing of the Tripolitan line sighted the lone American boat and began advancing on her, firing as they came. Somers held his fire until the Tripolitans were within point-blank range, then opened on them with grape and round shot. Still they came until, suddenly, when they were within fifty yards of Somers and the fight was at its hottest, they fled for shelter behind the rocks between the French Fort and the Molehead Battery. Somers followed them to within 300 or 400 yards of the fortifications and continued firing until Preble signalled all the gunboats and the ketches to disengage.

By three o'clock or a few minutes thereafter — about the time Gunboats Nos. 4, 2, and 6 were preparing to board the Tripolitan gunboats — the *Constitution* was within 1,800 feet of the Molehead Battery. From her quarterdeck Preble saw that the five Tripolitan gunboats that had retired through the western passage when Decatur fired on them had been reinforced by a galliot and another gunboat and were preparing to come out through the passage and surround the Decatur brothers and Trippe. The *Constitution* hoisted the signal "Cover the boats," and the *Enterprize, Nautilus, Argus, Syren,* and *Vixen* stood in close to the engaged Americans and opened fire on the Tripolitan boats that were attempting to debouch from the harbor. But the brigs' and schooners' guns were too light to have much effect. Real protection had to come from the *Constitution*. About the same time the *Constitution* hoisted the cover-the-gunboats signal, Preble fired three of his starboard bow guns and his bow chasers at the west wing of the Tripolitan gunboats, then wore the *Constitution*'s head to the westward and brought her port battery into action. The aft division concentrated its fire on the Tripolitan galliot and gunboat which were leading the gunboats out to capture the three engaged Americans. The center division aimed at the Pasha's Castle, while the forward division fired on the Molehead Battery and the Tripolitan gunboats farther to the west. The *Constitution* reloaded each of her port guns with two round shot and a stand of grape for a second broadside. This time she concentrated on the Molehead Battery and the Tripolitan gunboats, and her fire broke up the Tripolitan counterattack. The *Constitution*'s grapeshot were especially effective. Two shells from the bomb ketches burst over the Tripolitan gunboats, and Somers was beginning to fire on the western wing of the enemy gunboats, placing them in a cross fire. Tripoli's boats were milling about in confusion.

While she had been standing along parallel with the Tripolitan batteries, the *Constitution* had been able to silence each of them in succession. But as soon as the frigate had passed a battery the Tripolitan gunners would open fire again, harassing her with a continuous, heavy barrage. Only the French Fort had remained silent for any length of time. Luckily, the accuracy of the Tripolitan fire had not matched its volume: Nathaniel Haraden estimated that upwards of 200 shot fell within 60 feet of the *Constitution*, but only nine balls struck her. Most of the damage she received was in her rigging. Preble thought that the small number of hits scored on the *Constitution* could be attributed to poor marksmanship, to his policy of running in so close to the batteries that they overshot their mark, and to his use of grapeshot which made the Tripolitan gunners reluctant to expose themselves in serving and aiming the cannon.

At this point in the battle, Preble encountered a critical situation. Wind and sea were causing the *Constitution* to drift slowly to leeward, and she would soon be carried away from the combat. The solution was to haul off to the northward and reapproach the batteries from windward; but to do this the *Constitution* had to present her stern to the town, which made her extremely vulnerable. In this moment, more than in any other, Preble wished he had another frigate in his squadron to suppress the fire of the Tripolitan batteries while the *Constitution* carried out her maneuver.

Perhaps it was while the *Constitution* was hauling off and was exposed that Preble had his closest personal escape of the afternoon. Armed with signal book, spyglass, and speaking trumpet, he was standing in the gangway immediately forward of one of the quarterdeck 24-pounders when a Tripolitan shot entered the gunport and broke against the aft side of the gun, hurling pieces of iron about the quarterdeck. A Marine private, Charles Young, had his arm shattered by the fragments, but Preble got off with nothing more than some torn clothing.

For about half an hour the *Constitution* stood off to the northward, before she tacked, loosed a press of sail, and again stood in towards the center of battle. It was near four o'clock, and the scene on the *Constitution*'s spar deck was much the same as it had been all afternoon. A small group stood close by Preble: Nathaniel Haraden and Henry Wadsworth to execute the Commodore's instructions for maneuvering the ship, Midshipman Daniel S. Dexter to make signals to the squadron, and Ship's Clerk John Thompson to take notes for the log and for Preble's journal and dispatches. Nearby, Second Lieutenant of Marines Robert Greenleaf supervised his men stationed at two quarterdeck 24-pounders; amidships, Captain John Hall, USMC, commanded the Marines handling four other 24-pound cannon. And when Preble looked to the forecastle he could see that everything there was under the more-than-competent control of Boatswain John

N. Cannon, assisted by a midshipman and — of all people — Mrs. Cannon, who was bearing a hand with the lines and, when necessary, helping to get the foretack on board.

As the *Constitution* ran down towards Tripoli Preble saw three Tripolitan gunboats coming up to attack Stephen Decatur and John Trippe, and four others attempting to surround Richard Somers. Again, he made the signal, "Cover the boats." John Smith in the *Vixen* bore down in support of Somers, and the *Constitution* hove about and discharged her starboard battery at the Molehead fortifications and the advancing gunboats. The latter immediately abandoned their attempt to capture Somers and ran for shelter under the town's batteries. Then the *Constitution* wore to westward and sailed along parallel with the city walls. One broadside was aimed at the Castle and the Molehead Battery; the guns were reloaded and a second broadside was fired into the Molehead area, the retreating gunboats, and the French Fort. The Molehead Battery fell silent, gunners could be seen fleeing from the French Fort, and the fire of the remaining batteries was diverted from the U.S. flotilla to the *Constitution*. But the frigate was falling to leeward of Tripoli and, for the second time that afternoon, Preble was forced to stand off to the north and reapproach the city from windward. When the *Constitution* showed her stern to the batteries the Tripolitans went back to their guns.

No sooner had Stephen Decatur secured his prize gunboat, manned her, and sent her off, than he saw, immediately to leeward, a Tripolitan gunboat outside the rocks. Although manning his prize had left him shorthanded, he ran down and boarded her. Decatur, Midshipman Thomas Macdonough, and eight of their men fought the twenty-four Tripolitan defenders. It was a vicious battle. When the Americans finally secured the boat, twenty-one Tripolitans were dead or wounded, and three were taken prisoner. Two boarding actions that day had left Decatur with one man seriously wounded and three, including himself, slightly wounded. The savagery of Decatur's attacks is indicated by the fact that the Americans, only four of whom had been wounded, killed thirty-three Tripolitans and wounded nineteen.

By 4:30 p.m. all the remaining Tripolitan boats had either run into the harbor or taken shelter close under the fortifications. Between the Molehead Battery and the French Fort, Somers was still exchanging hot, though indecisive, gunfire with his opponents, but there was little more that could be done that day. The wind had freshened and was veering to the N.E. A heavy sea that was running would make it difficult for the American gunboats and their prizes to get offshore. The *Constitution* signalled the gunboats and bomb ketches, "Join company soon as possible," then sent her barge and jolly boat to help tow out the prizes.

THE BATTLE OF TRIPOLI, 3 AUGUST 1804, by MICHEL FELICE CORNÉ

Shortly after his return to the United States in 1805, Preble commissioned Corné to paint this representation of the high point of his Tripolitan campaign. The details of the battle in the painting do not correspond in every respect with those presented in this book. This is because the book is based on a correlation of all available accounts of the battle, while the painting conforms to Preble's perception of the conflict, as set out in his official dispatch.

From left to right, in the left and center foreground, are the *Enterprize*, the *Nautilus*, the *Argus*, the *Syren*, and the *Vixen*. Immediately above the *Vixen* and on the *Constitution*'s port quarter, Bomb Ketch No. 2 appears. Above and slightly to the right of Bomb Ketch No. 2, Gunboat No. 3 is shown — in conformity with Preble's conviction — a considerable distance from the heat of the action. Bomb Ketch No. 1 is just to the right of the *Constitution* and, at the extreme right, exchanging fire with five Tripolitan gunboats that have retreated under the shelter of the Molehead Battery, is Gunboat No. 1.

Courtesy of U.S. Naval Academy Museum

The two Tripolitan gunboats that Stephen Decatur chased into the harbor at the beginning of the action can be seen between the masts of the *Enterprize* and the *Nautilus*. To the right of these gunboats, inside the harbor rocks, are two three-masted galleys, and to the right of them, fourteen Tripolitan gunboats crowded into the western passage are closely engaged with, from left to right, U.S. Gunboats Nos. 4, 2, 6, and 5. The last is easily identified because her lateen yard has been cut in two and part of it is hanging down in disarray.

In the left and center background, two clouds of smoke on shore indicate, respectively, the English Fort and the New Battery. Three seagoing Tripolitan cruisers are anchored in front of the New Battery. The large squarish building directly above U.S. Gunboat No. 3 is, of course, the Pasha's Castle.

Preble presented the canvas to the Navy Department, where it was hung in the office of Secretary Robert Smith.

Some of the American commanders were already preparing to pull off when the *Constitution* made her signal. They all promptly began pulling quickly for the *Constitution*, the brigs, and the schooners. All, that is, except John Trippe. It will be remembered that, while he and ten of his crew were boarding the enemy, his gunboat drifted to leeward and, since Midshipman David Deacon was unable to work her back to windward, Trippe was left close by the western passage in his prize with twenty-two prisoners on his hands. Seriously wounded himself, he had only ten men, one of whom was also badly injured, to guard the prisoners and row the prize off, for she had no sails. Trippe soon fell far astern of the gunboats making for the *Constitution*. The Tripolitans were quick to spot his difficult situation. Two or three gunboats, obviously intending to come out and capture him, appeared in the passage. To make matters worse, the *Vixen* mistook Trippe's prize for a Tripolitan and fired a shot at her. Fortunately, Stephen Decatur saw the predicament and ordered Gunboat No. 5, Joseph Bainbridge, to check the advancing Tripolitans.

The *Constitution*, too, was coming down to cover the U.S. gunboats' withdrawal. As she swept by Trippe, Preble leaned over the netting and called, "Do you wish us to take you in tow?" No, answered Trippe, we shall make our own way out. The frigate tacked within half a mile of the Molehead Battery, and fired two broadsides which silenced the Pasha's Castle and, to the delight of all hands, one spectacular shot brought the minaret of a mosque crashing down. It was about 4:45 p.m. Preble could see that his gunboats and their prizes were out of range of the Tripolitan cannon. He signalled the brigs and schooners, "Tow the boats," the *Constitution* hauled off to take the bomb ketches in tow, and the squadron stood off to a position two or three miles north of Tripoli.

The ketches had kept their original stations throughout the afternoon, and not until they rejoined the squadron did Preble learn that their performance had been disappointing. Each had fired only seven shells, and apparently only one of the fourteen had carried as far as the city, though several had come tantalizingly close to the forts. The two commanders, Lieutenants Dent and Robinson, were distressed and puzzled. They had tried the mortars with American and with Neapolitan powder, but neither would throw the shells into the city.

Wherever the Americans gathered to talk over the day's events a prime topic was the peculiar behavior of Lieutenant Joshua Blake in Gunboat No. 3. At the opening of the battle, the American gunboats had chased the two Tripolitans at the east end of the enemy formation into the harbor and behind the sheltering rocks; then Gunboats Nos. 4, 2, 5, and 6 bore up to engage the Tripolitan gunboats moored to the westward. Instead of joining the other gunboats in their run to leeward, Blake in No. 3 remained to windward, firing at the two Tripolitans that had taken shelter behind the rocks. At most, he fired eight rounds with his bow gun, and perhaps twelve musket cartridges — substantially less ammunition than was expended by any other U.S. gunboat during the battle. After that no one remembered seeing No. 3 again until around 4:00 p.m. when Midshipman Deacon, in No. 6, saw her standing off, between Bomb Ketch No. 1 and the shore, and apparently unmanageable in the rough sea. Deacon hailed Blake, and asked him to go and help John Trippe extricate his prize. Blake seems to have complied as best he could. When Trippe was nearly out of grapeshot range of the batteries, Blake came within hail and threw him a line. Trippe missed it, and wind and sea carried No. 3 away before Blake could recover the line and throw it a second time.

Most of Preble's officers were calling Blake a coward for not closing with the enemy, but no one was more violent in his criticism or more active in stirring up feeling against Blake than his division commander, Richard Somers. He insisted he could have captured some of the Tripolitan gunboats opposing him if Blake had come to his aid. In his own defense, Blake claimed that the *Constitution* made confusing signals which he did not know how to obey; specifically, she had prematurely hoisted a signal of recall and followed it almost immediately with the annulling signal which latter signal had the effect of voiding all preceding signals. This may have been the case. Some evidence suggests that Preble's signal officer, Midshipman Dexter, did have difficulty in expressing the Commodore's intentions by means of the messages available in the two signal books. However, no other officer admitted to having seen the two signals that Blake insisted led him astray.

III

At nine o'clock on the morning after the battle, 4 August, the *Constitution* was some twelve or fourteen miles northeast of Tripoli when a lookout sighted an unidentified sail emerging from the harbor. "*Argus*: Chase to the S.W. by W.," Preble signalled. Four hours later the *Argus* returned with a vessel that proved to be the French privateer *Le Rusé*, 4 guns, Pierre Blaise Mercellise, master. *Le Rusé* had put in to Tripoli for water a few days earlier and had been in the port during Preble's bombardment. When the *Argus* went in chase of her, she was on her way out to the *Constitution* with a letter Bonaventure Beaussier had written Preble on 3 August before the attack began. "On the occasion of your approach with an offensive force I have submitted various considerations to the Pasha," Beaussier had written, "but he prefers to bury himself under the ruins of his country rather than subscribe to humiliating conditions. The whole city is in arms; each man is at his post day and night; the troops, the gunners and the bombardiers exhibit outwardly the greatest courage; women and children have been sent into the country."

After Richard O'Brien's abortive negotiations with the Pasha on 13 June, Preble sent William Bainbridge a message written in lime-juice ink, which was invisible until the paper was heated over a fire. He authorized Bainbridge to contact Sidi Mohammed Dghies, the prime minister, repeat Preble's peace offer of $40,000 ransom, $10,000 to influential Tripolitan officials, and a $10,000 consular present, and to inform Dghies that if he persuaded Yusuf to accept this offer he would receive a personal gift of $10,000 from the United States. This maneuver showed singularly poor judgment on Preble's part. Mohammed Dghies was aware both of his own importance and dignity and of the proper methods of conducting diplomatic business. He would not negotiate with a prisoner. Indeed, he told Bainbridge, the Pasha had resolved to accept no further communications from Commodore Preble or from any person sent by Preble: he would negotiate only with a fully-accredited representative sent directly from the United States. Dghies suggested casually — Bainbridge missed the significance of the hint — that if Preble were prepared to spend about $150,000 serious negotiations might be possible.

Furthermore, Preble should have known that Beaussier and Dghies were intimates and that Beaussier would find out immediately that Preble had made another attempt to circumvent him. This further inflamed the mutual distrust between Beaussier and Preble. Early in July Beaussier was certain that Preble had not received instructions from the United States since the loss of the *Philadelphia* had become known there, and that he was concealing his lack of instructions with bravado. Preble had said that additional frigates were on their way to the Mediterranean and that he would be coming with bomb ketches and gunboats to attack Tripoli, but Beaussier thought these were gross exaggerations, if not outright lies, and assumed that when Preble had new instructions from Washington he would make peace proposals more in line with Yusuf Caramanli's expectations.

Then, on the 24th of July, a courier brought the Pasha the news that Preble was coming with his whole squadron and eight gunboats or bomb ketches. Three days later the squadron appeared in the roads, and Beaussier was compelled to reconsider his opinion of Preble's truthfulness. But that same day a gale forced Preble to get away from the shore. The Tripolitans sighted the American squadron on the northern horizon on the 28th and again on the 30th, but on both occasions it disappeared again. The interval gave Beaussier an opportunity to reassess Preble's intentions.

If Preble thought that the mere appearance of his squadron would intimidate Yusuf into accepting his peace terms he was mistaken: sight of the enemy had raised Tripolitan morale. Still, looking at the situation as objectively as he could, Beaussier did not see how the Pasha could hope to prevent destructive bombardments of Tripoli, especially if more frigates arrived from America. Yusuf had only eighteen gunboats and they were badly handled. He did have 115 guns in the batteries — but in Beaussier's opinion the gunners were none too skillful. And, to complicate his search for peace, Beaussier had to admit that he did not understand Preble. How could he act so boldly when he had no instructions from his government based on the knowledge that the Pasha was holding three hundred American prisoners? "What opinion should one have," he asked Talleyrand, "of a commander who, without authorization from his government, commits the arms of his nation, hazards being dismissed himself, and exposes the lives of three hundred prisoners to the fanaticism and despair of these Africans?"

With admirable persistence, Beaussier decided to make one more attempt at mediation. On 27 July he appeared before the Pasha and presented him with a paper:

> Illustrious and Magnificent Lord:
> God keep me from advising Your Highness the least thing that could compromise the august name of the Caramanlis and the dignity of the regency, but the interest that the Emperor of France takes in the prosperity of your reign and the happiness of your subjects obliges me to submit the following considerations to you:
> If the American attack is not successful — of which I am assured by the courage and ardor of your troops — the war will be further prolonged to the great disadvantage of your revenue and your country, already well-impoverished by three years and three months of war. If it is successful, it is possible that the Commodore may demand, as his price for peace, the surrender of all the prisoners *without any ransom*. Then your expenses will have been totally lost, quite apart from the damage the city will have suffered. Certain it is that the continuance of the war matters little to the United States of America, because this new nation is forced to arm squadrons to train officers and seamen.
> These reflections, Illustrious and Magnificent Lord, are inspired by your own self-interest and by Bonaparte's desire to see you at peace with the Americans. I pray Your Highness to accept the homage of my profound respect,
> BEAUSSIER

Yusuf studied the document, thanked Beaussier for his efforts, then said with unmistakable determination: "I would rather bury myself under the ruins of my country than basely yield to the wishes of the enemy."[2]

There matters stood on the morning of 3 August when Beaussier wrote the letter that came out to Preble in *Le Rusé*. As Preble studied the letter, he seemed to detect a hint of an opening for further negotiations, and he was anxious to see if the Pasha's losses of the previous day had turned his thoughts more towards peace. In return for a generous supply of provisions from the *Constitution*'s storerooms and under strong pressure from Preble, Captain Mercellise agreed to return to Tripoli with the fourteen most seriously wounded Tripolitan prisoners and a letter from Preble to Beaussier. In the letter Preble suggested that if Beaussier thought Yusuf was at that moment at all interested in peace, Beaussier might tell him that Preble's offer of $40,000 for ransom, plus a $10,000 consular present would remain open until the four additional frigates arrived: he was expecting them any day and, once they had joined his squadron, the United States would never consent to give Tripoli one cent.

Le Rusé stood for Tripoli early on 5 August, and later that day the *Vixen* ran in towards the city to reconnoiter the batteries and the harbor. Her approach brought several Tripolitan gunboats out to the rocks, but no shots were exchanged. All the while carpenters and sailmakers were rerigging and refitting the three captured boats to join Preble's gunboat force, and the ships of the squadron were taking on provisions, water, and military stores from the *Constitution* in preparation for a second attack on Tripoli which Preble hoped to make on 6 August. These preparations were not completed until the early afternoon of the 6th. By that time the wind had shifted to N. by W. and clouds were rising over the northern horizon, promising not only an unfavorable onshore breeze, but the strong possibility of another gale. There could be no attack that afternoon. At dusk the wind died away to a dead calm, and *Le Rusé* was seen pulling out of the harbor towards the *Constitution*'s anchorage six miles N.N.E. of the city. Around 11:00 p.m. Captain Mercellise boarded the frigate and gave Preble another letter from Beaussier.

Preble had meant to be generous and humane in sending the wounded Tripolitans to Tripoli, where they could be cared for by their families and have the benefit of fresh food, which was in short supply in the American squadron. But Yusuf and Beaussier put the worst possible interpretation on what he had done. They thought he was trying to avoid the nuisance of having to care for wounded prisoners. In his anger, the Pasha considered ordering Mercellise to take them back to the *Constitution*.

Privately, Beaussier thought Preble was making a tactical mistake in seeking to negotiate at this time. He should, instead, be reinforcing the shock of 3 August with attack after attack until the Pasha himself asked for a parley.³ In spite of his misgivings, Beaussier spent most of the 5th and 6th with Yusuf and his council. He pointed to the defeat Tripoli had sustained a few days earlier, and suggested that there was much to be feared from future attacks. The Pasha assured Beaussier that he was anxious to be at peace with the United States, but he would not make peace on the dishonorable conditions Preble proposed. If, he said, Preble wanted peace as much as he did, then the American commodore would not hesitate to offer a little larger ransom: but if Preble's orders did not allow him to go any higher, then Yusuf would be forced to use every means at hand to defend himself against Preble's attacks, and the outcome would be ordained by Providence.

In the letter delivered by *Le Rusé*, Beaussier tried to tell Preble what the realities of the situation were. He was, he wrote, saying what he had to say not because he wished "to serve this regency, particularly at the expense of truth — a method that France has no need whatever to employ — but rather so that I will not leave you in ignorance of anything that can enlighten your operations and guide your conduct." He said he had persuaded the Pasha to entertain "reasonable conditions" of peace: "I conjure you, Monsieur le Commodore, to propose, as far as the honor and dignity of your nation will permit, a ransom more consistent with the number and rank of the prisoners." Finally, he told Preble that, if he wished to pursue the effort to negotiate, he should send a boat to the western passage under a flag of truce. Beaussier would guarantee the boat's safety.

Although he sensed a promising change in the Pasha's attitude, Preble did not send a flag of truce to the western passage. He was prepared for another attack. He had a new plan. And if one attack had inclined Yusuf towards peace, a second ought to make him even more pliable.

IV

Immediately to the west of the city of Tripoli the coast curved in to form a shallow bay that was masked from the batteries protecting Tripoli harbor. Led by Charles Stewart, the younger commanders of the squadron had been urging Preble to send the gunboats and bomb ketches into this bay, whence they would be able to bombard the city but the Tripolitans would be unable to reply. The young officers put particular faith in the effect of shells hurled by the bomb ketches from this snug anchorage. They pointed out that, if the Tripolitan gunboats were to come out of the harbor and run down and attack the American gunboats and ketches in the bay, Preble could move in with his brigs and schooners, cut the Tripolitans' line of retreat to the harbor, surround, and capture them. It appeared to be a good plan, since it would force the Pasha either to endure a severe bombardment without reply, or to risk the capture and, perhaps, total destruction of his gunboats. The more Stewart and his friends advocated their plan, the more it appealed to Edward Preble. He asked Richard O'Brien for his opinion. O'Brien said he favored another direct attack on the harbor and shipping: "I think a blow in the face is better than a kick in the stern." But Preble decided to try the Stewart scheme.

The morning of the 7th of August was calm and warm, with only occasional light airs from the S.E. Out where the *Constitution* rode at anchor, some six miles N.N.E. from Tripoli, a strong current was setting to the eastward and, in combination with the light wind, preventing the frigate from getting under way. Preble summoned all his gunboats under the *Constitution*'s stern, explained his plan of attack to the commanders, and, at ten o'clock, signalled them "Advance in a line abreast." Within thirty minutes the boats were in formation and rowing towards the shallow bay to the west of Tripoli. The gunboats went in first; behind them came the bomb ketches; and finally the *Syren, Argus, Enterprize, Nautilus,* and *Vixen*. All moved forward slowly, propelled by their sweeps. The *Constitution*, topsails and topgallant sails set, waited at anchor for the first good breeze.

As the nine American gunboats closed the distance to the bay they met something unexpected—a strong westerly current. It swept them far to leeward of the position they were trying to reach, and forced them to row back eastward, against the current, to gain the end of the bay adjacent to the city. While executing this maneuver, they attempted to form a new line abreast, but this proved almost impossible because the heavy, flat-bottomed boats were unmanageable in the current. As they rowed up towards their designated positions at the east end of the bay their formation was in considerable confusion.[4]

The day had slipped past noon. Lieutenant Thomas Robinson in Bomb Ketch No. 1 rode the contrary currents skillfully and reached a position off the northwest angle of the city walls, within a mile and a half of his target. At 1:00 p.m. he began firing shells to test the range. When the third or fourth shot landed on target, the ketch dropped anchor. She was in an excellent position, and most of the twenty-seven shells she fired from her mortar during the afternoon fell in the city. One shot dropped directly into the French Fort, where it burst and silenced all the guns for half an hour. Lieutenant John H. Dent in Bomb Ketch No. 2 had more difficulty with the currents, was swept westward, and finally forced to anchor about two miles west of Tripoli and, thus, at the extreme range of his mortar. Just a few of the nineteen shells No. 2 fired carried as far as the city walls.

While Lieutenant Robinson was still finding the range for his mortar,

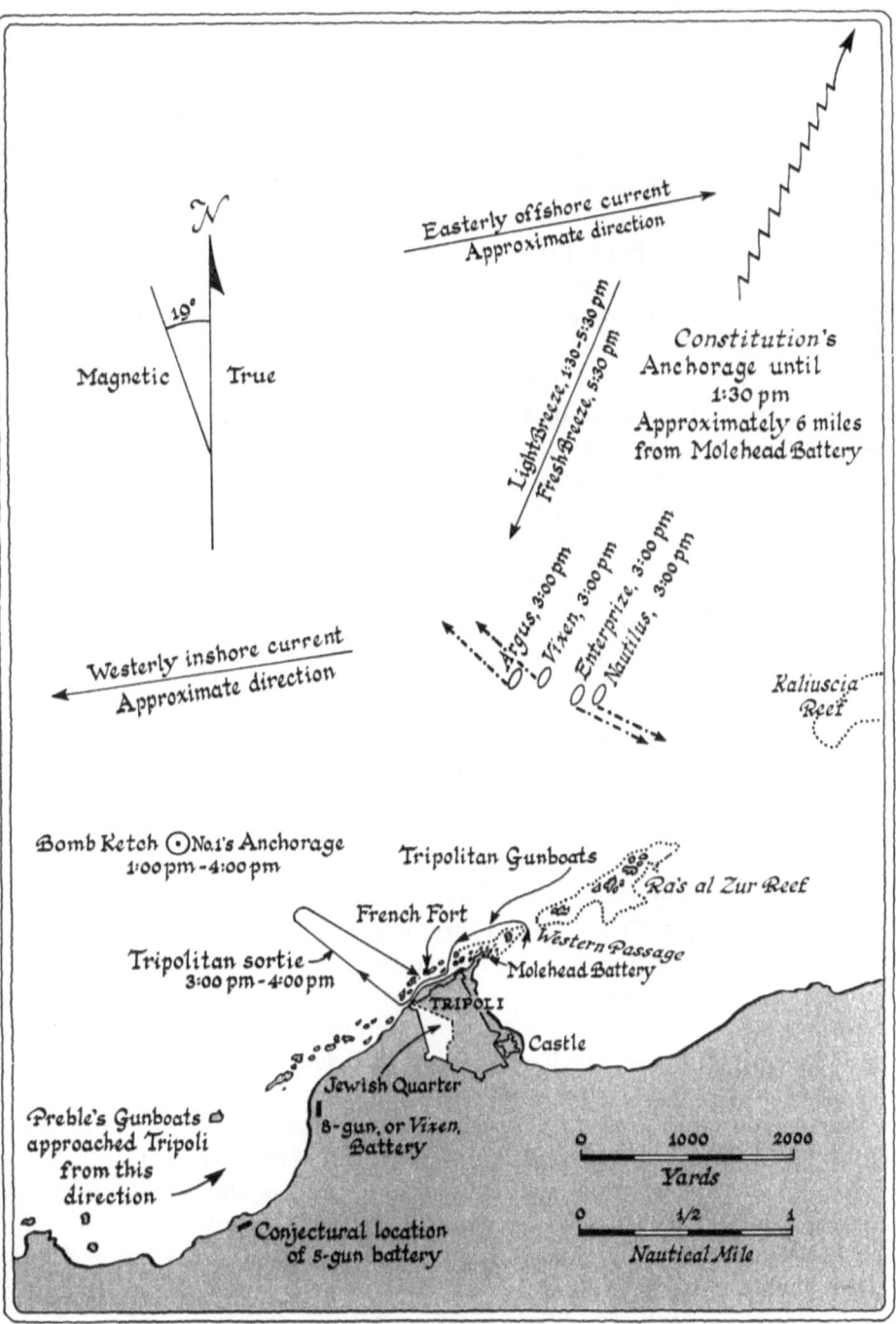

Bombardment of Tripoli from West of the City, 7 August 1804

about 1:30 p.m., a light breeze sprang up from the N.N.E. and enabled the *Constitution* to get under way. She stood in closer to Tripoli, but still lingered to windward of the western passage, well out of gunshot. Preble had already sent one of his boats with orders for the brigs and schooners to keep out of range of the Tripolitan batteries if the wind remained light. With the breeze onshore, Preble feared that if a Tripolitan shot disabled a mast, the crippled victim might drift inshore and be captured.

As the gunboats approached the eastern end of the bay, after four hours of hard rowing, they were greeted by a fierce cannonade from the shore. Unknown to Preble, the Tripolitans had, within the previous two or three days, constructed two new batteries — one of eight guns, the other of five — to cover the bay. The Americans returned the fire, but the Tripolitans derived considerable advantage from the disorder in which the gunboats had been caught. Nevertheless, the five-gun battery was soon knocked out of action. The eight-gun earthwork, nicknamed the *"Vixen* Battery" by the Americans, proved a tougher nut. The gunboats closed to within 200 yards of the *Vixen* Battery, concentrating their fire on it and on the western part of the city which lay beyond. During the afternoon's action the gunboats fired an average of fifty rounds apiece from their bow guns, although some boats — especially Stephen Decatur's No. 4 — had great difficulty in reaching suitable positions and got off fewer shots. Gradually, the walls of the *Vixen* Battery were smashed down. Twice the battery was silenced, only to come to life again in a few minutes. Finally, only one of its guns was firing, and that one the Americans never did put out of action.

Most of the shells that reached the city fell in its Jewish quarter.[5] A number of fires were set, and columns of smoke rose through the nearly motionless air. But Tripoli was a city of stone, mud and mortar, and the fires — although encouraging to American morale — did relatively minor damage. The impact of cannon ball and bomb shell was more serious: many buildings were battered and some were almost destroyed. Even so, an impartial observer would not have assessed the damage done Tripoli during this attack as either extensive or serious.

About 3:00 p.m., when the Americans were trying to smother the *Vixen* Battery and the *Syren* was close by, tacking and occasionally firing her bow chasers in support of them, the Tripolitan gunboats and galleys, fifteen in all, came out through the passages in the reef and maneuvered close under the Molehead Battery as though they were forming to attack the U.S. gunboats. Preble, hoping to lure the Tripolitans away from the protection of the batteries, ordered the *Vixen, Argus, Nautilus,* and *Enterprize,* which were approximately a mile N. and N.E. of the Tripolitan boats, to run to the east and south, as though frightened off by the innocuous shots which the Tripolitan gunboats were sending in their direction. The *Enterprize* and the *Nautilus* moved off to the S.E., but the *Argus* and the *Vixen* either did not see or misunderstood the signals: they tacked and stood to the N.W., assuming a position which clearly menaced the Tripolitan flotilla and, thus, defeated Preble's purpose.

Then, weaving through shallow, narrow channels among the offshore rocks, the Tripolitan gunboats worked their way westward until they suddenly emerged off the northwest angle of the city walls and advanced to attack Bomb Ketch No. 1, which was alone and unprotected. Lieutenant Robinson saw the threat. He raised anchor, and slowly and defiantly made sail to the west, rounding and firing his mortar as he went; when, at last, he was able to anchor again, he was near the U.S. gunboats in the bay, but beyond the effective range of his mortar. Bomb Ketch No. 1's contribution to the battle was finished. Meanwhile, the *Constitution*, with all sail spread in the light N.N.E. breeze, was bearing down on the northwest angle of Tripoli in an attempt to cut off and capture some of the Tripolitan gunboats that had gone out to attack Ketch No. 1. But the Tripolitans saw her coming. For them, the distance to safety was short. With oars and sails they raced back to the shelter of the offshore rocks near the French Fort. By the time the *Constitution* was within range, all that could be seen of the Tripolitan gunboats were their masts sticking up over the rocks.

While the Tripolitan sortie was taking place, one of the *Constitution*'s lookouts sighted a strange sail on the northeastern horizon. Was it the *Scourge* returning from Malta where she had gone to escort a storeship? Preble signalled the *Argus*, Lieutenant Isaac Hull, to come within hail, then sent her off under a crowd of sail to learn the stranger's identity.

Almost immediately, Preble's attention was diverted inshore again. Around half-past three there was a tremendous explosion. A cloud of smoke hid one of the U.S. gunboats that had been in the thick of the fight with the *Vixen* Battery. Bodies and parts of bodies could be seen hurtling above the smoke, then falling back into the sea. The Tripolitan batteries and the American gunboats alike fell silent; everyone stopped what he was doing and looked towards the site of the explosion. As the smoke cleared away, it could be seen that Gunboat No. 9, one of the captured Tripolitan boats, had blown up. Evidently her magazine had exploded, for her stern and midships sections had disintegrated. Only her bow remained above water, but it was sinking fast. Around the bow gun several men were coolly reloading to fire one more time. They did not make it: just as an officer was touching the match the wreck slipped under water. The small band of men gave three cheers as they went into the sea.

When all the survivors had been pulled from the water, the Americans found that of the twenty-eight officers and men on board No. 9, ten, including the boat's commander, Lieutenant James R. Caldwell, and Midshipman John S. Dorsey, had been killed, four men were dreadfully wounded, two less seriously hurt, and twelve were uninjured. Many of the American officers supposed that No. 9 had been blown up by a hot shot from the Tripolitan batteries. But, in point of fact, the Tripolitan gunners were not able to fire hot shot. The most objective observers in the American squadron, Nathaniel Haraden and Richard O'Brien, both blamed the accident on a piece of flaming wadding from one of the other American gunboats falling into No. 9's magazine.

The pause in the battle was only minutes long. The Americans fought in full fury to avenge their dead friends, while enemy resistance was invigorated by the destruction of the U.S. gunboat. Tripolitan gunners shot away No. 6's lateen yard. Stephen Decatur's No. 4 took a shot in her hull, and Gunboat No. 8, another converted Tripolitan, was more seriously damaged in the hull by a ball that also killed two seamen. The wind began to blow fresh from the N.N.E. at 5:30 p.m., making further inshore action hazardous. Preble signalled the gunboats and bombards to break off the attack and withdraw. The *Vixen*, *Nautilus*, and *Enterprize* had already moved in to give close support to the gunboats, and within an hour and fifteen minutes the mother ships had the gunboats and bomb ketches in tow and the whole squadron was standing off towards the N.W.

While the gunboats were rowing off, the *Argus*, which had gone to identify the strange sail more than two hours earlier, signalled the *Constitution*, "Strange ships in sight are friends." Somewhat later, experienced eyes recognized the large ship with American colors flying as the long-expected *John Adams*. At 9:00 p.m. the American squadron anchored five miles N.W. from Tripoli. As the *John Adams* came up under the *Constitution*'s stern, her men gave three cheers. A hail from Preble's ship determined that the *John Adams* was commanded by Master Commandant Isaac Chauncey and carried dispatches from Washington for the Commodore. A boat from the *Constitution* went alongside the newcomer with a request for Captain Chauncey to come on board the Commodore as soon as possible. Boats from the other ships were beginning to gather round the *John Adams*. Officers in the boats were calling to ask if she had any letters for them and what was the news from America?

Chauncey brought three letters for Preble from Robert Smith. They were tactfully worded, but their message was a harsh shock for a tired Preble. Word of the loss of the *Philadelphia* had caused a major change in the government's Barbary policy. The President had immediately determined to send to the Mediterranean "a force which would be able, beyond the possibility of a doubt, to coerce the enemy to a peace upon terms compatible with our honor and our interest." Consequently, Smith advised Preble, four frigates, the *President,* Samuel Barron, the *Congress,* John Rodgers, the *Essex,* James Barron, and the *Constellation,* Hugh G. Campbell, were on their way. In mid-June, when Preble had first heard that Samuel Barron was coming to the Mediterranean, his fear of being superseded had been eased by his understanding that Barron would command a separate squadron. Now, he learned that not only was his understanding on that point wrong, but a second officer who outranked him, John Rodgers, was also being sent out. Samuel Barron would, of necessity, wrote Smith, supersede Preble in command of the Mediterranean squadron. Soothing words from the Secretary were only a tiny compensation:

> Be assured, Sir, that no want of confidence in you has been mingled with the considerations which have imposed upon us the necessity of this measure. You have fulfilled our highest expectations, and the President has given it in an especial charge to me to declare that he has the highest confidence in your activity, judgment and valor. Through me, he desires to convey to you his thanks for the very important services which you have rendered to your country.
> I repeat to you the assurance that your whole conduct has received the unqualified approbation of the President of the United States and that his confidence in you remains unabated.

V

After the departure of Preble and his squadron for the Mediterranean during the summer of 1803, the Navy Department settled into a relaxed and somewhat somnolent routine that lasted into the following winter. While Preble, on the far side of the Atlantic, was becoming increasingly anxious over his need for reinforcements, the Jefferson administration was in an opposite frame of mind.

During August and September 1803 Robert Smith and the President corresponded at length about a plan — soon abandoned — to send the ratification of the treaty for the purchase of Louisiana to France in a naval vessel. Smith even began outfitting the *Essex* for the voyage, but at no time did he consider having her join Preble in the Mediterranean after performing her mission to France, although such word-of-mouth reports of the *Essex*'s preparations as reached Preble made it appear that she was to reinforce him.[6]

With the arrival of October, economy was the prevailing concern in Washington. The administration wanted to cut the proposed budget for the ensuing year so that the interest on the purchase of Louisiana could be paid from existing revenue sources. The President feared that a new tax would swing enough votes against the purchase to cause the treaty to fail of ratification. One place where he hoped to save money was in the cost of the Mediterranean squadron. At the suggestion of Secretary of the Treasury Gallatin, the President proposed that, should Preble fail to make peace during the summer of 1804, the Mediterranean squadron be cut to one frigate and three small cruisers.[7]

Commodore Richard V. Morris reached Washington in mid-November 1803, and what to do about him became the center of the Secretary of the Navy's concern. The two men had a personal confrontation, during which Robert Smith explained why the Commodore had been abruptly removed from his command and gave him an opportunity to defend his conduct. Although Morris's explanation failed to satisfy Smith,[8] no action was taken immediately. But, by January 1804, feeling was growing within the administration circle that additional investigation was in order. The public had expected the strong Morris squadron to end the Tripolitan War and they had been disappointed. Criticism was being directed at Commodore Morris and more particularly at the Republican administration. An official inquiry was the only way to quiet public dissatisfaction.[9] On 10 March Robert Smith summoned a court of inquiry which sat at Stelle's Hotel in Washington from 3 through 13 April. The court's opinion was that Morris had showed a lack of vigor in his official conduct and that he was censurable for his inactivity and his dilatory direction of operations in the Mediterranean.

Under normal procedure the next step would have been to summon a court-martial to try Morris. The President seemed mildly in favor of this action, but the Secretary of the Navy thought that enough evidence had been produced at the court of inquiry to permit the President to dismiss Morris from the Navy without a court-martial. Since Jefferson was almost as bitter against Morris as was Robert Smith, the Secretary had no difficulty in persuading the President to adopt the course of action he suggested: Morris's commission as a captain in the Navy was summarily revoked on 16 May 1804.[10]

Before the court of inquiry that had been called to investigate Morris's activities began its sessions, Preble's dispatches describing the loss of the *Philadelphia* reached Washington. One set of these dispatches was brought ashore at Boston on 9 March, to be followed four days later by the arrival of another set at the same port. But the mails must have been moving more slowly than usual for it was not until Monday, 19 March, that official Washington knew about the disaster in the Mediterranean. Midshipman Christopher Gadsden's passage from Gibraltar lasted seventy-six days and it was about 21 March when he landed at Georgetown, South Carolina, with the third set of dispatches.[11]

Immediate reaction in the administration was that preparations must be made to add at least two frigates to the Mediterranean squadron.[12] On Tuesday, 20 March, the President sent a message to Congress informing its members of the loss, and recommending an appropriation to enlarge the squadron in the Mediterranean Sea. The very next day, 21 March, the House Committee of Ways and Means reported out a bill that levied an additional import duty, revenue from which was to be used to equip and operate more frigates for the Mediterranean squadron; that provided for the building or purchase of two new vessels of war of 16 guns or less; authorized the President to hire or borrow gunboats in the Mediterranean; and increased the naval and related appropriations by $1,000,000.

Encouraged by the smooth and rapid progress of this measure through Congress, the Navy Department was — even before final enactment of the bill on 26 March — making plans to send four frigates, besides the *John Adams*, to the Mediterranean. Events had forced the President and his less bellicose cabinet members to come round to the position that Robert Smith had been maintaining alone for so long: vigorous use of a large force was the shortest, cheapest road to peace in the Mediterranean. The arguments that led to the decision to equip a large squadron were: A strong squadron appearing before Tripoli or actually attacking the city was the fastest way — other than agreeing to the Pasha's ransom demands — to release the captive Americans. A force of the size contemplated ought to be able to coerce Tripoli to make peace on American terms, an outcome thought the more necessary since the capture of the *Philadelphia* was believed to have caused a decline in American prestige in Barbary. As a result of this loss of prestige one or more of the Barbary States, Tunis especially, might be tempted to declare war on the United States. The presence of an impressive American squadron should discourage this unwanted expansion of the war.

The decision to send four frigates, instead of only two, automatically meant that Preble would have to be superseded as commander of the Mediterranean squadron, because only two of the captains available for service — James Barron and Hugh G. Campbell — were junior to him. When news of the *Philadelphia*'s capture reached the Navy Department, Samuel Barron and John Rodgers, as well as the younger Barron and Campbell, had already been called to Washington as members of, or witnesses before, the Morris court of inquiry. Robert Smith appointed the four of them to command the additional frigates.

In retrospect, the decision to supersede Preble may appear mistaken, but it must be remembered that when it was made, the government did not know of the burning of the *Philadelphia,* the borrowing of gunboats and bomb ketches, or the attacks Preble had made on Tripoli. It did, however, know about the loss of the *Philadelphia,* the greatest disaster the Navy had suffered since the Revolution. At least some slight shadow from this loss must have fallen on the commander of the squadron. And in December, when Preble was writing the dispatches on which the Navy Department's decision was based, his mood and predictions were gloomy. He asked for three more frigates, but was not certain that even if he had them he would be able to bring the Pasha to make peace without ransom.

On 26 May President Jefferson held a Cabinet meeting to consider what instructions should be issued governing the negotiation of a new treaty with Tripoli. The Cabinet regarded the enlargement of the Mediterranean squadron as a supreme and final effort to force Tripoli, during the summer of 1804, to release the prisoners without ransom and to make a new treaty without the payment of money. The administration was unwilling to continue the Tripolitan War into the indefinite future: if the enlarged squadron could not bring the war to a swift conclusion, then the government would use money to end it. Accordingly, Tobias Lear was instructed that the administration hoped peace could be concluded "without any price or pecuniary concession whatever." But, if circumstances unforeseen in Washington rendered Commodore Samuel Barron's campaign abortive, Lear was authorized to give Tripoli up to $20,000 for making peace, to promise an annuity of from $8,000 to $10,000, and to pay a ransom of up to $500 apiece for the officers and crew of the *Philadelphia.* These were maximum sums that were to be offered in the last extremity only. If a cash settlement must be made, the government expected Lear to negotiate for the smallest sums possible.

It was assumed that the Barron squadron would reach Tripoli in time to strike a decisive blow during the summer of 1804. By 21 June, its ships had assembled in Hampton Roads, and were expected to be ready to sail not later than 1 July. The *John Adams,* which Secretary Smith had told Preble would sail from the United States in season to reach Syracuse by about the end of April, had, for unexplained reasons, still not left. She, however, did not wait for the rest of the squadron, but got to sea on 26 June. Intended principally as a storeship, she mounted only eight 6-pounders and eight 12-pounders: the rest of her guns were stored in her hold and their carriages were distributed on board the frigates sailing with Barron. The *John Adams* leaked badly, sometimes making as much as six or eight inches of water an hour, and her deep draft made her difficult to steer, especially in a strong wind. For these reasons, it had been expected that she would be overtaken by the Barron squadron before she joined Preble. But when the *John Adams* anchored at Gibraltar on 22 July, there was no sign of the other frigates. During the three days she stayed there before sailing to join Preble off Tripoli, her commander, Isaac Chauncey, wrote a friend: "I arrived here in good health after a passage of twenty-six days, although we sometimes took a yaw of fifty or sixty miles before we could stop her, and then away she go as far the other way. However, we seldom let her come up to *blow* when we had any wind." [13]

And Chauncey brought Preble a private letter that expressed no doubts about the responsibility Preble bore. Writing on 5 March, Charles Washington Goldsborough said:

> I suppose this will reach you off Tripoli, when you possibly may be engaged in the blockade of that place. I wish you great glory because I esteem you and because I wish to see the time when the Navy shall be supported by all ranks of our citizens. The achievement of glorious deeds will render the Navy popular. If you return to this country covered with laurels, as I have no doubt you will do if an opportunity offers or can be made to acquire them, there will be but one pulse in America on the subject of a Navy. If, on the contrary, you should return without having seen the whites of the enemy's eye, I should not be surprised if the Navy should lose in popularity.

CHAPTER 15 AUGUST 1804–SEPTEMBER 1804

"I hope to finish the war with Tripoli first, and then the sooner he [Commodore Barron] arrives the better, as I am anxious to return home."

How much my feelings are lacerated by this supersedure at the moment of victory cannot be described and can be felt only by an officer placed in my mortifying situation," Preble wrote when he began to adjust to the news contained in Robert Smith's dispatches. His sense of frustration was heightened by the *John Adams*'s incomplete armament. Could she have mounted all her guns, he might immediately have delivered a final and decisive attack on Tripoli; and this would have led to the speedy conclusion of a treaty on terms acceptable to the United States.

To negotiate a peace treaty that would enhance, or at least not damage, his reputation, before he had to surrender his command to Barron, became Preble's goal. Bonaventure Beaussier had suggested that he send a flag of truce to the harbor if he wished further negotiations, a suggestion Preble had spurned on the morning of the very day he received his dispatches from Smith. The next afternoon, 8 August 1804, Preble and Richard O'Brien boarded the *Argus* and instructed Master Commandant Hull to run her close in with the harbor rocks. In his diary and elsewhere, Preble said he was reconnoitering the port, but as the *Argus* approached the harbor entrance she fired a gun and hoisted the tricolor at the fore, a signal for the French consul. Tripoli was not prepared for friendly overtures that afternoon: its batteries opened fire on the *Argus*. Before the brig could pull out of range, one heavy shot struck her below the waterline, about three feet from the place where Preble was standing, but, luckily, it did not penetrate her hull.

The following day, 9 August, Preble tried again to get in touch with the French consul. At 9:30 a.m. he and O'Brien again embarked in the

Argus, which, together with the *Vixen*, stood towards Tripoli. As they neared the batteries, both brig and schooner showed American colors and the French flag at the fore; the *Argus* fired a gun. No reply came from the shore, but the batteries remained silent. The brig and schooner stood off and on the harbor until 12:30 p.m., when the tricolor, with a white flag under it, appeared over the walls of Tripoli. The *Argus* and *Vixen* made the same signal, and Richard O'Brien was soon on his way into the harbor in the *Argus*'s boat. He was not allowed to land in the city, but Beaussier's messenger met him in the outer part of the harbor and handed him a note from the French consul explaining that the bearer would accept any letters the boat had for Beaussier; if a reply was expected, the boat should return the next morning. O'Brien handed the messenger a letter from Preble and was back on board the *Argus* by 2:30 p.m.

Preble's letter to Beaussier was bluff from beginning to end. It concealed the fact that Preble was about to be superseded as squadron commander. It identified the *John Adams* as one of a reinforcement of four frigates that had sailed from the United States together. The others, having stopped briefly at Algiers and Tunis, would be arriving any day now, and when they did, Preble would no longer be able to offer a single dollar for peace or ransom, for "Such a force, you must be sensible, will enable us to destroy all the seaport towns in Tripoli." He was making his final offer, one which he solemnly assured Beaussier he would never exceed: $80,000 for ransom and a $10,000 consular present. Preble, fearful that Barron's sails might be sighted on the northern horizon at any moment, pressed Beaussier for a quick decision. If the terms were to be accepted, it must be done by ten o'clock the next morning. The signal for peace was to be the white flag under the French flag and a white flag at the Castle.

A little after sunrise on 10 August excitement swept through the *Constitution*. Several flags had been hoisted around the walls of Tripoli. Two were flying from the Castle. One of them appeared to be white! By way of reply, every ship of the squadron immediately hoisted a white flag at the fore, and the *Vixen* stood towards Tripoli to investigate. At 8:00 a.m. she came back with disappointing news: the flag on the Castle was yellow and white.

A white flag below the tricolor was at last sighted in Tripoli at 11:30 a.m. The *Argus* and *Vixen* again ran in close to the harbor, and at 1:30 p.m. Consul O'Brien once more entered the port in the barge. Preble, Smith, and Hull all went over to the *Vixen* to idle away the time it would take the barge to go and come from the harbor. It was half-past two when Beaussier's reply was brought to Preble on board the *Vixen*.

Beaussier had received Preble's letter at about three o'clock on the afternoon of the 9th, and had set out for Sidi Mohammed Dghies's country seat to talk over Preble's latest offer with the prime minister before presenting it to the Pasha. "[Dghies] swore to me," Beaussier wrote, "that, since the effusion of blood had begun, his country breathed only war; that the Pasha, electrified more than ever by the determination of his council and the patriotic élan of all his people, wished to await the outcome [of battle] unless the sum offered were immeasurably increased; that the regency spoke of nothing less than two to three hundred thousand dollars."

Beaussier and Dghies agreed that, under the circumstances, it would be foolish to propose the $80,000 to the Pasha. He would reject it summarily. Preble's attack on 3 August had shaken Yusuf, but he had regained his self-confidence when he saw what little damage Preble inflicted on the 7th. He had taken Preble's measure and would stand up to the worst he could offer. However, Dghies and Beaussier thought that, if Preble would empower them to offer a ransom of $150,000, they could bring enough pressure to bear on the Pasha to persuade him to accept that amount and sign a new treaty. "This ransom, Monsieur le Commodore, is not at all dear, and could only be approved by your government if you desire to alter the intentions of the Pasha, who still persists in wishing to hazard all rather than compromise his dignity on this point. Moreover, what joy you would experience in setting your unfortunate countrymen free — without risking some catastrophe to them — and at a price which every power will call a reasonable one!" Would Preble authorize an offer of $150,000, asked Beaussier.

For Edward Preble this was summer's cruelest time. At last he was convinced that Beaussier was right: the United States could not hope to release its prisoners for less than $150,000. Tobias Lear had authorized Preble to pay this much ransom. But Isaac Chauncey told Preble that the government expected the enlarged squadron under Barron to release the prisoners without paying any ransom. In Preble's judgment this was the hour to move towards peace, yet if he gave $150,000 for ransom he would have forestalled Samuel Barron's chance of reaching a gratuitous peace settlement and the administration would be highly dissatisfied with him.[1] He would return to the United States more disgraced than Richard V. Morris, and would perhaps meet the same fate. The administration's vengeance against Morris — which Preble had heard about less than seventy-two hours earlier — was enough to make even the most resolute pause before exercising extraordinary discretion. If peace without a ransom was government policy, Preble would not hazard his reputation by paying $150,000 for the prisoners — even though his successor might end by giving just as much.

Without much enthusiasm, Preble returned to his writing desk to try one more combination of bluff, threats, and offers. One hundred and fifty thousand dollars could not be offered, he wrote Beaussier on 11 August, nor could any more time be lost in attempting to negotiate: the bombardment of the town must be resumed. From what he had already seen, said Preble, he was convinced that once the additional frigates arrived he would be able to reduce Tripoli "to a heap of ruins; the destruction of Derna and Benghazi will follow; and the blockade be constantly continued." In addition, William Eaton, the former U.S. Consul at Tunis, was coming out in one of the frigates with orders from the President to execute Eaton's long-meditated plan of assisting Hamet Caramanli to overthrow his brother Yusuf. To avoid these calamities, Tripoli should agree to the terms Preble now proposed — he was, he alleged, at the utmost limit of his instructions — $100,000 for ransom of the prisoners, a $10,000 consular present, and $10,000 in presents to Mohammed Dghies and other officials who used their influence to persuade the Pasha to sign a treaty on these terms. "If the terms now offered are accepted of, I wish you to hoist the white flag under the French flag at your staff by 5 o'clock this evening and come off, and I will send a boat to the rocks to receive you."

To reinforce this message Preble got his squadron under way and ran to within three or four miles of Tripoli; then with her main topsail to the mast, the *Constitution* brought to while Richard O'Brien took Preble's letter in to the harbor and returned. All through the afternoon of the 11th the ships stood off and on the town, waiting for a signal to be hoisted on the French flagstaff. At 4:00 p.m. Preble sent the *Argus* to stand by close to the town, ready to bring Beaussier off to the *Constitution*. Evening came, but no flag was hoisted at the French consulate.

II

In his report on the summer campaign, Preble gave the impression that he suspended his attacks for ten days or two weeks after the *John Adams*'s arrival so that, immediately upon Samuel Barron's appearance on the coast, his and Barron's squadrons could, together, make a decisive attack. In fact, after the suspension of negotiations on 11 August, Preble had no intention whatever of loyally waiting for Barron's topsails to appear over the horizon, as is shown in a letter he wrote a friend on 15 August: "You will have observed that Commodore Barron supersedes me in the command in the Mediterranean. I hope to finish the war with Tripoli first, and then the sooner he arrives the better, as I am anxious to return home."

For twelve days, beginning on 11 August, Preble made a series of attempts to launch a third attack on Tripoli. He was determined to try his luck with a night attack. He did not explain his reasons. Perhaps he thought that darkness would handicap the defenders more than it would the assailants; or he may have supposed that a night bombardment would have an especially demoralizing effect on the people of the city. Wind and sea frustrated his attempts, since, to approach Tripoli with a reasonable degree of safety and the assurance of a route of withdrawal when the time came, the wind had to be blowing from the southward of east and the sea had to be smooth.

When it became clear that Beaussier was not going to negotiate a new treaty on 11 August, Preble summoned all his captains on board the *Constitution* to complete plans for an attack as soon as darkness fell. But at 9:00 p.m. the wind veered from E. by N. to N.E. by N. and commenced to heave a swell on shore, precluding the possibility of action that night.

Two days later conditions for a night attack looked more favorable and, at sunset, the squadron formed up in close order, some three or four miles from Tripoli harbor, ready to push in when darkness came. By eight o'clock there were strong breezes from E. by N. Henry Wadsworth in Gunboat No. 6 was in difficulty: he fired a rocket, showed two lanterns, and burned a light-blue flame, known as a false fire, to signal his distress. The rising wind had carried away his lateen yard and was scattering the ships of the squadron and throwing them into confusion. Several attempts to form up anew failed, and at 9:00 p.m. another gunboat, No. 1, Richard Somers, lost her lateen yard. Preble realized the imprudence of making an attack that night and hoisted the signal, Prepare to anchor.

It was the evening of 16 August when Preble's ships again closed on the harbor. Fifteen Tripolitan gunboats, a three-masted galley, and a schooner were moored within the harbor rocks and under cover of grapeshot from the batteries. Between eight o'clock and 9:30 a light but favorable breeze enabled the squadron to move nearer to Tripoli. But by 9:45 p.m., with Tripoli in sight, bearing S. by W. ¼ W., the breeze had almost died away. The *Constitution* fired a rocket and hoisted three lanterns as a signal for the gunboats and bomb ketches to come within hail. She thereby revealed her position, and the Molehead Battery and the English Fort fired eleven guns at her, but all the shot fell short. A southwesterly current was rapidly carrying the squadron within range of the batteries, and the near calm would make it difficult for them to extricate themselves once engaged, particularly if any of the ships should be disabled. Preble decided to delay the attack. The squadron tacked to the N.N.E., then at 11:00 p.m. wore and stood in for the town again. This time, they were greeted with fourteen shot, but again all fell short. Midnight came and went, but the threat of total calm remained. Again, the attempt had to be abandoned.

After dark the following day, Preble sent Stephen Decatur and Isaac

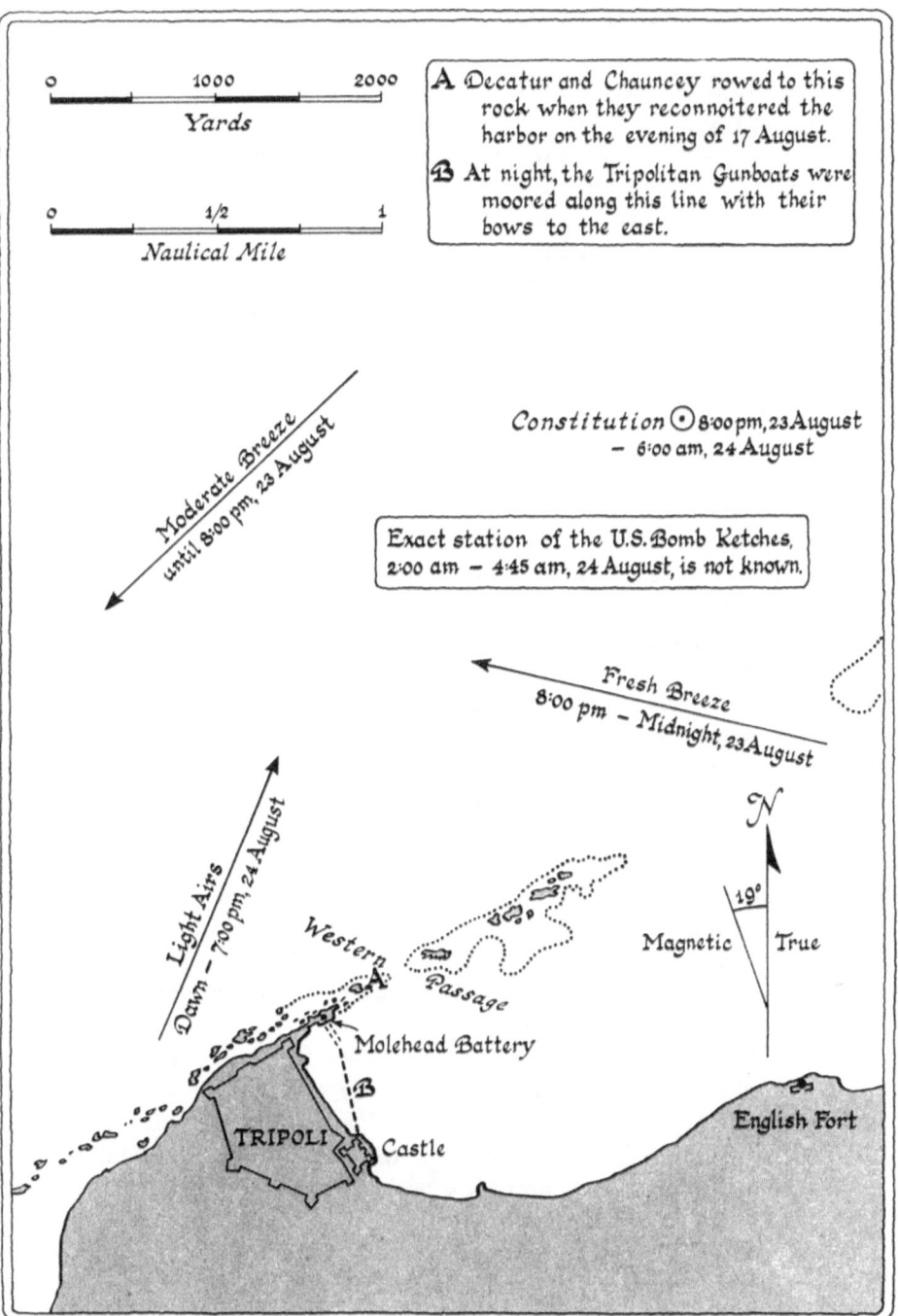

Reconnaissance of 17 August and Bombardment of 23/24 August 1804

Chauncey in two boats to discover where the Tripolitans moored their gunboats at night. The two officers rowed as far as the westernmost rock of the chain that formed the harbor, so close to the batteries that they could see the sentinels on the Castle. The Tripolitan gunboats, their bows pointed eastward, were moored in a line abreast extending from mole to Castle. At midnight, when Preble heard that report, he ordered the flotilla to move in to attack before daylight, but within the hour the wind shifted and dropped to light offshore airs. A strong current was setting to the westward. The gunboats and ketches would not be able to reach their stations before dawn. The attack must be deferred to another night.

On the evening of 22 August, it looked as though a bombardment could at last be brought off. The sky was cloudy and overcast, but the wind was from the right quarter. It varied between E. by N. and E.S.E. and gradually dropped in intensity until, at 11:30 p.m., it was nearly calm. This calm was less hazardous because the current set to the eastward, away from the batteries. At 11:45 p.m. the *Constitution* let go her small bower nearly two miles N.E. by N. from Tripoli. As the squadron cast loose the gunboats and ketches, a breeze sprang up from the northeast, practically dead onshore. All preparations had to be suspended. At 2:30 a.m., for the fifth time in twelve days, Preble abandoned hope of attacking.

The day before that last attempt, the Commodore had assessed the situation: there had been several periods of unsettled weather during the previous two weeks, and the gunboats were so hard to handle in the rough and open sea that he would not be able to keep his entire squadron off Tripoli any longer than another ten or twelve days, or until about the first of September. Unless the Barron squadron arrived within that time, or Preble could deliver so decisive a blow that it forced the Pasha to negotiate, the campaign would probably have to be abandoned for the year.

A chance for Preble to see what effect one more attack would have came at last during the night of 23/24 August.

In the afternoon the squadron was at anchor five miles N.E. by N. from Tripoli. As the sun began to drop towards the horizon, the ships got under way with a moderate N.E. breeze and stood in towards the city. When the *Constitution* anchored two miles from the English Fort and about two and a half miles from the batteries, with Tripoli bearing S.S.W., it was eight o'clock, and the wind had shifted to E. by S. and increased in force to a fresh breeze. The gunboats were cast off by the mother ships, and the whole squadron instructed by signal to remain within hail. But the breeze was too fresh for the gunboats to maneuver by themselves, and within the hour the brigs and schooners were ordered to take them in tow again. The *Constitution* put slip-buoys on her anchor cable and readied herself to go into action the moment the wind was favorable. About 10:00 p.m. Preble cast off the two bomb ketches and ordered the *Argus* and *Syren* to take them under tow, work inshore, and wait for his signal to attack the batteries.

By midnight the wind had started to drop away; at 1:00 a.m. there was a dead calm. The boats of the squadron were cast off to aid in towing the gunboats and bomb ketches into position for the attack. The role of the gunboats was to take up stations close by the ketches to protect them, should the Tripolitan gunboats attempt to capture them. At 2:00 a.m. the ketches reached what was assumed to be a favorable station and began throwing shells towards the town. No reply came from the Tripolitan batteries; not a light could be seen in the city or on the fortifications. Perhaps a total of fifteen or twenty shells had been thrown by 4:45 a.m., when, with dawn breaking, Preble signalled the gunboats and bomb ketches: "Discontinue firing on the batteries and retire as soon as possible out of gunshot of the batteries, to be taken in tow by the vessels you are attached to."

At 5:15 a.m., as the American flotilla was beginning to pull off, the Tripolitan gunboats came out from their anchorage within the mole and formed a line of defense. Snugly positioned inside the rocks and protected by the batteries, they presented no tempting target. The reassembled U.S. squadron stood off to an anchorage four miles N.N.E. of the Castle.

Compared to the battles of the 3rd and the 7th, this night bombardment may have seemed a rather lackluster affair. The participants told themselves that the shells must have damaged Tripoli heavily. One of them claimed that two Tripolitan gunboats and a galliot had been sunk. The usually accurate Nathaniel Haraden thought he saw a forty-foot breach in the wall of the Castle. Later, Preble confined himself to saying that the effects of the bombardment were uncertain. In point of fact, observers in Tripoli were unanimous in reporting that every American shell fell short: not one dropped inside the harbor; not one reached the Molehead Battery, the closest fortification. The Pasha was elated; and this ineffectual performance, added to the destruction of Gunboat No. 9 on 7 August, gave a fresh stimulus to the already keyed-up Tripolitan morale.[2]

III

Preble attempted a new daylight attack on 25 August, but strong easterly breezes frustrated him. Two and a half weeks of fickle weather and Preble was downcast. His luck seemed to be exhausted. By the morning of 27 August he may have been ready to give up the campaign. He learned from the master of the ketch *Eliza*, which had arrived from Malta the day before, that as late as 22 August not a single ship of the Barron squadron had touched at Malta. It was three weeks since the lumbering *John Adams* had arrived, supposedly with the other frigates on her heels. What had become of them? When Preble ordered the *John Adams* to hoist in the bow guns from several of the gunboats early on the 27th, many of his officers surmised that he was preparing to send the gunboats and bomb ketches back to Sicily, and to resume a simple blockade with a few of his ships. But if one hour Preble wanted to quit, by the next he had recovered himself and was full of fight. A letter from Sir Alexander Ball, brought by the *Eliza*, strengthened his spirit. "So eminent a display of bravery and enterprize," wrote Ball of the battle on 3 August, "cannot fail to impress the enemy with such an opinion of your countrymen as will make them sensible of their interest in cultivating peace with them, the result of which will stamp the highest honor on your naval character in having planned and so successfully executed such arduous operations." How could he give up after praise like that? By noon of 27 August the Commodore thought that the weather, which in the morning had been cloudy and overcast, with a N.N.W. wind and swell, was going to improve enough for another attack that night. He countermanded his order for disarming the gunboats.

Preble's assessment proved correct. By mid-afternoon the wind had become a pleasant E. by N. breeze. The squadron got under way and stood towards the town, while the senior officers assembled in the *Constitution*'s cabin to discuss plans for the night's attack. At 5:30 p.m., when the *Constitution* reached a position which Nathaniel Haraden calculated as two miles N. by E. ½ E. from the English Fort and two and a half miles N.E. by N. ½ N. from the Castle, she dropped anchor. The rest of the squadron remained under way, standing off and on the land. Preparations for the attack filled the hours till it was 8:00 p.m. Earlier in the day, a survey of Bomb Ketch No. 1 discovered that her mortar bed had given way and that she was leaking in a number of places. Preble ordered her five-ton mortar hoisted out and placed in the frigate's main hatchway, then sent her to moor near the *John Adams*, seven miles north of Tripoli.

As dusk deepened into darkness, sixteen or seventeen gunboats, two galleys, a schooner and a brig were counted at defensive positions within the shelter of the harbor rocks. A galliot and a ship lay at anchor deeper inside the harbor, but since neither had colors hoisted, Preble could not determine whether they were Tripolitan or not. The Americans assumed that once it was dark, all but two of the Tripolitan gunboats would follow their nighttime practice of retiring within the mole: the two left outside would serve as picket boats. By 8:30 p.m. a fresh E.S.E. breeze prevented immediate attack. The *Constitution* furled her sails and signalled the other vessels

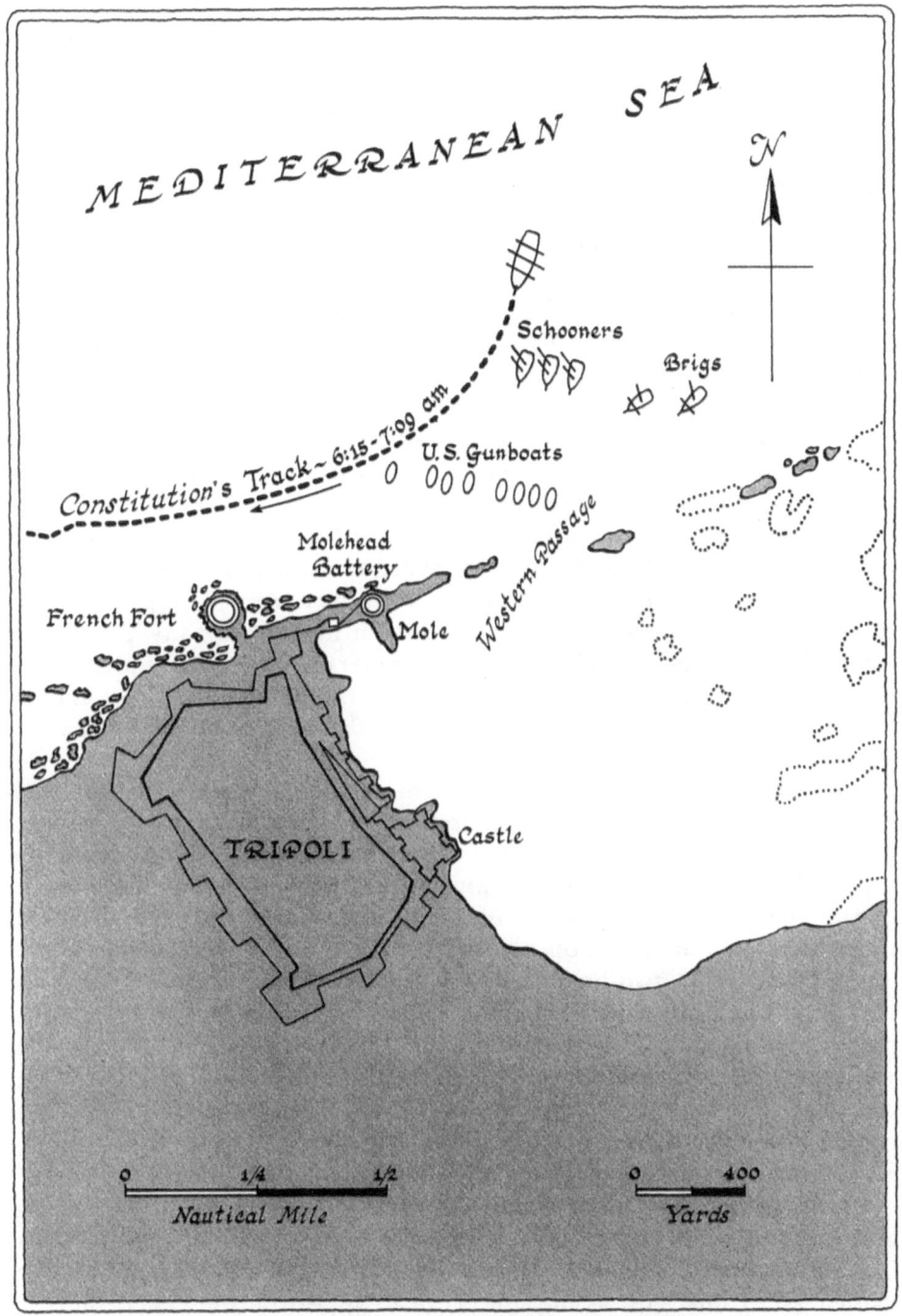

Attack on Tripoli by the U.S. Squadron and Flotilla
Commanded by Commodore Preble during the Morning of 28 August 1804

Redrawn from a Chart Made by Midshipman William Lewis

of the squadron to keep under way, but within sight, to windward. The wind had, by this hour, cleared away the clouds, and in the bright moonlight the movements of the U.S. squadron were visible from as far away as five miles. Occasionally the night was further brightened by false fires burning in the squadron or on shore. Now and then a signal gun was heard. Around midnight, the wind started to moderate, and at 1:15 a.m., although the sea was still rough, Preble signalled his gunboats and Bomb Ketch No. 2: "Advance to attack enemy's ships or batteries." All went well for perhaps half or three-quarters of an hour, that is, until Bomb Ketch No. 2 sprang a leak. The *Enterprize*, which had not yet cast her off, towed her out of range of the Tripolitan batteries, then rejoined the advance.

Preble directed his gunboats to a position that had been discovered by Midshipman Charles Morris when he had accompanied Richard O'Brien in one of the flags of truce earlier in the month. It was a station close to the western passage through the rocks, from which the American gunboats could fire on the city and shipping while remaining masked from some of the Tripolitan batteries defending the harbor. Armed ships' boats accompanied the gunboats in order to aid them in boarding any Tripolitans that might come out for close combat. The *Argus, Syren, Enterprize, Nautilus,* and *Vixen* took up positions offshore of the gunboats, but close enough in to cover them, to tow off any gunboats that might be disabled, or to cover a retreat.

Sometime between 2:30 and 3:15 a.m. Preble saw that the gunboats had reached their assigned position and had anchored with springs on their cables. For want of a precise night signal to deal with this situation, he repeated his signal to advance to attack the enemy's ships or batteries — a gun, a rocket arching through the night, and a false fire. The gunboats understood his intent and opened fire. In the course of the bombardment, which lasted about two hours, some of the boats fired as many as sixty or sixty-five rounds, principally 24-pound round shot, while one boat, for unexplained reasons, got off only eleven rounds. The average for all the gunboats was about forty-two rounds apiece. At first, no answering fire came from the shore, but soon every gun in the fortifications around Tripoli that could be brought to bear was in action. Tripolitan gunboats, firing at long range from their anchorage close under the Castle, joined the battle. Preble's gunboats proved poor targets, and the chief damage to them was cut rigging and torn sails. American fire battered down a part of the Molehead fortification, and the gunboat crews thought they saw a galliot and a three-masted galley sink. Just as the sun began to appear on the eastern horizon one of the largest Tripolitan gunboats came out through the western passage to attack the easternmost American boat. The U.S. boat waited until the Tripolitan had closed to about fifty yards, then fired a round shot from her bow gun, reloaded with grape, and fired again. The second round killed four Tripolitans and wounded two, whereupon the enemy boat pulled back within the rocks.

Even before this attack was repulsed, in the first weak light of dawn, Preble had seen thirteen Tripolitan gunboats and galleys, that had come out as far as the rocks, exchanging close-range fire with the American boats. Calculating that they were looking for an opportunity to attack the Americans and carry them by boarding, and that his own boats must have used up most of their ammunition, he decided to get under way. As the *Constitution*, aided by an ideal E. by S. wind, stood in towards the city, she came under fire from seventy-two shore-based Tripolitan guns which Nathaniel Haraden estimated covered her approach to the port.

"The Commodore's ship, when standing in and during the engagement, was the most elegant sight that I ever saw," wrote Purser Darby of the *John Adams*. "She had her tompions out, matches lit, and batteries lighted up, all hands at quarters, standing right in under the fort, and receiving a heavy cannonading from their battery."

When the *Constitution* was close to the harbor she signalled the gunboats to cease firing and retire out of gunshot as quickly as possible, there to be taken in tow by their mother ships. The gunboats began to haul off, and as the *Constitution* passed them, they started cheering her. At 6:15 the *Constitution* was within 1,200 feet of the harbor rocks and, with her bow guns, she opened fire on the Tripolitan gunboats and galleys that had been engaged with the American gunboats and were harassing them as they retreated. Observers in the *Constitution* credited her with sinking one Tripolitan boat and forcing two to run on shore to avoid a like end. Certain it was that all the enemy boats immediately retreated to safety deep in the harbor. The *Constitution* ran to leeward until she was 400 yards from the Molehead. There, she hove to, parallel with the seaward fortifications, and fired one broadside of round and grape after another until a total of nine broadsides, or about 225 rounds, had been discharged. With each broadside, a cloud of dust and stone fragments rose into the air and momentarily obscured the fortifications. The Castle and two of the batteries were completely silenced. As on the 3rd of August, the *Constitution* was working at such close range that most of the damage she sustained was to her rigging. Only nineteen Tripolitan round shot struck her, though after the battle a fair number of grapeshot were found lodged in her hull.

By the time the *Constitution* had fired her ninth broadside, all the gunboats were out of range and under tow of their mother ships. It was a little after 7:00 a.m. when she stood out for an anchorage four miles N.E.

by N. from the hostile batteries. As she did so, Tripoli's fortifications came to life and resumed their harassing fire.

IV

On the afternoon of 29 August Bonaventure Beaussier was drafting a letter to Preble when someone came in and told him that the brig *Argus* was off the harbor signalling for communication with him. He paused in his writing long enough to send a messenger off in a boat to meet the *Argus*'s barge and receive the dispatches the *Argus* had for him. Then he returned to his letter: "To my great astonishment and regret I heard that a brig of your squadron is advancing to parley. Whatever may be the motive, I think this step is most ill-advised and disastrous for the interests of your government, because it can only be interpreted to your disadvantage and raise the Pasha's pretensions."

Beaussier's letter summarized events in Tripoli since 11 August, when Preble had sent his dispatch saying that his "utmost" offer was $120,000 in ransom and presents.

Beaussier had been received in audience by the Pasha the day after receipt of that message, and thought he was making some progress towards a compromise acceptable to Preble and Yusuf. He was about to signal Preble to send a flag of truce on shore when the Pasha told him to hold off; he wished to see the results of Preble's next attack before he discussed negotiations further. That next attack was the ineffectual one of 23/24 August, when every shell thrown had dropped harmlessly into the sea. "The attack of the 27th/28th was more serious," Beaussier wrote Preble. "One 36-pound shot struck the Castle and penetrated the apartment of the [American officer] prisoners, another penetrated the sailors' prison, others struck a great many houses — notably those of the Spanish, Swedish, and Dutch consuls — while still other shot fell outside the city, where a camel was killed, and some even landed in the gardens. A Tunisian prize was sunk, and a Spanish vessel (with a pass from the United States consul at Tunis) that brought here a chiaus from the Grand Seignior was hulled. A corsair belonging to this regency lost four men killed by grapeshot."

It was difficult to fathom the Pasha's mind. Preble's incendiary shells alarmed him but, because buildings and batteries could be easily repaired, he was indifferent to the damage the round shot were doing Tripoli. In Beaussier's opinion, Preble was using the wrong tactic when he threatened: threats angered the Pasha and stiffened his resistance to negotiation. Sidi Mohammed Dghies and Beaussier had agreed to conceal from the Pasha the news that William Eaton was coming out to offer American aid to

Hamet Caramanli. Should Yusuf learn that the United States was making common cause with his brother, Dghies was certain it would destroy every hope for peace. For the present, Beaussier wrote before he heard that the *Argus* was bearing down on the town with the white and French flags flying, he did not intend to press Yusuf towards further negotiations: "I leave the Pasha to his own reflections. He is naturally mistrustful and suspicious. Were I to manifest any eagerness for a decision on his part he would only become more inflexible."

Two things accounted for the relatively light destruction in the city. First, the buildings were constructed almost exclusively of stone and mud, which are not as susceptible to damage as is wood. Second, only a small percentage of the shells thrown by the bomb ketches burst. This was probably a reflection of American inexperience with mortars: not a single officer in the U.S. Navy was a skilled bombardier. Preble had borrowed a Neapolitan bombardier officer, Don Antonio Massi, and he was training Preble's officers in the science of firing mortars, but the Americans apparently had not had enough battle experience to become adepts.

When Beaussier read the dispatch brought by the *Argus* late in the afternoon of the 29th, he found that Preble was proposing that forty-two Tripolitan prisoners on board the *Constitution* be exchanged for captive Americans in the Pasha's prisons. To this proposition Preble added: "I think it very probable, if I could see you on board, that such arrangements may be made as to effect the ransom of the whole of my countrymen." Apparently the Commodore was prepared to move a little closer to $150,000. But Beaussier's patience with what he considered Preble's lack of sensitivity to the Barbary mentality was wearing thin: cartels for the exchange of prisoners were simply never arranged between Muslims and Christians, and Preble's practice of finding excuses to send flags of truce on shore to take diplomatic soundings after each attack was weakening the Commodore's hand. The Pasha was growing weary of these unproductive negotiations, took them for a sign of weakness or perplexity on Preble's part, or for an indication that Preble *had* to make peace. Yusuf, feeling that he had the upper hand psychologically, grew more obstinate.

The Pasha was at his country home and Beaussier was not able to see him until 30 August. This audience proved as unproductive as Beaussier had feared. A prisoner exchange was instantly rejected. The Americans are neglecting nothing in their attempt to devastate my country and escape paying a just ransom for the three hundred prisoners, said Yusuf. Through all the months of negotiation, the Pasha had carefully avoided defining exactly what ransom he would accept for the *Philadelphia* prisoners. At this audience, however, he told Beaussier that the recent attacks had enabled him to gain an accurate idea of the power of the U.S. squadron — even of what it would be after the arrival of the four additional frigates — and, on the basis of that knowledge, he was formally setting the ransom at $400,000 plus gifts for himself and his ministers. He was holding his ransom demand down to this amount, Yusuf added, only because of his friendship for France; and he was not promising to stay within these limits in the future. If the Americans could not reach agreement with him now, perhaps they would next year.

Beaussier explained that it was beyond Preble's power to approach $400,000. The Pasha was impervious to argument or persuasion. Beaussier wrote to Talleyrand:

> Now Preble can hope for success only when his four additional frigates arrive — but this prince is not afraid of their guns either. Unless Preble succeeds in striking great blows, Tripoli will yet cause the United States to repent her vain attacks, and the regency will gain the glory of having resisted the reinforced squadron. This is what the Pasha desires most of all, that the powers of Europe and Africa may form a favorable opinion of his resources and his courage. From the outset, it would have been more appropriate and more adroit [for Preble] to have attacked vigorously and continuously, without entering into any negotiations. The Barbary regencies are skilled at putting up a good front with tiny means, but most especially when they see that one treats them with circumspection.[3]

Consul Beaussier reported the results of his audience to Preble by letter, and informed him that because of the unpromising outlook for negotiations, the Pasha was unwilling to let him go out to the *Constitution*. Then he added some reflections of his own:

> There remains for you, Monsieur le Commodore, only the sad alternative of attacking the town, and particularly the Castle, *without intermission,* unless you feel yourself authorized to approach the Pasha's demand. If you do not, it will be superfluous to reply. You must wait until the Pasha, harassed at all points, himself asks for a parley. Not having better news to give you is truly painful for me. I quite sincerely share all your anxiety and impatience, but I attribute this vexatious contretemps solely to the series of communications between us, which this prince takes for weakness and perplexity. . . .
> If I could think that it was in your power to approach it — or at least not deviate too much from it — I would say that I had reason to believe this business could be settled for $300,000. Ah, Monsieur le Commodore, if in reply to my letter of 10 August — which held out the hope of settling for $150,000 — if, instead of limiting the ransom to $100,000, you had had more confidence in me and in Sidi Mohammed Dghies, the prisoners should at this moment be free! The decision of the Pasha to see the outcome of the third attack [23/24 August] — which was, unhappily, nothing — and the small damage resulting from the fourth attack [27/28 August] have entirely changed the state of things.

These were the last communications between Beaussier and Preble. Their confrontation was Preble's most instructive and crucial personal relationship during his Mediterranean command. Instructive, because Preble's failure to get along with Beaussier shows how the same qualities that made him a strong executive and field commander, handicapped him in his duties as a diplomatist: when he lacked the moderating influences of Lear and Simpson, which had served him during the Moroccan negotiations, Preble's harshness and suspicion came to the fore. Crucial, since it is at least partially true to say that, because Beaussier and Preble did not trust one another, peace slipped through their fingers. But this last statement must be balanced against the realization that during the spring and summer of 1804 neither side was fully ready, mentally or emotionally, for peace negotiations.

V

It was easier for Beaussier to give advice than it was practical for Preble to carry it out: "Only the sad alternative of attacking the town, and particularly the Castle, *without intermission.* . . . wait until the Pasha, harassed at all points, himself asks for a parley."

By the 29th of August, the day of his final demarche to Beaussier, Preble had all but abandoned any expectation of ending the war during the summer of 1804. There was no news of Samuel Barron's four frigates. On their quick arrival depended the best chance of forcing a peace during the dwindling number of days of summer. When those few days were gone the gunboats, which even during August had been a nagging anxiety to Preble every time the wind rose or the swell built up, would have to return to Sicily. Whatever their seaworthiness, they would have to go into port soon, for their ammunition was nearing exhaustion. Moreover, the past five weeks on the enemy's coast — night after night of sleep lost in attacks or attempted attacks on Tripoli, the constant tension of being at an insecure anchorage in an open roadstead — had been expensive in terms of fatigue, and officers and men alike were worn out.

Despite the unpromising outlook, Preble was unwilling to give up his campaign. Concurrently with his last attempt at negotiation, he began, on 29 August, to prepare for two different types of attack: another bombardment of the city by the gunboats; and the sailing of a fire ship or, more precisely, an "infernal" into the midst of the Tripolitan gunboats and galleys at their night anchorage. Audacious and risky as the use of the latter device was, it was not a move inspired by desperation: as early as the preceding March Preble had written Robert Smith that he expected to use fire ships against Tripoli's defenses.

The ketch *Intrepid* had joined the squadron on 19 August with a cargo of water and provisions from Syracuse. During the morning of the 29th, even before he sent the *Argus* in towards Tripoli with his proposition for an exchange of prisoners, Preble began converting the *Intrepid* into a fire ship. All the squadron's carpenters were mobilized for the job and worked under Preble's personal inspection. They planked up a magazine in the hold, which magazine was then loaded with about five tons of powder. One hundred 13-inch shells and fifty 9-inch shells were placed on deck immediately above the powder. Two holes the size of a gun barrel were drilled in the bulkheads of the magazine, and into them were inserted gun barrels filled with fuses that would burn for eleven minutes before igniting the powder in the magazine. These fuses connected with a trough that ran to a scuttle near the *Intrepid*'s bow and aft to her companionway, permitting the train to be fired from the bow, the stern, or from both. A small room aft was filled with wood scraps and other combustibles, and was to be set afire when the fire ship reached her target. This blaze would touch off the train, and, it was hoped, would discourage the Tripolitans from boarding the *Intrepid* and defusing her while the American crew escaped in two of the squadron's swiftest boats.[4]

There was no shortage of volunteers for this dangerous mission, but Preble selected men who had so far been deprived of an opportunity to win some distinction, either by firing the *Philadelphia* or by serving in the gunboats. Command went to Richard Somers, who had been prevented by the poor sailing qualities of the *Nautilus* from participating in the gunboat battle on the 3rd of August. Although Henry Wadsworth had missed going on the expedition to destroy the *Philadelphia*,* some of his shipmates thought the Commodore was playing favorites in selecting him as Somers's principal assistant. Midshipman Joseph Israel, a protégé of Robert Smith, was chosen as the third officer. Somers selected four seamen from the *Nautilus*, and Wadsworth six from the *Constitution* to make up the *Intrepid*'s crew. The three officers announced their intention of blowing themselves up rather than permit the capture of five tons of powder, which, they had heard, was in critically short supply in Tripoli.

Chauncey's and Decatur's open-boat reconnaissance on the evening of 17 August had revealed thirteen gunboats, two galleys, a schooner, and a brig moored close alongside one another between the mole and the Castle, and subsequent observation confirmed that this was the nightly practice. Preble

---

* When the expedition left to destroy the *Philadelphia*, Henry Wadsworth was on the sick list with venereal disease. "The Devil, or rather my own imprudence, had decreed against me," he wrote. "I was too weak to walk and sat biting my fingers and consuming with vexation at the absence of my good genius which had suffered the Devil to gain a victory."

supposed that, if the *Intrepid* could be exploded in the middle of this shipping, most of the Tripolitan flotilla would be sunk or badly damaged, and he hoped the Castle and adjacent fortifications would be shattered by the force of the blast. Such a catastrophe would be the great blow that Beaussier said Preble must strike if the United States was to avoid an embarrassing defeat in the Mediterranean, and would almost surely force the Pasha to make peace.

The *Intrepid* was ready by the evening of 1 September. That afternoon the squadron stood down towards the harbor, but, to avoid arousing Tripolitan suspicions, the *Intrepid* did not accompany them. As the sun set, the *Constitution* anchored two and a half miles N.N.E. from Tripoli and above two miles from the English Fort. Through the twilight, the Tripolitan gunboats and galleys could be seen hauling into their nighttime berths between mole and Castle. When darkness was complete enough to conceal her movements, the *Intrepid* ran down to join the *Constitution*. The wind was E.S.E., a fair wind for her destination. From her deck, the mole bore S.S.W., two and a half miles away. At 10:30 p.m. Somers, Wadsworth, Israel, and the ten seamen relieved the men who had brought the ketch down. Half an hour later, they slipped her cable and she moved off towards the harbor. Everything went well until she came within 400 yards of the western passage, when suddenly the wind swung round to the south, taking the *Intrepid* dead aback and making it impossible for her to get into the harbor. So far as anyone could tell, her presence had not been detected by the Tripolitans. Master Commandant Somers turned back, and at 2:00 a.m. rejoined the squadron.

It was light, but the sun had not yet come up over the eastern horizon on 2 September, when twelve of the Tripolitan gunboats, two three-masted galleys, the brig, and the schooner hauled out from the inner harbor and assumed their defensive stations inside the line of rocks. They did not stay there long. During the forenoon, while Preble's vessels, scattered to leeward, were attempting to come within hail of the *Constitution*, in the face of light breezes veering between E.S.E. and E. by N. and a current setting to leeward, the Tripolitan gunboats and galleys worked to windward inside the harbor and anchored off the English Fort. They were under cover of grapeshot from that fortification. For once Preble admitted admiration for Tripolitan tactics: "This was certainly a judicious movement of theirs, as it precluded the possibility of our boats going down to attack the town without leaving the enemy's flotilla in their rear and directly to windward."

Behind the English Fort, which stood close to the water, there was a steep embankment on whose crest, about a quarter-mile to the west, stood the fortification known as the New Battery. Because the outer edge of the

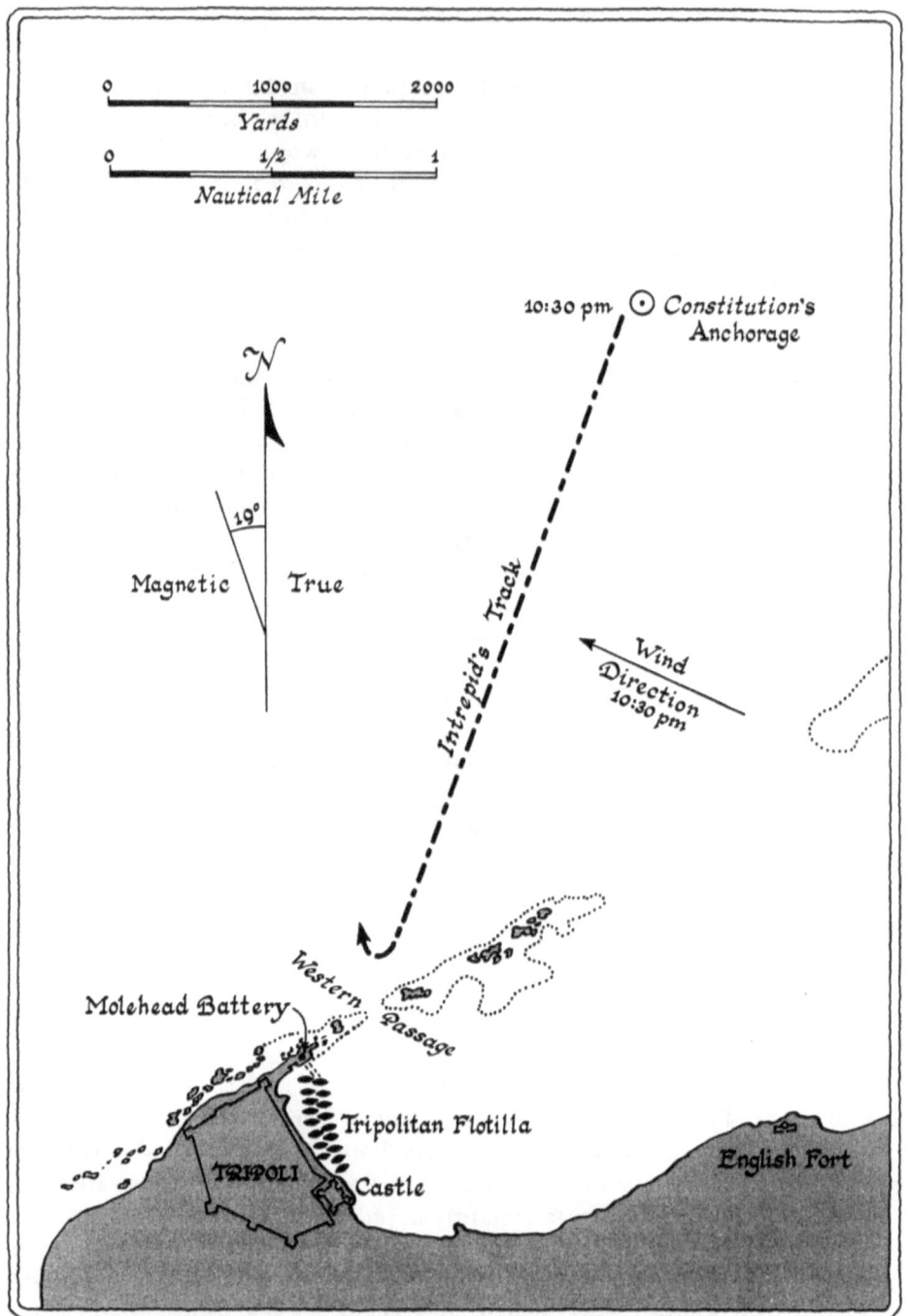

The *Intrepid*'s Attempt to Enter Tripoli Harbor, 1 September 1804

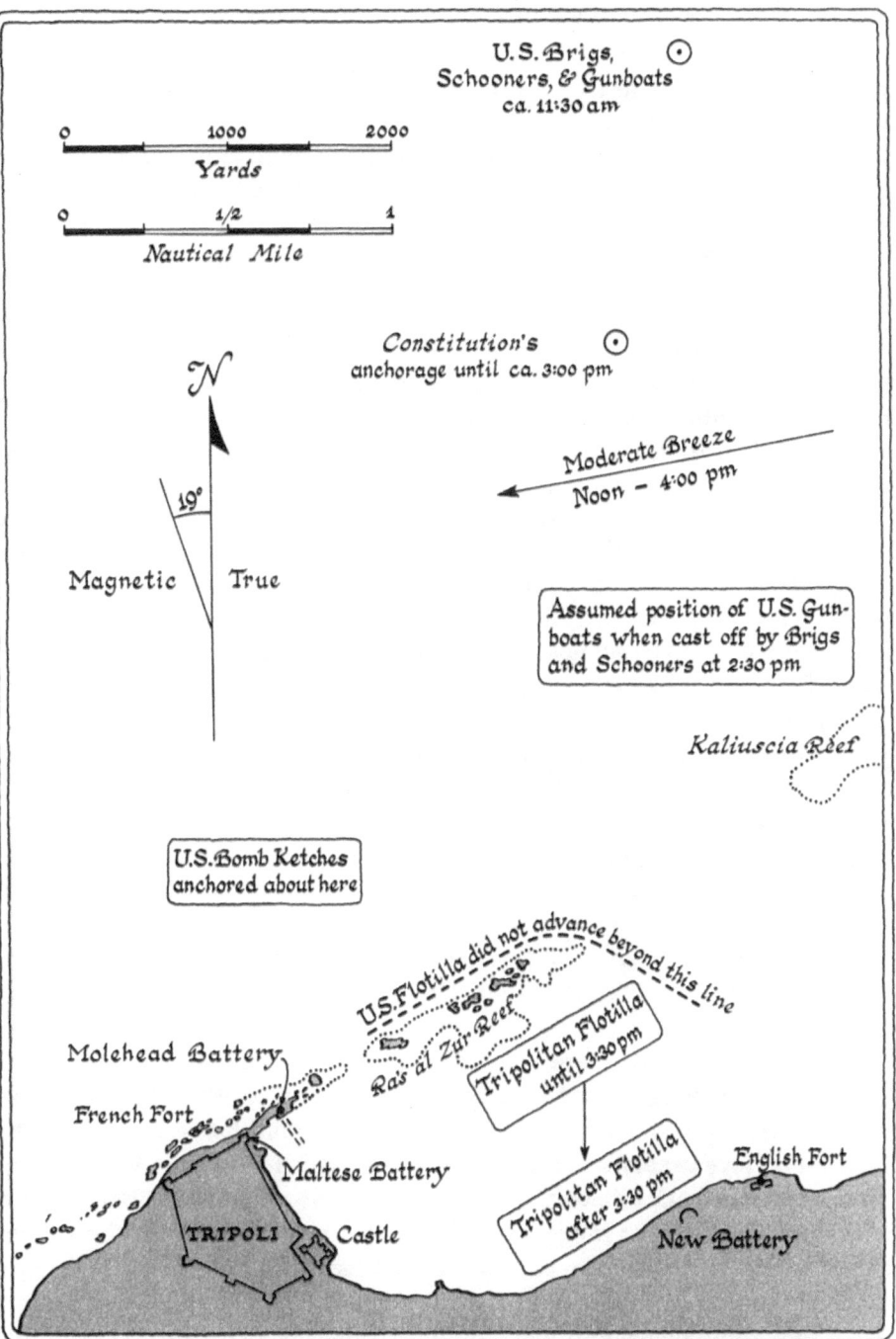

Attack on Tripoli and the Tripolitan Flotilla, 2 September 1804

Ra's al Zur Reef lay nearly a mile and a half offshore opposite the English Fort, it was impossible for the deep-draft *Constitution* to get in close enough to attack effectively either the fort or the small craft sheltering under its guns. To meet the Tripolitan dispositions, Preble decided to send his gunboats, supported by the brigs and schooners, to engage Tripoli's gunboats and galleys off the English Fort, while the *Constitution* and the bomb ketches attacked the city.

By 2:15 p.m. the brigs and schooners, towing the eight U.S. gunboats, had worked to windward of the enemy flotilla and were about two miles from the English Fort. The moderate breeze was from E. by N. In fifteen minutes, the gunboats had cast loose, and the *Constitution* signalled: "Advance, the first division, and attack the batteries or vessels of the enemy." Minutes later Preble made a similar signal to the second division.

Inside of an hour, the bomb ketches had found their range and were coming to anchor, the *Constitution* was running down towards the city, and the gunboats were within point-blank range of their targets and had begun firing. The Tripolitan flotilla and shore batteries were returning the fire, but when the American boats closed to less than 300 yards of the enemy craft, the latter broke formation and retired to a more secure station, close in with the beach and to the west of the English Fort. The U.S. gunboats pursued them as far as the rocks and the reef, but did not attempt to penetrate the harbor. One division of American gunboats, supported by the brigs and schooners, bombarded the English Fort; the other concentrated its fire on the galleys and gunboats. The action became a stalemate. During the hour between 3:30 and 4:30 p.m. Preble's gunboats fired an average of forty rounds apiece, but they were so far from the enemy flotilla that they received no damage save for some shot-through sails and cut rigging. Few Americans thought they had inflicted any more serious damage on the Tripolitans.

While the gunboats were engaged in this inconclusive duel, the bomb ketches were having their best day since 7 August. Both took up stations not more than a mile from the heart of the city. Bomb Ketch No. 1, Thomas Robinson, hove twenty-two shells, eighteen of which fell in the town. Fifteen of the nineteen shells thrown by Bomb Ketch No. 2, John H. Dent, landed in Tripoli. Their short range made the ketches prime targets for the gunners in the Castle, the Molehead and Maltese batteries, and the French Fort, and exposed them to occasional shot from the English Fort and the New Battery. No. 2 took some damage in her sails and rigging, but remained operational. Every piece of larboard rigging in No. 1 was cut, the recently repaired bed of her mortar gave way again under the impact of repeated firings, and two feet of water stood in her hold. She was soon totally disabled and out of action.

Preble saw Dent's and Robinson's danger, and decided to take the *Constitution* inshore of the ketches, so that she could draw most of the Tripolitan fire, while they continued to throw shells into the city. Eighty guns were aiming at the *Constitution* as she came on; shot fell into the sea around her, their spray wetting her sails nearly up to the lower yards. By 3:30 p.m. she was within 600 yards of Tripoli's fortifications, her port battery towards the city. There she remained for forty minutes, firing eleven broadsides into Tripoli and its batteries — 198 round shot, 21 stands of grape, and 14 double-head shot. But she was suffering, too: her rigging was severely damaged, and at 4:10 p.m. she withdrew to make emergency repairs.

The wind had freshened and was shifting from E. by N. round towards the northward. Preble saw the futility of attempting to accomplish anything more that afternoon, and at 4:30 p.m. he signalled the flotilla to break off the action.

Information about the effect on Tripoli of this attack is less conclusive than it is for any of the other bombardments. Bonaventure Beaussier said only that it was not any more successful or decisive than the earlier ones.[5] Dr. Jonathan Cowdery, an American prisoner in Tripoli who had an excellent opportunity of observing the battle, reported that shot from the *Constitution* penetrated the batteries and the Castle, and that the shells thrown by the two bomb ketches damaged several houses and — this would have delighted Preble's officers had they known it — completely demolished the residence of the Spanish carpenter who built the Pasha's gunboats. As best one can tell from the meager evidence, the damage on 2 September was too slight to bring Tripoli any closer to negotiations.

At 8:00 p.m., 3 September 1804, with the *Constitution*'s large cutter waiting nearby to raise and secure her anchor, the *Intrepid* again slipped her cable and stood towards Tripoli. The only light came from the stars. A moderate E. by N. breeze carried the ketch directly towards the harbor. Some distance to her rear, the *Argus*, *Vixen*, and *Nautilus* followed. Around 9:00 p.m. the *Argus* and *Vixen* hove to. The *Nautilus*, under the temporary command of Lieutenant George Washington Reed, ran on until she was about 700 yards from the western passage and three-fourths of a mile from the *Intrepid*'s target. There, she hove to.

When the *Intrepid* reached the western passage, she appeared to go through it. Two alarm guns were fired from the Tripolitan batteries; then there was silence. Ten minutes later there was a flash of light, followed by a tremendous report and a heavy shock. "How awfully grand!" wrote Midshipman Robert T. Spence. "Everything wrapped in dead silence made the

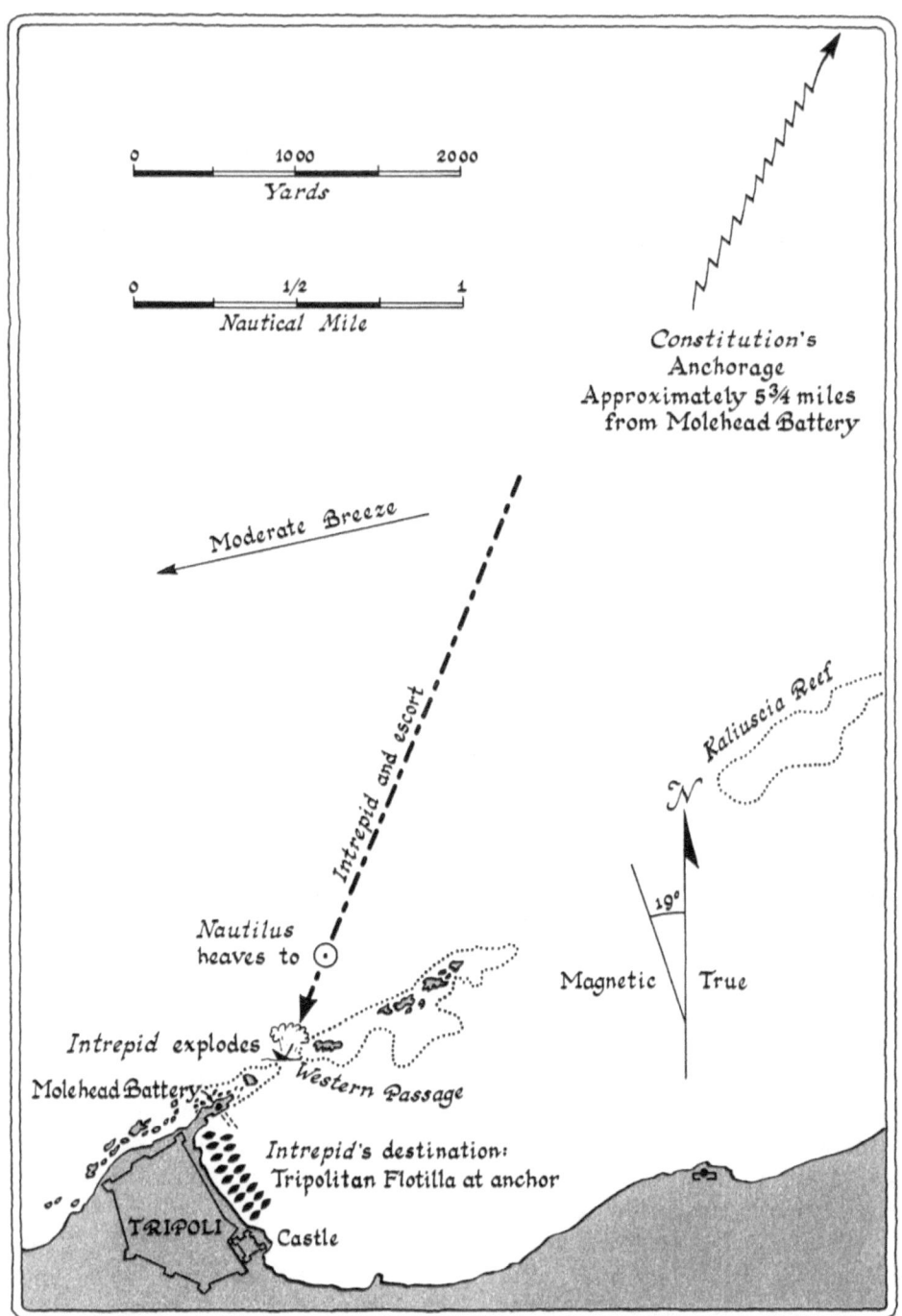

The *Intrepid's* Movements, Evening, 3 September 1804

explosion loud and terrible. The fuses of the shells, burning in the air, shone like so many planets. A vast stream of fire, which appeared ascending to heaven, portrayed the walls to our view." Nathaniel Haraden looked at his watch. It was 9:47.

Then silence returned, broken from time to time by Tripolitan batteries firing at the *Nautilus* as she waited to pick up Somers, Wadsworth, Israel, and the sailors in their two boats. Preble watched in vain for the rocket that Somers was to fire as a signal that the boats were safely out of the harbor. The plan was awry, and anxiety was rising. At 10:00 p.m. Preble ordered the *Constitution* to fire guns and rockets every ten minutes as a beacon for Somers and his companions. "The Commodore making repeated signal for Captain Somers, which was not answered," says a midshipman's journal. "Midnight. . . . The Commodore still making signals without being answered." Daylight came, a cloudy, overcast morning with a N.E. wind and an E.N.E. swell. Telescopes were trained towards Tripoli: the *Argus, Vixen,* and *Nautilus* were standing off and on shore near the port. Preble signalled the *Nautilus* to come within hail, but got no response. An hour later, at 7:30 a.m., he signalled: "*Nautilus*: Join company as soon as possible." A little before 9:00 a.m., his order still ignored, Preble repeated the signal: "*Nautilus*: Join company as soon as possible." This time, Lieutenant Reed stood off and came alongside the *Constitution*. Preble hailed to learn what had happened. Reed answered that he had been able to follow the *Intrepid*'s movements until two or three minutes before the explosion. She seemed to have reached her objective, but Somers, Wadsworth, Israel, and the ten seamen had vanished. Perhaps they were captured, perhaps dead. Lieutenant Reed could not say.

Eventually, Preble learned that all thirteen men had been killed in the explosion. Because three Tripolitan gunboats were hauled out for repairs and one other appeared to be missing, Preble chose to think that they were the ones that had been stationed ahead of the main anchorage, and that they had attempted to surround and capture the *Intrepid*, one of them coming up to board her. At that moment, Preble surmised, Somers touched a match where it would immediately fire the five tons of powder, and destroy both the *Intrepid* and the boarders.

Skeptics thought the powder had accidentally taken fire before Somers was ready.

Certain it is that the *Intrepid* exploded short of her target: otherwise, the Tripolitan flotilla would have been sunk or, at least, damaged. The explosion did only negligible injury to the city, and no one in Tripoli reported any vessels being destroyed by it, which makes it unlikely that Preble's theory was correct. Beaussier wrote Talleyrand: "During the night of [3/4

September] an infernal was sent in, doubtless to destroy a fort which had greatly distressed them. The explosion caused only a frightful noise and a general shock, felt well out into the countryside, without damaging the fort. However, she killed the persons charged with this perilous mission. Twelve drowned bodies were pulled from the water the next day, and afterwards one saw a number of scattered members along the shore." Preble never received the letter Beaussier wrote to him: "Your last effort was fatal only to yourselves. An infinity of bodies and scattered members has been found on the shore. Your design was, no doubt, to damage the fort that had troubled you the most or to introduce a fire ship into the port. The fort was not shaken, and the explosion caused only a general shock in the city and the countryside. In my own case I lost all the windows in my house."[6]

If Beaussier thought that Molehead was the fort the *Intrepid* was trying to blow up, the implication is that she exploded in or near the western passage. The fact that the bottom of her hull was found grounded on the north side of the harbor rocks, also seems to argue for a premature explosion inside or close to the western passage.

On the 6th of September the Pasha allowed William Bainbridge and Lieutenant David Porter to leave their prison and go down on the beach to examine some of the bodies that had been recovered after the explosion. In his journal Bainbridge reported:

> [We] there saw six persons in a most mangled and burnt condition lying on the shore, whom we supposed to have been part of the unfortunate crew of the fire vessel, the bottom of which grounded on the north side of the rocks near the round battery. Two of these distressed-looking objects were fished out of the wreck. From the whole of them being so much disfigured it was impossible to recognize any known feature to us, or even to distinguish an officer from a seaman. ...., who accompanied us, informed me that he saw six others yesterday on the shore to the southward, which were supposed to have come from the same vessel.[7]

VI

Preble's campaign was over.

By dawn of 5 September he had made up his mind to disarm the flotilla and send it back to Sicily. Late the following afternoon, he held a final conference with his senior officers. The *John Adams, Syren, Enterprize,* and *Nautilus* already had the eight gunboats and two ketches under tow and, at 6:30 p.m., Preble signalled them: "Make the best of your way for your intended port."

By daylight, the E.S.E. breeze had taken them out of sight. The *Constitution, Argus,* and *Vixen* stayed off Tripoli to keep up the blockade. The *Constitution* occupied a position about twelve miles north of Tripoli. During the daylight hours, the *Argus* was stationed to the east of the frigate, and the *Vixen* to the west, both at maximum effective signal distance from Preble: at sunset they closed on the *Constitution*. Preble intended to cruise on this station until he heard something from Samuel Barron or until weather forced him to leave.

Around noon on Sunday, 9 September, the *Constitution* was fifteen miles N.E. by N. from Tripoli when the *Argus* signalled: "Discovering strange ships N.E." A haze across the northern horizon hid the strangers from the *Constitution*, but she tacked towards the *Argus* and gave chase. Within the hour the haze cleared away, and Preble could see two strange ships, a long way off and dead to windward of the *Constitution*, which was still working towards them. When Preble excused himself at the end of his regular Sunday afternoon dinner as guest of the wardroom officers and went back on deck, the officer of the watch reported that the *Argus* had been exchanging signals with one of the strangers. Before long, the strangers were recognized as the *President* and the *Constellation*. As the *Constitution* came up with them, Edward Preble's broad pennant was struck and a boat was swung out so that her captain might call on the new squadron commander.

Barron's tardiness in reaching Tripoli was at last explained. His four frigates had sailed from Hampton Roads on 5 July. Steady, fair winds from the southwest had enabled them to sight Pico in the Azores at noon on 21 July. There, the wind abruptly swung ahead: they had to beat constantly to windward, and they did not reach Gibraltar Bay until 12 August. At Gibraltar, Samuel Barron found awaiting him a series of alarming letters from a nervous James Simpson: the activities of the Sultan of Morocco's ships were suspicious; it looked as though there would be a repetition of the previous fall's hostilities against the United States. Simpson importuned Barron to prevent this by leaving two of his frigates in the Straits of Gibraltar. The *Congress*, John Rodgers, and the *Essex*, James Barron, were detailed to keep a watch on Morocco until it could be determined whether or not the Sultan meant to break the peace. The *President* and the *Constellation* started up the Mediterranean on 16 August, again crawling to windward. A week later, they were still west of Cape Gata. Commodore Barron's last landfall, before sailing to Tripoli, was Malta, where he finally put in on 5 September.

Secretary Smith expected Preble would be willing to remain in the Mediterranean as a subordinate commander in Samuel Barron's squadron. Preble had no intention of doing so. He was going back to the United States. "Commodore Barron's arrival to supersede me in the command of the fleet has determined me to return," he wrote Mary, "as it is not expected by our government that I shall serve on any station again excepting as commander in chief or with a separate squadron, having served so long a time in that capacity and, as they acknowledge, with reputation to myself and honor to my country." He might have been willing to remain as second-in-command to Samuel Barron, who, at nearly 39 years of age,[8] was four years his junior and was rather easily dominated by forceful men of ideas and initiatives, such as Preble. However, John Rodgers was the second-ranking captain, and Edward Preble had no intention of subordinating himself to Rodgers as third-in-command of the squadron. The animosity between Rodgers and Preble had not abated in the past year. And to sweeten the idea of returning to the United States, there was a rumor about in the squadron that, in the spring of 1805, Preble was to be given command of a squadron in the West Indies, where the excesses of French and Spanish privateers were creating a need for American trade to have naval protection.[9]

From the 9th till the 13th of September, while the *Constitution* cruised off Tripoli with the *President* and the *Constellation*, Preble spent much of his time in conference with Samuel Barron. It was during these five days that he made his last contribution to the outcome of the Tripolitan War. William Eaton was a passenger in the *President*, and the new commodore had discretionary authority from the government to permit Eaton to execute his favorite plan of aiding Hamet Caramanli to regain the pashadom of Tripoli. Eaton's proposals were discussed at length by Preble, Barron, and Eaton. Although as recently as April Preble had jettisoned his own plans for cooperating with Hamet Caramanli, the idea must still have appealed to him, because he eagerly embraced Eaton's scheme.

Barron decided to let Eaton try it. In Eaton's presence, the new commodore gave Isaac Hull secret, oral orders that were bold, broad, and discretionary. Their tone, not characteristic of Samuel Barron, undoubtedly reflects the influence and ascendancy that Preble had over Barron at the conferences which led to their adoption. Hull, in the *Argus*, was to take Eaton to Egypt in search of Hamet Caramanli. When Hamet was found, the *Argus* was either to carry him and his adherents to Derna or any other suitable point on the Tripolitan coast, or to bring them to Samuel Barron off Tripoli. Hamet was to be assured that Commodore Barron would "take the most effectual measures with the forces under my command for cooperating with him against the usurper, his brother, and for reestablishing him in the regency of Tripoli."

At three o'clock on the cloudy afternoon of 13 September, the *Constitution* pulled away from the *President* and set course for Malta. Wrote Preble: "I presume [the effect of our operations against Tripoli] will be satisfactory to my country, having done all in my power to annoy the enemy and indeed all that so small a squadron could have effected."

CHAPTER 16   OCTOBER 1804–APRIL 1807

"The people are disposed to think that I have rendered some service to my country."

Preble could not simply tell his servant, Adam Smith, to pack the trunks in preparation for taking passage for the United States. There were accounts in Malta and Sicily that had to be closed, gunboats and military stores that had to be returned to the Neapolitan authorities, farewell parties to be given at Messina, Palermo, and Naples to repay social obligations or thank people who had helped the squadron. All this activity kept him shunting from one Mediterranean port to another for three and a half months after the change of command.[1]

It was in the course of carrying out these errands that Preble arrived at Malta from Syracuse on 23 October 1804. A few days later John Rodgers in the *Congress* anchored in Valletta harbor, and the feud between Rodgers and Preble reached its climax. In spite of his outbursts of temper and the harsh feelings he sometimes concealed, Preble truly wanted to be on a friendly footing with as many of his associates as possible. Usually, he would go out of his way to avoid hurting someone or to be conciliatory if he had offended. But there was one man with whom he just could not get along, and that was John Rodgers. "He never shall command me while I have command over myself," he once said. It was one of those unfortunate situations in which two good men could not abide one another. Friends of the two principals discouraged rather than promoted reconciliation. Preble's intimates were always eager to make the sparks fly by tendering some bad report about Rodgers, or to repeat something he was supposed to have said about Preble. Typically, Noadiah Morris hastened to acquaint Preble with Morris's opinion that Rodgers's "reputation as a fighting man has originated, I believe, in his black looks, his insufferable arrogance, and the frequent and unmerited assaults he has made on poor and inoffensive citizens."

All that is known about the incident that took place in Malta is contained in a note that Rodgers wrote Preble, apparently decided not to send, but carefully filed away among his papers:

> Sir:
> A respect I owe to my country prevented me *yesterday* from requiring of you to explain the cause of your observations on the comparative good order of the *Constitution* and *Congress* and other incoherent remarks, feeling sensible that any dispute between us (in the situation I am now placed) could not fail to be productive of injury to the service. When we meet in the United States you shall then be explicitly informed of my opinion of your conduct. I am, with consideration, your obedient servant,
>
> JNO. RODGERS[2]

By the time Rodgers got back to the United States he was involved in other quarrels that interested him much more.

Samuel Barron had placed the *John Adams,* commanded by Isaac Chauncey, at Preble's disposal for his return to the United States. In her Preble and several of his officers, including Noadiah Morris and Nathaniel Haraden, who thought their future careers were closely tied up with Preble's influence at the Navy Department, sailed from Malta on 4 November. After touching at Syracuse, Messina, and Palermo, on 1 December the *John Adams* stood towards Naples for the most important stop on Preble's itinerary. Samuel Barron's plans for 1805 called for the use of gunboats and bomb ketches, but he was too sick with a liver disease to travel to Naples and apply for a loan of such craft. Accordingly, he asked Preble to approach the Neapolitan government and see if they would lend him fifteen gunboats and six bomb ketches. Preble's informal talks with officials at Messina indicated that they would be willing to let the United States have that many ketches and up to twenty gunboats, though permission would have to come from Naples. At Palermo Sir John Acton, who had been forced from office by French pressure in May but whose influence at court was thought still to be considerable, told Preble that the Commodore would have no trouble in borrowing the craft, and armed him with a letter of introduction to King Ferdinand and Queen Maria-Carolina.

When the *John Adams* anchored off Naples during the night of the 6th of December, the Neapolitan court was at the summer palace at Portici, and Preble had to wait more than a week to present his introduction. The royal family "moved into their winter quarters last Sunday [16 December]," wrote the *John Adams*'s purser, John Darby:

As they passed the hotel where we lodged we had a full view of them and all their retinue, which was in great pomp and style. The Queen was drawn in her carriage [by] six elegant horses, and the other branches of the Royal Family, princes and princesses, dukes, barons, marquesses, etc., etc., were drawn in carriages with four horses, to the number of at least fifty, and they were about six days moving all the baggage. The King was not with the Family. He was at one of his country palaces about twelve miles out of town. A few days afterwards he came to town and we frequently saw him and queen and all the Royal Family at the grand Theatre of St. Carlos. He is a pleasant-looking old man and so is the Queen, but she has very much of the air of gallantry about her, and it is said she is fully equal in intrigues to her sister, Maria Antonetta, late Queen of France. Some of the young princesses are very beautiful women.

Within a few days of her return, Maria-Carolina granted Preble an audience, at which she told him that the Neapolitan government had only the friendliest feelings towards the United States. The ministers of state outdid one another in assurances that whatever Preble requested in the name of the United States would be granted. General Forteguerri, the minister of marine, asked Preble to go through one formality: draw up a petition that could be presented to the King for approval. Preble did so, but as days went by without any indication that the request was being acted on, he grew anxious, suspicious, and irritable. When his officers made up parties to visit Portici, Herculaneum, and Pompeii, and proposed to ascend Vesuvius, Preble declined invitations to join them. He preferred to be on hand when the reply came and, in the interim, to work to influence the decision.

On 21 December, after Preble had waited a week, General Forteguerri advised him politely that the Neapolitan government needed the vessels in question to protect its own coasts and coasting trade from Barbary cruisers, and would not lend them to the United States. "Some interest more powerful than ours has been working against us!" Preble exclaimed, surprised and disappointed, when he read Forteguerri's letter. His deep-rooted suspicions of the French led Preble to believe that they were responsible for this diplomatic defeat. He theorized that, since England and France were at war, it was to the interest of France to have the American blockade cutting off the flow of fresh provisions from Tripoli to Malta and making life difficult on that British island. With greater probability and less prejudice Preble also surmised that the British might be responsible for King Ferdinand's decision. Hugh Elliot, the British minister to the Neapolitan Court, had told Preble privately that Ferdinand had agreed to keep thirty-five gunboats and ketches constantly manned and ready at Messina as a precaution against a French invasion across the straits, but that so far less than one-third of that number had been provided. Elliot made no secret of the fact that he had been rather put out when he discovered that six gunboats and two ketches had been lent to Preble for the summer of 1804. Preble inferred that Elliot had protested the earlier loan and opposed a new one.

How was Samuel Barron to get the indispensable gunboats and bomb ketches? Perhaps, Preble suggested to Barron, he could purchase or hire suitable craft at Malta and fit them out as gunboats. Maybe he could get mortars and shells there, too, and mount the mortars on feluccas. Beyond those suggestions, Preble could only promise Barron that he would sail for the United States immediately so that the administration might learn as early as possible of the disarray to which their plans had been reduced: and when he got there, he would use his influence to stimulate prompt and vigorous action to provide Barron with reinforcement.

II

Whatever Preble's thoughts were as the *John Adams* carried him from port to port in the Mediterranean and out into the Atlantic on his passage home, he kept them to himself. They cannot have been cheerful. He had been superseded in the Mediterranean command before he had been able to bring the Tripolitan War to its inevitable successful conclusion. The supersedure had frustrated his one unrelenting ambition: to "acquire reputation" in the service of the United States. He was forty-three years old. Only two of the captains in the U.S. Navy who were actively employed at sea — Alexander Murray, forty-nine, and Hugh G. Campbell, about forty-four — were older. He was fast becoming an old man in a young man's Navy.

But when the *John Adams* reached New York on 25 February 1805, Preble discovered that he was a national hero. Before taking the road for Washington three days later to report to the Navy Department, he wrote Mary: "I cannot but be a little flattered with the reception I have met with here. The people are disposed to think that I have rendered some service to my country." The President had sent Preble's dispatches describing his attacks on Tripoli in August and September up to Congress on 20 February with a message that spoke of "the energy and judgment displayed by this excellent officer through the whole course of the service lately confided to him." Although it was 4 March 1805, Inauguration Day for Thomas Jefferson's second term in the Presidency, when Preble reached Washington, Robert Smith took him right over to call on the President. And Preble soon learned, if he did not already know, that Congress had adopted a resolution instructing the President to have struck and presented to him

Courtesy of U.S. Naval Academy Museum

PREBLE MEDAL

John Reich of Philadelphia engraved Preble's profile from a drawing by Rembrandt Peale. The drawing does not appear to be extant, but it and the oil portrait by Peale, reproduced as the frontispiece to this book, are the only likenesses for which Preble is known to have sat. Former President John Adams called the medal profile "an exact resemblance" of its subject and added, "the reverse will light up the fires of ambition in the breast of every American seaman."

a gold medal "emblematical of the attacks on the town, batteries, and naval force of Tripoli."

For the next two weeks Preble was the center of the sort of attention he loved. The Accountant of the Navy settled his complicated accounts with unprecedented speed. There were conferences with the Secretary of State. Preble was at the Navy Department almost daily, working with Robert Smith on plans for reinforcing Samuel Barron. On his second day in the capital, he was invited by the President to dine at the White House, and on the 12th he went to the Madisons' for dinner and an evening of cards.

Preble started north from Washington on 19 March and met similar adulation along the way. Aaron Burr, the retiring Vice-President, was only too happy to avoid the crowded stage and ride in the private carriage the Commodore had hired to take him from Washington to Baltimore.[3] In Philadelphia Charles Biddle, merchant and former Vice-President of the Supreme Executive Council of Pennsylvania, asked him to dinner. During the weekend of 23–25 March Rembrandt Peale drew his portrait for the medal authorized by Congress. Preble decided that his reputation was sufficiently established to justify sitting for a portrait in oils by Mr. Peale at the same time. When Preble was ready to leave Philadelphia, General Francis Gurney sent his carriage around to take him out to the home of Captain Stephen Decatur, Sr., in Frankford, where he was to stay for the night of 25/26 March. At Trenton, it was Governor Joseph Bloomfield of New Jersey who wanted him for a dinner guest; and when Preble got to Boston, Thomas Handasyd Perkins took him out to Quincy to call on former president John Adams.

At Philadelphia, New York, Boston, and Portland civic leaders arranged ceremonial dinners in his honor.[4] All these festivities followed a stylized pattern. They were presided over by a leading citizen, and two or three other worthies served as vice-presidents. During the meal, Preble would discreetly count the number of "respectable citizens" who had assembled in his honor, so that he could record it in his diary. Good taste forbade that the planned toasts, which followed the meal and were frequently punctuated by patriotic and nautical songs, mention the guest of honor, since he was still in the room. But when all the formal toasts had been made and Preble had saluted the host city — "The town of Boston! May wealth and happiness reward the industry and enterprise of its respectable inhabitants" — he would retire from the dining room. His withdrawal permitted someone, usually the presiding citizen, to toast his health: "Edward Preble! Our hero before Tripoli; may the laurels he has gained in the Old World be long the pride of the New." Thereafter, spontaneous toasts would come from the diners — "The whiskers of the Bashaw of Tripoli! May they have plenty of curling, twisting and powdering!" Thirty or forty such toasts must, at least partially, have accounted for "the most pleasing hilarity" which the press reported as characteristic of these occasions.

Additional evidence that the public regarded his year in the Mediterranean as the very opposite of a failure followed Preble north in the form of a rumor that Jefferson was about to appoint him Secretary of the Navy. This political gossip, which originated in Washington around 10 April 1805, was widely believed in the United States and among the officers of the Mediterranean squadron. Robert Smith wanted to become Attorney General. As a consequence, Jefferson offered the post of Secretary of the Navy to Congressman Jacob Crowninshield of Salem. Crowninshield, however, declined the appointment, and it was news of his declination that touched off the speculation about Preble for Secretary of the Navy.

In the end, Robert Smith agreed to stay on as Secretary of the Navy for another four years. Preble was never seriously considered for the position. He had to tell friend after friend who wrote to congratulate him: "I have not the vanity to imagine myself possessed of the necessary qualifications to discharge the duties of that important station with reputation either to myself or country. Of course, had I been actually appointed, I should not have accepted." The importance of this rumor is that it provides another clue to Preble's politics. Preble is a Federalist, said his Federalist friends; he would never accept the appointment: he detests the whole Jeffersonian system as much as we do. Preble did consider himself a nominal Federalist. But the fact that the rumor of his nomination as Secretary of the Navy could be so widely believed by newspaper editors — experts in the personalities of party politics — and by naval officers who knew him well, indicates that he was not identified as a partisan figure. Though he might not have admitted it, Preble was, in some ways, apolitical. His deep commitments were to preserving American independence and self-respect, and insuring the respect of other governments for the United States, rather than to the principles of a party.

When four hundred to five hundred Boston Federalists foregathered in Faneuil Hall on 4 July 1806, Preble was one of the honored guests. The toasts ranged from bitter to vitriolic: "The President of the United States! May the people be discerning, and history impartial!" "Such a National Administration as will not depend on trick for popularity nor on tribute for peace!" [5] Amid this party spleen, Preble's toast was conspicuously nonpartisan: "Our enterprising officers and hardy seamen engaged in the peaceful pursuit of commerce! May it ever be the pride and glory of their naval brethren-in-arms to protect and defend them." And Preble was careful to send the newspaper account of the dinner privately to Robert Smith so that the administration would have no doubts about his political neutrality.

Along with some other moderate Federalists — Senators William Plumer of New Hampshire and John Quincy Adams of Massachusetts — Preble was drifting towards Republicanism. He had dined and talked with the President often enough to know that he was the opposite of the ogre the Federalists imagined. Once, when thanking Jefferson for a gift, Preble went well beyond the dictates of simple politeness to speak of "the Chief Magistrate of our nation, whom I esteem and venerate," and added, "I beg leave to assure you of my ardent wishes that Heaven may preserve your health and long continue your valuable life, an honor to our country and to human nature." [6] What a sensation a copy of that letter would have made in certain circles in Boston!

III

Within days of his return to the United States from his Mediterranean command, Edward Preble became an important participant in an emotional political issue and the most controversial naval activity of President Jefferson's administration — the building of gunboat flotillas. All European navies of the Napoleonic period used gunboats, but the need for such shallow-draft vessels in the U.S. Navy did not come to the government's attention until late in the year 1802 when the Spanish authorities at New Orleans suddenly denied American citizens the privilege of depositing goods at that port without paying duty — a right guaranteed by Pinckney's Treaty of 1795 between the United States and Spain and one which was essential to Americans living along the western rivers. At that time the Navy consisted of thirteen frigates and the schooner *Enterprize;* in other words, the United States had no naval vessels suitable for enforcing its treaty rights on the Mississippi. To mend this gap in the defense system, an act of Congress, approved by the President on 28 February 1803, provided for the construction of not more than fifteen gunboats.* When Commodore Morris returned from the Mediterranean he brought a model of a Messina gunboat.[8] In December 1803 Secretary Smith ordered the construction of two experimental gunboats. No. 1 was built at Washington under the super-

---

* A Spanish retreat in the deposit controversy and the subsequent purchase of Louisiana from France obviated the necessity for immediately creating a naval force on the Ohio-Mississippi river system. However, before these events were known, the Navy Department had issued, on 11 April 1803, an invitation for bids to construct galleys at Pittsburgh, Marietta, and Louisville.[7] The proposed galleys were never built — probably because news of the purchase of Louisiana reached the President at Washington on 3 July 1803, which was only seventy-two hours after the closing date for the bids.

vision of John Rodgers, and No. 2 at Hampton, Virginia, supervised by James Barron. Both models were completed in the summer of 1804, whereupon the Navy Department set in motion the construction of eight more boats, Nos. 3 through 10. These eight boats, designed by Josiah Fox, the newly appointed Head Ship Carpenter and Naval Constructor, to be lighter than No. 1 and better suited for duty on the Mississippi River, were in various stages of completion when Preble returned to the United States in February 1805. On 2 March, two days before Preble reached Washington, the President signed a bill authorizing the construction of as many as twenty-five additional gunboats "for the better protection of the ports and harbors of the United States."

Official administration statements on the gunboat-building program stressed the boats' wartime role: they were to complement fortifications in protecting U.S. seaports from armed attack. In the early days of the program, however, the President assigned them duties more usually associated with a coast guard: protecting U.S. and foreign vessels in U.S. territorial waters from attack by privateers; maintaining law and order on rivers and in harbors; patrolling the lower Mississippi and Lake Pontchartrain; keeping an eye on U.S. interests at Mobile; checking smuggling and other illegal activities among the offshore islands and inlets of the coast; and assisting in the enforcement of health and quarantine regulations along the maritime frontier.[9]

That was as far as the gunboat program had gotten while Preble was abroad. What was Preble's attitude towards gunboats?* On 5 March 1805, the day after Preble got to Washington, General James Wilkinson sent him a copy of his paper, "Reflections on the Fortifications and Defence of the Sea Ports of the United States." [11] This paper, the key document in the administration's official justification of its gunboat-construction program, had been read to the House of Representatives.

Wilkinson advocated a fresh look at the type of protection most suitable for U.S. seaports. He suggested that the successful defenses of Forts Moultrie and Mifflin during the Revolution had led Americans to place excessive

---

* Years later brother Enoch Preble insisted that Edward detested the gunboat construction program. At the opposite pole, Howard I. Chapelle, the modern historian of naval construction, says: "It is impossible to draw any definite conclusion as to the importance of Preble in the development of the visionary gunboat theories of the Jeffersonian administration. Certainly he contributed something to the idea." Chapelle theorizes that Preble may have been a fanatical member of the Republican party who betrayed his objective professional preference for a blue-water Navy and "encouraged the administration to put its faith in gunboat flotillas rather than in a sound naval construction program." He adds that no real evidence has been found to confirm this supposition. "Rather, the indications are that Preble put excessive emphasis on gun vessels, which the administration seized upon to develop a political naval policy of its own." [10]

faith in fixed batteries, and to forget other battles of the Revolutionary War in which shore batteries had been ineffectual against British ships. In Wilkinson's view the only fixed batteries that were particularly effective were those adjacent to narrow crooked channels, which obliged the attackers to approach within point-blank range of the batteries and to tack under the guns. Most American seaports did not have such constricted approaches; aided by wind and tide, enemy warships could run past the protecting forts in no more than ten minutes, and would then be free to work their will on the exposed cities. And to build a system of even moderately effective fixed fortifications for the principal American ports would be enormously expensive. The cost of such a system might well be beyond the resources of the United States; certainly it would divert money from more important objects of national policy.

Coming to the heart of his argument, Wilkinson wrote:

> It may be asked whether we are to rest the safety of our commercial towns and shipping on the pacific disposition or good faith of foreign powers? To which we may reply in the negative and add that it is certainly our duty to seek for those places of defense within the compass of our abilities which may be found most economical, most durable, and most effectual.
>
> After as close a view of this question as can be expected from a man unskilled in naval affairs, I have formed a conclusion that, next to a superior navy, floating batteries will be found more effectual to the protection of our seaports and should, therefore, be preferred. But I speak with exception to long tidewater rivers and narrow channels, because they may be commanded by fixed batteries and chevaux-de-frise, yet cannot be secured by them against blockade.
>
> In determining on the size, form, and construction of such floating batteries regard must be had to the services to be performed and, after due experiment, the best models may be adopted for tidewater and uniform currents, for bays and harbors, narrow, wide, open, or sheltered from particular winds.
>
> The extent of our bays and inlets, the capacities of our harbors, and the water approaches to our great cities have determined my judgment in favor of these vessels calculated to be impelled with velocity by the more powerful combination of oars and sail to enable them to make rapid transitions and to take any requisite station with promptitude.
>
> In equipping armies and manning these vessels provision should be made to prevent their being boarded by light barges, and with submission I would recommend that they should carry battering pieces of the largest calibre and the lightest construction on their bows and sterns. I have strong prejudices in favor of a proportion of eight-inch howitzers, because one shell which takes effect will prove more destructive (generally speaking) than ten shot.
>
> I feel confident that, without extensive fortifications and proportionable military force to garrison them, that barges, galleys, or gunboats on the preceding or improved plan, with the cooperation of heavy movable batteries which may be expeditiously transferred from one part of a town or city to another by men and horses, will form our most economical, durable, and

effectual means of defense and afford the best security to the objects to be protected. And in support of this opinion I beg leave to offer the following considerations:

1st. Such vessels can either attack or defend, may prove as offensive in the retreat as pursuit, and can approach or avoid an enemy at discretion.

2nd. In calm their oars will enable them to take any station with safety which may be found most advantageous.

3rd. Their mobility will enable them in smooth water to hang on the bow or stern of a vessel and avoid its batteries.

4th. Their lowness in the water will enable them to deliver their shot on a horizontal range or at a small elevation, which will give them more certainty and effect.

5th. In calm weather they may without hazard approach a vessel at anchor in a stream to the point-blank [range] of 24-pounders, 650 yards, or of 32-pounders, 850 yards, and, preserving a steady station, may give effect to every shot without fail.

6th. In light breezes, with sails and oars, they may preserve the same distance on the bow of a vessel and, if pursued, may deliver as destructive a fire as if they were stationary.

7th. Should they be hard pressed, they may escape in shoal water and renew the action at discretion.

8th. In rough weather they may take station beyond the [range] of the guns of a ship, from whence the superior elevation of their own pieces may enable them to deliver their fire with effect.

9th. Taking advantages of circumstances, they may drive intruders from our bays, roads, or rivers; and, by forcing them to sea, may relieve a blockade or render it less close, constant, or pernicious.

10th. They may be employed during the calm season to transport stores or men from one port to another with safety, even should an enemy be waiting; and, lastly, in time of peace, eight out of ten may be laid up under cover, and, with due attention, instead of injury, may be improved by aid for a number of years.

Preble read Wilkinson's paper "with pleasure and satisfaction" he told the author. If he saw any fallacies or weaknesses in the argument, desire to avoid hurting anyone's feelings, which was always operative when he was not in a passion, may have kept him from mentioning them. "You have taken so clear and correct a view of the subject that I shall only beg leave to observe that my opinion perfectly coincides with your own, and I am convinced, when we have experimentally ascertained the best models for floating batteries destined for the defense or protection of our bays and harbors, that your system will meet with general approbation."

It is in the context of this experimental search for the best models for floating defenses, and of the Navy's need for small, handy vessels for shoal-water and river work, that the gunboat policy and Preble's part in it may best be understood. Preble never thought of gunboats as more important to the Navy than any other type of vessel: he advocated the building of a balanced naval force that would include ships of the line as well as a flotilla of shallow-draft vessels. Preble had an interest in, and an aptitude for, engineering and, like most men who commanded ships, he had ideas on how those ships should be built. Participation in the gunboat-construction program gave him a chance to get his hand into some mechanical work and to test his ideas on naval architecture.

IV

When Preble left Washington on 19 March he carried with him Robert Smith's instructions to contract, at either Boston or Portland, for the construction of two gunboats and two bomb ketches.

Design work on these boats was shared by Preble and Jacob Coffin, a master builder on the Merrimack, whom Preble retained on the recommendation of Ebenezer Stocker, the Newburyport merchant who had handled Preble's business affairs there since the 1790s. When Preble had decided what the general dimensions of the vessels should be, he had wooden models made to scale, and tested them to see what refinements were needed. At about this point, Coffin, having perhaps helped Preble to modify the design, drew the building plans.

Three of the five gunboat types for which Coffin drew up plans were smaller and less costly than the other two, and were for river and harbor use exclusively: they were to be built of light wood and armed with one long 24- or 32-pounder in the bow or two long twelves or eighteens amidships. Robert Smith intended that craft of these designs should be built in the Ohio River Valley. However, Preble was so slow about sending the drawings, which he designated as Plans Nos. 1, 3, and 5, to Washington that Smith, seeing the prime building season slipping away, decided to substitute a design by Josiah Fox.

The Preble-Coffin gunboat designs were derived, in part at least, from plans which James L. Cathcart had had drawn up at Leghorn late in 1803 or early in 1804, and which he had sent to Preble when the Commodore was looking for gunboats in the Mediterranean. In his cabin in the *Constitution* Preble kept models of the type of gunboat and ketch he borrowed at Messina; they, too, may have contributed something to the designs he and Coffin produced in May and June 1805.

Once the designs were settled, Preble proceeded to carry out Smith's instructions that he contract for two gunboats and two ketches to be constructed in New England.[12]

One gunboat, No. 11, based on plan No. 2, was built at Portland by Nathaniel Dyer, under a contract dated 1 July 1805. When finished she measured 73 feet 10 inches on deck, 18 feet 11 inches extreme beam, and 5 feet 3 inches deep in the hold. Although ready for launching by 24 October 1805, she was kept on the stocks throughout the winter of 1805-06 in order to season her timber before she went into the water. Rigged and equipped on the stocks, she was finally launched 3 May 1806. Because the gunboats were light and easy to careen, Preble did not have their hulls coppered: he had them sheathed with half-inch spruce boards, which he considered sufficient protection from worms even in subtropical waters.

Another Portland builder, William Moulton, Jr., received the contract, also dated 1 July 1805, for one of the bomb ketches. Preble named this vessel *Etna*; finished, she measured 83 feet 6 inches on deck, 24 feet extreme beam, and 8 feet deep in the hold. Both the *Etna* and her sister ship the *Vesuvius* were coppered. Preble planned to arm the *Etna* with one 13-inch mortar, two 8-inch brass howitzers, and eight long 9-pounders. Her hull was ready for launching by late October 1805, but, like Gunboat No. 11, she stayed on the stocks as long as practical and was not launched until 18 June 1806.

Gunboat No. 12, based on plan No. 4, and the bomb ketch *Vesuvius* were built at or near Newburyport by Jacob Coffin under contracts also dated 1 July 1805. The gunboat, launched 24 May 1806,[18] measured 67 feet 8 inches on deck, 19 feet 3½ inches extreme beam, and 5 feet 4 inches deep in the hold. In line with a suggestion made to Preble by James L. Cathcart, Gunboats Nos. 11 and 12 were schooner rigged aft and with a sliding gunter mast forward. Preble thought that this rig would be the easiest for rowing to windward; and he seems to have expected that boats would sometimes want to strike their foremasts when going into action to give the guns, which were mounted amidships, a clear field of fire forward.

The bomb ketch *Vesuvius* measured 82 feet 5 inches long on deck, 24 feet 5¾ inches beam, and 8 feet 4 inches deep in the hold. She was launched on Saturday, 31 May 1806, on which festive day, the *Newburyport Herald* of 3 June reported, "Gunboat No. 12, which lay off in the stream, was handsomely dressed for the occasion and exhibited quite a unique appearance." What the enthusiastic *Herald* neglected to mention was that the launching ways collapsed; the *Vesuvius* stuck part way down, and did not actually go afloat until 2 June. Her armament was planned to be one 13-inch mortar, two 24-pound carronades, and eight long 9-pounders.

Preble intended Gunboats Nos. 11 and 12 to be fast-sailing seagoing craft, capable of crossing the Atlantic, and thus available for foreign service. No. 11 was armed with two long iron 24-pounders, two 5½-inch brass howitzers, 20 muskets, 20 pairs of pistols, 20 cutlasses, 20 battle-axes, and 20 pikes. No. 12 carried the same weapons, save that two 24-pound brass carronades

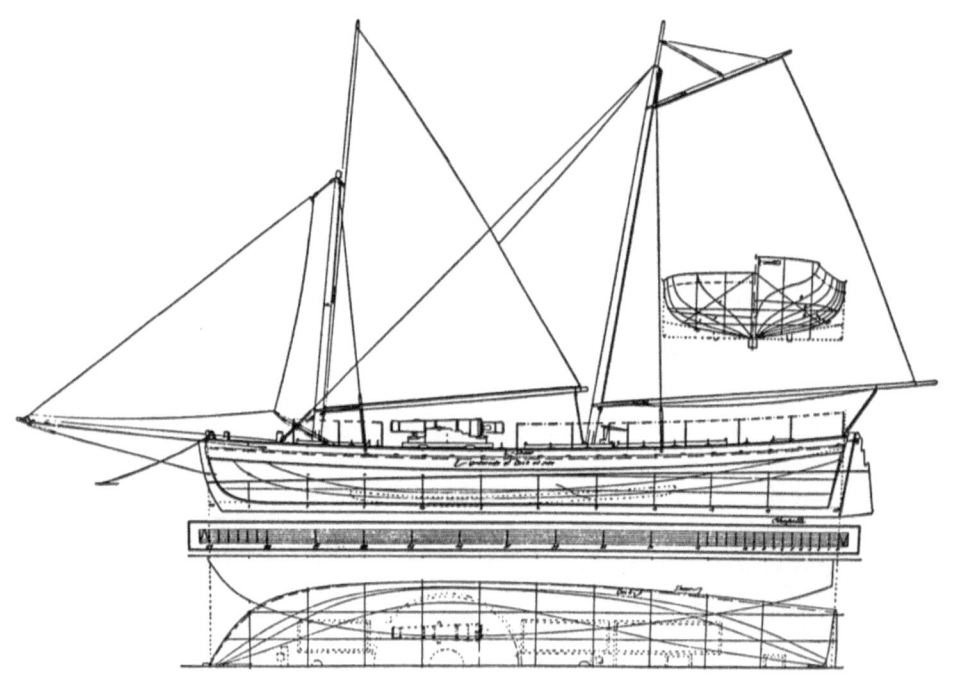

DESIGN OF GUNBOAT NO. 12

Preble-Coffin Plan No. 4

Note that the two long guns were mounted amidships on the horizontal wheel suggested by Henry Carbery and tested by Preble.

were substituted for the howitzers. The *Etna* and the *Vesuvius*, too, were designed as fast-sailers; Preble expected them to be equal to a winter passage across the Atlantic. Since the need for bomb ketches would be sporadic, Preble's design for the *Vesuvius* and the *Etna* allowed the mortar to be replaced by eight or ten heavy guns, so that the ketches could serve as cruisers in shallow coastal waters. Thus, their contracts specified top-timbers for a tier of gunports fore and aft of sufficient height for 24-pound carronades, with two stern-chase ports.

All four vessels sailed from Boston for New Orleans at the end of September 1806. As might be expected, Preble was proud of his work: the *Etna* "is as well-built and as handsome a vessel of her size as ever floated"; and, "No. 11 sails and works remarkably well and is a fine boat." [14] Their commanding officers were less enthusiastic. The *Etna* and *Vesuvius* are both reported to have been poor sailers because of faulty balance. Indeed, the *Etna*'s first commander was scarcely out of sight of land before he was contemplating alterations to her rig to improve her sailing. It is hard to know how much validity there was in these criticisms of Preble's designs because of a state of mind universal among the officers of the early Navy: never did an officer supervise the building of a ship without rating the finished product the finest, fastest thing ever put afloat; nor was there ever an officer who, on assuming command of a ship built under the supervision of someone else, did not see an urgent need for changes.

As contracting agent for the Navy Department Preble drove a hard bargain. Many constructors refused to work for the prices he would allow. The contract made, Preble watched the builder like a hawk. If the master builder was to receive so many dollars per ton for his work, the contractor's temptation was to make the boat a little bigger than the specifications called for, and so collect a few more dollars. "I have frequently heard him observe to them [the builders]," Preble's brother-in-law wrote, "that if they made them any larger [than the specified dimensions] it must be at their own expense, as the government would not pay them one cent." [15]

Although Preble was highly pleased with Jacob Coffin's design work, the two parted company after the completion of the *Vesuvius* and Gunboat No. 12. Coffin claimed that Preble had driven such a hard bargain in these contracts that he lost money on the two vessels. Among other things, he accused Preble of first insisting that they be put afloat by mid-October 1805 — causing Coffin to hire extra hands — then changing his mind and leaving them on the stocks till the spring of 1806. In a letter to Robert Smith, Preble dismissed Coffin's complaints in characteristic fashion:

Mr. Coffin is an excellent naval constructor, a good workman, and, I believe, a very honest man; but, unfortunately, he has the reputation of being a very indolent one. I have no doubt but he has lost money by his contract, but his loss must certainly have arisen from mismanagement and want of economy. I have heard no complaint from the man who built the *Etna*, which vessel cost considerably less than the *Vesuvius* and was every way equal to her. And I can at any time contract with any master builder, either here [Portland] or at Newburyport, to build vessels of the same description as the *Vesuvius* and No. 12 at the same rate that Mr. Coffin has been paid. Mr. Coffin's poverty has strong claims on your charity, and I sincerely wish that something could be done for him; but should his petition be granted, and what he states to be his loss allowed him, and it should become public, you may expect to be constantly troubled with applications of the same nature without regard to justice of claim.

Mr. Coffin is an excellent draftsman and has considerable taste in building, but is not fond of work himself; but, could you employ him in the Navy Yard at Washington as a second or third to Mr. Fox, he might be very useful.[16]

In providing naval supervision for, and liaison with, the civilian contractors and subcontractors Preble was assisted by a succession of lieutenants and midshipmen. But Purser Nathaniel Lyde, who joined Preble's staff in February 1806, quickly became the indispensable assistant: he ran the office and storerooms, copied the correspondence and contracts, kept the books, hired and paid workmen and sailors, collected supplies, and traveled to Boston and Portsmouth when Preble required a reliable person to transact some business.

Preble's interest in inventions and his adaptation and development of ideas first suggested by other men was well exemplified by the unusual gun mount he installed on Gunboats Nos. 11 and 12. When he was at Washington in March 1805 he saw in the Navy Department a model illustrating a proposal by General Henry Carbery, Navy Agent for Ohio and Kentucky, to mount on a horizontal wheel amidships two guns pointing in opposite directions. The theory was that when one gun was fired, the recoil would cause the wheel to turn 180°, bringing the other gun to bear. Thus, one gun could be loaded while the other was being discharged, and a much more rapid rate of fire would be attained than was possible from a single gun.

To test Carbery's theory, Preble had a prototype wheel constructed at the Charlestown Navy Yard during the summer of 1805. Preliminary tests run by First Lieutenant Newton Keene of the Marine Corps and Captain John Burbeck, Inspector of Military Stores for the state of Massachusetts, indicated that the idea might be feasible if modifications were made in the wheel. On receiving Keene's report, Preble went down to Boston from

Portland and experimented with the wheel on 24 August 1805. He described the results in a letter to Robert Smith:

> I have lately tried the experiment of mounting two guns on an horizontal wheel, agreeable to the plan which I saw on the model of a boat in your office at Washington, and find it will answer well. My wheel was twelve feet diameter, with iron rollers let into the wheel to travel on a circular plate of iron or copper let into the lower bed or deck of the vessel. On the verge of the wheel opposite to each other I mounted two long 9-pounders on carriages, the lower part of which was secured to the wheel by bolts or rivets, while the upper part was allowed to rise one inch parallel with the lower bed and recoil four inches on the hinges before it met with any resistance from the wheel. I fired sixteen rounds and every shot went in the direction given it so exactly that five in ten would have hit a man at three-quarter mile distance. Of course the four-inch recoil in the carriage is sufficient for the ball to leave the gun before any circular motion takes place. This has determined me to rig No. 11 and 12 as pilot boat schooners are rigged and carry the two heavy guns amidships with a light five-inch howitzer forward and aft. For the large guns neither tackle or breeching will be required, and the circular motion will take off all strain from the boat which the firing would otherwise occasion.

Secretary Smith at first proposed that experienced masters of merchantmen be brought into the Navy from civilian life, given appointments as sailing masters, and placed in command of the gunboats and ketches. This plan would, in effect, have created a distinct corps of officers to command this class of vessels. Preble, who strongly supported professionalism in the Navy, dissented:

> The bomb ketches will be a handsome command, such as any lieutenant or master in the Navy might be proud of, and the gunboats such as any of them would be glad to accept; and I hope you will pardon me for observing that, if respectable young officers who have been long in service and who are well acquainted with the regulations and discipline of the Navy should be appointed to command the four vessels building here, it would, in my opinion, add more to the respectability and reputation of the service among the people in this quarter and wherever the vessels may go than if they were commanded by masters of merchant vessels, totally unacquainted with order or discipline. I presume it would be best if every officer who commands a public vessel should first have served in a subordinate capacity in the Navy and made himself thoroughly acquainted with the duty of every grade of officer in our establishment.

Robert Smith had a high regard for Preble's opinions; he agreed and silently scuttled his own proposal.

Even before the *Etna*, the *Vesuvius*, Gunboat No. 11, and Gunboat No. 12 sailed for New Orleans in September 1806 Preble was busy with a new generation of gunboats. An act of 21 April 1806 had authorized the building and completion of up to fifty more gunboats, "for the protection of the harbors, coasts, and commerce of the United States." In its construction program under this authorization the Navy Department was concentrating on a few basic models that would be economical to build and designed for harbor service only. Of the forty or so boats built, Preble was responsible for nine, Nos. 29-37.

Preble's role in the building of the bomb ketches *Vesuvius* and *Etna* and Gunboats Nos. 11 and 12 was that of the Navy's professional supervisor and inspector of work done by civilian contractors. His involvement in the construction of Gunboats Nos. 29-37 was different: the Navy Department contracted directly with Edward Preble for nine boats, and he subcontracted the different parts of the job. The advantage to the Navy Department of contracting with Preble was that they were employing a person of known reliability and conscientiousness. There is also some evidence that such contracts were political plums awarded to persons who were considered "correct" in their "political principles." For Preble, this arrangement had two benefits. First, his role as middleman between the government and the subcontractors gave him the chance to make a modest profit. Second, and probably equally important to Preble, there was less paper work than when he had tediously to examine and approve the accounts of civilian contractors who were to be paid by the Navy Department. He was inordinately efficient in handling accounts and other paper work, but he found it an aggravating chore and preferred to be a contractor providing a gunboat at a fixed price.

All nine boats were built according to Preble-Coffin plan No. 3, one of those prepared for contractors in the Ohio Valley, but for which the Fox design had been substituted. Plan No. 3 was for a small boat intended for harbor or river use: Nos. 29-37 measured 55 feet between perpendiculars, 17 feet molded beam, and 4 feet 6 inches deep in the hold. Their rig, gun mounts, and armament were the same as in Nos. 11 and 12, except that they had no howitzers or carronades.

Three of the boats were subcontracted to William Moulton, Jr., of Portland, two to Eleazer Higgins of Portland, and three to Ephraim Hunt and Robert Giveen of Brunswick, Maine. All contracts for these eight gunboats were officially dated 25 August 1806, although preliminary agreements with the subcontractors had been reached on 13 August at Portland and on the 18th at Brunswick. The keel of the ninth boat was laid on 10 October 1806 at Portland by Eleazer Higgins under a later agreement.[17] Preble's initial contract with the Navy Department, which called for him to provide only the hulls, masts, and spars of nine boats, was fulfilled by the end of November 1806; but, because the winter of 1806-07 was severe, and great

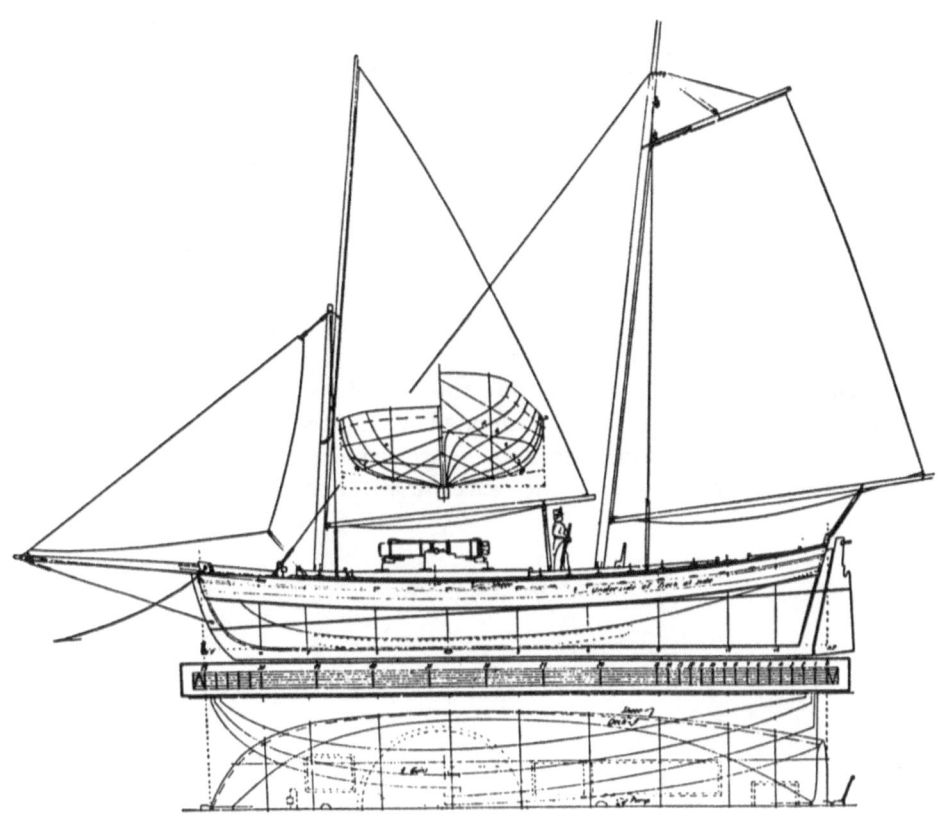

DESIGN OF GUNBOATS NOS. 29-37

Preble-Coffin Plan No. 3

When Gunboats Nos. 29-37 were actually armed in the summer of 1807, as a result of the *Chesapeake* crisis, only one 24-pounder was mounted on the horizontal wheel, rather than the two long guns shown on the original plan, above.

chunks of ice were floating in every part of Portland harbor, the boats were left on the stocks until spring.

A second contract concluded with the Navy Department in January 1807 authorized Preble to complete the nine gunboats by supplying cables and cordage, anchors, awnings and sails, blocks, yawl and oars, water casks, buckets, caboose and kitchen furniture, cabin and officers' furniture, and joiners' work in cabin, storerooms, magazine, and crew's accommodations. By late March, one boat was completely equipped as a prototype, and the others were lacking only water casks, kitchen and cabin furniture, and masters',* boatswains', carpenters', sailmakers', and coopers' stores. At that point the Navy Department discovered that its appropriation was insufficient to finish all the boats then under construction in the United States, and, on 20 March 1807, asked Preble to suspend the completion of his contract. Preble gradually wound up work in progress, and the boats, launched between early March and late April, were placed in ordinary at Portland: a dock was leased, and a carpenter, a caulker, and three hands were hired to keep them in repair. Equipment was placed in storage. Standing rigging, sails, and awnings went into a loft — the former laid out at full length, the latter folded, but opened, examined, and aired from time to time. Thus would Gunboats Nos. 29-37 remain until funds were available for their completion, or the government needed them for national defense.

---

* The master's stores for each of Gunboats Nos. 29-37 included a copy of Nathaniel Bowditch's *The New American Practical Navigator*.[18] This is the earliest mention of Bowditch's book observed among Preble's papers.

CHAPTER 17   SEPTEMBER 1804–JUNE 1807

*"So powerful an opposition as appeared in Congress
last session may for a while check the growth of the Navy,
but, unless the commercial spirit of our country dies,
it must rise into consequence."*

Samuel Barron's sickness created the atmosphere in which the final months of the Tripolitan War were spun out.[1] Soon after he relieved Preble off Tripoli on 9 September 1804, Barron developed a serious liver ailment. He was much too sick to live afloat — "God knows how it will end," he sighed — and early in November he moved ashore. There he stayed through the winter and on into the spring of 1805. At times, he was so ill that everyone thought he was dying; then he would seem to be on the mend, only to fall back to the edge of death again. But, sick as he was — and on some days he could not even attempt to write — Samuel Barron refused to give up command of the squadron and never stopped hoping that he would recover in time to lead his ships against Tripoli in the summer of 1805. He declined to delegate any but housekeeping responsibilities to his second-in-command, John Rodgers. By temperament Samuel Barron was likable, relaxed and easygoing. With such limited drive as he possessed drained away by disease, vigorous executive direction of the war was lacking: logistic buildup for the summer of 1805 and operations of the squadron were on a leisurely footing.

An intense power struggle developed around Barron's sickbed as three forceful personalities, John Rodgers, James Barron, and Tobias Lear, each tried to deflect policy in the direction he personally favored.

John Rodgers had chafed under Morris's command. Now, for the second time in two years, he was eating his heart out as second-in-command to an ineffectual commodore who would give little scope to Rodgers's large talents.

James Barron was his brother's closest confidant and, in his behalf, performed many executive functions in directing the activities of the squadron. As a counsellor and stand-in executive, James Barron was not a very happy choice, for he was a sensitive man, severely depressed by Samuel's illness; a man whose moods of black pessimism often psychologically crippled him to the point of inaction. At least some of the miasma of defeatism emanating from squadron headquarters was sponsored by James Barron.

Tobias Lear had come up from Algiers determined that the diplomatic arm of U.S. policy should play a more vigorous, a more adroit, and a more independent role under Barron than it had under Edward Preble.

The truly catalytic personality, William Eaton, was in another part of the Mediterranean developing his own offensive. After agreeing in mid-September to send Eaton to Egypt to cooperate with Hamet Caramanli, Samuel Barron apparently hedged on his decision; Eaton was kept drumming his heels in idleness for about two months while Barron tried to decide whether or not to use Hamet's aid. Early in November 1804, when Preble was still at Syracuse, Eaton enlisted Preble's help, as a result of which Samuel Barron finally sent the *Argus* off in search of Hamet. Although Samuel Barron, Edward Preble, and William Eaton thought they were in accord on plans, there was actually a major misunderstanding or difference among them on strategy. Barron expected the *Argus* to bring Hamet Caramanli to Syracuse, where a decision would then be made on how, or whether, Hamet was to be used. Eaton and Preble were thinking in terms of a more decisive strategy, an adaptation of Preble's old plan of cooperation with Richard Farquhar, Salvatore Busuttil, and Clemente Fama: Hamet and Eaton were to march from Egypt at the head of an army that had been raised there, capture Derna, and proceed to Benghazi. Ships of the U.S. squadron were to transport them across the Gulf of Sidra to Cape Misurata. Perhaps reinforced by detachments of the squadron's Marines, the army would then attack Tripoli from the rear while the squadron attacked by sea.

With this plan in mind, Eaton sailed from Syracuse for Egypt in the *Argus* on 14 November 1804. At Burg el Arab, thirty miles southwest of Alexandria, Eaton and Hamet assembled a heterogeneous army of some 300 Muslims, about 70 Greek and European soldiers of fortune, seven U.S. Marines, a Marine lieutenant, and a midshipman from the *Argus*. They captured Derna on 27 April 1805 with the aid of Isaac Hull, commanding the *Argus,* the *Nautilus,* and the *Hornet.*

Credit is due the courage and tenacity of purpose demonstrated by Eaton, but the march from Alexandria and the fighting at Derna revealed the feet — not to say the legs — of clay on which his scheme stood. Hamet Caramanli had repeatedly proved himself improvident, irresolute, craven, and subject to fits of despondency, as Bonaventure Beaussier and other men knowledgeable in Barbary affairs had all along been trying to tell the Americans. Nor were Hamet's followers, Arab sheiks and émigré Tripolitans, any more determined than their leader. The march from Alexandria was punctuated by quarrels among the Muslims, by Muslim threats to mutiny and massacre the Christians, by restiveness and incipient mutiny in the Christian column, and by panic among both leaders and followers whenever they heard rumors of Yusuf's forces moving against them. Time and again it was only the force of Eaton's character that kept them all, Hamet, sheiks, Muslims, and Christians, from abandoning the expedition forthwith.

Moreover, once Derna was captured there was no popular rallying to Hamet. At least one-third of the inhabitants of the city remained loyal to Yusuf, and there was an always-present threat that others would go over to that side. By 8 May Eaton's force was besieged in Derna by a column of Yusuf Caramanli's troops numbering between 900 and 1,000. Although Yusuf's army was turned back when it tried to attack Derna on 13 May, it was only Isaac Hull's naval guns that kept Eaton's enclave from being overrun. The defenders were too weak to attempt a counterattack, and the siege continued. Only substantial deliveries of money, supplies, and men from the Barron squadron could get the expedition out of Derna and on the march towards Tripoli.

Throughout, Samuel Barron fluctuated indecisively between hot and cold in his attitude towards Eaton's expedition. But one influential man, Tobias Lear, had opposed the adventure from the outset, and was satisfied to see Eaton stranded in Cyrenaica without much prospect of going any farther. In his opinion, if the United States was to be respected by the Barbary Powers, it must win peace with Tripoli on its own, and he considered the U.S. Mediterranean squadron strong enough to do that without enlisting Hamet's help. Furthermore, from what he had learned of the personalities of Yusuf and Hamet, Lear judged that if Yusuf were "well beaten into" peace, such a peace would be far more durable than one which resulted from the United States' placing Hamet in the pashadom. Or, as he put it to William Eaton: "We wished to make peace with a man who would have the ability to keep it." Lear had, in addition, developed a conviction that Yusuf would fight on indefinitely rather than give up the *Philadelphia* prisoners without the payment of at least token ransom. He held three times as many American sailors as the United States held Tripolitan subjects, and to surrender so many captives gratuitously would set a disastrous precedent for his relations with other small nations and might lead to a coup against him.

For all these reasons Lear was receptive in December 1804, when he began to get feelers from Tripoli. First, there were some vague hints from the Spanish consul at Tripoli that the Pasha was interested in terminating his war with the United States. Then a series of secret letters from William Bainbridge advised Lear and Barron that the people of Tripoli were more strongly attached to Yusuf, who was solidly entrenched in power, than to his miserable, effeminate, pusillanimous, fugitive brother, Hamet; that Hamet had further debased himself in Tripolitan eyes by allying himself with Christians against followers of Islam; that winter or spring might be excellent times to negotiate, since Yusuf was apprehensive about the planned summer attacks, and this fear might be more effective in bringing him to terms than an actual bombardment. Bainbridge also wrote that Sidi Mohammed Dghies had approached him privately to tell him that he, Dghies, intended to use his influence with the Pasha to promote a negotiated peace on moderate terms: Dghies hoped that Commodore Barron would soon send an accredited negotiator over to Tripoli. But none of these things led Bainbridge to believe that Tripoli would release the *Philadelphia* prisoners without some sort of ransom; that was a sine qua non.

Then Barron received a letter, dated in March, written by Nicholas C. Nissen, Danish consul at Tripoli, at the request of Mohammed Dghies. Through Nissen, Dghies said he intended to use his powerful influence to move the Pasha towards peace, and he wished that negotiations might be attempted before full hostilities were renewed. But, continued Dghies, his poor health would soon force him to leave the city and go to his country villa: once there, he would not return to participate in any negotiations. Unless talks began soon, his voice would not be heard in the Pasha's divan in support of a peaceful and speedy settlement of the war. Nissen, whose own integrity and reliability were beyond question, vouched for the sincerity of Dghies.

Lear's initial reaction to the several feelers was that it was up to Yusuf to make the demarche by giving the United States full assurances that he would negotiate on "honorable grounds which shall be compatible with the rising character of our nation and with a [prospect] of a permanent peace." These "honorable grounds" were, first, the United States would not be required to pay a cent for peace itself; second, if ransom were to be paid, it must be only for the number of "Philadelphias" in excess of the number of Tripolitans held by the United States; and, third, there must be reasonable assurance that the peace would be permanent. Nevertheless, Lear still did not see how permanency would be possible unless Yusuf were allowed a small, face-saving ransom.

When the Pasha's formal peace proposals, transmitted through the Spanish consul, reached Lear on 21 April 1805 they seemed to be extravagantly out of line: $200,000 for peace and ransom, and the United States to make full and gratuitous restitution of all Tripolitan prisoners and all captured Tripolitan property. After the first shock of these proposals passed, Lear realized that there remained convincing evidence of strong peace sentiment at Tripoli, and he grew confident that he would be able to negotiate successfully with the Pasha before the Barron squadron had a chance to fire a single gun at Tripoli. Following ample discussion of all these points, Samuel Barron and Lear decided, in the middle of May, that the Pasha's proposals were wholly unacceptable, but that he was probably ready to settle for much less. The only way to find out was by actual negotiation. Lear sailed for Tripoli in the *Essex* to discover what diplomacy could accomplish.

Two factors made Samuel Barron especially sympathetic to negotiations at that moment. In the first place, having finally realized that he was not going to recover in time to lead his squadron against Tripoli that summer, he was preparing to resign his command to John Rodgers. In the second, both he and his brother, James, had been taking a markedly defeatist attitude towards the summer's prospective operations because they had been unable to borrow bomb ketches or gunboats from the Neapolitan government, and it appeared that they would be no more successful in Venice. Their pessimism was wholly unjustified. Samuel Barron had prematurely written off as a failure Master Commandant Thomas Robinson's search for craft in the Adriatic: Robinson was actually in the process of purchasing four gunboats and two other small vessels. And an important dispatch from the Navy Department was on its way across the Atlantic. This dispatch, the first copy of which reached Malta on 26 May, announced the approach of nine gunboats and two merchantmen converted into bomb ketches — the reinforcement that Edward Preble had hurried home to secure for Barron.

Lear appeared before Tripoli on the morning of 26 May; serious negotiations began on the 29th. Early in the proceedings Yusuf sent an oral message to Rodgers, who by this time had succeeded Samuel Barron, and to Lear:

> I know that the exertions of your squadron this summer will be sufficient to reduce my capital; but recollect I have upwards of three hundred of your countrymen in my hands; and I candidly tell you that, if you persevere in driving me to the last extremity, I shall retire with them to a castle about ninety miles in the interior of the country, which I have prepared for their confinement and my own security. Money is not my object at present, but a peace on terms that will not disgrace me hereafter.

And that was the kind of peace Lear concluded. The preliminary articles were agreed upon on 3 June 1805. No money was paid for peace; no annuities were promised. The United States gave Tripoli $60,000 for the American prisoners in excess of the number of Tripolitans held — but Yusuf insisted that $60,000 was only a nominal, face-saving sum. The United States agreed to evacuate its forces from the enclave at Derna, and to attempt to persuade Hamet, in return for certain concessions to him by Yusuf, to withdraw from Cyrenaica.

Lear's treaty was a happy solution for both belligerents. The Tripolitans retained their vigorous and effective ruler, and were saved the civil disorders that almost certainly would have followed installation by the United States of the weak reed, Hamet Caramanli, as Pasha of Tripoli. The U.S. squadron, especially under Edward Preble, had shown so much spirit in maintaining national dignity that the United States was thereafter treated with high respect by Tripoli. By agreeing to a compromise peace and paying a face-saving ransom, rather than dictating a humiliating treaty at gunpoint, the United States almost certainly avoided a renewal of war with Yusuf: a humiliating treaty would have forced Yusuf to attempt to regain face once the United States had reduced its squadron in the Mediterranean. And, as Lear hoped, the peace was permanent.

II

When the earliest official naval reports of the Tripolitan peace treaty reached Washington early in September 1805 Robert Smith wrote the President: "Not having seen the communications from Colonel Lear, I would not form an opinion upon the treaty. But I must say I had expected a treaty of a different character. And informed as I now am, I wish that such a peace had not been made. However, it is possible their better knowledge of the condition of our captive countrymen may have induced them to accede to such terms." Ten days later, after he had read more dispatches and talked to officers returning from the Mediterranean, he wrote again:

> Many of the officers, late prisoners at Tripoli, have called upon me. They all say positively that, if Lear had persisted in not giving a ransom for them, peace would not have been made at all, and that the Bashaw had made up his mind to massacre them while our forces were laying waste his town. He admitted he was unable to cope with such a force, but that he might as well die under the ruins of his town as to be murdered by his own people, which would of course be the case should he deliver up the prisoners without ransom.* He again and again was heard to say that, having killed his father and a brother, he could not have any scruples in killing a few infidels.[2]

* Yusuf's claim is cast in some doubt by a letter dated 5/6 June 1805 in which Tobias Lear told his wife that, when he went ashore in Tripoli on the conclusion of the treaty,

Describing the peace the United States had concluded as the most favorable any nation at war with Tripoli had made for a century, Smith told Preble: "All Europe is giving us national reputation for this. But our own good folks will be busy in telling the world that we are, in fact, a very contemptible people."

In that prediction Smith was certainly correct. The fury of the hand-to-hand combat in the gunboat battle of 3 August 1804 was nothing compared to the fighting that broke out among the members of the Mediterranean high command as soon as the treaty was signed. The questions debated were: Should Lear have paid $60,000 in ransom before Barron's squadron had tested the effect of a summer campaign? Did the $60,000 ransom constitute a betrayal of the principles for which the United States had gone to war? Had the United States pledged to restore Hamet Caramanli to the pashadom and then broken faith by making peace with Yusuf?

William Eaton, armed with the most facile pen, was first on the field: he attacked the patriotism and integrity of Tobias Lear, Samuel Barron, and John Rodgers. Barron demanded and got a retraction of Eaton's charges against him. John Rodgers lashed back at William Eaton, and only last-minute good judgment kept him from entering a pamphlet war with Eaton — a contest in which the latter's literary ability would have made him a sure winner. Rodgers came near to fighting a duel with James Barron. The controversy spread to Congress, where Eaton's allies, if not large in number, were effective propagandists. Although it was ratified by the United States, 17 April 1806, Lear's treaty was one of the least popular ever concluded by the United States, and his reputation never recovered from the stigma with which it marked him.

Preble stayed out of these postwar quarrels and the national soul-searching. He had no taste for paper wars; but his abstention would more correctly be attributed to sound judgment and to self-discipline. He was determined to keep his opinions to himself. When he did draft an acidulous paragraph about some event that took place during the last nine months of the war, he usually toned it down or deleted it before he put the letter in the mail. Occasionally he gave a hint of his feelings, as when he spoke of "the ignominious Tripoline treaty" concluded by Lear "at the sacrifice of national honor." Preble did not enlarge on this opinion of Lear's treaty, but he made it clear that he considered the Barron squadron strong enough to dictate peace to Tripoli on any terms the United States wished to impose. It must have galled Preble intensely to see his successors, with all the

---

he "was met by thousands of people on the landing. . . . The people here are very much pleased with the peace, as they gain nothing but lose much by the war; and it matters not to them whether it be favorable to their ruler or not."

frigates he had wanted so badly, make the kind of peace he had reluctantly decided not to sign when he was given to understand that the terms were contrary to the administration's intentions. In October 1805, he wrote Eaton:

> The arduous and dangerous service you have performed has astonished not only your country but the world. If pecuniary resources and naval strength had been at your command, what would you not have done! . . . I have often wished we had left the United States together. Perhaps I am too selfish in this wish, for although an earlier acquaintance might have enabled me to render more service to my country while I was in command, and consequently to have acquired more glory, yet it could not have possibly increased your fame beyond its present zenith. You have gained immortal honor and established the military reputation of your country in the East. Should the United States be called to war with any of the European powers, it is my opinion that you would be called to fill the most important military post, and that you would have the unanimous vote of your country in favor of it.[3]

But Preble had no intention of spending the remaining years of his life refighting the Tripolitan War in his imagination, on paper, or with his old subordinates. A few of his former officers — Joshua Blake, for one — wrote to raise questions about accounts of actions in which they had been presented in an unfavorable light or about opinions expressed by Preble which did not seem to them to be fair. These were questions that could have led to endless feuds — if Preble had let them. But Preble always defused these potential quarrels: he was conciliatory; he said the kindest things he could about the questioner and his record; he carefully concealed what he had thought at the time of the incident; and he almost always satisfied the complainant.

Typical was the case of William Bainbridge. He decided that the sentences in Preble's published dispatch on the loss of the *Intrepid* which told how Somers, Wadsworth, and Israel had declared that they would blow themselves up rather than be captured were meant as a slap at him and his officers for surrendering the *Philadelphia*. In fact, at the time of the *Philadelphia*'s loss Preble did write, "Would to God that the officers and crew of the *Philadelphia* had, one and all, determined to prefer death to slavery!" But Bainbridge did not know Preble had written that; Preble may even have forgotten it; and Preble decided to bury the whole matter as quickly as possible. He wrote Bainbridge:

Portland, 3 October 1805.

Sir:
 I have this day received your letter of the 20th ultimo. It arrived here some days since, but being from home I could not reply to it sooner.

I regret extremely that any expressions in my official communications should have been construed, either by yourself or officers, into a reflection on your or their conduct in the loss of the *Philadelphia,* and I now declare that neither the expressions which have offended you nor any other made use of in my dispatches were ever intended to reflect, in any degree whatever, either on yourself or officers. I only quoted the expressions of Captain Somers as made use of by him the day before his death. The situation of yourself and Somers were very different. I never conceived that you were at liberty to destroy the lives of your officers and crew by blowing up your ship; nor do I conceive that your conduct could or would have been justified by your countrymen had you done it. Captain Somers' situation was very different. His associates in the daring expedition were but few, and they had entered into a mutual agreement never to return if unsuccessful. I again repeat that I did not mean to convey, nor do I imagine that any persons, excepting yourself and officers, ever supposed that I did, the smallest degree of censure on you or them by the expressions allud[ed] to in your letter or in any other part of my dispatches. I have taken from a newspaper the declaration of Captain Somers and enclosed it. I hope the explanation I have given may prove satisfactory, as I value your friendship and should regret that any circumstance should occur to deprive me of it. I am, with great regard, Sir, your obedient servant,

EDWARD PREBLE[4]

III

So by the fall of 1805 Preble was putting the Tripolitan War behind him. His mind and energy were committed to the Navy's new challenges, and he was involved in one of the first concerted efforts by a group of officers to influence naval legislation.

This lobbying activity received its initial stimulus in the late summer of 1805 when Robert Smith decided to press within the administration and in Congress for the resumption of work on the Navy's first ships of the line. During the Quasi-War with France, an excellent design for a 74-gun ship had been prepared by Joshua Humphreys. Frames, cannon, and much of the material for building six seventy-fours had been purchased and stockpiled at the projected construction sites: Portsmouth (New Hampshire), Boston, New York, Philadelphia, Washington, and Norfolk. But, because of the national reaction against heavy military expenditures at the end of the Quasi-War, construction had never begun. In Robert Smith's mind the First Session of the Ninth Congress, which would meet in December 1805, was the psychological moment to recommend construction of the seventy-fours. The previous May, negotiations to settle a number of issues with Spain — spoliation claims, the disputed southwestern boundary of Louisiana, navigation on the Mobile River, and the U.S. claim to West Florida — had ended in failure, and relations between the two countries were tense. Spain, Smith argued, was gambling that the United States would be reluctant to arm adequately for self-defense, and the construction of six — or, preferably, twelve — seventy-fours would force her to be more reasonable.

A second impetus came from James Barron, who, at the end of September 1805, wrote Preble, "The Navy wants so many reforms that my hopes are sinking fast to despair." By 15 October he had formulated at least two specific reforms toward which he thought the captains of the Navy should work: first, the pay of the captains ought to be increased; second, Barron and Thomas Tingey were interested in getting Congress to establish a Board of Navy Commissioners[5] to be composed of three men appointed by the President. The commissioners might be chosen from the captains of the Navy, former captains of the Navy — apparently a provision to get Thomas Truxtun on the Board — or civilians with nautical knowledge. As commissioners, all would be given the rank of captains in the Navy. The Board would meet from time to time, but the members would normally reside one at each of the principal navy yards, where they would superintend the building and major overhaul of all vessels. They were to introduce uniformity into masting, equipping, manning, and provisioning ships of war, in order to eliminate frequent, expensive, and time-consuming alterations in rig, armament, equipment, and even the basic structure of ships at the whim of their successive commanders. Other responsibilities proposed for the Board of Navy Commissioners were: advise the Secretary of the Navy on ship design; inspect and direct the work of Navy shore establishments; supervise ships in ordinary; handle procurement and issue of all stores and materials under the direction of the Secretary of the Navy; contract for and prove all guns cast for the Navy; and examine all midshipmen in their knowledge of navigation and seamanship before promotion to lieutenancies.

James Barron wanted several of the captains to come together as a body in Washington and exert their collective influence for the adoption of these reforms. Preble wrote Barron that he would not be able to go to Washington before February at the earliest, and the rest of his response was cheerless:

> What we are to do for a Navy God only knows. I do not believe we shall very soon have any large ships built notwithstanding [what is announced] in the newspapers about building seventy-fours. And, should we be suddenly involved in war, our commerce must go to the Devil without much chance for remuneration. . . . I think a Board of Commissioners are wanted and that the pay of the captains ought to be raised, but I doubt whether the government will consent to either — but it would be well to try. . . . Should a Board of Commissioners be appointed, I presume they ought to consist of three or five [of] the oldest captains. Five would be preferable to three, as it would generally enable a part to be occasionally absent to attend to their private concerns.

On 13 November William Bainbridge wrote Preble: "I hope that you will visit Washington this winter. In my opinion the ensuing session of Congress will be a very interesting epoch for the American Navy. If you will come on to Philadelphia, I will accompany [you] to Headquarters." By the time Preble replied to Bainbridge on the 29th, his attitude had changed and he had definitely embraced the lobbying plan:

> It is my intention to visit Washington this winter, and it will afford me great pleasure to be your traveling companion. I have a thousand interesting inquiries to make which it is in your power to satisfy. The pleasure of meeting my brother officers of our little squadron would be a sufficient inducement to me to take the journey, independent of the concerns of the Navy — which we all ought to attend to. I believe, if we could all meet at Washington the present session, that, by our joint endeavors, we might prevail on government to better our establishment.

Preble started out from Portland on 4 December. His trip south was not without excitement. As the stage was entering Philadelphia on 11 December, the horses suddenly bolted. Preble had to jump from the careening coach and, as he did so, hurt his right foot so badly that he was forced to stay over in Philadelphia for five days. He mitigated the tedium of his confinement by inviting half a dozen naval and Marine Corps officers — including his old Mediterranean associates, Bainbridge, Decatur, and Stewart — over for supper on the 14th. Two days later, his foot was well enough for him to get in and out of public conveyances, and he and Bainbridge took the road for Washington, where they arrived on the 18th and put up at Stelle's Hotel.

Fifteen days earlier, the President's annual message had been read to Congress. After delineating the difficulties faced by a small, peacefully-inclined nation in a world at war, the President made several recommendations touching on naval affairs. He suggested a substantial increase in the officer corps as a means of rewarding and retaining good officers through promotion; he wanted the section of the law that required six frigates to be kept in constant service to be amended so that the Navy Department would have flexibility in choosing between large and small vessels; and he recommended that seaport fortifications be strengthened and land fortifications supplemented by a "competent number of gunboats." Finally, with what might be interpreted as a certain lack of enthusiasm for the proposition, he reminded Congress that, "Considerable provision has been made, under former authorities from Congress, of materials for the construction of ships of war of seventy-four guns. These materials are on hand, subject to the further will of the Legislature."

When Bainbridge and Preble reached the capital, a select committee of the House of Representatives was considering those portions of the President's message, and within the week, had reported three resolutions as a basis for discussion by the House sitting as committee of the whole: the provision of $150,000 for repair and arming of fortifications; appropriation of $250,000 to build not more than fifty gunboats; and the designation of $660,000 for the construction of six line-of-battle ships. Since neither increased pay for captains nor establishment of a Board of Navy Commissioners was recommended to Congress by the Executive, all the professional expectations of the naval officers were concentrated on how Congress would react to the proposal to resume work on the seventy-fours.

Preble and Bainbridge probably found themselves somewhat handicapped in their attempt to present a picture of solidarity among the captains by the decision of the organizer, James Barron, not to join them in the capital. Barron attributed his absence to "a variety of adverse circumstances," but pessimism may once again have reduced him to a state of defeatism and moral paralysis: "From the present aspect of public affairs it appears that there is but little for naval men to expect," he wrote Preble from his home in Hampton, Virginia. Nevertheless, the two captains were certainly busy while they were in Washington. It is not surprising that there is no formal record of their activities, since Preble was convinced that his prestige and influence were more effectively used in personal interviews with the President, Secretary Smith, and members of Congress than in letters which could be filed away and ignored.

It is a matter of record that Preble enjoyed to the full the Washington social season. To Mary he wrote:

> The society here at present is agreeable enough. Yesterday I dined with the President. His only daughter, Mrs. [Martha] Randolph, and her five children are with him. Mrs. R. is considered as the first among women in this country for good sense and an improved mind. Her manners are so much like yours that I could not but admire her. I am to keep Christmas today with the British ambassador, of whose family I shall give you some account in my next. I know your contempt for the parade of large ceremonious dinner parties and shall say nothing of them. Tomorrow evening I am to attend the City Ball and shall, of course, be able to bring you an account of the fashions of the Capital.

On New Year's Day 1806 Preble and Bainbridge attended the President's levee. The Prebles were expecting a child in February, and Edward, concerned about leaving home at all during these last months, did not want to prolong his business in Washington. Consequently, that same night he caught a stage for Baltimore.

No action was taken on the committee report while Preble and Bainbridge were in town, but on 24 January the House formally called on the

President to report the amount of money spent on the Navy each year since its establishment, the cost of each ship, and the amount expended on each navy yard. A naval officer who was in Washington reported that, "It is conjectured by some that the object of obtaining the expenses *en masse* is to frighten the backcountry members, and my opinion is that their wishes in that respect will be realized, for the expenses are $13,600,000." Another officer studied opinion in Congress and found little reason to hope for an increase in the Navy: "Some of the gentlemen think the most economical plan is to let [the ships] rot; others to sell half for the repairs of three; and almost all are of opinion that six seventy-fours would ruin the country."

When the three resolutions on maritime defense were discussed on 28 February 1806 Speaker of the House Nathaniel Macon delivered a speech that attracted considerable attention in naval circles. He argued that, to have an adequate force of seventy-fours, the United States would have to build enough of them to meet Great Britain on the high seas, that is to say, forty or fifty, and she plainly could not afford to construct a fleet of that size: a squadron of six seventy-fours would be futile, for whenever the United States was at war with a major naval power, it would have to hide in harbor. "If we were now at war with any nation," Macon continued, "I think we should do well to lend our navy to another nation also at war with that with which we might be at war; for I think such nation would manage it more to our advantage than ourselves." One naval officer understood Macon to say "that in case of war it would be better to hire out our frigates to individuals to be employed as privateers than to man and officer them on account of government." The opinion of the House as indicated by the tone of debate, said this naval observer, was that, since the United States could not afford to build fortifications, more gunboats, *and* six seventy-fours, all at the same time, the emphasis should be on gunboats.

And so, indeed, it went. Defense measures came up for a vote on 25 March 1806: $150,000 was appropriated for fortifications and $250,000 for gunboats. But the proposal to spend $660,000 on building six seventy-fours was killed by a margin of more than two to one.[6]

From his home in Portland, where he arrived on 18 January, Preble followed the Congressional activity through newspapers and the letters of his friends, George Davis and Noadiah Morris, who were in Washington. In Preble's opinion, Lear's "unfortunate" treaty was partly to blame for the hostile attitude of Congress towards the Navy: after the Barron squadron had been equipped at great public expense on the assumption that it would release the *Philadelphia* captives without ransom, Lear had agreed to pay ransom.

"I believe," Preble told George Davis, "that the Navy is fast going to destruction and that Congress will not at present appropriate a sum sufficient to save it. But the day will come when they will be convinced that a government depending on commerce for the support of its civil establishment will find it necessary to protect the source from whence its existence springs." He was convinced that the United States would always be a seafaring, commercial nation, and that there would always be nations whose international relations could be controlled only by force and fear. Inevitably, then, the United States must some day have a great navy. These visceral convictions kept Preble from giving way completely to depression and even made him guardedly optimistic. "So powerful an opposition as appeared in Congress last session may for a while check the growth of the Navy," he told Charles W. Goldsborough late in the spring of 1806, "but, unless the commercial spirit of our country dies, it must rise into consequence. No great mercantile marine ever did, or ever can, exist without a correspondent military marine for its protection. It offers too powerful a stimulus to the avarice, to say nothing of jealousy and vindictive dispositions, of those powers whom nothing but force or the dread of it can restrain."

IV

Even before the overwhelming Congressional rejection of the seventy-fours, Preble sometimes talked wistfully of retiring from the Navy. In the fall of 1805, construction on the bomb ketches *Etna* and *Vesuvius* and on Gunboats Nos. 11 and 12 was in full swing, but in October he wrote: "I have lately been employed in building bomb ketches and gunboats, a business I am pretty well tired of. If no nobler game offers, I shall soon give up the chase."

Threats such as that were probably nothing more than a form of self-therapy. Preble loved the Navy. If pressed, he would probably have admitted that business and moneymaking did not really interest him. What he had said in 1798 — "I am particularly fond of naval service" — was still true seven or eight years later. It is difficult to imagine circumstances that would have driven Preble to give up his commission voluntarily, especially in view of the advice he gave William Bainbridge when the latter seriously considered quitting the Navy in 1807: keep your commission, Preble told him, as long as the Navy Department will grant you furloughs for merchant cruises when your active services are not required, and as long as it does not treat you with any marked neglect or disrespect.

But, if Preble remained in the Navy, how was the government going to make effective use of him? The answer seemed to be related to the problem of the economical administration of the naval establishment. Robert Smith was an excellent administrator, but the Navy Department had an Achilles' heel: the expense of its shore establishment, especially the principal navy yard, which was in Washington. A full analysis of this problem is beyond the scope of a biography of Edward Preble, but, in capsule, the difficulty was high costs in relation to the amount and the quality of work produced. This was a principal source of friction between Smith and Treasury Secretary Gallatin, and the target of a good measure of Congressional criticism of the Navy Department. The Department's top administrators, Smith and Goldsborough, were fully aware of the problem — but how to solve it?

In the summer of 1805, Goldsborough discussed the matter in a letter to Preble, and on 12 July Preble replied:

> I agree with you that our expenses in proportion to our establishment exceeds that of any other nation and that greater economy is absolutely necessary to its existence and increase. The wealth of the world would scarcely support the vast navy of England were it not for the excellent organization, system, and economy of its establishment, founded on long and expensive experience, which has enabled them to lop off all exuberances. We must follow their example, which we may soon be enabled to do by sending proper characters among them to acquire the necessary information on this subject.

Preble's hint about "sending proper characters among them" referred to a plan, which he and Robert Smith had been developing since the previous April, for Preble to make an extensive trip to Europe, in order to study and report on the establishments of the major naval powers. The idea originated with Robert Smith, but Preble picked it up enthusiastically:

> It has long been my opinion that such a measure would be judicious, as it would enable us, without the heavy expense of experiments, to gain a knowledge of all the improvements in naval affairs which has cost Europe millions of money. It would, in the event of an increase of our Navy, save immense sums of money to this country to be able to proceed on the most economical and best approved plans. . . . It would afford me the highest degree of satisfaction to be sent in pursuit of that knowledge which may [be] useful to my country.

Preble estimated that it would take him from twelve to eighteen months to find out all he wanted to know about how other nations cured timber; built, armed, and equipped ships; cast cannon of every caliber; cleaned hemp; tarred and laid cables; docked and careened vessels; laid out dockyards; preserved ships; and a variety of other information pertaining to naval rules and regulations. Finally, he suggested, "Would it not be well to collect a naval library, composed of a few of the most useful books, to be deposited at the Navy Office?"

Although Robert Smith had some misgivings about the way Preble proposed to handle his expense account, and the President considered a tour of twelve to eighteen months longer than necessary,[7] the basic idea was accepted and the plan was still very much alive in July 1805. After that, for unknown reasons, it was dropped — completely.

Another opportunity to involve Preble in the improvement of the Navy's shore establishment arose in the spring of 1806. At that time, Captain Thomas Tingey, the superintendent of the Washington Navy Yard, was apparently considering retiring in the fall, and the Navy Department unofficially asked Preble if he would be interested in the post. Word of the offer got out, and on 7 May James Barron wrote Preble:

> I find your friends very anxious to know whether you will accept the place you have been solicited to command or not. I have a hope that when you reflect on the *great good* you can do and how materially you may change the public opinion by your good management, that, if possible, you will make the sacrifice, if only for two years. In that time I am positively convinced you could put a very different face on naval affairs in this country. Is it not enough to disgust the people to see large sums of money expended and, in fact, nothing to show for it? For it is certain the ships that have been repaired at the city [Washington] (the *Chesapeake* excepted) have rather been injured than benefitted. Our excellent Secretary would then have confidence in your advice, and all would go on well.

Barron's persuasion seems to have been effective. When Preble wrote Goldsborough on the 25th of the month, he said:

> With respect to the navy yard at Washington, I beg leave to observe that it never can be for the interest of the United States to have such an establishment on a large scale at the head of a freshwater river, of difficult navigation for men-of-war, at so great a distance from the Atlantic. Ships will undoubtedly decay much faster in warm climates and fresh water than in salt. In salt water they will never decay below the light water line. In fresh water they generally decay there first; at least our merchants trading to the freshwater rivers of Africa, where their vessels lay at anchor for five or six months at a time, have generally found it so. There are many other objections, such as the difficulty of procuring seamen, the unhealthiness of the climate, etc., etc. But if it is determined to make that the principal establishment, exposed as it is to the observation of every member of Congress and curious visitor, the only method to make it respected and popular is by a systematical and judicious internal police founded on *correct* economical principles.
>
> I feel diffident of my own abilities either to give satisfaction to myself or the Navy Department as commandant of the navy yard at Washington; but if it should become vacant next autumn, and I should have the offer, I think it probable I may be induced to accept for a year or two in hopes, by unremitting exertions, to place it at least on a more respectable footing than it has hitherto been considered. But be assured the sacrifices I should make by

leaving this would be extremely great. Nothing but a hope of being serviceable would ever induce me to make them.

Nothing came of this proposition either. Tingey did not retire that fall: he stayed on as superintendent until 1829. But the administration was anxious to bring Preble to Washington in a high advisory post to the Navy Department. Preble wanted to come. It seemed to be only a matter of time before the right set of circumstances would provide the opportunity.

V

Hunting and fishing remained Preble's favorite sports, just as they had been when he was a boy, and there were family stories about his skill as a marksman in the field. The only one of these that has survived tells how, to win a bet, he brought down five swallows, one after another, with five shots. He purchased some hunting dogs in Sicily, but the winter voyage in the *John Adams* was too much for them, and all apparently died before the ship anchored at New York. Thanks to Samuel Taylor Coleridge, a hunting story that Preble told at Syracuse just before he left the Mediterranean has survived. It is a typical Preble story in that it is about someone else: Preble rarely served as raconteur of his own adventures.

On 19 October 1804, Coleridge wrote:

> This same morning Commodore Preble told me a most interesting story of his own knowledge of an American boy, not then quite eleven years old. Was following the men who were driving in the cattle to the fold, and had a gun, powder, balls, etc. The gun had been given him by [the] Commodore's brother who always favored the lad. His dog barked, and the boy thought a squirrel was treed, and then observed (it was evening) that the dog barked at the foot of a vast pine, hollow from top to bottom, and at the bottom open. . . . Walked up and saw the glare of the two eyes of an immense bear. He did not wait to put in a ball into the gun, but went up and discharged the powder and small shot full in the animal's face. Mad with pain and all bloody, the bear leapt out on the boy, but leapt beside him and was shuffling on in pursuit of what was behind him, when his dog attacked the bear and turned him. He then saw the boy and made at him, but the boy darted behind the tree and his dog again turned the bear; and during this time the boy had time to load and put a bullet in the gun. This done, he followed the bear, came up close to him, fired and broke his thighbone. The bear made at him, but was soon turned by the dog. The boy, again behind a tree, loaded again, but the bear now made off, as fast as three legs would carry him. The boy tracked him till he came to a great fern and furze brake. Still went on, oftentimes, from the nature of the ground, obliged to crawl on all fours, and it now being quite dusk. In three miles he came to the top of a very steep ascent at the bottom of which was the lake. Now the bear was halfway down (for when

wounded or hard pursued they take to the water). The boy now made sure, and turning the bear and irritating him, as he faced shot him through the heart. He twisted up and tumbled headlong down the hill upon the beach. The boy went on, took a pole and put his handkerchief on it to be seen at a distance, and went home to his alarmed family and told them his exploit. They went by a different and roundabout road (for the boy's road was not possible for a sledge) with two oxen and a sledge and brought home the animal that weighed eighty stone — larger than the largest cow the man had. This boy [the] Commodore put to school for two years, and wished the man to let him have the boy and make perhaps an admiral of him, but the father could not and would not part with him. He is now sixteen, a handsome and very clever boy.[8]

When Preble and the American-born British admiral, Sir Isaac Coffin, met during the latter's visit to New England in 1805, they discovered a mutual interest in fishing. On his return to England, Coffin sent Preble, "as a brother sailor and a fisherman," a trawl and dredge. In his letter of thanks, written on 18 April 1807, Preble said: "I have a gunboat of about forty tons fitted up in great style for the trawling business. I shall observe all your directions in the use of it and hope soon to be able to transmit to you an account of the thousands slain." And Coffin wrote to a mutual friend: "Commodore Preble has much engaged my attention. . . . Next *to myself* I consider him the best fisherman in America. By some of the spring ships I hope to be able to describe to him a net used in Scotland called a Few and Fike that will entrap all the fish in the lake he described to me. Offer him my best wishes. When we meet again at Boston I will show him where all the scallops are to be taken in Boston Harbor."

Farming evoked no more enthusiasm in Preble at this stage of his life than it had thirty years earlier when he threw down his hoe and marched off to sea. Only once a year, at apple cider season, did Preble's interest in the farm pick up. He used quantities of this home brew himself, and liked to ship it off to Bainbridge, Robert Smith, and other friends, along with a letter of instructions on how to treat it: "In order to preserve your cider good, as soon as you receive it put into each barrel one quart of French brandy, one pound brown sugar, and the whites of six eggs. Beat to a froth, roll it over a few times, then place in a quiet situation and in a fortnight or sooner it will be sufficiently refined for drawing. And if placed in a cool cellar, well bunged-up and vents stopped, it will keep good for two years."

At the beginning of February 1806, Bainbridge wrote Preble: "As the time is fast approaching to give you an heir, you have my wishes for *a boy* and that he may live to enjoy his father's well-acquired fame and establish his own equal to it." Preble replied: "I wish with you that the child may be a boy and that he may live to be useful to his country. Indeed, I think

Courtesy of Maine Historical Society

PREBLE MANSION, PORTLAND

Edward Preble was completing this mansion, long since demolished, at the time of his death. Its front entrance opened onto the thoroughfare known today as Preble Street.

males are generally better calculated to make their way good through this rough world than the other sex." On 22 February Edward Deering Preble, Edward's and Mary's only child, was born.

Preble turned out to be a doting father. When the boy was little more than two months old, Preble told Goldsborough, "My little son is healthy, playful, and pleasant. He affords me a vast deal of pleasure and anxiety."[9] And when on a visit to Boston, he wrote to Mary: "I long to see you and our darling boy. Every morning when I awake my imagination presents him to me, laid by my side on a pillow, smiling and innocent as an angel."

Edward Deering's birth apparently prompted his parents to commence the construction of a new and magnificent brick residence at what is now the corner of Congress and Preble streets. Floor plans scratched on the address leaves of letters Preble received during the winter and spring of 1806 indicate that the basic design and layout were his own work. Building began around the end of May 1806, with the digging of the cellar. On 13 July the walls started going up, and by mid-November the windows were in, the roof on, and the balustrade in place. Progress slowed down greatly during the bitterly cold winter that followed, but in the spring of 1807 workmen were busy on the interior. At midsummer that year the mansion house was approaching completion. Mary must have looked forward to the hours she would spend in the elegant library her husband had planned for her. But the new home was not quite ready for the Prebles to move in, and there was serious question whether the Commodore would ever live there.

CHAPTER 18 APRIL 1807–AUGUST 1807

"That the advice of his physicians and his own hopes may not prove to be delusive must be the fervent prayer of every American...."

Edward Preble's health had been erratic since 1800, when his digestion had first begun to give him trouble. From the end of 1800 until May 1802 he was not well enough for active duty. Thereafter, a year of careful convalescence restored him so fully that he was eager to accept the Mediterranean command when it was offered to him in March 1803. In the Mediterranean, the congenial combination of a challenging command and a mild climate completed the work begun by his year of rest, and he felt as well as he ever had.[1] To all appearances, his health remained sound for almost two years after his return to the United States. Then, in the winter of 1806-07, it collapsed.

Preble blamed the New England winter for his troubles. Henceforward, he said, he intended to spend the cold months farther south. Around the first of April 1807, he was planning to make a trip southward in May, in hopes that travel would initiate a recovery. He would break his journey at Perth Amboy and make a long visit with the Bainbridges. The two friends looked forward to seeing each other again, but the plan had to be given up. Preble's health was so shaken that, when the time came to go, he dared not travel even as far as New Jersey.[2]

No sooner had Preble's friends in the national capital heard about his declining health than they began a campaign to persuade him to move to Washington, where the temperatures might be more to his liking. "I am fearful your climate is too cold," wrote Lieutenant Colonel Franklin Wharton, the Commandant of the Marine Corps. "Had you not better then think of one more moderate, more in the center of the Union? This District may have charms with which you are unacquainted. Pray think of them."

Goldsborough wrote Preble about the "soul-reviving breezes" of the District of Columbia and described the good buys in the area. By the time Preble received Goldsborough's letter, he was thinking of making an extended visit to Washington:

Portland, April 29, 1807.

My Dear Sir:

I have received your favor of the 14th instant, and give me leave to say, friend Goldsborough, that thou canst flatter very agreeably and reason very powerfully. Indeed, you have almost convinced me that I ought to strike my tent and take up my line of march for Washington. At any rate, you have determined me to make you a visit in early autumn and pass the winter at Headquarters, which perhaps may lead to some establishment there.

Our summer climate here is delightful, but our winter does not agree with the constitution of those who have passed many winters in milder latitudes. You have correct ideas of this country, as much so indeed as though you had summered and wintered with us. Our sentiments with respect to property are perfectly congenial. Man never ought to sacrifice to wealth, although competency is necessary to enjoyment, beyond which I would not buffet a single snowstorm to acquire millions. It is not the acquirement of wealth that binds me here. It is a thousand local attachments which are almost insurmountable. I could, however, give up all if Mrs. P. would consent to accompany me, which by the way I am convinced I never shall be able to do, excepting on a visit, so long as her mother lives. She is an only daughter, and natural affection so strong between them that I verily believe, if the old lady could believe that we were determined to leave her and take up our residence at such a distance, that it would very soon occasion her death.

I could enjoy myself most perfectly at Washington, and no place on earth affords more agreeable society. Yours, my dear Goldsborough, I should always deem invaluable, and I am perfectly in love with that of our excellent Secretary and his amiable lady.

I am determined to be with you early in the autumn (God willing) and to spend the winter. We shall then have leisure for a thousand good plans. I shall endeavor to prevail on Mrs. P. to accompany me. In the meantime I pray you to present my most respectful compliments to Mrs. G. and believe me, with unfeigned esteem, yours most truly,

EDWARD PREBLE

Preble was sicker than his letters to Washington were admitting. Family and friends were worried. In the first days of June, he went to spend a week or so at Eben Preble's country place in Watertown. From there, he intended to go on to Ballston Springs in New York, and, should he not be restored to full vitality by the end of the summer, to spend the autumn in Washington and the winter in the south of France.

About 14 June Preble went from Watertown to see Dr. Samuel Danforth, one of Boston's ablest and most respected physicians. When Dr. Danforth had examined Preble, he was not too alarmed: he pronounced the ailment serious, but said it would not be fatal if Preble would take his medicines, which included arrowroot and ginseng; stick strictly to a diet that included apples, weak soups, pearl barley, beef tea, and chowder; avoid becoming involved in any business or active duty; and rest, cruise along the coast, or, better yet, go abroad.

But Preble's spirits sagged. Travel was hurting, not helping, him. The excursion to Ballston Springs must be abandoned. To Mary he wrote on 16 June: "My health is much as when I left home. I do not think it improved and shall endeavor to get home as soon as I conveniently can and go into the backcountry or take a voyage to sea." He had bought a few things for the new house, he wrote, but: "The fashionable furniture, etc., I shall leave for your own choice. I am not well enough to attend to them." The trip back to Portland was a torture. He arrived there on 23 June and the next day wrote to Robert Smith: "I was five days from Boston to this place, and it was with great difficulty and much suffering that I have been enabled to reach home. I am now confined to my room and incapable of bearing the fatigues of any sort of business."

Late June found Preble determined to follow doctors' orders. In one of the gunboats he sailed out into Casco Bay about 30 June for a two or three days' cruise. The clean salt air refreshed him. After three days at sea Preble felt better physically and his spirits were rising. As his gunboat headed back into Portland harbor on 2 July, he told himself that he was going to take coastwise cruises often: the doctors' recommendation was a good one. Once at his anchorage in the lower harbor, Preble instructed a sailor to hoist a signal summoning on board his brother-in-law, James Deering, with the mail and newspapers. Preble was lying on his cot when Deering arrived, bursting with news that had reached Portland only that morning: on 22 June the 50-gun British ship *Leopard* had attacked the *Chesapeake*, Commodore James Barron, off the Virginia Capes, forced her to strike her colors, and taken off four men claimed as deserters from the British Navy. To Deering it seemed as if the news was too much for Preble to cope with. He could not find the words to articulate the emotions that possessed him. One oath spewed out, then he fell back on his cot and refused to say another word to Deering.[3]

When Preble recovered his composure and looked at his mail, he found a letter from Robert Smith inquiring if he was well enough to travel to Hampton, Virginia, and preside at a court of inquiry into that naval disgrace. But Preble stuck by his determination to rest and devote his full attention to getting well again. He was sorry, he told Smith, but he could not go to Boston, let alone to Virginia. Edward Preble, who hated courts-martial and courts of inquiry and who certainly had no desire to sit in judgment on his friend James Barron, was probably relieved that he had a valid excuse for avoiding the duty. There seemed no chance that Barron would be able to avoid some degree of censure. "Great God! What an affair is this of the *Chesapeake*?" Noadiah Morris wrote Preble. "I should imagine that there is a dreadful responsibility to fall somewhere. Was it consistent, it would be gratifying to me to know your opinion of the apparent *shameful* management of that ship."

About 6 July Preble again went out on Casco Bay in his gunboat. Back in Portland by the 10th, he was extremely weak, but definitely better. He came ashore breathing fire over the *Chesapeake* business and the seeming inevitability of war with Great Britain. To Robert Smith, he wrote: "Should the late events lead to war, I pray you to order me early into actual service at sea, and I will cheerfully obey, even if my health should be such that I must be carried on shipboard in my cot." Sadly, for one who was working himself up into a mood to disregard his doctors' instructions, an opportunity to do just that soon presented itself. Preble's letters to the Navy Department should have left no doubt in Robert Smith's mind that the Commodore was seriously sick and had no business attempting any duty. But, when Preble returned from his cruise in early July, he found orders from the Secretary of the Navy instructing him to complete his contract for equipping Gunboats Nos. 29 through 37 and have them ready to turn over to Lieutenant James Lawrence, who would be responsible for getting them to New York.

Since the readying of the gunboats was connected with the nation's defense preparations for the threatened war with Britain, Preble threw himself into the job. Purser Nathaniel Lyde was the only naval officer in Portland with enough experience to help him, and, certainly, during the weeks that followed, Lyde was his strong right arm. Preble and Lyde had to order gun carriages and two hundred water casks: prepare a memorandum of military stores needed from Washington; revive orders already placed, but dormant since March, for buoys, buckets, kitchen equipment, and for masters', sailmakers', boatswains', carpenters', and coopers' stores; supervise lieutenants and midshipmen as they drifted in to Portland to take charge of the gunboats; and sign up seamen — no easy job, James Lawrence later reported, "almost every person in this small place being employed in the cod fishery."[4]

The effect that all this exertion had on Preble was predictable — a relapse. All the good he had drawn from his cruises on Casco Bay was wiped away. Within eight days of taking on the assignment, he was flat on his back and too weak even to hold his pen. Lyde had to be summoned to the Commodore's bedside to take down and write essential letters. Preble's doctors told him plainly that, if he did not stop work immediately, he would die. But it was not only work that had brought on the relapse. Eben Preble came up from Boston in July and was shocked to find that, sick as his brother was, he was wandering from his diet. "Pray attend to the kind of food you eat," Eben pleaded later in a letter. "I thought you was not prudent when I was at Portland." By 20 July Edward Preble had decided to adopt the therapy that family and doctors had been urging on him for weeks: charter a packet and sail to Madeira and Tenerife for six weeks or longer if necessary.

James Lawrence reached Portland on 26 July and called at the Preble home on Middle Street. The Commodore, who was in bed, plastered with poultices, said he expected to depart for Madeira in ten days or two weeks, and explained that he only awaited the Secretary of the Navy's permission to leave the country. In the meantime, Preble told Lawrence, he would receive him as frequently as his health permitted and would give him all the help and advice he could.

By the end of July, Robert Smith realized how sick Preble was, and instructed him to leave the gunboat business to Lieutenant Lawrence and go to Madeira or any other place that would help him. "All America is deeply interested in the restoration of the health of this valuable officer, and his acquaintance from personal considerations cannot but feel an additional solicitude," Smith wrote Secretary of War Henry Dearborn on 11 August. "That the advice of his physicians and his own hopes may not prove to be delusive must be the fervent prayer of every American and especially of his intimate acquaintance. In times like the present the value of such men is known and felt by all."[5]

Before Preble received Smith's solicitous urgings to go abroad he changed his mind again. British-American relations were in such a menacing state over the insult to the *Chesapeake* that he decided to use the 100-ton packet he had chartered for the voyage to Madeira to make short cruises along the New England coast. The first cruise was supposed to start on 2 August and last for two weeks, but the weather turned too stormy to permit sailing, and, when the skies cleared, Preble was too sick to go. Not until Sunday, 9 August, was he strong enough to begin his cruise. "He was carried on board at two o'clock this afternoon and sailed with a fine breeze from the S.W.," James Lawrence wrote Robert Smith that evening. "His physicians think it the only chance left him."

Four days later the packet returned to Portland. Edward Preble was desperately sick. He knew he was going to die, and on 18 August, with perfect self-control, called in Nathaniel Lyde and told him to write Robert Smith:

> Commodore Edward Preble made his attempt to take the sea air in a packet sloop on the 9th and returned here on the 13th instant extremely ill. And it is with great concern and sorrow I have to inform you, by his request, that he now lays so low as no hopes are entertained by himself, friends, or connections of a recovery. Two persons watch with him every night, and [he] appears to be senseless half the time. Indeed, unless some very extraordinary change should take place in favor shortly (not having taken any nourishment for one month of consequence to strengthen), nature must soon be exhausted.[6]

Mercifully, Preble's malady gave him very little pain.[7] Unable to eat, he simply grew weaker and weaker, and most of the time was comatose. During his short spells of consciousness, he fretted because his long periods out of contact were preventing him from closing out all his naval and personal business before the end. Purser Lyde came to sit at his bedside and Preble told him he was not afraid to die, but wished he might live for his country's and his family's sake. Enoch Preble stayed with his brother as much as possible during these summer weeks. "To die on bed of glory would be something," Edward said to him, "but to die of a stinking consumption is too bad."

It was Tuesday, 25 August. Here and there, isolated trees were beginning to show patches of autumn color. Earlier in the month a severe three-day gale had swept up the Maine coast from the southwest, warning that the September storms would soon follow. Late in the day Edward spoke to his brother: "Give me your hand, Enoch! I'm going. Give me your hand!" There was no struggle, no moan of pain. When life was gone from Edward's eyes, Enoch reached over and closed the lids. It was fifteen minutes after five in the afternoon.

BIBLIOGRAPHIC NOTES

ABBREVIATIONS

AAE	Archives du Ministère des Affaires Etrangères, Paris
Adm.	Admiralty Records, PRO
Barbary Wars	U.S. Office of Naval Records and Library. *Naval Documents Related to the United States Wars with the Barbary Powers.* Washington, 1939-45. 7 vols.
CC	Correspondance Consulaire, AAE
EPP	Edward Preble Papers, LC
FO	Foreign Office Records, PRO
HSPa	Historical Society of Pennsylvania, Philadelphia
LC	Library of Congress, Washington
MassArch	Massachusetts Archives Division, State House, Boston
MassHS	Massachusetts Historical Society, Boston
MeHS	Maine Historical Society, Portland
NA	National Archives, Washington
NYHS	New-York Historical Society, New York City
PRO	Public Record Office, London
Quasi-War	U.S. Office of Naval Records and Library. *Naval Documents Related to the Quasi-War between the United States and France.* Washington, 1935-38. 7 vols.
RG	Record Group, NA
RG 36	Records of the Bureau of Customs, NA
RG 45	Naval Records Collection of the Office of Naval Records and Library, NA
RG 59	Records of the Department of State, NA
RG 125	Records of the Office of the Judge Advocate General (Navy), NA
RG 127	Records of the United States Marine Corps, NA
RG 217	Records of the General Accounting Office, NA
RG 233	Records of the U.S. House of Representatives, NA
TJ Mss	Thomas Jefferson Papers, LC

BIBLIOGRAPHIC NOTES

CHAPTER 1

1. There are only three good biographies of Edward Preble. The earliest, *Life of Commodore Preble,* by John Thornton Kirkland, was published in *The Port Folio,* New [i.e. 3rd] ser., III (1810), 353–365, IV (1810), 531–549, and was also issued in a small printing as a separate 30-page pamphlet. James Fenimore Cooper's sketch of Preble in his *Lives of Distinguished American Naval Officers* (Philadelphia, 1846), I, 171–252, has a number of stories about the Commodore that were handed on in a word-of-mouth way among the officers who had served under him. Lorenzo Sabine, *Life of Edward Preble* (Boston, 1847), in Jared Sparks, ed., *The Library of American Biography* (Boston, 1834–48), 2d ser., XII, 1–192, is clearly the best of the three. The sole twentieth-century biography of Preble is in Fletcher Pratt, *Preble's Boys,* pp. 13–39 (New York, 1950); it offers some interesting insights and an astounding number of factual errors.

Edward Preble's personal papers are reasonably intact and are in the Manuscript Division, Library of Congress. The collection numbers nearly sixty volumes, but almost all of the records therein relate to the post-1798 portion of Preble's life. The Maine Historical Society, Portland, has a much smaller group of Edward Preble and Preble Family manuscripts. Rear Admiral Dundas Preble Tucker, USN (Ret.), of La Jolla, California — Edward Preble's great-great-grandson — holds certain papers, including Preble's letters to his wife Mary and Eben Preble's letters to his brother.

An important source for all periods of Edward Preble's life is a letter from George Henry Preble to James Fenimore Cooper, 22 Jan. 1843 (Yale University Library, Coll. of American Literature), which gives Enoch Preble's reminiscences of his older brother.

2. George Henry Preble, *Genealogical Sketch of the First Three Generations of Prebles in America* (Boston, 1868), remains the only general history of the Preble family. George Henry's account of Jedidiah Preble is supplemented by Winthrop Bell, *Brigadier-General Jedidiah Preble (1707–1784) and His Participation in Nova Scotia History* (Halifax, N.S., 1954).

3. William Willis, *History of Portland* (2d ed.; Portland, 1865), p. 371; *Sibley's Harvard Graduates* (Boston, 1873–), XIII, 498–500.

4. EPP: Edward Preble's account with Ebenezer Stocker, 26 Sept. 1795; John W. Ragle, *Governor Dummer Academy History, 1763–1963* (South Byfield, Mass., 1963); *Sibley's Harvard Graduates,* XII, 48–54. The Governor Dummer Academy archives are scanty for the earliest years of its history. Principal sources for that period are the Manuscript Catalogue, an alphabetical list of students who attended Dummer, 1763–1830; and the Hale Ledger, boarding accounts of Dummer students who lived with Joseph Hale. From these records it appears that Ebenezer Preble was a student there — but probably not later than 1772. Enoch Preble was definitely enrolled in Dummer School during the periods 1 May–6 July 1776, 17 August 1776–5 April 1777, and 10 May–25 October 1777.

5. MeHS, Preble Mss, "Old Deeds and Documents": James Frost, Deed to Jedidiah Preble, 31 Jan. 1776, Sarah Waldo, Deed to Jedidiah Preble, 30 July 1779; Maine Historical Society, *Documentary History of the State of Maine* (Portland, 1869–1916), XVI, 208.

6. Gardner W. Allen, *Massachusetts Privateers of the Revolution* ([Boston], 1927), p. 179.

7. This document is in the Preble Mss, MeHS. In the articles the sloop's name is spelled *Marimick*.

8. There is no detailed history of the operations of the Massachusetts state navy during the Revolutionary War. Gardner W. Allen, *A Naval History of the American Revolution* (2 vols.; Boston, 1913) is the best account, but — because Allen covers the entire Revolution — his treatment of Massachusetts's part in it is necessarily condensed. Charles O. Paullin, *The Navy of the American Revolution* (Cleveland, 1906), Chapter XI, "The Navy of Massachusetts," concentrates on administrative history. A series of short articles on individual ships of the Massachusetts navy by Frank A. Gardner appears in *Massachusetts Magazine,* I (1908), 103–107 *(Tyrannicide)*, 195–199 *(Hazard)*, 280–286 *(Massachusetts)*, II (1909), 45–47 *(Independence)*, 101–105 *(Freedom)*, 168–171 *(Republic)*, 234–236 *(Active)*, III (1910), 40–46 *(Diligent)*, 133–140 *(Machias Liberty)*, 181–183 *(Protector)*, 260–267 *(Mars)*, IV (1911), 43–48 *(Tartar)*, 110–116 *(Winthrop)*, 179–182 *(Rising Empire)*, 244–246 *(Lincoln Galley)*, V (1912), 36–37 *(Defence)*, 107–109 *(Nantes)*. Gardner's articles are not so much narrative histories of the vessels as sequences of extracts from the Massachusetts Archives, State House, Boston (and other sources) relating to the ships and the service records of their principal officers. The Massachusetts Archives Division is far and away the richest source of documents on the state navy; specific citations to important *Protector* and *Winthrop* manuscripts in MassArch will be given in the notes that follow. Some of these *Protector* and *Winthrop* documents in MassArch (herein cited from the originals) are printed in Maine Historical Society, *Documentary History of the State of Maine* (24 vols.; Portland, 1869–1916), XVIII–XX; these three volumes constitute the largest collection of published documents covering the latter years of the American Revolution as they affected Maine.

No log or journal of the *Protector*'s cruises (save the extracts mentioned in Note 13 below) appears to be available at this time. Around 1913 Franklin D. Roosevelt purchased a group of George Little papers which included a journal kept by First Lieutenant Little on board the *Protector,* 7 May–13 Aug. 1780. When Mr. Roosevelt's collection of Little manuscripts was inventoried in 1942 by the Franklin D. Roosevelt Library, Hyde Park, N.Y., the *Protector* journal could not be found — nor has it turned up since.

Two men who served in the frigate wrote their memoirs more than half a century later: Seaman Ebenezer Fox, *Adventures in the Revolutionary War* (Boston, 1848), and Midshipman Luther Little, "An American Sea Captain in the Revolution," *Journal of American History,* XI (1917), 409–420, XIII (1919), 217–252. A few copies of the 1848 printing of Fox's book were issued with six extra pages, 241–246, which contain copies of the *Protector*'s pay rolls. This is a particularly useful feature, since — as explained in Note 22 below — the originals in MassArch are not now accessible.

For the British view of the *Protector*'s activities, April–October 1780, the outstanding single source is University of Michigan, William L. Clements Library, Christopher Mason Letterbook, 1780–1795, especially: [Sir Richard Hughes] to

Mason, 26 July 1780; John Creighton to Hughes, 25 July 1780; and a series of dispatches from Henry Mowat, dated 3 Apr., 23 May, 9 July, 7 Aug., 7-9 Oct. 1780. Other highly useful British sources are: PRO, Adm. 51/23, pt. 5: Captain's Log, *Albany*, 9-14 Apr. 1780, Adm. 52/1552, No. 3: Master's Log, *Albany*, 22 June-20 July 1780, and Adm. 52/1883, No. 8: Master's Log, *Nautilus*, 1-15 Apr. 1780.

Legislative actions affecting the *Protector* and the *Winthrop* are to be found in *Acts and Resolves, Public and Private, of the Province of the Massachusetts Bay* (Boston, 1869-1922), XX-XXI, and *Acts and Resolves of Massachusetts, 1780-81, 1782-83* (2 vols.; Boston, 1890). Both series are well indexed. Service records of the officers and men of the Massachusetts navy are scrupulously compiled in Massachusetts, Secretary of the Commonwealth, *Massachusetts Soldiers and Sailors of the Revolutionary War* (17 vols.; Boston, 1896-1908).

The fullest biography of John Foster Williams is an anonymous one published in the *Army and Navy Register*, 2, 9, 16, 23 June 1883, under the title "Naval Yarns: Reminiscences of the Old Navy — Captain John Foster Williams, a Commander in the Continental Navy of the State of Massachusetts, and a Captain in the United States Revenue Marine Service." This sketch was based on printed and manuscript primary sources and is reasonably accurate, though far from definitive.

9. J. J. Currier, *History of Newburyport* (Newburyport, 1906-09), I, 587-590, is the fullest published account of the building of the *Protector*. During the winter and spring of 1781 the *Protector's* armament was twelve 12-pounders, eight 9-pounders, and six 6-pounders. (*Royal Gazette* [New York], 9 May 1781.)

10. MassArch, CLI, 505: Board of War to Williams, 26 Mar. 1780, CLIII, 345: Williams to Board of War, 31 Mar. 1780; *Boston Gazette*, 24 Apr. 1780; *Morning Chronicle & General Advertiser* (Boston), 20 Apr. 1780.

11. MassArch, CLI, 506-507: Board of War to Williams, May 1780.

12. MassArch, CCXXIX, 86: J. F. Williams to Council and House of Representatives, 8 Sept. 1780.

13. Basic source for the *Protector's* movements, 7 May-16 July, is NA, RG 45, Area 7 File: J. F. Williams to Board of War, 16 July 1780, enclosing "Extracts from the Journal of the Ship *Protector*," 7 May-10 July. This is a photostat of a document now missing from MassArch, CCII, 337-337b.

14. PRO, Adm. 51/982, pt. 9: Captain's Log, *Thames*, 1-2 July 1780.

15. Luther Little in *Journal of American History*, XIII (1919), 228; Yale University Library, Coll. of American Literature: George Henry Preble to James Fenimore Cooper, 22 Jan. 1843.

16. MassHS, Caleb Davis Papers, IXb: J. F. Williams to Caleb Davis and Gustavus Fellows, 20 July 1780; MassArch, CLIII, 385-386a: Williams to Board of War, 26 July 1780; *Boston Gazette*, 21 Aug. 1780.

17. *Boston Gazette*, 20 Nov. 1780; Gardner W. Allen, *Massachusetts Privateers of the Revolution*, p. 109.

18. MassArch, CCXXXII, 171-172: Caleb Davis to Senate and House of Representatives, 12 Apr. 1781; *Boston Gazette*, 19 Mar., 2 Apr., 30 Apr., 14 May, 2 July 1781; *Royal Gazette* (New York), 12 May 1781.

19. PRO, Adm. 1/486: Marriot Arbuthnot to Philip Stephens, 6 May 1781,

Adm. 51/573: Captain's Log, *Medea*, 3–9 May 1781, Adm. 51/796: Captain's Log, *Roebuck*, 3–8 May 1781; *Royal Gazette* (New York), 9 May 1781.

20. MassHS, Caleb Davis Papers, Xa: J. F. Williams to Caleb Davis and Gustavus Fellows, 12 May 1781, IXb: Same to same, 31 May 1780 [1781].

21. MassHS, George Henry Preble Papers, "Letters to Enoch Preble, 1781–1841."

22. No one who has written on the ships of the Massachusetts state navy attempts to describe the *Winthrop*'s characteristics, nor was any document found during research for this book that gives her dimensions. The advertisement for her sale by auction (23 June 1783) at the close of the Revolution describes her as "Burthen about 95 Tons." *(Independent Chronicle* [Boston], 19 June 1783.) She was definitely a sloop-rigged, single-masted vessel. This is confirmed both by the advertisement just quoted (wherein she is called: "That fast sailing, well-found SLOOP") and by the principal sails mentioned in her log (cited in Note 27 below): flying jib, jib, foresail, topsail, square sail, and mainsail. The *Winthrop*'s log indicates that she had only one boat. As for the number of guns she carried, the most authoritative contemporary source appears to be William Vernon's letter, 1 July 1782 (cited below, Note 23); Vernon calls her a "sloop of 12 guns." F. A. Gardner in *Massachusetts Magazine*, IV (1911), 111, synopsizes a document that implies that ten of these guns were 4-pounders. At least two of the *Winthrop*'s cannon were mounted in her cabin. (*Winthrop* Log, 25 Dec. 1782.) Paullin, *Navy of the American Revolution*, p. 342, says that she carried about 125 officers and men. Because the original muster and pay rolls in MassArch are in extremely fragile condition, they may not be examined; consequently, it was not possible to verify the size of the *Winthrop*'s company or to make an analysis of it.

23. MassArch, CCXCII, 1–179, 1–180: [John Hancock] to George Little, and to John Cathcart, 22 June 1782; William Vernon to Samuel Vernon, 1 July 1782, in Rhode Island Historical Society *Publications*, New ser., VIII (1900–01), 274.

24. NA, RG 45, Area 7 File: John Hancock to George Little, 8 July 1782; MassArch, CLXXXVIII, 99, 105: George Stillman to Senate and House of Representatives, 15 June 1782, Nathaniel Bosworth to Senate and House of Representatives, 4 July 1782, CCXCII, 1–181: Arbitration award of salvage on the *Swallow*, 7 Aug. 1782; MassHS: Increase Sumner, Notes of Evidence as Justice of the Supreme Judicial Court of Massachusetts, II, 95, [96], 193; Suffolk County Court House, Boston, Supreme Judicial Court of Massachusetts, Court Files, Suffolk, DCXX, 103133: Depositions of George Little, 17 Dec. 178[2], and Lemuel White, 20 Dec. 1782; *Boston Gazette*, 5 Aug. 1782; *Boston Evening-Post*, 10 Aug. 1782; *Independent Chronicle* (Boston), 12 Sept. 1782; additional data on some of the *Winthrop*'s prizes mentioned here and below is from Library of Congress, Manuscript Division, *Naval Records of the American Revolution, 1775–1788*, compiled by C. H. Lincoln (Washington, 1906), pp. 217–495: "Letters of Marque."

25. HSPa, Gratz Coll.: [John Hancock] to George Little, 8 Aug. 1782; MassArch, CCXCII, 2–181, 1–182, 2–182: Instructions to master of the *Ceres*, 28 Aug. 1782, and invoices of her cargo; *Boston Gazette*, 23 Sept. 1782; *Continental Journal* (Boston), 19 Sept. 1782; [John T. Kirkland], *Life of Commodore Preble*, pp. 3–4; Lorenzo Sabine, *Life of Preble*, pp. 23–24.

BIBLIOGRAPHIC NOTES

26. Franklin D. Roosevelt Library, Naval Mss, George Little Papers: Zebedee Hammond to Little, 31 Oct. 1782; MassArch, CCIV, 289: Little to Hancock, 3 Nov. 1782, CCXCII, 2-179: Appraisement of the schooner *Darby; Continental Journal* (Boston), 26 Sept., 3 Oct. 1782; *Independent Chronicle* (Boston), 7 Nov., 14 Nov. 1782; *Boston Gazette,* 11 Nov. 1782.

27. MassArch: *Winthrop* Log, 4 Dec. 1782–11 Apr. 1783.

28. William Willis, ed., *Journals of the Rev. Thomas Smith and the Rev. Samuel Deane* (Portland, 1849), p. 351.

29. MassArch, CXLII, 385-387: Hancock to George Little, 27 Dec. 1782, CLVIII, 274-275: Hancock, Message to House of Representatives, 6 Feb. 1783.

30. MassArch, CLVIII, 287-288: Hancock, Message to Senate and House of Representatives, 24 Mar. 1783, and Richard Devens to Hancock, 24 Mar. 1783, CCXXXIX, 413: George Little to Senate and House of Representatives, [Mar. 1783], CCXXXIX, 477-479: Convention of Selectmen and Committees from Most of the Principal Towns in the County of Cumberland to Senate and House of Representatives, 3 Feb. 1783.

CHAPTER 2

1. The few remaining Preble business papers in EPP, I, together with EPP, XXI, Letterbook and Accounts, 1793-95, give clues to where Preble was and what he was doing in a given year — at least for the period after 1791, the date of the earliest Edward Preble manuscripts, properly speaking, in that collection. With these documents as a starting point, the life of Edward Preble, merchant captain, has to be recovered from isolated manuscripts, newspaper shipping columns, customs records, and court files. Sources for each voyage or group of voyages (except papers in EPP, I) are enumerated in the notes which follow.

2. *Falmouth* [Maine] *Gazette,* 12 Nov., 26 Nov. 1785; information from Halifax, Nova Scotia, customs records, supplied by Dr. C. Bruce Fergusson, Provincial Archivist, Public Archives of Nova Scotia, Halifax. The *William* was at Halifax on 12 Sept. and 7 Dec. 1786.

3. Boston Public Library: Receipt from Preble to Thomas Fayerweather, 27 Jan. 1787; Yale University Library, Coll. of American Literature: George Henry Preble to James Fenimore Cooper, 22 Jan. 1843; North Carolina State Archives, Raleigh, Records of the Treasurer and Comptroller, Ports (Port Roanoke), Boxes 22-24, for North Carolina state customs records mentioning Preble, Feb. 1787–July 1789; NA, RG 36, Edenton Tonnage Record, 1790-97, fol. 4; *Massachusetts Centinel* (Boston), 20 Dec. 1786, 3 Feb. 1787; *State Gazette of North-Carolina* (Edenton), 21 May, 23 July, 20 Aug. 1789, 29 Oct. 1790, 22 Apr. 1791; A. B. Keith, ed., *John Gray Blount Papers* (Raleigh, N.C., 1952-), I, 480; Josiah Collins's orders to Preble, 9 Jan. 1788, in Southern History Association *Publications,* VI (1902), 26-27.

4. Essex Institute, *Ship Registers of the District of Newburyport, Massachusetts, 1789-1870* (Salem, Mass., 1937), pp. 182-183; Sabine, *Life of Preble,* p. 27; NA, RG 36, New York Abstract of Tonnage Duties Paid, 1789-95, under 22 June 1792.

5. *Neptune* accounts in EPP, XXI, Letterbook and Accounts, 1793-95; NA, RG

36: Boston Registers, 1792, No. 149; NA, RG 59, Consular Dispatches, Málaga: Michael Morphy to Thomas Jefferson, No. 2, 30 July 1793; *Columbian Centinel* (Boston), 17, 21, 28 Nov., 1, 8, 12, 15, 19 Dec. 1792, 28 Sept. 1793.

6. EPP, XXI, Letterbook and Accounts, 1793–95; NA, RG 36: Boston Registers, 1792, No. 35, and Boston Daily Record of Clearances, No. 6 (June–Dec. 1793), 13 Dec. 1793; *Columbian Centinel*, 14 Dec. 1793, 30 Apr., 18 June 1794.

7. MeHS, Fogg Autograph Coll., Revolutionary Celebrities.

8. EPP, XXI, Letterbook and Accounts, 1793–95; Dundas Preble Tucker Coll.: Preble to Comité Chargé de Traiter avec les Neutres, 13 Vendémiaire an 3 (4 Oct. 1794); NA, RG 36, Boston Daily Record of Clearances, No. 8 (Aug. 1794–Jan. 1795), 19 Aug. 1794, and Philadelphia Inward Foreign Entries, June 1795; *Columbian Centinel*, 3 Jan., 2 May, 8 July, 5 Sept., 30 Sept. 1795; *Dunlap and Claypoole's American Daily Advertiser* (Philadelphia), 20 June 1795.

9. Essex Institute, *Ship Registers of the District of Newburyport, 1789–1870*, p. 115; NA, RG 36, Boston Registers, 1795, No. 290, and Boston Daily Record of Clearances, No. 9 (Jan.–Nov. 1795), 24 Oct. 1795. *Massachusetts Mercury* (Boston), 5 Jan. 1796, mentions an (unidentified) Boston brig as being at St. Pierre, Martinique; this might be the *Jason*.

10. Sample press coverage of the activities of the Richery squadron: *Boston Price-Current*, 3, 13, 17, 20, 24, 31 Oct. 1796; *Columbian Centinel* (Boston), 5, 12, 15, 19 Oct. 1796.

11. NYHS, manuscript copy made for George Henry Preble. Because the copying was done by someone unfamiliar with Edward Preble's handwriting, a fairly large number of corruptions were introduced into the text. These have been corrected as far as possible. Other sources for the voyage of the *Success*: EPP: Gorham Parsons to Preble, 17 Oct. 1801; NA, RG 36, Boston Registers, 1796, No. 249, and Boston Daily Record of Clearances, No. 13 (Sept. 1796–May 1797), 14 Oct. 1796; *Columbian Centinel*, 15 Mar. 1797; *Salem Gazette*, 7 Mar. 1797.

12. Suffolk County Court House, Boston, Supreme Judicial Court of Massachusetts, Court Files, Suffolk, DCXCII, 107540, 107544.

13. NA, RG 36, Boston Registers, 1797, No. 101, and Boston Daily Record of Clearances, No. 14 (May–Nov. 1797), 6 June, 19 Sept. 1797; PRO, Adm. 51/1238, No. 9: Captain's Log, *Ceres*, 26 Sept., 7 Oct. 1797; Public Archives of Nova Scotia, Halifax, Manuscript Documents, Vol. 499½, p. 137: Proceedings of the Nova Scotia Court of Vice-Admiralty in re *Phenix*; *Columbian Centinel*, 8 July, 8 Nov., 25 Nov. 1797; *Boston Price-Current*, 14 Aug., 4 Sept. 1797; *Massachusetts Mercury*, 1 Sept. 1797.

14. NA, RG 123, Court of Claims Records, French Spoliation Cases, Nos. 28 and 1856; NA, RG 36, Boston Registers, 1796, No. 277, and Boston Daily Record of Clearances, No. 15 (Nov. 1797–Apr. 1798), 8 Mar. 1798; Dundas Preble Tucker Coll.: Edward Preble's account with Eben Preble and with the Freighters of the Ship *Dauphin*, 2 Feb. 1799; MassHS, Adams Papers, Microfilm ed., Reel 387: Preble to [Henry] Jackson, 12 Mar. 1798; *Columbian Centinel*, 30 June, 17 Nov. 1798; *Massachusetts Mercury*, 6 Nov. 1798. From this point on, the sources detailed in Chapter 3, Note 1, are also being drawn upon.

BIBLIOGRAPHIC NOTES

CHAPTER 3

1. MassHS, Adams Papers, Microfilm ed., Reel 386: [James] McHenry, Memorandum of proposed officers of *Constitution, United States, Constellation*, undated but located 14 frames from the end of the reel; U.S. Senate, *Journal of Executive Proceedings* (Washington, 1828–), I, 264–265, 268.

The chief sources for this chapter are EPP, XXII, Letterbook, 12 Apr. 1798–24 June 1799, and EPP, XXIX, 3–67: Pickering Journal, 31 Jan.–16 June 1799, kept by Sailing Master Joseph Ingraham. Many Preble documents for the years covered by this and the following chapter are published in U.S. Office of Naval Records and Library, *Naval Documents Related to the Quasi-War between the United States and France* (7 vols.; Washington, 1935–38). In making their selections from EPP the editors of *Quasi-War* were, unhappily, not as thorough as they might have been. Papers that deserved publication were overlooked. An example is the Preble Letterbook, 1798–99, just cited, which the staff of *Quasi-War* missed entirely.

2. American Historical Association, *Annual Report*, 1896, I, 805.
3. Yale University Library, Coll. of American Literature: George Henry Preble to James Fenimore Cooper, 22 Jan. 1843.
4. *Quasi-War*, III, 161–162, 559–560.
5. *Newport* [Rhode Island] *Mercury*, 18 June 1799.
6. *Quasi-War*, III, 423; EPP, II, 1039–1040: Edward Preble's account current with Eben Preble, 30 Mar. 1801; NA, RG 36, Boston Registers, 1799, No. 335.

CHAPTER 4

1. Preble's *Essex* command is covered by *Quasi-War*, IV–VII, and by these volumes in EPP: II–III, incoming correspondence, a few retained copies, etc.; XXIII, Letterbook, 20 Dec. 1799–16 Jan. 1801; XXXIV, Preble's "Journal Kept on Board the United States Frigate *Essex*," 31 Oct. 1799–4 May 1800; and XXXV, Sailing Master Rufus Low's Journal, Frigate *Essex*, 16 Dec. 1799–29 Nov. 1800, one of the less interesting journals in EPP. The editors of *Quasi-War* missed Preble's Journal, 1799–1800, and his *Essex* Letterbook, 1799–1801, in EPP and (unfortunately) took their texts of Preble's correspondence and diary from George Henry Preble, "The First Cruise of the United States Frigate *Essex*," *Essex Institute Historical Collections*, X, pt. 3 (1870); George Henry Preble's transcriptions are unreliable and he omits some material. The Essex Institute, Salem, Mass., has a photostatic copy of a journal kept by Lieutenant Richard C. Beale on board the *Essex*, 22 Dec. 1799–29 Nov. 1800; this contains information not in the Preble and Low journals cited above.

2. Adam Seybert, *Statistical Annals . . . of the United States* (Philadelphia, 1818), pp. 270, 272.
3. William Goold, *Portland in the Past* (Portland, 1886), pp. 415–416; but corrected against the manuscript letter in the Deering Papers, MeHS.
4. *American Neptune*, XVIII (1958), 183.
5. LC, James Sever Papers, fols. 202–203.

6. Preble's "Journal Kept on Board the United States Frigate *Essex*," cited above, ends with the nautical day of 4 May 1800; draft entries for nautical days 5–7 May are bound in EPP, XXXIX, *Essex* Stores, 1799–1801, fols. 310–312.

7. PRO, Adm. 51/1335: Captain's Log, *Arrogant*, 7, 9 May 1800.

8. MeHS, Wadsworth Family (of Hiram) Papers: Henry Wadsworth to Peleg Wadsworth, 28 Feb. 1800.

9. NA, RG 217, Letters Received by the Accountant of the Navy: Preble to Thomas Turner, 14 Jan. 1801.

10. NA, RG 127, Marine Corps, Letters Received: Porter to W. W. Burrows, 20 Jan., 5 Feb. 1801; Letters Sent by the Commandant of the Marine Corps: Burrows to Porter, 27 Jan. 1801.

CHAPTER 5

1. A few documents covering Preble's life between January 1801 and March 1803 are printed in U.S. Office of Naval Records and Library, *Naval Documents Related to the United States Wars with the Barbary Powers* (7 vols.; Washington, 1939–45), I–II. More significant for this biography are the incoming and outgoing letters in EPP, III–V, and a manuscript copy (made for George Henry Preble) of Edward Preble's Memorandum Diary, 27 Jan.–3 June 1802, in NYHS.

Barbary Wars, I–II, document the operations of the Richard Dale and Richard V. Morris squadrons. But it is impossible to understand the Jefferson administration's policy and strategy without studying the Thomas Jefferson Papers at LC. This collection was not exploited by the editorial staff of *Barbary Wars*. The correspondence in TJ Mss between Jefferson and his successive Secretaries of the Navy, Samuel Smith and Robert Smith, is a major source for the remainder of this book.

Commodore Dale's activities are well covered in *Barbary Wars*, but the inadequate selection of documents for the Richard V. Morris period printed in *Barbary Wars*, II, makes that volume the least satisfactory of the series. In an attempt to understand this most enigmatic phase of the Tripolitan War, six sources (besides TJ Mss and *Barbary Wars*, II) have been used: (1) The Commodore's published apologia: Richard V. Morris, *A Defence of the Conduct of Commodore Morris during His Command in the Mediterranean* (New York, 1804). (2) NA, RG 125, Records of General Courts-Martial and Courts of Inquiry, No. 600: "Minutes of Proceedings at a Naval Court of Enquiry . . . for Enquiring into the Conduct of Richard V. Morris," 3–13 Apr. 1804. This case file was overlooked by the editors of *Barbary Wars* because when Commodore Charles Morris, who borrowed it in the 1830s, returned the papers to the Secretary of the Navy's office (10 Sept. 1834) the clerks accidentally misfiled them 30 years out of sequence. Copies of Richard V. Morris's correspondence, 29 May–8 June 1803, during his negotiations at Tripoli are included in the court of inquiry case file. (3) HSPa, John Rodgers Papers: John Rodgers Letterbook, July 1799–Nov. 1803. (4) Mystic Seaport, Mystic, Conn., G. W. Blunt White Library: anonymous journal kept on board the *John Adams*, 22 Oct. 1802–9 Dec. 1803. (5) Franklin D. Roosevelt Library, Hyde Park, N.Y., Naval Mss: Journal, possibly kept by Jonathan Thorn, Frigate *Adams*, 11 June

1802–28 Feb. 1803, and Schooner *Enterprize,* 7 Apr.–12 Aug. 1803. (6) The dispatches of the French consul at Tripoli, Bonaventure Beaussier, in Archives du Ministère des Affaires Etrangères, Paris, Correspondance consulaire, Tripoli de Barbarie 31–32, which are the most easily accessible sources for the internal history of the Yusuf Caramanli regime and indicate how the Morris squadron was viewed from inside Tripoli.

2. Family traditions about Mary Preble from Dundas Preble Tucker.
3. P. L. Ford, ed., *Works of Thomas Jefferson* (New York, 1904–05), IX, 264–265.
4. Minutes of Jefferson's Cabinet meetings are printed in P. L. Ford, ed., *Works of Jefferson,* I, 363–430.
5. TJ Mss: S. Smith to Jefferson, 4 May 1801.
6. Reconstructed from EPP, III, 1192–1193, and IV, 1304.
7. [John T. Kirkland], *Life of Commodore Preble,* p. 29.
8. MeHS, Fogg Autograph Coll., Revolutionary Celebrities: Preble to Dearborn, 27 Apr. 1803.
9. NA, RG 59, Applications and Recommendations for Office, Jefferson's Administration, Nathaniel Fosdick File: Davis to Secretary of the Treasury, 5 Apr. 1803. Related papers are to be found in the Isaac Ilsley File. Carl E. Prince, "The Passing of the Aristocracy: Jefferson's Removal of the Federalists, 1801–1805," *Journal of American History,* LVII (1970–71), 563–575, is the most recent and most sophisticated study of that president's dismissals from office.
10. TJ Mss: Jefferson to Sterett, 1 Dec. 1801.
11. L. B. Wright and J. H. Macleod, *The First Americans in North Africa* (Princeton, 1945), p. 100.
12. TJ Mss: R. Smith to Jefferson, 19 Apr. 1805.

CHAPTER 6

1. NA, RG 217, Letters Received by the Accountant of the Navy: Trant to Thomas Turner, 14 Apr. 1802.
2. TJ Mss: S. Smith to Jefferson, 9 June [Aug.] 1802; Jefferson to R. Smith, 22 Aug. 1802; R. Smith to Jefferson, 27 Aug. 1802.
3. Henry Adams, ed., *Writings of Albert Gallatin* (Philadelphia, 1879), I, 91.
4. *Ibid.,* I, 86, 88.
5. TJ Mss: R. Smith to Jefferson, 20 Aug., 1 Sept., 14 Sept. 1802.
6. TJ Mss: Jefferson to R. Smith, 22 Aug., 30 Aug., 3 Sept. 1802; University of Virginia Library: Jefferson to R. Smith, 6 Sept., 20 Sept. 1802; Gallatin, *Writings,* I, 83.
7. TJ Mss: Jefferson to R. Smith, 16 Oct. 1802.
8. Franklin D. Roosevelt Library, Naval Mss.
9. NA, RG 217, Letters Received by the Accountant of the Navy: Preble to Thomas Turner, 30 Apr. 1802; Certificates of Settled Accounts, 1800–1805, No. 1028, 25 Nov. 1802; invitations in the collection of Dundas Preble Tucker; Preble to James Deering, 21 Nov. 1802, manuscript in Christopher McKee's possession.

10. EPP, XXXIII.

11. G. F. Martens, *Recueil de Traités* (2. éd.; Gottingue, 1817–35), VII, 422–424.

12. Gallatin, *Writings*, I, 118–119; Jefferson, *Works*, IX, 456.

13. TJ Mss, CXXX, 22552; CXXXI, 22561.

14. TJ Mss, CXXXI, 22651.

15. TJ Mss: Jefferson to R. Smith, 16 June 1803; R. Smith to Jefferson, 17 June 1803.

16. [R. Smith] to Rodgers, 21 June 1803. Letter in the possession of Mr. Frederick Rodgers who, in the spring of 1959, graciously permitted a copy to be made.

17. These dispatches in AAE, CC Tripoli de Barbarie 32 are the most useful for Morris's blockade-negotiation at Tripoli: Beaussier to Talleyrand, No. 22, 5 Floréal an 11 (25 Apr. 1803); No. 24, 26 Floréal (16 May); No. 25, 1 Prairial (21 May); No. 26, 22 Prairial (11 June); No. 27, 22 Prairial (11 June); and No. 30, 5 Messidor (24 June).

CHAPTER 7

1. From this point in Preble's life until his return to the United States at the end of his Mediterranean command the principal source is *Barbary Wars*, II–V. Those portions of EPP covering the same period, including material not published in *Barbary Wars*, are Volumes V through XIV, incoming correspondence, a few drafts, and other loose papers; XXIV–XXVII, four Letterbooks, May 1803–Mar. 1805; XXVIII, Preble's Diary, Mar. 1803–Aug. 1804; XLVIII, his memorandum Journal, Mar. 1803–Feb. 1806; XLIX, Order Book, May 1803–June 1805; and XXXIII, *Constitution*'s Logbook, May 1803–Oct. 1804, kept by Sailing Master Nathaniel Haraden. MeHS has Preble's interesting and important Pocket Account Book, 1803–1805. Letters from the Secretary of the Navy to Preble, not included in *Barbary Wars*, are in NA, RG 45, Letters to Officers, Ships of War, Oct. 1802–July 1805.

2. LC, Izard Family Papers. The leters from Ralph Izard, Jr., to Mrs. Alice Izard quoted in this chapter are dated 19 June, 26 June, 25 July and 31 July 1803.

3. NA, RG 233, 11th Cong., House, Committee on Claims (HR 11A-F1.1): Petition of William Hyler.

4. TJ Mss: R. Smith to Jefferson, 17 Mar. 1803; Jefferson to R. Smith, 29 Mar. 1803.

5. NA, RG 59, Instructions to Consuls, I, 158–160.

6. MeHS, Fogg Autograph Coll., Revolutionary Celebrities.

7. Charles Morris, *Autobiography* (Annapolis, 1880), pp. 20–21.

8. Letters to Officers, Ships of War, 1802–05: R. Smith to William Bainbridge, 12 July 1803.

9. TJ Mss: R. Smith to Jefferson, 17 Mar. 1803.

10. Free Library of Philadelphia, Rare Book Department. The letter is inserted in a special copy of the first edition of Kenneth Roberts's *Lydia Bailey* deposited at the Free Library by Mr. Roberts.

BIBLIOGRAPHIC NOTES

CHAPTER 8

1. Sources as in Chapter 7, Note 1, with these additions: (1) John Rodgers Letterbook, July 1799–Nov. 1803, John Rodgers Papers, HSPa; (2) James Simpson's dispatches in NA, RG 59, Consular Dispatches, Tangier, II, Jan. 1803–Oct. 1810, particularly No. 56, 14 May, No. 59, 9 July, No. 67, 15 Oct., No. 68, 17 Oct., and enclosures in No. 70, 4 Nov. 1803; (3) Henry Wadsworth Mss, Longfellow House, Cambridge, Mass.; and (4) *John Adams* Journal, Oct. 1802–Dec. 1803, G. W. Blunt White Library, Mystic Seaport, Conn.

2. Charles Morris, *Autobiography*, pp. 21–22; PRO: Adm. 52/3647, pt. 3, Master's Log, *Maidstone*, 11 Sept. 1803; John Marshall, *Royal Naval Biography* (London, 1823–35), II, pt. 2, 844–845.

3. Consular Dispatches, Tangier: No. 60, 28 July 1803, and enclosure.

CHAPTER 9

1. University of Michigan, William L. Clements Library, Tobias Lear Papers: Lear to Mrs. Lear, 13 Oct. 1803.

CHAPTER 10

1. With the shift of Preble's operations from the Straits of Gibraltar to waters near Tripoli, two new series of manuscripts become essential for understanding events and attitudes in Tripoli and for correcting the one-sided view of the war provided by American sources. These are the dispatches of the French consul, Bonaventure Beaussier, in Archives du Ministère des Affaires Etrangères, Paris, Correspondance consulaire, Tripoli de Barbarie 32; and the English consular dispatches in Public Record Office, London, FO 76/5. Of the two series, the French dispatches are by far the fuller and more informative for the general internal affairs of Tripoli, for American operations, and for negotiations which involved Beaussier.

2. British Museum, Add. Ms. 34920, fol. 378: Gore to Lord Nelson, 9 Oct. 1803. Bonaventure Beaussier reported that 170 members of the *Philadelphia*'s 307-man company were British subjects. (AAE, CC Tripoli de Barbarie 32: Beaussier to Talleyrand, No. 12, 4 Frimaire an 12 [26 Nov. 1803].)

3. EPP, XXXIII: *Constitution* Log, 22 Oct. 1803.

4. In addition to the documents in *Barbary Wars*, III, the loss of the *Philadelphia* is covered by AAE, CC Tripoli de Barbarie 32: Beaussier to Talleyrand, No. 4, 23 Vendémiaire an 12 (16 Oct. 1803); No. 8, 10 Brumaire (2 Nov.); and No. 10, 15 Brumaire (7 Nov.).

5. Dundas Preble Tucker Coll.: Henry Preble to Edward Preble, 4 Jan. 1804; Washington and Jefferson College Library: Edward Preble to Henry Preble, 18 Mar. 1804.

6. MeHS: Preble's Pocket Account Book, 1803–1805, 30 Nov. 1803.

7. HSPa, Dreer Coll.: Wadsworth to Porter, 15 Jan. 1804.

CHAPTER 11

1. Most of the basic sources on the destruction of the *Philadelphia* are printed in *Barbary Wars*, III, 399, 413–429, 431–432 and *passim*. One key document remains in manuscript: "Reminiscenses &c by Lewis Heermann Surgeon U.S. Navy – 1826" in NA, RG 233, 23rd Cong., House, Committee on Naval Affairs, Claims (HR 23A–D13.1, bundle 3), Claim of Susan Decatur. To these sources should be added Charles Morris, *Autobiography*, pp. 25–31, and Heermann's statement in Charles W. Goldsborough, *United States Naval Chronicle* (Washington, 1824), pp. 257–258. The entries for sea days 9 through 15 February 1804 in the journal kept by Midshipman F. Cornelius de Krafft on board the *Syren* are not published in *Barbary Wars*, but the manuscript journal is in NA, RG 45, and was consulted there.

Some interesting documents, not included in *Barbary Wars*, on the part taken by the *Syren*'s boats in the events of 16/17 Feb. 1804 will be found in U.S. Congress, *American State Papers; Documents, Legislative and Executive* (Washington, 1832–61), *Naval Affairs*, III, 178–189, 459–461. These papers are not wholly convincing. They were prepared more than twenty years after the event, and then only for the purpose of justifying the inclusion of the *Syren*'s officers and men in a proposed distribution of prize money for the destruction of the *Philadelphia*. In this biography only letters and documents of Charles Stewart that are demonstrably contemporary with the events to which they relate are accepted as evidence. Stewart lived a long time, and the recollections and anecdotes with which he frequently favored nineteenth-century historians are usually at variance with contemporary documents. Out of a host of examples that could be given on this point, see Merrill D. Peterson, *The Jefferson Image in the American Mind* (New York, 1960), pp. 208, 485; Irving Brant, *James Madison* (Indianapolis, 1941–61), VI, 38–39. The alleged letter from Stewart to Preble, 20 Feb. 1804, in *American State Papers, Naval Affairs*, III, 184, may be a later fabrication. Charles W. Goldsborough *(ibid.,* 183, 185–186) seems to have thought so; Christopher McKee agrees with Goldsborough.

2. PRO, FO 76/5: Brian McDonogh to Charles Yorke, 10 Mar. 1804.

3. *Barbary Wars*, III, 532; AAE, CC Tripoli de Barbarie 32: Bonaventure Beaussier to Talleyrand, No. 20, 26 Ventôse an 12 (17 Mar. 1804).

4. Parke-Bernet Galleries, Sale No. 1352 (27 May 1952), Item 254.

5. P. L. Ford, ed., *Works of Jefferson*, X, 78.

6. Schembri's activities are only partly covered by the references to him in *Barbary Wars*, III–IV, *passim;* essential supplementary sources are AAE, CC Tripoli de Barbarie 32: Beaussier to Talleyrand, No. 18, 6 Ventôse an 12 (26 Feb. 1804), and NA, RG 59, Diplomatic Dispatches, France, IX: Beaussier to Stephen Cathalan, Jr., 25 Ventôse an 12 (16 Mar. 1804), enclosed in R. R. Livingston to Secretary of State, No. 107, 19 June 1804.

7. AAE, CC Tripoli de Barbarie 32: Beaussier to Talleyrand, No. 30, 17 Messidor an 12 (6 July 1804).

8. AAE, CC Tripoli de Barbarie 32: Beaussier to Talleyrand, No. 19, 10 Ventôse

BIBLIOGRAPHIC NOTES

an 12 (1 Mar. 1804); see also PRO, FO 76/5: Brian McDonogh to Charles Yorke, 10 Mar. 1804.

9. AAE, CC Tripoli de Barbarie 32: Rapport au premier Consul, [early Jan. 1804]; Talleyrand to Beaussier, 6 Pluviôse an 12 (27 Jan. 1804).

10. There is a long account of this incident in HSPa, John Rodgers Letterbook, July 1799–Nov. 1803: Rodgers to Robert Smith, 6 Apr. 1803.

11. The most detailed narrative of Preble's visit to Tunis, particularly the diplomatic maneuverings on shore, is NA, RG 59, Consular Dispatches, Tunis: George Davis to Secretary of State, 8 Apr. 1804.

12. AAE, CC Tripoli de Barbarie 32: Beaussier to Talleyrand, No. 19, 10 Ventôse an 12 (1 Mar. 1804).

CHAPTER 12

1. Reconstructing the daily routine in the *Constitution* under Preble's command poses a problem. The normal source would be the general orders for the government of the *Constitution* which Preble issued on 25 Aug. 1803 (EPP, XXVIII, Diary, Mar. 1803–Aug. 1804), but a copy of these orders could not be found during research for this book.

The manuscript published in *Barbary Wars*, III, 32–41, and there described as "Internal Rules and Regulations for U.S. Frigate *Constitution*, 1803–1804, by Captain Edward Preble," is not a Preble document. This manuscript, now in the Huntington Library, San Marino, Calif., was among Edward Preble's papers before 1907 and was identified, probably by George Henry Preble, as the *Constitution*'s rules and regulations. However, there are two reasons for concluding that they are, rather, William Bainbridge's rules and regulations for the *Philadelphia:* (1) they contain no reference to the *Constitution,* whereas Rule 99 mentions the *Philadelphia;* (2) they are in the handwriting of Bainbridge's clerk in the *Philadelphia,* William Anderson, of which there are numerous examples in EPP. How a copy of Bainbridge's general orders found its way into Preble's papers can only be guessed. Perhaps Preble borrowed the volume and forgot to return it.

Even lacking Preble's own general orders for the government of the *Constitution,* existing sources make it possible to construct a reasonably accurate picture of daily life in a U.S. ship of war of that era. In addition to Bainbridge's rules for the *Philadelphia,* already mentioned, there are the "General Orders for the Government of the U.S. Frigate *President* under the Command of Capt. William Bainbridge," ca. 1809 (MeHS, in Alexander S. Wadsworth, Journal, Frigate *Chesapeake*, 9–27 May 1807); Captain Rodgers's "Standing General Orders to be Particularly Attended to on board the United States Ship of War *John Adams* under My Command," 1802–03 (HSPa, John Rodgers Papers); and James Sever's "Rules and Regulations to be Observed on board U.S. Frigate *Congress*," 22 May 1800 (*Quasi-War*, V, 546–550). The law regulating shipboard life, "An Act for the Better Government of the Navy of the United States," 23 Apr. 1800, will be found in *Quasi-War*, VII, 462–473. *Naval Regulations, Issued by Command of the President of the United States of America, January 25, 1802* ([Washington, 1802]) are reprinted in *Barbary Wars*, II, 29–40. However, the earlier *Marine Rules and Regulations* ([Philadelphia:] Printed by John Fenno, 1798), issued while the Navy was administratively part of the War Department, are more useful to the historian searching out the details of Navy life during these years.

Information on many of the practices in Preble's *Constitution* is to be found in Nathaniel Haraden's unusually full and candid logbook, May 1803–Oct. 1804. Excerpts from that document are published in *Barbary Wars*, II–V, but for some of the most important entries the manuscript version (EPP, XXXIII) must be consulted. Some material in this chapter is drawn from EPP, XXXII, *John Adams* Logbook, Oct. 1804–Feb. 1805, selectively printed in *Barbary Wars*, V. This log embraces the period of Preble's command of the *John Adams*. Details of the sailors' dress are from EPP, XLIV, *Constitution* Clothing and Stores, 1803–04. A few of the reports of the *Constitution*'s surgeon will be found in MeHS, Edward Preble Mss. One of Marine Captain John Hall's printed morning reports is displayed on board the frigate *Constitution* at Boston.

2. HSPa, Gratz Coll.: Henry Wadsworth to David Porter, 27 Mar. 1804.

3. Edward Cutbush, *Observations on the Means of Preserving the Health of Soldiers and Sailors* (Philadelphia, 1808), pp. 126–128.

4. EPP, VIII, 2065: "Memorandum of books belonging to E. Preble on board the *Constitution*"; Preble to James Deering, 19 July 1803 (photocopy in Christopher McKee's possession). "John Thompson," the name by which the *Constitution*'s clerk was known to Preble and to all Navy records, was an alias; his real name was David Wright. (EPP, X, 2421: David Wright to Preble, 25 Mar. 1805.)

5. Preble's copy (Newburyport: Edmund M. Blunt, 1799) is owned by Mr. William B. Jordan, Jr., of Portland, Me.

6. Thomas Truxtun, *Remarks, Instructions, and Examples Relating to the Latitude & Longitude* (Philadelphia, 1794), Appendix, p. xvii.

7. MeHS, Edward Preble Mss: *Constitution*'s Daily Reports of Prisoners, Jan.–June 1804. Harold D. Langley, *Social Reform in the United States Navy, 1798–1862* (Urbana, 1967), particularly pp. 209–269, discusses the problem of drunkenness among sailors of the early Navy.

8. Principal sources for Syracuse as an American naval base are NA, RG 45, Subject File OM: John Darby, Journal kept on board the *John Adams*, June–Dec. 1804, especially pp. 137–147, 159, 196–197, 205; Washington Irving, *Journals and Notebooks*, ed. by Nathalia Wright (Madison: University of Wisconsin Press, 1969–), I, 179–195, 518–524; Samuel Taylor Coleridge, *Collected Letters*, ed. by E. L. Griggs (Oxford: Clarendon Press, 1956–), II, 1150–1156; and Coleridge, *Notebooks*, ed. by Kathleen Coburn (New York: Pantheon Books, 1957–), II, entries 2227, 2230, 2261, 2492. Henry Wadsworth Mss are essential.

9. C. O. Paullin, "Dueling in the Old Navy," *United States Naval Institute Proceedings*, XXXV (1909), 1155–1197; Nicholson–de Krafft duel at p. 1165. The aftermath of this duel is covered in *Barbary Wars*, V, 42, 57, 344, 376–377, 493, 504, but the following description of the event itself, from NA, RG 45: F. C. de Krafft, Journal, Aug. 1803–Feb. 1805, entry for 18 Sept. 1804, is omitted from *Barbary*

BIBLIOGRAPHIC NOTES

Wars: "[Morning.] Received a note from William Nicholson, midshipman, to meet him, for an insult gave him. . . . At 6 p.m. Mr. Nicholson's corpse was brought on board (from shore). At 9 [p.m.] I was arrested for dueling with Mr. Nicholson."

10. NA, RG 45, Letters Received by the Board of Navy Commissioners from Commandants, Several Stations, 1815–1820.

11. NA, RG 217, Letters Received by the Accountant of the Navy: George Dyson to Robert Smith, 20 Jan. 1808.

CHAPTER 13

1. EPP, XXV, Letterbook, Dec. 1803–Apr. 1804, pp. 165–166: F. Degen & Co. to Preble, 15 Feb. 1804.

2. AAE, CC Tripoli de Barbarie 32: Beaussier to Talleyrand, No. 30, 17 Messidor an 12 (6 July 1804).

3. NA, RG 59, Applications and Recommendations for Office, Jefferson's Administration, Frederic Degen File.

4. MeHS: Preble's Pocket Account Book, 1803–1805.

5. AAE, CC Tripoli de Barbarie 32: Beaussier to Talleyrand, No. 21, 13 Germinal an 12 (3 Apr. 1804); No. 26, 4 Prairial (24 May).

6. PRO, FO 76/5: W. W. Langford to Charles Yorke, 10 July 1804.

7. AAE, CC Tripoli de Barbarie 32: Beaussier to Talleyrand, No. 27, 25 Prairial an 12 (14 June 1804).

CHAPTER 14

1. *Barbary Wars,* IV–V, contain the bulk of the basic documents for Preble's operations against Tripoli, 25 July–13 September 1804, but there are other essential sources. William Eaton's pamphlet, *Interesting Detail of the Operations of the American Fleet in the Mediterranean, Communicated in a Letter from W. E., Esq., to His Friend in the County of Hampshire* (Springfield, Mass. [1805]), is valuable because Eaton joined the Preble squadron on 9 September and had ample opportunity to talk with Preble and other officers before writing his *Interesting Detail* early in November. For the 3 August battle the most important new source to come to light since the printing of *Barbary Wars* is the transcript of the Blake Court of Inquiry, published as "An Inquiry into the Conduct of Joshua Blake," Linda and Christopher McKee, eds., *American Neptune,* XXI (1961), 130–141. An important Charles Stewart letter, 9 Aug. 1804, is in the Washington *National Intelligencer,* 5 Dec. 1804. Richard O'Brien's "Narrative of the Attacks on Tripoli, the 3d and 7th of August 1804, with Remarks and Observations thereon, by O'Brien" is printed in *Barbary Wars,* IV, 341–343, but from the fragmentary copy — about one-fourth of the full text — in the William Eaton Mss, Huntington Library, San Marino, California. A complete O'Brien "Narrative" was found in British Museum, London, Add. Ms. 34925, fols. 8–21b. The British Museum copy is one sent to Lord Nelson by Sir Alexander Ball.

EPP contain a small number of unpublished papers for this period, the most important of which are the French originals of Beaussier's letters to Preble. Thomas Truxtun's pseudonymous printed letter to the President (TJ Mss, CXLIII, 24907–24908) gives his ideas on the proper method for assaulting Tripoli; it is a contemporary analysis of the tactical problems of an attack on Tripoli by the Navy's first major theoretician.

The general signal code used by the Navy at this time was *A Set of Signals Presented to the Navy of the United States of America by John Barry, Esq., Senior Officer* (Norfolk, Va., 1800). Midshipman Robert T. Spence's copy, now at the Boston Athenaeum, was the most useful of several surviving copies: Spence apparently used it only during his service with the Preble squadron, so it gives the exact state of the general signal book in the spring and summer of 1804, including distinguishing flags of the vessels of Preble's squadron and a 15-page manuscript addition, "Directions for Using the Signals by Night." For his attacks on Tripoli Preble supplemented the general code with additional signals addressed particularly to the bomb ketches and gunboats. Two copies of the gunboat and bomb ketch signals are in EPP, LIII, Signal Book, 1803–1804, fols. 68–78, 83–89.

Most of the battle diagrams in this book are, of necessity, reconstructions. There are only two contemporary manuscript charts showing American and Tripolitan dispositions. One, drawn by Midshipman F. C. de Krafft, is in LC, Map Division; it is reproduced in *Barbary Wars*, IV, btwn. 336–337, and more legibly in United States Naval Institute *Proceedings*, V (1878–79), btwn. 50–51. De Krafft's chart is concerned chiefly with the action of 3 August. The other chart, by Midshipman William Lewis, is in EPP, XIII, 3002. This depicts the burning of the *Philadelphia*, 16/17 February 1804, and the night bombardment, 27/28 August.

2. AAE, CC Tripoli de Barbarie 32: Beaussier to Talleyrand, No. 30, 17 Messidor an 12 (6 July 1804); No. 31, 15 Thermidor (3 Aug.); also TJ Mss: Beaussier to his brother at Marseilles, 3 Aug. 1804.

3. AAE, CC Tripoli de Barbarie 32: Beaussier to Talleyrand, No. 32, 14 Fructidor an 12 (1 Sept. 1804).

4. Charles Morris, *Autobiography*, p. 32; also *Barbary Wars*, IV, 512.

5. AAE, CC Tripoli de Barbarie 32: Beaussier to Talleyrand, No. 32, 14 Fructidor (1 Sept.).

6. TJ Mss: Jefferson to R. Smith, 23 Aug., 5 Sept. 1803; R. Smith to Jefferson, 28 Aug., 10 Sept. 1803.

7. Gallatin, *Writings*, I, 162; TJ Mss: Jefferson to R. Smith, 10 Oct. 1803.

8. C. W. Goldsborough, *United States Naval Chronicle*, p. 205.

9. HSPa: Levi Lincoln to Robert Smith, 17 Jan. 1804.

10. Jefferson, *Works*, X, 77–78; TJ Mss: R. Smith to Jefferson, 16 May 1804.

11. LC, Izard Family Papers: Christopher Gadsden, [Jr.], to Ralph Izard, [Sr.], 21 Mar. 1804; Dundas Preble Tucker Coll.: Eben Preble to Edward Preble, 10 Mar. 1804; *Columbian Centinel* (Boston), 10 Mar., 14 Mar. 1804.

12. TJ Mss: R. Smith to Jefferson, 19 Mar. 1804.

13. Frederick Rodgers Coll.: Chauncey to John Rodgers, 25 July 1804.

CHAPTER 15

1. Charles Biddle, *Autobiography* (Philadelphia, 1883), pp. 300–301; *Barbary Wars*, IV, 301, 394, V, 544, VI, 26–27.
2. *Barbary Wars*, IV, 64, 480; AAE, CC Tripoli de Barbarie 32: Beaussier to Talleyrand, No. 32, 14 Fructidor an 12 (1 Sept. 1804); William Bainbridge's prison journal, paraphrased in J. F. Cooper, *History of the Navy* (2d ed.; Philadelphia, 1840), I, 394 note.
3. AAE, CC Tripoli de Barbarie 32: Beaussier to Talleyrand, No. 32, 14 Fructidor (1 Sept.).
4. Internal arrangements of the *Intrepid* reconstructed from *Barbary Wars*, IV, 305–306, 493, 499, 506, V, 141, and Cooper, *History of the Navy*, I, 400–401.
5. AAE, CC Tripoli de Barbarie 32: Beaussier to Talleyrand, No. 33, 30 Fructidor an 12 (17 Sept. 1804).
6. Earl Gregg Swem Library, College of William and Mary, Barron Papers 33.a, Item 27: Beaussier to Preble, 1 Nov. 1804.
7. Quoted in Cooper, *History of the Navy*, I, 411–412 note; but for correct date and identification of Lieutenant Porter as the person who accompanied Bainbridge see H. A. S. Dearborn, *Life of William Bainbridge* (Princeton, 1931), pp. 74–75.
8. J[ames] B[arron], "Commodore Samuel Barron," *Virginia Historical Register*, III (1850), 198–204.
9. EPP: Ralph Izard, Jr., to Preble, 19 Sept. 1804.

CHAPTER 16

1. *Barbary Wars*, V–VI, include only a limited selection of Preble-related documents for the period subsequent to his departure from the Mediterranean, January 1805. Lorenzo Sabine, *Life of Preble*, pp. 165–179, quotes from and summarizes a number of especially interesting letters not now in EPP. In the main, however, the story of the final three years of Preble's life, as recounted in this and the following two chapters, is drawn from manuscript sources. The backbone collections are: EPP, XIII–XX, incoming correspondence and drafts of a fair number of outgoing letters; NA, RG 45, Captains' Letters, May 1805–Aug. 1807, for Preble's official letters to Robert Smith; and NA, RG 45, Letters to Officers, Ships of War, Oct. 1802–Dec. 1807, and Letters to Officers Commanding Gunboats, Dec. 1803–Dec. 1808, for official letters from the Secretary of the Navy to Preble. Letters from Preble to Thomas Turner, Accountant of the Navy, Apr. 1805–Apr. 1807, are in NA, RG 217, Letters Received by the Accountant of the Navy. Preble's day-to-day movements are recorded in EPP, XLVIII, memorandum Journal, 7 Mar. 1803–20 Feb. 1806; but for Preble's memorandum diary, 23 Nov. 1805–13 Dec. 1806, one has to use the manuscript copy (made for George Henry Preble) in NYHS.
2. LC, Rodgers Family Papers.
3. Preble's activities are frequently mentioned in MassHS, Adams Papers, Microfilm ed., Reel 30: John Quincy Adams Diary, under the dates 12, 19–23 Mar., 1–5, 9–10 Apr. 1805.

4. *Poulson's American Daily Advertiser* (Philadelphia), 26 Mar. 1805; *New-York Herald*, 3 Apr. 1805; *Columbian Centinel* (Boston), 13 Apr. 1805; *Eastern Argus* (Portland), 19 Apr. 1805; *Gazette* (Portland), 22 Apr. 1805.

5. *Columbian Centinel* (Boston), 5, 9 July 1806.

6. TJ Mss: Preble to Jefferson, 30 July 1805.

7. NA, RG 45, Subject File AC, Box 9.

8. Peabody Museum, Salem, Mass., Plan File, P-392: "A Plan of the Messina Gun Boats," is almost certainly one of the drawings circulated by the Navy Department to its constructors and officer-superintendents for study in the early stages of the U.S. gunboat-construction program. For details of deck arrangement, gun mount, and location of living spaces, P-392 is also the most accurate known representation of the six gunboats which Preble borrowed from the Neapolitan government in 1804.

9. On the origins and philosophy of the gunboat policy see — in addition to *Barbary Wars* and NA, RG 45, Letters to Officers Commanding Gunboats, Dec. 1803–Dec. 1808 — these sources: TJ Mss: Jefferson to R. Smith, 15 June, 4 July 1804, R. Smith to Jefferson, 17 June, 3 July, 14 Sept. 1804, printed letter of Thomas Truxtun to Timothy Pickering, 27 Nov.–8 Dec. 1807, the last another important paper by this service intellectual; U.S. Naval Academy Museum: Jefferson to [Joseph H.] Nicholson, 29 Jan. 1805; C. W. Goldsborough, *United States Naval Chronicle*, pp. 322–329; U.S. Congress, *American State Papers; Documents, Legislative and Executive* (Washington, 1832–61), *Naval Affairs*, I, 163–164.

10. Yale University Library, Coll. of American Literature: George Henry Preble to James Fenimore Cooper, 22 Jan. 1843; Howard I. Chapelle, *The History of the American Sailing Navy* (New York: Norton, 1949), pp. 207–208. Chapelle's Chapter Four, "The Gunboat Navy" (pp. 179–241, also pp. 513–514), is the pioneer study of that subject and sets the terms for all subsequent scholarly analysis.

11. EPP, IV, 1322–1329.

12. EPP, L and LI, contain important memoranda, inventories, and accounts covering the construction of the *Etna*, the *Vesuvius*, and Gunboats Nos. 11–12, 29–37.

13. Launch date of No. 12: *Columbian Centinel* (Boston), 31 May 1806; contracts and bill of sale for the *Vesuvius* and No. 12 are in NA, RG 45, Contract Book, I, 242–251; the contracts for all other vessels built under Preble's supervision are in EPP.

14. NA, RG 45, Miscellaneous Letters: Preble to Robert Smith, 18 June 1806.

15. NA, RG 45, Miscellaneous Letters: Preble to Smith, 22 July 1806; James Deering to Smith, 11 Dec. 1807.

16. NA, RG 45, Miscellaneous Letters: Jacob Coffin to Smith, 12 Aug. 1806; Jacob Crowninshield to Smith, 2 Sept. 1806; Preble to Smith, 8 Dec. 1806.

17. EPP, L, "Contract Gun Boats Accounts," at 27 Oct. 1806.

18. MeHS, Edward Preble Mss: Inventory of stores for a gunboat.

CHAPTER 17

1. This analysis of the final months of the Tripolitan War is developed principally from *Barbary Wars*, V–VI, but on a number of crucial points it draws on

BIBLIOGRAPHIC NOTES

John Rodgers's unpublished reply to William Eaton's pamphlet, *To the Honorable Secretary of the Navy of the United States* [1806?]. Mr. Frederick Rodgers made his great-grandfather's manuscript reply to Eaton available for copying and quotation. The Tobias Lear Papers, William L. Clements Library, University of Michigan, include a series of seven letters from Lear to Mrs. Frances Lear, 27/29 Jan.–24 June 1805, which supplement the documents in *Barbary Wars* covering the negotiation of peace with Tripoli.

2. TJ Mss: R. Smith to Jefferson, 9 Sept., 19 Sept. 1805.
3. HSPa, Gratz Coll.: Preble to Eaton, 28 Oct. 1805.
4. Haverford College Library, Charles Roberts Autograph Coll.
5. Information on James Barron's proposals is derived from the draft (EPP, IV, 1284) of Preble's reply to Barron's letter of 15 Oct. 1805 and from an undated, unsigned draft, in Thomas Tingey's handwriting, of a bill establishing a Board of Navy Commissioners. The latter document is bound at the end of NA, RG 45, Captains' Letters, 1805, III.
6. U.S. Congress, *Annals of Congress*, XV (9th Cong., 1st sess.), especially 11–16, 258, 301–302, 377–397, 447, 475, 523–531, 842–848, 1029–1052, 1075–1078, 1272–1273, 1287; *American State Papers, Naval Affairs*, I, 140–142, 147–155.
7. TJ Mss: R. Smith to Jefferson, 28 May 1805, Jefferson to R. Smith, 31 May 1805.
8. Coleridge, *Notebooks*, ed. by Kathleen Coburn (New York: Pantheon Books, 1957–), II, entry 2228.
9. NYHS: Preble to Goldsborough, 29 Apr. 1806.

CHAPTER 18

1. EPP: Noadiah Morris to Preble, 30 July 1807.
2. Huntington Library, HR 318: Preble to Bainbridge, 31 May 1807.
3. Sabine, *Life of Preble*, pp. 175–176; *Eastern Argus* (Portland), 2 July 1807.
4. NA, RG 45, Officers' Letters: Lawrence to Smith, 9 Aug. 1807.
5. Indiana University, Lilly Library, War of 1812 Mss: Smith to Dearborn, 11 Aug. 1807.
6. NA, RG 45, Officers' Letters: Lyde to Smith, 18 Aug. 1807.
7. "Extract of a letter from Portland," *Poulson's American Daily Advertiser* (Philadelphia), 1 Sept. 1807; *Gazette* (Portland), 31 Aug. 1807; NA, RG 45, Officers' Letters: Lyde to Smith, 10 Sept. 1807; Yale University Library, Coll. of American Literature: George Henry Preble to James Fenimore Cooper, 22 Jan. 1843.

INDEX

Edward Preble is abbreviated EP

Abercromby, James, 3
Accountant of the Navy, 80, 105, 237, 314
Acton, John, 235, 237–38, 310
Adams: retained in Navy, 83; operations with Morris squadron, 93, 104, 107, 110, 113–14, 115–22; EP commands, 96–101; R. V. Morris returns to U.S. in, 146, 158; takes J. L. Cathcart to Tunis, 146; Gordon ordered to, 224*n*
Adams, John: EP calls on, 314; mentioned, 50–57 *passim*, 64
Adams, John Quincy, 316
Admiral Duff, 11–12, 16
Aetna. See Etna
Albany, 9–10, 16
Alcoholism: Geddes victim of, 68, 80; in *Constitution*, 217, 222–23
Algiers: captures U.S. vessels, 36–37; treaty with, 41; dissatisfied with cash annuity, 111; refuses J. L. Cathcart as consul, 115; threatens war with U.S., 122; described by H. Wadsworth, 177–78; described by EP, 178–79
Algiers, Dey of, 176–77
Alknomack, 76–77
Allegiance, 20
Allen, David, 22
Allen, Mayhew, 28
Alliance (brig), 32
Alliance (Continental frigate), 37
Allies, Stephen, 52, 57
Amazon, 179
Amory, Thomas C., 64, 65
Amphion, 174
Argus: to be part of EP's squadron, 128; operations during Moroccan crisis, 146, 148; operations, Oct. 1803–July 1804, 175, 183, 201, 209–10, 245–46, 247–50; in attacks on Tripoli, 256, 261, 264–65*illus*, 267, 272, 274–75, 276, 282–83, 285, 289, 292, 294, 295, 298, 303–05, 306–07; Brooke transferred to, 226–27; and Eaton-Hamet Caramanli expedition, 308, 330
Arrogant, 74–75, 78
Ayscough, Thomas, 223

Bagaduce: center of British and Loyalist activity in Maine, 8, 9–10, 20–21, 22, 24; Mowat's operations out of, 9–10, 16; *Merriam* captured at, 23–24; Winthrop looks into harbor, 28
Bagaduce, 9–10
Bainbridge, Joseph, 257, 260, 266
Bainbridge, William: takes command of *Essex*, 88; to command *Philadelphia*, 128; and capture of *Mirboha*, 139, 141–43; sent to blockade Tripoli, 148–49; and loss of *Philadelphia*, 179–82, 336–37; EP's opinion of, 181–82, 336–37; negotiates with Dghies, 268; views bodies from *Intrepid*, 306; urges peace with Tripoli, 332; offended by EP's dispatches, 336–37; joins EP in lobbying for Navy, 339–40; considers retiring from Navy, 342; mentioned, 346, 349
Baker, Lawrence, 31
Baldwin, Thomas, 226
Ball, Alexander John, 186, 203, 220, 233, 237, 290
Baltimore, 53
Bangs, Mehetable. *See* Preble, Mehetable (Bangs) Roberts

377

INDEX

Barbary States. *See* Algiers; Morocco; Tripoli; Tunis

Barron, James: as member of Morris squadron, 110, 111–12; commands *Essex* in S. Barron squadron, 277, 279, 307; builds Gunboat No. 2, 317; personality of, 329–30, 340; pessimism about securing gunboats and bomb ketches, 333; quarrels with Rodgers, 335; advocates reforms in Navy, 338; declines to join lobbying effort, 340; urges EP to accept Washington Navy Yard, 344; and *Leopard-Chesapeake* affair, 351–52; N. Morris's opinion of, 352

Barron, Samuel: compared with EP and Rodgers, 146; supersedes EP, 246, 277, 279, 280–81, 307; EP attempts to end war before Barron's arrival, 282, 283, 285; EP concerned over non-arrival of, 289–90, 297; and cooperation with Hamet Caramanli, 308, 330, 331; EP influences, 308, 330; EP seeks gunboats and bomb ketches for, 310–12, 314, 333; illness of, 310, 329–30; refuses to give up command of squadron, 329; agrees to negotiations, 332–33; resigns command of squadron, 333; attacked by Eaton, 335

Barry, John, 50, 59, 60, 64, 128
Bartell, John, 174
Bartlet, William, 33
Bartlett, Nicholas, 44
Barton, Samuel, 36
Beale, Richard C., 72, 74
Beaussier, Bonaventure: dispatches as source for history of Tripolitan War, viii; reports movements of Tripoli's cruisers, 120*n*; assists R. V. Morris's negotiations, 121; authorized to mediate between Tripoli and U.S., 201–02; conference with EP, 204–07; EP's opinion of, 206, 243–44; negotiates with Tripolitan authorities, 241–44, 269–71, 283–84, 294–96; EP and O'Brien attempt to circumvent, 242–43, 268; communications with EP, 243, 267–68, 270–71, 282–85, 294–97, 306; on effectiveness of blockade of Tripoli, 249; relationship with EP, 297; on 2 Sept. 1804 attack on Tripoli, 303; on explosion of *Intrepid*, 305–06; on number of British subjects in *Philadelphia*, 367*n*2 (Chap. 10)

Berryman, Charles, 215–16
Bertozzi, Cecilia Fontana, 230
Bickerton, Richard, 186

Biddle, Charles, 314
Blackie, James, 22
Blake, Charles, 56
Blake, Joshua, 123, 135–36, 257, 266–67, 336
Blockade: instructions to Dale, 88; Dale's opinions on, 92–93, 104; in instructions to R. V. Morris, 93–95; Murray on effectiveness of, 108–09; Jefferson favors, 128

of Tripoli by EP: affects U.S. relations with Tunis, 245–46; by small cruisers described, 210, 247–50; effectiveness of, 249–50; resumed, 306–07

Bloomfield, Joseph, 314
Board of Navy Commissioners. *See* Navy Commissioners, Board of
Bomb Ketch No. 1: in attacks on Tripoli, 256, 264–65 *illus*, 266, 267, 272, 275, 302–03; damaged, 290
Bomb Ketch No. 2: in attacks on Tripoli, 256, 264–65 *illus*, 266, 272, 302–03; out of action, 292
Bomb ketches. *See also* Etna; Gunboats and bomb ketches; *Vesuvius*
Bonnevie, Emmanuel, 119, 120*n*
Boot topping, 25
Bordeaux: economic conditions in described by EP, 40, 41
Boston: retained in Navy, 83; reputed battle with Tunisian squadron, 101–02, 104; to blockade Tripoli, 104*n*; rumored coming to reinforce EP, 193
Boston Gazette, 246–47
Bowditch, Nathaniel, *New American Practical Navigator,* 328*n*
Bowen, Richard, 142
Boys, Elias, 41
Bribes. *See* Gifts and bribes; Preble, Edward, Personal characteristics, practices bribery
Bridge, Mathew, 34–41 *passim*
British Navy. *See* Great Britain, Navy
Brooke, Samuel B., 226–27
Brown, Moses, 33
Brown, Thomas, 259
Brunswick, Maine: gunboats built at, 326
Bryant, Captain, 38
Bullock, Isaac, 43
Burbeck, John, 324
Burchard, John, 222
Burr, Aaron: Goldsborough's opinion of, 83; travels with EP, 314
Burrows, William W., 81
Busuttil, Salvatore, 187–88, 210–12, 330

378

INDEX

Caldwell, James R., 276
Camilla, 41
Campbell, Hugh G.: reports EP's courtship, 84; takes command of *Adams*, 101; in action, 119, 120; takes command of *New York*, 158; dines with EP, 163; commands *Constellation*, 277, 279; mentioned, 312
Campbelltown, Maine. *See* Bagaduce
Cannarella, Baron, 228
Cannon, John N., 214–17 *passim*, 262–63
Cannon, Mrs. John N., 216, 263
Capisic, 7
Caramanli, Hamet: relations with brother Yusuf, 112–13, 186–87; EP cooperates with, 186–88, 203, 205, 210–12; Beaussier's opinion of, 241, 330–31; Yusuf Caramanli's opinion of, 241; Eaton cooperates with, 112–13, 285, 294–95, 308, 330–31, 334; personality of, 330–31; W. Bainbridge's opinion of, 332
Caramanli, Yusuf: declares war on U.S., 86, 91; interested in negotiating with Dale, 91; relations with brother Hamet, 112–13, 186–87; Rodgers attempts to negotiate with, 120–21; gets possession of W. Bainbridge's papers, 180; welcomes French mediation, 205; refuses to exchange prisoners, 205, 295; supervises defenses, 206; rejects peace terms, 241, 243, 244; Beaussier's opinion of, 244, 294–95, 296; attitude on attacks, 267–68, 269–70, 271, 284; learns of EP's approach, 268; refuses to negotiate, 268; misinterprets EP's humane action, 270; effect of attacks on, 289, 294; effect of negotiations on, 295; sets peace terms, 295–96; permits prisoners to view bodies from *Intrepid*, 306; Lear's opinion of, 331; W. Bainbridge's opinion of, 332; determination to save face, 333, 334. *See also* Tripoli
Carbery, Henry, 324; circular gun mount, 322*illus*, 327*illus*
Careening, description of, 123–27, 136–37
Cargoes (EP's merchant career): *William*, 30, 31; *Elizabeth*, 31, 32; *Alliance*, 32; *Polly*, 33; *Neptune*, 34, 35; *Katy*, 36, 38; *Helena*, 38; *Camilla*, 41; *Jason*, 42; *Success*, 43; *Phenix*, 48; *Dauphin*, 50
Castine, Maine. *See* Bagaduce
Catalano, Salvador, 189–90, 196–97
Cathcart, James L.: and outbreak of Tripolitan War, 86–87; authorized to negotiate, 94–95; to attempt negotiations, 110; urges cooperation with Hamet Caramanli, 112–13; dispute with R. V. Morris, 115, 129, 132; instructions for negotiations with Tripoli and Tunis, 129; replaced by Lear, 129; Tunis refuses to receive, 146, 200; on gunboat construction, 320, 321
Cathcart, John, 20
Cederström, Rudolf, 92–93, 108
Celia, 142, 151, 156, 157
Ceres (sloop), 23
Ceres (British frigate), 48
Chapelle, Howard I., 317*n*
Chauncey, Isaac: dines with EP, 163; as commander of *John Adams*, 276, 281, 310; advises EP of government's intentions, 284; reconnoiters Tripoli harbor, 286–88, 298
Chesapeake: retained in Navy, 83; operations with Morris squadron, 93, 104, 107, 109–12, 113, 115; recall from Mediterranean, 104, 109, 110, 111; repaired, 344. *See also* Great Britain, friction with U.S., *Leopard-Chesapeake* affair
China, 75–76, 78
Clemente, Mr. *See* Fama, Clemente
Cod fishery, 43, 135, 352
Codman, Statira (Preble), 4
Codman, Stephen, 48
Coffin, Isaac, 346
Coffin, Jacob, 320–21, 323–24
Coleridge, Samuel T., 220, 233, 345–46
Collins, Isaac, 58
Collins, Josiah, 30–32
Columbia (ship, NW Coast pioneer), 58
Columbia (ship, 1800), 78
Columbian Centinel, 34, 35–36, 46, 48
Comité Chargé de Traiter avec les Neutres, 40, 41
Commissioners, Navy. *See* Navy Commissioners, Board of
Confiance, 76–78
Congress. *See* U.S. Congress
Congress: consort of *Essex*, 66–72 *passim*, 75; dismasted, 78–79; retained in Navy, 83; to Mediterranean, 193, 246, 277; to watch Morocco, 307; EP contrasts with *Constitution*, 309–10
Constellation: launched, 49; officers for, 50; escorts *Dauphin*, 53; retained in Navy, 83; operations with Morris squadron, 93, 107–110, 112; recall from Mediterranean, 104, 109, 110; to Mediterranean, 246, 277; off Tripoli, 307–08

INDEX

Constitution: launched, 49; officers for, 50–51; EP ordered to, 54; officers criticized by Higginson, 55–56; EP avoids duty in, 56–57; retained in Navy, 83; EP promised command of, 106; fits for sea at Boston and sails, 123–38; operations during Moroccan crisis, 139–72 *passim;* British seamen in, 135–36, 173–74; passage from Gibraltar to Syracuse, 175–82 *passim;* captures future *Intrepid,* 183–85, 233–34; and expedition to destroy *Philadelphia,* 190, 193; cruises, 199–212 *passim,* 213, 237–39, 240–47 *passim;* life in, 214–27, 307; EP's library in, 219–21; EP increases armament of, 238n; in attacks on Tripoli, 250–308 *passim;* EP contrasts with *Congress,* 310

Consuls, U.S. *See* Cathcart, James L.; Davis, George; Eaton, William; Elmslie, John; Gavino, John; Lear, Tobias; Mathieu, John S. M.; Morphy, Michael; O'Brien, Richard; Simpson, James

Continental Navy. *See* Navy, Continental

Convoy: in Quasi-War, 60; EP's and Sever's attitude towards, 69–70; in instructions to R. V. Morris, 93; in event of war with Morocco, 105n; Jefferson's opposition to, 113

Cordis, John B., 55
Corné, Michel Felice, 264–65
Cowdery, Jonathan, 303
Cox, John S. H., 142
Crocillo, Pietro F., 185
Crofton, Ambrose, 44
Crowninshield, Jacob, 315
Crutch, George, 222
Curtis, John, 22
Curtis, Roger, 71
Cutter, William, 62
Cygnet, 63

Dale, Richard: orders for command of Mediterranean squadron, 87–88; operations in Mediterranean, 91–92, 101; on strategy for Tripolitan War, 92–93, 104, 130; resigns from Navy, 128; uses Malta as base, 175
Danforth, Samuel, 350–51
Darby, 24
Darby, John, quoted, 227, 228, 229, 230, 293, 310–11
Darling, David, 215
Dauphin, 50-53, 55, 56–57
Davis, Daniel, 90–91

Davis, George, 207–09, 210, 212, 245–46, 341–42
Davis, Isaac P., 50, 51
Daylie, John, 24
Deacon, David, 259, 266, 267
Deane (Continental frigate), 7, 50
Deane (Massachusetts privateer), 17
Dearborn, Henry: EP's relations with, 89–90; EP writes to, 130, 136–37, 137–38; advises EP to govern his temper, 138; EP asks for reinforcements, 200–01; R. Smith writes to regarding EP's health, 353
Decatur, James, 257, 259, 261
Decatur, Stephen, Sr., 314
Decatur, Stephen, Jr.: to command *Argus,* 128; takes command of *Enterprize,* 175; reconnoiters Tripoli harbor, 184, 286–88, 298; and destruction of *Philadelphia,* 190–99; in Syracuse, 228, 231; letter to, from G. F. Leckie, 232n; in attacks on Tripoli, 257–59, 260, 261, 263, 264–65 *illus,* 266, 274, 276; dines with EP, 339; mentioned, 223
Decay, in ships, 215, 344
Deering, Dorcas, 67–68, 350
Deering, James: friendship with EP, 67; and removal of Fosdick, 90–91; EP describes Washington trip to, 106; on EP and civilian contractors, 323; tells EP of attack on *Chesapeake,* 351; mentioned, 84
Deering, Mrs. James, 89, 90n
Deering, John, 90
Deering, Mary. *See* Preble, Mary (Deering)
Defence, 22
Defiance, 22
Degen, Frederic, 237n
de Kraft, F. Cornelius, 228, 370–71n9
Democratic-Republicans. *See* Republican Party
Dent, John H.: sent ashore at Malta, 179; commands *Scourge,* 210; and Bertozzi, 230; sent on mission to Messina, 236; in attacks on Tripoli, 266, 272, 302–03
Derby, Richard, 66
Desertion: from *Neptune,* 34; from EP's squadron, 173–74, 222, 223, 225, 230–31; not encouraged at Malta, 186
Desfourneaux, Etienne, 62
Dexter, Daniel S., 262, 267
Dghies, Mohammed: negotiates with R. V. Morris, 121; O'Brien neglects, 242–43; W. Bainbridge attempts to negotiate

INDEX

with, 268; confers with Beaussier, 283–84, 294–95, 296; urges early peace negotiations, 332
Dimensions of vessels: *Polly*, 33; *Neptune*, 34; *Katy*, 36; *Jason*, 41–42; *Success*, 43; *Phenix*, 48; *Massachusetts*, 64; Gunboat No. 11, 320–21; *Etna*, 321; Gunboat No. 12, 321; *Vesuvius*, 321
Discipline: in *Essex*, 81n; in *Constitution*, 218, 221–27
Donegal, 141
Dorsey, John S., 276
Dorsey, John W., 229
Drunkenness. *See* Alcoholism
Dueling, 228, 370–71n9
Dummer School, 5–6, 7, 32, 357n4
Dundas, Francis, 71
Dutch East India Company, 64
Dyer, Nathaniel, 320
Dyson, George, 233–34

Eaton, William: asks for meeting with Morris and Cathcart, 111; debt at Tunis, 208; and Hamet Caramanli, 112–13, 285, 294–95, 308, 330–31, 334; attacks S. Barron, Lear, and Rodgers, 335; EP's opinion of, 336
Elbert, Samuel, 225
Eliza (ship), 46
Eliza (ketch), 289–90
Elizabeth, 31–32
Elliot, George, 141
Elliot, Hugh, 311–12
Ellwell, Henry, 8
Elmslie, John, 71
Elphinstone, Charles, 71
En flûte, defined, 209n
Enterprize: retained in Navy, 87, 108, 316; operations with Dale squadron, 87, 91–92; battle with Tripolitan polacre, 91–92; operations with Morris squadron, 93, 104, 104–05n, 107, 111, 113–14, 115–22; to be part of EP's squadron, 128; operations during Moroccan crisis, 154; operations, Oct. 1803–July 1804, 175, 190, 210, 230, 231, 236, 247–50; and capture of future *Intrepid*, 183–85; in EP's attacks on Tripoli, 256, 261, 264–65*illus*, 272, 274–75, 276, 292, 306
Eolus, 9
Essex: EP commands, 66–81, 86, 88, 98; EP's opinion of, 68; sailing qualities of, 68, 75; retained in Navy, 83; operations with Dale squadron, 87, 91; EP may be given command of, 105; to Mediterranean, 193, 246, 277; to watch Morocco, 307; Lear sails for Tripoli in, 333
Etna, 321–26 *passim*
Experiment, 87, 108

Fair American, 61
Falmouth, Maine. *See* Portland, Maine
Fama, Clemente, 211–12, 330
Fame, 45, 47, 48
Farquhar, Richard, 187–88, 189, 204, 210–12, 330
Federalist Party: concern with political affiliation of naval officers, 56; EP a member of, 88, 315–16; Fosdick as member of, 89–91; EP guest of, 315–16
Ferdinand, King of the Two Sicilies, 310–11
Fisher, Samuel S., 52
Fletcher, Patrick, 60–63 *passim*
Flogging: in *Essex*, 81n; in *Constitution*, 221–24; not permitted by Murray, 224n
Forteguerri, General, 238, 311
Fosdick, Nathaniel, 89–91
Fox, Josiah, 108, 317, 320, 324
France: mediates between Sweden and Tripoli, 112; as mediator between U.S. and Tripoli, 201–02, 206–07; and U.S. vessels of war in her ports, 235–36; EP suspects of intrigue, 311. *See also* Beaussier, Bonaventure
   Friction with U.S.: activities of privateers, 45–46, 49, 52, 308; causes of Quasi-War, 49; capture of *Dauphin*, 51–52, 57; capture of French armed vessels authorized, 52; U.S. naval operations in Quasi-War, 52–79 *passim*; U.S. strategy in Quasi-War, 59, 66–67; attitude of Guadeloupe authorities during Quasi-War, 62; peace treaty, 82–83
France, Isle of, operations of French privateers from, 67, 72–75, 76–78
Francis (brig), 38
Francis (schooner), 61–62
Friend, William, 7–8
Friends, 72–75

Gadsden, Christopher, Jr., 183, 193, 278–79
Gallatin, Albert: and removal of Fosdick, 90–91; opposition to Mediterranean naval operations, 102–03, 278; Murray criticizes R. V. Morris to, 112; Jefferson

INDEX

expresses dissatisfaction with R. V. Morris to, 113; and naval shore establishment, 343
Gallatin, Hannah, 133
Gavino, John, 112, 143, 193
Geddes, Simon W., 68, 80
General Greene, 83
George, Fort. *See* Bagaduce
George Washington, 60–63 *passim*
Gerry, Elbridge, 49
Gifts and bribes in diplomatic negotiations, 164, 171, 242, 268, 285, 296
Giveen, Robert, 326
Goldsborough, Charles W.: sketched, 82; on reduction of Navy in event of peace with France, 82–83; on presidential election of 1800, 83; on EP's courtship, 84; attempts to persuade EP to resign from Navy, 100–01; on strategy for war with Morocco, 105; summarizes dispatches from Mediterranean, 113; wishes EP success in Mediterranean, 281; EP writes regarding future of Navy, expense of shore establishment, and Washington Navy Yard, 342–45; E. D. Preble described to, 347; urges EP to move to Washington, 350; EP's opinion of, 350; mentioned, 135
Good Design, 17–18
Gordon, Charles, 216, 224n, 225
Gore, John, 173–74
Governor Dummer Academy. *See* Dummer School
Governor Parry, 51
Graves, Samuel, 6
Graving, 25
Gray, Robert, 58
Great Britain, Commissioners for Taking Care of Sick and Wounded Seamen, 72
Great Britain, friction with U.S.: detention of *Three Friends*, 40–41; capture of *Phenix*, 48; capture of *Dauphin*, 51; over EP's prize, *Friends*, 74–75; British seamen in EP's squadron, 135–36, 173–75, 367n2 (Chap. 10); over loan of Neapolitan gunboats and bomb ketches to S. Barron, 311–12; *Leopard-Chesapeake* affair, 351–53
Great Britain, Navy: EP's relations with officers of, 44, 71–72, 74–75, 140–41, 173–75, 186, 346; influence on U.S. Navy, 71–72, 219–20, 343
Greenleaf, Robert, 217, 262
Gregorio, Marcello de, 182, 230–33
Greyhound, 97

Grivegnée & Co., 36–38
Grog, 124, 217, 218
Guadeloupe: U.S. merchantmen captured by privateers from, 45–46, 49; *Pickering* and *George Washington* cruise off, 61–62, 63; Joseph Ingraham's mission to, 62–63
Gunboat No. 1 (Neapolitan): in attacks on Tripoli, 254, 257, 260–61, 263, 264–65 *illus*, 286
Gunboat No. 1 (U.S.), 316–17
Gunboat No. 2 (Neapolitan), 257, 259, 261, 263, 264–65*illus*, 266
Gunboat No. 2 (U.S.), 316–17
Gunboat No. 3 (Neapolitan), 257, 264–65*illus*, 266–67
Gunboat No. 4 (Neapolitan): in attacks on Tripoli, 257–59, 261, 263, 264–65*illus*, 266, 274, 276
Gunboat No. 5 (Neapolitan), 257, 260, 264–65*illus*, 266
Gunboat No. 6 (Neapolitan): in attacks on Tripoli, 257, 259–60, 261, 263, 264–65 *illus*, 266, 276, 286
Gunboat No. 8 (ex-Tripolitan), 276
Gunboat No. 9 (ex-Tripolitan), 275–76
Gunboat No. 11, 320–26 *passim*
Gunboat No. 12, 321–26 *passim*
Gunboats Nos. 3–10 (U.S.), 317
Gunboats Nos. 29–37, 326–28, 352–53
Gunboat program, U.S., 316–28, 339–41
Gunboats and bomb ketches: Dale on employment of, 92–93; EP seeks 176, 188, 192, 206, 210, 213, 235–39; EP shows Beaussier models of, 205; Congress authorizes acquisition of, 237; Neapolitan boats, 239, 252, 272, 297; organization table, for EP's 3 Aug. 1804 attack, 254; S. Barron seeks, 310–12, 333. *See also* individual boats and ketches
Gurney, Francis, 314

Hale, Joseph, 6
Hall, John, 216, 217, 262
Hambleton, Captain, 46
Hammond, 23
Hammond, Zebedee, 24
Hancock, 136
Hancock, John: L. Little reports to, 18; cruising instructions for *Winthrop*, 20, 21–22, 25–26; naval strategy of, 26
Hannah (brig), 150, 154, 155, 156, 163, 166
Hannah (coasting sloop), 32

382

INDEX

Haraden, Nathaniel: quotations from logbook kept by, 106–07n, 126, 127, 137, 153, 157, 159, 161, 162–63, 169–70, 171, 191, 214, 215, 217n, 252; commands *Constitution* in ordinary, 106; and heaving down of *Constitution*, 123–25; EP's opinion of, 125n; on EP's anxiety to get to sea, 137; on homosexuality, 153; on navigational difficulties, 157; on events at Tangier, 161, 162–63, 169–70, 171; describes daily life in *Constitution*, 214, 215, 217n; prepares entries for logbook, 217; opinion of own ability, 220; and attacks on Tripoli, 262, 276, 289, 290, 293, 305; returns to U.S., 310
Harmony, 53
Harrison, Alexander C., 226–27
Harvard College, 5, 7
Hashash, Abd al-Rahman, 143–58 *passim*, 167, 171
Hatch, Crowell, 34, 35
Hazard, 7
Health: in *Protector*, 12, 16; in *Chesapeake*, 110; Hyler paralyzed, 127; in *Constitution*, 215, 216, 218. *See also* Preble, Edward, health; Venereal disease
Heaving down. *See Constitution*, fits for sea at Boston
Heermann, Lewis, 197–98
Helena, 38–39
Henley, John D., 259
Herald, 57, 59–60
Higgins, Eleazer, 326
Higginson, Stephen, 55–56, 58, 64, 65
Hillar, Benjamin, 58, 65
Hinman, Elisha, 17
Hodshon (John) & Son, 40
Homosexuality, 153
Hope (William Friend, commander), 7–8
Hope (Joseph Ingraham, commander), 58
Hornet, 330
Houlton harbor, Nova Scotia, described by EP, 43
House of Representatives, U.S. *See* U.S. Congress
Hughes, Victor, 45
Hull, Isaac: in R. V. Morris's attacks on Tripolitan vessels, 118–20; commands *Enterprize*, 128; sent off Mogador, 154; ordered to remain near Gibraltar, 175; ordered to remain in central Mediterranean, 209–10; use of flogging, 224; captures boat near Old Tripoli, 245; in EP's attacks on Tripoli, 275, 282–83;

and Eaton-Hamet Caramanli expedition, 308, 330–31
Humphreys, Joshua, 337
Hunt, Ephraim, 326
Hurd, Joseph, 36–41 *passim*
Hyler, William, 127

Ibn Abdallah, Muhammed, 145
Ilsley, Augusta, 90n
Ilsley, Isaac, 89–91
Indians, Nova Scotian, mentioned by EP, 43
Industry, 52, 53
Ingraham, Joseph (commander, *Lincoln Galley*), 9
Ingraham, Joseph (sailing master, *Pickering*): sketched, 58; journal of, quoted, 58, 60, 63; mission to Guadeloupe, 62–63
Insurance, marine, 52n, 145
Insurgente, 146
Intrepid: captured by *Constitution*, 183–85, 233; and destruction of *Philadelphia*, 189–99; employed as infernal, 297–99, 303–06; destruction of, 303–06, 336–37
Irving, Washington, 227–28, 230
Isabella, 22
Israel, Joseph, 298–99, 305, 336
Izard, Ralph, Jr.: describes heaving down of *Constitution*, 124, 127; opinion of EP, 132–33; sent by EP to New York, 136; accompanies EP to Tangier, 163–68 *passim*; visits Algiers with EP, 177; accompanies EP to Malta, 185–86; describes poverty in Syracuse, Sicily, 229

Jack, 139, 142
Jackson, Henry, 39, 50-51, 55
Jackson, Joseph, 48
Jamisen, Saunders, 24
Japan, EP misses opportunity to make voyage to, 64–65
Jason, 41–42, 47, 362n9
Java: U.S. trade with, 64, 66–67, 75–76; EP's operations near, 72–79
Jefferson, Thomas: lack of research into naval policy of, viii; as Secretary of State, 35; Goldsborough's opinion of, 83; sends Dale squadron to Mediterranean, 87; on annuities for Barbary States, 87, 128; abused by Federalists at Portland and Boston, 89–90, 315; praises

Sterett, 91–92; fiscal retrenchment program and Mediterranean operations, 94; attempts to compromise Cabinet differences over strategy, 103-05; meets EP, 106, 312, 314, 340; and dismissal of R. V. Morris, 113–14, 278; EP's opinion of, 130, 316; Maulay Sulaiman writes to, 167, 169, 170, 171; against French mediation of Tripolitan War, 201; rejects Tunis's request for frigate, 212; will cut size of Mediterranean squadron, 278; adopts R. Smith's program, 279; naval recommendations to Congress, 279, 339; Cabinet meeting to consider peace terms, 280; sends EP's dispatches to Congress, 312; offers to make Crowninshield Secretary of Navy, 315; R. Smith writes to regarding peace with Tripoli, 334; and EP's proposed mission to Europe, 344. *See also* Gunboat program, U.S.; Strategic policy, U.S.

Jeffersonian Republicans. *See* Republican Party

Jeffry, John, 22
Jersey, 18
Jews, Tripolitan, 236, 243, 249, 274
John, 17
John Adams: retained in Navy, 83; operations with Morris squadron, 104, 110–12, 113–14, 115–22; operations during Moroccan crisis, 146, 148, 149–51, 156–57, 158, 161, 163, 166, 226; joins EP's squadron, 209, 212, 246, 276, 279, 280–81, 285; sailing qualities of, 280–81; and EP's attacks on Tripoli, 282, 283, 290, 293, 306; EP returns to U.S. in, 310–12, 345
Josiah, James, 76, 78
Junkins, Martha. *See* Preble, Martha (Junkins)

Katy, 36–38
Keene, Newton, 324
Kelapa Island, described by EP, 72
Knox, Henry, 39
Knox, Thomas, 124

Lamb, James, 47
Landolina, Saverio, 227
Lawrence, James, 352–53
Lear, Frances D. (Henley), 176, 177, 178
Lear, Tobias: appointed Consul General at Algiers, 129–30, 131; R. Smith's opinion of, 132; boards *Maimona*, 139–40; advises EP during negotiations with Morocco, 149, 158, 162–172; discusses Moroccan crisis with prisoners in *Constitution*, 152; takes up duties at Algiers, 175–79 *passim;* to deal with *Paulina* claim, 208–09; unable to assist EP in negotiations with Tripoli, 210; new instructions to regarding peace with Tripoli, 280; as moderating influence on EP, 297; concludes peace treaty with Tripoli, 329, 330, 331–35; and Eaton, 331, 335; EP's opinion of, 335, 341
Lebas, M., 46
Leckie, Gould Francis, 231–32
Leckie, Mrs. Gould Francis, 231–32
Lee, Benjamin, 50, 55
Lee, George G., 72, 74
Leonard, Peter, 219
Leopard. See Great Britain, friction with U.S., *Leopard-Chesapeake* affair
Leverett, Thomas, 12, 16, 18
Lewis, William, 216
Lincoln Galley, 8, 9
Linzee, S. H., 71
Little, Edward Preble, 20n
Little, George, 11, 13, 20–29
Little, Luther, 13, 17–18
Little, Rachel, 20n
Liverpool, 22
Livingston, Robert R., 201
Livingston, William, 135–36
Lobbying, by officers of U.S. Navy, 337–42
Low, Rufus, 75
Lubarez, Ibrahim: captured by *Philadelphia*, 142–43, 144; as prisoner in *Constitution*, 149, 152–53, 163, 169; orders to, 155
Ludlow, Charles, 98
Lundström, Olof, 38–39
Lyde, Nathaniel, 324, 352–54

Mac, 48
McCormick, Hugh, 222
McDonogh, Brian, 203, 244
Macdonough, Thomas, 263
McHenry, James, 51, 53–54
M'Lean, John, 36–41 *passim*
McNeill, Daniel, 101–02, 104
Macon, Nathaniel, 341
Madison, James, 106, 129, 314
Maidstone, 140–41
Maimona: EP meets, 139–40, 167; W. Bainbridge searches for, 142; fits for sea, 144; EP threatens to sink, 145, 157;

Rodgers and EP search for, 151, 156; shelters at Lisbon, 158n

Maine: conditions in during Revolutionary War, 7, 20–21; EP's opinion of climate, 350

Majabagaduce. *See* Bagaduce

Malbone, Edward Greene, 85

Malta: social life at, 186; EP permits to trade with Tripoli, 204; U.S. officers prefer to Syracuse, 230

Maria-Carolina, Queen of Naples, 310–11

Marines: in *Protector*, 11; in *Pickering*, 58; in *Essex*, 80–81; in *Constitution*, 124, 133, 153, 216, 217, 222, 262; in *Syren*, 207; in Eaton-Hamet Caramanli expedition, 330

Marquizeaux, Captain, 74

Mars, 22

Marshall, John, 49

Marshall, Samuel R., 99

Mary, 193

Massachusetts, 64–65

Massachusetts Board of War, 10

Massachusetts General Court: Jedidiah Preble's service in, 4; and *Protector*, 8, 9; naval strategy of, 10, 26; votes to sell *Winthrop*, 29; makes slave trade illegal, 33

Massachusetts state navy: EP joins, 8, 9; strategic policy, 10, 26; last cruise of, 25–29; disbanded, 30. *See also* Prize money; *Protector*; *Winthrop*

Massi, Antonio, 295

Mathieu, John S. M., 237n

Mauritius. *See* France, Isle of

Medea, 17–18

Medusa, 173

Melville, Herman, 58

Mentor, 40

Mercellise, Pierre Blaise, 267, 270

Merriam, 23–24, 190, 259

Merrill, Orlando B., 64

Merrimack, 8

Meshuda: blockaded, 91, 101, 107, 110, 115; captured, 116, 122, 143–44, 146; captains of, in *John Adams*, 149, 150; Hashash gives orders to, 155; in negotiations between U.S. and Morocco, 155, 156, 166–67, 169; as prison ship, 159; restored to Morocco, 170–71

Miller, Edward, 99

Miquelon. *See* St. Pierre and Miquelon

Mirboha: captured by *Philadelphia*, 142–43, 151, 157; fits for sea, 144; officers, as prisoners in *Constitution*, 149–50, 152–53, 163, 169; in negotiations between U.S. and Morocco, 155, 156, 159, 160, 166–67, 169; described by EP, 169; desertions from prize crew of, 173–74

Mogador: *Hannah* detained at, 150, 155, 156, 163; U.S. trade with, 154

Moody, Samuel, 6

Morale: in *Protector*, 11; in *Neptune*, 34–35; in *Essex*, 80–81; in *Intrepid*, 194

Morocco: diplomatic relations with U.S., 37; declares war on U.S., 101; naval force of, 102, 105n, 144; strategic advantages of, 102, 157; difficulties with adjusted, 107; fear of war with, 122; EP and Sept.-Oct. 1803 crisis with, 139–173; Isaac Hull to watch, 175, 210; threatens hostilities, 307

Morocco, Sultan of. *See* Sulaiman, Maulay

Morphy, Michael, 35

Morris, Anne (Mrs. Richard V.), 107, 122

Morris, Charles, 133, 292

Morris, Noadiah: goes ashore at Tangier with EP, 163–64, 167, 170; goes ashore at Algiers with EP, 177; goes to Malta with EP, 186; aids EP as purser, 219; returns to U.S., 310; reports activities in Congress to EP, 341; on *Leopard-Chesapeake* affair, 352

Morris, Richard V.: reasons for studying his Mediterranean command, viii; orders for conduct of operations against Tripoli, 93–95, 107, 113, 116; operations during war with Morocco, 101, 104, 107; operations, Aug. 1802–May 1803, 107, 109–12, 115–16; court of inquiry on and dismissal from Navy, 109, 111, 116, 278, 284; on impossibility of winter operations against Tripoli, 110–11; reasons for taking squadron to Gibraltar, 111–12; dismissal from Mediterranean command, 113–14, 122; dispute with J. L. Cathcart, 115, 129, 132; attacks on Tripolitan shipping, 116–20, 142; relations with Rodgers, 116, 147; negotiations with Tripoli, 121; abandons operations off Tripoli, 121–22; Simpson warns, 144; compared with EP and Rodgers, 146; returns to U.S., 146, 158, 316; promises release of *Meshuda*, 166; uses Malta as base, 175; intrigues with Hamet Caramanli, 187; and *Paulina* affair, 200; arrested at Tunis, 208; seeks to borrow gunboats from Kingdom of the Two Sicilies, 235; brings model of gunboat from Mediterranean, 316

Morris, Robert, 29
Mortars, performance of, 266, 289, 294, 295
Moulton, William, Jr., 321, 326
Mowat, Henry, 3, 6–7, 9–10, 16
Mumford, William, 68, 80
Murray, Alexander: commands *Constellation* in Mediterranean, 107–08; opinions on blockade and on U.S. Barbary policy, 108–09; returns to U.S., 109, 110; criticizes R. V. Morris, 112–13, 129; compared with EP and Rodgers, 146; Gordon's and R. Smith's opinions of, 224*n*; lenient approach to discipline, 224*n*; mentioned, 312

Naples, described by EP, 238. *See also* Two Sicilies, Kingdom of the
Nautilus (British sloop of war), 9–10
Nautilus (U.S. schooner): carries order recalling R. V. Morris, 114; to be part of EP's squadron, 128; recruiting for, 135; operations during Moroccan crisis, 146, 148–49, 160, 166; operations, Oct. 1803–May 1804, 175, 183, 231, 239; in EP's attacks on Tripoli, 250, 254–56, 257, 260, 261, 264–65*illus*, 272, 274–75, 276, 292, 298, 303–05, 306; and Eaton-Hamet Caramanli expedition, 330
Naval policy, U.S. *See* Gunboat program, U.S.; Ships of the line; Strategic policy, U.S.
Navy, Accountant of the. *See* Accountant of the Navy
Navy, Continental, 37, 76
Navy, Massachusetts. *See* Massachusetts state navy
Navy, Secretary of the. *See* Smith, Robert; Smith, Samuel; Stoddert, Benjamin
Navy, U.S. *See* U.S. Navy
Navy Commissioners, Board of, proposed, 338, 340
Navy Department. *See* U.S. Navy Department
Nelson, Horatio, 177–78, 186
Neptune, 34–36, 37
New Orleans, right of deposit at, withdrawn, 316
New York: retained in Navy, 83; operations with Morris squadron, 104, 110–12, 113–14, 115–22; operations during Moroccan crisis, 146, 148, 153, 158, 161, 163, 166

Newburyport: EP's association with, 32; Gunboat No. 12 and *Vesuvius* built at, 321
Newburyport Herald, 321
Nicholson, John B., 226
Nicholson, Joseph, 134, 226
Nicholson, Joseph Hopper, 133
Nicholson, Samuel: recommends officers for *Constitution*, 50, 55; EP's relations with, 51, 54, 57, 133–34; criticized by Higginson, 55–56; compared with EP and Rodgers, 146
Nicholson, William R., 228, 370–71*n*9
Nissen, Nicholas C., 120–21, 332
Norman, Captain, 101

Oakes, Hildebrand, 186
O'Brien, Richard: stays at Algiers, 176, 177; H. Wadsworth's opinion of, 178; negotiates at Tunis, 210, 212; negotiates at Tripoli, 242–43, 244, 268; learns Tripolitans may try to capture blockader, 248–49; opposes attack on Tripoli from the west, 272; on explosion in Gunboat No. 9, 276; carries dispatches into Tripoli harbor, 282–85 *passim*, 292
O'Bryen, James, 44
Officers, selection and training of. *See* U.S. Navy, selection of officers for; Professionalism
Ohio River Valley, construction of galleys and gunboats in, 316*n*, 317, 320, 326
Oiseau, 71
Old Tripoli, actions near, 119–20, 245–46, 248
Orpheus, 74–75, 78
Osborn, Edward O., 74–75
Otty, William, 51
Oxnard, Martha (Preble), 4

Page, Octavius A., 225
Parker, Captain, 48
Parker, Isaac, 48
Parkman, Samuel, 50, 51
Parsons, Eben, 41, 42–43, 47
Parsons, Gorham, 41, 42–43
Patten & Walker, 61
Paulina, 200, 208–09, 210, 212
Peace terms with Barbary States: outlined to J. L. Cathcart, 94, 129; stated by Jefferson, 103–04; Murray on, 108–09;

INDEX

offered by R. V. Morris, 121; proposed by Tripolitan officials, 121, 284, 295–96, 332–33; EP and, 199, 202, 204, 205–06, 240, 241, 242, 244, 268, 270, 283, 284–85, 335–36, 341; Beaussier on, 205–06, 284, 296; French Foreign Ministry on, 207; Lear authorizes EP to offer, 240, 284; new, sent to Lear, 280, 284; Lear on, 331–33; agreed to, 334; R. Smith on, 334–35; Tripolitan people and, 334–35n; postwar quarrels over, 335–36

Peale, Rembrandt, *frontis*, 85, 313, 314
Pepperrell, William, 3
Perkins, James, 64, 65, 86
Perkins, Thomas Handasyd, 64, 65, 86, 314
Petite Vertu, 51–52, 57
Phenix, 48–49
Philadelphia: retained in Navy, 83; operations with Dale squadron, 87, 91; to be part of EP's squadron, 128; operations during Moroccan crisis, 139, 141–43, 146; captured by Tripoli, 148, 179–83, 185, 189–90, 201, 278–79, 280, 336–37; number of British seamen in, 173, 367n2 (Chap. 10); EP's efforts to release crew of, 183, 199, 203–05, 240, 242–43, 244, 295; proposals to exchange, 188–89, 202–03; destruction of, 194–99, 207, 249, 280, 298; Lear's efforts to release crew of, 331–34

Phillips, Isaac, 53
Phipps, David, 68
Phips, David, 20
Pickering: EP commands, 57–65; EP's opinion of, 58–59
Pickering, Timothy, 55
Pinckney, C. C., 49
Plover, John, 174
Plumer, William, 316
Pluto, 44
Political parties. *See* Federalist Party; Republican Party
Polly (brigantine), 35
Polly (letter of marque ship), 17
Polly (storeship), 59–60
Pomroy, Richard, 23–24
Pope, Alexander, 220–21
Porter, David, 58, 216, 306
Porter, James, 80–81
Portland, Maine: in EP's youth, 3; destroyed by Mowat, 6–7; merchant fleet destroyed, 21; gunboats and *Etna* built at, 320–21, 326; described by Lawrence, 352

Collector of Customs at. See Fosdick, Nathaniel; Ilsley, Isaac
Poverty: in St. John's, Newfoundland, 44; in Tangier, 171; in Syracuse, Sicily, 228–29
Preble, Eben: birth, 4; at Dummer School, 6, 357n4; commands *Hazard*, 7; owner of *Dauphin*, 50, 51; owner of *Massachusetts*, 64, 65; and EP's health, 96, 209, 350, 353; and Joshua Preble's death, 189; mentioned, 53; 85*illus*
Preble, Edward

Youth and merchant service: birth and childhood, 3–5; education, 5–6, 7; runs away to sea, 7–8; midshipman in *Protector*, 9–19; encounter with sea serpent, 13–16; prisoner of war, 18–19; first lieutenant of *Winthrop*, 20–29; capture of *Merriam*, 23–24; accidentally wounds self, 25; sent to St. Christopher in prize, 28; enters merchant service, 30; commands *William*, 30–31, 361n2; moves to Edenton, North Carolina, 30; commands *Elizabeth*, 31–32; commands *Alliance*, 32; commands *Hannah*, 32; returns to Massachusetts, 32; makes voyage to Africa in *Polly*, 33; commands *Neptune*, 34–36, 37; describes activities of Spanish and British fleets for *Columbian Centinel*, 35–36; commands *Katy*, 36–38; supercargo of *Helena*, 38, 39; commission agent in Bordeaux, 39–41; sails to Philadelphia in *Camilla*, 41; owner and master of *Jason*, 41–42, 362n9; supercargo in *Success* and *Fame*, 42–46; assaults Lamb, 47; in Havana trade, 47–49; commands *Dauphin*, 50–53, 55, 56–57

Commission in Navy and Quasi-War with France: seeks commission in U.S. Navy, 38–39, 40, 41, 49; seeks berth in *Constitution*, 50–51; receives appointment in Navy, 53–54; asks leave of absence from *Constitution*, 56–57; commands *Pickering*, 57–65; considers resigning from Navy, 63–65; promoted to captain, 64–65; commands *Essex* on voyage to Java, 66–81, 98; courts Mary Deering, 67–68, 79–80

Tripolitan War years: marries Mary Deering, 84; resumes command of *Essex*, 84–86; gives up command of *Essex*, 88; selected to command Mediterranean squadron, 89, 106, 127–28; removal of Fosdick, 89–91; commands *Adams*, 96–

INDEX

Preble, Edward (Continued)
101; attempts to resign commission, 98–100; fits *Constitution* for sea, 123–38; orders for command of Mediterranean squadron, 127–28, 130; criticized in Washington, 136; Moroccan crisis, 139–72; encounter with *Maimona*, 139–40; encounter with *Maidstone*, 140–41; learns of hostilities between Morocco and U.S., 141–45; takes tough line with Morocco, 145–46, 151, 154–55, 157; thinks trade with U.S. more profitable for Morocco than war, 152, 168; treatment of Moroccan prisoners, 152–53; analyzes success in resolving crisis, 157–58; precautions against surprise, 161, 162, 163, 172, 207; negotiates settlement with Morocco, 163–72; conflict with British over deserters, 173–75; need for reinforcements, 175–76, 183, 192–93, 200–01, 209, 246–47; visits Algiers, 175–79; loss of *Philadelphia*, 179–82, 280, 336–37; establishes base at Syracuse, 182–83; captures *Intrepid*, 183–85; plans destruction of *Philadelphia*, 184, 189–91; relations with Schembri, 188–89, 202–04; at Malta in *Vixen*, 185–89; and threats of hostile action by Tunis, 199–201, 207–09, 212, 245–46; negotiations with Tripoli, 204–07, 240–45, 267–71, 282–85, 294–97; cooperation with Hamet Caramanli, 186–88, 203, 205, 210–12, 308, 330; day-to-day activities in *Constitution*, 214–18 *passim;* dictates to government of Syracuse, 230–34; acquisition of permanent naval bases in Mediterranean, 232n; borrows gunboats and bomb ketches from Kingdom of the Two Sicilies, 235, 236–39; rejects Lear's advice on peace settlement with Tripoli, 241

Conduct of Tripolitan War: strategy in Mediterranean operations, 130–31, 175–76, 180–81, 182, 183, 188, 192–93, 200–01, 202, 205, 210–12, 237–38, 247, 249, 285; attitude towards Barbary States, 145–46, 151, 157, 176, 201, 202, 213, 243. *See also* Preble, Edward, Attacks on Tripoli, Tactics

Attacks on Tripoli: Tactics, 237–38, 247, 252–53, 254, 261–62, 271–72, 285–86, 288, 292, 298–99, 299–302; effects of weather on, 247, 286, 288; preliminary movements, 51–53; 3 Aug. 1804, 253–67; orders no quarter in hand-to-hand com-

Preble, Edward (Continued)
bats, 259; escapes injury, 262, 282; 7 Aug. 1804, 271–76; superseded by S. Barron, 276–77, 279–80, 282, 307–08; attempts to end war before Barron's arrival, 282, 283, 285; abortive attacks, 11–22 Aug. 1804, 285–88; considers abandoning attacks, 288, 289–90; 23/24 Aug. 1804, 288–89; 27/28 Aug. 1804, 290–94; abandons hope of ending war in summer of 1804, 297; fatigue as factor in, 297; *Intrepid* employed as infernal, 297–99, 303–06; 2 Sept. 1804, 299–303; expresses admiration for Tripolitan tactics, 299; resumes blockade, 306–07. *See also* Tripoli

Final years: may be given command in West Indies, 308; final months in Mediterranean, 309–12; return to U.S., 312–14; honored at public dinners, 314–15; may be appointed Secretary of Navy, 315; gunboat program, 317–28; interest in Carbery's circular gun mount, 324–25; relationships with civilian contractors, 323–24; on professionalism in Navy, 325; avoids postwar quarrels, 335–37; lobbies on behalf of Navy, 337–42; views on future of Navy, 338, 341–42; considers retiring from Navy, 342; proposed mission to study naval affairs in Europe, 343–44; considered for command of Washington Navy Yard, 344–45; constructs new house, 347–48, 351; and *Leopard-Chesapeake* affair, 351–53; final illness and death, 349–54

Health: accidentally wounds self, 25; begins to fail, 81; forces resignation from command of *Essex*, 88; difficulties with, during command of *Adams*, 96–101; improves in summer of 1802, 105; illness in Sept. 1803, 157; fever in Apr. 1804, 209; injuries suffered in stagecoach accident, 339; during Mediterranean command, 349; terminal illness, 349–54

Personal characteristics: frontis, 7; significance of career, vii; reasons for rise to prominence, vii-viii; aptitude for military life and seamanship, 4; efficiency, 4, 326; reserve, formality, and courtliness, 4, 46, 232; sense of humor, 4, 160–61, 227, 244; single-mindedness, 4, 189; temper, 4–5, 46–47, 133, 138, 140–41, 162, 223, 225, 231, 244; love of hunting and fishing, 5, 13–16, 60, 101,

INDEX

Preble, Edward (Continued)
345–46; adopts promising boys, 6, 346; attitude towards education, 6; dislike of farming, 7, 346; cultivation of influential and socially prominent persons, 18–19, 44, 65, 71, 86, 89, 152, 163, 182, 186, 314; self-possession and self-discipline, 23–24, 44–45, 70, 181, 335; absence of adventurous spirit during merchant career, 33; refusal to participate in slave trade, 33; relations with seamen and Marines, 34–35, 80–81, 133, 221–24; pets, 35; financial affairs, 36, 41, 47–48, 64–65, 84, 326, 350; practices bribery, 37, 182, 234, 238; powers of persuasion, 40; engages in deceptive practices, 45, 48, 174, 190; use of physical violence, 47, 81*n*, 221–24; love of naval service, 57, 342; ambition, 64–65, 78, 89, 128, 137–38, 172, 312; relationships with subordinate officers, 58, 68, 80–81, 98, 132–33, 141, 174, 224–27, 233, 248–49, 307; influence of British Navy on, 71–72, 219–20; decisiveness and independence, 72, 75, 133, 236–37, 240–41; experiences frustration, 77–78; attitude towards others, 80, 133–34, 297; political affiliation, 88–89, 315–16, 317*n*, 326; patriotism, 57, 89, 221, 225, 315, 352; interest in engineering and inventions, 106–07, 320, 324–25, 347; operates at high level of competence, 134; religious sentiments, 138, 182; optimism, 154, 157, 173, 199, 239; social relations with officers of Navy, 163, 307, 339; satisfaction with successes, 172, 308, 312; charitable activities, 177, 270; pessimism, 181–82, 239, 280, 312; anxiety, insecurity, and sensitivity, 136, 193, 235, 282; eating habits, 204–05, 353; drafts own letters, 219; reading interests, 219–21, 343; attitudes towards discipline, 221–27, 233; singing, 221; dislike of courts-martial and courts of inquiry, 224, 351–52; boasting, 237; handicaps as a negotiator, 297; conciliatoriness, 147–48, 309, 336; drives hard bargain, 323; dislike of paper wars, 335; on future of U.S. as seafaring nation, 342; lacks interest in business, 342; thinks only force and fear can restrain some nations, 342; thinks men have better lives than women, 346–47; as father, 347; attitude towards death, 354

Opinions of EP: Ball, Alexander John, 290; Beaussier, Bonaventure, 241–42, 244, 268, 269, 270–71, 294, 295, 296;

Preble, Edward (Continued)
Caramanli, Yusuf, 243; Coffin, Jacob, 323; Higginson, Stephen, 56; Izard, Ralph, Jr., 132–33; Jefferson, Thomas, 277, 312; Lear, Tobias, 240–41; Morris, Charles, 133; Porter, James, 81; Rodgers, John, 146–48, 308, 309–10; Smith, Robert, 353; Stoddert, Benjamin, 64; Trant, James, 98; Wadsworth, Henry, 177, 189, 231

Preble, Edward Deering, 84, 340, 346–47
Preble, Enoch: recollections of EP, 3, 7–8, 57, 317*n*4; birth, 4; at Dummer School, 6, 357*n*4; goes to sea, 7; at EP's deathbed, 354
Preble, George Henry, 57; mentioned, 313
Preble, Henry, 4, 7, 181
Preble, Jedidiah, 3–4, 5, 7, 19, 84
Preble, Jedidiah, Jr., 4
Preble, John, 4, 22, 28
Preble, Joshua: birth, 4; becomes a mate, 7; in *Protector*, 17; marries, 32; captured by French 61–62, 63; death, 189
Preble, Lucy. *See* Webb, Lucy (Preble)
Preble, Martha. *See* Oxnard, Martha (Preble)
Preble, Martha (Junkins), 4
Preble, Mary (Deering): EP's courtship of, 67–68, 79–80, 84; description of, 84, 85*illus;* EP's relationship with, 235; and construction of new house, 347–48, 351; will not leave Portland, 350

Letters from EP about: his illness at New York, 98, 99; his ambitions, 128; sailing to Mediterranean, 138; Moroccan crisis, 172; strategic outlook in Mediterranean, 176; Algiers, 178–79; loss of *Philadelphia*, 181–82; Syracuse, Sicily, 182–83; search for gunboats, 235; Naples, 238; mood on eve of attacks on Tripoli, 239, 240, 247; his intention of returning to U.S., 307–08; his reception at New York, 312; Washington social life, 340; Edward Deering Preble, 347; his health, 351

Preble, Mehetable (Bangs) Roberts, 4
Preble, Samuel, 4
Preble, Statira. *See* Codman, Statira (Preble)
Preble, William, 4
President, 83, 87, 91, 246, 277, 307–08
Prize money, Massachusetts state navy and, 10, 26
Professionalism in U.S. Navy, 60, 131–32, 325

INDEX

Profits: on voyage of *Polly*, 33; on voyage of *Dauphin*, 52
Protector: building and outfitting, 8; midshipmen for, 8–9; cruises of, 9–18; officers and crew of, prisoners, 18–19; armament of, 359n9; mentioned, 39, 60
Public opinion, effect of naval actions on, 278, 281

Quasi-War with France. *See* France, friction with U.S.

Rajah, 156
Randolph, Martha (Jefferson), described by EP, 340
Recruiting: for *Pickering*, 57–58, 59; for *Constitution*, 134–36; for *Nautilus*, 135; for *Vixen*, 135; of Maltese sailors and pilots, 186, 236
Reed, George Washington, 303–05
Reed, William, 55–56
Reich, John, 313
Republican Party: W. Reed a member of, 55; S. Nicholson a member of, 56; J. F. Williams a member of, 56; wins election of 1800, 82, 83; EP and, 88–89, 316, 317n; and removal of Fosdick, 89–91
Richery, Joseph de, 42, 43
Rider, Samuel, 38
Roberts, Mehetable (Bangs). *See* Preble, Mehetable (Bangs) Roberts
Robinson, Thomas, 266, 272, 275, 302–03, 333
Rodgers, John: as leading officer of U.S. Navy, vii; at Morris court of inquiry, 111, 116; R. Smith criticizes R. V. Morris to, 114; and capture of *Meshuda*, 116, 143, 146, 149; views on squadron needed to defeat Tripoli, 118; in action of 27 May 1803, 119; attempts to negotiate with Tripoli, 120–21; relations with EP and S. Barron, 146–48, 308, 309–10, 329; operations with EP during Moroccan crisis, 148–71 *passim;* views on punishment, 224; commands *Congress*, 277, 279; to watch Morocco, 307; N. Morris's opinion of, 309–10; builds Gunboat No. 1, 316–17; takes command of Mediterranean squadron, 333; quarrels with Eaton and J. Barron, 335
Roebuck, 17–18

Roxbury, 21
Royal Navy. *See* Great Britain, Navy
Rusé, 267, 270, 271
Russell, Charles C., 57

Sabratha. *See* Old Tripoli
St. John's, Newfoundland, described by EP, 44
Saint-Pierre, Bernardin de, 221
St. Pierre and Miquelon, described by EP, 43
St. Tammany, 46
Salem Gazette, 46
Sally, 17
San Marco, Baron, 234
Sapitapa (Tunis), 209, 212
Schembri, Gaetano Andrea, 188–89, 202–04, 205, 210
Scourge, 210, 231, 245, 247–50, 275
Selawy, Mohammed, 145, 155–71 *passim*
Senate, U.S. *See* U.S. Congress
Sever, James, 66–72 *passim*, 75, 78–79
Sex, extra-marital, 186, 229, 230, 298n
Shark, 44
Shays's Rebellion, 30
Shield (Richard) & Co., 36, 38
Shipboard life. *See* U.S. Navy, life in *Pickering*, in *Constitution*
Ships of the line, 337–41
Sigourney, Captain, 46
Simpson, James: notified of declaration of war by Morocco, 101; reports difficulties with Morocco adjusted, 107; and Moroccan crisis of 1803, 139–72 *passim;* moderating influence on EP, 297; fears new difficulties with Morocco, 307
Simpson, Mrs. James, 172
Sinclair, Captain, 193
Siren. *See Syren*
Skinner, Thomas, 44
Slave trade, 33
Smith, Adam (EP's servant), 97, 309
Smith, John: to command *Vixen*, 128; arrives in Mediterranean, 146; sent to re-establish blockade of Tripoli, 148; borrows books from EP, 220; cannot persuade Gregorio to restore deserter, 230; and blockade of Tripoli, 248; in EP's attacks on Tripoli, 263, 283
Smith, Margaret (Mrs. Robert): EP's opinion of, 350
Smith, Robert: correspondence as source for study of naval policy, viii; appointed

390

INDEX

Secretary of Navy, 93; orders to R. V. Morris, 93–95, 107, 113, 116; relies on discretion of naval commanders, 94; and EP's health, 98, 99–101, 105, 351–54; policy for dealing with Barbary States, 103, 104–05, 128, 279; EP's opinion of, 106, 350; will give Mediterranean command to Dale, 106; Murray writes to regarding Mediterranean affairs, 108–09; dissatisfaction with and dismissal of R. V. Morris, 113–14, 278; orders EP to command *Constitution*, 123; authorizes EP to remove Haraden, 125n; instructions to EP for Mediterranean command, 128, 130, 131, 132, 236; on selection and training of officers, 131–32, 325; EP complains about S. Nicholson to, 133–34; and recruiting for EP's squadron, 135; optimism on fitting out *Constitution*, 136; Rodgers complains to regarding EP, 147, 148; EP explains attitude towards Morocco to, 151; EP asks for reinforcements, 175–76, 183, 201; EP reports loss of *Philadelphia* to, 183, 184; EP urges cooperation with Hamet Caramanli on, 188; EP promises to send papers for *Intrepid*'s condemnation, 190; EP reports hostile Tunisian attitude to, 199; notifies EP that *John Adams* will join him, 209; on condition of Murray's ship, 224n; EP reports conduct of Baldwin to, 226; tells EP he is to be superseded by Barron, 276–77, 282; prepares *Essex* for voyage to France, 277; selects officers for Barron squadron, 279; EP tells of plans to use fire ships, 297; thinks EP will remain as subordinate to S. Barron, 307; takes EP to call on President, 312; EP confers with on reinforcing Barron squadron, 314; EP tells of own political neutrality, 315–16; wishes to be Attorney General, 315; and gunboat program, 316–28 *passim;* on Tripolitan War peace terms, 334–35; urges construction of ships of the line, 337–38; and EP's proposed mission to Europe, 343–44; J. Barron's opinion of, 344; mentioned, 346

Smith, Samuel, 86–88, 90, 101, 108

Sodomy. *See* Homosexuality

Somers, Richard: to command *Nautilus*, 128; on convoy duty, 148–49; detained by Gregorio, 231; in attacks on Tripoli, 257, 260–61, 263, 267, 286; and *Intrepid*, 298–99, 305, 336–37

Spain, friction with U.S., 308, 316, 337–38

Spence, Robert T., 303–05

Sterett, Andrew, 91–92, 105n, 193

Sterne, Laurence, 221

Stewart, Charles: to command *Syren*, 128; ordered on convoy duty, 158; dispute over deserters, 173–74; EP sends to Leghorn and Algiers, 175; and destruction of *Philadelphia*, 190–99, 368$n1$; meets hostile Tunisian at sea, 199; friction with EP, 226–27; and blockade of Tripoli, 247–48; urges attack on Tripoli from west, 271–72; dines with EP, 339

Stocker, Ebenezer, 64, 65, 320

Stoddert, Benjamin: appointed Secretary of Navy, 52; EP asks for leave of absence, 56–57; orders to EP regarding *Pickering*, 57, 59; EP writes to regarding complement of *Pickering*, 58; strategy in Quasi-War with France, 59, 66–67; concern over resignations from Navy, 63–64; acts to keep EP in Navy, 64–65; orders to EP for cruise in *Essex*, 66, 70, 72; EP describes strategic situation in Sunda Strait to, 78; grants EP leave of absence, 79–80; EP writes to regarding Mumford, 80; Goldsborough as clerk to, 82; advises sending of squadron to Mediterranean, 87; views on composition of Navy, 108; assigns S. Nicholson to shore duty, 133; mentioned, 81

Strachan, Richard, 141

Strategic policy, U.S.: in Quasi-War with France, 59, 60, 66–67; effect of Peace Establishment Act on, 83–84, 87; as embodied in orders to Dale, 87–88; Dale's views on, 92–93, 104, 130; as embodied in orders to R. V. Morris, 93–95; effect of fiscal considerations on, 94, 131, 135, 277–78; conflicts within Cabinet over, 102–05; in event of war with Morocco, 104–05n, 105; Murray disagrees with, 108–09; as embodied in orders to EP, 128, 130; effects of loss of *Philadelphia* on, 276–77, 278–80; effect of purchase of Louisiana on, 277–78. *See also* Blockade; Gunboat program, U.S.; Massachusetts state navy, strategic policy; Peace terms; Preble, Edward, Conduct of Tripolitan War; Ships of the line; Vessels, small

Stromboli, described by EP, 238–39

Success, 43–45, 47

Sulaiman, Maulay, 101, 140–72 *passim;* described by Izard, 166. *See also* Morocco
Surcouf, Robert, 76–78
Sutton, Samuel, 174
Swallow, 22
Sweden, cooperates with U.S. in Tripolitan War, 92–93, 104n, 107–08, 112
Syracuse, Sicily: as EP's base, 175, 182, 185, 227–34; described by EP, 182–83
Syren: to be part of EP's squadron, 128; operations during Moroccan crisis, 146, 148, 158, 166; operations, Oct. 1803–July 1804, 175, 199, 207–09, 231, 247–50; and destruction of *Philadelphia,* 190–99; sailing masters for, 226–27; in EP's attacks on Tripoli, 251, 253, 256, 261, 264–65*illus,* 272, 274, 289, 292, 306

Tacklenborg, Frans, 40
Talleyrand-Périgord, Charles Maurice de, instructions to and reports from Beaussier, 201–02, 207, 269, 296, 305–06
Tangier: described by Izard, 168; described by Lear, 171–72
Tarbell, Joseph, 159
Tartar, 20
Termagant, 174
Thacher, George, 39
Thames, 12–13, 18
Theft, in *Constitution,* 222–23
Thompson, John, 219, 262, 370n4
Three Friends, 40–41
Tibbets, John, 22
Tingey, Thomas, 338, 344, 345
Transfer. See Scourge
Trant, James, 98
Treasury, Secretary of the. *See* Gallatin, Albert; Wolcott, Oliver
Tripoli: war with U.S., sources for Tripolitan side of conflict, viii; U.S. has no treaty with, 37; naval force of, 118, 120n, 206, 241, 251–52, 269; defenses of, 206, 251–52, 269, 274, 299–302; internal conditions during EP's attacks, 249–50; damage to, during EP's attacks, 274, 284, 289, 294, 295, 303, 305–06; war with U.S., results of, 334
See also Bainbridge, William; Barron, Samuel; Beaussier, Bonaventure; Blockade; Caramanli, Hamet; Caramanli, Yusuf; Cathcart, James L.; Dale, Richard; Dghies, Mohammed; *Intrepid;* Lear, Tobias; *Meshuda;* Morris, Richard V.; Murray, Alexander; O'Brien, Richard; Peace terms; *Philadelphia;* Preble, Edward, Attacks on Tripoli; Preble, Edward, Conduct of Tripolitan War; Preble, Edward, Tripolitan War years; Rodgers, John; Sweden
Tripoli, Old. *See* Old Tripoli
Trippe, John, 257, 259–60, 261, 263, 266, 267
Truxtun, Thomas: during Quasi-War with France, vii; recommends officers for *Constellation,* 50; escorts *Dauphin,* 53; and command of Mediterranean squadron, 86, 87; on character of seamen, 221; may be made Navy Commissioner, 338
Tunis: U.S. has no treaty with, 37; thought to be at war with U.S., 101–02, 104; threatens war with U.S., 111, 122, 180–81, 199–201, 207–09, 212, 245–46; asks U.S. for frigate, 154, 200; naval force of, 200; to trade two xebecs for *Philadelphia,* 202–03
Bey of: expects EP to call on him, 207–08; audiences with G. Davis, 208–09, 245
See also Blockade; Cathcart, James L.; Davis, George; Eaton, William; Lear, Tobias; Morris, Richard V.; O'Brien, Richard; *Paulina;* Peace terms; Preble, Edward, Tripolitan War years; Sapitapa
Turner, Thomas. *See* Accountant of the Navy
Two Friends, 10
Two Sicilies, Kingdom of the: EP borrows gunboats and bomb ketches from, 176, 235, 236–39; declines to lend gunboats and bomb ketches to S. Barron, 232n, 311-12, 333; quality of U.S. consular representation to, 237n; loans sailors to EP, 239. *See also* Ferdinand; Maria-Carolina; Naples
Two Sisters, 46
Tyng, William, 19

Uniform, of sailors in *Constitution,* 214
Union (schooner), 62
Union (sloop), 17
United States, 49, 50, 83, 246
U.S. Congress: authorizes establishment of Navy, 38; construction and employment of frigates, 41, 49; and officer nominations, 50, 55; legislation on size of Navy,

INDEX

52, 83–84; authorizes capture of French vessels, 52; Senate and treaty ending Quasi-War, 82–83; authorizes operations against Tripoli, 93; Jefferson and discretion authorized by, 104; and composition of Navy, 108; authorizes acquisition of gunboats, 237; provides for expanded Mediterranean operations, 279; authorizes medal for EP, 312–14; authorizes gunboat construction programs, 316, 317, 325–26, 339–41; and Wilkinson's paper, 317; and treaty with Tripoli, 335; and reform and expansion of Navy, 337, 338, 339–42; and naval shore establishment, 343, 344
United States, friction with France. *See* France, friction with U.S.
United States, friction with Great Britain. *See* Great Britain, friction with U.S.
United States, friction with Spain. *See* Spain, friction with U.S.
U.S. Marine Corps. *See* Marines
U.S. Navy: opposition to establishment of, 37; authorized by Congress, 38; selection of officers for, 38–39, 49–50, 56, 131–32, 325; construction of first frigates, 41, 49; Congress authorizes increase of, 52; life in *Pickering*, 60; life in *Constitution*, 123–27, 214–27, 307; resignation of officers, 63–64; operations before 1800, 66; uncertainty and transition, 82; reduction of, 83–84; operations against Tripoli authorized, 93; cruisers sold, 108; discipline in, 221, 222; overseas bases, 232n; pay of captains in, 338, 340; expense of shore establishment, 342–43, 344. *See also* Great Britain, Navy, influence on U.S. Navy; Gunboat program, U.S.; Lobbying, by officers of U.S. Navy; Navy, Continental; Ships of the line; Strategic policy, U.S.
U.S. Navy Department: authorized, 52; mishandles supplies, 111–12; EP proposes to collect books for, 343. *See also* Accountant of the Navy; Goldsborough, Charles W.; Navy Commissioners, Board of; Smith, Robert; Smith, Samuel; Stoddert, Benjamin
U.S. War Department, 38, 41, 50. *See also* Knox, Henry; McHenry, James

Vaillant Bonaparte, 119
Venereal disease, 298n

Vessels, small, and conduct of Tripolitan War: *Enterprize* and *Experiment* retained in Navy, 87, 108; Dale on, 92–93, 104, 130; Murray on, 108; sale of, 108; R.V. Morris needs, 122; four added to Navy, 128; EP proposes to acquire in Mediterranean, 130–31. *See also* Gunboats and bomb ketches
Vesuvius, 321–26 passim
Vickers, Joel, 76–77
Villettes, William A., 186
Vinall, John, 47
Viper, 24
Vixen: to be part of EP's squadron, 128; recruiting for, 135; operations during Moroccan crisis, 146; and loss of *Philadelphia,* 148, 179, 181; operations, Jan.–July 1804, 186, 189, 210, 230, 247–50; Page transferred to, 225; in attacks on Tripoli, 250, 253, 256, 261, 263, 264–65 illus, 266, 270, 272, 274–75, 276, 283, 292, 303–05, 306–07

Wadsworth, Henry: describes dismasting of *Congress,* 79; sketched 163–64; describes audience with Maulay Sulaiman, 164–66; describes Algiers, 177–78; describes social life at Malta, 186, 189; on Mrs. Cannon, 216; describes EP's quarrel with Gregorio, 231; on evasion of quarantine at Syracuse, 233; in *Scourge,* 245; in blockade of Tripoli, 248; in EP's attacks on Tripoli, 262, 286; contracts venereal disease, 298n; and *Intrepid,* 298–99, 305, 336; mentioned, 167
Wadsworth, Peleg, 9, 16, 79
Wallace, James, 223
Wallace, John, 38
War Department. *See* U.S. War Department
War, Secretary of. *See* Knox, Henry; McHenry, James
Wars, European (French Revolution and Napoleonic Empire): EP makes first contact with, 35–36; Spain changes sides in, 48; EP on benefits to U.S. from, 130, 201; effect on recruiting for EP's squadron, 134–36. *See also* France, friction with U.S.; Great Britain, friction with U.S.; Spain, friction with U.S.
Washington, 46
Washington, George, 38, 39, 168, 178
Washington, D.C.: social life, described by

393

INDEX

EP, 340; Navy Yard, 343-45; EP urged to move to, 349-50
Watts, Bellingham, 40-41
Weather. *See* Preble, Edward, Attacks on Tripoli
Webb, Jonathan ("Pithy"), 5
Webb, Lucy (Preble), 4, 5
Wells, James, 215, 216
Wharton, Franklin, 349
White, Lemuel, 22
Wilkie, Patrick, 202
Wilkinson, James, 317-19
William, 30-31, 361n2
Williams, John Foster, 8-18, 56
Williams, Joseph W., 150

Wilson, William, 90
Winthrop: cruises of, 19-29; logbook described, 25; sailing qualities of, 27; described, 360n22; mentioned, 39, 60, 259
Wiswell, John, 47
Wolcott, Oliver, 48
Women: in ships of U.S. Navy, 216, 263; Italian, 228-29; EP thinks have more difficult lives than men, 346-47
Woodrop Sims, 209
Wright, David. *See* Thompson, John

Yonge, George, 71
Young, Charles, 262

ABOUT THE AUTHOR

CHRISTOPHER MCKEE is Samuel R. and Marie-Louise Rosenthal Professor and Librarian of the College at Grinnell College, Iowa. He is the author of *A Gentlemanly and Honorable Profession: The Creation of the United States Naval Officer Corps, 1794–1815,* published by the Naval Institute Press in 1991, and is currently at work on a history of enlisted men in the United States Navy between 1798 and 1860.

CLASSICS OF NAVAL LITERATURE
JACK SWEETMAN, SERIES EDITOR

Autobiography of George Dewey, by Admiral of the Navy George Dewey. Introduction and notes by Eric McAllister Smith

Away All Boats, by Kenneth Dodson. Introduction by Robert Shenk

The Big E, by Edward P. Stafford. Introduction by Paul Stillwell

Bluejacket: An Autobiography, by Fred J. Buenzle and A. Grove Day. Introduction and notes by Neville T. Kirk

The Buccaneers of America, by Alexander Exquemelin. Introduction and notes by Robert C. Ritchie

The Caine Mutiny, by Herman Wouk. Introduction by Noël A. Daigle

The Commodores, by Leonard F. Guttridge and Jay D. Smith. Introduction by James C. Bradford

The Cruel Sea, by Nicholas Monsarrat. Introduction by Edward L. Beach

Delilah, by Marcus Goodrich. Introduction by C. Herbert Gilliland Jr.

Fix Bayonets! by John W. Thomason Jr. Introduction by Edward R. Crews

The Good Shepherd, by C. S. Forester. Introduction by J.D.P. Hodapp Jr.

John Paul Jones; A Sailor's Biography, by Samuel Eliot Morison. Introduction by James C. Bradford

Journal of a Cruise Made to the Pacific Ocean by Captain David Porter in the United States Frigate Essex *in the Years 1812, 1813, and 1814,* by Capt. David Porter. Introduction and notes by Robert D. Madison and Karen Hamon

The Life of Nelson, by Robert Southey. Introduction and notes by Robert D. Madison

Man-of-War Life, by Charles Nordhoff. Introduction and notes by John B. Hattendorf

Master of Sea Power: A Biography of Fleet Admiral Ernest J. King, by Thomas B. Buell. Introduction by John B. Lundstrom

Midway: The Battle That Doomed Japan, by Mitsuo Fuchida and Masatake Okumiya. Edited by Clarke H. Kawakami and Roger Pineau, introduction by Thomas B. Buell

Mr. Midshipman Easy, by Frederick Marryat. Introduction and notes by Evan L. Davies

Mister Roberts, by Thomas Heggen. Introduction by David P. Smith

My Fifty Years in the Navy, by Rear Adm. Charles E. Clark. Introduction and notes by Jack Sweetman

The Naval War of 1812, by Theodore Roosevelt. Introduction by Edward K. Eckert

Ned Myers; or, A Life Before the Mast, by James Fenimore Cooper. Introduction and notes by William S. Dudley

The Quiet Warrior: A Biography of Admiral Raymond A. Spruance, by Thomas B. Buell. Introduction by John B. Lundstrom

Raiders of the Deep, by Lowell Thomas. Introduction and notes by Gary E. Weir

Recollections of a Naval Officer, 1841–1865, by Capt. William Harwar Parker. Introduction and notes by Craig L. Symonds

The Riddle of the Sands, by Erskine Childers. Introduction and notes by Eric J. Grove

The Rise of American Naval Power, 1775–1918, by Harold and Margaret Sprout. Introduction by Kenneth J. Hagan and Charles Conrad Campbell

Running the Blockade, by Thomas E. Taylor. Introduction and notes by Stephen R. Wise

Run Silent, Run Deep, by Edward L. Beach. Introduction by Edward P. Stafford

Sailing Alone Around the World, by Joshua Slocum. Introduction by Robert W. McNitt

A Sailor's Log, by Robley D. Evans. Introduction and notes by Benjamin Franklin Cooling

Samurai! by Saburo Sakai with Martin Caidin and Fred Saito. Introduction by Barrett Tillman

The Sand Pebbles, by Richard McKenna. Introduction by Robert Shenk

Sea Devils: Italian Navy Commandos in World War II, by J. Valerio Borghese. Introduction by Paolo E. Coletta

The Sinking of the Merrimac, by Richmond Pearson Hobson. Introduction and notes by Richard W. Turk

Two Years on the Alabama, by Arthur W. Sinclair. Introduction and notes by William N. Still Jr.

The Victory at Sea, by Rear Adm. William S. Sims and Burton J. Hendrick. Introduction and notes by David F. Trask

White-Jacket; or, The World in a Man-of-War, by Herman Melville. Introduction by Stanton B. Garner

With the Battle Cruisers, by Filson Young. Introduction and notes by James Goldrick

With the Old Breed: At Peleliu and Okinawa, by E. B. Sledge. Introduction by Joseph H. Alexander

The **Naval Institute Press** is the book-publishing arm of the U.S. Naval Institute, a private, nonprofit society for sea service professionals and others who share an interest in naval and maritime affairs. Established in 1873 at the U.S. Naval Academy in Annapolis, Maryland, where its offices remain today, the Naval Institute has almost 85,000 members worldwide.

Members of the Naval Institute receive the influential monthly magazine *Proceedings* and discounts on fine nautical prints, ship and aircraft photos, and subscriptions to the bimonthly *Naval History* magazine. They also have access to the transcripts of the Institute's Oral History Program and get discounted admission to any of the Institute-sponsored seminars offered around the country.

The Naval Institute's book-publishing program, begun in 1898 with basic guides to naval practices, has broadened its scope in recent years to include books of more general interest. Now the Naval Institute Press publishes about 100 titles each year, ranging from how-to books on boating and navigation to battle histories, biographies, ship and aircraft guides, and novels. Institute members receive discounts of 20 to 50 percent on the Press's nearly 600 books in print.

Full-time students are eligible for special half-price membership rates. Life memberships are also available.

For a free catalog describing Naval Institute Press books currently available, and for further information about U.S. Naval Institute membership, please write to:

Membership Department
U.S. Naval Institute
118 Maryland Avenue
Annapolis, Maryland 21402-5035
Telephone: (800) 233-8764
Fax: (410) 269-7940

www.ingramcontent.com/pod-product-compliance
Lightning Source LLC
Chambersburg PA
CBHW030509080526
44586CB00011B/121